Evidence

Sixth Edition

RODERICK MUNDAY

MA, PhD (Cantab), Bencher of Lincoln's Inn

Fellow of Peterhouse, Cambridge

Reader in Law, University of Cambridge

Series editor

NICOLA PADFIELD

Fitzwilliam College, Cambridge

OXFORD
UNIVERSITY PRESS

OXFORD
UNIVERSITY PRESS

Great Clarendon Street, Oxford OX2 6DP

Oxford University Press is a department of the University of Oxford.
It furthers the University's objective of excellence in research, scholarship,
and education by publishing worldwide in

Oxford New York

Auckland Cape Town Dar es Salaam Hong Kong Karachi
Kuala Lumpur Madrid Melbourne Mexico City Nairobi
New Delhi Shanghai Taipei Toronto

With offices in

Argentina Austria Brazil Chile Czech Republic France Greece
Guatemala Hungary Italy Japan Poland Portugal Singapore
South Korea Switzerland Thailand Turkey Ukraine Vietnam

Oxford is a registered trade mark of Oxford University Press
in the UK and in certain other countries

Published in the United States
by Oxford University Press Inc., New York

© Oxford University Press 2011

The moral rights of the author have been asserted

Database right Oxford University Press (maker)

Contains public sector information licensed under the
Open Government Licence v1.0 (http://www.nationalarchives.gov.uk/doc/
open-government-licence/open-government-licence.htm)

Crown Copyright material reproduced with the permission of the
Controller, HMSO (under the terms of the Click Use licence).

Third edition 2005
Fourth edition 2007
Fifth edition 2009

British Library Cataloguing in Publication Data
Data available

Library of Congress Cataloging in Publication Data
Data available

Typeset by Newgen Imaging Systems (P) Ltd, Chennai, India
Printed in Great Britain
on acid-free paper by
Clays Ltd, St Ives plc

ISBN 978–0–19–960050–2

10 9 8 7 6 5 4 3 2 1

Preface to sixth edition

This new edition of *Evidence* incorporates many developments that have occurred over the past two years. In the realm of statute, notably the provisions of the Coroners and Justice Act 2009 have replaced and expanded the Criminal Evidence (Witness Anonymity) Act 2008, as well reducing restrictions on the admission of complaints by victims of crime. In the realm of case law, hardly any area of the Law of Evidence has remained immune from noteworthy decisions. The Court of Appeal has handed down significant guidance on the competence of child witnesses and on facial mapping evidence; it has reviewed the conditions of admissibility of 'low template' DNA evidence and re-drawn the boundaries of the exception to the rule against narrative dealing with charges of concoction. The courts have continued to churn out cases on hearsay evidence and on defendants' bad character, as well as delivering a pair of important decisions elucidating the principles underlying the admission of non-defendants' bad character under s 100 of the Criminal Justice Act 2003. Additionally, the book notes rulings the courts have delivered on such matters as privilege, the rape shield provision set forth in s 41 of the Youth Justice and Criminal Evidence Act 1999, and confessions. Further reform may be just over the skyline: the Law Commission has published a consultation paper on the admissibility of expert evidence in criminal proceedings. New suggested readings have also been added to this volume.

At the time of going to press, there remains one conspicuous piece of unresolved business. The case of *Horncastle v UK* has invited the Grand Chamber of the European Court of Human Rights to reconsider the earlier decision in *Al-Khawaja and Tahery v UK* (2009) and to determine whether a trial will be held in breach of Article 6 of the European Convention if 'the sole or decisive prosecution evidence' is made up of hearsay. Following the lead of the Court of Appeal ([2009] 2 Cr App R 15), the Supreme Court ([2010] 2 WLR 47) struck what the Grand Chamber may have interpreted as a combative posture. Lord Phillips of Worth Matravers, more emolliently, expressed the hope that the Supreme Court's judgments might initiate 'valuable dialogue between this court and the Strasbourg Court.' Not often is the right reason of Euro-judges challenged quite so directly. Those claiming to be in the know originally expressed confidence that the Strasbourg Court's decision would be handed down in the late autumn of 2010. This was not to be. The 2011 crop of spring crocuses, snowdrops and woodland aconites is already in full flower, and the Grand Chamber's decision is still eagerly awaited. As and when that decision is delivered, an annotation will go up on the website that now accompanies this book. For the time being, as the cosmologist Carl Sagan observed, 'Somewhere, something incredible is waiting to be known.'

Peterhouse, Cambridge
St Valentine's Day 2011

Contents

Table of cases

Table of statutes

Table of international instruments

Introduction

'I have pondered much on the nature of truth, my way having lain in courts of justice, where men deal in an inferior substitute called "evidence".'

A Lieck, *Narrow Waters* (1937)

The noted American writer on evidence, Wigmore, once wrote: 'at the trial of Warren Hastings in 1794, Edmund Burke is reported to have said that he knew a parrot who could learn the rules of evidence in a half-hour and repeat them in five minutes' (*A Treatise on the Anglo-American System of Evidence* (1923, 2nd edn, I.237)). It will be disheartening for twenty-first century students to learn that this golden age, if ever it existed, is long past. The law of evidence, it should be said from the outset, is complex—sometimes it is said, unnecessarily so. Modern scholars have variously suggested that the rules of evidence are 'arcane' (Brian W Simpson in John H Langbein, *The Origins of Adversary Criminal Trial* (2003, p v)) or 'even more bizarre and complex than the game of cricket' (W Twining, *Rethinking Evidence* (1994, p 178)). The law of evidence, it could be added, is also rapidly evolving. All the same, since it determines the critical issue, which items of proof are parties actually permitted to produce before a court in support of their contentions, it would be difficult to exaggerate the importance of the subject. Certainly, lawyers in practice worth their salt cannot afford to ignore the law of evidence.

Despite the title of this book, it is to an extent misleading today to speak of the law of evidence as though the subject enjoyed a strong intellectual unity. In fact, while there remain some areas where civil and criminal proceedings do share broadly common principles, the two domains have grown apart. Some of today's best-known rules of evidence only ever did apply in criminal cases: for instance, the admissibility of confessions, now governed by the Police and Criminal Evidence Act 1984, s 76 (Chapter 10). Others, such as the rules affecting the admissibility of evidence of a defendant's other misconduct, now regulated in criminal cases by Part 11 of the Criminal Justice Act 2003, always possessed greater importance in the criminal context and follow principles quite distinct from those that obtain in civil cases when 'similar fact evidence' is adduced before the court (Chapter 7). Another great exclusionary rule, the hearsay rule, which once applied in criminal and civil proceedings alike with almost equal vigour, for some while has had little role to play in civil cases: successive Civil Evidence Acts, passed in 1968, 1972 and 1995, buttressed by provisions in the recent Civil Procedure Rules 1998, have virtually rendered the hearsay rule devoid of significance in civil cases. The hearsay rule in criminal cases is regulated by its own separate legislation—the Criminal Justice Act 2003, ss 114–136—which, it is true, does now share some features with the legislation affecting civil evidence (Chapter 9). To paint the picture with an impressionistic brushstroke, the empire of civil evidence has been progressively shrinking; in contrast, whilst many of the principles of criminal evidence seem to be in retreat, the subject itself, if anything, is in expansion.

This transformation is obvious if one only pauses to examine the sources of the law of evidence. Until comparatively recently, the law of evidence was largely a case-law subject. Today, not only does statute play a leading role in delineating the rules of evidence, but it also alters those rules at a giddy pace. In the last decade and a half, one can count amongst the major legislation that has transformed key areas of criminal evidence such bagatelles as the Criminal Justice and Public Order Act 1994 (which introduced radical changes to the right of silence: Chapter 11), the Youth Justice and Criminal Evidence Act 1999 (which introduced detailed rules designed to protect vulnerable and intimidated witnesses, as well as modifying existing rules relating to the evidence of children and spouses, and to computer evidence: Chapters 3 and 4) and a Brobdingnagian Criminal Justice Act 2003 which has re-jigged, hip and thigh, the rules governing the admission of both evidence of bad character and that perennial thorn in the lawyer's side, the hearsay rule. The fact is that the law of evidence, and criminal evidence in particular, is in a state of almost perpetual transition. Most recently, the Coroners and Justice Act 2009 has both renewed earlier legislation regulating the admission of the testimony of witnesses whose identities are concealed and created a further regime of 'investigation anonymity orders' designed to protect the identities of those who assist the police or the Serious Organised Crime Agency in certain types of homicide enquiry.

Outside the common law world legal systems tend not to have developed laws of evidence. (But see, Damaška, *Of Hearsay and its Analogues*, 76 Minn L Rev 425 (1992).) Although some decisions of the European Court of Human Rights in Strasbourg have arguably induced Continental systems to adopt what almost begin to resemble common law rules of evidence, such as a semblance of a hearsay rule,

European jurisdictions do not in truth possess meaningful counterparts to the great exclusionary rules of the English law of evidence. The law of evidence, then, is a distinctive feature of common law systems.

The origins of a law of evidence

There is disagreement over the origins of many of the English rules of evidence. A substantial body of legal historians believes that the emergence of a number of the major exclusionary rules of criminal evidence coincided with and was prompted by the advent of meaningful legal representation of accused persons in criminal trials in what became increasingly adversarial proceedings during the course of the eighteenth century (eg, Langbein, 'The Criminal Trial before the Lawyers' 45 U Chi L R 263 (1978); 'Shaping the Eighteenth-Century Trial: A View from the Ryder Sources' 50 U Chi L R (1983) at p 86; *The Origins of Adversary Criminal Trial* (2003, Oxford)). Indeed, the 'crucial impulse' for, if not the very origins of, many of these exclusionary rules may be traceable to historical developments that took place in the English criminal courts (Gallanis, *The Rise of Modern Evidence Law*, 84 Iowa L Rev 499 (1999)). Other scholars would portray much of the law of evidence as having evolved as a means of buttressing humanistic policies, and more particularly of protecting the individual's rights rather than simply ensuring factual accuracy (eg, Richard Friedman, 'Anchors and Flotsam: Is Evidence Law "Adrift"?' 107 Yale LJ 1921 (1998)).

Another breed of writer endeavours to explain the law of evidence in pronouncedly theoretical terms. Whereas Leubsdorf has argued that evidence can be viewed as a complex system of incentives and disincentives affecting people's behaviour in anticipating, conducting, litigating and settling future disputes ('Evidence Law as a System of Incentives', 95 Iowa L Rev 1621 (2010)), in his study, *Foundations of Evidence Law* (2005, Oxford), Alex Stein works with a cocktail of insights derived from probability theory, economic analysis, epistemology, and moral philosophy. Stein argues that in examining the probabilistic deductions to which the tribunal of fact must inevitably resort in reaching its decisions, and in resolving the sometimes paradoxical conclusions to which probabilistic deduction can lead, it is necessary to distinguish between 'probability' and 'weight'. Although it may in turn be overridden by notions of social utility, Stein contends that fact-finders cannot make a finding against a person when the evidence they employ is not susceptible to individualised testing—what he terms 'the principle of maximum individualisation.' The concern of the law of evidence, Stein contends, is the allocation of risk of error. Moreover, this process of risk-allocation operates via three vehicles: a principle of cost-efficiency, which requires the tribunal to minimise the total cost of errors as well as the total cost of error-avoidance; (in civil cases) a principle of equality, according to which both claimant and defendant share equally in the cost of apportioning risk; and, finally, (in criminal cases) an 'equal best' principle, which requires the state both to exert itself to protect the defendant against the risk of wrongful conviction and to ensure that others are not afforded greater protection. These three principles, which together conduce to allocating the risk of error within the justice system, are said to explain many of the leading rules of the law of evidence.

Other writers, again, incline to the more conventional view that many of the law of evidence's exclusionary rules represent an attempt by the judges to control the activities of autonomous juries, whose members, if uncontrolled, might otherwise be tempted to pay undue regard to irrelevant or prejudicial material. In the words of the great American scholar, Thayer, the law of evidence can in this sense be viewed as 'the child of the jury system' (*A Preliminary Treatise on Evidence at Common Law*, 1898, p 296).

This latter outlook, which would link a law of evidence with the presence of a jury, endures. Because lay persons lack the expertise of the professional lawyer, jurors need to be protected from evidence that might prejudice or enflame them (see, eg, *R v South Worcestershire Magistrates, ex p Lilley* [1996] 1 Cr App R 420 *per* Rose LJ). The most radical solution is to exclude such evidence entirely from jurors' consideration. An alternative strategy is to accompany such evidence with warnings or instructions as to how jurors must use it.

True, the courts may now be retreating from an attitude of strong distrust. In *Mirza* [2004] 1 AC 1118, a case concerned with the extent to which juror misconduct can properly be investigated by the courts, Lord Rodger of Earlsferry strongly defended the lay presence in criminal trials:

> The risk that those chosen as jurors may be prejudiced in various ways is, and always has been, inherent in trial by jury. Indeed, only the most foolish would deny that judges too may be prejudiced, whether, for example, in favour of a pretty woman or a handsome man, or against one whose dress, general demeanour or lifestyle offends. The legal system does not ignore these risks: indeed it constantly guards against them. It works, however, on the basis that, in general, the training of professional judges and the judicial oath that they take mean that they can and do set their prejudices on one side when judging a case. Similarly, the law supposes that, when called upon to exercise judgment in the special circumstances of a trial, in general, jurors can and do set their prejudices aside and act impartially. The recognised starting-point is, therefore, that all the individual members of a jury are presumed to be impartial until there is proof to the contrary.
>
> (at [52])

More generally, it is now noticeable that appellate judges often articulate the view that the whole criminal justice system is 'premised on the basis that juries will be loyal to and will understand the judge's directions when difficult matters...arise as they frequently do in the course of trials' (eg, *Isichei* (2006) 1790 JP 753 at [50] *per* Auld LJ). Nevertheless, one encounters suggestions in some quarters that jurors are less qualified than judges to adjudicate certain matters and, therefore, the law of evidence should take account of this when determining which evidence is actually placed before the tribunal. One possible corollary is that exclusionary rules might be operated more loosely, even disregarded, if no jury is present. The degree to which such suggestions are justified is open to question. (See Munday, 'Case Management, Similar Fact Evidence in Civil Cases, and a Divided Law of Evidence' (2006) 10 E & P 81. Also, Schauer, 'On the Supposed Jury-Dependence of Evidence Law', 155 U Pa L Rev 165 (2006), who has concluded that 'it is hardly self-evident that the practices of so many trial judges [in the USA] in assuming that the rules of evidence are for other and lesser people is as beyond reproach and beyond remedy as is currently believed. More broadly, it is far from clear that the increasing academic and judicial momentum in favor of some form of Free Proof rests on solid empirical or conceptual foundation'.)

Regardless of where the truth lies, the student will discover that the law of evidence, as elaborated over the decades largely by the judiciary, has a strong, negative quality. Lord Phillips of Worth Matravers MR referred critically to this characteristic in *Lambert, McGrath and Brown* [2006] 2 Cr App R (S) 105, as though it were become a thing of the past:

> For a long time our criminal procedure has been encumbered, and we use that word advisedly, with a mass of jurisprudence and legislation dealing with what can and cannot be put before the jury and what should be said to the jury about the evidence put before them. Much of this is designed to assist the jury in drawing conclusions from the evidence which are essentially matters of common sense. Sometimes the relevant rules are, or were, designed to prevent the jury from seeing relevant material, or drawing logical conclusions from such material, because they could not be trusted to accord to the material no more weight than it deserved.
>
> (at [55]).

Taking up Lord Phillips' point, the hearsay rule, for instance, forbids parties from adducing evidence of a statement not made in oral evidence in the proceedings as proof of any matter stated: in the round, witness A may not testify to the facts in place of witness B. It could be said that this rule prevents unschooled jurors from being misled by unreliable tittle-tattle and gossip. The rules that restrict the introduction of evidence of an accused's bad character, again, could be portrayed as having been designed to keep from the jury evidence which, although it may be relevant and hence probative, could simply prejudice them against the accused, preventing them from judging the case solely on the evidence. It is also certain that even if the rules of evidence did not originate in judicial distrust of juries, such distrust has unquestionably played a role in English law's retention of these rules. Their purpose in criminal cases was to ensure that defendants received a fair trial. (In civil cases, too, until the last century jury trial was of course the order of the day.) However, as Lieck pointed out:

> The English law of evidence can sometimes, by its very attempt at fairness, succeed more effectually in suppressing the truth.... Our law of evidence has been built up by generations of judges distrustful of the capacity of juries, and it has ended by holding the judges themselves in fetters.
>
> (*Trial of Benjamin Knowles* (1933, Notable British Trials, pp 22–23))

Properties of the law of evidence

Whatever their origins, the rules of the law of evidence developed several unfortunate properties:

First, they became highly complex. For some, the gradual and serendipitous accretion of judicial decisions that is the common law contrasts unfavourably with the temptingly sleek lines of legislation. Indeed, for thinkers like Bentham, an obsessive devotee of codification, not only was the subject a jumble, but in addition, the rules of evidence turned the lawyer into a keeper of the mysteries, being 'at once the engines of a [lawyer's] power, and the foundation of his claim to the reputation of superior wisdom, and recondite science' (*Rationale of Judicial Evidence*, II.48). In fact, great tracts of the law of evidence have been overhauled in recent years by legislation, and most notably by the Criminal Justice Act 2003. Legislation has done little to reduce the complexity of the law of evidence. On the contrary, if Rose LJ's *cri de coeur* in *Bradley* [2005] 1 Cr App R 24 is representative, the very opposite would appear to be the case:

> It is more than a decade since the late Lord Taylor of Gosforth CJ called for a reduction in the torrent of legislation affecting criminal justice. Regrettably, that call has gone unheeded by successive governments. Indeed, the quantity of such legislation has increased and its quality has, if anything, diminished. The 2003 Act has 339 sections and 38 schedules and runs to 453 pages. It is, in pre-metric terms, an inch thick. The provisions which we have considered have been brought into force prematurely, before appropriate training could be given by the Judicial Studies Board or otherwise to approximately 2,000 Crown Court

and Supreme Court judges and 30,000 magistrates. In the meantime, the judiciary and, no doubt, the many criminal justice agencies for which this Court cannot speak, must, in the phrase familiar during the Second World War "make do and mend". That is what we have been obliged to do in the present appeal and it has been an unsatisfactory activity, wasteful of scarce resources in public money and judicial time.

(at [39])

Nor has the entry into force of this legislation always been managed especially stylishly (see, eg, *R (CPS) v City of London Magistrates' Court* [2006] EWHC 1153 (Admin) at [13] and [32] *per* Maurice Kay LJ).

Following enactment of the Criminal Justice Act 2003, one might have assumed that the Benthamite school's appetite for legislation had been temporarily sated. However, in March 2005 the Law Commission gave codification of the law of criminal evidence pride of place in its forthcoming Ninth Programme of Law Reform. The Commissioners informed us that 'the law of criminal evidence consists of a jumble of statutes and common law rules, lacking clarity and coherence. This project would seek to clarify and improve the law.' The projected codification will be led by the Home Office at a date to be appointed. It is little short of outlandish that no recognised evidence scholar's name appears in the long list of persons consulted by those responsible for assembling the Ninth Programme. Nor was the project mentioned in Sir Roger Toulson's otherwise comprehensive lecture in May 2006 on *Law Reform in the Twenty-First Century* (2006) 26 LS 321. One does just wonder how this project found its way into the programme, not least because one Law Commissioner with whom I conversed seemed decidedly unclear on its genesis. More recently, the codification project was described, hesitantly, in an undated consultation document, as a project 'not started that will be considered for priority alongside potential new projects' for the Tenth Programme, which commenced two years ago in April 2008.

One consequence of the law of evidence's growing complexity is that the Judicial Studies Board, the body responsible for training our judiciary, published a *Crown Court Bench Book* which carried specimen directions intended to assist judges to tailor suitable directions on the law to juries. The specimen directions were subject to several important failings (see Munday, *'Exemplum habemus*: Reflections on the Judicial Studies Board's Specimen Directions' [2006] J Crim Law 27.) As Lord Judge CJ acknowledged in the Foreword to the March 2010 edition, they could sometimes be 'incanted mechanistically and without any sufficient link with the case being tried' (p v). The new *Crown Court Bench Book—Directing the Jury*, which brings the materials up to date, is claimed to move away from the perceived rigidity of specimen directions towards a fresh emphasis on the responsibility of the individual judge, in an individual case, to craft directions appropriate to that case. It now provides 'thorough exposition of the summary of the relevant law, bullet-pointed ingredients for directions, some essential, most calling for a judgment as to relevance, and illustrative examples, it guides the judge in the crafting of directions, and should be a useful starting point of reference on the Bench.' Although they will no longer be updated, Lord Judge recognises that it would be 'unrealistic to attempt an instant cross-over from specimen directions to self-crafted directions.' The directions are not therefore being 'withdrawn'. Although this author was a declared foe of the specimen directions, in this book reference will occasionally be made to them when it is thought useful. The student will have to consult pre-March 2010 editions of the *Bench Book* for the relevant texts.

Secondly, in the past it was possible to say that the rules of evidence had a tendency to become too rigid, often serving to exclude evidence contrary to the plain dictates of common sense. In recent years, thanks to numerous legislative and judicial interventions, the significance of this failing has diminished. Judges do sometimes refer to the phenomenon, but more often than not in order to stress how in modern times our outlook has altered, for the better:

> On occasions, issues are raised in criminal proceedings which appear to be rooted in a belief that the criminal process of our courts is an obstacle course for the prosecution and that the defendant is a bystander at the spectacle. It has to be emphasized that the rules of evidence and procedure which have been developed in our courts are there to prevent unfairness and to further justice.
>
> *(R (Cox) v DPP* [2005] EWHC 2694 (Admin) at [10] *per* Newman J)

Interestingly, a similar sea change is visible in the courts' approach to rules of criminal procedure. In *Ashton* [2006] 2 Cr App R 15, an important decision, Fulford J noted:

> The prevailing approach to litigation is to avoid determining cases on technicalities (when they do not result in real prejudice and injustice) but instead to ensure that they are decided fairly on their merits. This approach is reflected in the Criminal Procedure Rules and, in particular, the overriding objective. . . . [A]bsent a clear indication that Parliament intended jurisdiction automatically to be removed following procedural failure, the decision of the court should be based on a wide assessment of the interests of justice, with particular focus on whether there was a real possibility that the prosecution or the defendant may suffer prejudice. If that risk is present, the court should then decide whether it is just to permit the proceedings to continue . . .
>
> (at [9])

Thirdly, a curious feature of the law of evidence is that, although in practice the jury has dramatically declined in importance, rules of evidence that evolved in the particular context of jury trial often apply with equal vigour in magistrates' courts, where there is no jury—and, increasingly often, no lay magistrates either. The jury, it should be noted, is now virtually extinct in civil cases, and attempts are regularly made to restrict its use even in criminal cases by governments anxious to be seen to be cutting costs or getting tough on crime. As Damaška has pointed out:

> ... [T]he relative marginalization of jury trials has so far failed to bite deeply into the common law orthodoxy and produce shifts in mainstream thinking about evidence; jury trials continue to be employed both as the institutional background for reflection on evidence and as a benchmark for shaping evidentiary rules.
>
> (*Evidence Law Adrift* (1997, p 128))

Fourthly, in criminal cases the rules of evidence have often come to be seen as tilting too far in favour of accused persons. The *bien-pensants* frequently argue that the balance needs to be redressed. This critique looks less convincing today. In particular, following enactment of the Criminal Justice Act 2003, it is not so easy to argue that the system is heavily tilted in favour of those accused of crime. Under the last-mentioned enactment the situations in which the prosecution may adduce evidence of a defendant's bad character have been considerably expanded and the defendant's opportunities to attack the prosecution's witnesses have considerably diminished; the constitution of the jury has been transformed—even to the extent of compelling members of the judiciary to serve as jurors; the range of cases triable without a jury has been extended to include certain fraud trials, cases where there is a danger of jury tampering, and rare cases where 'the complexity of the trial or the length of the trial (or both) is likely to make the trial so burdensome to the members of a jury hearing the trial that the interests of justice require that serious consideration should be given to the question of whether the trial should be conducted without a jury' (*Twomey et al* [2010] 1 WLR 630); the exceptions to a now re-written hearsay rule are extremely wide-ranging; acquitted defendants may be re-tried in a variety of circumstances, and so on. Even the definition of the overriding objective of the criminal trial and the need to deal with cases justly, set out in the Criminal Procedure Rules, includes a reference to 'dealing with the prosecution and the defence fairly' (Part 1.1(2)(b)): the ordering of the parties in this key provision might be counted significant.

Fifthly, for long the law of evidence was assumed by many to be largely impervious to thoroughgoing reform. Writing in the press in 1992, a former Lord Chancellor, Lord Hailsham, emphasised how resistant the English law of evidence has shown itself to fundamental re-modelling:

> [L]et nobody suppose that a serious attempt to introduce into our law of evidence a general rule in favour of common sense would be either popular or acceptable to either

> House of Parliament. . . . There are more sacred cows in our law of criminal evidence and
> procedure than would fill Smithfield market in a decade.
>
> (*The Sunday Times*, 19 January 1992)

The distinguished criminal lawyer and judge, Fitzjames Stephen, writing in the previous century, had similarly commented morosely on the English law of evidence's general resistance to change:

> It would be as impossible to get in Parliament a really satisfactory discussion of a Bill codi-
> fying the law of Evidence as to get a Committee of the whole House to paint a picture.
>
> (*A Digest of the Law of Evidence* (1874))

The welter of recent legislative reforms in the field demonstrate that such fears were misplaced.

In keeping with diminishing confidence in the merits of our system, which is evident in other contexts, and as a response to the criticisms to which the law of evidence has been subjected, a small but vociferous group of lawyers, both academics and practitioners, has sought sanctuary in the belief that in place of an adversarial procedure, where responsibility for adducing proof in the case rests predominantly with the parties, English law ought to adopt a putatively more efficient, inquisitorial model, with the court taking a more prominent role in proceedings. This line of attack has led other writers to put forward some interesting defences of common law adversarial procedure. One of the most ambitious has been Richard A Posner's attempt to apply economic analysis to the law of evidence. Although this does nothing approaching full justice to his arguments, Posner has set out to compare the relative merits and demerits of adversarial and inquisitorial trial procedures in terms of overall cost efficiency. His analysis of American evidence law, which makes extensive use of Bayes' theorem (see *post*, paras **8.46–8.48**), acknowledges that 'superficially' inquisitorial systems can appear to be more economically efficient than adversarial systems, particularly if one restricts one's attention to the process of evidence-gathering where inquisitorial systems do indeed facilitate the amassing of an optimum amount of evidence. Other *desiderata*, however, ought to be taken into consideration when assessing the respective overall efficiencies of common law and civilian systems of trial in relation not only to evidence-gathering but also to the presentation and evaluation of evidence. Notably, Posner argues, when one takes into account American law's greater public visibility and widespread use of plea-bargaining, the superior efficiency of inquisitorial systems begins to look less self-evident. Moreover, having examined a number of specific rules of evidence, many of which have close counterparts in English law, Posner concludes that American adversarial procedure does not simply sacrifice efficiency to a number of non-economic values but is actually quite efficient in itself and conceivably superior to Continental, inquisitorial systems in that respect. Although these findings, some of them highly debatable, cannot necessarily be transposed unadjusted into an English setting, Posner's writings nevertheless serve as a warning that those who decry adversarial method may be assuming too readily the correctness of the beguiling claims sometimes made on behalf of inquisitorial modes of trial—claims which are all too often made by their more uncritical exponents. (*An Economic Approach to the Law of Evidence*, 51 Stan L Rev 1477 (1999). See also Hodgson, *The Future of Adversarial Justice in 21st Century Britain*, 35 NCJ Int'l & Com Reg 319 (2010))

Recent years have witnessed a transformation in the law of evidence. In criminal cases, legislation has unquestionably tipped the scales more in favour of the prosecution. Alongside the examples already mentioned, legislation has restricted the right of silence under the controversial provisions of the Criminal Justice and Public Order Act 1994, just as it has also dramatically altered the legal system's attitude towards classes of vulnerable witnesses, such as child victims (see Criminal Justice Act 1988, as amended) and vulnerable or intimidated witnesses (Youth Justice and Criminal Evidence Act 1999 and Criminal Justice Act 2003). The courts, too, have relaxed some of the exclusionary rules in favour of the prosecution. Indeed, one occasionally detects a fresh spirit in the courts' judgments, with judges calling for the abandonment of 'ancient rules' and their replacement by a more pragmatic approach (eg, Lord Steyn in *Mills v R* [1995] 3 All ER 865). The Law Commission's reports on the hearsay rule (1997) and on bad character evidence (2001)), and Sir Robin Auld's *Review of the Criminal Courts* (2001), each played their part in stimulating the government to bring forward proposals for reconstruction of some of criminal evidence's central topics. The reforming process within the law of evidence is often portrayed as the law's lowering the barriers to truth. For long many have believed that the law of evidence is in need of this variety of 'rationalisation'.

Sixthly, little more than a passing familiarity with the law of evidence will alert us to the fact that this is an area where the Human Rights Act 1998 exerts considerable influence. It has occasionally been suggested that the general effect of the 1998 Act has been relatively minimal. In an interview in 2002, Lord Phillips of Worth Maltravers MR, speaking of leading cases in the Civil Division of the Court of Appeal, proffered the opinion that 'Looking back across the board, I don't think the Human Rights Act has made an enormous difference to their result' ('The Master of All that He Surveys', Counsel, April 2002, p 8). This may be broadly correct in civil cases. In the criminal arena, however, matters have proceeded differently. The consequences of the Act are visible in a vast number of cases. Indeed, to judge the situation simply by the extent to which the 1998 Act has led to altered results in the cases tried before the courts is to apply altogether the wrong yardstick. What counts is that the advent of the Human Rights Act has led judges and lawyers fundamentally to alter their discourse. To the extent that all lawyers have had to adjust to a new intellectual framework, it is difficult to imagine the occurrence of any greater change to the system. As Lord Woolf CJ pointed out in *R (S) v Chief Constable of South Yorkshire Police* [2003] 1 Cr App R 16 at [2], a case concerned with the retention of fingerprints and DNA samples taken from citizens who have not been convicted of criminal offences, the Human Rights Act has more obviously than before imposed on courts the role of 'holding the balance between the rights of the individual and the rights of the State.'

Even before the Act was brought into force, decisions of the European Court of Human Rights had caused English law to modify the rules governing the permissible inferences that might now be drawn from a suspect's exercise of the right of silence (see Youth Justice and Criminal Evidence Act 1999, s 58). The Convention, and more especially the presumption of innocence enshrined in Art 6, must have been a factor in the government's decision in the Terrorism Act 2000 (s 118(2)) and in the Regulation of Investigatory Powers Act 2000 (s 53(3)) to impose only an evidential rather than a legal burden of proof on defendants charged with certain offences under those statutes (see generally, Chapter 2). Prior to the enactment of Part 11 of the Criminal Justice Act 2003, there had also been broad acknowledgement that the rule against hearsay, and indeed some of its exceptions, were unlikely to pass muster under the Convention. As Lord Hope of Craighead pointed out in *R v DPP, ex p Kebilene* [2000] 2 AC 326 prior to the Act's entry into force:

> It is now plain that the incorporation of the European Convention on Human Rights into our domestic law will subject the entire legal system to a fundamental process of review and, where necessary, reform by the judiciary.
>
> (at 374–5)

Subsequently, in *Lambert* [2002] 2 AC 545 at [6] Lord Slynn put us on notice: 'It is clear that the 1998 Act must be given its full import and long or well-entrenched ideas may have to be put aside, sacred cows culled.' Later, in a brief dissenting speech in *Harrow LBC v Qazi* [2004] 1 AC 983, Lord Steyn twice referred to 'the new landscape' created by the Human Rights Act 1998 (at [27] and [32]).

How, then, is the Convention to be applied? Lord Woolf CJ outlined the manner in which courts ought to approach the Convention in *Lambert, Ali and Jordan* [2002] QB 1112. Notably, he declared:

> In [applying it] it is necessary to have in mind the nature of the Convention as an instrument for the protection of fundamental rights. This justifies the approach vividly described by Lord Wilberforce in relation to the provisions of a written constitution in *Minister of Home Affairs v Fisher* [1980] AC 319, 329. It involves giving a broad and purposive approach not a rigid approach to the language of the Convention, an approach which will make the

Convention a valuable protection of the fundamental rights of individual members of the public as well as society as a whole.

This would suggest that the instrument is open to some interpretative manipulation. Such has proven to be so in a number of evidence cases. In *Lambert* [2002] 2 AC 545 and in *A (No 2)* [2002] 1 AC 45 (see *post*, paras **2.41–2.51** and **4.76–4.81**), the House of Lords has delivered sharp reminders that the Human Rights Act did introduce an entirely novel mechanism, permitting the courts to give domestic legislation very ample constructions simply in order to maintain the legislation's compatibility with European human rights law. To this end, s 3 of the 1998 Act requires that 'so far as it is possible to do so, primary legislation... must be read and given effect in a way which is compatible with the Convention rights'. The section introduces a distinctive form of statutory interpretation, which Lord Steyn in *A (No 2)* explained as follows:

In accordance with the will of Parliament, as reflected in s 3, it will sometimes be necessary to adopt an interpretation which linguistically may appear strained. The techniques to be used will not only involve the reading down of express language in a statute but also the implication of provisions.

(at 1563)

Section 3 therefore may 'require the court to subordinate the niceties of the language of the (impugned Act)... to broader considerations'. This technique, previously alien to English judges, is one that ought rarely to be necessary. As the South African Constitutional Court warned in *State v Zuma* (1995) 4 BCLR 401, 412 *per* Kentridge JA, 'If the language used by the lawgiver is ignored in favour of a general resort to "values" the result is not interpretation but divination.' The English higher judiciary has come to appreciate the risks. Lord Steyn, who penned a number of the more ambitious human rights judgments, appeared to alter tack in his opinion in the Privy Council in *HM Advocate v R* [2003] 1 WLR 317. His Lordship began by quoting a passage from L'Heureux-Dubé J's judgment in *O'Connor* [1995] 4 SCR 411, where, speaking of the Canadian Charter of Rights and Freedoms, she had said:

It is now important to recognise that the Charter has... put into judges' hands a scalpel instead of an axe—a tool that may fashion, more carefully than ever, solutions taking into account the sometimes complementary and sometimes opposing concerns of fairness to the individual, societal interests, and the integrity of the judicial system.

(at [69])

Lord Steyn then observed, significantly, 'The moral authority of human rights in the eyes of the public must not be undermined by allowing them to run riot in our justice systems' (at [18]). The law of evidence affords a commanding vantage point from which to survey this process.

Finally, mention needs to be made of the advent of active case management, and more precisely of the fundamental procedural changes wrought by both the Civil Procedure Rules and the Criminal Procedure Rules 2005 (now 2010). Rules have been introduced in recent years, in both civil and criminal procedure, which can have the effect of restricting the volume of evidence admitted at trial. The Civil Procedure Rules, which came into force first, formally introduced the concept that every trial judge is responsible for the efficient husbanding of court resources via 'active case management'. When, on 4 April 2005, the Criminal Procedure Rules were brought into force, they too adopted this concept. Like their civil counterparts, the Criminal Procedure Rules 2010 exert significant impact on the evidence admitted in criminal trials, both in terms of quantity and even in terms of substance, through this medium of 'active case management'.

Lord Woolf CJ's original foreword to the Criminal Procedure Rules shows that they were intended to precipitate a sea-change in criminal practice:

> Most importantly of all, [the Rules] promote a culture change in criminal case management. They introduce new rules, written in plain English, that give courts explicit powers and responsibilities to manage cases actively, and to reduce the numbers of ineffective hearings that cause avoidable distress to witnesses and inconvenience and expense to everyone.

Today, these 'explicit powers and responsibilities' are considered 'of the first importance' (*R (Kelly) v Warley Magistrates' Court* [2008] 1 WLR 2001 at [4] *per* Laws LJ).

The overriding objective of criminal procedure, as stated in the Rules, includes the court's 'dealing with the case efficiently and expeditiously' (Part 1.1(2)(e)), and 'in ways that take into account...the complexity of what is in issue' (Part 1.1(2)(g) (ii)). The overriding objective applies with equal force to the conduct of trials before both Crown Court, magistrates' courts (eg, *Robinson v Abergavenny Magistrates' Court* (2007) 171 JP 683) and appellate courts (*Siddall and Brooke* [2006] EWCA Crim 1353 at [57]–[58]). All parties who are involved in any way with a criminal case must now 'conduct the case in accordance with the overriding objective' (Part 1.2(1)). Moreover, 'the court must further the overriding objective in particular when...interpreting any rule' (Part 1.3(c).). Part 3 of the Criminal Procedure Rules requires that 'the court must further the overriding objective by actively managing the case', and, after the manner of its civil counterpart, 'active case management' includes such things as 'ensuring that evidence, whether disputed or not, is presented in the shortest and clearest way; discouraging delay, dealing with as many aspects of the case as possible on the same occasion, and avoiding unnecessary hearings; [and] encouraging the participants to co-operate in the progression of the case' (Part 3.2(2)(e), (f), and (g)). 'Each party must actively assist the court in fulfilling its duty' (Part 3.3.). These Rules could quite readily be construed to confer on criminal trial judges and case management judges the power to deliver directions that restrict the volume of admissible evidence, even according to the type of tribunal before which the case is ultimately to be tried (see further Munday, 'Case Management …' *cit supra*). They certainly foster a degree of openness—where parties must be 'prepared to put their cards face up' (*Hayes* [2008] EWCA Crim 1998 at [13] *per* Toulson, LJ)—which before was largely alien to English criminal procedure.

The notion that the trial judge must retain control over the conduct of proceedings is by no means new. Its formal integration into the Rules, however, lends this judicial responsibility added force. The judge's role is now very much to ensure that attention is focused single-mindedly on what really counts; iterative and tangential evidence is to be avoided. As Pill LJ observed in *Sylvester* [2005] EWCA Crim 1794:

> The danger about letting in peripheral and collateral matters is in one thing leading to another, as happened in this case. The trial lasted four days and a great deal of material was admitted the relevance of which to the charge before the jury was at best extremely limited, even if properly admitted. There is a real danger … that the jury were distracted from the central issue in the case. If justice is to be done, trials must be kept within reasonable bounds. The central issue must not so be overlaid with consideration of peripheral matters that the judge and the jury are likely to lose sight of the central issue.
>
> (at [44])

Tuckey LJ made similar points in *Caley-Knowles* [2006] 1 WLR 3181 at [29], noting that 'robust but reasonable use of this power is the way to ensure that a trial is not side-tracked into consideration of matters which are not as a matter of law relevant to the issues which the jury has to decide.' Unmindful of the caution that case management powers are to be exercised robustly but reasonably, judges occasionally exercise them over-enthusiastically. In *FB* [2010] EWCA Crim 1857, for example, the Court of Appeal had to check a judge who, wishing to spare the public purse, made it his practice to quash indictments in cases which he did not believe ought to have been brought before the Crown Court. As Leveson LJ pointed out, '… the Rules do not either expressly or by necessary implication include a power to alter the established constitutional position. … It is not … for judges to short circuit or ignore well established principles of law in the name of efficiency' (at [29] and [34]). (See also *SH* [2010] EWCA Crim 1931 esp at [53]–[60].)

As Sir Igor Judge P pointed out in *K and others* [2006] EWCA Crim 835 at [6], a judge nevertheless enjoys considerable discretion in such matters: 'We are not prescribing any particular method of approach. Case management decisions are case specific.' They may even lead to the exclusion of otherwise admissible defence evidence.

Musone [2007] 1 WLR 2467 represents a particularly powerful application of the Criminal Procedure Rules in so far as they prevented an accused from adducing evidence in his defence. M had failed to comply with rules of court which require that notice be given whenever a defendant intends to introduce evidence of his co-accused's bad character. As a tactical ploy, M had deliberately chosen to seek to adduce evidence of a co-accused's confession very late in the day. The Court of Appeal declared that the requirements of fair trial, enshrined in art 6 of the European Convention, were met by the proper application of the Criminal Procedure Rules. By failing to give notice, as required, M had deliberately manipulated the trial process in order to ambush his co-defendant and to deprive the latter of an opportunity of dealing properly with the allegation. All of which led Moses LJ to conclude, in upholding the trial court's decision to exclude the evidence altogether:

> It is not possible to see how the overriding objective can be achieved if a court has no power to prevent a deliberate manipulation of the rules by refusing to admit evidence which it is sought to adduce in deliberate breach of those rules.
>
> (at [59])

Case management often takes pride of place in Judicial Studies Board judicial training sessions. Its consecration in the Criminal Procedure Rules 2010 will mean that the notion of what is relevant, the central tenet of a law of evidence (see *post*, Chapter 1), as well as what is fair, will need to be clearly delineated, will be at the forefront of all parties' minds, and in future will be strictly enforced in criminal as well as civil cases. (See further, HHJ Roderick Denyer QC, *Case Management in the Crown Court* (2008).)

Envoi

If one elects to write a textbook in a subject in which legal rules develop and mutate at bewildering speed, contents are bound to have a restricted shelf life. As on previous occasions, this latest edition has involved considerable re-writing of the text. Some small part of this relates to common law rules of evidence; by far the greater part, however, is necessitated by case law that would elucidate recent legislation. There is a persistent fantasy amongst law reformers that legislation simplifies the law. The short, and selfish, point I would make is that if one sets out to write on the law of evidence, then one finds oneself shooting at a rapid-moving target. In his 'prudently chaotic' but wholly ungeographic work, *Atlas* (New York: E P Dutton, 1984), Jorge Luis Borges wrote about his friend, the Argentine mystic and painter, 'Xul-Solar', who

> had...invented...a kind of complex duodecimal chess which took place on a board boasting one hundred and forty-four squares. Every time [Xul] explained it to me he would decide it was too elementary, and would proceed to enrich it with new ramifications, with the result that I never learned it.
>
> (p 80)

Borges could almost have been referring to the relationship between us, long-suffering students of the law of evidence, and successive governments that simply cannot let well alone. It might be agreeable to imagine that, following enactment and progressive implementation of the Criminal Justice Act 2003, the law of evidence would have been allowed to enjoy brief respite from the process of reform, and be granted time to consolidate. Such has not been the case. All the same, despite the panoply of new rules with which the subject is persistently enriched, the writer expresses the hope that, with this book, the reader may be enabled to learn something of the laws of the game.

Cambridge
February 2011

1

Relevance and admissibility of evidence

SUMMARY

- The respective functions of judge and jury
- The concept of relevance
  - Lifestyle evidence and drugs charges
  - Fingerprint evidence
- The so-called 'best evidence principle'
- Matters of which proof is unnecessary
  - Judicial notice
    - *Omnia mutantur, nos et mutamur in illis*
  - Formal admissions
- Judicial findings as evidence
  - Estoppel
  - Defence evidence of previous acquittals
  - Convictions of non-defendants as evidence of commission of offences: Police and Criminal Evidence Act 1984, s 74
- Prejudicial evidence, unfairly obtained evidence and suspect witnesses
  - Judicial discretion to exclude relevant evidence
  - The discretion to exclude evidence in criminal cases
    - Common law discretion
    - Police and Criminal Evidence Act 1984, s 78
    - Abuse of process and the discretion to exclude evidence
  - The discretion to exclude evidence in civil cases

- The judicial discretion in criminal cases to warn of the dangers of relying on the evidence of suspect witnesses: *Makanjuola* directions and cell confessions
- 'Cell confessions'
- Prosecutions brought after substantial delay
  - Evidence excluded as a matter of public policy
    - Intercepted communications: the Regulation of Investigatory Powers Act 2000 (RIPA)

But at the far end of the cart, with its back to him, sat a little yellow dog with a little pointed nose over which it was gazing, with an indescribably solemn and meditative expression, back along the way it had come. It was an exquisite and highly amusing little dog, worth its weight in gold; unfortunately however it is irrelevant in the present context, and we must therefore ignore it.

Thomas Mann, *The Road to the Churchyard* (1900)

1.1 The law of evidence is concerned to regulate what evidence may be admitted at trial, and under what conditions such admissible proofs are to be admitted. Before it can be admitted, evidence has to clear two hurdles. The foundational requirement is that evidence can only be admitted if it is relevant. From the outset, it is therefore necessary to have an understanding of what the law means by 'relevant'. However, even if legally relevant, the admission of evidence at trial may still be problematic. In the first place, relevant evidence may be excluded altogether because it falls foul of one of English law's exclusionary rules of evidence. These exclusionary rules— which notably include the hearsay rule, the opinion rule and the rules concerning the accused's bad character—will be considered separately in later chapters. At this stage it can be pointed out that some rules of evidence apply to both civil and criminal cases with equal force; some apply exclusively in criminal proceedings; and others again, like the hearsay rule, apply more rigorously in criminal cases than in civil proceedings—and even now operate under different notions of what actually constitutes hearsay. In addition to the settled exclusionary rules, predominantly in criminal cases the courts also enjoy discretion to exclude technically admissible evidence in a variety of circumstances (see *post*, paras **1.47–1.54**). However, even if evidence is technically admissible, having cleared all these hurdles, particularly in criminal cases its admission may be subject to a requirement that the court issues a particular form of direction, either restricting or affording guidance on the way in which the evidence is to be employed. As we shall see below, such directions may be demanded for instance in cases where prosecutions are brought after substantial delay or where the Crown relies upon the testimony of a witness whose evidence, for some reason, is considered to be of suspect quality (see *post*, paras **1.64–1.71**). Further examples of such mandatory directions occur throughout this book.

The respective functions of judge and jury

1.2 The English mode of trial has evolved from trial by jury. This fact has served to shape many aspects of procedure. In particular, it has necessitated a division of functions between judge and jury. Basically, matters of law fall within the province of the judge and matters of fact are the exclusive preserve of the jury. Thus, the judge is responsible for determining questions of admissibility of evidence. In cases that are being tried with a jury, the judge determines these questions in the absence of the jurors. Obviously, if there is a possibility that the judge will exclude a contested item of evidence, it is preferable that the jury should not even be aware of its existence. While matters of admissibility are the judge's concern, the jury—or tribunal of fact, as it is often known—has the task of evaluating the weight of the admissible evidence and of deciding whether or not the party who bears the burden of proving its case has actually done so. Although the majority of criminal and civil cases today are heard without juries, this historical division of labour between judge and jury has still left its mark on the English form of trial.

1.3 The law/fact dichotomy is not always easy to operate. On the one hand, some matters of law are treated as though they were matters of fact. Thus, English law traditionally treats rules of foreign law not as questions of law for the judge but as matters of fact on which evidence must be called. Indeed, it was only in 1920 that in jury cases the task of determining questions of foreign law was taken from the jury by the Administration of Justice Act, s 15. These matters are now decided by judge alone, after hearing evidence. The rule regarding proof of foreign law does not admit of exceptions. Thus, in *Okolie* (2000) Times, 16 June a handling conviction was quashed because the trial judge had accepted, without proof, that the four luxury cars in the case were stolen goods in terms of German law. As Henry LJ made clear, 'Foreign law must be proved strictly. It should be proved... by calling a properly qualified expert in that law, who will give evidence himself unless his testimony is agreed or no issue is taken.... foreign law cannot be the subject of judicial notice' (at [11]). A similar procedure, it might be noted, applies to questions affecting the meaning or effect of Community Treaties under the European Communities Act 1972, s 3(1). On the other hand, judges sitting with or without juries are sometimes required to entertain questions of fact when determining the admissibility of evidence. One example will perhaps suffice. If the admissibility of an accused's confession is contested under s 76 of the Police and Criminal Evidence Act 1984 (PACE) (see *post*, Chapter 10), before admitting the confession in evidence the judge must conduct a trial within a trial (also known as a *voire dire*). The trial within a trial is conducted in the absence of the jury. After hearing the evidence presented by the prosecution and by the defence, the judge will be required to deliver a ruling on the mixed question of law and fact as to whether the Crown has established beyond reasonable doubt that the confession was not obtained in ways that infringe s 76. This proceeding occasionally can make for a complex division of functions. As the opinion in the Privy Council case of *Timothy v R* [2000] 1 WLR 485 makes clear, if a defendant claims *both* that he did not make a particular confession to the police *and* that he was ill-treated by the police, two issues are raised: the first, a question of fact, and the second, a mixed question of law and fact. In such a case, the judge must initially resolve, in the absence of the jury, whether or not the confession was extracted from the defendant by unlawful means. If it cannot be shown that the confession was not obtained unlawfully, the confession must not be admitted. If it passes this test, the confession is admitted and it is then left to the jury to resolve the further question of pure fact, whether or not the confession was actually made at all (see *post*, Chapter 10).

1.4 A judge can exert control over the jury in a number of ways. Most dramatically, the judge may form the view that there is insufficient proof of a particular matter to justify leaving a question to the jury. Hence, in the nineteenth-century civil case of *Metropolitan Railway Co v Jackson* (1877) 3 App Cas 193 the House of Lords held that the trial judge ought not to have left a question of negligence to the jury at all since it could see no evidence to support the contention that the claimant's injuries were ascribable to the defendant's fault. This procedure still obtains when civil claims are tried by judge and jury. The vast majority of civil cases today, however, are tried by judge alone. In these cases, a party may submit that he has no case to answer, but the judge may only deliver a ruling on the submission if the party making it elects not to call evidence. In criminal cases, although a judge may remove a case from the jury of his own motion, it is more usual for the defendant to submit at the close of the prosecution case that there is no case to answer. Under the test laid down by the Court of Appeal in *Galbraith* [1981] 2 All ER 1060, if the judge feels that, taking the evidence adduced by the prosecution at its highest, a properly directed jury could not reasonably convict, the judge must withdraw the case from the jury (see *post*, para **2.27**).

1.5 Removing a case from the jury is an extreme measure, only applicable in situations where the prosecution's or a claimant's case is seriously deficient. A more subtle pressure is exerted on the jury by the rules of evidence, which variously exclude certain categories of evidence from the jury's consideration altogether or seek to restrict the use that the jury makes of it. Subtler still is the summing-up, which the judge delivers to the jury at the close of the case, immediately before the jurors retire to deliberate on their verdict. The summing-up is an event of great importance, as the Court of Appeal is apt sometimes to scrutinise what a judge has said to the jury with considerable particularity. Owing to the increasing complexity of the directions judges are required to deliver to juries, the Judicial Studies Board, the body responsible for the training of English judges, at one time issued a set of 'specimen directions', which was updated from time to time, setting out recommended forms of jury directions (see now *Crown Court Bench Book: Directing the Jury* (March 2010) <http://www.judiciary.gov.uk/).

1.6 Some of the directions judges are called upon to deliver—such as the direction on joint enterprise in criminal law—concern such complex areas of law that the modern approach is for judges to record their oral directions on the law in writing and, before they retire, to present those written directions to the jury. In one case, whilst upholding the convictions, the Court of Appeal made clear that the fact that the judge had directed the jury orally, at a slow dictation speed, which would have given the jury an opportunity to make full notes, was not a satisfactory alternative to presenting jurors with a text: *Small* [2006] EWCA Crim 495. Judicial attempts meaningfully to assist jurors can be carried even further than mere written directions, whether or not amplified by further oral directions in the summing-up. Take *Fury* [2006] EWCA Crim 1258, a case of affray and murder involving multiple defendants, which gave rise to knotty issues of joint enterprise and manslaughter. In this particular case Hooper LJ felt that even written directions were inadequate to the task:

> In our respectful view the jury would have been much assisted by a question and answer flowchart personalised for each defendant. This is often referred to in the criminal courts as 'The Steps to Verdict'. The jury could then have used the appropriate flowchart/Steps to Verdict when considering each defendant's case. Rather than applying the general principles of primary and secondary liability, the jury would simply have had a series of questions to answer, questions which would have incorporated the relevant principles.
>
> (at [24])

In a recent study, published by the Ministry of Justice, the author argued that her study showed that jurors greatly benefit from written instructions and that the judiciary should reconsider implementing Sir Robin Auld's recommendation for issuing jurors with written *aide-mémoires* on the law in all cases (Thomas, *Are Juries Fair?* (February 2010) pp 38–9.)

1.7 Rose LJ explained what a trial judge is required to do in his summing-up in *Curtin* [1996] Crim LR 831:

> It is a judge's duty, in summing up to a jury, to give directions about the relevant law, to refer to the salient pieces of evidence, to identify and focus attention upon the issues, and in each of those respects to do so as succinctly as the case permits. It follows that as part of this duty the judge must identify the defence.

The judge is therefore required to put to the jury the respective contentions that have been presented in a fair and balanced manner. Strong expressions of personal opinion are now discouraged (*Culpepper v Trinidad and Tobago* (2000) 20 December, PC Appeal no 68 of 1999 *per* Lord Bingham of Cornhill), although a judge is not forbidden to comment, even quite robustly, upon the evidence, if such comment is truly justified. In the words of Lord Clyde, it is the judge's responsibility:

> . . . to place before the jury all the possible conclusions which may be open to them on the evidence which has been presented in the trial whether or not they have all been canvassed by either of the parties in their submissions. It is the duty of the judge to secure that the overall interests of justice are served in the resolution of the matter and that the jury is enabled to reach a sound conclusion on the facts in light of a complete understanding of the law applicable to them.
>
> (*Von Starck v R* [2000] 1 WLR 1270, 1275)

Should a judge deliver an unfair or unbalanced summing-up, the Court of Appeal may quash the conviction on the ground that it is 'unsafe' within the terms of the Criminal Appeal Act 1968, s 2(1) (eg, *Winn-Pope* [1996] Crim LR 521).

The concept of relevance

1.8 The concept of relevance is deceptively simple. 'Relevance' simply refers to any item of proof that renders more probable or less probable the existence of a fact in issue in the case. The great Victorian jurist and judge, James Fitzjames Stephen, whose formulation won Lord Oliver's approbation in *Kearley* [1992] 2 AC 228, 263, explained relevance in the following terms:

> Any two facts to which it is applied are so related to each other that according to the common course of events one either taken by itself or in connection with other facts proves or renders probable the past, present, or future existence or non-existence of the other.
>
> (*Digest of the Law of Evidence* (1936) 12th edn, p 3)

In broadly similar vein, Lord Simon of Glaisdale in *DPP v Kilbourne* [1973] AC 729 declared, 'Evidence is relevant if it is logically probative or disprobative of some matter which requires proof'. Significantly, his Lordship added:

> I do not pause to analyse what is involved in "logical probativeness", except to note that the term does not of itself express the element of experience which is so significant of its operation in law, and possibly elsewhere.

Lord Steyn possibly expressed the matter in a more practical way in *Randall* [2004] 1 WLR 56 when he stated:

> A judge ruling on a point of admissibility involving an issue of relevance has to decide whether the evidence is capable of increasing or diminishing the probability of the exist-ence of a fact in issue. The question of relevance is typically a matter of degree to be determined, for the most part, by common sense and experience.
> (at [20])

1.9 Relevance is by no means an exact science. Take *Wilson* [2008] EWCA Crim 1754, [2009] Crim LR 193, for example. W was charged with seven counts of robbery and one of unlawful wounding. W, who denied these offences, had been apprehended by the police in possession of a kitchen knife and a telephone, and at his home property was found belonging to three of the complainants. At trial, evidence was given by a witness responsible for monitoring crime in Islington, who testified that she had performed various computer searches in her database and had concluded that between the date of the last offence (W was arrested just three days later) and May 31, 2007 (approximately, the date of W's trial) no similar offences had been committed in the Islington area. Was this evidence sufficiently relevant? Did it contribute meaning-fully to showing that W was the culprit? Alternatively, in the words of the defence, was the evidence irrelevant being too 'nebulous and prejudicial' (at [7])? Whilst the Court of Appeal adjudged that this information could have been 'helpful if the jury were speculating as to whether robberies might have continued after [W's] arrest' (at [9]) and upheld the trial judge's ruling, one can see that the absence of similar crimes committed by a young, lone, white male robber wearing a mask and carrying a knife could be attributable to several causes—the perpetrator might have been hospitalised, detained or imprisoned on other charges or died, victims might not have reported sub-sequent offences, or indeed the true culprit might have diverted to nearby Hornsey as the appellant tried vainly to show (at [12]). No calibrated scale exists telling courts at what exact point the utility of a piece of evidence becomes too speculative to justify its admission. Experience and common sense may provide the key.

1.10 Experience does indeed play an important role in differentiating what is from what is not evidentially relevant. Nevertheless, from time to time the courts also attempt to provide guidance on what sort of evidence is to be treated as relevant and admissible in particular contexts. These decisions underline the difficulty encountered whenever one tries to pin down exactly what is meant by 'relevant' evidence. Two examples will perhaps suffice: the admission of evidence relating to a defendant's general lifestyle in prosecutions for drugs offences and the Court of Appeal guidelines setting out the criteria that fingerprint evidence must satisfy in order to be admitted.

Lifestyle evidence and drugs charges

1.11 A veritable blizzard of decisions has considered the admissibility of cash and lifestyle evidence in criminal cases where the defendant is charged with possession of drugs, with or without intent to supply. Indeed, so vexed did this particular question become that the Judicial Studies Board took the step of issuing a specimen direction to assist judges when directing juries on how to use such evidence. *Guney* [1998] 2 Cr App R 242 is an instructive authority on this topic. G was charged with possession of almost five kilos of heroin with intent to supply. Although G maintained that the drugs were not his and had been planted, one question which the Court of Appeal addressed was the relevance, and hence the admissibility, of G's having also been found in possession of a substantial sum of cash. £24,815 had in fact been found by the police under some towels in the selfsame wardrobe in G's bedroom in which they had also found the drugs and a firearm. Substantial holdings of cash tend to go hand-in-hand with drug dealing, as do unexplained trappings of wealth. Two points, however, need to be considered.

- *First*, there may be other plausible explanations for both possession of substantial amounts of cash and for high living. Thus, the relevance of lifestyle evidence may be questionable.

- *Secondly*, evidence that a defendant is in possession of money that may be the proceeds of previous drug dealing could be prejudicial because it tends to show the commission of other offences not charged in the current proceedings.

1.12 In *Guney* the Court of Appeal noted that previous case law drew a broad distinction between two types of drug charge. On the one hand, where a defendant is charged with simple possession, or where the only issue in the case is whether he possessed the drugs, it is most unlikely that cash and lifestyle evidence will be relevant. While it cannot be said that such evidence will never be relevant, it is most improbable that one could deduce from the circumstance that an accused possesses a substantial bundle of money that he must therefore have possessed drugs. In the words of Judge LJ:

> Evidence of possession of cash will often lack any probative value. The defendant's pos-
> session of a large sum of cash, or enjoyment of a wealthy lifestyle, does not, on its own,
> prove anything very much, and certainly not possession of drugs.
>
> (p 266)

In contrast, this species of circumstantial evidence is more likely to be relevant in cases where the issue is whether the defendant had *intent* to supply. Here Judge LJ considered,

> There are numerous sets of circumstances in which cash and lifestyle evidence may be
> relevant and admissible to the issue of possession itself, not least to the issue of know-
> ledge as an ingredient of possession.
>
> (p 267)

However, as *Guney* itself shows, it is dangerous artificially to separate these two issues: in all cases 'the question whether evidence is relevant depends not on abstract legal theory but on the individual circumstances of each particular case'. In *Guney*, G claimed not to know about the drugs and the gun, which, he asserted, had been planted in the wardrobe by his enemies. Realistically, there could be no issue so far as intent to supply was concerned. Defence counsel conceded that, in view of the large quantity of heroin discovered, if G was found to have possessed the drug, then it would have to be assumed that G had possessed it with intent to supply. G, how-ever, denied possession. As Judge LJ pointed out, the fact that a large sum of cash, ill-concealed like the drugs and the gun, was found in the same place 'was . . . rele-vant to how the drugs and the firearms both remained undiscovered when the cash was placed in the wardrobe on the evening before the arrest'. The coincidence that G's cash was physically close to firearms and drugs, which, G claimed, belonged to someone else, was obviously a relevant factor for the jury to take into account in deciding whether G knowingly had possession of the drugs. Thus, in this case, most unusually, the possession of a large sum of money was found to be relevant to the issue of whether G consciously had possession of the drugs. (Significantly, G's conviction has since been quashed, following a reference from the Criminal Cases Review Commission: 'The reasons for that conclusion are set out . . . in . . . a sensitive document which has been made available to the court, but not to counsel acting on behalf of [G]': [2003] EWCA Crim 1502 *per* Kennedy LJ. For more on G's rocam-bolesque brushes with the law, see <http://erkinguney.com/>.)

1.13 Regarding the potential prejudice admission of lifestyle evidence can arouse, it has been argued that if the Crown reveals that the accused possesses a lot of cash this may constitute evidence of criminal propensity which could induce the jury to infer from the fact that D has dealt in drugs in the past and that he currently possesses drugs with intent to supply. In principle, evidence suggestive of other misconduct by an accused—indicating a propensity to deal in drugs—is only admissible if it satisfies rules laid down in the Criminal Justice Act 2003 (see *post*, Chapter 7). The courts do not always overcome this objection convincingly. They have sometimes argued that because this form of evidence was admissible prior to the advent of the 2003 Act (eg, *Morris* [1992] 2 Cr App R 69) and 'the distinction between treating [other misconduct] (a) as evidence that [D] is a drug dealer, or (b) as evidence that [D] has dealt in drugs and has a propensity to do so, is fine', it would be 'highly artificial' to treat lifestyle evidence as evidence of bad character under the 2003 Act (*Graham* [2007] EWCA Crim 1499; *Green* [2009] EWCA Crim 1688). In contrast, Judge LJ, in *Guney*, signalled that provided that the evidence indicative of previous drug-dealing was admissible under other misconduct evidence principles, the prejudice generated would not entail the exclusion of the lifestyle evidence. The latter, it is suggested, is the more orthodox response. To summarise, the following propositions, accepted by Clarke LJ in *Wright* [2004] EWCA Crim 1546 at [24], succinctly encapsulate the relevant principles:

1. Evidence of cash/lifestyle is only admissible in case of drug trafficking in order to prove an issue in the case, ie possession or intent to supply (*Gordon* [1995] 2 Cr App Rep 61);

2. Such evidence will frequently lack probative value in proving possession (*Guney*);

3. To be admissible to prove an intention to supply the evidence has to be relevant, meaning that it must be logically probative of that intention (*Gordon*);

4. The judge must direct the jury as to the precise relevance and probative force of such evidence (*Gordon*); and

5. Evidence that may lead a jury to conclude that the defendant has been or has propensity to be a drug dealer and that he is therefore more likely to be guilty of the instant offence is objectionable and involves an inadmissible chain of reasoning (*Guney*), unless it satisfies the rules governing the admission of evidence of bad character (see *post*, Chapter 7).

Fingerprint evidence

1.14 Even in the realm of scientific evidence one finds the courts wrestling with the question, at what point on the scale does circumstantial evidence purportedly identifying the defendant as the culprit become sufficiently relevant to be admitted? Fingerprint evidence provides a case in point. Following a series of cases in which the Court of Appeal appeared to have operated different criteria of admissibility, Rose LJ comprehensively reviewed this important species of evidence in *Buckley* (1999) 163 JP 561. The central question is: given that at present there exists no agreed criterion other than the numerical test, how many ridge characteristics must coincide between the accused's print and that found at the scene of crime to justify the admission of this form of evidence and for the fingerprint expert to be allowed to testify that, in his opinion, the scene-of-crime print belongs to the accused? At one time, a minimum of 16 similarities was required. Although it made their opinions unassailable, experts for long felt that this number was too high, not least thanks to the discovery that Alphonse Bertillon's samples, upon which the number 16 was in part based, were forgeries. In more recent times courts behaved inconsistently, sometimes admitting prints with as few as eight similar characteristics. In *Buckley*, therefore, Rose LJ proffered general guidance. Looking to best practice for inspiration, his Lordship suggested:

- If there are fewer than eight similar ridge characteristics, it would be most exceptional for a judge to admit fingerprint evidence.
- If there are eight or more, exercise of the judge's discretion to admit such evidence will depend on all the circumstances of the case. These should include:
  - the witness's experience and expertise;
  - the number of similar ridge characteristics;
  - the size of the print relied upon, bearing in mind that the smaller the fragment, the more significant the number of characteristics will be; and
  - the quality and clarity of the print, taking into account such factors as smearing and contamination.

Although the Court has set out guidelines, on close examination it can be seen that, as in the case of lifestyle evidence, inevitably a lot is left to judicial appreciation. In the case of fingerprint evidence, the judge is left to assess what is the appropriate minimum requirement in the circumstances of each individual case. Relevance, then, is by no means a cut-and-dried concept. Nor, it should be added, is fingerprint evidence infallible. It is only as good as the experts who interpret it. In February 2006, without admitting liability for negligence or malicious prosecution, the Scottish Executive entered into an out-of-court settlement with Shirley McKie, a former Strathclyde police officer who, in 1999, had been unsuccessfully prosecuted for perjury for truthfully asserting that a fingerprint, found at a murder scene in 1997—and identified as hers by the Scottish Criminal Records Office in its finest hour, belonged to someone else.

The so-called 'best evidence principle'

1.15　In addition to being relevant, it used sometimes to be claimed that evidence can only be admitted by a court if it is 'the best that the nature of the case will permit' (*Omychund v Barker* (1745) 1 Atk 21, 49 *per* Lord Hardwicke). Although a number of older authorities do make reference to a best evidence principle, as Jonathan Parker LJ observed in *Springsteen v Masquerade Music Ltd* [2001] EMLR 654 at [64], 'even in its heyday, the best evidence rule was not an absolute rule'. In the twentieth century its influence waned perceptibly. In *Garton v Hunter* [1969] 2 QB 37 at 44, for instance, Lord Denning MR dismissed the principle almost out of hand with the words, 'That old rule has gone by the board long ago...Nowadays we do not confine ourselves to the best evidence', while in *R v Pentonville Prison, ex p Osman* [1990] 1 WLR 277 the Divisional Court declared itself 'more than happy to say goodbye to the...rule', noting that 'the little loved best evidence rule has been dying for some time'. Ackner LJ, it should be said, in *Kajala v Noble* (1982) 75 Cr App R 149, 152 had claimed that one vestige of the rule survived:

> The old rule, that a party must produce the best evidence that the nature of the case will allow, and that any less good evidence is to be excluded, has gone by the board long ago. The only remaining instance of it is that, if the original document is available in one's hands, one must produce it.

In *Springsteen v Masquerade Music Ltd*, however, the Court of Appeal extinguished even this final flicker of the rule:

> The authorities...establish that by the mid-nineteenth century, if not earlier, the so-called "best evidence rule" was recognized by the courts as no more than a rule of practice to the effect that the court would attach no weight to secondary evidence of the contents of a document unless the party seeking to adduce such evidence had first accounted to the satisfaction of the court for the non-production of the document itself....For my part, I would not even recognize the continuing existence of that "remaining instance" of the application of "the old rule".
>
> ([2001] EMLR 654 at [76] and [79]. See also *post*, para **13.8**)

This judgment seems finally to have dispelled any lingering notion that it is a condition of admissibility that evidence proffered must be the best that the nature of the case will admit. Nevertheless, judges continue to employ the expression 'best evidence' from time to time, if only to signify that there may have existed more immediate or compelling means of establishing a particular fact than the evidence actually adduced (eg, *JF* [2002] EWCA Crim 2936 at [32] *per* Bell J). It was perhaps in this sense that, in *Okolie* (2000) Times, 16 June, Henry LJ speculated that the present-day rule that foreign law must be proven by evidence (see *ante*, para **1.3**) is 'due no doubt to the development of the law through the best evidence rule' (at [6]). Generally, speaking, however, the position is well expressed in a recent dictum of a Scots judge, who declared, 'the "best evidence rule" is not a general exclusionary rule of evidence but a counsel of prudence' (*Haddow v Glasgow City Council*, 2005 SLT 1219 at [14] *per* Lord Macphail).

Matters of which proof is unnecessary

1.16 Although courts will not normally find a matter proven in the absence of positive evidence, in some situations they do dispense with the need for evidence. Some facts are considered so self-evident that it would be pointless to insist upon the adduction of evidence and, thus, judicial notice is taken of them. Alternatively, it is open to parties in both civil and criminal cases to make formal admissions which, again, absolve the opposing side from the duty of adducing evidence in support of whatever fact or facts have been conceded in the formal admission.

Judicial notice

1.17 To the delight of the press, the judiciary sometimes displays a baffling unworld-liness. Harman J once famously asked, 'Who is Gazza?', while Popplewell J required instruction in the significance of 'Linford Christie's lunchbox'. A magistrate, trying a case of ticket touting in 2000, requested positive evidence that Arsenal is a pre-mier league football club, remarking that he always discarded the sports section of the newspaper. According to *The Daily Mirror* (16 April 1975), when trying a case arising out of the cancellation of a Frank Zappa concert in the Albert Hall, Mocatta J had to be enlightened on the meanings of the expressions 'groupies' and 'underground rock band', and a judge at St Albans, puzzled by the concept of a sofa bed, asked: 'How can a bed be turned into a sofa?' (*The Times*, 13 December 2005) A judge at Carlisle Crown Court in 1999, however, took the biscuit, affecting total ignorance of those icons of our national culture, the Bafta-winning Teletubbies. Judicial notice, thankfully, is concerned with the opposite end of the spectrum. It allows the court to employ its general knowledge of the world. As Coleridge J said in *Lumley v Gye* (1853) 2 E & B 216, 267:

> Judges are not necessarily to be ignorant in court of what everybody else, and they themselves out of court, are familiar with; nor was that unreal ignorance considered to be an attribute of the bench in early and strict times. We find in the Year Books the judges reasoning about the ability of knights, esquires, and gentlemen to maintain themselves

without wages; distinguishing between private chaplains and parochial chaplains from the nature of their employments; and in later days we have ventured to take judicial cognisance of the moral qualities of Robinson Crusoe's Man Friday.

Buxton LJ was therefore confident that a court was entitled judicially to notice that 'when corporal punishment was in general use in English schools, direct involvement of the parents was not the general practice' (*R (Williamson) v Secretary of State for Education and Employment* [2003] 3 WLR 482, 490). In like vein, in *Morris v KLM Royal Dutch Airlines* [2001] 3 WLR 351, 359, a case in which a 15-year-old girl, travelling unaccompanied, sought compensation for 'bodily injury' suffered when she was groped by another passenger on a flight from Kuala Lumpur to Amsterdam, Lord Phillips MR declared:

> Judges do not travel exclusively in first-class seats and can take judicial notice of the fact that those who travel in economy have to accept relatively cramped conditions which bring them into close proximity with their neighbours.
>
> (at [29])

Similarly resorting to his personal experience, Rimer J explained why he was rejecting a witness's evidence, saying, 'I propose to take judicial notice, based on my own experience of wheelchair users, of the fact that the occupation of a wheelchair provides no obstacle to writing' (*Reynolds v Reynolds* [2005] EWHC 6 (Ch) at [122]).

1.18 The doctrine of judicial notice allows the court to dispense with the need to prove notorious facts. Some facts are simply so well known that it would be both wasteful of court time and bring the law into ridicule were parties put to proof of them. A party does not therefore have to prove that rain falls (*Fay v Prentice* (1845) 14 LJCP 298); that cats are kept for domestic purposes (*Nye v Niblett* [1918] 1 KB 23) or that a goldfinch is a British bird (*Hughes v DPP* (2003) 167 JP 589); that steamrollers and traction engines are made mainly of iron and steel (*McKenna* (1956) 40 Cr App R 65); that it costs more to eat in London than in the provinces (*Drummond v Wace Morgan* (21 December 1992, unreported, QBD); that Elvis Presley 'must be counted amongst the most well known, popular musicians this century' (*Re Elvis Presley Trade Marks* [1997] RPC 543 *per* Laddie J); that butterfly knives are offensive weapons made or adapted for use for causing injury (*DPP v Hynde* [1998] 1 All ER 649); that Thailand and Jamaica are areas of drug dealing and supply (*R v Crown Court at Isleworth, ex p Marland* (1997) 162 JP 251) and that 'Amsterdam, unfortunately, has an international reputation as a centre for drug trafficking. It is a well-established, if sad, fact and needs no evidence to prove it' (*Butt v Customs and Excise Comrs* (2002) 166 JP 173 at [33]); that the postal system is not infallible (*Sloan Electronics Ltd v Customs and Excise Comrs* (7 May 1999, unreported)); that 'banks do not do anything for nothing'

(*IRC v Mallender* [2001] STC 514); that 'by mid-1996 the style of restaurants in London had greatly changed' and, sadly, 'the era of minimalist decorations and almost minimalist cuisine had begun' (*Campbell v Crabtree* [2001] All ER (D) 81 (Jul), case no C2890/00 at [138] *per* Patten J); or that the secondhand car market follows a seasonal pattern (*Poole v Smith's Car Sales (Balham) Ltd* [1962] 2 All ER 482). Although a dyed-in-the-wool Cambridge man might prefer to reserve his position, Coleridge J even judicially noticed that Oxford University was 'a national institution created for a great national purpose, the advancement, namely, of religion and learning through the nation' (*The Case of the Oxford Poor Rate* (1857) 8 E & B 184). The facts judicially noticed may sometimes assume some complexity. In *R v Z (Att Gen for N I's Reference)* [2005] 2 AC 645 at [13] Lord Bingham of Cornhill reported:

> The Court of Appeal took judicial notice of certain facts which [counsel] for the acquitted person, did not challenge as inaccurate. (1) Until 1969 an organisation calling itself the IRA existed as a cohesive unit dedicated to unification of the 32 counties of Ireland, to which end it resorted to occasional violence . . . (2) In about 1969 a major split occurred in the ranks of the IRA. Some members, claiming to be the true inheritors of the mantle of the IRA, in effect declared a ceasefire in 1972. They became known as the Official IRA. Other members (becoming known as the Provisional IRA) continued to assert their right and intention to use violence for the purpose of achieving unification. The two organisations existed independently of each other thereafter . . . (3) In 1994 and again in 1997 the Provisional IRA declared a ceasefire. Dissident groups within the Provisional IRA opposed these moves, and in late 1997 one group (calling itself the Real IRA) dissociated itself from the leadership of the Provisional IRA and declared that the ceasefire was over . . . (4) The Real IRA claimed responsibility for a number of acts of violence, most notably the bombing of Omagh in August 1998 . . . (5) When the 2000 Act was passed, Parliament was well aware of the existence and activities of the Real IRA . . .

1.19 What is notorious, however, will vary over time. It is improbable in the extreme that a court today could assume that a jury in a libel case would be so familiar with Aesop's fables as to appreciate the sting of a reference to a 'frozen snake' (cf *Hoare v Silverlock* (1848) 12 QB 624, the moral of Aesop's tale being that the greatest kindness will not bind the ungrateful). Similarly, one might question whether Slesser LJ's views in the libel case *Youssoupoff v MGM Pictures Ltd* (1934) 50 TLR 581, 587 would hold true today, namely:

> One may, I think, take judicial notice of the fact that a lady of whom it has been said that she has been ravished, albeit against her will, has suffered in social reputation and in opportunities of receiving respectable consideration from the world.

Omnia mutantur, nos et mutamur in illis

1.20 The courts sometimes use the concept of judicial notice more speculatively. Thus, in *Home Office v Dorset Yacht Co Ltd* [1970] AC 1004 Lord Diplock said:

> It is common knowledge, of which judicial notice may be taken, that borstal training fails to achieve its purpose of reformation, and that trainees when they have ceased to be detained in custody revert to crime and commit tortious damage to the person and property of others.

Meanwhile, in *Burns v Edman* [1970] 2 QB 541 the court took notice that the life of a criminal is not a happy one, whilst the Court of Appeal in *Yap Chuan Ching* (1976) 63 Cr App Rep 7 judicially noticed that most jurors are generally familiar with televised re-constructions of trials and know something of the burden and standard of proof before they go into the jury box. Not everyone would instinctively consider these to be propositions beyond dispute.

1.21 Possibly reflecting Scrutton LJ's complaint that 'it is difficult to know what judges are allowed to know, though they are ridiculed if they pretend not to know' (*Tolley v JS Fry & Sons Ltd* [1930] 1 KB 467, 475), the courts are often cautious to treat comparatively well-known facts as proven in the absence of evidence. In *Westminster City Council v Croyalgrange Ltd* [1986] 2 All ER 353, for instance, Lord Bridge doubted whether he could take judicial notice that typical sex establishments are managed by front men while the parties really running these businesses remain concealed, and in *Miliangos v George Frank (Textiles) Ltd (No 2)* [1976] 3 All ER 599, 603 Bristow J declined to take judicial notice of the cost of borrowing Swiss francs in Zurich. In *North Yorkshire County Council v Laws* (1996) 2 February, unreported, the Employment Appeal Tribunal refused judicially to notice that teachers 'do in fact do actual work during the summer holiday'. More extraordinarily, in *Rackstraw v Douglas* 1917 SC 284 a Scots court even refused to take judicial notice of the fact that women of 81 and 78 were past childbearing. The courts may be right to display caution. Occasionally, they have been over-eager to employ judicial notice. In *McQuaker v Goddard* [1940] 1 KB 687, for example, the court accepted that camels are domestic animals, a fact which was anything but beyond dispute. Yet, even if the ruling in *McQuaker v Goddard* may be questionable, the Court of Appeal's approval of a passage from Stephen's *Digest of the Law of Evidence* setting out the procedure the court follows when judicially noticing a notorious fact is important:

> No evidence of any fact of which the court will take judicial notice need be given by the party alleging its existence; but the judge, upon being called upon to take judicial notice thereof, may, if he is unacquainted with such fact, refer to any person or any document or book of reference for his satisfaction in relation thereto, or may refuse to take judicial

notice thereof unless and until the party calling upon him to take such notice produces any such document or book of reference.

1.22 Although the doctrine of judicial notice undoubtedly sounds in common sense, not every commonsensical conclusion is to be treated as the application of judicial notice. Hence, in *Police v Kristnamah* (1993) 12 July, Privy Council Appeal No 55 of 1992, where K appealed against a drugs conviction arguing that his 180-line 'confession' could not possibly have been taken down 'in a painstaking handwriting' and read over to him in 50 minutes, as the police claimed, Lord Slynn said that 'this is not a matter...of judicial notice in a formal sense. It was a matter of common sense which the court was not required to abandon when deciding on credibility.'

1.23 Courts can be said judicially to notice a number of other matters after inquiry. Thus, when so informed by the Secretary of State, a court is duty-bound to accept the Secretary's statement regarding the sovereignty of a foreign state (*Duff Development Co v Government of Kelantan* [1924] AC 797). If they have been regularly recognised in the past in judicial decisions, there comes a point at which the courts can judicially notice the existence of particular customs. And when it comes to the meaning of words, courts regularly refer to dictionaries to elucidate what is meant, just as recourse is also had to standard works of history and so on in order that the court inform itself about facts of a public nature. *McQuaker v Goddard* (*ante*, para **1.21**) was such a case, where the trial judge informed himself by means of both books and witnesses in order to determine whether camels are tame or wild animals. Here, judicial notice served in lieu of evidence because, as the Court of Appeal put it, the judge was entitled to take judicial notice having 'form(ed) his view as to what the ordinary course of nature in this regard in fact is, a matter of which he is supposed to have complete knowledge.' Similarly, the judge in *United Biscuits (UK) Ltd v Asda Stores Ltd* [1997] RPC 513, a case in which the claimant, who manufactured 'Penguin' biscuits, sought to prevent the defendant from marketing a rival 'Puffin' biscuit, displayed a prodigious knowledge of the *spheniscidae* family and *fratercula arctia*, thanks to an assortment of reference books, which enabled the court to take 'judicial notice of relevant ornithology'.

1.24 Statutes also make provision for the taking of judicial notice on a range of matters. In this way, public Acts of Parliament are to be judicially noticed (Interpretation Act 1978, s 3), as are the European Communities treaties, the Official Journal of the Communities and the decisions of the European Court of Justice (European Communities Act 1972, s 3(2)).

1.25 While the courts may dispense with proof in what might be loosely termed matters of general public knowledge, in principle courts may not make use of their personal knowledge. Distinguishing between these two types of knowledge is not always easy, not least because facts which are notorious within a given locality may be the subject of judicial notice. This problem often arises in magistrates' courts, where justices will be familiar with their own local area. By way of illustration, in *Paul v DPP* (1989) 90 Cr App R 173, a kerb-crawling case, although there was no evidence that P's activities had caused a nuisance to residents, as required by the Criminal Justice Act 1985, the justices used their local knowledge of this heavily populated, residential area of Luton to supply the missing element in the prosecution case. The courts occasionally take this principle too far. In *Ingram v Percival* [1969] 1 QB 548, for instance, justices were held to have been entitled to use their personal knowledge of where tidal waters ebbed and flowed in a case involving unlawful netting of salmon and migratory trout. It is doubtful whether this fact was generally notorious within the locality; it does look suspiciously like private and personal knowledge, and the defendant could feel justly aggrieved that his conviction rested in part upon the magistrates having acted as silent witnesses for the Crown.

1.26 An allied problem is that magistrates will sometimes possess personal professional knowledge which has a bearing on the case they are trying. In *Wetherall v Harrison* [1976] QB 773 one justice, who was a doctor, gave his colleagues the benefit of his professional opinion on the likely genuineness of the defendant's claim that he suffered from 'needle phobia', which was intended to explain why he had failed to supply a specimen in a drink-driving case. The court held that a justice, unlike a professional judge, could draw on his specialised knowledge in evaluating evidence in the case and, *if asked to do so*, was entitled to tell his fellow justices how his specialised knowledge had caused him to look at the evidence.

1.27 When employing local knowledge the courts enjoin magistrates to display restraint. In *Waite v Taylor* (1985) 149 JP 551 justices, trying a busker who had been juggling with fire-sticks on a charge of obstruction of the highway, had used their local knowledge. The Divisional Court suggested that justices should disclose whenever they proposed to take judicial notice of local conditions to enable the parties to comment and/or call evidence on the matters in question. That magistrates ought not to make use of their personal knowledge and experience of the world in place of evidence was illustrated in *Carter v Eastbourne Borough Council* (2000) 164 JP 273. C had been convicted of uprooting five trees which, it was claimed, were protected by a preservation order. The Crown had not called evidence to show that the trees were at least four years old and thus in existence when the order had been made. The justices, however, viewed photographs of the uprooted trees (which included a yew, one of the slowest-growing trees on the planet) and 'from our own experience in our own gardens and woodlands' concluded that the trees must have been at least four years of age. Lord Bingham, CJ held that they had not been entitled to do this. Alluding to *Preston-Jones v Preston-Jones* [1951] AC 391, a case in which the House of Lords had held that a court could not assume in the absence of proof that a child born 360 days after husband and wife had last indulged in *coitus* was not the child of the husband, Lord Bingham observed 'how cautious the courts are in treating a factual conclusion as obvious, even though the man in the street would unhesitatingly hold it to be so'. The age of the trees should therefore have been the subject of evidence and not of personal undisclosed belief on the part of the justices.

Formal admissions

1.28 Largely in order to save time, in both civil and criminal cases parties may make formal admissions in which they concede certain facts to be the case, thereby sparing their adversary the need to prove them. To this end, in criminal cases the Criminal Justice Act 1967, s 10 sets out a procedure which allows a party to make a formal admission in writing either before or during the proceedings regarding 'any fact of which oral evidence may be given'; any such admission 'shall as against that party be conclusive evidence in those proceedings'.

1.29 Parties may make similar formal admissions in civil cases. Under Part 14 of the Civil Procedure Rules, 'A party may admit the truth of the whole or any part of another party's case' (r 14.1). Such an admission may be made in writing either in the party's statement of claim or in a letter, thereby dispensing with the need to adduce evidence to establish the issue in question—unless the court accedes to a party's request to amend or retract that admission (r 14.5).

Judicial findings as evidence

1.30 Where a matter has been previously litigated, in order to maintain consistency and to prevent issues from being forever reopened rules of evidence may require subsequent courts to treat earlier judicial findings as binding. Two contexts in which this issue regularly arises are estoppel, on the one hand, and the proof of previous convictions under s 74 of PACE, on the other.

Estoppel

1.31 Although detailed treatment of this subject is beyond the scope of an introductory work, it is important to be aware that the law sometimes ordains that parties in both civil and criminal cases may not even seek to prove or disprove certain things, but are bound to accept them as established. These situations can generally be referred to as estoppels. The underlying idea is that issues ought not to be continually reopened and that disputes ought not to be litigated more than once. The civil and criminal rules must be treated separately.

1.32 Estoppels come in two forms: estoppels *in rem* and estoppels *in personam*. An estoppel *in rem* has been authoritatively defined as:

> A judgment of a court of competent jurisdiction determining the status of a person or thing, or the disposition of a thing (as distinct from a particular interest in it of a party to the litigation). (*Lazarus-Barlow v Regent Estates Co Ltd* [1949] 2 KB 465, 475 *per* Evershed LJ)

Judgments giving rise to estoppels *in rem* are conclusive against all parties. For this reason, if a court issues a decree pronouncing a couple divorced, unless someone is seeking to have the judgment set aside on the ground that it was procured by fraud or suchlike, its status must be treated as settled and no one may reopen the question in any subsequent litigation. Estoppels *in personam*, on the other hand, refer to all other estoppels.

1.33 In civil cases, estoppels, so far as they are relevant to the law of evidence, can be divided into two types, 'cause of action estoppels' and 'issue estoppels'. Cause of action estoppel, perhaps more properly known as estoppel *per rem judicatam*, simply signifies that no one may sue twice on the same cause of action. Once a claimant has litigated a particular set of facts, he may not do so again. In the leading case, *Conquer v Boot* [1928] 2 KB 336, C successfully sued B for £24 for breach of contract in failing to build a bungalow 'in a good and workmanlike manner'. Less than a year later C brought a fresh claim virtually identical in its terms against B for £81, once again for failing to build a bungalow 'in a good and workmanlike manner'. The court held that the cause of action was the same in both actions and that since the question had been decided in the first action, the matter was *res judicata* and the claimant could not recover further damages. This form of estoppel produces a situation in which it can be justifiably claimed:

> It is a fundamental rule of our procedure, sometimes known as the rule in *Conquer v Boot*, that parties to litigation must, in all ordinary circumstances, bring forward the whole of their case at one and the same time. (*Gardiner v Michael Sallis & Co Ltd* (1991) 8 May, unreported, *per* Lloyd LJ)

Issue estoppel, in contrast, was broadly defined by Lord Diplock in *Mills v Cooper* [1967] 2 QB 459, 469 as follows:

> A party to civil proceedings is not entitled to make, as against the other party, an assertion ... the correctness of which is an essential element in his cause of action or defence, if the same assertion was an essential element in his previous cause of action or defence in previous civil proceedings between the same parties ... and was found by a court of competent jurisdiction in such previous proceedings to be incorrect ...

As Lord Diplock went on to explain, the effect of issue estoppel is that there is no issue left to be decided in the subsequent proceedings to which the evidence would be relevant. The doctrine is 'a particular application of the general rule of public policy that there should be finality in litigation'.

1.34 Do the forms of estoppel that operate in civil cases possess obvious counterparts in the criminal law? The principle of finality, as we shall see, does resemble a rule of criminal procedure which lays down that no one may be tried twice for the same offence. The rule against double jeopardy, as it is known, could be described as a counterpart to cause of action estoppel such as operates in civil cases. But what of issue estoppel? In *DPP v Humphrys* [1977] AC 1, although the facts of the case did not necessarily require it to do so, the House of Lords considered whether issue estoppel had a role to play in English criminal law. The case concerned a charge of perjury. At his first trial on a charge of driving a motorcycle while disqualified H had testified that although he had been disqualified at the relevant time, he had not in fact been the driver seen by the police officer. H went on to claim that S, a third party, had actually been driving the motorcycle on that occasion. The justices acquitted H. Subsequent police enquiries, however, suggested that H had in fact been the driver of the motorcycle. H was therefore prosecuted for perjury, and the police officer who had testified at the first trial repeated his evidence that he had observed H driving the motorcycle while disqualified. H argued that since the sole issue at the first trial had been whether H had been the driver and he had been acquitted, this question had been finally determined at the first trial and could not therefore be reopened at the subsequent perjury hearing. The House of Lords rejected this contention.

1.35 One question the House of Lords considered was whether the civil doctrine of issue estoppel has any role to play in the criminal law. The House acknowledged that even if it did, it could not be used to prevent prosecutions for perjury being brought against defendants who lied on oath at their trials. Given that the prosecution must prove its case to the high standard of 'beyond reasonable doubt', and also given that the verdicts of criminal courts are handed down without reasons in the form of inscrutable dooms, it is impossible to maintain that a verdict (other than that rarely used procedure of a special verdict, where the jury is called upon to pronounce upon a specific factual question) settles any particular point of fact, other than guilt. In consequence, criminal law recognises only the more restricted doctrine, the formal pleas in bar of *autrefois convict* and *autrefois acquit*.

1.36 The *autrefois* pleas are intended to protect defendants against double jeopardy. Double jeopardy means that if an accused has once been convicted or acquitted of a particular offence, he cannot subsequently be retried for that offence or, indeed, for any lesser included offence which forms part of the offence originally charged and in respect of which he was at risk at his original trial. Hence, if the defendant has been tried and acquitted of murder, he cannot later be re-indicted either for that murder or for attempted murder or manslaughter. Attempted murder and manslaughter are lesser included offences, in the sense of being offences in respect of which the jury could have returned a verdict at the defendant's first trial. The protection afforded against double jeopardy in fact extends beyond the technical limits of the *autrefois* pleas because the House of Lords in *Connelly* [1964] AC 1254 recognised that the trial judge has a discretion to stay proceedings when they would constitute an abuse of the process of the court. Therefore, even if the charge does not technically amount to a lesser included offence, the court is entitled to hold a second prosecution brought against the defendant on substantially the same facts as the first indictment to be oppressive and an abuse of process. Proceedings, in such cases, will therefore be stayed.

1.37 The double jeopardy principle, it should be said, is not absolute in criminal cases. Recent statutes have made limited inroads on the principle. Under the Criminal Procedure and Investigations Act 1996, ss 54–57, it is possible to apply to the High Court to quash an acquittal tainted by intimidation and then to bring fresh proceedings. Provided that someone has subsequently been convicted of an administration of justice offence involving interference or intimidation of a witness or juror, and provided that the convicting court is also satisfied that there is 'a real possibility' that the defendant in the earlier proceeding would not have been acquitted but for that interference or intimidation, the convicting court may issue a certificate to that effect. The certificate is then laid before the High Court, which in turn must determine whether or not to quash the acquittal and thereby to permit fresh proceedings to be brought against the acquitted defendant. These provisions will obviously only apply in a very restricted class of cases. Part 10 of the Criminal Justice Act 2003 contains a reform that punctures the double jeopardy principle to a more meaningful degree. By virtue of s 75 of that Act, with the consent in writing of the Director of Public Prosecutions, the Crown may now apply to the Court of Appeal in cases where there is 'new and compelling evidence' against an acquitted person in relation to a qualifying offence (as defined in s 78) to have the acquittal quashed and a re-trial ordered. The court may make such an order provided that it considers both that (i) there is new and compelling evidence (meaning, evidence that appears to be reliable, substantial and, in the context of the outstanding issues, highly probative of the case against the acquitted person (s 78); such new evidence does not need to be direct evidence: *Andrews* [2009] 1 WLR 1947) and that (ii) it is in the interests of justice to make such an order (s 79). In determining whether or not it is in the interests of justice to order a re-trial, the appellate court must have particular regard to:

(a) whether existing circumstances make a fair trial unlikely;

(b) ... the length of time since the qualifying offence was allegedly committed;

(c) whether it is likely that the new evidence would have been adduced in the earlier proceedings against the acquitted person but for a failure by an officer or by a prosecutor
to act with due diligence or expedition;

(d) whether, since those proceedings…any officer or prosecutor has failed to act with
due diligence or expedition.

(s 79(2))

These are demanding criteria (*G(G) and B(S)* [2009] EWCA Crim 1207).
Nevertheless, in September 2006, William Dunlop, pleaded guilty to a murder
committed in 1989 for which he had been acquitted in 1991. Two convictions in
2000 for perjury, relating to evidence he had given at trial in 1991, provided the
new and compelling evidence that sealed his fate. More recently, in May 2009
Mario Celaire, a Maidstone United footballer, who had originally been acquitted
of the homicide of a former girlfriend in 2002, was convicted of her manslaughter
following a confession made to a later victim.

Defence evidence of previous acquittals

1.38 The retreat of the double jeopardy principle is also evident in criminal case law.
Sometimes an accused will wish to adduce evidence of a previous acquittal as
part of his case. At one time, there were suggestions that such evidence could
operate as conclusive evidence of the defendant's innocence, for all purposes. By
way of example, in *Hay* (1983) 77 Cr App R 70, H had confessed in writing to
two unconnected offences, arson and burglary. H was tried separately on each
count. At his first trial for arson, H's confession was admitted in evidence but
all references to the burglary were edited out. H adduced evidence of alibi and
also claimed that the police had fabricated his statement. He was acquitted of
the arson. Having subsequently been convicted of burglary, it was held that H
had been wrongly prevented by the trial judge from introducing into evidence his
entire confessional statement and the fact of his previous acquittal. As O'Connor
LJ observed:

> The jury ought to have been told of the acquittal and directed that it was *conclusive evi-*
> *dence* that the appellant was not guilty of arson, and that his confession to that offence
> was untrue. The jury should have been directed that in deciding the contest between the
> appellant and the police officers as to the part of the statement referring to the burglary,
> they should keep in mind that the first part must be regarded as untrue.
>
> (p 75)

The notion that a previous acquittal might constitute 'conclusive evidence' of innocence was reinforced by the famous declaration of Lord Macdermott in *Sambasivam*

v Public Prosecutor, Federation of Malaya [1950] AC 458, 479 that:

> The effect of a verdict of acquittal pronounced by a competent court on a lawful charge and after a lawful trial is not completely stated by saying that the person acquitted cannot be tried again for the same offence. To that must be added that *the verdict is binding and conclusive* in all subsequent proceedings between the parties to the adjudication.

The House of Lords' decision in *Z* [2000] 2 AC 483, however, has since dispatched the latter assertion in relation to acquittal evidence adduced by the prosecution. The reason for this is that Lord Macdermott's proposition confuses the rule against double jeopardy (ie, the foundational principle that a defendant ought not to be put more than once at risk of conviction for the same offence) with the separate question of the admissibility and treatment of evidence, which was relevant to a charge of which an accused has been acquitted, and which also has relevance to another charge for which the accused is subsequently being tried (see *post*, paras **7.32–7.36**). Does similar reasoning apply to acquittal evidence adduced by the defence? The Court of Appeal considered this question in *Terry* [2005] 3 WLR 379.

1.39 In *Terry*, T appealed against conviction on assorted counts of burglary, handling and theft. At trial, T had been formally acquitted on four charges because, in the absence of other evidence confirming his presence at the relevance location, a voice recognition expert was not prepared to identify T's voice with certainty as the one she had heard on certain police tape recordings. On appeal, the question was whether the trial judge had been correct to refuse to direct the jury that these four acquittals had to be employed as conclusive evidence that T was not in the relevant spot at the operative time. Auld LJ was visibly unimpressed with the argument that an acquittal amounted to a declaration of positive innocence. The preferred general principle was to be derived from Lord Lowry's opinion in *Hui Chi-Ming* [1992] 1 AC 34, where the latter had said that 'some exceptional feature is needed before it will be considered relevant (and therefore admissible) to give evidence of what happened in earlier cases arising out of the same transaction.' In most cases, therefore, 'the verdict reached by a different jury (whether on the same or different evidence) in the earlier trial was irrelevant and amounted to no more than evidence of the opinion of that jury.' Auld LJ considered that the expression 'conclusive evidence' in O'Connor LJ's judgment in *Hay* could no longer stand (at [15]). Three principal points can be made.

- First, as in the case of acquittal evidence adduced by the Crown following *Z* [2000] 2 AC 483 (see para **7.33**), 'an acquittal is not conclusive evidence of innocence unless by that word it is meant "not guilty in law of the alleged offence to which it relates". Nor does it mean that all relevant issues have been resolved in favour of a defendant' (at [16]).

- Secondly, because the reasoning of the House of Lords in *Z* is equally applicable to acquittal evidence adduced by the defence, it is important to distinguish the double jeopardy rule from the issue of the admissibility of evidence of facts alleged in respect of another charge, notwithstanding that that charge resulted in an acquittal: 'Finality of a verdict of acquittal does not necessarily prevent the institution of proceedings or the tender of evidence, which might have the incidental effect of casting doubt upon, or even demonstrating the error of, an earlier decision'
  (at [18]).
- Thirdly, the issue of fairness needs to be considered, too. As Lord Hobhouse stressed in *Z*,

Fairness requires that the jury hear all relevant evidence....Any prejudice to the defendant arising from having to deal a second time with evidence proving facts which were in issue at an earlier trial is simply another factor to be put into the balance. The fact that the previous trial ended in an acquittal is a relevant factor in striking this balance but it is no more than that.

(p 510)

Plainly, it would be wrong were a jury to be compelled to reach a conclusion that did not accord with the merits of the evidence. In *Terry* it would have made no sense had the judge been obliged to direct the jury that T could not have been at the relevant location when the incriminating statements were made simply because there was no evidence other than that of the voice recognition expert directly locating him there at those times. It would also have been unfair had T been allowed to suggest to the jury the conclusiveness of his innocence on the counts on which he had been acquitted because of the expert's unsupported evidence on those charges, so as to unseat her supported evidence on the remaining charges.

Convictions of non-defendants as evidence of commission of offences: Police and Criminal Evidence Act 1984, s 74

1.40 The so-called rule in *Hollington v Hewthorn* ([1943] KB 587) used to hold that a conviction in former proceedings was inadmissible as proof of guilt in subsequent criminal proceedings. This gave rise to the absurd situation that if D was charged with handing stolen goods, proof that X had been convicted of the theft of those goods was not admissible to show that the goods were in fact stolen goods. This had to be proven afresh at the subsequent handling trial. To remedy this situation, Parliament passed PACE, s 74. That section (as amended) provides:

> (1) In any proceedings the fact that a person other than the accused has been convicted of an offence by or before any court in the United Kingdom...shall be admissible in evidence for the purpose of proving that that person committed the offence, where evidence of his having done so is admissible, whether or not any other evidence of his having committed that offence is given.

1.41 Section 74 successfully reversed the rule in *Hollington v Hewthorn* and, to take the handling example, the Crown can now introduce in evidence X's conviction for theft of the goods and, under the terms of s 74(2), at D's trial for handling X 'shall be taken to have committed that offence unless the contrary is proved (by D)'. Moreover, s 75 renders admissible:

> ...without prejudice to the reception of any other admissible evidence for the purpose of identifying the facts on which the conviction was based—
>
> (a) the contents of any document which is admissible as evidence of the conviction; and
>
> (b) the contents of the information, complaint, indictment or charge-sheet on which the person in question was convicted.

This legislation, particularly when one takes into account reversal of the burden of proof (s 74(2)), greatly eases the Crown's task in cases like our handling example. However, because it constitutes proof of 'bad character' of a non-defendant, such evidence will only be admissible if specifically sanctioned by a statute or, more generally, if it is admissible under the restrictive terms of s 100 of the Criminal Justice Act 2003. In essence that will mean that, in the absence of the agreement of all the parties to the proceedings, a non-defendant's convictions must either constitute 'important explanatory evidence' within the meaning of the 2003 Act or must have substantial probative value in relation to a matter which is a matter in issue in the proceedings, and is of substantial importance in the context of the case as a whole, as required by s 100(1). In the former case, this will signify that without the evidence, the court or jury would find it impossible or difficult properly to understand other evidence in the case, and its value for understanding the case as a whole is substantial. In the latter case, s 100 lays down a number of factors restricting the admissibility of such evidence (see *post*, paras **4.22–4.35**).

1.42 Soon after its enactment it became apparent that, owing to the inclusion of the words (now repealed) 'relevant to *any* issue in those proceedings', s 74 was of much wider significance than just cases of handling—which was all government ministers and MPs referred to during the Bill's original passage through Parliament. Lord Lane CJ in *Robertson* (1987) 85 Cr App R 304, 311 noted that 'the word "issue"...is apt to cover not only an issue which is an essential ingredient in the offence charged...but also less fundamental issues, for instance evidential issues arising during the course of the proceedings'. It is essential, nevertheless, that the evidence of non-defendants' convictions is actually relevant to an issue in the case. In *Downer* [2009] EWCA Crim 1361, for example, D was charged with aggravated burglary on the basis that, in company with others, he was already armed when he entered the relevant premises. His co-accuseds' pleas of guilty, founded on their having acquired the weapons inside the premises, were therefore of no probative value and ought not to have been admitted in evidence against D.

1.43 Although the wording of PACE, s 74 is now different, and s 100 of the 2003 Act will additionally control the admissibility of such evidence, it is plain that s 74 operates in many circumstances to permit the admission of evidence of a non-defendant's conviction without the need to call the non-defendant as a witness. Let us consider a pair of cases decided under the old formulation of s 74. In *Gummerson and Steadman* [1999] Crim LR 680 four co-accused were jointly charged with robbery and grievous bodily harm. The Crown case rested to a significant degree on voice identification evidence. One of the four defendants, D1, had pleaded guilty, but the others denied guilt and contested the witness's ability to recognise them by their voices. The judge was held to have correctly admitted in evidence D1's conviction because it was relevant to an issue in the case, namely, the rebuttal of the other co-defendants' contention that the witness could not identify anyone by voice alone. Provided that the jury is told that D1's conviction has been admitted solely for this restricted purpose, it is unobjectionable that s 74 now allows for the admission of previous convictions of third parties in a wide variety of contexts. This evidence would, in all likelihood, still be admissible today under s 100 as evidence having substantial probative value in relation to a matter which is a matter in issue in the proceedings, and which is of substantial importance in the context of the case as a whole (s 100(1)(b)). Similarly, the case of *Dixon* (2000) 164 JP 721, where D had been jointly charged along with two other parties, J and C, on counts of attempted burglary, would almost certainly produce the same result under the new law. The police claimed to have seen three people, including D, near a door that someone had tried to kick open. J and C pleaded guilty. It was D's contention that throughout the attempted burglary she had been in the company of J and that they had been nowhere near the relevant door. It was held that the trial judge had been perfectly entitled to allow the prosecution to prove J's conviction because, if accepted at face value, it demonstrated that D's account of what had happened was untrue.

1.44 In *Dixon*, in the course of his judgment, Mantell LJ remarked that courts have indicated many times before that 'the discretion to allow in evidence of this sort should be used sparingly.' To put it more accurately, it used to be that only on rare occasions would the courts not exercise discretion under PACE, s 78 (see *post*, paras **1.47–1.54**) to exclude s 74 conviction evidence on account of the prejudice it is prone to engender. The fact is that the use to which the Crown seeks to put s 74 is not always unobjectionable. Most frequently, a problem arises in cases where the prosecution is alleging a conspiracy. In *Robertson* the Court of Appeal pondered the difficulties. R was charged in two counts with conspiring with P and L to burgle premises. P and L entered pleas of guilty to 16 counts of burglary. At R's trial on the two conspiracy counts, evidence of the guilty pleas of P and L was admitted because it tended to establish the existence of a conspiracy to burgle. Provided that the existence of a conspiracy can be kept distinct from the question whether R was a party to that conspiracy, the admission of this evidence is unobjectionable. In *Robertson* itself Lord Lane CJ held that evidence of the guilty pleas had been properly admitted as there was no danger that the jury would conclude from P's and L's confessions that they had committed the burglaries and that R was therefore a party to the conspiracy. However, he did warn that, owing to the danger of jurors conflating the two issues in such cases, s 74 should be 'sparingly used' (at p 312). Farquharson J reinforced this warning in *Curry* [1988] Crim LR 527 stating that 'where the evidence expressly or by necessary inference imports the complicity of the person on trial it should not be used'.

1.45 In *Kempster* [1989] 1 WLR 1125 the Court of Appeal took these counsels of prudence to heart. There was ambivalent evidence connecting K with various robberies and burglaries and, in particular, only sketchy identification evidence of the four suspects. K's three co-accused entered guilty pleas. Having admitted evidence of these convictions under s 74, the trial judge's summing-up left it open to the jury to use the convictions to assist them generally in determining K's guilt. The Court of Appeal allowed K's appeal on the ground that the judge's failure to consider the adverse effects admission of this evidence might have exerted on the fairness of the proceedings constituted a material irregularity. In this, and in many subsequent cases, the role of the court's discretion to exclude unfair evidence under s 78 of PACE has been stressed. In *O'Connor* (1986) 85 Cr App R 298, for example, where two accused were jointly indicted of conspiring together, the Court of Appeal deemed it unfair to have admitted evidence of one defendant's guilty plea as this may have suggested to the jury that the other must therefore also necessarily have been party to that conspiracy. Similarly, in *Clarke* (1999) 11 February, case no 9803390/W2, the guilty plea of one of two co-accused charged with conspiracy to pervert the course of justice was held to have been wrongly admitted: this evidence by express or necessary inference imported the complicity of the second defendant and, although technically admissible under the terms of s 74, should have been excluded by the judge under s 78 of PACE.

1.46 There are two reasons for thinking that Lord Lane's warning, in *Robertson*, offers a wise counsel. *First*, as has already been argued, unless the judge can clearly circumscribe the use to which evidence of a third party's convictions is put and there is no serious risk of the jury concluding guilt simply by association, counsels of prudence ought to prevail and evidence of doubtful value ought always to be excluded under s 78. For this reason, it is vital that in the summing-up the trial judge identifies the precise relevance of the conviction (eg, *Girma* [2009] EWCA Crim 912 esp at [62] *per* Goldring J). Secondly, given that s 75 reverses the burden of proof and that in practice a defendant will often have no opportunity to cross-examine the non-defendant whose conviction is being employed against him, the unfairness s 74 potentially can occasion is all the more acute. Take *Mattison* [1990] Crim LR 117. M appealed successfully against his conviction for gross indecency with D. Having previously pleaded guilty, D's conviction was led at M's trial, supposedly to give the jury the background to the case. As Saville J observed, the problem here is that 'if A commits an act of gross indecency with B, it is a strong inference that the converse is also true in the absence of special circumstances to indicate otherwise'. The unfairness is obvious. The simple fact is that s 74 can all too easily jeopardise a defendant's entitlement to a fair trial.

Prejudicial evidence, unfairly obtained evidence and suspect witnesses

Judicial discretion to exclude relevant evidence

1.47 The mere fact that evidence is relevant and does not fall foul of any of the great exclusionary rules does not guarantee its admissibility. In both criminal and civil cases the court possesses a residual discretion to exclude otherwise admissible evidence. In each category of case, exercise of this discretion is intended to reinforce overriding notions of fairness. However, because completely distinct factors govern these respective notions of fairness, judicial discretion to exclude evidence in criminal and civil cases will be considered separately.

The discretion to exclude evidence in criminal cases

Common law discretion

1.48 At common law it has for long been recognised that trial judges enjoy a general discretion to order the exclusion of technically admissible evidence if they feel that its prejudicial effect exceeds its probative value (see *Christie* [1914] AC 545). Indeed, in *Sang* [1980] AC 402 the House of Lords unanimously held that in order to fulfil the overarching duty to ensure that an accused receives a fair trial a trial judge may refuse to admit technically relevant evidence. The discretion, which applies in virtually all situations, is intended to prevent the tribunal of fact from hearing evidence which is either so prejudicial that it could cloud the tribunal's judgment or which might deceive the tribunal into attributing to the evidence more weight than it merits. By way of example, in cases where the prosecution has succeeded in showing beyond reasonable doubt at a trial within a trial that a confession has not been extracted from a defendant by illicit means, contrary to PACE s 76, the judge may still decide that the prejudicial weight of the evidence exceeds its probative value and may therefore exclude that technically admissible confessional evidence. Similarly, a court would be within its rights to exclude gratuitously gruesome evidence on the ground of its extreme prejudicial effect if, in the words of one American court, 'the minute peg of relevance' is 'entirely obscured by the quantity of dirty linen hung upon it' (*State v Bucanis*, 138 A 3d 739 (NJ 1958). See, eg, Pill LJ's judgment in *Shankly* [2004] EWCA Crim 1224 at [20] ff).

1.49 Prior to the enactment of PACE, it was unclear whether under the common law discretion a judge was entitled to exclude evidence on the ground that it had been obtained by unfair means. While some Court of Appeal *dicta* did suggest that this was permissible if prosecution evidence had been obtained by means of a trick, by misleading the defendant or by employing oppressive or unfair means (eg *Jeffrey v Black* [1978] QB 490), in *Sang* [1980] AC 402 the House of Lords gave less than clear guidance on whether the common law discretion extends to such situations. The advent of s 78 of PACE, however, has thankfully disposed of much of this controversy.

1.50 Although in practice almost entirely superseded by the statutory discretion now conferred on courts by s 78, s 82(3) of PACE expressly preserves the common law discretion. The relationship between these two discretions to exclude evidence which the court considers prejudicial is somewhat mysterious. However, the courts do still employ their common law discretion from time to time. Ognall J, for instance, relied on common law discretion as well as PACE s 78 to exclude evidence obtained by an undercover policewoman in somewhat provocative circumstances at the trial of Colin Stagg. 'A careful appraisal of the material,' the judge observed at the conclusion of the pre-trial submissions, 'demonstrates a skilful and sustained enterprise to manipulate the accused, sometimes subtly, sometimes blatantly' (*The Times* (1994) 15 September, p 1. See Stagg & Kessler, *Who Really Killed Rachel?* (1999) Ch 14 for full text of Ognall J's impeccable ruling). The House of Lords, too, had developed a taste for referring to both forms of discretion in its judgments in leading cases like *H* [1995] 2 AC 596, *Z* [2000] 2 AC 483 and *Hasan* [2005] UKHL 22.

1.51 Although it raises complex issues, one further aspect of the common law discretion will be briefly mentioned. It is sometimes asked whether or not, in trials involving co-defendants, a judge possesses discretion at common law to exclude defence evidence. Evans LJ canvassed this question in *Thompson, Sinclair and Maver* [1995] 2 Cr App R 589, arguing that a discretion that permitted the judge to disallow evidence D1 seeks to adduce against D2, where its probative value is slight but its likely prejudicial effect to D2 is substantial, might prove a useful alternative to the more costly existing option of ordering separate trials. Although he admitted that there was no authority to support its existence, Evans LJ said that he would not like to be thought to suggest that such discretion could never exist. Two comments might be made. First, given that the statutory discretion to exclude prejudicial evidence conferred by s 78 of PACE (see *post*, paras **1.52–1.54**) only relates to evidence upon which the prosecution intends to rely, any discretion to exclude defence evidence must found in common law. Secondly, the problem with such a discretion would be that its exercise would be likely to convey the impression that the judge was taking sides. It is a serious matter to exclude evidence that D1 wishes to call. The judicial role is not to hamper and embarrass defendants in the conduct of their defence. By intervening, the judge could convey the appearance of tipping the scales in favour of one of the two co-defendants. Inevitably, in cases where co-accused are running cut-throat defences, what is of advantage to D2 will be of disadvantage to D1. A discretion to exclude a co-defendant's evidence could create the impression that the judge, no matter how well intentioned, was stepping into the arena. This seems undesirable (cp *Lawson* [2007] 1 WLR 1191 at [31] *per* Hughes LJ).

Police and Criminal Evidence Act 1984, s 78

1.52 Section 78 of PACE now provides:

> In any proceedings the court may refuse to allow evidence on which the prosecution proposes to rely to be given if it appears to the court that, having regard to all the circumstances, including the circumstances in which the evidence was obtained, the admission of the evidence would have such an adverse effect on the fairness of the proceedings that the court ought not to admit it.

This provision, which confers upon the judge a broader discretion to exclude prosecution evidence than previously existed at common law (*Cooke* [1995] Crim LR 497), is often invoked. It is commonly used in cases where evidence has been obtained in breach of the PACE Codes of Practice, which notably regulate the way in which the police question suspects, conduct identification parades and so on. If the court concludes that breaches of these rules have been 'significant and substantial' (*Keenan* [1990] 2 QB 54)—and this does not necessarily mean that there must have been police impropriety—then it will exclude the evidence if it is considered that its admission would reflect adversely on the fairness of the proceedings.

1. 53 What is meant by 'fairness' in this context? Traditionally, it signifies fairness to the accused, which normally means that in deciding whether or not to exclude particular evidence the court primarily will see if serious procedural breaches of rule have occurred which deprive an accused of important rights (eg *Nathaniel* (1995) 159 JP 419, where DNA evidence obtained in breach of PACE Code C was excluded by Lord Taylor CJ). Alternatively, however, 'the fairness of the proceedings' is stated to mean 'both fairness to the accused person and fairness to the public good, as represented by the Crown' (eg, *Cooke* [1995] Crim LR 497 *per* Glidewell LJ, where DNA evidence obtained in breach of Code C was admitted primarily on grounds of its inherent reliability). When taken in this wider sense, in exercising its discretion the court naturally inclines to treat the reliability of the evidence as the determining factor. The latter interpretation of 'fairness' will have received a fillip from the entry into force of the Criminal Procedure Rules, whose overriding objective of dealing with cases justly imposes the judicial requirement of 'dealing with the prosecution and the defence fairly' (Part 1.1(2)(b)).

1.54 There is strong reason to think that, unlike its common law counterpart, the statutory discretion permits a court to exclude improperly obtained evidence. Not only does s 78 expressly invite the court to consider 'the circumstances in which the evidence was obtained' when assessing whether the evidence would reflect adversely on the fairness of the proceedings, but such an approach is also buttressed by the Human Rights Act 1998. ECtHR case law holds that the right to a fair trial, guaranteed by art 6 of the Convention, extends not merely to the trial itself but also to the pre-trial phase of proceedings (eg, *Edwards v UK* (1992) 15 EHRR 417). Since s 3 of the 1998 Act requires courts to interpret English legislation so far as possible in a manner compatible with the Convention, this means that in determining whether evidence ought to be excluded on grounds of unfairness courts will have to take into account the fact that it may have been obtained in breach of the accused's Convention rights. This aspect of the judicial discretion to exclude admissible evidence was considered by the Court of Appeal in *Shannon* [2001] 1 WLR 51, a case involving entrapment. S, a television actor, appealed against a conviction for drug dealing on the ground that he had been induced to commit the offence by an *agent provocateur*, an undercover reporter from the *News of the World*, who had lured him to the Savoy Hotel by posing as an Arab sheikh with a craving for drugs. (This intrepid reporter also succeeded in entrapping the Earl of Hardwicke with the same ploy and with identical legal consequences: *Hardwicke* [2000] All ER (D) 1776. He met his nemesis, however, in March 2006 in the person of George Galloway MP.) The Court of Appeal reaffirmed that there is no general defence of entrapment in English law. Nevertheless, Potter LJ did acknowledge that in cases where a party applies to have evidence excluded under s 78 on the ground that he was entrapped, although the principal focus of the court will be the procedural fairness of the proceedings, the opportunity the defendant has had to deal with the prosecution evidence and the reliability of the Crown evidence, the court will also take into account the facts and circumstances of the entrapment. Indeed, in an appropriate case, Potter LJ said, such facts and circumstances might prove decisive. Thus, if there was good reason to doubt the credibility of the *agent provocateur* and these doubts were not susceptible to being properly or fairly resolved in the course of the proceedings from available admissible, untainted evidence, the judge would in likelihood feel impelled to exclude the *agent*'s evidence. Merely feeling that it was just unfair that the evidence had been obtained by the particular method adopted by the investigators, however, would not be sufficient on its own to justify exclusion under s 78.

Abuse of process and the discretion to exclude evidence

1.55 Entrapment, it should be said, is something of a special case, particularly in view of the recent rise to prominence of the concept of abuse of process. Abuse of process arises where the circumstances in which a prosecution has come to be brought are such as to amount to what Lord Steyn in *Latif* [1996] 1 WLR 104, 112 designated 'an affront to the public conscience' or what Lord Bingham in *Nottingham City Council v Amin* [2000] 1 WLR 1071, 1076 called matters 'deeply offensive to ordinary notions of fairness'. Although the concept remains somewhat ill-defined, entrapment involves agents of the state luring or enticing persons to commit offences or otherwise instigating crime. As Lord Nicholls explained in *Looseley* [2001] 1 WLR 2060, a case in which the House of Lords helpfully reviewed the law governing abuse of process and the relationship between this concept and the discretion to exclude evidence,

> It is simply not acceptable that the state through its agents should lure its citizens into committing acts forbidden by the law and then seek to prosecute them for doing so.
> ([2001] 1 WLR 2060 at [11])

Therefore, if a court finds that there has been an abuse of process, rather than simply excluding individual items of otherwise admissible evidence, it will actually stay the entire proceedings against the defendant. This is because in cases where a defendant complains that he has been lured into committing an offence, he is not just arguing that particular evidence ought not to be admitted at trial, but rather that he should not be tried at all (eg, Lord Hoffmann in *Looseley* at [42]). 'Different tests are applicable to these two decisions,' declared Lord Nicholls (at [18]). In the majority of cases in which entrapment is alleged the appropriate course will be for the accused to apply for a stay of proceedings on the ground of abuse of process rather than merely seeking the exclusion of certain evidence by exercise of the judicial discretion conferred by PACE, s 78. However, as Lord Hutton explained,

> If [the defendant's] application is refused, it will still be open to him to seek to exclude the evidence under s 78...But...if a later application to exclude evidence under s 78 is, in substance, an application to stay on the ground of entrapment, a court should apply the principles applicable to the grant of a stay.
>
> (at [104])

1.56 Both the Court of Appeal in *Shannon* [2001] 1 WLR 51 and the House of Lords in *Looseley* [2001] 1 WLR 2060 additionally measured the question of entrapment against the yardstick of European human rights law. Notably, the courts referred to the leading European decision of *Teixeira de Castro v Portugal* (1998) 28 EHRR 101. Apart from repeating its oft-heard message that rules regulating the admissibility of evidence are essentially matters for individual national jurisdictions, therefore falling within the margin of appreciation (see, eg, *Schenck v Switzerland* (1988) 13 EHRR 242), the ECtHR in *Teixeira de Castro* drew a broad distinction between the covert investigation of crime and the positive instigation of offences. The former was permissible; the latter could not be countenanced. Therefore, as Lord Hoffmann explained in *Looseley*, the ECtHR in *Texeira de Castro* concluded that the evidence of two police officers who had not merely operated undercover but had actually instigated serious crime, without following the customary procedure in Portugal of conducting their investigations under judicial or police supervision, ought not to have been admitted because it violated de Castro's right to a fair trial.

1.57 From this, it will be seen that the mere fact that evidence has been obtained by what is sometimes termed 'pro-active policing' will not automatically mean that under the European Convention evidence ought to be excluded or proceedings stayed. Broadly speaking, the appropriate test for entrapment is whether or not the police's law enforcement methods were part of a *bona fide* investigation as opposed to being merely a means of 'preying on the weakness of human nature to create crime for an improper purpose' (*per* Lord Hoffmann at [58]). This approach appears to be consistent with ECtHR rulings in other domains. If one takes the broadly analogous case of illegally obtained evidence, in *Khan v UK* (2000) 8 BHRC 310 it is notable that the Strasbourg court held that the fact that a listening device had been unlawfully applied to the wall of a suspect's house in breach of art 8, violating K's right of privacy, did not of itself render K's trial unfair under art 6. As the House of Lords explained subsequently in *R v P* [2001] 2 WLR 463, 475,

> [T]he direct operation of arts 8 [right of privacy] and 6 [fair trial] does not…alter the vital role of s 78 as the means by which questions of the use of evidence obtained in breach of art 8 are to be resolved at a criminal trial. The criterion to be applied is the criterion of fairness in art 6 which is likewise the criterion to be applied by the judge under s 78.

1.58 Applying these principles, in *Rosenberg* [2006] EWCA Crim 6, [2006] Crim LR 540, where R faced a number of charges involving Class A drugs, a trial judge was held to have properly admitted film taken by a surveillance camera 'of the most ostentatious type' mounted on top of a pole on R's neighbours' property. The camera had been directed into R's home. The police were aware of its existence and had even warned the neighbours that their actions amounted to a violation of R's right to privacy. Having reviewed and balanced the circumstances of the case, which 'included intrusion, but intrusion which was openly practised, the complicity of the police in the surveillance, and the seriousness of the crime involved', Pill LJ concluded that admission of the evidence did not render R's trial unfair. Similarly, in *Harmes and Crane* [2006] EWCA Crim 928 H and C appealed against a trial judge's decision not to stay proceedings brought against them for conspiracy to supply cocaine. They claimed that they had been entrapped by undercover police officers. The police had initially supplied the accused with soft drinks in exchange for an ounce of cocaine. Following this modest transaction, H boasted of his ability to import the drug in bulk and the undercover officers ordered a large quantity. The Court accepted that the police had committed criminal acts, notably by suggesting that they be supplied with cocaine in exchange for soft drinks, but considered that this was not so seriously improper as to require the court to intervene to stay the prosecution for conspiracy. As the House had held in *Looseley*, 'undercover officers, seeking to expose drug dealers, must show enthusiasm and a degree of persistence to provide protection for their undercover activities':

> [T]he conduct of the police officers was not exceptional and did not go beyond that which was necessary to show their willingness to deal in drugs. An exchange of a small amount of cocaine triggered the revelation that these defendants were not only happy to import very substantial quantities of cocaine but had the ability to do so. The officers' activities pale into insignificance in comparison to the offers made by H to import, on their behalf, large amounts of cocaine of a high value.
>
> (at [52] *per* Moses LJ)

1.59 Some indication of what will qualify as entrapment can be gleaned from the House of Lords' view of the Court of Appeal's decision in *A-G's Reference (No 3 of 2000)* [2001] 1 WLR 2060. In the latter case the Court of Appeal had determined that the trial judge had wrongly stayed proceedings against a drug dealer, with a previous record of dealing in soft drugs, who had twice obtained and supplied heroin at the insistent request of undercover police officers. The Court emphasised that, when deciding whether an abuse of process has occurred, the judge must bear in mind that there exists a spectrum of possibilities: at one end, there is the defendant who has simply been offered the market price for drugs—who can hardly argue that he has been entrapped; towards the other extreme, a judge might view in a different light the perspective of police officers dangling large sums of cash under the nose of someone in urgent need of money, thereby persuading that person to do something that he might not otherwise have done. *Texeira de Castro*, it was urged, has to be considered in the context of its particular facts and of Portuguese criminal procedure. In *A-G's Reference (No 3 of 2000)* the Court of Appeal had concluded that the police had done no more than give the accused an opportunity to breach the law, of which he had freely availed himself. In the view of the House of Lords, however, the trial judge had been entitled to stay proceedings in that case: the accused had never before dealt in heroin and he had been induced to procure heroin by the prospect of a profitable trade in smuggled cigarettes—something not normally associated with the commission of this offence. The judge could therefore justifiably take the view that the police had caused the accused to commit an offence that he would not otherwise have committed (cf *Loosely*, at [81] and [116] *per* Lords Hoffmann and Hutton). Similarly, in *Moon* [2004] EWCA Crim 2872, an addict, with no previous history of dealing in drugs, had been approached on four separate occasions by an undercover police officer posing as someone suffering from withdrawal symptoms. The officer eventually persuaded M to acquire and to sell to her a small quantity of heroin. The Court of Appeal held that, particularly bearing in mind that the Crown accepted that M had not been a dealer, in this case the police had caused M to commit the offence rather than having simply provided her with an opportunity to act in a way in which she would have acted anyway had the business been proposed to her by another purchaser.

1.60 Finally, reverting to s 78, it might be noted that in the context of s 78 the word 'discretion' has a slightly restricted meaning. As the Court of Appeal observed in *Chalkley* [1998] 2 Cr App R 79, 105, once a judge determines that admission of an item of evidence would reflect adversely on the fairness of proceedings, the evidence *must* be excluded. It is 'discretion' in a peculiar sense of that word.

1.61 Cases in which s 78 is invoked are also distinguishable from abuse of process cases in another important respect. The trial judge's decision on whether or not particular evidence reflects adversely on the fairness of proceedings under s 78 is largely unreviewable: in essence, an appellate court will only intervene if the trial judge's exercise of discretion can be characterised as *Wednesbury* unreasonable. When it is argued on appeal that proceedings ought to have been stayed as an abuse of process, however, the appellate court will exercise its own judgement as to whether the prosecution ought to be stayed. It is not simply for the appellate court to review exercise of the trial judge's discretion; its duty is to determine whether the prosecution ought to have been allowed to go ahead at all (*Harmes and Crane* [2006] EWCA Crim 928).

The discretion to exclude evidence in civil cases

1.62   It used to be widely accepted that civil courts do not enjoy discretion to exclude relevant evidence on account of its potential prejudicial effect. Thus, it was said that a judge in a civil proceeding could not decline to receive evidence proffered by a party on the ground that it had been obtained unlawfully (*Helliwell v Piggott-Sims* [1980] FSR 356, 357). The Civil Procedure Rules (CPR), however, have altered the position and Part 32 now expressly provides:

(1) The court may control the evidence by giving directions as to—

(a) the issues on which it requires evidence;

(b) the nature of the evidence which it requires to decide those issues; and

(c) the way in which the evidence is to be placed before the court.

(2) The court may use its power under this rule to exclude evidence that would otherwise be admissible.

On the face of it, the new discretion appears to be an unfettered 'case management power designed to allow the court to stop cases getting out of hand and hearings becoming interminable because more and more admissible evidence, especially hearsay evidence, is sought to be adduced' (*Post Office Counters Ltd v Mahida* [2003] EWCA Civ 1583 at [24] *per* Hale LJ). However, as Potter LJ pointed out in *Grobbelaar v Sun Newspapers Ltd* (1999) Times, 12 August, in exercising this discretion courts must not lose from sight that the stated 'overriding objective' of the CPR is to enable cases to be dealt with justly. This means that so far as is practicable, courts must ensure that the parties are on an equal footing, that expense is spared, and that cases are handled proportionately to the amount of money involved, the importance and complexity of the case, and the financial positions of the parties. Courts must also deal with cases expeditiously and fairly, allotting to them an appropriate share of court time (CPR, r 1.1). Clearly, it would not be open to courts to employ their discretion, say, to prevent litigants from putting forward allegations central to their defence, but they can now use Part 32 to control the manner in which cases are presented, notably preventing prolixity and the waste of court time and costs (see Lord Woolf's lucid account of the CPR's aims in *McPhilemy v Times Newspapers Ltd* [1999] 3 All ER 775, esp at 793–794).

1.63 In fact, CPR, Part 32 can now give rise to complex issues, particularly when a party to civil litigation wishes to introduce evidence obtained by improper means. This is vividly illustrated in Lord Woolf MR's judgment in *Jones v University of Warwick* [2003] 1 WLR 954, esp at [28]–[30]. The defendant employer had been permitted at trial to contest the *bona fides* of J's claim for damages following an injury suffered at work by adducing in evidence two videotapes, secretly filmed by an enquiry agent who had gained entry to J's home by posing as a market researcher. In the course of reviewing the trial court's decision to receive the tapes, Lord Woolf observed that, in deciding whether or not to admit evidence obtained, in this instance in violation of ECHR, art 8 (J's right to a private life), '[t]he court must try to give effect to what are here...two conflicting public interests. The weight to be attached to each will vary according to the circumstances. The significance of the evidence will differ as will the gravity of the breach, according to the facts of the particular case. The decision will depend on all the circumstances.' On the one hand, it would often look ridiculous for a civil court deliberately to close its eyes to relevant evidence:

> Here, the court cannot ignore the reality of the situation. This is not a case where the conduct of the defendant's insurers is so outrageous that the defence should be struck out. The case, therefore, has to be tried. It would be artificial and undesirable for the actual evidence, which is relevant and admissible, not to be placed before the judge who has the task of trying the case.

On the other hand, plainly uncomfortable with the idea that a court should, without more ado, receive evidence obtained by questionable or unlawful means, thereby endorsing or even encouraging such underhand tactics, Lord Woolf went on to say that, irrespective of whether the evidence in this case could have been obtained by other means, 'the fact that the insurers may have been motivated by a desire to achieve what they considered would be a just result does not justify either the commission of trespass or the contravention of the claimant's privacy which took place.' On balance, the court nevertheless held the evidence to have been properly admitted. However, Lord Woolf did add that a judge must still consider the impact of his rulings on litigation generally and, indeed, should mark his disapproval and seek to discourage similar inappropriate conduct in the future. 'Excluding the evidence,' Lord Woolf explained, 'is not...the only weapon in the court's armoury. The court has other steps it can take...In particular it can reflect its disapproval in the orders for costs which it makes,' say, by declining in its discretion to allow recovery of the costs of the enquiry agent.

The judicial discretion in criminal cases to warn of the dangers of relying on the evidence of suspect witnesses: *Makanjuola* directions and cell confessions

1.64 In a criminal case, even if the judge does not feel it necessary to go so far as to exclude evidence because its admission would reflect adversely on the fairness of the proceedings, an obligation to deliver a warning to the jury may nevertheless arise. Sometimes a witness may appear unreliable. The witness, for instance, may bear the defendant a grudge, or may have admitted to having previously told a pack of lies. Alternatively, the supposed victim of an offence may have made false complaints of a similar type in the past. In such a case, following Lord Taylor CJ's ruling in *Makanjuola* [1995] 1 WLR 1348, the trial judge may be required to deliver to the jury a warning, whose intensity will vary according to the extent of the risk, cautioning them against relying too readily upon the evidence of that suspect witness.

1.65 At one time the law imposed rigid corroboration rules. In some cases the law demanded that, in order to secure a conviction, the evidence of a particular class of witness (eg, a child giving unsworn evidence) actually had to be corroborated. In other situations the law merely required the judge to warn the jury to view the evidence of a certain class of witness with caution and to recommend that the jury look for corroboration—that is, other evidence, independent of the suspect witness, confirming the latter's evidence in a material particular. The three classes of witness who fell into this latter category were complainants in sexual cases, accomplices, and children who gave sworn testimony. The corroboration rules attracted widespread criticism for their artificiality and inflexibility. As Lord Hobhouse has observed in relation to sexual complainants, the rule of practice that formerly obtained 'had led to inappropriate and discriminatory directions being given which confused juries and created unfairness as between the prosecution and the defence and undermined rather than supported the safety of the juries' verdicts' (*Gilbert* [2002] 2 WLR 1498 at [14]). The rules of practice were eventually abolished by statute, notably by the Criminal Justice and Public Order Act 1994, s 32(1).

1.66 The result is that, but for a few exceptional legislative provisions, English law today has no general principle that a defendant cannot be convicted on a single piece of uncorroborated evidence. Figuring amongst the best-known exceptions to that principle, however, are the Perjury Act 1911, s 13 (which forbids conviction for perjury offences 'solely upon the evidence of one witness as to the falsity of any statement alleged to be false': eg, *Cooper* (2010) 174 JP 265) and the Road Traffic Regulation Act 1984, s 89 (which prevents a person charged with speeding offences from being convicted 'solely on the evidence of one witness to the effect that, in the opinion of the witness, the person prosecuted was driving the vehicle at a speed exceeding the speed limit').

1.67 Although the regimented corroboration requirements may well have been consigned to the past, the Court of Appeal in *Makanjuola* did recognise that trial judges still enjoy discretion whether or not to deliver warnings in a wide range of situations. Lord Taylor CJ, however, made clear that any attempt to re-impose the straitjacket of the old corroboration rules or to resurrect the old categories of suspect witnesses would be strongly deprecated. Moreover, whenever a question arises at trial as to whether a *Makanjuola* warning is appropriate, it is desirable that the matter first be discussed between judge and counsel in the absence of the jury. Otherwise, the Court of Appeal has left the question very much at large:

> Whether, as a matter of discretion, a judge should give any warning and if so its strength and terms must depend upon the content and manner of the witness's evidence, the circumstances of the case and the issues raised. The judge will often consider that no special warning is required at all. Where, however, the witness has been shown to be unreliable, he or she may consider it necessary to urge caution. In a more extreme case, ...the judge may suggest that it may be wise to look for some supporting material before acting on the impugned witness's evidence....[J]udges are not required to conform to any formula and this court will be slow to interfere with the exercise of discretion by a trial judge. (*Makanjuola* [1995] 1 WLR 1348, 1351)

1.68 *Walker* [1996] Crim LR 742 supplies a good example of a case where a strongly worded warning was warranted. A girl complained to the police that her mother's boyfriend for two years had been having intercourse with the daughter. The daughter later retracted this story, but subsequently retracted her retraction. No reference was made to these circumstances in the judge's summing-up. Not surprisingly, Ebsworth J felt that this situation 'cried out' for application of the *Makanjuola* principles. As Lord Taylor CJ made clear, it is in the discretion of the judge to determine in each individual case whether a warning ought to be given and, if so, how strong that warning should be. The Court of Appeal will only interfere with exercise of this discretion if the judge's decision is wholly unreasonable. Appellate interventions will therefore be rare. In *W (Dennis)* [2002] EWCA Crim 1732 the Court, however, did unusually intervene. W had been convicted of indecent assaults committed on three boys. Although medical evidence had been given by an expert witness called by the Crown which indicated that W suffered from a medical condition that probably rendered him physically incapable of engaging in the type of sexual activity described by one of the boys, no warning had been delivered putting the jury on their guard to view this boy's evidence with particular care. Kennedy LJ held that a *Makanjuola* warning ought to have been delivered in these circumstances and quashed the relevant convictions.

'Cell confessions'

1.69 In like manner, a pair of cases before the Privy Council has highlighted another context in which a judicial warning may be especially desirable: cases involving what are known as cell confessions—that is, admissions that are claimed to have been made by one prisoner to another during their joint detention. In *Pringle v R* [2003] UKPC 9 at [31], although the Board declined to set down any fixed rules requiring judges to deliver a particular form of warning in such cases, Lord Hope was anxious that trial judges should be particularly vigilant 'where an untried prisoner claims that a fellow untried prisoner confessed to him that he was guilty of the crime for which he was then being held in custody'. This situation, it was said, 'raises an acute problem which will always call for special attention in view of the danger that it may lead to a miscarriage of justice'. A prisoner yet to face trial might all too easily have a strong interest of his own to serve in testifying against a defendant.

> The indications that the evidence may be tainted by an improper motive must be found in the evidence.... Where such indications are present, the judge should draw the jury's attention to these indications and their possible significance. He should then advise them to be cautious before accepting the prisoner's evidence.
>
> (at [31])

Lord Hope reiterated the points he had made in *Pringle*, if anything, with greater force in the subsequent case of *Benedetto v R* [2003] 1 WLR 1545, esp at [27]–[37]. Similar issues arose in *Stone (Michael)* [2005] EWCA Crim 105, where S's convictions for murder and attempted murder rested substantially on a cell confession S was alleged to have made to a drug-addicted prison inmate with whom he had shared a cell. The Court of Appeal repeated that where there is a cell confession, the judge is 'not trammelled by fixed rules':

> [T]here will generally be a need for the judge to point out to the jury that such confessions are often easy to concoct and difficult to prove and that experience has shown that prisoners may have many motives to lie. If the prison informant has a significant criminal record or a history of lying then usually the judge should point this out to the jury and explain that it gives rise to a need for great care and why. The trial judge will be best placed to decide the strength of such warnings and the necessary extent of the accompanying analysis. But not every case requires such a warning ... If an alleged confession, for whatever reason, would not have been easy to invent, it would be absurd to require the judge to tell the jury that confessions are often easy to concoct.
>
> (at [83]–[84])

Prosecutions brought after substantial delay

1.70 In recent years offences are quite frequently prosecuted many years after their commission. Increasingly, stale offences—and, in particular, sexual offences committed many years in the past—are now being pursued. As Holland J explained in *Percival* (1998) 19 June, case no 9706746/X4:

> A developing concern with, and understanding of, sexual abuse is reflected in a growing experience of cases featuring delays that at one time would been regarded as intolerable. That experience and the underlying problem of unreported abuse has encouraged experienced judges to be more liberal in their concept of what is possible by way of a fair trial in the face of delay

Holland J went on to say:

> [B]ut . . . there is a price, namely safeguarding the defendant from unacceptable resultant prejudice by a pro-active approach in terms of directions.

But judicial directions delivered in such circumstances need not be wholly favourable to the defendant. As Toulson LJ pointed out in *Breeze* [2009] EWCA Crim 255:

> Cases involving allegations of historical sexual abuse are always difficult, especially where there is no material independent evidence to support either side. It is proper for the judge to remind the jury . . . that there may be understandable reasons why child abuse does not come to light until many years afterwards, and the fact that a complaint is unsupported by other evidence is not of itself an indication that the evidence is untrue. . . . [B]alance has to be preserved.
>
> (at [23])

The judge nevertheless may need to alert jurors to the danger of real prejudice to the defendant when trials explore events that occurred many years ago. Jurors should be told to ask themselves through whose fault matters did not come to light sooner, to take into account the fact that memories fade over time, to consider how a defendant may find it harder to meet a charge long after the event, and even to give greater weight to the defendant's good character if years have gone by and there has been no repetition of the offence (on good character directions, see *post*, paras **6.16–6.33**). The judge's direction on delay is meant to counteract the disadvantages under which a defendant may labour whenever considerable time has elapsed between the alleged offending and the date of trial. The fact, say, that a defendant, of otherwise good character, is not even questioned about allegations of sexual misconduct until between 28 and 37 years after the events complained of does not mean that it will be deemed unfair to try him on those counts provided that a suitably worded warning is delivered to the jury: eg *Ely* [2005] EWCA Crim 3248.

1.71 Lord Bingham CJ, in *Lloyd* (1998) 30 November, case no 9802447/Z5, considered that it would be 'unduly prescriptive' to require judges to deliver warnings in every case of long-delayed prosecution. Indeed, as his predecessor, Lord Taylor CJ, noted in *E (John)* [1996] 1 Cr App R 88, 92–93:

> We are not saying that as a matter of law or as a matter of invariable practice whenever there has been some delay in the case coming to trial the judge must give the jury direction as to the difficulties in which the defence find themselves. Much must depend upon the length of the delay, the cogency of the evidence and the circumstances of the case.

Nevertheless, although this matter is within the appreciation of the trial judge, a warning will usually be deemed desirable, imposing a 'clear, unequivocal stamp of the court's authority on the issue of delay' (*GY* [1999] Crim LR 825).

1.72 In addition to requiring the delivery of a warning to the jury, extreme delay may create a situation in which a defendant can claim that the proceedings against him ought to be stayed on the ground of abuse of process (see *ante*, paras **1.55–1.61**). However, the mere fact that delay—even culpable delay—has occurred somewhere along the line, will not automatically mean that an abuse of process has occurred. In *Massey* [2001] EWCA Crim 2580, for example, there were long delays before the police got around to taking statements from the three minors who claimed that M had sexually assaulted them. The Court of Appeal nevertheless declined to hold that proceedings against M ought to have been stayed on grounds of abuse of process. Even if criticism could justifiably be levelled at the police for omitting to prosecute the enquiry with proper dispatch, the appellant had still failed to show that he had suffered such a degree of prejudice as to render his trial on 16 counts of indecent assault unfair. Again, in *A-G's Reference (No 2 of 2001)* [2001] EWCA Crim 1568, [2002] Crim LR 207 the Court of Appeal considered a further case where the police had delayed charging a suspect for a considerable time. Lord Woolf CJ stressed that proceedings in which delay had occurred ought only to be stayed where there has actually been an abuse of the court. If the accused has suffered no specific prejudice, other remedies—such as a reduction in sentence or even compensation—are more appropriate.

1.73 At one time there was an occasional tendency to treat abuse of process submissions in cases of delay as though they raised an evidential issue, with the defendant being first required to satisfy an evidential burden of raising the matter and with the Crown then having to disprove abuse of process beyond reasonable doubt (eg, *EW*

[2004] EWCA Crim 2901. See further Chapter 2). As Rose LJ has since made clear in *S* (2006) 170 JP 434, this approach is mistaken:

> The discretionary decision whether or not to grant a stay as an abuse of process, because of delay, is an exercise in judicial assessment dependent on judgment rather than on any conclusion as to fact based on evidence. It is therefore potentially misleading to apply to the exercise of that discretion the language of burden and standard of proof, which is more apt to an evidence-based fact-finding process.
>
> (at [20])

Moreover, in *S* Rose LJ laid down five principles to guide judges in such cases:

- Even where delay is unjustifiable, a permanent stay should be the exception rather than the rule;
- In the absence of fault on the part of the complainant or the prosecution, a stay will rarely be granted;
- In the absence of serious prejudice to the defence such that no fair trial can be held, no stay should be granted;
- When assessing possible serious prejudice, judges should bear in mind their power to regulate the admissibility of evidence and the fact that the trial process itself should ensure that all relevant factual issues arising from delay will be placed before the jury for their consideration in accordance with appropriate judicial directions; and
- If, having considered all these factors, a judge's assessment is that a fair trial will be possible, a stay should not be granted.

1.74 Claims of abuse of process in cases of delay have grown so common that in *Smolinski* [2004] 2 Cr App R 40 Lord Woolf CJ questioned the wisdom of counsel routinely resorting to abuse of process, particularly before any evidence had been called in the case. Because the Crown can normally be relied upon to have considered carefully whether or not to proceed with stale charges:

> In the normal way we would suggest that it is better not to make an application based on abuse of process. It will take up the court's time unnecessarily. Unless the case is exceptional, the application will be unsuccessful... If an application is to be made to a judge, the best time for doing so is after any evidence has been called... [I]t seems to us that on the whole it is preferable for the evidence to be called and for a judge then to make his decision as to whether the trial should proceed or whether the evidence is such that it would not be safe for a jury to convict.
>
> (at [8]–[9])

The Court was anxious to make two, not always easily reconcilable, points: first, that it wished to discourage applications based on abuse in delay cases; and secondly, that whenever evidence was given after a long period of years, it still urged the trial court to scrutinise the circumstances with great care at the end of the evidence to see whether or not the case was safe to be left to jury:

> We are certainly not indicating that it is not right to bring prosecutions in the appropriate circumstances merely because of the period that has elapsed.... Justice must be done of course to a defendant, but the court must also be mindful of the position of the alleged victims.
>
> (at [13])

Evidence excluded as a matter of public policy

Intercepted communications: the Regulation of Investigatory Powers Act 2000 (RIPA)

1.75 Generally speaking, English law holds logically probative evidence admissible. Leaving to one side evidence excluded under s 78 of PACE (*ante*, paras **1.47–1.54**), along with the law governing confessions (which, regardless of their probative force, may be excluded under s 76 of PACE if the party seeking to rely upon them cannot establish that they were obtained lawfully: see *post*, Chapter 10), the Regulation of Investigatory Powers Act 2000 (RIPA), which is the successor to the Interception of Communications Act 1985, affords a notable exception to English law's general principle of admissibility. The 1985 Act was passed hot upon the heels of *Malone v United Kingdom* (1984) 7 EHRR 14, a case in which the European Court of Human Rights had criticised the inaccessibility, imprecision and lack of formal safeguards in the area of communications intercepts in the UK. Although the 1985 White Paper, which preceded that Act, stated its objects clearly enough, the House of Lords only settled the meaning of the Interception of Communications Act at the third attempt in *Morgans v DPP* [2001] 1 AC 315.

1.76 Briefly, s 1(1) of RIPA declares that it is an offence for anyone:

> ...intentionally and without lawful authority to intercept, at any place in the United Kingdom, any communication in the course of its transmission by means of:
>
> (a) a public postal service; or
>
> (b) a public telecommunication system.

Section 1(2) also makes it an offence to intercept communications transmitted via private telecommunication systems. However, the Act then states that an offence is not committed in certain situations: for example, if the interception was effected under warrant from the Home Secretary (s 5) or if the interceptor had reasonable grounds to believe that the sender and the intended recipient of the communication had consented to the interception of the communication (s 3). Section 5 enumerates the circumstances in which a warrant may issue. In particular, it permits the Home Secretary to do so 'for the purpose of preventing or detecting serious crime' (s 5(3) (b)). There are further exemptions from criminal liability, not relevant for present purposes. Section 17(1) provides:

> [N]o evidence shall be adduced, question asked, assertion or disclosure made or other thing done, for the purposes of or in connection with any legal proceedings which (in any manner)—
>
> (a) discloses, in circumstances from which its origin in anything falling within subs (2) may be inferred, any of the contents of an intercepted communication or any related communication data; or
>
> (b) tends (apart from any such disclosure) to suggest that anything falling within subs (2) has or may have occurred or be going to occur.

Section 17(2) lists five categories of information about the provenance of communications which may not be revealed: essentially, these relate to the fact that offences of unlawful interception may have been committed, that a warrant to intercept has been issued or that such a warrant may have been applied for. Although the effect is to exclude a great deal of otherwise relevant evidence from criminal trials, strictly speaking, the 2000 Act does not render intercept evidence inadmissible; technically, it only forbids its disclosure (see, eg, *Scotting* [2004] EWCA Crim 197 at [14] *per* Latham LJ). The consequences, however, are to all intents indistinguishable.

1.77 It perhaps needs to be emphasised that not all police monitoring of suspects that reveals the contents of telephone conversations will necessarily fall foul of the Act's restrictive evidentiary provisions. In *E* [2004] 1 WLR 3279, for example, in the course of a drugs enquiry, the police placed a listening device in X's car. As well as conversations X conducted with other occupants of the car, the listening device picked up what X said to other people in calls that he made over his mobile telephone. The listening device, however, did not register the replies and conversation of the people to whom X was telephoning. The Court of Appeal rejected the argument that evidence of what X had had to say on these occasions was inadmissible on the ground that it fell within the restrictions imposed by the 2000 Act. Rix LJ observed in particular that in defining what constitutes an 'interception' in s 17(2) and s 17(8) of RIPA the legislation variously refers to communications 'in the course of transmission' or 'whilst being transmitted':

> ...the natural meaning of the expression "interception" denotes some inference [*sic*] or abstraction of the signal, whether it is passing along wires or by wireless telegraphy, during the process of transmission. The recording of a person's voice, independently of

the fact that at that time he is using a telephone, does not become interception simply because what he says goes not only...into the recorder, but, by separate process, is transmitted by a telecommunications system.

(at [20])

The court therefore concluded that what was being recorded was not the transmission but the words of X taken from the sound waves in the car. The evidence was therefore admissible evidence for the Crown.

1.78 Although the 1985 Act has been replaced, Lord Mustill's explanation of the purpose behind this general prohibition on disclosure of materials obtained via an intercept, delivered in *Preston* [1994] 2 AC 130, still holds good:

The purpose of [s 17] can be seen as the protection, not of the fruits of the intercepts, but of information as to the manner in which they were authorised and carried out... [T]he defendant was not to have the opportunity to muddy the waters at a trial by cross-examination designed to elicit the Secretary of State's sources of knowledge or the surveillance authorities' confidential methods of work. Evidently, the proscription of questioning on the existence of warrants was seen as an economical means of achieving this result.

(p 167)

The policy of the statute, therefore is to protect the methods and sources of information of bodies engaged in surveillance by excluding all reference to them in proceedings. In the words of Lord Bingham of Cornhill,

The obvious purpose of this prohibition was to preserve the secrecy of what had, to be effective, to be a covert operation.

(*A-G's Reference (No 5 of 2002)* [2004] 3 WLR 957 at [6])

1.79 Given the counter-intuitive quality of this area of the law, students coming fresh to the topic will be bemused by the wholesale exclusion of telecommunications intercept evidence in the supposed interests of methodological secrecy. True, a few provisions expressly exempt proceedings from the ambit of this prohibition. Section 18(1)(e) of the Anti-terrorism, Crime and Security Act 2001, for instance, under which the Special Immigration Appeals Commission hears appeals against decisions to certify and detain suspected international terrorists, has 'disapplied' s 17 of RIPA and allows the tribunal to receive evidence of intercepted communications. But more significantly, with growing concern at the difficulties encountered in convicting major criminals and terrorists, this 'policy choice' on the part of the Home Office to conceal details of the extent and methods of police surveillance of criminals, even at the cost of excluding valuable prosecution evidence, has come under intense scrutiny. In July 2003 the Prime Minister ordered a review to be undertaken (the fifth such review in the space of 10 years) which was to examine the benefits and risks of using intercepted communications as evidence to secure more convictions of organised criminals and terrorists. The Home Secretary delivered a written report in January 2005, concluding that the risks which would be incurred in allowing the use of intercept evidence remained too great to permit removal of the prohibition, but promised that the matter would be kept under review. In October 2005 Lord Lloyd of Berwick introduced an Interception of Communications (Admissibility of Evidence) Bill into the House of Lords. This Bill would have allowed the Crown to apply to the court for permission to introduce intercept evidence for the purpose of conducting a criminal prosecution for serious crime or offences relating to terrorism. After receiving a second reading, the Bill proceeded no further.

1.80 The 2000 Act is an intricate enactment by any standards. Indeed, in *A-G's Reference (No 5 of 2002)* Clarke LJ actually admitted that it is 'a particularly puzzling statute', adding for good measure that, like the 1985 Act before it, it is 'a difficult statute (if somewhat longer)' ([2003] 1 WLR 2902 at [98]). In the House of Lords, Lord Bingham, too, comparing RIPA with its predecessor, said:

> [T]he 2000 Act is both longer and even more perplexing. The trial judge and the Court of Appeal found it difficult to construe the provisions of the Act with confidence, and the House has experienced the same difficulty.
>
> ([2004] 3 WLR 957 at [9])

The confusing nature of RIPA is brought out by the question eventually posed before the House of Lords in this last-mentioned case. Whilst all would have agreed that the contents of intercepts made from private telecommunications systems were admissible in evidence, it was seriously questioned whether it was open to a criminal court actually to investigate whether intercept material relied upon by the Crown had in fact been obtained by tapping a private as opposed to a public telecommunications system. In short, if a dispute arose, it was suggested that any judicial inquiry into the question would infringe the general prohibition on disclosure imposed under this legislation. Lord Bingham commented that such a situation would be 'absurd' (at [20]), Lord Nicholls of Birkenhead favoured the term 'bizarre' (at [28]), whilst Lord Steyn confined himself to politely noting that 'the Act creates a linguistic difficulty' (at [31]). Thankfully, the House of Lords bulldozed through the statutory verbiage, concluding with disarming simplicity:

> Given the obvious public interest in admitting probative evidence...and the absence of any public interest in excluding it, I am satisfied that a court may properly enquire whether the interception was of a public or private system and, if the latter, whether the interception was lawful. If the court concludes that it was public, that is the end of the enquiry. If the court concludes that it was private but unlawful, that also will be the end of the

enquiry. If it was private but lawful, the court may (subject to any argument that there may be) admit the evidence.

([2004] 3 WLR 957 at [20] *per* Lord Bingham)

1.81 Although RIPA only expressly forbids the disclosure of information concerning the methods and sources of intercept information, this does not mean that the prosecution can rely upon the contents of intercepts provided that the sources are not alluded to. The Human Rights Act 1998 militates against the drawing of this distinction. As Lord Hope explained in *Morgans*, even if the prosecution can introduce its evidence without alluding to the intercept, the defendant will almost certainly wish to explore this forbidden territory. By preventing him from testing the evidence, s 17 deprives the defendant of proper safeguards and, owing to a consequent inequality of arms, infringes his right to fair trial under art 6 of the European Convention. Therefore, the unsurprising conclusion drawn by Lord Hope was that:

> Evidence of material obtained by the interception by the persons mentioned in [the legislation] of communications of the kind described in...that Act...will always be inadmissible. It is not possible to say that [s 17] of the Act provides for this in express language. But, in the context of the Act as a whole, the prohibitions which it contains lead inexorably to that result.

1.82 It does perhaps need to be stressed that s 17 of the Act only excludes evidence of *intercepted* communications. As Rose LJ was at pains to emphasise in *Hardy and Hardy* [2003] 1 Cr App R 30, s 17 only renders inadmissible the product of interceptions properly so-called, whether authorised by the Home Secretary or effected illegally. Unlike its legislative predecessor, RIPA defines what is meant by 'interception'. Section 2(2) specifies:

> A person intercepts a communication in the course of its transmission by means of a telecommunications system if, and only if, he—
>
> (a) so modifies or interferes with the system, or its operation,
>
> (b) so monitors transmissions made by means of the system, or
>
> (c) so monitors transmissions made by wireless telegraphy to or from apparatus comprised in the system,
>
> as to make some or all of the contents of communication available, while being transmitted, to a person other than the sender or intended recipient of the communication.'

This definition requires that the contents of the communication be made available to a third person 'while being transmitted'. Thus, in *Hardy and Hardy*, when an undercover police officer tape-recorded his conversation with one of the drug traffickers, this was not 'interception' within the meaning of RIPA and the tape recording was subsequently admissible at H's trial. Similarly, in *Allsopp et al* [2005]

EWCA Crim 703 Gage LJ held that a face-to-face conversation between A and K, picked up by a telephone-like apparatus in A's car and transmitted to the police, was not a 'communication' between two individuals within the meaning of RIPA, and, therefore, was not an intercepted communication. The conversation between the first and second defendants, quite simply, had not been drawn into the telecommunications system. In contrast, 'the position of a telephone conversation which is intercepted and overheard by a third party, unknown to either of the parties to it, is different. That is what is separately provided for as "interception" for the purposes of the 2000 Act' ([2003] 1 Cr App R 30 at [34]).

1.83 More generally, if the communication falls outside the statute, intercept evidence is generally admissible. Thus, in *P* [2002] 1 AC 146 the House of Lords upheld a judge's ruling that telephone intercept evidence lawfully acquired by the authorities in a foreign jurisdiction could be used at the appellants' trial on serious drug charges in England. The English legislation is concerned only with intercepts effected within the United Kingdom. In similar fashion, in *Scotting* [2004] EWCA Crim 197 the Court of Appeal had no difficulty in holding that evidence of intercepted telephone calls made from a prison, in the first instance arranging the delivery of drugs to the prison and later endeavouring to set up a false defence of duress for the supplier, were admissible. Section 18(4) of the Act explicitly permits the disclosure of certain categories of intercept, including those effected under rules made under the Prison Act 1952.

1.84 Of course, even if disclosure of the evidence is not forbidden, a court might still exclude it under PACE, s 78 if its admission was felt to reflect adversely on the fairness of those proceedings (*ante*, paras **1.47–1.54**). In *P*, however, where this question was considered, the House of Lords rejected P's claim that art 8 of the ECHR, which guarantees respect for private life, inevitably predicated the exclusion of intercept evidence not covered by RIPA. Deriving support from the ECtHR's decision in *Khan v UK* (2000) 8 BHRC 310 (*ante*, para **1.57**), Lord Hobhouse robustly declared:

> Questions of the admissibility of evidence are not governed by art 8. The fair use of intercept evidence at a trial is not a breach of art 6 even if the evidence was unlawfully obtained. It is a cogent factor in favour of the admission of intercept evidence that one of the parties to the relevant conversation is going to be a witness at the trial and give evidence of what was said during it.
>
> (p 472)

Moreover, the House expressly dismissed the notion that there is any principle requiring the exclusion of intercept evidence independent of the relevant legislation.

1.85 Given the generous breadth of the prohibition imposed by the Interception of Communications Act 1985, it was argued in *Sargent* [2003] 1 AC 347 that there was 'an implied statutory prohibition' against the use of transcripts of intercepts even by the police when they interviewed suspects. This was said to arise from the fact that the police's entitlement to withhold favourable intercept material from the defence on these occasions would contravene both the common law's concept of fairness and the principle of 'equality of arms', guaranteed under the ECHR (eg, *Jasper v UK* (2000) 30 EHRR 441). In *Sargent*, S had been convicted of conspiring to commit arson with intent to endanger life. By chance his victim, P, worked for a telephone company, a circumstance that enabled him to monitor and record telephone calls. Without his company's authorisation, P recorded one call made by S to P's former wife in which S made incriminating statements. P made a transcript of this conversation and passed both transcript and recording to the police. The police interviewed S, who, when told of the recording and the transcript, made admissions. Although the House of Lords found that, in light of *Morgans v DPP*, the trial judge had been wrong to allow the Crown to adduce the intercept evidence, Lord Hope went on to hold that there was no reason in addition to outlaw the use by the police of inadmissible intercept evidence at interview. Such an approach, first, would go against English law's tradition of admitting illegally obtained evidence provided that it is relevant. Second, any such rule would apply indiscriminately even to cases like *Sargent* itself where, as it happened, the police had made full disclosure of the entire transcript to the defendant, thereby evading any accusation involving 'inequality of arms' or unfairness. Further, s 78 of PACE was felt to afford defendants ample protection against any unfairness that the use of intercept material might occasion. More generally, Lord Hope recalled the words of Lord Steyn in *A-G's Reference (No 3 of 1999)* [2001] 2 AC 91, 118 to the effect that the purpose of the criminal law is to permit everyone to go about their daily lives without fear or harm to person or property and that crime should be effectively investigated and prosecuted.

FURTHER READING

Carter, 'Judicial Notice: Related and Unrelated Matters', in Waller and Campbell (eds), *Well and Truly Tried* (1982, Sydney), pp 88ff

Grevling, 'Fairness and the Exclusion of Evidence under s 78(1) of PACE' (1997) 113 LQR 667

Mirfield, 'Shedding a Tear for Issue Estoppel' [1980] Crim LR 336

Mirfield, 'Regulation of Investigatory Powers Act 2000: Evidential Aspects' [2001] Crim LR 91

Munday, 'Gruesome Photographs' (1990) 154 JP Jo 19

Munday, 'Proof of Guilt by Association under Section 74 of the Police and Criminal Evidence Act 1984' [1990] Crim LR 236

Munday, '*Exemplum habemus*: Reflections on the Judicial Studies Board's Specimen Directions' [2006] J Crim Law 27

Ormerod and Birch, 'The Evolution of the Discretionary Exclusion of Evidence' [2004] Crim LR 767

Ormerod and McKay, 'Telephone Intercepts and their Admissibility' [2004] Crim LR 15

Spencer, 'Intercept Evidence–the Case for Change' (2008) 172 JP Jo 651 and 671

SELF-TEST QUESTIONS

1. When, if ever, may the Crown adduce evidence of an accused's extravagant lifestyle when prosecuting offences involving the possession of drugs (a) with, and (b) without intent to supply?

2. What rules, if any, govern the admissibility of fingerprint evidence?

3. To what extent does English law still respect a 'best evidence rule'?

4. What do you understand by the term 'judicial notice'? How does it differ from the situation where justices make use of their personal knowledge?

5. What do you understand by the principle of 'double jeopardy'? Does issue estoppel have any role to play in the criminal law?

6. Despite the generous wording of PACE, s 74, when do the courts in practice allow the Crown to adduce evidence of a third party's convictions?

7. When ought a trial judge to exclude prosecution evidence under PACE, s 78 on the ground that the accused may have been induced to commit the offence charged?

8. When ought a trial judge to look to abuse of process rather than to exercise of discretion to exclude evidence under PACE, s 78?

9. Explain why the prosecution is generally prevented from adducing evidence derived even from lawful intercepts under the Regulation of Investigatory Powers Act 2000. What use, if any, can be made of information acquired in this way?

10. What is the significance of Lord Woolf CJ's judgment in *Smolinski* [2004] 2 Cr App R 40?

2

Presumptions and the burden of proof

SUMMARY

Criminal and civil burdens of proof

The 'legal burden of proof' and the 'evidential burden'

The 'tactical burden'

The prosecution's legal burden of proof in criminal cases

When the defendant in a criminal case bears the legal burden of proof

- The exceptions to the general rule: at common law the defence of insanity imposes a burden of proof on the accused

- The exceptions to the general rule: statute may expressly decree that the defence bears the legal burden of proof

- The exceptions to the general rule: statute may impliedly cast the burden of proof on the defendant

The standard of proof

The evidential burden

The judge's 'invisible burden'

The burden of proof when establishing the admissibility of evidence

Presumptions and the incidence of the burden of proof

Reversal of the burden of proof and the ECHR

- *R v Lambert* and the 'reading down' of reverse burdens of proof

- Reverse burdens of proof after *R v Lambert*

- *R v Lambert*, *R v Johnstone*, and *Sheldrake v DPP*

- Criminal offences properly so-called and regulatory legislation

---

FAY: You must prove me guilty. That is the law.

TRUSCOTT: You know nothing of the law. I know nothing of the law. That makes us equal in the sight of the law.

FAY: I'm innocent until I'm proved guilty. This is a free country. The law is impartial.

TRUSCOTT: Who's been filling your head with that rubbish?

Joe Orton, Loot (1966)

2.1 Given that it is decisive to the determination of the contested issues in civil and criminal cases, one might expect the burden of proof to be a straightforward topic. Sadly, such is not the case. The topic has spawned a considerable literature, and commentators have adopted a number of different terminologies. It seems appropriate for an introductory work to avoid being drawn into too many of the (possibly unnecessary) intricacies of the subject. This chapter, therefore, will concentrate upon outlining the leading principles before focusing on the impact the Human Rights Act 1998 has exerted on the incidence of the burden of proof in criminal cases. Indeed, the entire chapter will concentrate largely upon the burden of proof as it affects criminal cases.

Criminal and civil burdens of proof

2.2 Since a trial involves the determination of the relative strength of two competing contentions, it is vital to know which party bears the burden of proving what. Unfortunately, the very expression 'burden of proof' is the subject of terminological confusion. From the outset, it is necessary to distinguish between two different types of so-called 'burden'. On the one hand, there is the true burden of proof—variously called the 'legal burden', the 'persuasive burden' or the 'onus of proof'. When this legal burden of proof rests with a party, that party has the duty of proving its case to the trier of fact to the standard stipulated by law. The law imposes different standards of proof according to whether the case is criminal or civil.

- In a criminal case the legal burden normally rests with the Crown, which will have to prove the accused's guilt to the jury (if the case is indictable) or the magistrates (if the case is tried summarily) beyond reasonable doubt.

- In a civil case, in contrast, the party bearing the legal burden need only establish its case on a balance of probabilities, demonstrating that the existence or non-existence of a particular fact or facts in issue is more probable than not. There have been persistent *dicta* suggesting that the burden of proof in civil cases ought to vary according to the gravity of the misconduct alleged or the seriousness of the consequences for the party concerned. This so-called 'heightened civil standard of proof' has been advocated in cases either where proceedings defined as 'civil' entail such serious consequences that it is felt that a more demanding standard of proof ought to be imposed (eg, the imposition of sex offender orders: *B v Chief Constable of Avon and Somerset Constabulary* [2001] 1 WLR 340 or sexual offences prevention orders: *R (Cleveland Police) v Haggas* (2010) 174 JP 1332), or where the inherent improbability of an event means that unusually powerful evidence is required in order to persuade the tribunal that it is more probable than not that the event occurred (eg, allegations of fraud: *Hornal v Neuberger Products Ltd* [1957] 1 QB 247, 266 *per* Morris LJ). The House of Lords, however, has firmly rejected this notion, and insists that the burden of proof in civil cases is always on the balance of probabilities. The point was made in *re H (Minors)(Sexual Abuse: Standard of Proof)* [1996] AC 563, 586, a case involving allegations of sexual abuse of a child, and was subsequently endorsed and explained in *re B (Children)* [2009] 1 AC 11. Whilst there may well be certain classes of civil proceedings in which the criminal standard of proof, properly so called, ought to be imposed, the civil standard of proof does not deviate. Speaking in *re B* of care proceedings in which numerous unpleasant allegations had been made, Baroness Hale said,

> Neither the seriousness of the allegation nor the seriousness of the consequences should make any difference to the standard of proof to be applied in determining the facts. The inherent probabilities are simply something to be taken into account, where relevant, in deciding where the truth lies.
>
> (at [70])

Reflecting more generally, Lord Hoffmann declared:

> I think that the time has come to say, once and for all, that there is only one civil standard of proof and that is proof that the fact in issue more probably occurred than not....Common sense, not law, requires that in deciding this question, regard should be had, to whatever extent appropriate, to inherent probabilities. If a child alleges sexual abuse by a parent, it is common sense to start with the assumption that most parents do not abuse their children. But this assumption may be swiftly dispelled by other compelling evidence of the relationship between parent and child or parent and other children. It would be absurd to suggest that the tribunal must in all cases assume that serious conduct is unlikely to have occurred.
>
> (at [13] and [15])

The 'legal burden of proof' and the 'evidential burden'

2.3 Whereas the 'legal' or 'persuasive burden' is in a true sense a burden of proof in that it involves a party establishing something to the satisfaction of the trier of fact, the 'evidential burden' is not really a burden of proof at all. As a Canadian judge, Dickson CJC, explained:

> I prefer to use the terms "persuasive burden" to refer to the requirement of proving a case or disproving defences and "evidential burden" to mean the requirement of putting an issue into play by reference to evidence before the court. The party who has the persuasive burden is required to persuade the trier of fact, to convince the trier of fact that a certain set of facts existed. Failure to persuade means that the party loses. The party with an evidential burden is not required to convince the trier of fact of anything, only to point out evidence which suggests that certain facts existed.
>
> (*Schwartz* (1988) 66 CR (3d) 251, 270)

On account of the very different roles fulfilled by the two species of 'burden', there is strong reason to avoid referring to the 'evidential burden' in language that might suggest that it operates as a burden of proof. As Dickson CJC went on to say:

> The phrase "onus of proof" should be restricted to the persuasive burden, since an issue can be put into play without being proven. The phrases "burden of going forward" and "burden of adducing evidence" should not be used, as they imply that the party is required to produce his or her evidence on an issue. As we have seen, in a criminal case the accused can rely on evidence produced by the Crown to argue for a reasonable doubt.

2.4 Lord Devlin, in *Jayasena* [1970] AC 618 at 624, expressed similar concern at the confusion the expression 'evidential burden' can engender, noting that 'it is misleading to call it a burden of proof, whether described as legal or evidential or by any other adjective, when it can be discharged by production of evidence that falls short of proof'. Lord Ackner was to voice similar concerns in *Hunt* [1987] AC 352, 385, observing that 'the discharge of an evidential burden proves nothing—it merely raises an issue'. In *Lynch v DPP* [2003] QB 137 at [22], Pill LJ even suggested that 'it is better not to speak of an evidential burden of proof', praying in aid the practical consideration that:

> ...the so-called burden may not in substance be a burden on the defendant at all. Evidence raising the issue will often emerge from the evidence, direct and circumstantial, called by the prosecution. A defendant is entitled...to have that evidence scrutinised by the court.
>
> (at [23])

Not all judges, however, have sought to outlaw use of the term. Clarke LJ observed in *Sheldrake v DPP* [2004] QB 487 at [47] that 'it is...sensible to continue to use it provided that it is recognised that all that is required to discharge the burden is to identify evidence raising the issue'. More recently, addressing the question with customary clarity, Lord Bingham explained what is meant by an evidential burden resting on a defendant:

> An evidential burden is not a burden of proof. It is a burden of raising, on the evidence in the case, an issue as to the matter in question fit for consideration by the tribunal of fact. If an issue is properly raised, it is for the prosecutor to prove, beyond reasonable doubt, that that ground of exoneration does not avail the defendant.
> (*Sheldrake v DPP* [2004] 1 AC 264 at [1])

(Sadly, from time to time, a court will still misapply the expression: see, eg, *Sewell* [2004] EWCA Crim 2322 at [20] *per* Scott Baker LJ; *Malinina* [2007] EWCA Crim 3228 at [11] *per* Longmore LJ.)

2.5 The 'evidential burden', therefore, is simply the obligation borne by a party to show the court that there is sufficient evidence to raise an issue. Wigmore, perhaps most helpfully, describes the evidential burden as the duty of 'passing the judge'. This latter expression is felicitous because it brings out the fact that two different dynamics are at work, according to whether the burden is legal or evidential. The evidential burden refers to the initial hurdle a party faces, to adduce enough evidence to prevent the judge from withdrawing an issue from the court's consideration. The legal burden, in contrast, refers to a party's obligation to prove the existence or non-existence of a fact in issue to the requisite standard to the satisfaction of the trier of fact. As Wigmore explained in relation to jury trials:

> The important practical distinction between these two senses of "burden of proof" is this: the risk of non-persuasion operates when the case has come into the hands of the jury, while the duty of producing evidence implies a liability to a ruling by the judge, disposing of the issue without leaving the issue open to the jury's deliberations.
> (*Evidence in Trials at Common Law* (1981) ed Chadbourn, vol IX, para 2487, p 299)

The 'tactical burden'

2.6 At the risk of complicating matters further, reference is sometimes made to another species of burden, the 'provisional burden'. This 'burden' (which is also called, more aptly perhaps, the 'tactical burden') simply signifies the fact that when party A has satisfied his evidential burden, if party B does not adduce any evidence in rebuttal B runs the risk that the court will find against him on that issue. So, to the extent that there is such a thing as a provisional burden, its significance is strategic. It is in the main recognition that, as a matter of common sense, party B might be acting ill-advisedly if he does not adduce some evidence. Although the extent of B's imprudence, should he elect not to call evidence, will normally vary according to the relative strength of the evidence A has amassed, the operation of the tactical burden is revealed most clearly in cases where a presumption of fact comes into play.

2.7 A presumption of fact is an inference that it is permissible for the tribunal of fact to draw if certain facts are established. Take a straightforward example—a trial for handling stolen goods. The prosecution has the legal burden of proving three things: that the goods are stolen; that D handled the goods in one of the ways referred to in the Theft Act 1968; and that D had the requisite *mens rea*. There is a rule at common law that if the Crown can prove beyond reasonable doubt that D has handled *recently* stolen goods but adduces no evidence to show that D knew or believed those goods to be stolen goods, then the jury, if it wishes, may nevertheless presume guilty knowledge and convict D. As Lord Reading CJ explained in *Abramovitch* (1916) 11 Cr App R 45 at 49:

> Where the prisoner is charged with [handling stolen] property, when the prosecution has proved the possession by the prisoner, and that the goods had been recently stolen, the jury should be told that they may, not that they must, in the absence of any reasonable explanation, find the prisoner guilty.

The jury does not have to draw this inference, but it is at liberty to do so if it feels that such a course is appropriate. The jury's decision whether or not to do so will turn on its willingness to make the commonsensical assumption that it is likely that someone who has handled *hot* stolen goods ought to have a pretty shrewd idea of their likely provenance. In such circumstances, D does not of course carry any legal burden; D does not have to prove an absence of guilty knowledge. Equally, D does not bear an evidential burden; D does not have to call any evidence at all. However, given that the jury is entitled to draw an inference that D had guilty knowledge, and might choose to do so and convict, D can be said to have a tactical/provisional burden, in the sense that D runs the risk of the issue of guilty knowledge being decided against him in the event of his not calling evidence. In this sense, the tactical burden is a matter of practical strategy, not of legal obligation.

2.8 Particularly in this context, one finds judges sometimes speaking of the 'shifting' of the burden of proof. But since one cannot be sure what impact the evidence called by one party may have had on the minds of the tribunal of fact, it is not really possible to determine when a 'tactical' burden may actually have arisen. The use of the expression 'shifting of the burden' is misleading. Burdens do not shift as such. Such language is best avoided.

> Our fathers claimed, by obvious madness moved,
> Man's innocent until his guilt is proved.
> They would have known, had they not been confused,
> He's innocent until he is accused.
>
> Ogden Nash, 'Period I' in *You Can't Get There from Here* (1957) p 123

The prosecution's legal burden of proof in criminal cases

2.9 Probably the most celebrated principle of English criminal law is that the accused is initially presumed innocent and it is for the prosecution to prove the guilt of an accused person beyond reasonable doubt. Thus, English law does not merely presume defendants innocent, but it also insists upon the prosecution discharging a heavy onus before accused persons can be adjudged guilty. As the court put it in *Hobson* (1823) 1 Lew CC 261, 'it is a maxim of English law that ten guilty men should escape rather than one innocent man should suffer'. This article of faith was emphatically endorsed in *Woolmington v DPP* [1935] AC 462. W had been charged with murdering his wife. His defence was that he had shot her accidentally. The trial judge had instructed the jury that while it was for the Crown to prove that W had shot and killed his wife, it was for W then to show that there were circumstances in the evidence either which reduced the offence to one of manslaughter or which excused the killing entirely. In short, the defendant bore the burden of establishing any defence he wished to advance. The House of Lords, however, rejected this approach and held that, save in certain exceptional cases, the prosecution bore the burden of proving all the elements of the crime *and* of negativing any defences advanced by the accused. In the resounding words of Viscount Sankey LC:

> Throughout the web of the English criminal law one golden thread is always seen, that it is the duty of the prosecution to prove the prisoner's guilt subject to...the defence of insanity and subject also to any statutory exception. If, at the end and on the whole of the case, there is a reasonable doubt, created by the evidence given by either the prosecution or the prisoner, as to whether the prisoner killed the deceased with a malicious intention, the prosecution has not made out the case and the prisoner is entitled to an acquittal. No matter what the charge or where the trial, the principle that the prosecution must prove

the guilt of the prisoner is part of the common law of England and no attempt to whittle it down can be entertained.

(at 481–2)

This 'golden thread', which imposes the entire legal burden on the prosecution, is not as ancient a concept as this passage might suggest. While the notion that the Crown must prove its case beyond reasonable doubt can be traced back to the mid-nineteenth century (eg *White* (1865) 4 F & F 383), before 1935 it was at least moot which party carried the burden of proving or disproving defences. The House of Lords in *Woolmington*, therefore, can take credit for having settled that the prosecution bears the entire burden in criminal cases.

2.10 There are several reasons why the Crown ought to bear this substantial burden of proof. Firstly, as Fitzjames Stephen argued, 'society...is so much stronger than the individual, and is capable of inflicting so very much more harm on the individual than the individual as a rule can inflict upon society, that it can afford to be generous' (*History of the Criminal Law*, vol I, 354). Not surprisingly, this idea only emerged in the latter portion of the nineteenth century, once the English criminal justice system had grown reasonably effective, with a professional police force, a reasonably organised prosecution system and so on. Secondly, and perhaps most importantly, by reducing the risk of wrongful convictions, it is said that a heavy burden of proof reinforces the legitimacy of the criminal justice system. As we have learned to our cost, there is nothing more demoralising for the criminal justice system than a succession of miscarriages of justice. Moreover, correcting such errors can involve a profligate waste of time and money. Thirdly, taking into account the profound inequality between the resources available to the state and those available to the individual, a basic sense of fairness would suggest that the balance ought to be tipped in favour of the individual. Additionally, it has been argued that a heavy onus borne by the prosecution can serve a symbolic function within the criminal justice framework. It demonstrates the gravity of criminal convictions and thereby enhances their moral force and, more wishfully, even augments their deterrent effect.

2.11 Whilst in criminal cases it falls to the prosecution to disprove the majority of defences raised by an accused—such as loss of control (under the Coroners and Justice Act 2009, s 54), alibi, duress and self-defence—it might be noted, in contrast, that in civil proceedings, where defendants may sometimes rely upon similar defences, the burden of proof operates quite differently. In *Ashley v Chief Constable of Sussex Police (Sherwood intervening)* [2008] 2 WLR 975, a son and father sued the police under the Fatal Accidents Act 1976 and the Law Reform (Miscellaneous Provisions) Act 1934 in respect of the death of their relative, who had been shot in the course of an armed police raid on premises that were suspected of being used for drug dealing. In respect of the claimants' allegations of assault and battery the police denied liability, pleading self-defence. In the Court of Appeal Sir Anthony Clarke MR, in his conclusions on the relevant law, with which Auld and Arden LJJ agreed, crisply stated:

> In criminal proceedings the burden of negativing self-defence is on the prosecution. By contrast, in civil proceedings the burden is on the defendant to establish self-defence.
>
> ([2007] 1 WLR 398 at [82]; and again at [170])

This distinction is potentially significant. Although the other members of the Court of Appeal saw matters differently, it is suggested that there is some force in the point made both by Auld LJ (see at [176] ff) and by the trial judge, Dobbs J, that a defendant to a civil claim for battery who relies upon self-defence is in a worse position forensically than a similar defendant in criminal proceedings. This could matter. If a claimant has some ulterior motive for pursuing the civil claim—for instance, his claim is employed as proxy for a public inquiry—questions must arise as to whether the claim amounts to an abuse of the process of the court and, more specifically, whether the judge needs to invoke appropriate trial management powers, notably the power to strike out the claim because it puts a civil defendant to proof of a contention that is not genuinely at issue in the case (Civil Procedure Rules, r 3.4(2)(b)).

When the defendant in a criminal case bears the legal burden of proof

2.12 How frequently does the defendant bear the burden of proof? Upon reading the excerpt from Viscount Sankey LC's speech in *Woolmington* quoted *ante* (para **2.9**), the uninitiated might run away with the idea that it is extremely rare for English law to impose a burden of proof on an accused person. Such, however, is not the case. In a study published in 1996 Ashworth and Blake leafed through *Archbold*, noting all indictable offences in which the legislature at some point imposed a legal burden on the defendant. Disturbingly, they discovered that in approximately 40 per cent of indictable offences, the defendant may come to bear a legal burden of proof at some point. On closer examination, therefore, we discover that the 'golden thread of the English criminal law' looks a trifle frayed (see [1996] Crim LR 306). Further, it should be remembered that Ashworth and Blake's study only examined the more serious criminal offences, triable on indictment before the Crown Court. Were one to conduct a similar experiment with summary offences, there is little doubt that one would find that the percentage of those offences triable before magistrates' courts which cast a legal burden on the defendant would be considerably higher.

2.13 The required standard of proof is less exacting in cases where, exceptionally, an accused bears the legal burden of proof. Although a body of opinion would support the proposition that the defendant ought only ever to bear an evidential, not a legal burden, it is incontrovertibly established that the defendant bears a legal burden in a variety of situations. However, whereas the Crown bears the heavy burden of establishing guilt beyond reasonable doubt, the burden imposed on the defendant is less onerous, being on a balance of probabilities. In the words of Humphreys J in *Carr-Briant* [1943] KB 607 at 612:

> ...in any case where, either by statute or at common law, some matter is presumed against an accused person "unless the contrary is proved", the jury should be directed that it is for them to decide whether the contrary is proved, that the burden of proof required is less than that required at the hands of the prosecution in proving the case beyond reasonable doubt, and that the burden may be discharged by evidence satisfying the jury of the probability of that which the accused is called upon to establish.

The exceptions to the general rule: at common law the defence of insanity imposes a burden of proof on the accused

2.14 As Viscount Sankey LC pointed out in *Woolmington*, the defence of insanity is the only exception to 'the golden thread' at common law. It can be traced back to the advisory opinions of the judges in *M'Naghten's Case* (1843) 10 Cl & Fin 200. Whenever the accused raises the insanity defence, therefore, it is for him to establish on a balance of probabilities that at the time of the offence he was labouring under such a defect of reason, from disease of mind, as not to know the nature and quality of his act or if he did know it, that he did not know he was doing what was wrong.

The exceptions to the general rule: statute may expressly decree that the defence bears the legal burden of proof

2.15 Not infrequently, Parliament specifically provides that the defendant will bear the burden of proving some particular fact or issue. Examples abound. The Homicide Act 1957, s 2(2), which defines the defence of diminished responsibility, states that:

> On a charge of murder, it shall be *for the defence to prove* that the person charged is by virtue of this section not liable to be convicted of murder.

The language of s 2(2) plainly signifies that it is for the defendant to establish on a balance of probabilities that he was suffering from diminished responsibility at the time of commission of his offence. Similarly, as we have already seen, PACE, s 74 renders admissible the convictions of persons other than the accused where evidence of their having committed them is admissible. In all cases where such evidence is admitted, s 74(2) provides that that person 'shall be taken to have committed that offence *unless the contrary is proved*' (see *ante*, paras **1.40–1.46**). Finally, to take a more contentious, contemporary example, s 1 of the Terrorism Act 2006 has created the offence of encouragement of terrorism. The offence, which forms part of a raft of repressive offences introduced in the wake of the 7 July 2005 London bombings, consists in the glorification of the commission or preparation of certain acts or offences, provided that members of the public could reasonably be expected to infer that what is being glorified is being glorified as conduct that should be emulated by them in existing circumstances. An offence is committed whenever someone publishes a statement 'that is likely to be understood by some or all of the members of the public to whom it is published as a direct or indirect encouragement or other inducement to them to the commission, preparation or instigation of acts of terrorism', provided that the accused intends that, or is reckless as to whether, members of the public will be directly or indirectly encouraged or otherwise induced by the statement to commit, prepare or instigate acts of terrorism. Section 1(6) of the Act provides a defence to such charges:

> In proceedings for an offence under this section against a person in whose case it is not proved that he intended the statement directly or indirectly to encourage or otherwise induce the commission, preparation or instigation of acts of terrorism or Convention offences, *it is a defence for him to show—*
>
> (a) that the statement neither expressed his views nor had his endorsement...; and
>
> (b) that it was clear, in all the circumstances of the statement's publication, that it did not express his views and... did not have his endorsement.
>
> (emphasis added)

By using the words 'it is a defence for him to show' Parliament has made explicit its intention that the defendant must shoulder the burden of establishing on a balance of probabilities the two elements set out in paragraphs (a) and (b). Section 1(6), it should be explained, was intended to provide a protection for news broadcasters and the press who might otherwise fall within the literal wording of the enactment simply by relating the views of those who are committing s 1 offences.

The exceptions to the general rule: statute may impliedly cast the burden of proof on the defendant

2.16 As the House of Lords has held in *Hunt* [1987] AC 352, the 'statutory exceptions' to which Viscount Sankey referred in *Woolmington*, include not only statutes which expressly cast the burden of proof on the defendant but also those that only impose a burden on him by implication. So far as summary offences are concerned, the relevant rule is set out in the Magistrates' Courts Act 1980, s 101, which provides:

> Where the defendant...relies for his defence on any exception, exemption, proviso, excuse or qualification,...the burden of proving [that defence]...shall be on him.

This is potentially a very broad provision. Section 101 in fact originated in the common law. Lawton LJ explained in *Edwards* [1975] 1 QB 27 that:

> [O]ver the centuries the common law, as a result of experience and the need to ensure that justice is done both to the community and to defendants, has evolved an exception to the fundamental rule of our criminal law that the prosecution must prove every element of the offence charged. This exception, like so much else in the common law, was hammered out on the anvil of pleading. It is limited to offences arising under enactments which prohibit the doing of an act save in specified circumstances or by persons of specified classes or specified qualifications or with the licence or permission of specified authorities. Whenever the prosecution seeks to rely on this exception, the court must construe the enactment under which the charge is laid. If the true construction is that the enactment prohibits the doing of acts, subject to provisos, exemptions and the like, then the prosecution can rely upon the exception.

This principle of interpretation, Lawton LJ emphasised, does not proceed upon the fact or the assumption that the defendant had peculiar knowledge enabling him to prove the position of any negative averment—although the House of Lords in *Hunt* did recognise that this consideration is of somewhat greater significance. As Lawton LJ went on to explain:

> Two consequences follow...as to the evolution and nature of this exception. First, as it comes into operation on an enactment construed in a particular way, there is no need for the prosecution to prove a *prima facie* case of lack of excuse, qualification or the like; and secondly, what shifts is the *onus*: it is for the defendant to prove that he was entitled to do the prohibited act. What rests on him is the legal, or, as it is sometimes called, the persuasive burden of proof. It is not the evidential burden.

2.17 When it comes to the application of this principle, the precedents are not always easy to reconcile. However, s 101 has often been applied in cases where under regulatory legislation the defendant requires a licence or a permit to carry on some activity. To take a typical example, in *Gatland v Metropolitan Police Commissioner* [1968] 2 QB 279 the court held that G, who was charged with depositing a metal hopper on a highway 'without lawful authority', bore the burden of proving that he indeed possessed lawful authority to place a skip on the highway where it had caused an accident. The words in the relevant statute, 'without lawful authority', were thought by Lord Parker CJ to show that it was for G 'to raise and prove lawful authority or excuse'.

However, as Auld LJ warned in *Environmental Agency v M E Foley Contractors Ltd* [2002] 1 WLR 1754, a case which necessitated construction of the Environmental Protection Act 1990, each statute has to be individually construed:

> There should...be a case-specific approach rather than the adoption of a blanket s 101 approach to complex offence-creating statutory provisions involving exceptions and, as here, exceptions to exceptions.
>
> (at [30])

It is therefore for the court in each case to construe the relevant piece of legislation to determine whether or not it creates an exception, exemption, proviso, excuse or qualification casting the burden on the defendant.

2.18 It is often claimed that the meanings of the terms 'exception, exemption, proviso, excuse or qualification' are clarified by Lord Pearson's speech in the Scots case of *Nimmo v Alexander Cowan & Sons Ltd* [1968] AC 107 where, for instance, it was pointed out that exceptions, exemptions or provisos are easy to detect simply from the drafting of the statute: according to Lord Pearson, this is because 'an exception would naturally begin with the word "except" and a proviso with the words "provided always that"'. 'Excuses', however, bear 'no usual formula', whilst a 'qualification', according to Lord Pearson:

> ...more probably...means some qualification, such as a licence, for doing what would otherwise be unlawful...You have to look at the substance and the effect of the enactment, as well as its form, in order to ascertain whether it contains an "excuse or qualification" within the meaning of the section.

Therefore, whereas the words of the statute may sometimes provide a decisive clue to Parliament's intention, in other cases it will be very much for the court to interpret the individual piece of legislation. *DPP v Barker* (2004) 168 JP 617 affords a relatively straightforward application of s 101. B was charged with driving whilst disqualified. One of the conditions attaching to his earlier disqualification was that he had to pass an extended driving test before he could hold a driving licence again. At the time of the alleged offence, G's period of disqualification had elapsed. Given that G had admitted the driving, the question for the court was: Did the Crown then bear the burden of showing that G had not taken the extended test, or was the burden upon G to prove that at the relevant time he had a provisional licence and was driving a car that bore 'L' plates? Section 37 of the Road Traffic Offenders Act 1988 provides:

> ...a person disqualified...under s 36 of this Act is...entitled to obtain and to hold a provisional licence and to drive a motor vehicle in accordance with the conditions subject to which the provisional licence is granted.

Collins J was clear (i) that this provision created an exemption under s 101 of the 1980 Act, and (ii) that the defendant's consequent burden of establishing on a balance of probabilities that he possessed a provisional licence and was driving in accordance with the terms of that licence was entirely proportionate (at [9]–[10]).

2.19 Whilst s 101 of the Magistrates' Courts Act 1980 sets out in textual form the rule regarding reversal of the burden of proof in the case of summary offences, it is accepted that an identical rule applies at common law to indictable offences. Thus, in *Edwards* [1975] QB 27, where E was charged on indictment with selling liquor without a justices' licence contrary to the Licensing Act 1964, the Court of Appeal held that the onus lay on E to show that he held a licence. As the House of Lords later explained in the leading decision of *Hunt* [1987] AC 352, in the case of indictable offences the wording of the statute may provide a guide to what Parliament intended in the sense that legislation 'which prohibit[s] the doing of an act save in specified circumstances or by persons of specified classes or with specified qualifications or with the licence or permission of specified authorities' (*per* Lord Pearson in *Nimmo v Alexander Cowan*) will tend to impose the burden of proof on the defendant; but before the burden is held to lie on the defendant, the court must take other considerations into account. *Hunt* illustrates this process. H was charged with possession of morphine, a controlled drug, contrary to the Misuse of Drugs Act 1971, s 5(2). The Crown failed to adduce evidence of the proportion of morphine in the substance the police had found at H's house. Because under the Misuse of Drugs Regulations 1973 any morphine preparation containing not more than 0.2 per cent of morphine compounded with other ingredients was excepted from the operation of the Act, the prosecution successfully argued before the trial judge and the Court of Appeal that it was for H to prove that he fell within this statutory exception. The House of Lords came to the opposite conclusion. The House acknowledged that a statute could indeed impose a burden on a defendant by necessary implication, but insisted that it is necessary to construe the particular legislation. When construing legislation, a court should bear in mind certain policy considerations. Speaking generally, in cases where Parliament's intention is unclear, a court should be slow to infer that Parliament intended to impose an onerous duty on D to prove his innocence in a criminal case. As Lord Griffiths pointed out:

> I regard this last consideration as one of great importance for surely Parliament can never lightly be taken to have intended to impose an onerous duty on a defendant to prove his innocence in a criminal case, and a court should be very slow to draw any such inference from the language of a statute. When all the cases are analysed, those in which the courts have held that the burden lies on the defendant are cases in which the burden can be easily discharged.
>
> (at 374)

2.20 Applying this approach to *Hunt* itself, we can immediately see that whilst the dispute boiled down to whether or not the Misuse of Drugs Act 1971 imposed a burden on the Crown to prove *both* that the compound in H's possession contained morphine *and* that the morphine was not within the permissible level specified in the 1973 Regulations—ie made up of not less than 0.2 per cent of that compound—various issues of policy also needed to be taken into account. First, it was significant that the offence with which H was charged was a serious one. This should have caused a court to hesitate before imposing a legal burden on H. Additionally, H would not necessarily have had ready access to the scientific facilities required for analysis of the compound found in his possession in order to determine the proportion of morphine present: it would have been easier for the Crown to acquire this sort of scientific evidence. This, again, was a relevant factor, militating against the imposition of a legal burden on H. Thus, fortified by these policy considerations, the House of Lords concluded that the 1971 Act did not impose a burden on H to prove that there was less than 0.2 per cent morphine in the compound; the Crown bore the onus of establishing both that H possessed morphine and also that it made up not less than 0.2 per cent of that compound.

2.21 More recently, these factors came into play in the Court of Appeal in *Clarke* [2008] EWCA Crim 893 esp at [28] when construing upon whom the burden rested under s 84(2) of the Immigration and Asylum Act 1999. This provision penalises the provision of immigration services by unqualified persons. Taking into account the practical considerations identified by the House of Lords in *Hunt*, the Court of Appeal resolved that once the Crown had discharged its burden by proving beyond reasonable doubt that C had provided immigration services, it was then for C to show on a balance of probabilities that he had been duly qualified at the relevant time. The burden on C was hardly onerous. In contrast, it would have been highly complex for the Crown to prove lack of qualifications because there were many routes to qualification under the Act.

2.22 To illustrate the way in which the courts combine the *Edwards/s* 101 and *Hunt* approaches in concrete cases, let us finally examine *R (on the application of Grundy & Co Excavations Ltd) v Halton Division Magistrates' Court* (2003) 167 JP 387, especially at [27]–[31]. The Divisional Court was required to construe the Forestry Act 1964, s 9, which, broadly speaking, makes it an offence to fell any growing tree subject to the Act without a licence. Construing the statute, Clarke LJ held that s 9 created an exception, thereby imposing a legal burden on the defendant to show that he possessed the requisite licence. Why? Firstly, the Act actually refers to 'exceptions' on two occasions—both in the context of commissioners being granted power to make regulations creating 'additional exceptions' (s 9(5)(a)) and where the Act refers to 'the exception in subs 3(b)' (s 9(5)(c)); secondly, as required by

Edwards and *Hunt*, the structure of the statute is such that it plainly prohibits the doing of certain acts subject to exemptions or exceptions; and thirdly, the practical considerations which Lords Griffiths and Ackner highlighted in *Hunt* lead to the same conclusions—that is, if no burden were imposed on a defendant, the Forestry Commission would have to negative all conceivable factual situations, which would be a nigh impossible task. Clarke LJ added for good measure that such a conclusion also tallied with the general principles laid down in *Hunt*, in as much as the facts would in great likelihood be within a defendant's sphere of knowledge and, if true, would be easy enough to prove.

The standard of proof

2.23 As already noted, the standard of proof resting on the Crown in criminal cases is normally proof *beyond reasonable doubt*. In cases where the accused bears the legal burden of proof, and in civil cases where either party bears a legal burden, the standard is proof on *a balance of probabilities*. If a case involves a jury, neither expression probably ought to be employed in any judicial instructions. Neither 'reasonable doubt' nor 'balance of probabilities' is readily intelligible; and, in the case of proof beyond reasonable doubt, the expression is not even in common usage outside a court of law. The question therefore arises: how ought one to direct a jury on these concepts, which, after all, embody the principal dynamic of proof underlying the trial?

2.24 In those exceptional cases where a defendant bears the burden of proving a defence 'on a balance of probabilities', the recommended Judicial Studies Board formula (former specimen direction no 2) proposes that D must show that it is 'probable, which means more likely than not' that his defence is made out. As the Court of Appeal noted in *Swaysland* [1987] BTLC 299, expressions like 'more likely than not' or 'more probable than not' will make more sense to a jury than the phrase 'on a balance of probabilities'.

2.25 The concept of proof 'beyond reasonable doubt' is more problematical. What, if anything, ought one to say in order to explain to the jury what is meant by this expression? English courts are not alone in having had to wrestle with this question. The Canadian Supreme Court in *Lifchus* (1997) 150 DLR (4th) 733, for example, determined that jurors need to be given a detailed explanation of what is meant by 'reasonable doubt'. This explanation has to make clear that the expression has a specific meaning in a legal context; that it is inextricably linked with the presumption of innocence ('as closely linked as Romeo with Juliet or Oberon with Titania', *per* Cory J); that a reasonable doubt is not an imaginary or frivolous one, or one based on sympathy or prejudice; that it does not equate with absolute certainty; and so on. The United States Supreme Court, too, has pronounced on this matter. The Fourteenth Amendment, guaranteeing due process and notably that guilt must be established beyond reasonable doubt, does not actively require courts to define 'reasonable doubt' or to employ any particular form or words. American jurisdictions, nevertheless, follow pattern instructions not dissimilar to the specimen directions formerly issued by our own Judicial Studies Board. The Supreme Court has ruled that jurors must be carefully instructed in what 'reasonable doubt' means so as to avoid the risk that a jury might convict on a lesser standard (*Victor v Nebraska*, 511 US 1 (1994)). English law, in contrast, has taken the opposite and, arguably, the simpler route, maintaining that a trial judge is wise to avoid employing the expression altogether. When summing up, a judge is often advised simply to instruct jurors that they must be 'sure that the defendant is guilty' and that if they are not sure of his guilt, they must find the defendant not guilty (see former specimen direction no. 2). It is true that in *Bentley (Derek)* [2001] 1 Cr App R 326 Lord Bingham suggested that a jury should be directed in terms of 'reasonable doubt':

> The jury must be clearly and unambiguously instructed that the burden of proving the guilt of the accused lies and lies only on the Crown, that . . . there is no burden on the accused to prove anything and that if, on reviewing all the evidence, the jury are unsure of or are left in any reasonable doubt as to the guilt of the accused that doubt must be resolved in favour of the accused. Such an instruction has for very many years been regarded as a cardinal requirement of a properly conducted trial. The courts have not been willing to countenance departures from it.
>
> (at [49])

In *Blackford* [2009] EWCA Crim 1684 at [17], however, it was pointed out that the Judicial Studies Board's preferred direction did not in fact coincide with Lord Bingham's rendering.

2.26 Even if the thrust of the Judicial Studies Board's advice is that trial judges should eschew the expression 'beyond reasonable doubt'—and the Court of Appeal considers it 'very well established that the jury should be told that they have to be satisfied so that they are sure of guilt before they convict' (*Stephens* [2002] EWCA Crim 1529 at [13]), the case law establishes two things. Firstly, it is still open to the judge to instruct the jury in the traditional terms of proof beyond reasonable doubt. Indeed, the House of Lords on more than one occasion, and notably in *Woolmington v DPP* [1935] AC 462, has sanctified 'beyond reasonable doubt'. Secondly, if the judge does choose to amplify the meaning of this expression, several formulae have gained acceptance. Thus, in *Walters v R* [1969] 2 AC 26 the Privy Council approved a direction that invited jurors to equate a reasonable doubt with one such as might influence them in dealing with matters of importance in their own affairs, whilst in *Ching* (1976) 63 Cr App R 7 the Judicial Committee was even content with a judge's drawing an analogy with a person contemplating taking out a mortgage. Some judicial formulations, however, have incurred appellate disapproval. For instance, in *Gray* (1973) 58 Cr App R 177 the Court of Appeal censured a direction in which the jury was told that a reasonable doubt was 'the sort of doubt which might affect you in the conduct of your everyday affairs'. Courts have also expressed disapproval of formulations like 'the sort of doubt to which jurors can ascribe a reason' or 'the kind of doubt that would stop them eating or sleeping'. The use of the word 'satisfied' similarly should be avoided. In *Stephens*, meanwhile, the court counselled strongly against a judge telling the jury that they had to be sure but did not need to be certain of guilt before convicting: 'most people would find it difficult to discern any difference between the two', Keene LJ noted at [15]. As Lord Goddard CJ concluded in *Hepworth and Fearnley* [1955] 2 QB 600: 'the explanations given as to what is and what is not a reasonable doubt are so very often extraordinarily difficult to follow and it is very difficult to tell a jury what is a reasonable doubt.' However:

> One would be on safe ground if one said...: "you must be satisfied beyond reasonable doubt", and one could also say, "you the jury, must be completely satisfied", or better still, "you must feel sure of the prisoner's guilt".

The key thing is that whatever the judge says must convey to the jury that they cannot return a verdict against the accused unless the prosecution has made them sure of his guilt: 'then whether the judge uses one form of language or another is neither here nor there'. (*Kritz* [1950] 1 KB 82, 89 *per* Lord Goddard CJ.)

The evidential burden

2.27 As was explained above, the 'evidential burden' is the duty borne by a party to adduce sufficient evidence to put a matter in issue. In a criminal case, both prosecution and defence may have a burden of adducing evidence. For the prosecution, this takes the form of an obligation to establish a *prima facie* case. What is meant by a *prima facie* case is laid down in the Court of Appeal's decision in *Galbraith* [1981] 1 WLR 1039, which concerned the question when a judge must rule that the defendant has no case to answer. At the close of the Crown case, it is open to a defendant to submit to the court (normally in the absence of the jury, if the case is tried on indictment) that the prosecution has not established a case to answer. If there is no evidence that the defendant committed the offence or if, taking the prosecution's evidence at its highest, he feels that no properly directed jury could reasonably convict, the judge must rule that there is no case to answer and will normally direct the jury to acquit the defendant. (In fact, the judge is not always obliged to take a 'not guilty' verdict from the jury immediately. In *Livesey* [2007] 1 Cr App R 35, for example, the Court of Appeal upheld L's conviction when a jury had brought in a 'guilty' verdict for an alternative offence after the trial judge had refused to take a 'not guilty' verdict at the close of the Crown case in respect of the original count in the indictment.) Reverting to the test in *Galbraith*, it will be seen that the judge's task is not to trespass on the jury's task and to assess the strength of the evidence; it is merely to determine that there is sufficient evidence upon which a jury *could* convict. The test, therefore, is not especially demanding (eg, *B v DPP* [2010] EWHC 1301 (Admin)). Very occasionally, if the judge feels that the prosecution evidence is so weak or self-contradictory that any reasonable tribunal would conclude that it was unreliable, here too his duty is to withdraw the case from the jury (see, eg, *Shippey* [1988] Crim LR 767; *Ciro Gallo* [2005] EWCA Crim 242). Although the obligation to establish a *prima facie* case is not exactly the same thing as the 'evidential burden', in a sense the Crown's obligation to adduce a certain quantum of evidence by the close of its case serves a similar function.

2.28   A defendant, however, does have an 'evidential burden' if he invokes a defence. In essence, whenever he introduces a new element into the case, as for instance by pleading alibi, or duress, or loss of control, or non-insane automatism, or self-defence at a trial on indictment, the defendant must present sufficient evidence to persuade the judge that he is obliged to leave the issue to the jury. It is obvious that the Crown could not reasonably be expected, as a matter of course, to rebut every possible defence that the accused might conceivably seek to advance. Therefore, the law requires that:

> The accused, either by the cross-examination of prosecution witnesses or by evidence called on his behalf, or by a combination of the two, must place before the court such material as makes duress (or whatever defence the accused seeks to put forward) a live issue, fit and proper to be left to the jury.
>
> (*Gill* (1963) 47 Cr App R 166, 172 *per* Edmund Davies J)

Once the defendant has produced this modicum of evidence, however, the judge is under a duty to leave the issue to the jury. In the case of certain defences, the courts additionally require that this evidence take a particular form. Thus, in the case of automatism, it has been held that the defendant must lay 'a proper foundation' for this defence, meaning that the defendant's testimony alone will rarely suffice in the absence of medical evidence (*Bratty v A-G for Northern Ireland* [1963] AC 386).

2.29   How much evidence is required to satisfy this evidential burden? To the extent that the courts have ruled on this matter, a defendant discharges the evidential burden if there is evidence of a reasonable possibility of the existence of the relevant defence (*Jayasena* [1970] AC 618, 624 *per* Lord Devlin). A mere speculative possibility will not therefore suffice. As Lord Steyn made clear in the context of the former defence of provocation, where the now-repealed s 3 of the Homicide Act 1957 referred to cases 'where . . . there is evidence on which the jury can find that the person charged was provoked':

> If there is such evidence, the judge must leave the issue to the jury. If there is no such evidence, but merely the speculative possibility that there had been an act of provocation, it is wrong for the judge to direct the jury to consider provocation. In such a case there is simply no triable issue of provocation.
>
> (*Acott* [1997] 2 Cr App R 94,102)

The wording of the new statutory defence to a murder charge, loss of control, makes clear how the evidential burden mechanism operates. The requirements for loss of control are set out in the Coroners and Justice Act 2009, s 54: notably, the accused's loss of control requires 'a qualifying trigger' and must be judged according to how someone of that person's sex and age might normally have reacted (s 54(1)). Section 54(5) states:

> [I]f sufficient evidence is adduced to raise an issue with respect to the defence under subs (1), the jury must assume that the defence is satisfied unless the prosecution proves beyond reasonable doubt that it is not.

Subsection (6) explains:

> For the purposes of subs (5), sufficient evidence is adduced to raise an issue with respect to the defence if evidence is adduced on which, in the opinion of the trial judge, a jury, properly directed, could reasonably conclude that the defence might apply.

Whilst it would obviously be wrong for a judge to leave a defence too readily to the jury in the absence of more than a speculative possibility that it was present, given that the courts, when in any doubt, traditionally lean in favour of the accused, in practice one suspects that they will opt to leave a defence to the jury if there is any credible evidence whatever to support it.

The judge's 'invisible burden'

2.30 The effect of a defendant's satisfying the evidential burden is to impose a duty on the court to leave his defence to the jury. Normally, this will have come about through the defendant's actively asserting the defence. However, evidence may sometimes emerge at trial suggesting the presence of a defence not actually put forward by the accused. In *von Starck* [2000] 1 WLR 1270 Lord Clyde stated with clarity the duty which weighs on a judge to place these issues too before the jury, the judge's so called 'invisible burden'. As his Lordship explained, 'for tactical reasons counsel for a defendant may not wish to enlarge upon, or even mention, a possible conclusion which the jury would on the evidence be entitled to reach.' If there is evidence to support such a defence, however, the judge must be alert to place that defence also before the jury:

> The judge is required to put to the jury for their consideration in a fair and balanced manner the respective contentions which have been presented. But his responsibility does not end there. It is his responsibility . . . to place before the jury all the possible conclusions which may be open to them on the evidence which has been represented in the trial whether or not they have been canvassed by either of the parties in their submissions. It is the duty of the judge to secure that the overall interests of justice are served . . . and that the jury is enabled to reach a sound conclusion on the facts in light of a complete understanding of the law applicable to them. If the evidence is wholly incredible, or so tenuous or uncertain that no reasonable jury could reasonably accept it, then of course the judge is entitled to put it aside.
>
> (p 1275)

For this reason, in *Calvert* (2000) 1 December, case no 9906511/W4, the Court of Appeal quashed C's conviction for rape because, even though C had not contested the charge on this basis, the evidence revealed a possible defence of honest mistaken belief which the judge had omitted to place before the jury.

2.31 In *Coutts* [2006] 1 WLR 2154 the House of Lords had cause to revisit the scope of a judge's duty in this matter, following a Court of Appeal judgment which suggested that a judge has only to direct on defences not specifically raised by the parties 'when it is in the interests of justice for this to happen' (see [2005] 1 Cr App R 31 at [84] *per* Lord Woolf CJ). C was charged with having murdered a woman. He claimed that her death had occurred accidentally during consensual asphyxial sexual activity. In conformity with the wishes of both prosecution and defence, the trial judge had deliberately omitted to direct the jury upon a possible alternative verdict of manslaughter, despite the fact that parts of C's own testimony would have justified such a course. The prosecution had taken the view that it would have been wrong to direct the jury on manslaughter because the case had been conducted on the basis that this was either a deliberate killing or an accident. The defence, for purely tactical reasons, preferred that the judge did not direct the jury on the possibility of manslaughter. Only after conviction did C contend that the judge had been wrong not to deliver a manslaughter direction. Excluding summary proceedings from his analysis—on the ground that they do not engage the public interest to the same degree as trials on indictment—in Lord Bingham of Cornhill's view,

> The public interest in the administration of justice is . . . best served if in any trial on indictment the trial judge leaves to the jury, subject to any appropriate caution or warning, but

> irrespective of the wishes of trial counsel, any obvious alternative offence which there is
> evidence to support.
>
> (at [23])

What Lord Bingham meant by 'any obvious alternative offence' was:

> alternatives which should suggest themselves to the mind of any ordinarily knowledge-
> able and alert criminal judge, excluding alternatives which ingenious counsel may identify
> through diligent research after the trial.'
>
> (at [23])

2.32 The outcome of a case, the House affirmed, ought not ultimately to depend either upon how the prosecution chooses to present it or upon the strategic ploys of the accused. As Lord Hutton put it:

> the interests of justice require...that the jury should be able to reach a sound conclusion
> on the facts in the light of a complete understanding of the law applicable to them'.
>
> (at [43])

Not only must courts trust jurors to understand and to act upon the instructions they receive from the judge, it can be seen that the range of alternative verdicts open to the tribunal of fact will affect the way in which the jurors approach the delibera-tions. In the latter regard the Law Lords took their cue from Callinan J's reasoning in *Gilbert v R* (2000) 201 CLR 414 at [101], to the effect that as a matter of human experience, a choice of decisions may be affected 'by the variety of choices offered, particularly when ... a particular choice [is] not the only or inevitable choice'. Lord Rodger of Earlsferry, for instance, felt that in reality:

> in the course of their deliberations, a jury might well look at the overall picture, even if
> they eventually had to separate out the issues of murder, manslaughter and accident. So,
> introducing the possibility of convicting of manslaughter could have changed the way the
> jury went about considering their verdict'.
>
> (at [89])

There may well be some exceptional cases in which it could undermine the fairness of a trial were a particular alternative verdict left to the jury. For instance, one of the parties might be prejudiced because,

> if they had realized that the alternative verdict was going to be left to the jury, they would
> have examined or cross-examined the witnesses differently or would have led other evi-
> dence. If the prejudice was significant and could not be avoided or mitigated at that stage,
> the overall interests of justice might mean that the duty to direct on the alternative verdict
> would not apply.

Similarly, the alternative verdict might be so trivial that the jury would be unlikely to be misled by not knowing about it and the public interest would not suffer if the defendant were not convicted of the offence (esp at [84] *per* Lord Rodger of Earlsferry).

2.33 Subsequently, the Court of Appeal, in *Foster* [2008] 1 Cr App R 38, has stressed that a judge is not automatically required to leave an alternative verdict to a jury if such a verdict would not properly reflect the facts of the case, when judged realistically, or would not do justice to the gravity of the case. Whether it is necessary to leave such a verdict, even when legally available as an alternative, will depend on the facts of each individual case. As Keene LJ made clear in *Hodson* [2008] EWCA Crim 1590, [2010] Crim LR 248:

> If it is a realistically available verdict on the evidence, as an interpretation properly open to the jury, without trivialising the offending conduct, then it should be left.
>
> It is . . . particularly important that this is done where the offence charged requires proof of a specific intent and the alternative offence does not. Even then there may be circumstances where the issue of specific intent does not truly arise. For example, if a man is shot at point-blank range in the head and the defence is simply that the defendant was not present, there is no requirement on the judge then to leave the alternative of manslaughter by way of killing without the necessary intent for murder. However, there will be cases . . . where it is necessary to leave the lesser offence as an alternative to avoid the dangerous situation where the jury is faced with the stark choice of convicting for the serious offence or acquitting altogether. That may give rise to a miscarriage of justice.
>
> (at [10] and [11] *per* Keene LJ)

In the great generality of cases, therefore, whenever an obvious alternative verdict presents itself in respect of some more than trifling offence and can without injustice be left for the jury to consider, the trial judge should in fairness ensure that this is done, even if the alternative only arises on the defence case in circumstances where as a matter of law there should, apart from that alternative, be a complete acquittal (see *Coutts* at [100] *per* Lord Mance).

The burden of proof when establishing the admissibility of evidence

2.34 In general, the burden of establishing the admissibility of evidence rests upon the party who seeks to adduce it. In some instances, legislation has explicitly stipulated the nature of this burden. Thus, under PACE, s 76 the prosecution must establish the admissibility of a confession beyond reasonable doubt, if its admissibility is contested by the accused or by the court (see *post*, Chapter 10). Indeed, as a general rule, if the prosecution seeks to have evidence admitted whose admissibility turns on any issue of fact, it will have to establish any such matter to the criminal standard of proof. Another statutory provision which lays down a standard of proof, the Youth Justice and Criminal Evidence Act 1999, s 54(2), provides that, when required to do so, a party calling a witness must satisfy the court on the balance of probabilities that its witness is competent to testify (see *post*, para **3.5**). There is, however, one major exception to this approach: namely, the judge's discretion, conferred by PACE, s 78, to exclude otherwise admissible prosecution evidence if its admission would reflect adversely on the fairness of the proceedings (see *ante*, paras **1.52–1.54**). In *R v Governor of Brixton Prison, ex p Saifi* [2001] 1 WLR 1134, for example, a court, debating the admissibility of a translated document in extradition proceedings, was considering whether to exercise this discretion. Rose LJ rejected the analysis that s 78 proceeded upon the basis that a party contesting the appropriateness of admitting certain evidence carried an initial evidential burden of establishing the primary facts which gave rise to potentially unfair circumstances and that the prosecution then bore a legal burden of rebutting those facts beyond reasonable doubt. The concept of burden of proof has no role in the exercise of this discretion. As Rose LJ made clear:

> The purpose of the section is to enable the court to achieve fairness in the conduct of its proceedings, not by reference to the particular character or type of evidence but by having "regard to all the circumstances". The exercise of the power is unlikely to achieve its aim if encased in a rigid framework.
>
> (at [50])

Each party simply seeks to persuade the court of the fairness or otherwise of admitting the evidence; from the point of view of burdens of proof, therefore, the position under PACE, s 78 is neutral.

Presumptions and the incidence of the burden of proof

2.35 Presumptions—that is, those assumptions which the law sometimes requires a tribunal to make (eg, the presumption of innocence)—are closely linked with the burden of proof. Thus, the existence of a presumption of innocence in criminal cases has the consequence that the burden of proving a defendant's guilt rests upon the prosecution (see *ante*, para **2.9**). Another important common law presumption is the presumption of sanity, whereby the law will presume a defendant to be sane. If an accused wishes to rely upon a defence of insanity, he bears the legal burden of establishing that he is insane within the meaning of the *M'Naghten* rules (see *ante*, para **2.14**). This presumption makes good, practical sense. Indeed, in *Lambert, Ali and Jordan* [2002] QB 1112 Lord Woolf CJ described the presumption of sanity, alongside Lord Sankey's famous 'golden thread', as 'another equally glittering thread of English law'. The presumption of sanity runs in tight tandem with the presumption of innocence. As Lord Woolf explained, 'the commission of any offence requires the existence of a guilty mind and the ability to prove this depends on courts being able to rely upon the presumption of mental capacity in the absence of evidence to the contrary'. (Lord Woolf, it would seem, is not alone in wishing to extend the tapestry imagery of the criminal law. In *Lifchus* (1997) 150 DLR (4th) 733, too, Cory J proclaimed: 'If the presumption of innocence is the golden thread of criminal justice then proof beyond reasonable doubt is the silver and these two threads are forever intertwined in the fabric of criminal law.')

Reversal of the burden of proof and the European Convention on Human Rights

2.36 In criminal cases, the House of Lords in *Woolmington* may have conveyed the impression that the burden of proof invariably rests throughout proceedings upon the prosecution. However, in truth legislation makes frequent use of the device of reversal of the burden of proof. In the main, however, reverse burdens of proof have tended either to be confined to minor offences or to have affected only a single element within any given offence. There is nevertheless a temptation to employ reversal of the burden of proof as a weapon in the fight against serious crime. As the South African judge, Sachs J, pointed out in a ringing judgment in *State v Coetzee* 1997 (3) SA 527, 612:

> There is a paradox at the heart of all criminal procedure, in that the more serious the crime and the greater the public interest in securing convictions of the guilty, the more important do constitutional protections of the accused become. The starting point of any balancing enquiry where constitutional rights are concerned must be that the public interest in ensuring that innocent people are not convicted and subjected to ignominy and heavy sentences, massively outweighs the public interest in ensuring that a particular criminal is brought to book...Hence the presumption of innocence, which serves not only to protect a particular individual on trial, but to maintain public confidence in the enduring integrity and security of the legal system. Reference to the prevalence and severity of a certain crime therefore does not add anything new or special to the balancing exercise.

The perniciousness of the offence is one of the givens, against which the presumption of innocence is pitted from the beginning, not a new element to be put into the scales as part of a justificatory balancing exercise. If this were not so, the ubiquity and ugliness argument could be used in relation to murder, rape, car-jacking, drug smuggling, corruption...the list is unfortunately almost endless and nothing would be left of the presumption of innocence, save, perhaps, for its relic status as a doughty defender of rights in the most trivial cases.

2.37 Article 6(2) of the European Convention on Human Rights provides:

Everyone charged with a criminal offence shall be presumed innocent until proved guilty according to law.

This provision immediately poses the question as to whether, under human rights law, it is ever permissible for the law to cast a legal burden of proof on a person accused of crime or whether such rules are now outlawed because they infringe the fundamental principle of the presumption of innocence. Three members of the House of Lords, and Lord Hope in particular, first gave thought to this question in *R v DPP, ex p Kebilene* [2000] 2 AC 326. The case arose out of a charge brought under the Prevention of Terrorism (Temporary Provisions) Act 1989, s 16A (since repealed), which stated that:

...if [the accused] has any article in his possession in circumstances giving rise to a reasonable suspicion that the article is in his possession for a purpose connected with the commission...of acts of terrorism...*it is a defence for (D) to prove* that at the time of the alleged offence the article in question was not in his possession for such a purpose...

European Convention organs have had occasion in the past to consider specimens of English legislation that impose a legal burden on the accused. In the rather elderly case of *X v UK* (1972) 42 CD 135 the Commission first ruled that the pimping provision in the Sexual Offences Act 1956 (since repealed) did not infringe the Convention. Similarly, the common law rule that an accused must prove the defence of insanity on the balance of probabilities was not held to contravene Article 6(2) in *H v UK* (4 April 1990, unreported), whilst in *Bates v UK* [1996] EHRLR 312 the more extreme provision of the Dangerous Dogs Act 1991, s 5(5), which states that:

...if in any proceedings it is alleged by the prosecution that a dog is one to which [this Act] applies, it shall be presumed that it is such a dog unless the contrary is shown by the accused by such evidence as the court considers sufficient...

also passed muster.

2.38 The European Court of Human Rights has provided guidance on how Article 6(2) is to be approached on at least two occasions: in *Salabiaku v France* (1988) 13 EHRR

379 and, to a lesser degree, in *Hoang v France* (1992) 16 EHRR 53. In *Salabiaku*, which concerned a provision in the French Customs Code and where the court held that the applicant's rights had not been infringed, the Court first observed that not all provisions that impose a burden of proof on an accused will compromise the presumption of innocence:

> Presumptions of fact or of law operate in every legal system. Clearly, the Convention does not prohibit such presumptions in principle.

But even if Article 6(2) does not forbid such provisions outright:

> It does, however, require the Contracting States to remain within certain limits in this respect as regards the criminal law...Article 6(2) does not...regard presumptions of fact or of law with indifference. It requires States to confine them within reasonable limits which take into account the importance of what is at stake and maintain the rights of the defence.
>
> (at [28])

Although Article 6(2) may appear to be expressed in absolute terms, these ECtHR decisions make plain that rules which reverse the burden of proof are far from being absolutely forbidden. In each case, as Lord Hope explained in *Ex p Kebilene* [1999] 3 WLR 972, 'a fair balance must be struck between the demands of the general interest of the community and the protection of the fundamental rights of the individual' (at 997). How is this balance to be achieved? Lord Hope suggested (especially at 998–9) the following:

- The first issue to address is, how much does the Crown have to prove before the onus is transferred to the defence? Is the defendant being required to disprove an essential element of the offence? If so, the provision may be difficult to justify. If the defendant is only being asked to establish a special defence or exception, that will be less objectionable.

- Second, what is the burden imposed on the defendant? Is it something that he is likely to find difficult to prove or does it relate to something likely to be within his knowledge to which he has ready access?

- Finally, one must take account of the nature of the threat faced by society that the particular provision was intended to combat. (Subsequently, Lord Woolf CJ in *Lambert, Ali and Jordan* [2001] 2 WLR 211, 219 amplified this point, stressing that: ' it is also important to have in mind that legislation is passed by a democratically elected Parliament and therefore the court, under the Convention are entitled and should, as a matter of constitutional principle, pay a degree of deference to the view of Parliament as to what is in the interest of the public generally when upholding the rights of the individual under the

Convention.' Lord Bingham was later to question whether the courts truly needed to be so deferential to the will of Parliament: *Sheldrake v DPP* [2005] 1 AC 264.)

2.39 These general directions have subsequently been adopted, and then refined, in further decisions of the House of Lords. Notably, in *Johnstone* [2003] 1 WLR 1736 Lord Nicholls expressed the opinion that in reverse burden cases the courts enjoy simply a power of review, and ought only to differ from Parliament when it is apparent that the latter has attached insufficient importance to the fundamental right of an individual to be deemed innocent until proved guilty (at [51]). His Lordship also noted that the courts' approach to reverse burdens of proof needed to be 'coloured' by an appreciation of the fact that 'if an accused is required to prove a fact on the balance of probability to avoid conviction, this permits a conviction in spite of the fact-finding tribunal having a reasonable doubt as to the guilt of the accused' (at [50]). The former observations, in particular, were seized upon by a five-man Court of Appeal in *A-G's Reference (No 1 of 2004)* [2004] 1 WLR 2111, which argued that Lord Nicholls' observations concerning the courts' power of review over Parliament's handiwork were at variance with, and were to be preferred to, an earlier decision of the House in *Lambert*. Lord Bingham, however, dispelled this unnecessary complication in an important speech in *Sheldrake v DPP* [2005] 1 AC 264, in which he made clear that wherever a reverse burden of proof is contested, the following general philosophy was to be borne in mind:

> The overriding concern is that a trial should be fair, and the presumption of innocence is a fundamental right directed to that end. The Convention does not outlaw presumptions of fact or law but requires that these should be kept within reasonable limits and should not be arbitrary. It is open to states to define the constituent elements of a criminal offence, excluding the requirement of *mens rea*. But the substance and effect of any presumption adverse to a defendant must be examined, and must be reasonable. Relevant to any judgment on reasonableness or proportionality will be the opportunity given to the defendant to rebut the presumption, maintenance of the rights of the defence, flexibility in application of the presumption, retention by the court of a power to assess the evidence, the importance of what is at stake and the difficulty which a prosecutor may face in the absence of a presumption. Security concerns do not absolve member states from their duty to observe basic standards of fairness. The justifiability of any infringement of the presumption of innocence cannot be resolved by any rule of thumb, but on examination of all the facts and circumstances of the particular provision as applied in the particular case.
>
> (at [21])

R v Lambert and the 'reading down' of reverse burdens of proof

2.40 In *Ex p Kebilene*, the House of Lords did not have to resolve whether the Prevention of Terrorism (Temporary Provisions) Act 1989 was compatible with the Convention—although Lord Hope did consider that this question was 'still open to argument'. The House of Lords, Court of Appeal and Divisional Court, however, have all subsequently had many opportunities to consider the applicability of Article 6(2) to a wide range of criminal offences. The following selection will convey an impression both of the general technique the courts employ and of the essential intractability of some of the questions the courts have to address. It will not escape readers' attention that in two of the three House of Lords cases since *Ex p Kebilene*—in *Lambert* and *Sheldrake v DPP*—the House has handed down majority decisions.

2.41 In *Lambert, Ali and Jordan*, a decision which was later reversed in part in the House of Lords, the Court of Appeal had thought to apply Lord Hope's approach to two provisions which were traditionally assumed to impose legal burdens of proof on accused persons, the Homicide Act 1957, s 2(2) (diminished responsibility) and the Misuse of Drugs Act 1971, ss 5(4) and 28 (proving lack of knowledge when charged with possession of drugs with intent to supply). Neither provision, the Court of Appeal held, infringed Article 6(2). The case of the Misuse of Drugs Act 1971 was by far the more problematical. In the Court of Appeal Lord Woolf CJ had found, first, that under the statute the Crown had clearly to establish identifiable *actus reus* and *mens rea*: the prosecution had to show that the defendant was in possession of the controlled drug and that he had the intention to supply. While the Crown might not have to show that the defendant actually knew what was in any particular container, it did have to show that he knowingly possessed the container itself. The provision did not impose additional ingredients that had to be proved to complete the offence, but merely provided a means of avoiding liability for what would otherwise be an offence. Defendants could all too easily claim that they did not know that packages in their possession contained drugs, but believed that the packages contained gemstones, precious metals or even pornography. It is notoriously difficult for the prosecution to rebut such claims. Therefore, it was obvious why Parliament had deliberately elected to present defendants with a special defence in this particular legislation enabling them to avoid liability. The social objective behind the legislation—namely, the need to curb the trade in illicit drugs, had also to be taken into account, and this too objectively justified the course that the legislature had taken in the Misuse of Drugs Act in imposing a legal burden of proof on the defendant.

2.42 In *Lambert*, appeal was taken to the House of Lords against the ruling that the Misuse of Drugs Act 1971 reverse onus provisions were compatible with Article 6(2) of the European Convention ([2002] 2 AC 545). The Court of Appeal's ruling was reversed by a majority of 4–1. Contrary to received wisdom, four members of the court concluded that when s 28(2) of the Misuse of Drugs Act 1971 states:

> . . . it shall be a defence for the accused to *prove* that he neither knew of nor suspected nor had reason to suspect the existence of some fact alleged by the prosecution which it is necessary for the prosecution to *prove* if he is to be convicted of the offence charged . . .

the statute does not impose a legal burden of proof on the defendant. And this, despite the fact that the selfsame subsection uses the verb 'prove' in precisely this sense when referring to the burden borne by the prosecution. (Normally, there is a presumption that, when used in more than one place within a single statute, let alone within a single subsection, a word will bear an identical meaning: see, eg, *Hounslow LBC v Thomas Water Utilities Ltd* [2004] QB 212 at [70] *per* Scott Baker LJ.) *Lambert* neatly illustrates the unpredictability of the human rights notion of proportionality. Even if one ignores the Crown Court judge, what is remarkable in *Lambert* is that four appellate judges confidently stated that s 28(2) is compatible with Article 6 of the European Convention and represents a proportionate response to a social scourge; an equal number of appellate judges, however, espoused the opposite opinion with matching assurance. What lies at the root of the case, of course, is differing perceptions of the degree to which the state is entitled to deprive defendants of their customary protections in the interests of protecting society against the baneful effects of drug dealing. This constitutes a legal question in a rather peculiar sense. In situations like *Lambert*, European human rights law arguably becomes an instrument enabling the courts to appraise and even override what have traditionally been considered quintessentially political decisions.

2.43 In *Lambert*, powerful points could be made on both sides of the argument. The dissenting judge, Lord Hutton, perhaps, had a fuller grasp of the implications of the majority's decision that it would be incompatible with the European Convention were s 28 of the 1971 Act held to impose a legal burden on the defendant. In diametrical opposition to his colleagues, and partly echoing Lord Woolf's speech in the Court of Appeal, Lord Hutton warned of the ease with which a defendant would now be able to resist a charge under the Act and of the resultant difficulty that would be experienced by prosecutors:

> All that a defendant would have to do to discharge [his evidential] burden would be to adduce some evidence to raise the issue that he did not know that the article in the bag or the tablets on the table were a controlled drug, and the prosecution would then have to

destroy that defence in such a manner as to leave in the jury's mind no reasonable doubt that the defendant knew that it was a controlled drug...In my opinion, it would be easy for a defendant to raise the defence of lack of knowledge by an assertion in his police statement or by adducing evidence (which could be from a third person)...[T]he threat of drugs to the wellbeing of the community and the peculiar difficulty of proving knowledge in such cases justifies an exception to the general principle...In my opinion, it is not unprincipled to have regard to practical realities where the issue relates to knowledge in a drugs case.

(at [192]–[194])

Taking his lead from the Commission's decision in *X v UK* (*ante*, para **2.37**), Lord Hutton's view was that s 28 was justifiable: it was restrictively worded, requiring first that the prosecution establish the basic factual elements of the offence, and then imposed a presumption that was neither irrebuttable nor unreasonable.

2.44 In contrast, the majority concluded that the imposition of a legal burden on a defendant under the 1971 Act amounted to a disproportionate response, which dispensed too readily with hallowed protections customarily enjoyed by defendants facing serious criminal charges. The majority stressed the fact that certain offences under the Misuse of Drugs Act actually carry a penalty of life imprisonment. Taking their cue from a variety of sources—including Canadian and South African human rights cases (Lord Steyn), the Privy Council's opinion in a case like *Vasquez v R* [1994] 1 WLR 1304, Glanville Williams' celebrated article on the burden of proof ([1988] CLJ 261) and the views of the *Eleventh Report of the Criminal Law Revision Committee*—the majority depict a legal world retreating from the idea that legal burdens should lightly be placed on a defendant. Lord Steyn, for example, felt that the potential evidential difficulties faced by the prosecution were overstated (especially at [39]). For the majority, what really mattered was that when a legal burden is imposed on the defendant:

...it would be possible for an accused person to be convicted where the jury believed he might well be innocent but not have been persuaded that he probably did not know the nature of what he possessed. The jury may have a reasonable doubt as to his guilt in respect of his knowledge of the nature of what he possessed but still be required to convict...[T]he proper way by which that harshness should be alleviated is to recognise that the accused should have the opportunity to raise the issue of his knowledge but to leave the persuasive burden of proof throughout on the prosecution. Respect for the "golden thread" of the presumption of innocence deserves no less.

(at [156]–[157] *per* Lord Clyde)

Just as a unanimous House of Lords had done a few weeks earlier in *A (No 2)* [2002] 1 AC 45 (see *post*, paras **4.77–4.80**), the majority had recourse to s 3 of the Human Rights Act 1998, which requires that 'so far as it is possible to do so, primary legislation... must be read and given effect in a way which is compatible with the Convention rights'. The four Law Lords decided that only an evidential burden represented a proportionate response to the evil of drug dealing in view of the risk of miscarriages of justice occurring were a legal burden of proof to be imposed upon defendants. They therefore resolved to give s 28(2) an intrepid construction, dissociated from its literal wording (cf Lord Clyde at [157]), and to 'read the words "to prove" in s 28(2) as if the words used in the subsection were "to give sufficient evidence"... The effect which is to be given to this meaning is that the burden of proof remains on the prosecution throughout' (*per* Lord Hope at [94]).

Reverse burdens of proof after *R v Lambert*

2.45 At first, it was quite difficult to discern the long-term implications of *Lambert* for statutes that purport on their face to reverse the legal burden of proof, not least because the majority did not speak with one voice. At one extreme, Lord Clyde claimed that even without the aid of s 3 of the Human Rights Act 1998, this was ' a construction to which [he] would in any event have inclined', involving 'no straining of the language of s 28 to construe the references to proof as intending an evidential burden' (at [157]). Quite how his Lordship proposed squaring this particular circle remains something of a mystery. Lord Slynn, meanwhile, spoke airily of the 1998 Act requiring the courts to cull sacred cows (at [6]). (Was it not Abbie Hoffman, the notorious Yippie of the 1960s who stood trial as one of the 'Chicago Seven', who taught us that 'sacred cows make the tastiest hamburgers'?) Lord Hope's approach, in contrast, involved arguing that because other recent statutes had specifically imposed only evidential burdens on the defence, 'it is not unreasonable to think that, if Parliament were now to have an opportunity of reconsidering the words used in s 28(2) and (3) of the 1971 Act, it would be content to qualify them in pre-cisely the same way' (at [93]). This argument, I would suggest, is both speculative and misconceived.

2.46 Lord Hope is of course correct to point out that on a number of recent occasions Parliament has gone out of its way to specify that only an evidential burden rests on a defendant. Thus, the Terrorism Act 2000, s 118(2) states that, to defend against a charge of possessing an article for terrorist purposes:

> If [an accused] adduces *evidence which is sufficient to raise an issue* with respect to the matter the court or jury shall assume that the defence is satisfied unless the prosecution proves beyond reasonable doubt that it is not.

Similarly, this device features in the Sexual Offences Act 2003, where s 75(1) sets up an evidential presumption of absence of consent, in circumstances enumerated in s 75(2):

> If in proceedings for an offence to which this section applies [eg, rape] it is proved:
>
> (a) that the defendant did the relevant act,
>
> (b) that any of the circumstances specified in subsection (2) existed, and
>
> (c) that the defendant knew that those circumstances existed,
>
> the complainant is to be taken not to have consented to the relevant act *unless sufficient evidence is adduced to raise an issue* as to whether he consented, and the defendant is to be taken not to have reasonably believed that the complainant consented unless sufficient evidence is adduced to raise an issue as to whether he reasonably believed it.

2.47 Although occasionally enacting what are obviously evidential defence burdens, Parliament at the same time has continued to impose express legal burdens on defendants in other enactments in time-honoured fashion. The Private Security Industry Act 2001, for example, which sets out to regulate the activities of club bouncers, wheel clampers and other private sector enforcers, provides that where a person commits an offence under s 5, 'it shall be a defence for that person to show...' The Gangmasters (Licensing) Act 2004, s 13(2) looks to impose an express legal burden on defendants charged with entering into arrangements with unlicenced gangmasters. The late Labour government's flagship legislation, the Hunting Act 2004, in s 4 incorporates a reverse legal burden of proof, as by implication do a number of sections in the Female Genital Mutilation Act 2003. A defendant charged with possession of extreme pornographic images under s 63 of the Criminal Justice and Immigration Act 2008 has a defence if he can 'prove' one of a number of specified matters (eg, that he 'had a legitimate reason for being in possession of the image concerned': s 65). The Bribery Act 2010, s 13 also imposes a legal burden on defendants seeking to rely upon the defence that their conduct was necessary for either the proper exercise of any function of an intelligence service, or the proper exercise of any function of the armed forces when engaged on active service. And so on. It will be recalled that reverse burdens were retained for certain offences under the Terrorism Acts of 2000 and 2006 (*ante*, para **2.15**). However, as *Sheldrake v DPP* showed, this may not have been a judicious policy. Although the Court of Appeal upheld the reverse burden imposed on a defendant by s 11(2) of the Terrorism Act 2000, requiring him to show that an organisation to which he had belonged had not been proscribed at the time he joined and that he had not taken any part in its activities at a time when it was actually proscribed, the House of Lords determined, by a bare majority of 3–2, that this burden was incompatible with ECHR, Article 6(2) (see now

[2004] 3 WLR 976). The majority considered that, if a legal burden rested upon the defendant, there was a risk that the offence created under s 11 might cover conduct that was not blameworthy or such as to attract criminal sanctions. Lords Rodger of Earlsferry and Carswell, it should be said, delivered powerful, and coherent, dissenting judgments.

2.48 Parliament continues to impose a legal or an evidential burden on an accused, as it sees fit. There is no reason to believe that the legislature now systematically dilutes legislation and only imposes evidential burdens on those accused of criminal offences. Nor is there any reason to assume, as Lord Hope may have suggested we should, that if Parliament took the opportunity to reconsider the Misuse of Drugs Act 1971, it would inevitably impose only an evidential burden on those accused of serious drugs offences—although it has been boldly suggested by one commentator that *Lambert* implies in a more general way that if any criminal statute 'pre-dates the Human Rights Act 1998, or at least the 1997 general election, courts should be slow to draw any conclusions about Parliament's conclusions on human rights unless the debates show that the issue was addressed' (Ashworth, 'Criminal Proceedings after the Human Rights Act' [2001] Crim LR 855, 863).

2.49 Before leaving the case of *Lambert*, Lord Steyn's speech deserves mention. His Lordship advised 'a healthy scepticism...about practised predictions of an avalanche of dire consequences likely to flow from any new development' which otherwise will impede 'the orderly development of convention principles in our country' (at [30]). In this context, he adopted reasoning broadly similar to that of Dickson, CJC in the Canadian Supreme Court in *Whyte* (1988) 51 DLR (4th) 481, 493. This approach, which also tallies with portions of Lord Hope's speech, amongst other things would outlaw legal burdens in cases where the defence bears directly on the moral blameworthiness of the accused, as in:

> ...cases where the defence is so closely linked with *mens rea* and moral blameworthiness that it would derogate from the presumption to transfer the legal burden to the accused, eg the hypothetical case of transferring the burden of disproving [*sic*] provocation to an accused.
>
> (at [35])

2.50 As can be seen, there was scarcely unity of approach amongst their Lordships in *Lambert*. Nevertheless, in practice the courts will now look at the relevant legislation, seeking to identify 'the gravamen of the offence'. Only if the statute absolves the Crown of the need to prove part of these central elements of the offence can the statute be said to derogate from the presumption of innocence (eg, *Sheldrake v DPP*, cited *supra*, especially at [37]).

2.51 Two contrasting cases adjudicating upon different provisions of the Insolvency Act 1986 give some indication of how problematical many decisions on individual statutes can prove. In *Carass* [2002] 1 WLR 1714 the Court of Appeal held that, contrary to its express wording, s 206(4) of the Insolvency Act 1986 only imposes an evidential burden on a defendant. This subsection *ex facie* imposes a legal burden on a company officer to prove that he had no intention to defraud if the Crown can once show that that officer, within the 12 months preceding an order that the company be wound up, concealed company property. While admitting that 'it is necessary to examine each case on its merits' (at [41]), the court concluded that 'it is unrealistic to argue that an intent to defraud is not also an element of the offence and, indeed, an important element of the offence of conspiring to defraud the creditors of the company' (at [59]). A heavy onus, therefore, was said to rest on those seeking to justify the reversal of the legal burden if the effect of the provision is to compel the defendant to disprove a presumed element of the offence. Like the majority in *Lambert*, the Court of Appeal was persuaded that in this instance, 'common sense dictates that if concealment is proved the evidential burden will itself be quite a difficult burden for the defendant to surmount' (at [61]). If a defendant can surmount this difficult hurdle, it would simply be wrong that he could be convicted if the tribunal of fact was still not sure that he had an intention to defraud. In *Daniel* [2002] EWCA Crim 959, on the other hand, the Court of Appeal indicated that it would have reached an opposite conclusion in respect of the Insolvency Act 1986, s 352. This section lays down that a bankrupt does not conceal a debt due to him 'if he proves that, at the time of the conduct constituting the offence, he had no intent to defraud or to conceal the state of his affairs'. Auld LJ argued, first, that the relevant offence provided for in s 354 carries a *mens rea* in that the prosecution has to show that the bankrupt deliberately concealed a debt. When he is made bankrupt, a party is made aware that the law imposes duties upon him, that he must make full disclosure and that the legal regime is designed to protect his creditors.

> In such circumstances, an act of concealment cannot be equated with conduct of an everyday nature by an innocent person...[W]here a bankrupt, knowing what is required of him, conceals a debt,...if he inadvertently 'concealed' the debt he will not be guilty of an offence under s 354, regardless of the defence provided by s 352, because of lack of intent. Why should it be unreasonable to require a person, who has deliberately concealed a debt in circumstances where he knows he was obliged to disclose it, to prove that he did not intend to defraud or to conceal the state of his affairs? Such a burden does not seem to us...to contravene Article 6(2).
>
> (at [30]–[31])

This area of law, however, is built on shifting sands and courts can diverge sharply in their interpretation of the legislation. A five-man Court of Appeal in *A-G's*

Reference (No 1 of 2004) [2004] 3 WLR 1153 subsequently reconsidered *Carass*, and declared that the case had been wrongly decided (at [52]). The five-man Court's judgment on *Carass* was unanimously endorsed by the House of Lords in *Sheldrake v DPP* [2005] 1 AC 264 at [32]. Even if there exists a passing resemblance between them, individual provisions will need to be analysed with great care.

R v Lambert, R v Johnstone, and *Sheldrake v DPP*

2.52 The most significant difference of opinion yet to have surfaced in the domain of reverse burdens has concerned the construction to be put upon the two principal House of Lords decisions to date: *Lambert* [2002] 2 AC 545 (*ante*, paras **2.41–2.44**) and *Johnstone* [2003] 1 WLR 1736 (*ante*, para **2.39**). In the judgment handed down by the five-man Court of Appeal in *A-G's Reference (No 1 of 2004)* [2004] 1 WLR 2111 Lord Woolf CJ had stated that the Court detected a significant difference of approach between the judgments handed down by the House on these two occasions. More specifically, the Court of Appeal proceeded to declare that Lord Nicholls's approach in *Johnstone* was to be preferred to that of Lord Steyn in *Lambert*. The Court of Appeal went so far as to suggest that, in future, courts ought strongly to discourage reference to any cases other than *Johnstone* and *A-G's Reference (No 1 of 2004)*. The principal features of the judgments—and, in particular, that of Lord Steyn—in *Lambert*, have been outlined above. In the case of *Johnstone*, however, a case concerned with the possession of bootleg recordings and breach of the Trade Marks Act 1994, the Court of Appeal identified what it termed a 'significant difference in emphasis' between Lord Nicholls's judgment in that case and the speech of Lord Steyn in *Lambert*. Notably, the Court of Appeal highlighted that in the course of upholding the reverse burden in *Johnstone*, Lord Nicholls had said of the method courts ought to pursue in assessing the compatibility of reverse burden provisions with human rights law:

> In evaluating these factors the court's role is one of review. Parliament, not the court, is charged with the primary responsibility for deciding, as a matter of policy, what should be the constituent elements of a criminal offence...The court will reach a different conclusion from the legislature only when it is apparent the legislature has attached insufficient importance to the fundamental right of an individual to be presumed innocent until proved guilty.
>
> (at [51])

2.53 In *Sheldrake v DPP* [2005] 1 AC 264, in a judgment in which the other four members of the House (significantly, including Lord Steyn) concurred, Lord Bingham rejected outright Lord Woolf's analysis of these two speeches. Lord Bingham made clear both that the two previous House of Lords cases were not inconsistent with one another in their elaboration of the general principles that inform this area of law and, further, that 'the opinions of the House in these cases…must, unless and until revised or supplemented, be regarded as the primary domestic authority on reverse burdens' (at [32]). Lord Bingham explained:

> Both *Lambert* and *Johnstone* are recent decisions of the House, binding on all lower courts for what they decide. Nothing said in *Johnstone* suggests an intention to depart from or modify the earlier decision, which should not be treated as superseded or implicitly overruled. Differences of emphasis (and Lord Steyn was not a lone voice in *Lambert*) are explicable by the difference in the subject matter of the two cases.
>
> (at [30])

To avoid further possible misunderstanding concerning the courts' role in this enterprise, Lord Bingham added:

> The task of the court is never to decide whether a reverse burden should be imposed on a defendant, but always to assess whether a burden enacted by Parliament unjustifiably infringes the presumption of innocence.
>
> (at [31])

2.54   In addition to scotching the notion that *Lambert* and *Johnstone* were at odds with one another, Lord Bingham also doubted the Court of Appeal's analysis in one further respect. His Lordship doubted that the Court had been correct to posit that a reviewing court ought not lightly to assume that Parliament had insufficient reason to impose a reverse burden on defendants in a particular enactment:

> It may nonetheless be questioned whether (as the Court of Appeal ruled in [2004] 1 WLR 2111 at [52D]) "the assumption should be that Parliament would not have made an exception without good reason". Such an approach may lead the court to give too much weight to the enactment under review and too little to the presumption of innocence and the obligation imposed on it by section 3 [of the Human Rights Act].
>
> (at [31])

In *Keogh* [2007] 1 WLR 1500 a strong Court of Appeal, invoking these passages from Lord Bingham's speech in *Sheldrake*, has since held that two provisions in the Official Secrets Act 1911 that purport to impose a legal burden on an accused to show that he had 'no reasonable cause to believe, that the information, document or article [disclosed] related to defence or that its disclosure would be damaging' within the meaning of the Act are 'disproportionate and unjustifiable' and must be read down under s 3 of the Human Rights Act 1998 so as to impose only an evidential burden on a defendant. (See also, *Webster* [2010] EWCA Crim 2819.)

Criminal offences properly so-called and regulatory legislation

2.55 In one bid to ease the task of analysis in this area, the courts have sought to distinguish between two types of criminal statute—criminal legislation properly so-called and regulatory legislation, by which is meant those 'primary mechanisms employed by governments...to implement public policy objectives'. In the latter class of legislation, it is said, the courts will be far more disposed to uphold reverse burden provisions as justified, necessary and proportionate according to the dictates of human rights law. The Canadian Supreme Court, it would seem, first exploited the possibilities of this distinction in *R v Wholesale Travel Group* (1991) 3 SCR 154, when wrestling with similar problems. As Cory J pointed out in that case:

> The objective of regulatory legislation is to protect the public or broad segments of the public...from the potentially adverse effects of otherwise lawful activity. Regulatory legislation involves a shift of emphasis from the protection of individual interests and the deterrence and punishment of acts involving moral fault to the protection of public and societal interests. While criminal offences are usually designed to condemn and punish past, inherently wrongful conduct, regulatory measures are generally directed to the prevention of future harm through the enforcement of minimum standards of conduct and care.
>
> It follows that regulatory offences and crimes embody different concepts of fault. Since regulatory offences are directed primarily not to conduct itself but to the consequences of conduct, conviction of a regulatory offence may be thought to import a significantly lesser degree of culpability than conviction of a true crime. The concept of fault in regulatory offences...does not imply moral blameworthiness in the same manner as criminal fault. Conviction for breach of a regulatory offence suggests nothing more than that the defendant has failed to meet a prescribed standard of care...
>
> (at 219)

2.56 In *Lambert* [2002] AC 545, too, Lord Clyde distinguished between what he termed matters 'truly criminal' and those regulated in the public interest, suggesting that the courts should adopt a more permissive attitude to the imposition of a legal burden on defendants in the case of the latter species of criminality:

> A strict responsibility may be acceptable in the case of statutory offences which are concerned to regulate the conduct of some particular activity in the public interest. The requirement to have a licence in order to carry on certain kinds of activity is an obvious example. The promotion of health and safety and the avoidance of pollution are among the purposes to be served by such controls. These kinds of cases may properly be seen as not truly criminal. Many may be relatively trivial and only involve a monetary penalty. Many may carry with them no real social disgrace or infamy.
>
> (at 609)

This dichotomy subsequently found favour with Tuckey LJ in the Court of Appeal in *Davies* [2003] ICR 586. Tuckey LJ concluded that in a case brought under the Health and Safety at Work Act 1974, ss 3(1) and 33(1), where it was stated to be for the employer to prove that it was not reasonably practicable to do more than had been done to satisfy his duty to ensure that those not in his employment were not exposed to risks to their health and safety:

> ...in the regulatory context there is nothing unfair about imposing that onus; indeed it is essential for the protection of our vulnerable society...The reversal of the burden of proof takes into account the fact that duty holders are persons who have chosen to engage in work or commercial activity (probably for gain) and are in charge of it. They are not therefore unengaged or disinterested members of the public and in choosing to operate in a regulated sphere of activity they must be taken to have accepted the regulatory controls that go with it.
>
> (at [15]. See also *Clarke* [2008] EWCA Crim 893 esp at [30])

Such a distinction, however, has not found universal favour (eg Cooper and Antrobus (2003) 153 NLJ 352). Nothing in the ECHR suggests that the presumption of innocence does not extend to regulatory offences.

The utility of human rights instruments other than the European Convention

2.57 Does a comparative approach to questions of domestic human rights law convey helpful insights? More than any other member of the court in *Lambert*, Lord Steyn looked to other jurisdictions for inspiration, claiming that 'comparative experience in constitutional democracies underlines the vice inherent in transfer of legal burden provisions, and the utility, in appropriate contexts, of evidential presumptions' (at [40]). There are readily identifiable dangers in this course. The world's human rights instruments are not all identical legal clones. They more closely resemble a comparative law patchwork. Lord Steyn's speech opens with a quotation from the South African judge, Sachs J, in which the latter argues the more reviled their crimes, the greater ought to be the protection society affords to those accused of them (see *ante*, para **2.36**). This, it is suggested, is not quite the philosophy upon which *Salabiaku v France* reposes (see *ante*, para **2.38**). There, the European Court of Human Rights stated that '[the Convention] requires States to define [presumptions of fact and law] within reasonable limits *which take into account the importance of what is at stake and maintain the rights of the defence*' (emphasis supplied). *Salabiaku* predicates balance and compromise; in the passage quoted from *Coetzee* Sachs J seems to advocate a rather different optic when he declares that, when assessing the compatibility of particular legislation with human rights values:

> Reference to the prevalence and severity of a certain crime...does not add anything new or special to the balancing exercise. The perniciousness of the offence is...not a new element to be put into the scales as part of a justificatory balancing exercise.

2.58 In *Sheldrake v DPP* [2005] 1 AC 264, Lord Bingham made telling reference to this issue. Whilst courteously acknowledging that 'on a number of occasions the House has gained valuable insights from the reasoning of Commonwealth judges deciding issues under different human rights instruments: see, eg, Lord Steyn in *Lambert*, at [34], [35] and [40], and Lord Nicholls in *Johnstone*, at [49]', Lord Bingham was rightly anxious to warn again overenthusiastic recourse to this source of authority:

> Some caution is...called for in considering different enactments decided under different constitutional arrangements. But, even more important, the United Kingdom courts must take their lead from Strasbourg. In the United Kingdom cases I have discussed our domestic courts have been trying, loyally and (as I think) successfully, to give full and fair effect to the Strasbourg jurisprudence.
>
> (at [33])

A summary

2.59 One ought not to run away with the idea that *Lambert*, and subsequent decisions, have led to wholesale abandonment by the courts of the idea that Parliament can legitimately cast a legal burden of proof on a defendant. In *L v DPP* [2003] QB 137, to take one example, the Divisional Court decided that s 139(4) of the Criminal Justice Act 1988, as amended, legitimately places a legal burden on an accused 'to prove that he had good reason or lawful authority for having [an offensive weapon] with him in a public place'. In the course of his judgment, Pill LJ laid bare a further fallacy in the House of Lords' decision in *Lambert*. In that case, Lord Hope (at [94]) had taken up an extravagant argument which Glanville Williams had discreetly tucked away in a footnote to an article on *Hunt* (see *ante*, para **2.44**). In that paper Glanville Williams had advanced the following proposition:

> If, where an evidential burden lies on the defendant, the jury acquit, this is because they feel at least a reasonable doubt whether the defendant is guilty. It does not appear to be wholly discordant with ordinary language to say that, in such a case, at least a reasonable doubt as to guilt has been established; and if "established" why not "proved"? It may not be the best use of words, but if there is a reasonable possibility that this is how the words "prove" and "proof" have been intended, and if this interpretation diminishes the likelihood of miscarriages of justice, we should accept it.
>
> (see [1988] CLJ 261, 265)

With all due respect to Glanville Williams' memory, this argument uncomfortably resembles Humpty-Dumpty's petulant outburst that a word meant whatever he chose it to mean and that it was simply a question of who was to be the master (*Alice through the Looking-Glass*, ch 6: '"When I make a word do a lot of work like that," said Humpty Dumpty, "I always pay it extra"'). The argument scarcely carries great force. Indeed, Pill LJ elegantly dispatches it, observing:

> Better, in my view, to look to incompatibility than to treat the English language in that way. The fact that on the evidence a doubt is present as to whether a proposition is proved does not prove a proposition directly contrary to it.
>
> (at [23])

The Divisional Court, in *L v DPP*, distinguished the Misuse of Drugs Act 1971, which the House of Lords had examined in *Lambert*, on a number of grounds. Notably, the Divisional Court took account of the following factors:

(i) that a fair balance has to be struck between the rights of the defendant and those of society at large;

(ii) that, unlike the Misuse of Drugs Act, where the defendant must prove that he did not know that he had drugs in his possession, under the 1988 Act before any burden falls upon the defendant the prosecution must first prove that the defendant knowingly had the offensive weapon in his possession;

(iii) that the burden imposed by the Criminal Justice Act 1988 was not especially fierce given that the defendant was being asked to prove something peculiarly within his personal knowledge; and

(iv) that a democratically elected legislature is entitled to recognise the strong public interest in bladed articles not being carried in public without good reason.

Moreover, as Poole J mischievously pointed out (at [29]), neither counsel had been able to produce any empirical, or even anecdotal, evidence that the 1988 Act had ever occasioned injustice to a single defendant:

> [N]either the young apprentice carrying his tools to work, nor the grandmother carrying her knitting needles to her daughter's...have anything to fear, I believe, from the reverse onus reading of this section, which I would regard as a proportionate measure, weighed by Parliament, and well within reasonable limits.
>
> (at [31])

The Court of Appeal has since upheld the Divisional Court's interpretation of the Criminal Justice Act 1988, s 139: see *Matthews* [2004] QB 690.

2.60 Is it possible to summarise the law in this confusing, and still expanding, domain? Although the majority's decision has since been unanimously overturned by the House of Lords (see *Sheldrake v DPP* [2005] 1 AC 264), the approach adopted by Clarke LJ, and approved by Jack J, in *Sheldrake v DPP* [2004] QB 487 probably still represents conventional orthodoxy. The reasoning adopted by the courts follows four distinct phases.

- The first question is: *Does the impugned statutory provision actually reverse the burden of proof, thereby potentially infringing the presumption of innocence enshrined in Article 6(2) of the ECHR?* This is a matter of statutory construction. It should be emphasised, however, that, in interpreting the particular statute, the court must have regard to the substance of the provision rather than simply the form of the enactment. As Lord Steyn explained in a memorable passage in *Lambert* [2001] 3 WLR 206 at [20]:

  The distinction between constituent elements of the crime and defensive issues will sometimes be unprincipled and arbitrary. After all, it is sometimes simply a matter of which drafting technique is adopted: a true constituent element can be removed from the definition of the crime and cast as a defensive issue whereas any definition of an offence can be reformulated so as to include all possible defences within it. It is necessary to concentrate not on technicalities and niceties of language but rather on matters of substance.

- Secondly, the court must ask itself: *Is the derogation from the presumption of innocence justified?* This means that the court will require objective justification for Parliament's having interfered with the burden of proof. The prosecution will have to persuade the court that, by reversing the burden of proof, the legislature was pursuing a legitimate aim. Furthermore, if it were held that there was no objective justification for the reverse onus provision, the appropriate course might even be for the court to make a declaration of incompatibility under the Human Rights Act 1998, s 4, bearing in mind Lord Hope's observation in *Lambert* that 'a declaration of incompatibility is a measure of last resort' (at [44]).

- The third question runs: *If the reverse onus provision is justified, does it also represent a proportionate response?* The exact formulation of this question appears to have altered over time. The current general understanding derives from a passage in Lord Hope's speech in *Lambert* in which he said:

  It is now well settled that the principle which is to be applied requires a balance to be struck between the general interest of the community and the protection of the fundamental rights of the individual. *This will not be achieved if the reverse onus provision goes beyond what is necessary to accomplish the objective of the statute.*

  (at [88], emphasis added)

This has been taken to mean that:

> The proper approach has to be that if a reverse burden is to be imposed on an accused it must be justified and *in particular it must be demonstrated why a legal or persuasive rather than an evidential burden is necessary.*
>
> (*Sheldrake* at [25], *per* Clarke LJ, emphasis added)

In his study of reverse onuses and the presumption of innocence, Dennis ([2005] Crim LR 901) concluded of this proportionality requirement that 'analysis of the case law shows considerable disagreement and inconsistency'. The writer itemised six factors that may come into play when courts deliberate upon this question, these being:

– limited judicial deference to the democratically elected legislature (see Lord Hope in *ex p Kebilene* at 326);

– the distinction between true criminal offences and regulatory legislation (see *Davies, ante* para **2.56**);

– the desirability of the prosecution having to establish all the essential elements of an offence;

– the nature of the penalty a defendant risks upon conviction;

– the ease with which a defendant can satisfy his legal burden of proof and, more specifically, whether the defence lies within his peculiar knowledge; and

– the significance of a presumption of innocence either as a general procedural safeguard, as a 'morally substantive conception', or even as a normative standard committed to avoiding wrongful convictions.

We have of course seen all these various factors at work in the cases described above. However, it is difficult to discern any clear overall pattern in their operation. In view of this, Dennis proffered the following observation:

> If no broader principles for applying the relevant factors can be identified, the decisions as to the justifiability of particular reverse onuses will continue to resemble a forensic lottery. A search for principle suggests that issues of moral blameworthiness should be proved by the prosecution.
>
> (927)

This echoes sentiments expressed by Lord Bingham in *Sheldrake v DPP* [2005] 1 AC 264, especially at [49]–[51], where it was suggested that if Parliament drafts an offence so widely as to include within its purview defendants who are not blameworthy, a reverse onus to prove lack of culpability should be held to be disproportionate. However, it is not obvious that even this criterion affords an altogether satisfactory antidote to the uncertainties of the proportionality test.

- The fourth, and final question is: *If the provision is not a proportionate response, can it nevertheless be 'read down' under the Human Rights Act 1998, s 3 as only imposing an evidential burden on the accused?* If it is not possible to 'read down' the provision, a court's only remaining option is to issue a declaration of incompatibility under the Human Rights Act 1998, s 4.

2.61 Although it may be possible to reduce the exercise to this deceptively simple format, three further observations seem called for.

- *Firstly*, whenever construing a statutory provision that would purport to impose a legal burden of proof upon a defendant, the court will find itself wandering in Tennyson's 'wilderness of single instances' (see *Aylmer's Field*). Precedents in this field can be of only very limited assistance. Given that each individual statutory provision will involve different considerations, cases decided under different statutes concerned with different subject matters are unlikely to provide helpful guidance.

- *Secondly*, one must be reconciled to the fact that, given the impressionistic nature of the questions a court has to address, judicial views on the correct construction of a statute may vary wildly, ultimately resting on only a fragile foundation of logic. *Sheldrake* was originally heard by a two-man Divisional Court, but Latham LJ and McCombe J were unable to agree and directed a rehearing before a three-man court. Even at the rehearing one of the three judges, Henriques J, dissented. In short, the decision in *Sheldrake*—when heard by the Divisional Court—could be said in a sense to have been reached by a bare majority of 3–2. Students who encounter difficulty in determining what interpretation to put upon any given statutory provision will therefore be heartened to know that in that respect they are in good, and numerous, company. Ultimately, five Law Lords overturned the Divisional Court's interpretation, finding that the reverse burden imposed by the Road Traffic Act 1988, s 5 did not go beyond what was necessary ([2005] 1 AC 264 at [41]).

- *Thirdly*, an important constitutional issue arises once one accords the courts the freedom to rewrite the text of statutes. In the 2005 supplement to his celebrated work, *Statutory Interpretation*, Francis Bennion observes that 'reading down' is a misleading expression, being simply a euphemism for 'strained construction'. The late Sir John Smith made the point strongly in his 2002 Judicial Studies Board Annual Lecture:

[S]urely, we ought to be able to rely on statutes meaning what they plainly say. I thought this was one of the primary objects of codification. For this reason, in my opinion, section

3(1) of the Human Rights Act 1998 is a dangerous provision insofar as it invites courts to give a meaning to statute that no ordinary reader would think it had...[*Lambert*] offends an even more fundamental principle than does the reversal of onus of proof; it falsifies the words of a statute so that it becomes a source of deception instead of enlightenment.

(*Judge, Jurist, and Parliament*, 6–7)

Statutes that create irrebuttable presumptions

2.62 The statutes mentioned thus far have concerned rebuttable presumptions. Statutes, however, continue to create irrebuttable presumptions. Section 76 of the Sexual Offences Act 2003, for instance, provides:

(1) If in proceedings for an offence to which this section applies [eg, rape] it is proved that the defendant did the relevant act and that any of the circumstances specified in subsection (2) existed, it is to be conclusively presumed—

(a) that the complainant did not consent to the relevant act, and

(b) that the defendant did not believe that the complainant consented to the relevant act.

(2) The circumstances are that—

(a) the defendant intentionally deceived the complainant as to the nature or purpose of the relevant act;

(b) the defendant intentionally induced the complainant to consent to the relevant act by impersonating a person known personally to the complainant.

The courts have had occasion to consider whether this practice is consonant with the principles of fair trial enshrined in the ECHR. In *Parker v DPP* (2000) 165 JP 213, the Divisional Court had to determine whether s 15(2) of the Road Traffic Offenders Act 1988, which creates an *irrebuttable* presumption that the quantity of alcohol present in a drink-driving motorist at the time of driving 'was not less than in the specimen' he provided in compliance with the Act, is compatible with Article 6(2) of the Convention. Waller LJ emphasised the underlying social objective of the legislation—namely, preventing the consumption of alcohol before a motorist drives—as a reason for concluding that 'it is simply not to rebut the presumption of innocence to assume that the quantity of alcohol shown up on the breath test or the blood specimen carried out at the police station is the quantity which the motorist has in his blood at the time that he would be driving...'. Alternatively, he reasoned, 'having regard to the importance of what is at stake, the assumption [made in s 15(2)] is a reasonable one and well within limits'. Thus, it would seem, even irrebuttable presumptions that work against a defendant may be compatible with the Convention. It is difficult to know whether *Parker v DPP* would satisfy the House of Lords, following *Lambert, Johnstone, and Sheldrake v DPP*.

Statutes that impose strict liability

2.63 It is tempting to see a link between offences that reverse the burden of proof and offences that impose strict liability. In both categories of situation, it could be said, the prosecution has been absolved from establishing an element of an offence. In the latter case it is actually relieved of the need to prove *mens rea*. Although there is a strong initial presumption that the legislature has not sought to create offences of strict liability (eg *Gammon (Hong Kong) Ltd v A-G of Hong Kong* [1985] AC 1, 14 *per* Lord Scarman), such offences are plentiful, and largely regulatory in character. The question is whether the same principles that apply to statutes that reverse the burden of proof ought to apply also to statutes that create offences of strict liability. In *Barnfather v Islington Education Authority* [2003] 1 WLR 2318, B had been successfully prosecuted under the Education Act 1996, s 444 because her child, who was of compulsory school age, had failed to attend school. This offence is one of strict liability. Traditionally, in the case of absolute offences a defendant's absence of knowledge has only been treated as relevant to mitigation of sentence (eg *Bath and NE Somerset DC v Warman* [1999] ELR 81). On appeal to the Divisional Court in *Barnfather*, however, it was argued that because s 444 does not make provision for proof of knowledge or fault, it is not actually compliant with the ECHR, Article 6(2). B contended that in *Salabiaku v France* (*ante*, para **2.38**) the ECtHR had declared that, in addition to creating presumptions of fact and law that reverse the burden of proof:

> ... contracting states may, under certain conditions, penalise a simple or objective fact as such, irrespective of whether it results from criminal intent or from negligence
>
> (at [27])

provided that such things are kept 'within reasonable limits'. Opposing counsel, however, maintained that strict liability offences are the concern of substantive criminal law, which is exclusively a matter for national legislatures. They therefore remain unaffected by ECHR, Article 6(2), which is concerned solely with proof of whatever elements of an offence the national legislature chooses to prescribe. Maurice Kay and Elias JJ each pointed out that offences of strict liability are not founded upon any reversal of the burden of proof—defendants are not being required to disprove anything; strict liability offences simply reflect the legislature's decision to eliminate *mens rea* requirements from particular criminal acts. The prosecution must establish all other elements of the offence beyond reasonable doubt in the customary manner. Although it is obviously incongruous that a court can question a statute on the ground that the defence it provides is too restrictive but cannot do so if the statute provides for no defence whatsoever, as Elias J correctly pointed out, 'this inevitably follows from the principle that the purpose of Article

6 is to ensure that a trial is conducted fairly...Strasbourg has no power to question the substance of the laws unless they contravene some specific Convention article' (at [46]). (Interestingly, both judges went on to consider whether, had they decided otherwise, the strict liability offence created by the Education Act 1996, s 444 could be justified in this case. On this point, as is all so often the case in this area of judicial endeavour, they each arrived at diametrically opposed conclusions.)

2.64 In *R v G* [2006] 1 WLR 2052, the Court of Appeal had again to consider whether criminal offences of strict or absolute liability were compatible with the ECHR, given that a defendant charged with such an offence will be liable to conviction even if he has done nothing blameworthy. G had been convicted of raping a child under the age of 13, contrary to the Sexual Offences Act 2003, s 5. It was unsuccessfully argued that whilst *Salabiaku v France* does not render offences of strict liability in violation of Article 6, an evidential presumption that is irrebuttable is more likely to infringe Article 6 than one that is merely rebuttable. Lord Phillips of Worth Matravers CJ took the view that:

> An absolute offence may subject a defendant to conviction in circumstances where he has done nothing blameworthy. Prosecution for such an offence and the imposition of sanctions under it may well infringe articles of the Convention other than Article 6. The legislation will not, however, render the trial under which it is enforced unfair, let alone infringe the presumption of innocence under art 6.2.
>
> (at [33])

Whilst recognising that such sentiments might seem to contradict passages in Lord Bingham's speech in *Sheldrake v DPP* [2005] 1 AC 264, especially at [49]–[51], the Lord Chief Justice stressed that in the latter case Lord Bingham had been solely addressing the question of the standard of proof. As has often been observed, Article 6 of the ECHR does not guarantee any particular contents of civil rights:

> The presumption of innocence is a presumption that one is not guilty of whatever may be the elements of a criminal offence. One must not confuse innocence of a criminal offence with innocence of blameworthy conduct. This is not, of course, to decry the normal presumption of statutory interpretation that mens rea is a necessary ingredient of a criminal offence.
>
> (at [36])

2.65 Even if the fairness of a State's substantive law is not a matter to be measured by the yardstick of Article 6, this does not mean that other Articles of the ECHR may not be engaged. Thus, in *G*, Lord Phillips CJ conceded that in a case where the rape had been committed by a child and the intercourse was consensual on the victim's part, a prosecution under s 5 of the 2003 Act might 'produce consequences that amount to an interference with the child's art 8.1 right that are not justified under art 8.2' (at [46]). But even in these circumstances, the Court stressed, the judge's wide powers of sentencing could allow for the reduced gravity of the child's conduct and render the proceedings compliant with Article 8. This approach appears to have been followed in *Deyemi and Edwards* (2008) 172 JP 137, where it was held that s 5(1) of the Firearms Act 1968 creates a strict liability offence of possessing firearms. However, because she was persuaded that the defendants honestly believed that the electric stun gun in the possession of D and E was merely a torch, the judge only imposed twelve-month conditional discharges.

Envoi

2.66 The case law shows clearly that, whereas the literal wording of art 6(2), enshrining the presumption of innocence, might appear to afford an absolute bar to rules of criminal law that would place a legal burden of proof on defendants, in point of fact neither the ECtHR nor the English courts will inevitably find that art 6(2) is infringed in such cases. Additionally, it is evident that it would be an error to imagine that the human rights protection enjoyed by accused persons facing charges under such legislation is crisply delineated. As Lord Woolf CJ acknowledged in *Benjafield* [2001] 3 WLR 75, when assessing whether or not a particular enactment is in breach of Art 6:

> *It is very much a matter of personal judgment* as to whether a proper balance has been struck between the conflicting interests . . . and it is always necessary to consider all the facts and the whole history of the proceedings in a particular case to judge whether a defendant's right to a fair trial has been infringed or not.
>
> (paras [88] and [95]: emphasis added)

What is now clear is that the presumption of innocence, as embodied in the Convention, does not enable the courts to adopt Glanville Williams' suggestion that statutes employing such language as 'unless the contrary is proved' should always be taken to mean 'unless sufficient evidence is given to the contrary', which in turn only requires 'evidence that, if believed, and on the most favourable view, could be taken by a reasonable jury to support the defence' ([1988] CLJ 261, 265). Indeed, in *Sheldrake v DPP* [2005] 1 AC 264 Lord Bingham commented upon this proposal, which had found its way into the Eleventh Report of the Criminal Law Revision Committee (1972, Cmnd 4991, para 140):

> Whatever the merits of this sweeping proposal, its adoption is not mandated by Strasbourg authority as it now stands. Lord Griffiths' observation in *Hunt* [1987] AC 352, 376 remains apposite:

"My Lords, such a fundamental change is, in my view, a matter for Parliament and not a decision of your Lordships' House."

(at [42])

Not all rules that impose a legal burden on defendants, therefore, are intrinsically offensive to European human rights law. Provided that in the context of the given case they can be justified as a proportionate response to a defined social evil, statutory provisions whose literal wording imposes a legal burden on defendants will not automatically be downgraded to impose only evidential burdens.

FURTHER READING

Ashworth and Blake, 'The Presumption of Innocence in English Criminal Law' [1996] Crim LR 306

Birch, 'Hunting the Snark: The Elusive Statutory Exception' [1988] Crim LR 221

Cornish and Sealy, 'Juries and the Rules of Evidence' [1973] Crim LR 208

Dennis, 'Reverse Onuses and the Presumption of Innocence: In Search of Principle' [2005] Crim LR 901

Doran, 'Alternative Defences: The Invisible Burden on the Trial Judge' [1992] Crim LR 878

Lewis, 'The Human Rights Act 1998: Shifting the Burden' [2000] Crim LR 667

McBride, 'Is the Civil "Higher Standard of Proof" a Coherent Concept?' (2009) 8 Law, Probability and Risk 323

Mirfield, 'The Legacy of *Hunt*' [1988] Crim LR 19

Mirfield, 'An Ungrateful Reply' [1988] Crim LR 233

Roberts, 'The Presumption of Innocence Brought Home? *Kebilene*' (2002) 118 LQR 41

Stumer, *The Presumption of Innocence: Evidential and Human Rights Perspectives* (2010)

Glanville Williams, 'The Logic of Exceptions' [1988] CLJ 261

Wolchover and Heaton-Armstrong, 'Reasonable Doubt' (2010) 174 CL & J 484

SELF-TEST QUESTIONS

1. What do you understand by the terms 'legal burden of proof', 'evidential burden' and 'tactical burden'?

2. What is meant by the judge's 'invisible burden'?

3. When does the defendant in a criminal case bear the legal burden of proof?

4. Following *Lambert* (2001), *Johnstone* (2003) and *Sheldrake v DPP* (2005), when will a court accept that when Parliament in legislation has specified that a defendant must

'prove' or 'establish' or 'demonstrate' something, this is actually intended to impose a legal burden on the accused?

5. Blaster is appealing a conviction for supplying adult fireworks to Simplex, a person under the age of 18, contrary to the Fireworks Act 2003 and the Fireworks Regulations 2004 (SI 2004/1836). Section 11(8) of the Act provides:

> In proceedings against any person for an offence of contravening a prohibition imposed by fireworks regulations made by virtue of section 3(1) it is a defence for that person to show that he had no reason to suspect that the person to whom he sup-plied . . . the fireworks was below the age specified in the regulations.

At trial, Blaster's defence was that he had no reason to suspect that Simplex was only 17 years of age. The judge directed the jury that Blaster had to prove his lack of belief on a balance of probabilities. On appeal, Blaster contends that this was a misdirection as s 11(8) only imposes an evidential burden on a defendant. Discuss.

6. 'If, where an evidential burden lies on the defendant, the jury acquit, this is because they feel at least a reasonable doubt whether the defendant is guilty. It does not appear to be wholly discordant with ordinary language to say that, in such a case, at least a reasonable doubt as to guilt has been established; and if "established" why not "proved"? It may not be the best use of words, but if there is a reasonable possibility that this is how the words "prove" and "proof" have been intended, and if this inter-pretation diminishes the likelihood of miscarriages of justice, we should accept it.'

(Glanville Williams [1988] CLJ 261, 265)

Discuss.

3

Witnesses: competence, compellability and various privileges

SUMMARY

The competence of witnesses in civil and criminal cases

- Competence to testify in a civil case
- Competence to testify in a criminal case

The compellability of witnesses

- The accused
- The accused's spouse or civil partner

Sworn and unsworn evidence

Privileges enjoyed by certain classes of witness

- The privilege against self-incrimination
- Legal professional privilege
  - Legal advice privilege
  - Litigation privilege
  - Legal professional privilege in general
- Common interest privilege
- 'Without prejudice' privilege

Public interest immunity

> I am an only child; and I was twenty-one years old at my last birthday. On coming of age I inherited a house and lands in Derbyshire, together with a fortune in money of one hundred thousand pounds. The only education which I have received was obtained within the last two or three years of my life; and I have thus far seen nothing of Society, in England or in any other civilized part of the world. I can be a competent witness, it seems, in spite of these disadvantages. Anyhow, I mean to tell the truth.
>
> Wilkie Collins, 'Miss Bertha and the Yankee' in *Little Novels*
> (1887, London: Chatto & Windus)

3.1 Historically, English law used to disqualify all manner of witnesses from testifying in civil cases, notably if they had any personal interest in the cause. This disability, of course, has now ceased to apply. In criminal cases, too, there were restrictions. Notably, it was not until 1898 that accused persons became competent witnesses in all criminal proceedings brought against them. In recent times the trend, particularly in criminal cases, has been to enlarge as far as possible the classes of competent witnesses. Thus, whereas the law used once to assume that, *prima facie*, the evidence of children was to be distrusted and placed obstacles in the way of free reception of their testimony, legislation has now reversed the position. Today, even though most restrictions on competence have disappeared, it remains the case that:

(i) not everyone is considered competent to testify;

(ii) not everyone can be compelled to give evidence; and

(iii) certain classes of witness enjoy privileges not to testify to particular matters.

Competence and compellability in civil and criminal cases have to be considered separately.

The competence of witnesses in civil and criminal cases

Competence to testify in a civil case

3.2 Civil and criminal cases used to follow the same principles when determining whether or not a particular witness was competent—that is, the question was whether the witness had sufficient understanding to give evidence in court. In civil cases, the traditional common law test still applies. The judge has to be satisfied that a witness is both:

- capable of speaking coherently; and

- understands not only what it means to speak the truth, but also the solemnity of the occasion and the added obligation to speak the truth in a court of law (*Hayes* (1977) 64 Cr App R 194).

It used to be that, if they were to take the oath, witnesses into whose competence the court inquired—and this notably applied to children—were required to display a rudimentary belief in the deity. Incredible as it may sound, as recently as 1976 a criminal trial was adjourned in order for a young girl to receive religious instruction from a clergyman before being allowed to testify on oath against her father, who was charged with committing an assault upon her (*Fawcett* (1976) *Daily Telegraph*, 20 and 27 November). *Hayes*, however, heralded the abandonment of such practices, redolent of a bygone era.

Competence to testify in a criminal case

3.3 The rules applicable in criminal cases are governed by the Youth Justice and Criminal Evidence Act 1999. This Act presumes that 'at every stage in criminal proceedings all persons (whatever their age) are competent to give evidence' (s 53 (1)). Further, it sets out the general test applicable in criminal cases when a witness's competence is called into question:

> A person is not competent to give evidence in criminal proceedings if it appears to the court that he is not a person who is able to—
> (a) understand questions put to him as a witness, and
> (b) give answers to them that can be understood.
>   (s 53(3))

As Scott Baker LJ observed in *Powell* [2006] 1 Cr App R 6:

> Section 53 makes clear that the age of a witness does not determine whether he or she is competent to give evidence. It cannot therefore be said that below a particular age a witness is too young to give evidence. Rather, the test is as set out in s 53(3) whether the witness is able (a) to understand the questions put to him or her and (b) give answers that can be understood. It is for the court to make a judgement on this.
>   (at [18])

In *Powell*, for example, the complainant had been three-and-a-half years old at the time of the alleged assault and just over four years old at the time of the trial. In *B* [2010] EWCA Crim 04 a child, who had been under three at the time she claimed to have been anally raped and who was only four-and-a-half years old when she testified, was held to have been properly ruled competent.

3.4 Whilst s 53(3) refers to the need for a person to 'understand questions put to him as a witness', that person does not actually need to be aware of his status as a witness. The expression is treated as equivalent to 'understand questions asked of him in court'. Therefore, in *MacPherson* [2006] 1 Cr. App. R. 30 the Court of Appeal explained that an infant who could only communicate in baby language with its mother would not ordinarily be competent, whereas a young child, such as the complainant in the instant case, who could speak and understand basic English with strangers, would be competent to testify.

3.5 It is open both to a party, and to the court of its own motion, to question the competence of any witness (s 55(1)). It is then for the party calling that witness to satisfy the court 'on a balance of probabilities' (see *ante*, paras **2.23–2.24**), and in the absence of the jury if there is one, that it is more likely than not that the witness does meet the criteria set out in s 53(3). It may be moot exactly how demanding these criteria are intended to be. In *Sed* [2004] 1 WLR 3218, for example, Auld LJ did remark, *obiter*:

> It should be noted that s 53 does not, in terms, provide for 100 per cent mutual comprehension of material exchanges giving rise to potential evidence....[D]epending on the length and the nature of the questioning and the complexity of the matter the subject of it, it may not always require 100 per cent, or near 100 per cent, mutual understanding between questioner and questioned as a pre-condition of competence...It is thus for the judge to determine the question of competence almost as a matter of feel, taking into account the effect of the potential witness's performance as a whole, whether there is a common and comprehensible thread in his or her responses to the questions, however patchy— bearing always in mind that, if, on critical matters, the witness can be seen and heard to be intelligible, it is for the jury and no-one else to determine matters of reliability and general cogency.
>
> (at [45]–[46])

Although the practice will not be routine—save in cases of clinical mental disorder—expert evidence can be heard on the question of whether the witness meets the statutory criteria (s 54(5)). And just to add a speculative quality to the judicial enquiry, s 54(3) enjoins the court, when ruling on competence, to 'treat the witness as having the benefit of any (special measures) directions made under s 19 which the court has given, or proposes to give, in relation to the witness' that are likely 'to improve, or to maximize so far as practicable, the quality of evidence given by the witness' (s 19(3)) (see *post*, paras **4.88–4.101**).

3.6 In *B* [2010] EWCA Crim 4 Lord Judge CJ gave additional guidance on how courts should approach the question of child competence in criminal cases—or, for that matter, the question of the competence of the infirm or those of unsound mind. Amongst the points he made:

- Competence is always witness-specific: there should be no presumptions, no preconceptions. A witness does not need to understand or to give an intelligible answer to every question. However, a child witness called by the Crown must also broadly be able to understand questions put by the defence and give intelligible answers to them.

- This will be a matter of judgement in every case. Judges ought not to import additional criteria based on the old law. Although the chronological age of the child will inevitably help to inform the judicial decision about competency,

ultimately the decision concerns the individual child and his or her competence to give evidence in a particular trial.

- A witness's age is not determinative of his ability to give truthful and accurate
  evidence. Although due allowance must be made for children's more limited
  attention spans, none of the special measures applicable to them under the
  Youth Justice and Criminal Evidence Act 1999 (see *post*, paras **4.88–4.95**)
  should convey the stigma that children are inherently less reliable than adults.
  The child witness starts off on the basis of equality with every other witness.
  The child's credibility is then for the jury.

- Cross-examination of children ought not to be too lengthy, should take the
  form of short, clear questions, etc.

- A child's competence may properly be reviewed after that child has given evidence. This is part of a defendant's entitlement to a fair trial.

- Delay in cases involving children should be kept to a minimum, for obvious
  reasons. As Richards LJ made clear in *Malicki* [2009] EWCA Crim 365 at [22],
  'cases involving such young complainants must be fast-tracked. The proper
  administration of justice requires it. It is the responsibility of all concerned—
  prosecution and defence—to bring the need for expedition to the attention of
  the court... and it is the responsibility of the court to ensure that such expedition is provided.' However, unless the delay amounts to an abuse of process
  it will not operate as some special sort of defence; nor are applications under
  PACE, s 78 bound to succeed in cases of delay (see *ante*, paras **1.52–1.54**).

- '[I]t is open to a properly directed jury, unequivocally directed about the dangers and difficulties of doing so, to reach a safe conclusion on the basis of the
  evidence of a single competent witness, whatever his or her age, and whatever
  his or her disability' ([2010] EWCA Crim 4 at [51]).

The compellability of witnesses

3.7 As a general rule, competent witnesses are also treated as compellable—that is,
they may be constrained to testify, whether they wish to or not. There are statutory
procedures whereby witnesses may be summoned to court to testify and penalised if
they refuse to comply. Once in court, if they then refuse to give evidence, they may
be prosecuted for contempt of court. The reason for such principles is not far to seek.
As Rose LJ pointed out in *Yusuf* [2003] 2 Cr App R 32, referring to the obligation
of witnesses to testify before criminal courts:

> The role of the courts, in seeking to provide the public with protection against criminal
> conduct, can only properly be performed if members of the public co-operate with the

courts. That co-operation includes participation in the trial process... Witnesses who may have important evidence to give must come to court if... formally directed to do so. If they choose to ignore a summons, they are in contempt of court and can expect to be punished because their failure to attend is likely to disrupt the trial process and, in some cases, undermine it entirely.

(at [16])

3.8 Certain parties, such as the sovereign and diplomatic agents (and, to some extent, their family members), are not compellable in any proceedings. There are occasional signs that civil courts retain some right to hold particular witnesses non-compellable if it would be oppressive to insist that they testify. Thus, in *Morgan v Morgan* [1977] Fam 122, where a wife applied for a lump sum payment from her former husband, the court held that it would be 'oppressive and wrong' to compel her wealthy father, whose sole heir she was likely to be, to divulge evidence to the court about his assets and his intentions in regard to them. The great majority of exceptions to the compellability principle, however, are found in criminal cases.

The accused

3.9 The accused's position is special in two principal respects. *First*, unless he 'is not, or is no longer, liable to be convicted of any offence in the proceedings'—eg, he has pleaded guilty or has benefited from a *nolle prosequi*—'a person charged in criminal proceedings is not competent to give evidence in the proceedings for the prosecution' (Youth Justice and Criminal Evidence Act 1999, s 53(4) and (5)). Section 53(5), let it be noted, refers only to a witness's liability to be 'convicted'. There is no requirement that, if convicted, the witness must also have been sentenced prior to testifying. One might imagine that after the embarrassments suffered in 'supergrass' trials, where convictions obtained in reliance upon the testimony of witnesses who had something to gain by testifying vigorously for the Crown against former confederates were set aside (eg *Treadaway* [1997] CLY 1134), there would now be a requirement that the defendant had been both convicted and sentenced before becoming a compellable witness for the Crown. The dominant opinion, however, appears to be that Lawton LJ's ruling in *Turner* (1975) 61 Cr App R 67 remains good law. In his view, the fact that the defendant retains an interest in the prosecution does not disqualify him from testifying; but the judge retains a discretion to exclude his evidence under PACE, s 78. *Second*, while a defendant is competent to testify for the defence, he is not compellable and gives evidence only 'upon his own application' (Criminal Evidence Act 1898, s 1(1)).

3.10 An accused, however, differs from other witnesses in at least four further respects.

(i) Unlike most other witnesses, the accused does not enjoy a privilege against self-incrimination but must answer questions notwithstanding that they might tend to incriminate him (Criminal Evidence Act 1898, s 1(2)).

(ii) If he gives evidence, the defendant will normally be the first witness called by the defence (PACE, s 79).

(iii) Whereas all witnesses, apart from expert witnesses, are required to remain outside the courtroom until it is their turn to testify, the defendant is entitled to be present throughout proceedings.

(iv) Finally, as we shall discover, Part 11 of the Criminal Justice Act 2003 restricts what evidence may be introduced regarding people's bad character, regardless of whether or not they are participants in the trial. Non-defendants follow one regime (see Criminal Justice Act 2003, s 100 and *post*, paras **4.22–4.35**), the accused another (see Criminal Justice Act 2003, ss 101–108 and *post*, Chapter 7).

The accused's spouse or civil partner

3.11 There are restrictions on the compellability of an accused's spouse. The rationale for this exception to the general principle of compellability, however, may well have altered over time. It used once to be 'a well-established maxim of the law that husband and wife are one person. For many purposes, no doubt, this is a mere figure of speech, but for other purposes it must be understood in its literal sense' (*Phillips v Barnet* (1876) 1 QBD 436, 440 *per* Lush J). Obviously, the idea that someone could testify against him- or herself would make no sense. But as Maule J once remarked, in a judicial aside, 'It is all nonsense; I do not believe that, under the most favourable circumstances, [husband and wife] can be considered less than two' (Serjeant Robinson, *Bench and Bar* (1889) at 123). In *O'Connor v Marjoribanks* (1842) 4 Man & G 435, 445, the same judge explained the rule on an alternative footing:

> The text-books generally give, as the reason for the rule as to excluding the testimony of husband or wife, the necessity of preserving the confidence of the conjugal relation; and that may be so. But it by no means follows that the rule is co-extensive with the reason given in support of it…A rule may be a very good rule, though the reason on which it is founded may not be applicable to every case which is governed by the rule.

In more recent times, in *Hoskyn v MPC* [1979] AC 474, 488 Lord Wilberforce explained that the privilege had been recognised owing to 'the identity of interest between husband and wife and because to allow [the wife] to give evidence would give rise to discord and to perjury, and would be, to ordinary people, repugnant.'

3.12 Spousal privilege is of course capable of being abused. Students of English literature will recall that a central feature of the plot in Graham Greene's 'entertainment', *Brighton Rock*, first published in 1938, is Pinkie's cynical marriage to Rose, contracted simply to prevent her testifying against him in any eventual homicide trial. A present-day defendant might still marry a potential witness in order to render her non-compellable (subject to PACE, s 80(3), discussed below). Indeed, as Waller LJ made clear in *R (Crown Prosecution Service) v Registrar General of Births, Deaths and Marriages* [2003] QB 1222, s 80 of PACE clearly points to the fact that Parliament intended that, once married, spouses should enjoy the privilege against being compelled to testify against one another. In this particular case, the Crown Prosecution Service sought judicial review of the registrar's decision to authorise a prisoner, who was awaiting trial on two counts of murder, to marry the principal prosecution witness. Although there was a justified 'apprehension of a significant risk that the proposed marriage [was] based on a desire that [the detainee] should avoid conviction and an intention that, to that end, the jury should be denied the probative evidence of [the girlfriend]' (at [10]), Waller LJ concluded that the registrar had been right to allow the marriage to go ahead, adding for good measure that the registrar's act in allowing the marriage to proceed did not offend against public policy:

> ... [I]t is such a very obvious argument that it should not be right that somebody should be entitled to take advantage of the non-compellability provision by marrying two days before the trial and after the offence was committed, that Parliament must be taken to have had that factor in mind... [T]hey chose to pass the section that they did. It seems to me that, simply to take advantage of s 80 once the husband and wife are married, cannot be said to be unlawful or contrary to public policy, although if the husband is in fact guilty but acquitted, obviously in one sense the husband has avoided liability for serious crime. It seems to me difficult to see how marrying when one objective may be to achieve the protection of s 80 can be said to be unlawful or contrary to public policy.
>
> (at [19])

It is true that *Phipson on Evidence* (2000, 15th edn, para 8.25) did once argue that an English court could ignore a marriage if it were shown to be a complete sham. Unfortunately, *Phipson's* supporting authorities, a US Supreme Court decision in which three of the most able members of the Court (Jackson, Black and Frankfurter JJ) dissented and a Canadian decision containing somewhat qualified *dicta*, both concern the old common law rule and seem completely inapplicable to the English situation, which now is precisely regulated by statute. In any case, there exists no mechanism whereby a court can measure the genuineness of parties' marital intentions.

3.13 The non-compellability rule applies to 'lawfully wedded spouses' and to those who have contracted civil partnerships under the Civil Partnership Act 2004, but not to those who are merely cohabiting or who have contracted either bigamous marriages or marriages which are of no effect under English law (*Khan* (1986) 84 Cr App R 44). There are of course other persons to whom it might appear plausible to extend this privilege. In *Pearce* [2002] 1 WLR 1553 it was argued that, in view of ECHR, Article 8, which guarantees a right to respect for family life, the category of non-compellable near-and-dear ought to be expanded. P had been convicted of murdering his brother. At his trial both P's daughter and the woman with whom P had lived for 19 years, and who had borne him three children, had been declared hostile witnesses (see *post*, paras **4.10–4.15**). It was argued that, in recent years, when determining whether or not a relationship exists between parties, the courts have increasingly looked to substance as well as to form. In 2001, it was said, a marriage certificate ought no longer to be treated as 'the touchstone of compellability'. The court rejected these contentions, pointing out both that Parliament had reviewed the terms of s 80(1) of PACE as recently as 1999, and that respect for family life did not, of necessity, entail that a cohabitee could not be compelled to testify against a defendant:

> This is plainly...an area where the interests of the family must be weighed against those of the community at large, and it is precisely the sort of area in which the European Court defers to the judgment of...domestic courts....[I]f the concession were to be widened it is not easy to see where logically the widening should end.
>
> (at [12])

In any case, Article 8(2) allows an exception to the right to respect for private life when it is '*necessary*...for the prevention of...crime'—a word whose meaning, as Lord Griffiths explained in the analogous context of Article 10 in *Re an Inquiry* [1988] AC 660, 704, 'lies somewhere between "indispensable" on the one hand and "useful" or "expedient" on the other'. *Pearce* underlines English law's restrictive approach to the privilege against testifying. In contrast, it might be noted that in the state of Victoria, Australia relevant legislation was amended to give the court discretion to exempt certain members of the accused's family—the mother, father and children—from being compelled to testify against him (Vict Crimes Act 1958, s 400 (3)–(6)). Similarly, in many other legal systems there are further classes of witness, beyond the family, whose relationships to the parties are privileged. Prime examples would include doctor and patient, and priest and penitent. Strictly speaking, in English law a priest is a compellable witness, although one knows full well that, even under compulsion, a priest would refuse to violate the seal of the confessional.

3.14 *Police and Criminal Evidence Act 1984, s 80.* In recent years the legislature has pursued a policy of eroding the traditional exclusionary principle that applies to spouses in English law, and has rendered spouses compellable in an increasingly wide range of circumstances. The relevant law today is found in PACE, s 80, as amended by the Youth Justice and Criminal Evidence Act 1999. This legislation represents an attempt to reconcile two conflicting policies: on the one hand, the law wishes not to sow discord between husband and wife, thereby undermining the institution of marriage; on the other, it seeks to uphold the interests of justice in ensuring that those who commit serious criminal offences can be effectively brought to book. PACE, s 80 regulates the competence and compellability of husbands and wives in respect of both their spouses and their spouses' co-defendants.

3.15 Although the statute refers to both husband and wife (and although under the Civil Partnership Act 2004, s 84 identical rules now apply in respect of civil partners), if only for simplicity of exposition the following précis of the rules will assume that the defendant is the husband and that the testifying spouse is his wife.

- A wife is competent (PACE, s 80(1)), but is not normally compellable to give evidence on behalf of the Crown against the husband or the husband's co-defendant.

- Section 80(2A)(b), however, provides that in the case of certain 'specified offences' a wife is compellable for the Crown.

3.16 An offence is a 'specified offence' within the definition of s 80(3) if:

(a) it involves an assault on, or injury or a threat of injury to, the wife or husband or a person who was at the material time under the age of 16;

(b) it is a sexual offence [defined in s 80(7)] alleged to have been committed in respect of a person who was at the material time under that age; or

(c) it consists of conspiring or attempting to commit, or of aiding, abetting, counselling, procuring, or inciting the commission of, an offence falling within para (a) or (b) above.

Section 80(3) is not necessarily as straightforward as at first might appear, and its exact scope may yet be subject to legal interpretation. To take a simple example, let us imagine that a wife has information concerning her husband, who is charged with burglary. The Crown alleges that the husband broke into a house with intent to inflict grievous bodily harm upon the 15-year-old occupant. Is the wife compellable for the Crown? While this form of burglary does not fall within para (b), the more intriguing question is whether the offence 'involves ... a threat of injury to ... a person who was at the material time under the age of 16' within para (a). The word 'involves' is not the most precise of terms. It may be that, faced with this question, a court would have to choose whether to interpret para (a) to signify that the threat of injury actually has of necessity to constitute a formal element of the offence itself, as in the cases of threats to murder contrary to the Offences against the Person Act 1861, s 16 or the intimidation of witnesses, jurors etc contrary to the Criminal Justice and Public Order Act 1994, s 51. These crimes always incorporate a threat of injury to a person (albeit not necessarily a person under 16). Alternatively, the court might wish to give full effect to the purpose which plainly underlies s 80(3): namely, to accept that there is strong reason to put the interests of young victims of violent or potentially violent crime before the more abstract interest of upholding a marriage where, if the charge is brought home, the husband will turn out to have been a violent criminal. To take a parallel case, the Court of Appeal in *McAndrew-Bingham* [1999] 1 WLR 1897 generously assumed that, even though not every case might comprehend the use or even the threat of physical force against a child, in order to fulfil Parliament's intention every child abduction under the Child Abduction Act 1984 should be taken to comprehend an assault for the purposes of the Criminal Justice Act 1988, s 32(2)(a) (which renders admissible a video recording of a child's statement and her cross-examination and re-examination by live link). The Court left open the question whether the operative words, 'an offence which involves an assault on, or injury or a threat of injury to, a person', referred solely to the technical components of the offence charged in the indictment or whether the Court had also to have regard to the evidence supporting the charge in the particular case (see esp p 1903). Since the 1988 Act and PACE, s 80(3)(a) are identically worded, the courts might well be tempted to give an ample, purposive construction to s 80(3) (a) and look to the social reality of the offence charged and the furtherance of child protection, concluding without too much difficulty that burglaries committed with intent to inflict grievous bodily harm (or even to do unlawful damage to a building or its contents, also contrary to the Theft Act 1968, s 9(2)) 'involve... a threat of injury'. Were the latter analysis preferred, it can be seen that 'specified offences', as defined in s 80(3), form a very broad category of offences in which the spouse may find herself a compellable witness.

3.17 Another interpretational difficulty surfaced in *RL* [2008] 2 Cr App R 18. RL was charged with a number of offences suggesting that over a prolonged period he had sexually abused his daughter. Some of the offences were alleged to have occurred long before she had attained the age of 16 (these were undoubtedly specified offences), others occurred afterwards. Had RL's wife agreed to testify for the Crown, her evidence would primarily have related to one count in the indictment that was not a specified offence because the victim at that time was over the age of 16. The wife refused to testify, and the trial judge accepted that she was non-compellable. Although the Court of Appeal did not need to determine the question, it did consider it 'a nice point' (at [22]) whether it could be argued that because s 80(3)(b) refers to a spouse's evidence 'in respect of' a person who was at the material time under 16, the wife in RL could in fact have been treated as a compellable prosecution witness on the basis that her evidence was also of relevance to counts relating to earlier specified offences.

3.18 PACE, s 80 lays down further rules where criminal charges relate to 'specified offences':

- If the offence charged is a 'specified offence', the wife is compellable not only against the husband but also against a co-defendant, 'but only in respect of any specified offence with which any person is charged in the proceedings' (s 80(2A)(b)).

- If the offence with which the husband's co-defendant is charged is a 'specified offence' within the meaning of s 80(3), a wife is also compellable on behalf of the co-defendant but 'only in respect of any specified offence with which that other person is charged' (s 80(2A)(a)).

3.19 Finally, PACE, s 80 makes clear that spousal privilege extends only to compulsion to testify on behalf of the Crown or a co-accused. Thus,

- Unless they are jointly charged with an offence, the wife is both competent and compellable to testify on behalf of the husband (s 80(2)).

Moreover, the privilege only endures as long as the marriage (or civil partnership) endures:

- If the parties cease to be married, the spouse becomes fully compellable 'as if that person and the accused had never been married' (s 80(5)).

3.20 *Procedure in court.* According to *Pitt* [1983] QB 25, in cases where she is not a compellable witness, it is a desirable practice for the judge to explain to the spouse, in the absence of the jury, that she is not obliged to give evidence. As the court explained, 'she retains the right of refusal up to the point when, with full knowledge of that right, she takes the oath in the witness box'. However, once the spouse has taken the stand, whether or not in full knowledge of her right not to testify, and has indicated her willingness to testify by taking the oath, she is treated like any other witness and cannot go back on her decision: 'Once the wife has started upon her evidence, she must complete it…Justice should not allow her to give evidence which might assist, or injure, her husband and then to escape from normal investigation'. Thus, once she begins to testify, if she displays an unwillingness to cooperate with the prosecution, the wife may be declared a hostile witness and cross-examined accordingly (*Pitt, supra*; see also *post*, paras **4.10–4.15**). *Nelson* [1992] Crim LR 653 confirms that, no matter how fitting a warning might be, it is only desirable, not mandatory that the court delivers a warning to the spouse that she does not have to give evidence. Thus, convictions will not be adjudged unsafe merely because a spouse testified in ignorance of the fact that she was actually free to decline to give evidence against the other spouse. Given that English law is prepared to admit even illegally obtained evidence, such a solution is not perhaps surprising. One might also assume that if, once she has begun testifying, the spouse becomes aware for the first time that she is entitled not to give evidence, the court would not allow her to break off from her testimony. It has, however, been stated in *Birmingham Magistrates' Court, ex p Shields* (1994) 158 JP 845 that the case would be altered if, before testifying, the spouse had indicated to the prosecutor an unwillingness to give evidence and the prosecutor did not act upon this information. In such a case, the prosecutor has an obligation to alert both the defence and the court of the spouse's reluctance. In these circumstances, the court could be expected to deliver a warning; and its failure to do so could then amount to an irregularity of which an appellate court would take notice.

3.21 The New Zealand courts have taken matters further. In *Nati v Police* (1993) 10 CRNZ 404, invoking the circumstance that under the New Zealand Bill of Rights courts both recognise, enforce *and facilitate* the exercise of rights conferred thereunder, Heron J declared:

> . . . if a right is available it should be able to be exercised and not defeated by a misunderstanding or technicality . . . There will be . . . cases . . . where the spouse has been made aware of her right and has, through a misunderstanding, not exercised it. I think it is beholden on the Court to ensure that those cases do not arise . . . I leave this case with the general cautionary note that where the circumstances suggest that this particular right might be exercised it should be facilitated by the judge before the evidence begins . . . It is in the interests of the proper administration of justice that the exercise of rights such as this be freely and fully available to the individual in whom it resides . . .
>
> (at 409–10)

3.22 *Comment.* It is provided that the failure of a spouse to give evidence 'shall not be made the subject of any comment by the prosecution' (PACE, s 80A). The law on this point has alternatively been described as 'not particularly present to the minds of many people in criminal trials' (*Marsh* [2008] EWCA Crim 1816 at [32] *per* Hughes LJ) and also as 'clear, of long standing and mandatory'. Any infringement of s 80A on the part of prosecuting counsel is likely to be treated as a material irregularity, almost inevitably requiring the trial judge to deliver a clear instruction to the jury to ignore Crown counsel's comments (*Davey* [2006] EWCA Crim 565 *per* Aikens J, esp at [20]). But whilst the Crown is forbidden to comment, technically s 80A does not prevent the judge from passing some observation. A judge, it is suggested, ought to display restraint and normally the best policy by far will be to say nothing.

3.23 *Placing a spouse's testimony before the court by other means.* The refusal of one spouse to testify against another does not necessarily mean that no evidence of what that spouse might have testified to will be available to the Crown. In *RL* [2008] 2 Cr App R 18, at his trial on multiple counts of indecent assault and rape committed against his daughter, the prosecution called RL's wife as a witness. She declined to testify, and was declared non-compellable. The prosecution thereupon successfully applied to the trial judge to adduce a statement the wife was alleged to have made to the police, undermining the husband's defence on one of the counts in the indictment. Her statement was admitted in the interests of justice under the statutory exception to the hearsay rule, s 114(1)(d) of the Criminal Justice Act 2003 (see further *post*, paras. **9.70-9.80**). In addition to determining that PACE, s 80 does not impose an automatic legal bar on a spouse's statement being admitted in these circumstances in the interests of justice under s 114(1)(d), Lord Phillips of Worth Matravers CJ also declined to hold that the police were under any duty to warn a spouse from whom they were taking a statement that he or she was not a compellable witness. This, it was said, 'could inhibit the investigation of crime' (at [31]). His Lordship went on to say, however, that in some cases the police might be well advised to do so:

> If a question is raised, as it has been in this case, as to whether it is in accordance with the interests of justice to admit a wife's statement, the prosecution's hand is likely to be strengthened if they can show that the wife made her statement voluntarily, having been expressly informed that she was under no obligation to make it.
>
> (at [33])

Statements spouses make to the police, it should be noted, will not automatically be admissible whenever a spouse declines to take the stand. In each case the prosecution will have to show that, on balance, it is in the interests of justice to admit the evidence, taking into account the factors enumerated in s 114(2) of the 2003 Act (see *post*, paras **9.72–9.79**). In *RL*, where the accused was alleged to have subjected his daughter to a lengthy course of abuse, the Court of Appeal was clear that 'the public interest was served by the admission of [the wife's] evidence' (at [36]).

Sworn and unsworn evidence

3.24 In criminal cases a witness may not be sworn unless:

(a) he has attained the age of 14 years, and

(b) he has sufficient appreciation of the solemnity of the occasion and of the particular responsibility to tell the truth which is involved in taking an oath. (s 55(2))

If a witness is capable of giving 'intelligible testimony', which is defined in s 55(8) in terms of someone who:

(a) understands questions put to him as a witness, and

(b) gives answers to them which can be understood,

it is initially presumed that that person fulfils the conditions laid down in s 55(2). It is for the opposing party in the first instance to adduce evidence to the contrary. If such evidence is forthcoming, then the party calling the impugned witness must show that it is more likely than not that he does in fact meet those standards.

3.25 Witnesses in civil and criminal cases usually take the oath in the form laid down in the Oaths Act 1978, s 1. However, a witness who objects to taking an oath is allowed to make a solemn affirmation in the form set out in s 6 of that Act. Non-Christian witnesses also are permitted to take oaths in appropriate form (s 55(3) and (4)). Witnesses who do satisfy the criteria laid down in s 55(2) may give their testimony unsworn (s 56(4)), and wilful lies told whilst unsworn attract similar penalties for perjury to those applying in the case of sworn evidence (s 57(2)).

3.26 The form of oath or affirmation does not matter. What counts is that the witness has positively indicated an intention to be bound upon his or her conscience. Therefore, a failure to observe the formalities of the Oaths Act to the letter will not render a witness's testimony invalid (*Chapman* [1980] Crim LR 42, where C's son failed to take the Testament in his hand, as required by the Oaths Act 1978, s 1; *Hussain* [2005] EWCA Crim 1815, where a Muslim wife took her oath on the New Testament rather than the Koran). Moreover, s 56(5) of the Youth Justice and Criminal Evidence Act 1999 provides that the mistaken admission of unsworn testimony from a witness who ought to have been sworn does not render a conviction unsafe.

Privileges enjoyed by certain classes of witness

3.27 Although the general rule is that a compellable witness cannot decline to answer questions, witnesses enjoy certain privileges entitling, or sometimes even obliging, them to refuse to testify to certain matters. English law, it could be argued, is not particularly generous in according these privileges to witnesses. Unlike a number of other jurisdictions, it does not recognise a general relationship of confidentiality as between, say, doctor and patient, or even between confessor and penitent. Leaving to one side the case of the accused, which will be discussed further in the chapter on the admission of bad character evidence (see *post*, Chapter 7), the principal privileges to note are the privilege against self-incrimination, and the cluster of privileges associated with litigation: legal professional privilege, common interest privilege and 'without prejudice' privilege. Legal professional privilege, in particular, has been subject to a certain turbulence in recent times.

The privilege against self-incrimination

3.28 Virtually any witness to legal proceedings, other than the accused in a criminal case, is entitled to refuse to answer questions put which might tend to incriminate him. More specifically, if in the opinion of the judge there appears a risk that a witness's answers to particular questions might expose him to a criminal charge, or the infliction of a penalty or (in criminal cases only) a forfeiture under UK law, the witness may be excused from answering those questions. In the case of civil proceedings, the detailed rules governing the privilege against self-incrimination are set out in the Civil Evidence Act 1968, s 14. Linking up with the discussion of spousal competence and compellability, it might be noted that s 14(1)(b) prescribes that the privilege:

> ...shall include a like right to refuse to answer any question or produce any document or thing if to do so would tend to expose the husband or wife of that person to proceedings...

The privilege may come to be invoked in one of three ways. As Sedley LJ explained in *Institute of Chartered Accountants, ex p Nawaz* [1997] PNLR 433, often counsel will ask a question but instruct the witness not to answer until the judge has had a chance to explain the position to him. Otherwise, the judge may either interject to tell a witness that he need not answer counsel's question or the witness himself may enquire of the court whether he has to answer the question (at [34]).

3.29 There are two rival formulations of the test the courts ought to apply in determining whether a witness is entitled to claim this privilege. In *Boyes* (1861) 1 B & S 311, 330 Cockburn CJ referred to the need for only a 'reasonable ground to apprehend danger to the witness' and spoke of this danger having to be 'real and appreciable, with reference to the ordinary operation of law in the ordinary course of things'. Subsequently, Goddard LJ in *Blunt v Park Lane Hotel* [1942] 2 KB 253, 257 devised a seemingly more stringent test, stating that the risk to the witness had to be 'reasonably likely'. More recently still, Templeman LJ stated that 'in any legal proceedings a person, whether a party to the proceedings or not, cannot be compelled to answer any question or produce any document or thing if to do so would tend to expose him to proceedings for an offence' (*Rank Film Distributors Ltd v Video Information Centre* [1980] 2 All ER 273, 288). No matter how the test is expressed, the purpose of the privilege is to protect witnesses against 'a real risk of incrimination or material increase of an existing risk' (*Khan v Khan* [1982] 1 WLR 513, 518 *per* Stephenson LJ). Therefore, if a witness has already incriminated himself independently of any evidence he might be constrained to give in the proceedings, *ex hypothesi* the privilege is no longer available to him. In *Khan* [2007] EWCA Crim 2331 K appealed against a conviction for contempt of court arising out of his refusal to answer questions in the course of giving evidence on behalf of a co-accused charged with terrorist offences. K, who had earlier pleaded guilty to conspiring to make available money or other property for terrorist purposes, claimed privilege against answering questions on matters which the court found fell within the scope of that guilty plea. As Moses LJ pointed out, dismissing K's appeal,

> It must be emphasised that the privilege is designed to provide protection in relation to questions which might incriminate. If the danger of incrimination has already arisen and is independent of any questions which a person is required to answer, it is not possible to see why that person should be entitled to any protection at all. If his position is made no worse by answering a question, then there can be no basis for him to invoke the privilege.
>
> (at [31])

Some uncertainty also surrounds the question of whether or not the privilege against self-incrimination only attaches to legal proceedings. Although Lord Denning MR stated the principle in expansive terms, Roskill LJ in *Rio Tinto Zinc Corpn v Westinghouse Electric Corpn* [1978] AC 547 reserved the question. Five members of the High Court of Australia, however, did consider the matter in *Sorby v Commonwealth of Australia* (1983) 152 CLR 281, four of whom concluded that the privilege does attach to executive inquiries, too. Sedley LJ in *Ex p Nawaz* (*ante*, para **3.28**) ventured a similar opinion.

3.30 Witnesses are accorded a privilege against self-incrimination because it is felt that no one ought to be compelled to answer questions under threat of a penalty. Indeed, as we shall see in the chapter dealing with the accused's right of silence (*post*, Chapter 11), in *Saunders v UK* (1996) 23 EHRR 313 the European Court of Human Rights held that, when used by the Crown in subsequent proceedings, answers which DTI inspectors had lawfully obtained from S under threat of prosecution infringed S's right to fair trial under Article 6 of the Convention (see *post*, paras **11.65** ff). Some statutes, however, deprive witnesses of this privilege in certain forms of proceedings. In view of the paramount importance accorded to the interests of children who are the subject in such proceedings, the Children Act 1989, s 98(1), for example, lays down that:

> In any proceedings in which a court is hearing an application for [a care or supervision] order..., no person shall be excused from
>
> (a) giving evidence on any matter; or
>
> (b) answering any question put to him in the course of his giving evidence,
>
> on the ground that doing so might incriminate him or his spouse of an offence.

The Act goes on to provide, as a 'counter-balance' (*Re Y and K* [2003] 2 FLR 273 at [33] *per* Hale LJ), that any statements or admissions made as a result of being compelled to testify or answer particular questions under this provision cannot be used in criminal proceedings instituted against that witness or his spouse, save if there is a prosecution for perjury (s 98(2). See also Fraud Act 2006, s 13; *JSC BTA Bank v Ablyazov* [2010] 1 WLR 976). The Child Support Act 1991, s 14(A), too, provides that the privilege against self-incrimination is not available to a party who is the subject of a request for information (eg, *Child Maintenance Enforcement Commission v Forrest* [2010] 2 FCR 631.) Such exceptions to the privilege, however, remain rare. Nevertheless, an increasing number of judges would question whether the law ought to show such indulgence to witnesses. It might also be noted that the courts do sometimes interpret the privilege against self-incrimination in a restrictive manner, or impose limitations on its exercise. Lord Templeman, for example, in *AT & T Istel Ltd v Tully* [1993] AC 45 declared:

> It is difficult to see any reason why in civil proceeding the privilege against self-incrimination should be exercisable so as to enable a litigant to refuse relevant and even vital documents which are in his possession or power or which speak for themselves...I regard the privilege against self-incrimination in civil proceedings as an archaic and unjustifiable survival from the past...
>
> (at 53)

Lord Griffiths in the same case declared: 'The privilege against self-incrimination is in need of radical reappraisal.'

3.31 The privilege against self-incrimination, it should be stressed, attaches to the witness, not to the evidence. Therefore, even though it may not be possible to extract a particular piece of evidence from testimony because the relevant witness successfully claims privilege, a party is not debarred from proving the same matter by other means. Admittedly, matters can become a little more complicated where prosecuting authorities are actually contemplating bringing criminal proceedings against a defendant already engaged in a civil action. In such cases, the court will need to bear in mind both the interests of the claimant to the civil claim as well as the risk of unfairness to the defendant at any eventual criminal trial. In *Versailles Trade Finance Ltd v Clough* [2001] EWCA Civ 1509; [2002] CP Rep 8, for example, C sought to resist summary judgment being given against him in respect of a claim for over £11m. C, who, at the time, risked prosecution for fraudulent trading—an eventuality that later materialised—argued that he was unable to plead to the claimant's allegation: if he did so, he might thereby incriminate himself. The Court of Appeal emphasised that the privilege against self-incrimination cannot operate either as a defence to a civil claim or, more pertinently, as a reason for outright refusal to plead a defence. Its purpose is restricted to preventing people from being compelled under threat of punishment to provide information that might subsequently be used against them. Hence, if it can be demonstrated that what would emerge at the civil trial—were C to plead to the allegation—might have an adverse impact on the fairness of the criminal trial, then the civil court has discretion to grant a stay, an adjournment or a postponement of the civil proceedings. The civil court, however, is not obliged to indulge the defendant. Indeed, in the *Versailles* case it was held that, because C had not demonstrated any real prospect of successfully defending the civil claim or any serious likelihood of suffering prejudice at any subsequent criminal trial, there was no reason to exercise discretion in his favour or for summary judgment not to be given against him.

3.32 Finally, if it is held on appeal that the court at first instance wrongly refused to grant a witness this privilege in respect of part of his testimony, recognition of this error by no means guarantees that the lower court's judgment will be overturned on appeal.

Legal professional privilege

3.33 In a now oft-quoted statement in *R v Derby Magistrates' Court, ex p B* [1996] AC 487, 507 Lord Taylor CJ gave voice to the following resounding article of faith:

> The principle that runs through [the law] . . . is that a man must be able to consult his lawyer in confidence, since otherwise he might hold back half the truth. The client must be sure that what he tells the lawyer in confidence will never be revealed without his consent. Legal professional privilege is thus much more than an ordinary rule of evidence, limited in its application to the facts of a particular case. It is a fundamental condition on which the administration of justice as a whole rests.

As late as the nineteenth century, powerful voices had been raised against the recognition of legal professional privilege—notably, those of Lord Langdale MR and Wigram V-C. Their opposition reflected the Benthamite view that any such privilege merely conduced to false defences. This selfsame viewpoint also argued that a rule that deterred a guilty person from seeking legal advice was no bad thing, particularly since an innocent person would not be so discouraged. Such, however, was not the thinking of the majority of nineteenth-century lawyers. Knight Bruce V-C in *Pearse v Pearse* (1846) 1 De G & Sm 12, 29, for example, argued:

> Truth, like all other good things, may be loved unwisely—may be pursued too keenly— may cost too much. And surely the meanness and the mischief of prying into a man's confidential communications with his legal adviser, the general evil of infusing reserve and dissimulation, uneasiness, and suspicion and fear, into those communications which must take place, and which, unless in a condition of perfect security, must take place uselessly or worse, are too great a price to pay for truth itself.

3.34 From the turn of the twentieth century, dissident voices were largely quelled, and the Earl of Halsbury LC in *Bullivant v A-G for Victoria* [1901] AC 196, 200, could speak of legal professional privilege as an established principle of public policy. This 'fundamental condition on which the administration of justice as a whole rests' today is indeed far-reaching—indeed, so far-reaching that Laws LJ, in *Grant* [2005] 3 WLR 437 at [54], considered that 'it is unnecessary to multiply authority to demonstrate the importance which the law attaches to legal professional privilege', that Brooke LJ in *Bowman v Fels* [2005] 1 WLR 3083 especially at [85]–[87] concluded that only legislation expressed in the clearest terms could override the privilege, and that Lord Taylor CJ, in *ex p B*, could declare that legal professional privilege amounted to a basic human right guaranteed under the European Convention. Lord Taylor's view has since been echoed by Lord Hoffmann in *R (Morgan Grenfell & Co Ltd) v Special Commissioner* [2003] 1 AC 563 at [7]. Certainly, it is a durable privilege, for the watchword has always been 'once privileged always privileged' (*The Aegis Blaze* [1986] 1 Lloyd's Rep 203, 210 *per* Croom-Johnson LJ). Nevertheless, this generous view of privilege (illustrated by the facts of *Calcraft v Guest* [1898] 1 QB 759; see *post*, para **3.45**) was doubted *obiter* by Lord Nicholls in *Derby Magistrates' Court, ex p B* (cited *ante*, at 512–13). Indeed, there is some force in Lord Nicholls's observations for, as the High Court of Australia also observed in *Grant v Downs* (1976) 135 CLR 674:

> The existence of the privilege reflects, to the extent to which it is accorded, the paramountcy of this public interest over a more general public interest, that which requires that in the interests of a fair trial litigation should be conducted on the footing that all relevant documentary evidence is available.
>
> (at 685)

In fact, the great challenge posed by legal professional privilege resides in finding a happy point of equilibrium that successfully balances the 'two opposing imperatives, making the maximum, relevant material available to the court of trial and avoiding unfairness to individuals by revealing confidential communications between their lawyers and themselves' (*Three Rivers DC v Governor and Company of the Bank of England* [2004] 3 WLR 1274 at [86] *per* Lord Carswell).

3.35 It is possible that the absolute nature of legal professional privilege under English law, broadcast by the House of Lords in *Derby Magistrates' Court, ex p B*, may need to be reviewed one day. Although operating under a different human rights regime, it is significant that the Supreme Court of Canada in *McClure* [2001] SCC 14 has now held that, despite its unquestioned importance, legal professional privilege is not absolute. In limited circumstances where innocence is at stake—more specifically, where core issues going to the guilt of the accused are involved and there is a genuine risk of a wrongful conviction—a court may order disclosure, granting the defendant access to materials in the hands of a third party which normally would be considered privileged. The right of fair trial guaranteed under Article 6, one might suggest, could so easily predicate that a defendant ought to be allowed access even to a legally privileged document in the possession of a third party, of the existence of which he has become aware, if it would in likelihood reinforce his claim that he is innocent. More generally, the House of Lords has recently indicated that, because legal professional privilege is a creation of an adversary system of trial, at least in the context of civil proceedings, which, since the introduction of the CPR have to a great extent lost their adversarial character, the privilege may one day need to be reconsidered (*Three Rivers DC v Governor and Company of the Bank of England* [2004] 3 WLR 1274 at [29] *per* Lord Scott of Foscote, and at [53] *per* Lord Rodger of Earlsferry).

3.36 The potential scope of legal professional privilege can be readily gleaned from PACE, s 10(1), which defines 'items subject to legal privilege' as:

(a) communications between a professional legal adviser and his client or any person representing his client made in connection with the giving of legal advice to the client;

(b) communications between a professional legal adviser and his client or any person representing his client or between such an adviser or his client or any such representative and any other person made in connection with or in contemplation of legal proceedings and for the purposes of such proceedings;

(c) items enclosed with or referred to in such communications and made—

(i) in connection with the giving of legal advice; or

(ii) in connection with or in contemplation of proceedings and for the purposes of such proceedings,

when they are in the possession of a person who is entitled to possession of them.

As this definition shows, the privilege consists of two related but separate elements: what are known as '*legal advice privilege*' and '*litigation privilege*'. Legal professional privilege therefore attaches not only to confidential communications between lawyer and client in the course of the client's seeking legal advice but also, whenever litigation is pending or in prospect, it extends to communications between lawyer and client provided that the main purpose of the communication is either to obtain advice relating to that future litigation or to collect evidence for use in that litigation. Hence, the privilege can potentially be claimed for a broad range of documents relating to prospective litigation—correspondence, reports, etc (s 10(1)(c)).

Legal advice privilege

3.37 In *Three Rivers DC v Governor and Company of the Bank of England (No 6)* [2004] 3 WLR 1274, a decision of very considerable importance, the House of Lords took the opportunity to review legal advice privilege. Although impeded by its own Appeals Committee's puzzling decision not to hear the appeal in *Three Rivers DC v Governor and Company of the Bank of England (No 5)* [2003] QB 1556, the House's views can be largely deduced. Also, the alarm spread by certain of the Master of the Rolls' *dicta* in the Court of Appeal in *Three Rivers (No 6)* [2004] QB 916 is evident from the fact that the Attorney-General, the Bar Council and the Law Society all felt prompted to intervene in the House of Lords hearing, in which Lord Scott of Foscote justified the existence of legal advice privilege, independent of litigation, in the following manner:

> [I]t is necessary in . . . a society in which the restraining and controlling framework is built upon a belief in the rule of law, that communications between clients and lawyers, whereby the clients are hoping for the assistance of the lawyers' legal skills in the management of their [the clients'] affairs, should be secure against the possibility of any scrutiny from others, whether the police, the executive, business competitors, inquisitive busy-bodies or anyone else . . . It justifies, in my opinion, the retention of legal advice privilege in our law, notwithstanding that as a result cases may sometimes have to be decided in ignorance of relevant probative material.
>
> (at [34])

Such a philosophy necessitates that 'legal advice privilege must cover . . . advice and assistance in relation to public law rights, liabilities and obligations' (at [36])—for, as Lord Hoffmann explained in *R (Morgan Grenfell & Co Ltd) v Special Commissioner* [2003] 1 AC 563, 607, the privilege is 'a necessary corollary of the right of any person to obtain skilled advice about the law'.

3.38 Even though other professionals may offer their clients advice that is legal in character, 'legal advice privilege' only attaches to advice given by members of the legal profession (*R (Prudential plc) v Special Commissioner of Income Tax* [2011] 2 WLR 50: accountants advising client on taxation issues). Until recently, it was widely believed that 'legal advice privilege' would not only cover communications between lawyer and client, but might also extend to communications between lawyer or client and third parties, provided that the dominant purpose of the communication was either to obtain advice relating to that future litigation or to collect evidence for use in that litigation. This interpretation of the rule, however, has now been abandoned by the Court of Appeal in *Three Rivers District Council v Governor and Company of the Bank of England (No 5)* [2003] QB 1556. The *Three Rivers* litigation arose out of the closure of the BCCI bank. During the course of Lord Bingham's inquiry into the bank's collapse, the Governor of the Bank of England appointed three officials to oversee communications between BCCI and the inquiry. BCCI's liquidators and creditors commenced proceedings against the Bank of England for misfeasance in a public office for having failed properly to supervise BCCI's affairs. The Bank of England claimed legal advice privilege over masses of documents that originated after BCCI had been closed down but before the Bank of England had made its final submissions to Lord Bingham's inquiry. The liquidators and creditors of BCCI claimed that such privilege could only extend to actual communications between solicitor and client. The Court of Appeal upheld this contention. Longmore LJ declared that the 'dominant purpose test' applied only to litigation privilege (see *post*, paras **3.40** ff) and could not therefore extend to any of the documents and internal memoranda generated by the Bank of England's employees or former employees whilst supervising the passage of communications between BCCI and the inquiry, even if their intention had been to send these papers on to the Bank of England's legal advisers. The only concession Longmore LJ was prepared to envisage might arise in respect of documents which solicitor or client intended to communicate to one another, but for some reason (eg death) failed so to do. This decision is significant because it now means that unless litigation is in prospect, if a party's employee prepares a document which is to be sent to the employer's lawyers, it will only be non-disclosable provided that the court considers that in effect it amounts to the employer's communication with the legal adviser for the purpose of taking legal advice. Most surprisingly, the House of Lords' Appeals Committee declined to hear an appeal from this far-reaching decision.

3.39   In *Three Rivers (No 6)* the House of Lords was required to consider another question regarding the scope of legal advice privilege: namely, whether it extends to presentational advice with which a lawyer might be requested to furnish his client. It was held, unanimously, that the privilege did indeed cover presentational advice. As Lord Scott made clear:

> Presentational advice or assistance given by lawyers to parties whose conduct may be the subject of criticism by the inquiry is advice or assistance that may serve to avoid the

> need to invoke public law remedies. It would be—or should be—readily accepted that, once an inquiry's conclusions have been reached and communicated to the sponsors of the inquiry, advice from lawyers to someone criticised as to whether a public law remedy might be available to quash the critical conclusions would be advice that qualified for legal advice privilege. It makes no sense at all ... to withhold the protection of that privilege from presentational advice given by the lawyers for the purpose of preventing that criticism from being made in the first place.
>
> (at [37])

Lord Carswell, *inter alios*, echoed this opinion:

> [A]ll communications between a solicitor and his client relating to a transaction in which the solicitor has been instructed for the purpose of obtaining legal advice will be privileged, notwithstanding that they do not contain advice on matters of law or construction, provided that they are directly related to the performance by the solicitor of his professional duty as legal adviser of his client.
>
> (at [111])

This does not mean that every piece of advice a solicitor offers his client will be privileged. Lord Scott, for instance, stressed, 'there must be a "relevant legal context" in order for the advice to attract legal professional privilege' (at [38]). Lord Rodger of Earlsferry made plain what really counted in this particular case, where the Bank of England's Bingham Inquiry Unit had sought the presentational advice of its solicitors:

> In relation to legal advice privilege what matters today remains the same as what mattered in the past: whether the lawyers are being asked *qua* lawyers to provide legal advice ... [T]he [Unit] was asking [the solicitors] to put on legal spectacles when reading, considering and commenting on the drafts. In other words it was asking them to consider, as lawyers, how the Bank's evidence could be most effectively presented to Bingham LJ, given that he was inquiring into the Bank's discharge of their legal responsibilities under the Banking Acts.
>
> (at [58] and [60])

Litigation privilege

3.40 'Litigation privilege' arises only from the moment that litigation is pending or in prospect. Lord Rodger of Earlsferry defined it thus in *Three Rivers (No.6)* [2005] 1 AC 610:

> Litigation privilege relates to communications at the stage when litigation is pending or in contemplation. It is based on the idea that legal proceedings take the form of a contest

in which each of the opposing parties assembles his own body of evidence and uses it to try to defeat the other, with the judge or jury determining the winner. In such a system each party should be free to prepare his case as fully as possible without the risk that his opponent will be able to recover the material generated by his preparations. In the words of Justice Jackson in *Hickman v Taylor*, 329 US 495, 516 (1947), "Discovery was hardly intended to enable a learned profession to perform its functions either without wits or on wits borrowed from the adversary."

(at [52])

The notion of litigation 'pending or anticipated', to take Denning LJ's well-known formulation (*Jarman v Lambert & Cooke Contractors Ltd* [1951] 2 KB 937, 946), is far from clear. Indeed, as the Court of Appeal has confessed when endeavouring to apply this criterion, 'Some concepts are difficult to express in words' (*US v Philip Morris Inc* [2004] 1 CLC 811 at [25]). From the moment that litigation is pending, however, privilege attaches to any confidential communications passing between lawyer and client if the 'dominant purpose' is either the giving of advice or the assembling of evidence for prospective use in litigation. Sir John Donaldson MR compressed the general import of this privilege into a single, neat sentence in *Lee v South West Thames Regional Health Authority* [1985] 1 WLR 845:

The principle is that a [party] or potential [party] shall be free to seek evidence without being obliged to disclose the result of his researches to his opponent.

(at 850)

3.41 Unlike legal advice privilege, litigation privilege is not restricted to matters passing between the lawyer and his client but may extend to documents emanating from third parties (see *Wheeler v le Marchant* (1881) 17 Ch D 675). The requirement of 'dominant purpose', originally borrowed from Barwick CJ's judgment in the Australian High Court in *Grant v Downs* (1976) 135 CLR 674, was applied by the House of Lords in *Waugh v British Railways Board* [1980] AC 521. In seeking to establish that her husband's death in a railway collision between two locomotives had been occasioned by the Board's negligence, W sought disclosure of an internal inquiry report into the collision. The report had been commissioned for two reasons: it served both railway safety purposes and also had been composed with a view to seeking legal advice. The House of Lords determined that the dominant purpose of the report was not the seeking of advice. In this case, this purpose had been of no more than equal rank and weight with that of establishing for the railway the cause of the accident. Therefore, litigation privilege did not attach to it. Wide though it undoubtedly is, litigation privilege applies to confidential communications between lawyer and client. It does not attach to communications passing between claimant and defendant. Thus, if a solicitor has made notes of a meeting he attended or of a telephone conversation he held with the opposing side's solicitor, such notes are not privileged from disclosure (*Parry v News Group Newspapers* (1990) NLJR 1719).

3.42 Although the detailed debate is beyond the scope of an introductory text, the precise scope of litigation privilege is currently disputed. In brief, the orthodox understanding appears to have been that the privilege extends beyond legal advice to what is known as 'materials for evidence', that is to any materials which come into existence wholly or mainly for the purpose of preparing a case. Scott V-C's judgment in *Re Barings plc* [1998] 1 All ER 673, 681–2 would suggest, on the contrary, that litigation privilege centres uniquely upon protecting the lawyer–client relationship:

> ... There [is] no general privilege that attache[s] to ... documents brought into existence for the purposes of litigation independent of the need to keep inviolate communications between client and legal adviser. If documents for which privilege was sought did not relate in some fashion to communications between client and legal adviser, there was no element of public interest that could override the ordinary rights of discovery and no privilege. So, for example, an unsolicited communication from a third party, a potential witness, about the facts of the case would not, on this view, have been privileged. And why should it be?

For the time being, the matter is unresolved. It is, nevertheless, of very considerable practical importance.

Legal professional privilege in general

3.43 What is the exact relationship between the two forms of legal professional privilege discussed above? According to Lord Nicholls of Birkenhead in *Re L (a minor)* [1997] AC 16 at 33, legal advice privilege and litigation privilege simply constitute integral parts of a single privilege. In *Three Rivers (No 6)*, too, Lord Carswell expressed similar sentiments:

> [T]he cases establish that, so far from legal advice privilege being an outgrowth and extension of litigation privilege, legal professional privilege is a single integral privilege, whose sub-heads are legal advice privilege and litigation privilege, and that it is litigation privilege which is restricted to proceedings in a court of law in the manner which the authorities show.
>
> (at [105])

The point is significant because it has been sought in the past to suggest that if legal advice privilege is simply an outcrop of litigation privilege, then it may only attach to advice relating to rights and obligations where there is some risk of litigation (eg *16th Report of the Law Reform Committee* (1967) esp para 19). To recognise the independent existence of legal advice privilege is to liberate the concept from impending or potential litigation and to grant legal advisers and their clients a privilege against disclosure in a very wide range of legally motivated circumstances.

3.44 Putting this debate to one side, however, a number of general principles affecting legal professional privilege in general need to be mentioned. Legal professional privilege, it must be noted, is restricted to communications that pass between legal adviser and client. It does not extend to factual matters. For this reason, a lawyer may not be entitled to decline to say whether certain papers are in his possession, even if he cannot be compelled to disclose their contents (*Dwyer v Collins* (1852) 7 Exch 639). Again, it has been held that a person's name, address and contact details provided prior to advice being proffered cannot be regarded, without more, as having been made in connection with legal advice and do not therefore automatically attract legal professional privilege (*R v Manchester Crown Court, ex p Rogers* [1999] 1 WLR 832). Similar reasoning has been applied to a solicitor's record of a client's mobile telephone number, which the latter claimed did not belong to him (*R (Miller Gardner) v Minshull Street Crown Court* [2002] EWHC 3077).

3.45 The privilege may be bypassed if the matters to which it relates can be proved by other secondary evidence. In the classic case of *Calcraft v Guest* [1898] 1 QB 759, Mrs D and G were involved in a trespass action relating to a fishery. The original copies of certain privileged documents, relating to an assault action brought over a century earlier by one of C's predecessors in title, had by chance come into G's possession. Although they had been privileged in the proceedings that had taken place in 1787, the court held that copies of these documents made by the lawyers acting for Mrs D and G before they were handed back to C were admissible at the later trial. Therefore, if an opposing party comes into possession of the other side's privileged information lawfully, under English law it would appear that privilege is lost and that the evidence can be introduced. In *Tompkins* (1977) 67 Cr App R 181, for example, prosecuting counsel was held to be entitled to make use in cross-examination of the contents of a note that T had passed to his counsel. The note had been found lying on the floor of the courtroom by a legal assistant in the chief prosecuting solicitor's office. Ethically speaking, this is a dubious decision, and it is not surprising that some jurisdictions have rejected it. In *Uljee* [1982] 1 NZLR 561, 572, a New Zealand case, a policeman, standing guard outside a house, happened to overhear through the kitchen window a conversation between U and his solicitor. Richardson J declared:

> Our society expects that certain standards will be set for the conduct of criminal investigations and will ordinarily be met in practice. In turn the individual is entitled to expect

> those standards to be adhered to and that he may act accordingly...Solicitor and client
> should be able to act in the belief that what they legitimately discuss in the interview is
> confidential.

A case like *Tompkins* in fact looks vulnerable from a human rights point of view, particularly were the court not to proceed upon the benevolent assumption that the finding of the note was 'fortuitous'. Notably, in *S v Switzerland* (1991) 14 EHRR 670 the Strasbourg Court has declared:

> The Court considers that an accused's right to communicate with his advocate out of
> hearing of a third person is part of the basic requirements of a fair trial in a democratic
> society and follows from art 6(3)(c) of the Convention. If a lawyer were unable to con-
> fer with his client and receive confidential instructions from him without surveillance, his
> assistance would lose much of its usefulness, whereas the Convention is intended to
> guarantee rights that are practical and effective...
>
> (at [48])

It would be no bad thing were the *Tompkins* principle to be rejected. After all, any claim that the image of the Crown's agents, scrabbling around on their hands and knees on the floor under defence counsel's bench in quest of incriminating notes, equates with any sort of dignified notion of fair trial looks pretty implausible. (Cf *McE v Prison Service of NI (NI Human Rights Commission intervening)* [2009] 1 AC 908.)

3.46   It is important to emphasise that not all communications between client and solicitor are privileged. In *R (Howe) v South Durham Magistrates' Court* (2004) 168 JP
424 H, who declined to give evidence, denied having driven whilst disqualified. H
claimed that he had not been previously disqualified in 2000, as the prosecution
alleged. In the absence of other means of proving H's identity as the person who
had been convicted and disqualified in 2000, on the application of the CPS the justices issued a witness summons under the Magistrates' Courts Act 1980, s 97 to the
solicitor who was acting for H, and who had also acted for the person who had been
convicted on the earlier occasion, ordering the production of the attendance note of
the earlier hearing with a view to establishing the identity of the person disqualified in 2000 and the identification of H as being that same person. Although the
justices made clear in their reasons that the evidence they hoped the solicitor would
give had to be limited to what had happened in the public courtroom and that he
would not be asked to reveal anything which had passed privately between him
and his then client, the summons was contested on the ground that the attendance
note was subject to legal professional privilege. Although it will obviously occasion
professional embarrassment whenever a solicitor is summonsed to give evidence
against his client—the solicitor will have to withdraw—provided that questions

are restricted to resolving these identity issues, the Divisional Court did not accept that the summons would infringe H's legal professional privilege. As David Clarke J pointed out:

> The witness is not being called in his capacity as the claimant's solicitor, but as a person who was present in court at the relevant time. The evidence he will be asked to give, and the questions which will be put to him, will not enter the territory of solicitor and client communication.
>
> (at [23])

Although this procedure, which, if widely practised, could undermine the confidence between client and solicitor that is considered so important in the administration of criminal justice, ought to be 'of last resort' (at [42] *per* Rose LJ), the *Howe* case illustrates the fact that there do exist situations where matters that pass between client and solicitor may fall outside the realm of legal professional privilege.

3.47 Being for his benefit, legal professional privilege belongs to the client, not to the lawyer. Only the client, therefore, is entitled to waive legal professional privilege. Moreover, if the client does decide to waive privilege, the lawyer retains no right to assert it for his own benefit. Waiver, however, may sometimes be forced upon the client to all practical intents, if he is the defendant in a criminal case. In Chapter 11 there is discussion of those troublesome provisions, introduced by the Criminal Justice and Public Order Act 1994, and notably of s 34, which now circumscribe the accused's right of silence. If an accused seeks to justify a failure to mention facts upon which he subsequently relies at trial on the ground that he was acting upon legal advice, whilst his mere statement that he received such advice will not of itself be taken as a waiver of his privilege, the court will expect the accused to produce rather more information than that. The law, it would seem, cannot accept that it is inherently reasonable for a suspect in custody blindly to follow his lawyer's advice on how to approach questions put to him by his interrogators. Therefore, details of the lawyer's advice in all likelihood will need to be given to the court in order to enable the tribunal of fact to gauge the reasonableness or otherwise of the suspect's reticence and to determine therefrom whether or not it is appropriate to draw adverse inferences from the accused's omission to mention particular facts. The practical effect of a provision like s 34 frequently is to pressurise D into waiving his legal professional privilege (see *post*, paras **11.16** ff and *Seaton* [2011] 1 Cr App R 2).

3.48 Legal professional privilege has traditionally been generously construed. Thus, it applies to any lawyers, provided that they are exercising their professional skill. It has occasionally been held to include those who do not have practising certificates, and even those who are mere trainees. Conversely, however, if a lawyer is not acting in his professional capacity, his communications do not attract privilege. In *Blackpool Corporation v Locker* [1948] 1 All ER 85, correspondence carried on both within the town council and with the Minister of Health by a town clerk, who was a qualified solicitor, was held not to be privileged because at the relevant time the town clerk was acting in his executive rather than his legal capacity. More generally, however, it has for some time been unclear exactly what communications between lawyers and client the law will treat as privileged. As Taylor LJ observed in *Balabel v Air India* [1988] Ch 317, at pp 330 and 332, while the test is whether the communication or other document was made confidentially for the purposes of legal advice, 'those purposes have to be construed broadly' and the answer 'must depend on whether they are part of that necessary exchange of information of which the object is the giving of legal advice as and when appropriate'. *C v C (Privilege: Criminal Communications)* [2002] Fam 42 illustrates the difficulties posed by the law's lax approach to this key question. A husband and wife were going through a bitter divorce. The husband's solicitors wished to be rid of their awkward client. They secretly taped conversations between the husband and his solicitor in which he complained of the solicitors' proposed charges for handling the eventual sale of the matrimonial home and, more particularly, in which he threatened to 'rip someone's throat out'. In what Thorpe LJ indulgently characterised as 'the sort of minor aberration that happens, even in the best conducted solicitors' office', transcripts of these conversations were mistakenly sent to the wife's solicitors. Understandably, the wife wished to use the transcripts in the divorce hearing as evidence of her husband's abusive and violent attitude towards her. The husband argued that the transcripts were subject to legal professional privilege and therefore should not be so used. Whereas Thorpe LJ was clear that the communications between the husband and his solicitor could not remotely be said to be connected with the obtaining of legal advice, but had to do with the husband's seeking to get a better deal and to press the solicitors to move things along (at [11]), Hale LJ declined to take this line. Although she would not hold that the communications fell outside the purview of legal professional privilege, Hale LJ nevertheless agreed with Thorpe LJ's alternative conclusion that the husband's communications were not covered by privilege owing to the fact that they fell within the exception established in *Cox and Railton* (1884) 14 QBD 153, which excludes from the scope of the privilege communications 'criminal in themselves, or intended to further any criminal purpose'. (See further, *R (Hallinan Blackburn-Gittings and Nott (a firm)) v Middlesex Guildhall Crown Court* [2005] 1 WLR 766; also, *Kuwait Airways Corporation v Iraqi Airways Co* [2005] 1 WLR 2734, which holds that, subject to certain qualifications, the fraud exception applies to both litigation privilege and legal advice privilege.) The issues here are highly sensitive. Once one accepts that such a privilege deserves to exist at all, even small inroads made into the notion of what may properly be considered legal professional communications are potentially of great concern. Hale LJ accepted this point in the course of argument, noting:

> The spectre was raised of solicitors being asked to disclose the demeanour of their clients when they came to seek advice. One example was personal injury solicitors dealing with their client, who might then be asked whether the client had come in with a limp that he claimed that he suffered as a result of his accident. That would of course be a spectre that would haunt these courts for years to come.
>
> (at [23])

3.49 Legislation, it could be added, has occasionally extended the privilege to communications with other classes of person. The Copyright, Designs and Patents Act 1988, s 280, for instance, provides that any communication between a party and his patent agent relating to the protection of inventions, designs, technical information or trademarks or to any matter involving passing off 'is privileged from disclosure in legal proceedings...in the same way as a communication between a person and his solicitor'.

3.50 Legal professional privilege, one senses, is a subject in flux. It is significant that in *Three Rivers (No 5)* [2004] 2 WLR 1065, esp at [28], in the Court of Appeal, Lord Phillips MR expressed dissatisfaction with the current state of the law. In *Three Rivers (No 6)* [2004] 3 WLR 1274, the House of Lords, too, evinced concern, not least at some of the implications of the Court of Appeal's decision in *Three Rivers (No 5)*. Notably, Lord Carswell (at [118]), who—like his brethren—declined to express an opinion on the correctness of that case, nevertheless went out of his way to make clear that he was 'not to be taken to have approved of the decision in *Three Rivers (No 5)'*. There can be little doubting that the House of Lords will need to revisit this subject ere too long.

Common interest privilege

3.51 Owing to its obvious links with legal professional privilege, brief mention needs to be made of common interest privilege. In essence, this privilege may arise whenever, at the time a document is created, two or more parties who share a common interest in anticipated litigation exchange information. Documents received for this purpose are treated as privileged in the hands of the recipient. As Lord Denning MR explained in *Buttes Gas and Oil Co v Hammer (No 3)* [1981] QB 223, 243:

> It often happens in litigation that a plaintiff or defendant has other persons standing alongside him—who have the self-same interest as he—and who have consulted lawyers on the self-same points as he—these others have not been made parties to the actions. Maybe for economy or for simplicity or which you will. All exchange counsel's opinions. All

collect information for the purpose of litigation. All make copies . . . . In all such cases . . . the courts should—for the purposes of discovery—treat all the persons interested as if they were partners in a single firm or departments in a single company. Each can avail himself of the privilege in aid of litigation.

The essence of this privilege is that the parties must have a common interest in advancing proceedings brought or contemplated against another person or in defending such proceedings. As a corollary, where claimants had been opponents, enjoying no such common interest, prior to settling their litigation, in subsequent criminal proceedings common interest privilege could not be claimed over affidavits sworn by them in the course of their civil litigation (*Trutch and Trutch* [2001] EWCA Crim 1750).

'Without prejudice' privilege

3.52 It is recognised to be in the public interest that parties should compromise their disputes rather than fight them out in court to final judgment. (Certain institutions of civil procedure, such as the payment into court, are obviously designed to encourage parties to settle rather than litigate.) All communications, whether oral or written, which pass between the parties during their negotiations with the purpose of seeking a settlement are therefore treated as privileged. Plainly, it would act as a damper were parties forever to be concerned lest things they said or wrote during attempts to reach a compromise might later be used against them, were the negotiations ultimately to prove fruitless. As Oliver LJ put it in *Cutts v Head* [1984] Ch 290:

> [Parties] should . . . be encouraged fully and frankly to put their cards on the table. . . . The public policy justification, in truth, essentially rests on the desirability of preventing statements or offers made in the course of negotiations for settlement being brought before the court of trial as admissions on the question of liability.
>
> (at 306)

However, as Lord Walker of Gestingthorpe recently pointed out in *Olofue v Bossert* [2009] AC 990:

> In England the rule has developed vigorously (more vigorously, probably, than in other common law jurisdictions, and more vigorously than some overseas scholars, notably J H Wigmore approved . . .)
>
> (at [57])

3.53 Although 'without prejudice' documents will very often be generated once litigation has commenced, the privilege is more extensive than this. Whilst the ambit of the rule ought not to be extended further than is necessary to foster the public interest objective of aiding the settlement of disputes, a dispute may engage the rule notwithstanding that litigation has not yet begun. The validity of any claim to the privilege will turn on the subject matter of the dispute, the crucial consideration being whether in the course of negotiations the parties contemplated or might reasonably have contemplated litigation, should they not reach agreement. Thus, in *Barnetson v Framlingham Group Ltd* [2007] 1 WLR 2443, where a senior employee was in dispute with his employer over his dismissal, the Court of Appeal held that in view of the large sums of money involved and the fact that the parties were plainly aware at the time of the disputed exchanges that litigation was likely to ensue if they failed to agree terms, the defendants were entitled to the benefit of the formula 'without prejudice' which had been written on a draft compromise agreement that was ultimately rejected by the claimant.

3.54 The common practice is to mark documents or to state that conversations are being conducted 'without prejudice'. This prima facie means that it was intended to be a negotiating document' (*South Shropshire DC v Amos* [1986] 1 WLR 1271, 1277 *per* Parker LJ; *Olofue v Bossert* [2009] AC 990 at [2] *per* Lord Hope). However, the privilege attaches whenever communications between the parties form part of a *genuine* attempt to reach settlement in a legal dispute, whether or not they have made this explicit beforehand (*Rush & Tompkins v GLC* [1989] AC 1280, 1299 *per* Lord Griffiths). Communications which attract without prejudice privilege may only be admitted by the court in a limited range of circumstances—for example, to explain why there may have been delay in prosecuting a claim or even to establish whether or not the parties' negotiations actually ripened into a full contractual settlement of their dispute. Equally, they may become admissible if they contain 'an unambiguous admission of impropriety' by one of the parties. However, the strength of that perceived public interest in the promotion of settlements, captured in Oliver LJ's *dictum* in *Cutts v Head* (*ante*, para **3.52**), is such that the courts are very hesitant to admit otherwise privileged communications under this exception (eg, *Oceanbulk Shipping & Trading SA v TMT Asia Ltd* [2010] 3 WLR 1424 at [30] *per* Lord Clarke of Stowe-cum-Ebony).

Public interest immunity

3.55 On occasion, the law forms the view that the disclosure of certain evidence may operate against the public interest. Such evidence may involve a document or the identity of a witness or person who has assisted the authorities in the detection of crime which one party seeks to conceal from the other side. Plainly, if a party to civil or criminal proceedings is allowed to withhold potentially helpful evidence from its opponent or to deprive the latter of the opportunity of cross-examining someone with material information, injustice could result. While a detailed treatment of this complex topic is beyond the scope of an introductory work, it is an important area of the law where two great public interests can conflict: the public interest affecting, say, the security of the state or the proper functioning of the public service, on the one hand, and a competing public interest in the due administration of justice. In cases where it is sought to avoid disclosing evidence on grounds of public interest immunity, although it is normally the interested party who lays claim to this immunity, the court, too, is under a duty to raise the matter if the parties omit to do so (*Rogers v Secretary of State for the Home Department* [1973] AC 388, 400 *per* Lord Reid). Once it has allowed an application requesting non-disclosure on grounds of public interest immunity, a court must continue to monitor its decision, throughout the course of the hearing, in case the public interest in non-disclosure is subsequently eclipsed by a competing interest that militates in favour of disclosure (*Davis* [1993] 1 WLR 613).

3.56 At one time it was considered sufficient for the Crown simply to claim what was known as 'Crown privilege' for an individual document or even for an entire class of documents. Once such a claim was made in due and proper form, the courts would then refrain from enquiring further into the Crown's claim and would not order disclosure (*Duncan v Cammell Laird & Co Ltd* [1942] AC 624). In *Conway v Rimmer* [1968] AC 910, however, the House of Lords altered tack. It held that where a party claims public immunity privilege, the court is entitled in appropriate cases to view the document. It must then balance the harm which might potentially be done to the public interest by disclosure of the material against the competing public interest which holds that the administration of justice ought not to be frustrated by the party's withholding the production of evidence. In *Conway v Rimmer* itself, a malicious prosecution case, the House, having inspected the documents, which were reports filed by a police officer's superiors at various points during his career, concluded that these reports contained nothing that in any way threatened the public interest and therefore ordered their disclosure to the claimant. As Lord Reid emphasised in the subsequent *Rogers* case (*ante*, para **3.55**):

> The real question is ... whether [the] public interest is so strong as to override the ordinary right and interest of a litigant that he shall be able to lay before a court of justice all relevant evidence.
> (at 400)

There may still be cases where public interest immunity can be claimed for an entire class of documents, although it will impose 'a heavy burden of proof on any authority who makes such a claim' (*Conway v Rimmer* [1968] AC 910; see, eg, *Taylor v Anderton* [1995] 1 WLR 447). Normally, public interest immunity claims are restricted to the particular documents before the court.

3.57 Rather than survey the field in its entirety, before turning to consider the impact of human rights law in this domain, we shall focus upon just one variety of public immunity claim: namely, applications by the prosecution to withhold from the defence the identity of informers and the location of police observation posts in criminal cases. In *Conway v Rimmer*, Lord Reid observed:

> The police are carrying on an unending war with criminals many of whom are today highly intelligent. So it is essential that there should be no disclosure of anything which might give any useful information to those who organise criminal activities.
> (at 953–4)

Lord Reid went on to say that it would generally be wrong to require disclosure in a civil case of anything which might be material in a pending prosecution; but after a verdict has been given or it has been decided to take no proceedings, there is not the same need for secrecy.

3.58 In criminal proceedings, too, it is recognised that police sources may be justifiably excluded from evidence by virtue of public interest immunity. This principle, however, is subject to the proviso that the information is not necessary in order to establish the innocence of the defendant. As Lord Esher MR acknowledged in *Marks v Beyfus* (1890) 25 QBD 494:

> If upon the trial of a prisoner the judge should be of the opinion that the disclosure...is necessary or right in order to shew the prisoner's innocence, then one public policy is in conflict with another public policy, and that which says that an innocent man is not to be condemned when his innocence can be proved is the policy that must prevail.
> (at 498)

3.59 In the criminal context, the police informer furnishes a classical example of public interest immunity at work. Police informers will often have passed information on to the police on the understanding that their identities will be kept secret; they may have legitimate grounds to fear reprisals from those on whom they have informed; additionally, their continuing utility to the police may depend upon their identities remaining concealed. The courts appreciate the need to protect informers' identities both for their own safety and in order to ensure that the flow of information does not dry up. They therefore hold that it is for the defence to demonstrate that disclosure of the informant's identity is necessary to enable the defence properly to present its case (*Hennessey* (1978) 68 Cr App R 419). The judge must weigh the competing interests and determine whether the interest of the informer to remain concealed is exceeded by 'an even stronger public interest in allowing a defendant to put forward a tenable case in its best light' (*Agar* (1990) 90 Cr App R 318, 324 *per* Mustill LJ). The consequence of a judge ruling in favour of the defence and ordering that an informer's identity be revealed will invariably be that the Crown desists from prosecuting, preferring to protect its sources rather than persist with a prosecution. The judge, however, when ruling on a public interest immunity application, is not to take into account such matters as the intransigence of the police or the likelihood that a prosecution will crumple if disclosure is ordered (*Vaillencourt* [1993] Crim LR 311).

3.60 In *Rankine* [1986] QB 861 the Court of Appeal extended the protection afforded to informers to those who allow premises they occupy or own to be used for surveillance purposes. The court was of the view that public interest immunity extended even 'to the identification of the premises themselves'. This is a wide category of claim. As was suggested in *Johnson* [1988] 1 WLR 1377, before granting such an application the Crown may need to establish a particularly strong need for the location of a particular observation post and the identity of its owner or occupier to be withheld. The court in the latter case proposed, in some detail, the evidence which needed to be placed before the court in cases where the Crown sought to exclude evidence that might tend to reveal the location of its observation posts and the identities of their occupiers:

> The minimum evidential requirements seem to us to be the following:
>
> (a) The police officer in charge of the observations to be conducted, one of no lower rank than a sergeant should usually be acceptable for this purpose, must be able to testify that beforehand he visited all observation places to be used and ascertained the attitude of occupiers of premises, not only to the use to be made of them, but to the possible disclosure thereafter of the use made and facts which could lead to the identification of the premises thereafter and of the occupiers. He may of course in addition inform the Court of difficulties, if any, usually encountered in the particular locality of obtaining assistance from the public.
>
> (b) A police officer of no lower rank than a chief inspector must be able to testify that immediately prior to the trial he visited the places used for observations...and ascertained whether the occupiers are the same as when the observations took place and whether they are or are not, what the attitude of those occupiers is to the possible disclosure of the use previously made of the premises and of facts which could lead at the trial to identification of premises and occupiers.
>
> (at 1385–86)

The susceptibilities triggered when a court privileges such evidence is plain from the guidelines.

3.61 To the extent that it allows one party to withhold information from the other, it is obvious that any grant of public interest immunity is liable to have serious human rights implications. Under the principle of 'equality of arms' the ECtHR holds that prosecuting and investigating authorities have an obligation to disclose to the defence information in their possession, or to which they have access, that could assist either in exonerating the defendant or securing a reduction in his sentence (*Jespers v Belgium* (1981) 27 DR 61 at [54]; *Edwards v UK* (1992) 15 EHRR 417 is to similar effect, although the European Court there found that this defect had been cured by the Court of Appeal's subsequent inquiry into the safety of E's conviction). The most significant decision on this question, perhaps, is *Rowe and Davis v UK* (2000) 30 EHRR 1, where the ECtHR first declared, as an article of faith:

> It is a fundamental aspect of the right to a fair trial that criminal proceedings...should be adversarial and that there should be equality of arms between the prosecution and defence. The right to an adversarial trial means, in a criminal case, that both prosecution and defence must be given the opportunity to have knowledge of and comment on the observations filed and the evidence adduced by the other party.
>
> (at [60])

This right, however, is not absolute. The court went on to recognise that other countervailing interests, such as 'national security or the need to protect witnesses at risk of reprisals or keep secret police methods of investigation of crime', have to be weighed against the interests of the accused. Therefore, 'in some cases it may be necessary to withhold certain evidence from the defence so as to preserve the fundamental rights of another individual or to safeguard an important public interest' (at [61]). Courts must therefore be concerned 'to ascertain whether the decision-making procedure applied in each case complied, as far as possible, with the requirements of adversarial proceedings and equality of arms and incorporated adequate safeguards to protect the interests of the accused' (at [62]).

3.62 From the perspective of domestic law, what measures will prove adequate to meet the demands of human rights law will vary from one situation to another. Although not a case of public interest immunity *stricto sensu*, the Youth Justice and Criminal Evidence Act 1999, for example, seeks to assure the fairness of the procedure which prohibits a defendant from cross-examining in person the complainant in a sexual offence (s 34) by providing for the appointment of special counsel. In the specific context of public interest immunity, it would seem that the involvement of the judge will often save the situation. Thus, in one case it was questioned whether the police actually had grounds for reasonable suspicion before taking a sample of the defendant's hair without his consent, and, in consequence, whether the DNA evidence deriving from this procedure ought not to have been excluded under PACE, s 78. The Court of Appeal held that in determining this question it was open to the Court to take into account sensitive evidence that had been excluded under public interest immunity. This was held to be so even though the evidence has been excluded following an *ex parte* application at which the defence had been kept in ignorance not only of the precise nature of the sensitive material but also of the category of material involved (*Smith (Joe)* [2001] 1 WLR 1031). It is obviously more doubtful that such a ruling would be compliant with human rights requirements in those highly exceptional cases, referred to by Lord Taylor CJ, where the prosecution does not even let the defence know that an application has been made, for fear that this would 'let the cat out of the bag', thereby stultifying the application (*Davis* [1993] 1 WLR 613).

FURTHER READING

Munday, 'Sham Marriages and Spousal Compellability' [2001] J Crim Law 338

Murphy, 'The Innocence at Stake Test and Legal Professional Privilege: A Logical Progression for the Law . . . but not for England' [2001] Crim LR 728

Scott, Sir Richard, 'The Acceptable and Unacceptable Use of Public Interest Immunity' [1996] PL 427

Spencer and Flin, *The Evidence of Children: The Law and the Psychology* (2nd edn, 1993, London), especially chs 9–14

Tapper, 'Privilege and Confidence' (1972) 35 MLR 83

Tomkins, 'Public Interest Immunity: Freedom of Information and Judicial Discretion', in Leyland and Woods (eds), *Administrative Law Facing the Future: Old Constraints and New Horizons* (1997, London), 321

Zuckerman, 'Legal Professional Privilege—The Core of Absolutism' (1996) 112 LQR 535

SELF-TEST QUESTIONS

1. Apart from a very few limited exceptions, English law proceeds upon the assumption that all witnesses are competent and compellable. In what ways do the rules governing competence and compellability differ in the cases of:

    (a) the accused in a criminal case;

    (b) the spouse of an accused; or

    (c) children?

2. Mr Stalker is appealing against a conviction for putting a 15-year-old neighbour in fear of violence contrary to the Protection from Harassment Act 1997, s 4. Mrs Stalker, his wife, was called by the Crown to testify against Mr Stalker. During her testimony,

the justices informed her for the first time that she was not obliged to give evidence against her husband, that it was most unfortunate that no one had troubled to tell her this before, but that since she had started, she now had to finish.

(a) Were the justices correct that Mrs Stalker was not a compellable witness?

(b) If they were correct and if the prosecution also acknowledges that it knew that, given the chance, Mrs Stalker would prove a most reluctant witness, does Mr Stalker have a valid ground of appeal?

(c) Would any of your answers be different if Mr Stalker had instead been prosecuted for publicly displaying indecent photographs of young children in his art gallery contrary to the Indecent Displays (Control) Act 1981?

(d) Would any of your answers to the above questions be different if, by the time of trial, Mr and Mrs Stalker were:

(i) living apart; or

(ii) living apart, but Mrs Stalker has also since gone through a bigamous form of marriage with Mr Right; or

(iii) divorced?

(e) Would any of your answers differ if 'Mr' and 'Mrs' Stalker were in fact a same-sex couple who had contracted a civil partnership under the Civil Partnership Act 2004?

3. During a break in proceedings in Barsetshire magistrates' court, Leak, who is seated in a cubicle in the public lavatories, overhears a hushed conversation between the defendant, Gormless, and his solicitor, Seed, during which Gormless makes a number of significant admissions. Leak reports what he has heard to the Crown prosecutor, Vindict. Advise Vindict, who now wishes to call Leak to testify to what he overheard.

4. What is the significance of the House of Lords decision in *Three Rivers DC v Governor and Company of the Bank of England (No 6)* [2004] 3 WLR 1274?

5. What protection does the law afford to informers and to those who assist the police in criminal cases?

6. What do you understand by the following terms:

(a) 'litigation privilege';

(b) 'common interest privilege'?

4

The course of the trial

SUMMARY

The right to begin

The role of the judge

The judge's right to call a witness

Examination-in-chief

Hostile witnesses

- Reluctance to testify

- Hostile witnesses and unfavourable witnesses

Cross-examination

- Introducing evidence of non-defendants' bad character: Criminal Justice Act 2003, s 100

- The defendant who alleges that a third party was the true culprit

- Issue and credit, and the principle of collateral-finality

Re-examination

Calling evidence relating to witnesses' veracity

The Crown's right to reopen its case

Special protections extended to various classes of witness in criminal cases

- Restrictions on the cross-examination of sexual complainants on their previous sexual histories

- Protection of sexual complainants, child witnesses and others from cross-examination by the defendant in person

- The provision made for protecting the welfare of children and young persons tried in the Crown Court

- 'Special measures directions' available to assist vulnerable and intimidated witnesses
- Criminal trials of children

His Lordship: As head of this court a terrible responsibility rests upon me. Indeed, 'devolves upon me' would be a better term. I cannot run the risk of hearing irrelevant evidence. I must therefore interview the lady in the privacy of my chamber. She will now be conducted there, and the court must be adjourned until to-morrow.

Mr Juteclaw: I protest, my Lord. This is most irregular.

His Lordship: Protest away.

Flann O'Brien, *The Best of Myles* (1968) 144

4.1 This and the next chapter will examine the principal rules affecting the way in which witnesses give evidence at trial. The present chapter will concentrate on describing features of the examination, cross-examination and re-examination of witnesses, as well as considering the protection the law now affords to various classes of intimidated or vulnerable witness. This brief account can only present a general outline. Many of the rules apply to civil and criminal proceedings alike. However, as elsewhere in this book, the accent in this chapter will be on rules of criminal evidence.

The right to begin

4.2 Although the Civil Procedure Rules have altered matters to the extent that the judge in a civil case now has far-reaching powers to regulate how the evidence is given (CPR, r 32.1(1): 'The court may control the evidence by giving directions as to...the way in which the evidence is to be placed before the court'), traditionally, unless the defendant bears the burden of proving all the issues in the case, it is for the claimant to open the case and to present his evidence first (*Mercer v Whall* (1845) 5 QB 447). In criminal cases, too, the normal order of events, whenever the defendant pleads not guilty, is for the prosecution to open the case, since the Crown will carry the burden of proving all, or almost all of the issues in the case. (On the burden of proof, see *ante*, Chapter 2.) As between co-accused in a criminal trial, the order in which they cross-examine the other parties' witnesses and present their evidence in the case is essentially dictated by the order in which they appear in the indictment, the indictment being drafted by the prosecution. In trials at the Crown Court, typically the prosecution makes a brief opening speech outlining what it intends to prove and then calls its witnesses. If the defence chooses to call no evidence, the prosecution delivers a closing speech, which is then followed by the defence closing speech. If the defence does call witnesses, the Crown's closing speech follows the defence evidence and is in turn followed by the closing speech for the defence. In all cases, the defence has the final word (see notably, the Criminal Procedure (Right of Reply) Act 1964).

The role of the judge

4.3 The ideal of the common law judge in both civil and criminal cases is of someone who remains above the battle throughout proceedings. Denning LJ described the situation in memorable terms in *Jones v National Coal Board* [1957] 2 QB 55, 62 ff. In *Jones* a judge trying a civil case was alleged to have participated too freely in the questioning of witnesses and thereby to have prevented the appellant from properly presenting his case. In upholding this complaint, Denning LJ outlined the proper role of the judge:

> In the system of trial which we have evolved in this country, the judge sits to hear and determine the issues raised by the parties, not to conduct an investigation or examination on behalf of society at large . . . Even in England, however, a judge is not a mere umpire to answer the question "How's that?" Was it not Lord Eldon LC (in *ex p Lloyd* (1822) Mont 70, 72n) who said in a notable passage that "truth is best discovered by powerful statements on both sides of the question"? . . . If a judge, said Lord Greene, MR (in *Yuill v Yuill* [1945] P 15), should himself conduct the examination of witnesses, "he, so to speak, descends into the arena and is liable to have his vision clouded by the dust of conflict." . . . The judge's part in all this is to hearken to the evidence, only himself asking questions of witnesses when it is necessary to clear up any point that has been overlooked or left obscure; to see that the advocates behave themselves seemly and keep to the rules laid down by law; to exclude irrelevancies and discourage repetition; to make sure by wise intervention that he follows the points that the advocates are making and can assess their worth; and at the end to make up his mind where the truth lies. If he goes beyond this, he drops the mantle of a judge and assumes the robe of an advocate; and the change does not become him well.

Broadly similar principles apply in criminal cases. Indeed, one upshot of decisions like *Jones v NCB* was that for a while appeals were regularly lodged in criminal cases by counsel who had simply totted up the number of questions asked by an interventionist judge. It is of course true, as Cumming-Bruce LJ acknowledged in *Gunning* [1980] Crim LR 592, that:

> The judge is not an advocate. Under the English . . . system of criminal trials he is much more like the umpire at a cricket match. He is certainly not the bowler, whose business is to get the batsman out.

From time to time, trial judges have been criticised for intervening excessively during the examination of witnesses (eg *Webb and Simpson* (2000) 23 October, case no 99/03785/S3, where the judge asked 175 questions at the close of W's evidence, sometimes assuming the role of prosecutor and refusing to allow W's counsel to correct his various factual errors; *Khalid Rabani* [2008] EWCA Crim 2030). The Court of Appeal, however, has disapproved of an exclusively numerical approach to this question for, as Henry LJ explained in *Frixou* [1998] Crim LR 352, 'ultimately it is the *quality* of the interruptions which counts', not simply their frequency. Indeed, the necessity for judges to try defendants fairly and not take over counsel's questioning has gained added force since *Kartal* (1999) 15 July, case no 98/04147/X5, a case in which the Court of Appeal stressed that this 'key principle' of fair trial is now enshrined in the European Convention on Human Rights, Art 6. (See also *CG v UK* (2001), application no 43374/98 at [22], [2002] Crim LR 313, where the ECtHR in turn quotes this portion of Clarke LJ's judgment in *Kartal*.)

The judge's right to call a witness

4.4 One consequence of English law's stance is that it is primarily left to the parties to decide which witnesses to call, and in which order. In civil cases the judge may only call a witness if both parties consent to his so doing. In criminal cases, however, the situation is in one respect more restrictive, in another a little more flexible. The restriction is that the defendant is not at liberty to give his evidence at whatever point in proceedings he chooses. If the defendant testifies, PACE, s 79 requires that normally he give his evidence before the other witnesses for the defence are called. The relaxation in criminal cases is that a judge may sometimes be under a duty to call a witness whom neither the prosecution nor the defence has elected to call. The judge must consider the overall interests of justice, being alert not to give the appearance of stepping in to assist the prosecution. As Taylor LJ pointed out in *Grafton* [1992] 4 All ER 609, 613, a case in which the court found that 'the judge was not only supplementing the prosecution; he was in effect taking it over', the judge's power to call a witness should be used most sparingly and rarely exercised. In short, the judge must avoid at all costs the appearance of descending into the arena. But sometimes this power has to be exercised in order to achieve the ends of justice and fairness. In *Haringey Justices, ex p DPP* [1996] QB 351, for example, two co-defendants were charged with threatening and assaulting two police officers. Owing to the fact that one of the officers had been suspended from duty on an unconnected charge by the time of trial, the Crown decided not to call him. Since that officer would have been a key witness—indeed, one of the two complainants in the case—Stuart-Smith LJ held that the justices ought to have called him themselves, given that the Crown had omitted to do so.

4.5 Because it is the parties who invariably determine whom to call as witnesses in the case, in criminal trials the jury ought not to speculate on why a particular witness has not been called. In *C(T)* (2000) 14 January, case no 98/01431/Y3, for example, the defendant was charged with raping his daughter. It was obvious to everyone in court that C's wife had been present in the public gallery throughout the trial, but that the defence had not called her to testify. (As it happened, the defence knew that the wife would have said that she did not allow C to bath their daughter because of her concerns about him.) After retirement, the jury returned into court specifically to ask if there was any legal reason why the wife had not been called. The Court of Appeal quashed C's conviction, primarily because the judge had not instructed the jury not to speculate upon the reasons for the wife's absence from the witness box, a circumstance from which they evidently were prepared to draw an adverse inference.

Examination-in-chief

4.6 When a witness enters the witness box, typically he is first questioned by his own side, then may be questioned by the opposing side and, finally, may be questioned again by the side that called him. These three phases are known respectively as examination-in-chief, cross-examination and re-examination. Examination-in-chief, therefore, is the term given to the initial questioning of one's own witness. As might be anticipated, the purpose of examination-in-chief is to obtain from the witness evidence favourable to the side calling him or her. This can prove a delicate operation. Apart from the need to avoid inducing the witness to give inadmissible evidence in breach of one of the exclusionary rules of evidence (which are detailed in other chapters of this book), as a general rule one may not ask witnesses 'leading questions' during examination-in-chief.

4.7 Leading questions are of two types. Most commonly, a leading question is one that suggests to the witness the desired answer. Thus, in an assault case arising out of a bar room brawl it would be improper to ask the barmaid who had witnessed the attack: 'Did you see the accused deliberately smash a bottle over the victim's head?' Examination-in-chief is supposed to proceed in a more neutral mode. The purpose is to allow the witness to tell her own story and not for counsel to put words into her mouth. Alternatively, a leading question may be one that simply assumes disputed facts. Although there have been occasional suggestions that answers given to leading questions are inadmissible as evidence (see, eg, *Wilson* (1913) 9 Cr App R 124), this is not so. Answers elicited by leading questions simply carry less weight. The prohibition on leading questions, it should be noted, is not absolute. The exceptions cannot be stated exhaustively, but broadly speaking leading questions are acceptable when they relate to introductory matters such as the witness's name and occupation, when they concern matters that are not contested, or when they are simply designed to direct a witness's attention to the precise issue on which he or she is to give evidence. As we shall see, leading questions are also allowed in the event that one's witness is declared hostile (on 'hostile witnesses', see *post*, paras **4.10–4.15**). Leading questions, however, are not permitted as prompts for witnesses whose memories prove defective in court. Again, as we shall see in the next chapter when we consider previous consistent statements and the rule against narrative, there are specialised rules governing the manner in which, and the extent to which, witnesses may refresh their memories (see *post*, paras **5.29 ff**).

Hostile witnesses

Reluctance to testify

4.8 The reluctance of witnesses to come forward to assist the police or to testify in court is a persistent problem. Yet even when witnesses have come forward, they may subsequently resile from their statements, modify their testimony, refuse to testify or simply develop chronic amnesia in the witness box. This may be attributable to many causes. Despite the fact that the Bar's Code of Conduct enjoins counsel not to put questions that are simply intended to insult or annoy, witnesses in general may be rightly apprehensive of the treatment they will receive in court. Rape complainants, it is widely accepted, in the past received a raw deal in the courts, not infrequently having to submit to embarrassing cross-examination on their sexual relationships with other partners despite the supposedly tight restrictions on such questioning imposed by the (since repealed) Sexual Offences (Amendment) Act 1976, and more recently by the provisions of the Youth Justice and Criminal Evidence Act 1999 (see *post*, paras **4.66 ff**). However, perhaps the most worrying feature of reluctance amongst witnesses to give evidence today is the extent of intimidation, particularly in cases involving serious crime. The 1998 British Crime Survey uncovered the disturbing fact that 8 per cent of all incidents led to witness intimidation, and that this figure rose to 15 per cent if one focused on cases where there was obvious potential for intimidation—as, for example, where the victim knew the offender (Home Office Research, Development and Statistics Directorate, Research Findings, no 124). The Home Office acknowledges 'there has been relatively little research into the extent and nature of victim and witness intimidation', but it is known that in 2005 there were 783 convictions for various forms of 'witness nobbling', as compared with 366 in 1996 (*The Times*, 5 April 2008, p 4). This could indicate either that 'nobbling' is on the increase or, more improbably, that the authorities are suppressing it more effectively. In a bid to deter such conduct, the Criminal Justice and Police Act 2001 created two criminal offences, one of intimidation of witnesses with intent to obstruct, pervert or interfere with the course of justice (s 39) and the other of harming persons who have appeared as witnesses (s 40), each punishable on indictment by a sentence of up to five years' imprisonment.

4.9 The courts can employ various devices to overcome the problem of witness intimidation and reluctance to face the ordeal of testifying. Screens may be erected in the courtroom shielding a witness from the view of the accused, and even of the public gallery. The court may be cleared during a witness's testimony—apparently, even if a witness merely feels uncomfortable giving evidence in public (*Richards* (1999) 163 JP 246). Alternatively, the court may grant witnesses varying degrees of anonymity, by allowing them to use pseudonyms or by disguising their voices or concealing their features. Such devices used to be simply matters within the court's discretion. However, following the House of Lords' decision in *Davis* [2008] 3 WLR 125, Parliament intervened, now regulating matters by means of Part 3 of the Coroners and Justice Act 2009 (see post, paras **9.104–9.114**). If it can be shown that a witness has made a statement but does not testify through fear, that witness's written statement may be admitted in evidence as an exception to the hearsay rule under the Criminal Justice Act 2003 (see *post*, paras **9.24–9.29**). But whereas this cluster of rules is designed to alleviate problems experienced by witnesses, coercion is also possible. A recalcitrant witness may be prosecuted for contempt of court. In the courtroom, however, it is not uncommon for counsel to apply to have a reluctant or recalcitrant witness declared hostile.

Hostile witnesses and unfavourable witnesses

4.10 Witnesses who fail to give evidence as expected fall into two categories: hostile witnesses and unfavourable witnesses. An unfavourable witness is one who is endeavouring to be truthful but simply fails to testify in the way his counsel anticipated. There is little counsel can do if a witness proves unfavourable. Whatever facts the witness was called to establish can be proven if counsel can call another witness or other evidence, if available. However, the court may declare hostile any witness who is obstructive, who stands mute or who obviously will not tell the truth. Hostility is often evidenced by the attitude of the witness, or by an inconsistency between a witness's statement to the police and his evidence in court (eg *Prefas and Pryce* (1987) 86 Cr App R 111). In order to justify the judge in ruling a particular witness hostile, an inconsistency does not have to be overt. It has been stated that, in appropriate cases, even 'an omission is capable of constituting an inconsistency' (*Jobe* [2004] EWCA Crim 3155 at [23] *per* Potter LJ). Thus, in the latter case, J, who was charged with two counts of rape, had called a witness, S, who claimed that one of the complainants had flirted with J and made certain sexually provocative remarks. Remarkably, S had made no reference to these remarks in either of his police interviews. The evidence was of critical importance and ran contrary to the tenor of S's earlier statements. This justified the court in treating S as a hostile witness.

4.11 Customarily, counsel will apply to the judge to have a particular witness declared hostile—very occasionally, this application may even be made during a witness's re-examination (*Greene* [2009] EWCA Crim 2282 at [67] *per* Scott Baker LJ). Alternatively, a judge may intervene of his own motion (eg Lord Goddard CJ in *The Trial of Ley and Smith* (1947) *Notable British Trials*, at 119). Two consequences customarily flow from a witness being declared hostile. The witness may be asked leading questions—something counsel is not generally entitled to do with his own witness. More importantly, the hostile witness may be questioned about any previous inconsistent statements he or she may have made. (Naturally, counsel may also call further witnesses or other evidence to contradict the hostile witness' testimony.)

4.12 Section 3 of the Criminal Procedure Act 1865 lays down the procedure for questioning the hostile witness about previous inconsistent statements:

> A party producing a witness shall not be allowed to impeach his credit by general evidence of bad character, but he may in case the witness shall in the opinion of the judge prove adverse contradict him by other evidence or by leave of the judge prove that he has made at other times a statement inconsistent with his present testimony, but before such last mentioned proof can be given the circumstances of the supposed statement sufficient to designate the particular occasion must be mentioned to the witness and he must be asked whether or not he has made such a statement.

Although the 1865 Act refers to witnesses who 'prove adverse', it is settled law that in s 3 'adverse' means hostile (*Greenough v Eccles* (1859) 5 CBNS 786).

4.13 It may happen that production of his previous statement brings a witness to heel, reviving his recollection of the earlier version of events reflected in the statement. If a witness adopts his previous statement, this will constitute evidence of the facts. Thus, in *Allen, Sampson and Howlett* (2000) 10 November, case no 90/6882/W2, when questioned about her previous statement, a witness continued to maintain that she could remember nothing but accepted that anything she had said in her statement had to be true. The court held that, although her credibility was still adversely affected by her change of story, it was open to the jury to place reliance upon her readopted version of events. Indeed, when a witness, who has been declared hostile, does revert to the story that it was originally anticipated he would recount, 'although no magic formula need be followed', it has been suggested that jurors should be warned 'that there was a special need for caution when considering evidence which had been elicited in that way' (*Ugorji* (1999) 11 June, case no 98/6131/W3 *per* Tuckey LJ. Cp *Middleton* [2005] EWCA Crim 692 at [24], where Keene, LJ said that what is required will vary greatly from case to case). More commonly, however, the witness will continue to dissociate himself from his earlier statement, in which case the court is presented with a dilemma: the witness maintains one thing, but the jury will have heard another version of events, now rejected by the witness. Section 119 of the Criminal Justice Act 2003 provides that where a previous statement has been proved by virtue of s 3 of the Criminal Procedure Act 1865, 'the statement is admissible as evidence of any matter stated in it of which oral evidence by that person would be admissible'. Section 119 will come into play whenever a witness maintains that the contents of a prior statement are not true (*Gibbons* (2009) 173 JP 260). It will then be for the tribunal of fact to choose which, if any, of the various versions of events they believe.

4.14 A delicate question used to arise whenever counsel was aware that if he called a particular witness, there was a strong likelihood that that witness would prove hostile. Was it even proper for counsel to call a witness, knowing that the witness's previous statement was likely to become admissible? This question—which had a particular urgency before the Criminal Justice Act 2003, s 119 made the previous statement evidence of the facts, and not merely evidence going to the witness's credit—arose in *Honeyghon and Sayles* [1999] Crim LR 221. Prosecution witnesses in a murder case were called to give evidence, even though it was not at all unlikely that they would prove hostile once in the witness box. Deriving comfort from the possibility that a reluctant witness, or indeed one who stands deliberately mute, may change his attitude if faced with an earlier statement, the Court of Appeal held that the prosecution was perfectly entitled to call these witnesses. It was for the judge to weigh the likelihood of the witnesses changing their stance against the risk of prejudice of a statement being put to them which the jury ought not to treat as evidence of the facts. The judge in such circumstances, it was said, might even hold a *voire dire* (a trial within a trial conducted in the absence of the jury: see further *ante*, para **1.3**) to resolve the question in those rare cases where such a procedure was deemed appropriate (*Khan* [2002] EWCA Crim 945 at [34] *per* Kay LJ; [2003] Crim LR 428). The important consideration was that 'evidence should not be led or statements made whose value in proof of the issues the jury have to decide is substantially outweighed by the prejudice they are likely to cause'. Given that the central concern, prior to the entry into force of the 2003 Act, was that the jury might wrongly use the contents of the hostile witness's previous statement as evidence of the facts, now that the previous statements of hostile witnesses may be so used, prosecutors will be less inhibited in calling as witnesses individuals whom they strongly suspect are likely to prove uncooperative.

4.15 The 1865 Act refers to cross-examining the hostile witness on 'a statement inconsistent with his present testimony'. This might suggest that one cannot use previous statements if the witness gives no evidence but merely stands mute in the witness box. In *Thompson* (1976) 64 Cr App R 96, however, it was held that a witness who stood 'mute of malice' could be declared hostile at common law. The Court of Appeal upheld the judge's decision to allow cross-examination on her earlier statement because the judge enjoys a discretion in settling the modalities for questioning a witness declared hostile at common law. Under the old law this created a serious complication, and in *Honeyghon and Sayles* (*ante*, para **4.14**) Beldam LJ conceded that the witness who refuses to speak at all presents a tricky problem. Obviously, there was a considerable risk that unless the witness changed her mind and adopted the contents of her statement, the jury might well act upon a statement which they would have been told was solely relevant to the credibility of a witness whose credibility was not even in issue, given that she had not given any testimony. As mentioned already, the Criminal Justice Act 2003, s 119 dissolves this problem away to the extent that, where a court resolves to admit the previous statement of a witness who stands mute of malice, that statement is admissible 'as evidence of any matter stated of which oral evidence by him would be admissible'. It may not always operate very fairly, however. Let us imagine that, very much as in *Thompson*, a daughter, who claims to have been sexually abused by her father, refuses to say a single word in court. Her statement is proved under s 3. Cross-examination fails, too, because she continues to refuse to say anything. There is no other evidence in the case. Would one be content were the accused convicted solely on the witness statement of the daughter? (For further discussion of this class of situation from the point of view of European human rights law, see *post*, paras **9.95** ff).

Cross-examination

4.16 The purpose of cross-examination is twofold: first, it permits the opposing party to put questions that are designed to extract evidence helpful to its cause from the other side's witnesses; second, it allows the opposing party to ask questions designed to undermine the credit of the other side's witnesses. This second object may be achieved either by showing that the witnesses have made other statements inconsistent with their present testimony or by showing that they are of bad character and therefore unworthy of belief. The Criminal Justice Act 2003, s 100 tightly regulates the cross-examination of witnesses on their bad character, in criminal cases; in civil cases, in contrast, this form of cross-examination will be subject to the court's general duty to manage the case (CPR, r 1).

4.17 The form of questioning alters when cross-examination takes place. In particular, the cross-examiner may adopt a more aggressive form of questioning and ask leading questions. Although in most cases cross-examination is rather more prosaic, there is still some truth in Hoffmann LJ's statement in *Libby-Mills v Metropolitan Police Commissioner* [1995] PIQR 324 that:

> Attacking the credit of a witness by dramatic confrontation in the witness box is so much part of the English forensic tradition, so hallowed in history and fiction, that lawyers are naturally reluctant to be deprived of the chance to ambush the opposing party with some devastating piece of cross-examination.
>
> (at 328)

More realistic, possibly, is the Judicial Committee's observation in *A-G of Hong Kong v Wong Muk Ping* [1987] AC 501:

> There may, of course, be extreme cases where a witness under cross-examination is driven to admit that his evidence-in-chief was false. Such triumphs for the cross-examiner are more frequently seen in fictional courtroom dramas than in real life.

4.18 As we shall see, if a witness in cross-examination denies making a previous inconsistent statement, it may be permissible for the cross-examiner to prove that the statement was in fact made (*post*, para **4.44**). Moreover, once the tribunal learns of the existence of the previous inconsistent statement, s 119 of the Criminal Justice Act 2003 now provides that:

> ... the statement is admissible as evidence of any matter stated of which oral evidence by him would be admissible.

This contrasts sharply with the position pre-2003 when it used to be held that previous inconsistent statements were only admissible to assist the tribunal to determine whether the witness was likely to be giving truthful evidence. This obscure distinction, between evidence going to issue and evidence going solely to credit, has now ceased to have effect in this context. When a previous inconsistent statement is proved, it will be open to the tribunal of fact to determine which, if any, of the alternative versions of events presented via the witness's testimony and his or her previous statements they wish to believe.

4.19 Following the enactment of s 119, it will often be the case that documents will be placed before the court, once it has been shown that a witness has made a previous inconsistent statement. Section 122 of the 2003 Act stipulates that whenever such a document is adduced as an exhibit in the case, normally it ought not to accompany the jury when they retire to consider their verdict. The exhibit may only accompany the jurors to the jury room in two circumstances. *First*, it may do so if 'the court considers it appropriate' (s 122(2)(a)). The Act gives no further guidance on when a court might judge it 'appropriate' to make such an order. Trial judges will clearly enjoy considerable latitude. *Secondly*, if all parties to the proceedings are agreed that this should happen, the exhibit may accompany the jury in their deliberations.

4.20 Although cross-examination will tend to be more robust and testing for witnesses than examination-in-chief by their own counsel, the Bar Council has promulgated rules in its Code of Conduct designed to prevent against the very worst excesses— questions intended only to insult and annoy, unsupported attacks on the credibility of an opponent's witnesses, and so on. More generally, however, in criminal cases the judge has discretion to curtail prolonged or vexatious cross-examination. This does not mean that cross-examination, even of an accused, may not be rigorous. Thus, in *Jisl, Tekin and Konakli* [2004] EWCA Crim 696, a drugs case involving the illegal importation of diamorphine with a street value in excess of £7m, even though it had lasted *in toto* some forty hours, the Court of Appeal held that T's cross-examination had been fair, particularly in view of the fact that his examination-in-chief had been extremely long and his own conduct and forceful personality had contributed to prolonging the cross-examination. It is, then, all a question of context.

4.21 In civil cases, too, it might be noted that the Civil Procedure Rules (CPR, r 32.1(3)) provide that 'the court may limit cross-examination'. The Court of Appeal acknowledged in *Watson v Chief Constable of Cleveland Police* [2001] EWCA Civ 1547 that the CPR do not indicate how this discretion is to be exercised. The police authority was appealing against a civil jury verdict under which W had been granted substantial damages for an assault committed on him while in police custody. The judge had permitted W to be cross-examined about his 31 previous convictions for offences of dishonesty, but had disallowed questioning on W's 27 further convictions for other offences, including affray and obstructing the police. The ruling was upheld, primarily because counsel had sought to introduce these latter offences in order to show W's propensity to commit acts of violence rather than upon the basis of their relevance to W's credibility. The decision in *Watson* can be defended on the ground that only previous convictions relevant to the witness's credibility ought to be admissible in cross-examination. Nevertheless, it is worth bearing in mind Patten J's judgment in *Re Stardella* (2000) 11 October, unreported, with its reminder that, even when justified by the circumstances of the case, judicial interventions in this context can all too easily appear to 'verge on the heavy-handed'.

Introducing evidence of non-defendants' bad character: Criminal Justice Act 2003, s 100

4.22 One way of undermining the opposing side's witnesses is to cross-examine them in order to show that they are of bad character or to introduce evidence of their previous convictions. Since the entry into force of the Criminal Justice Act 2003, it is necessary to draw a distinction between civil and criminal trials. In civil trials, it remains the case that, subject to any order made by the judge under CPR, r 32.1(3), opposing witnesses may be cross-examined as of right on all of their criminal convictions (*Clifford v Clifford* [1961] 1 WLR 1274, 1276 *per* Cairns J), save those that are spent under the Rehabilitation of Offenders Act 1974. (Under the 1974 Act, a witness in a civil case may only be cross-questioned about spent convictions with the leave of the court.) The criminal records (and general bad character) of witnesses in criminal cases, however, are only admissible in restricted circumstances. If a witness denies or refuses to acknowledge a particular conviction, the Criminal Procedure Act 1865, s 6 allows the opposing party 'to prove such conviction'. In criminal trials, however, the Court of Appeal's decision in *Taylor and Goodman* [1999] 2 Cr App R 163 in some cases will have spared the defendant the need to introduce a witness's previous convictions. For, in that case, Judge LJ declared that it ought to be the universal practice of prosecuting counsel to offer to disclose to the jury the convictions of any accomplices who testify for the Crown.

4.23 *The purpose of s 100.* Just as the Criminal Justice Act 2003 has considerably modified the rules governing the admissibility of evidence of a defendant's bad character (*post*, Chapter 7), so too s 100 of the 2003 Act severely restricts the extent to which evidence of a *non*-defendant's bad character may be introduced in criminal cases. 'Non-defendants' will often be the opposing side's witnesses. But not necessarily so. Section 100 prevents the introduction of the bad character of anyone other than the defendant—in short, any person whatsoever. As Pitchford LJ explained in *Miller* [2010] 2 Cr App R 19,

> One of [s 100's] intended effects is to eliminate kite-flying and innuendo against the character of a [non-defendant] in favour of a concentration upon the real issues in the case.
>
> (at [20])

By way of illustration, in *R v S (David)* [2006] EWCA Crim 2325 S appealed against his convictions for indecency with a child and for three rapes. One ground of appeal was that the trial judge had refused S leave to cross-examine the victim on her previous convictions for some elderly offences of dishonesty. The Court of Appeal held that not only did it not follow that a previous conviction for dishonesty was synonymous with untruthfulness, but s 100 requires that, to be admissible, evidence of bad character must have 'substantial probative value', which was simply not present in this case. If evidence does not attain the threshold set by s 100, cross-examination on, or the introduction of, evidence of bad character will simply be impermissible.

4.24 *Evidence of 'bad character'.* The restrictions imposed by s 100 only apply to evidence of 'bad character' *stricto sensu*, which, if one conflates ss 98 and 112 of the Act, is defined as 'evidence of, or of a disposition towards...the commission of an offence or other reprehensible behaviour' (see further *post*, paras **7.28–7.30** and [2005] Crim LR 24). 'Reprehensible behaviour' is not further defined in the statute. Nevertheless, if what is being alleged does not amount to 'bad character' within the meaning of the Act, provided that the evidence is relevant, and not otherwise inadmissible), it may be introduced.

4.25 *Admissible evidence of a non-defendant's bad character.* Section 100(1) provides that evidence of a witness's bad character—or for that matter, evidence of any other person's bad character—is only admissible in three situations:

> (1) In criminal proceedings evidence of the bad character of a person other than the defendant is admissible if and only if—
>   (a) it is important explanatory evidence,
>   (b) it has substantial probative value in relation to a matter which—
>   (i) is a matter in issue in the proceedings, and
>   (ii) is of substantial importance in the context of the case as a whole, or
>   (c) all parties to the proceedings agree to the evidence being admissible.

4.26 *Leave of the court.* Unless all the parties have consented, the Act stipulates that leave of the court must be sought before any such evidence may be admitted (s 100(4)).

4.27 *Exercise of judgement.* The three conditions set out in s 100(1) mirror provisions that we will encounter when considering the admissibility of a defendant's bad character (*post*, Chapter 7). Clearly, the principal question is, how far do they restrict a defendant's ability to introduce third parties' bad character? In the final analysis, s 100 remains a matter for judicial interpretation. Thus, in *Carr* [2008] EWCA Crim 1283 at [25] Dyson LJ spoke of 'the relatively generous band given to a judge exercising a discretion whether or not to allow cross-examination in relation to bad character' under s 100. Nevertheless, it is plain that the conditions of admissibility prescribed by the statute were designed to supplant the freewheeling approach to cross-examination to credit that had previously been the norm in criminal cases. Indeed, in a recent case the Court of Appeal has insisted: 'section 100(1) requires…not discretion but judgement on the part of the judge' (*Braithwaite* [2010] 2 Cr App R 18 at [12] *per* Hughes LJ).

4.28 Section 100 is not expressed in a wholly felicitous manner. It refers to the admission of evidence of bad character generally, without referring specifically to cross-examination. The Court of Appeal, however, has acknowledged that '[a]lthough cross-examination is not mentioned in terms, it cannot be doubted that leave must be sought to cross-examine about matters of bad character' (*V* [2006] EWCA Crim 1901 at [23] *per* Crane J).

4.29 Often, but not always, evidence of a non-defendant's bad character will be directed either towards the propensity of that person to behave in a particular way or towards that person's credibility (*Braithwaite*, at [12]). Both evidence relating to credibility and evidence of propensity may have 'substantial probative value' in relation to 'a matter in issue in the proceedings' (s 100(1)(b)(i)). Thus, cross-examination designed to undermine a witness's credibility may be permissible under s 100, provided always that one of the three specified conditions of admissibility listed in s 100(1) has been met. As Kennedy LJ noted in *Weir et al* [2006] 1 Cr App R 19:

> In our view, s 100(1) does cover matters of credibility. To find otherwise would mean that there was a significant *lacuna* in the legislation with the potential for unfairness.
> (at [73])

4.30 A non-defendant's criminal propensity, too, may become admissible under s 100. In *H* (2010) 174 JP 203, where H accused HH of having committed a robbery of an off-licence with which H stood charged, the Court of Appeal held that evidence that HH had racked up a conviction for theft at the very same premises a few weeks previously ought to have been admitted. Again, in *S (Andrew)* [2006] 2 Cr App R 31 the Court of Appeal concluded that evidence of a complainant's bad character met the requirements of s 100(1)(b)(i) because it showed her propensity to act in a particular way. S, who was charged with indecently assaulting a prostitute, claimed that after performing an agreed sex act for £10 the woman had demanded more money of him, had threatened to accuse him of rape, and had tried to snatch a gold chain from around his neck. Whilst agreeing with the trial judge that the complainant's relatively elderly previous convictions for going equipped for theft, handling and burglary—to all of which charges she had pleaded guilty—were not admissible as going towards her credibility as a witness under s 100(1)(b)(i), the Court of Appeal held that these convictions did betray a propensity on the complainant's part to behave in the way in which S claimed that she had and that this was a matter of 'substantial probative value' within the terms of s 100. As Laws LJ remarked:

> Section 100 contains no analogue to s 103(1)(a), but...it can hardly be doubted...that a complainant's propensity to act in the way the defendant asserts he or she acted must likewise be part of 'the matters in issue'.
>
> Here the appellant's case was to the effect that the complainant demanded money with menaces and tried to take his property. Her persistent criminal record of offences of dishonesty, notwithstanding their antiquity, might...very well be said to possess substantial probative value upon this issue: Did she have a propensity to act dishonestly?
>
> (at [14]–[15])

4.31 *Conditions of admissibility.* Turning to the conditions of admissibility of non-defendants' bad character in s 100(1)(a)–(c), if one examines the concept of 'important explanatory evidence' mentioned in s 100(1)(a), the Act goes on to specify that a witness's bad character will only satisfy this criterion provided that 'without it, the court or jury would find it impossible or difficult properly to understand other evidence in the case, *and* its value for understanding the case as a whole is substantial' (s 100(2)). These requirements are demanding. (See further *post*, paras **7.41–7.46**) 'Important explanatory evidence' is not intended to provide an easy vehicle for the introduction of non-defendant's bad character.

4.32 Section 100(1)(b), which permits evidence of a non-defendant's bad character to be introduced if it has 'substantial probative value in relation to...a matter in issue in the proceedings', also sets a demanding standard of admissibility. Paragraph (b), it will be noted, requires additionally that such evidence is 'of substantial importance in the context of the case as a whole'. The question whether a person's bad character may be introduced as a means of undermining their credibility as a witness is most likely to fall to be considered under s 100(1)(b). By way of example, in one of the appeals heard together in *Renda et al* [2006] 1 Cr App R 24 O had been charged with robbing £200 from a public house. O contested that a robbery had never taken place and suggested that the publican, C, had fabricated this tale in order to cover up his own defalcations. One of the issues was whether a defence witness, W, whose evidence undermined C's claim that he had been a victim of violence on the night in question and reinforced O's claim that this was a trumped-up charge, could be cross-examined by the Crown about a recent conviction for an offence of serious violence. Judge LJ declared:

> The evidence of the conviction fell within s 100, particularly germane to the fundamental question whether or not a robbery had taken place. Without knowing of W's character, the jury would have been deprived of important evidence of substantial probative value in relation to the issue of the credibility of W's evidence on the vital question whether

Mr C had fabricated his complaint, or whether in truth he was rightly to be regarded as a victim.

(at [59])

Judge LJ could see no principled reason to interfere with the judge's ruling, and although the trial judge's reasoning was described as 'over-parsimonious compliance with the duty of the court under s 110(1) to give reasons for any rulings made under s 100' (at [60]), the ruling was upheld. In order to pass the admissibility threshold, s 100(1)(b) requires both that the bad character severely damages the credibility of the particular witness, *and* that that witness's evidence plays a prominent part in the overall case.

4.33 Section 100(3) explains how the court should set about determining whether a non-defendant's bad character has 'substantial probative value' in relation to a matter which is 'a matter in issue in the proceedings', and 'is of substantial importance in the context of the case as a whole'. This subsection provides:

> In assessing the probative value of evidence for the purposes of subsection (1)(b) the court must have regard to the following factors (and to any others it considers relevant)—
>
> (a) the nature and number of the events, or other things, to which the evidence relates;
>
> (b) when those events or things are alleged to have happened or existed;
>
> (c) where—
>> (i) the evidence is evidence of a person's misconduct, and
>> (ii) it is suggested that the evidence has probative value by reason of similarity between that misconduct and other alleged misconduct,
>
> the nature and extent of the similarities and the dissimilarities between each of the alleged instances of misconduct.

This list of factors is not exhaustive; the court must additionally consider 'any others it considers relevant'. A court, then, must consider the nature, number and timing of events as well as the extent of their similarity to other alleged misconduct if that is said to be the source of its probative value. If it is advocated that the evidence is such as to show that the non-defendant committed the offence being tried (s 100(3)(d); see *post* paras **4.40–4.41**), the extent to which the totality of the evidence tends to show that the same person was responsible for both the bad character event and the offence being tried must be assessed to determine whether it possesses 'substantial probative value' for that particular purpose. Section 100(3), therefore, 'emphasises that the test of "substantial probative value" is a test of the force of the evidence which it is sought to adduce' (*Braithwaite*, at [16]).

4.34 It will be a matter of deciding whether particular bad character evidence is sufficiently probative to the particular matter in issue raised in each individual case. In *Braithwaite* [2010] 2 Cr App R 18, for example, B, who pleaded self-defence to a charge of murder, wished to introduce the bad characters of the deceased's companions, a number of whom testified against him. The trial judge admitted evidence of their bad characters to the extent that it consisted of conduct resulting in convictions, cautions and (by the Crown's concession) penalty notices, but he declined to admit material contained in police CRIS reports which merely indicated that some third party had made an allegation against the witness or that the witness had been investigated in respect of some offence without being tried or convicted. The Court of Appeal said that when adjudicating upon such applications, all of which necessarily are fact-sensitive, a judge must consider *seriatim*:

 a) the issue to which the evidence goes (s 100(1)(b)(i)),

 b) whether that issue is of substantial importance in the context of the case as a whole (s 100(1)(b)(ii)), and

 c) whether the evidence has substantial probative value in relation to that issue (s 100(1)(b)).

 (at [12](iv))

The probative value of proffered bad character evidence has to be assessed in the context of the case as a whole, which may mean that in some cases the court has to consider whether it adds significantly to other more probative evidence directed to the same issue. In *Braithwaite*, Hughes LJ held that the witnesses' convictions and cautions (which comprise either findings of guilt or admissions of guilt) had been properly admitted. The trial judge had also been 'right to direct himself that a mere police report indicating that an allegation had been made, which remained unproven, was most unlikely to have substantial probative value' (at [20]). Indeed, the Court also doubted whether, in the absence of an acknowledgement of guilt, penalty notices issued under the Criminal Justice and Police Act 2001, s 2(1)—which, in most cases, will simply provide evidence that a policeman has reason to believe someone guilty of an offence—would carry 'substantial probative value' as to that person's guilt.

4.35 Pitchford LJ, in *Brewster and Cromwell* [2010] 2 Cr App R 20, has provided important guidance on how s 100 is to be applied when a non-defendant's bad character is invoked to call his credibility into question:

 [T]he trial judge's task will be to evaluate the evidence of bad character...for the purpose of deciding whether it is reasonably capable of assisting a fair-minded jury to reach a view whether the witness's evidence is, or is not, worthy of belief. Only then can it properly be said that the evidence is of substantial probative value on the issue of credit-worthiness.... It does not seem to us that the words "substantial probative value", in their s.100(1)(b) context, require the applicant to establish that the bad character relied on amounts to proof of a lack of credibility of the witness when credibility is an issue of substantial importance, or that the convictions demonstrate a tendency towards untruth-fulness. The question is whether the evidence of previous convictions, or bad behaviour, is sufficiently persuasive to be worthy of consideration by a fair-minded tribunal upon the issue of the witness's creditworthiness....

The first question for the trial judge under s. 100(1)(b) is whether creditworthiness is a matter in issue which is of substantial importance in the context of the case as a whole. This is a significant hurdle. Just because a witness has convictions does not mean that the opposing party is entitled to attack the witness' credibility. If it is shown that credit-worthiness is an issue of substantial importance, the second question is whether the bad character relied upon is of substantial probative value in relation to that issue. Whether convictions have persuasive value on the issue of creditworthiness will... depend principally on the nature, number and age of the convictions. However, we do not consider that the conviction must, in order to qualify for admission in evidence, demonstrate any tendency towards dishonesty or untruthfulness. The question is whether a fair-minded tribunal would regard them as affecting the worth of the witness' evidence.

(at [22] and [23])

4.35 *No further judicial discretion to refuse leave.* Pitchford LJ added that once a judge has resolved that the non-defendant's bad character is of substantial probative value in relation to an issue of substantial importance in the context of the case as a whole, he retains no additional residual discretion to exclude the evidence, save under his general case management powers (at [24]; *Braithwaite* [2010] 2 Cr App R 18).

4.36 *Evidence which has to do with the alleged facts of the offence.* Not all non-defendants are covered by the restrictions imposed on bad character evidence by s 100. Section 98(a) of the Criminal Justice Act 2003 specifically provides that the bad character provisions do not apply to:

evidence which has to do with the alleged facts of the offence with which the defendant is charged.

Therefore, allegations of bad character concerning those who, for example, participated in the offence are admissible. Thus, if, in answer to a charge of assault occasioning grievous bodily harm, D pleads that he only assaulted the victim because he was attempting to fend off the latter's unprovoked attack, then—assuming that an unprovoked attack is deemed to amount to evidence of bad character—such evidence will be admissible without leave because it has to do with the alleged facts of the offence. In *Machado* (2006) 170 JP 400 M had been convicted of robbery and possession of a bladed article in a public place along with two co-accused, T and R. The victim, H, testified that the robbery had taken place as he was walking home in the three defendants' company. When arrested, M was found in possession of H's mobile telephone and a lock-knife. M's version of events was that, when he had merely touched H, the latter had fallen to the ground. M had noticed a wallet had fallen from H's pocket, but before he could return it to him H had run off. During the trial, the judge ruled that M might not put questions in cross-examination to H alleging that in the course of their encounter H had offered to supply M with drugs and that H had also told M that he had taken an ecstasy tablet. On appeal, the question was whether the judge had been correct to uphold the Crown's argument that any evidence tending to show that H had taken drugs or offered to supply them ought not be admitted as it constituted evidence of H's bad character and thereby fell within the restrictive terms of s 100 of the Criminal Justice Act 2003. The Court of Appeal held that s 98(a) of the Act, which excludes from the ambit of 'bad character' 'evidence which has to do with the alleged facts of the offence with which the defendant is charged', makes clear that evidence of bad character is evidence of misconduct other than evidence which has to do with the alleged facts of the offence. In this case M wished to give evidence of (and, had this been allowed, to adduce evidence from witnesses of) the very circumstances in which the offence charged had occurred. All the matters were in effect contemporaneous with and closely associated with the alleged facts of the offence. Applying the simple English of the provision, these matters were to do with the alleged facts of the offence and, therefore, did not constitute evidence of 'bad character' within the meaning of s 98 of the Act.

4.37 *Evidence of misconduct in connection with the investigation or prosecution.* Additionally, s 98(b) of the 2003 Act excludes from the definition of 'bad character':

> evidence of misconduct in connection with the investigation or prosecution of that offence.

Thus, if the defendant alleges that the police fitted him up by concocting evidence or that prosecuting counsel has bribed his witnesses or deliberately withheld evidence exculpating him, these matters fall outside the Act's definition of bad character and will not be subject to s 100. They will be admissible provided that they are considered relevant. In contrast, if the defendant wishes to explore a police officer's bad character more generally, enquiring into disciplinary proceedings to which he may have been subject or asking about other cases in which, say, he may have falsified evidence (*Edwards* [1991] 1 WLR 207), s 100 will apply. However, as in *Braithwaite* [2010] 2 Cr App R 18,

> [T]he mere fact that a complaint or allegation has been made, or that a person who is a witness has been charged with some offence of disciplinary behaviour, is not of itself a

sufficient foundation for cross-examination as to credit and, by the same token, acquittal at a previous trial in which reliance was placed on the evidence of a particular witness does not of itself confer a right of cross-examination—though it will do if, in exceptional cases, the acquittal, by the circumstances in which it comes about, demonstrates rejection of the evidence of the prosecution witness.

(*Twitchell* [2000] 1 Cr App R 373 at 382–3)

4.38 *According credit to police officers.* Although, strictly speaking, this is not directly relevant to the introduction of evidence questioning police officers' credibility, it might just be noted in addition that courts have sometimes inclined in the opposite direction, suggesting that police officers, as a class, are likely to prove reliable witnesses. This creates a rather different problem. In a few cases where the prosecution has relied substantially on identification evidence (see *post*, Chapter 12), it has been suggested that the evidence of police officers, as trained observers, may be more worthy of credence than that of ordinary members of the public. In *Tyler* [1993] Crim LR 60, for example, the Court of Appeal held that the trial judge had been entitled to make restrained comment to this effect in his summing-up in relation to police witnesses who had been caught up in a poll tax demonstration. They had been observing the crowd and particularly looking out for those who were throwing things at them. The training police officers received, it was held, could be mentioned to the jury in these circumstances. Such comments, however, it is suggested, must not be made too readily. In the notorious case of *Bentley (deceased)* [2001] 1 Cr App R 21, where the Court of Appeal quashed B's murder conviction 45 years after he was hanged, one criticism levelled at Lord Goddard CJ's summing-up at the original trial of Craig and Bentley was precisely that he had suggested to the jury that police officers were likely to be more reliable witnesses than defendants. As Lord Bingham CJ observed:

> The courts have in recent years deprecated judicial comments which suggest that police officers will be professionally ruined if a defendant is acquitted (*Culbertson* (1970) 54 Cr App R 310) or which place police officers in a different position from other witnesses (*Beycan* [1990] Crim LR 185)...There is an obvious risk of injustice if a jury is invited to approach the evidence on the assumption that police officers, because they are police officers, are likely to be accurate and reliable witnesses and defendants, because they are defendants, likely to be inaccurate and unreliable. This is the pitfall into which the trial judge, for all his vast experience and authority, fell.
>
> (at [53])

4.39 *Deceased non-defendants.* A further point might be mentioned. Section 100(1) forbids the introduction of evidence of the bad character of 'a person other than the defendant'. It might be legitimately asked, was this provision meant to cover the case of dead non-defendants? The language employed by the legislature does not necessitate such a construction. The writer is unaware of any statute in which the word 'person' has been used to denote a deceased. Further, English law is not noted for its willingness either to protect the reputations of the dead or the feelings of the kith and kin of the departed. However, it could just about be argued that an affirmative answer would coincide with the legislature's overall purpose when enacting s 100 (see further Munday 'The Quick and the Dead' [2007] 71 J Crim Law 238).

The defendant who alleges that a third party was the true culprit

4.40   Section 100(1)(b), again, may permit defendants to cross-examine Crown witnesses on their bad character or to adduce evidence of another person's bad character, provided that 'it has substantial probative value in relation to a matter which is a matter in issue in the proceedings, and is of substantial importance in the context of the case as a whole' in order to allege that that other party was the true culprit. If one imagines a sexual assault case where the accused wishes to suggest that, by reason of the nature of the offence and of a third party's particular record of offending, that third party was responsible for committing this offence, one might have assumed that such evidence was admissible independently of s 100 on the ground that it is 'evidence which has to do with the alleged facts of the offence with which the defendant is charged' (s 98(a)). However, this seems not to be the case, when one examines the language of s 100(3)(d), which contemplates that in these circumstances too the evidence must satisfy the standard imposed by s 100(1)(b). In such cases, the court is instructed by s 100(3) to take into account a number of specific factors (see *ante*, para **4.33**), such as the number, the nature, the time span and, if relevant, the similarity between the misconduct and other alleged misconduct.

4.41   As was mentioned above, s 100(1)(b) allows evidence of the bad character of someone other than the accused to be adduced if 'it has substantial probative value in relation to a matter which is a matter in issue in the proceedings, and is of substantial importance in the context of the case as a whole'. Plainly, evidence suggesting strongly that a person other than the accused is likely to be the true culprit is liable to satisfy this test. How readily will such evidence be admitted? Section 100(3) sets out how a court is to determine whether the non-defendant's bad character has 'substantial probative value' under s 100(1)(b). The Act provides a detailed list of factors that must be taken into account by the court when adjudging whether particular items of evidence suggestive of a non-defendant's bad character are in fact admissible. Section 100(3)(d) additionally provides:

(d) where—
    (i) the evidence is evidence of a person's misconduct,
    (ii) it is suggested that that person is also responsible for the misconduct charged, and
    (iii) the identity of the person responsible for the misconduct charged is disputed,
  the extent to which the evidence shows or tends to show that the same person was responsible each time.

It will be apparent that a judge's discretion to admit such evidence is quite tightly circumscribed. Indeed, the exceptions outlined in both s 100(2) and (3) are intentionally narrow. Clearly, save where there the non-defendant consents to the disclosure of his bad character, the legislature's intention is to restrict such evidence to a minimum of cases in which the evidence is strong and is also of prime importance in the context of the case. In all cases in which it is sought to adduce evidence of bad character (apart from cases where the parties all agree to the admission of such evidence), it bears repeating that the leave of the court must be sought (s 100(4)).

Issue and credit, and the principle of collateral-finality

4.42 As a general principle, when a witness is cross-examined on a matter going to credit, the witness's answers have to be taken as final and evidence may not be called by the cross-examining party to rebut the witness's answers. The reason for this is that the trial should remain focused on the principal issues at stake and not be sidetracked into the pursuit of questions entirely collateral to the litigation. This is often referred to as the 'collateral-finality principle'. Like most legal principles, however, it is subject to exceptions, the majority of which derive from statute.

4.43 The distinction drawn between matters going to issue and matters going simply to credit is critical. How does one distinguish between the two? The authoritative test was laid down by Pollock CB in *A-G v Hitchcock* (1847) 1 Exch 91 in the following terms:

[I]f the answer of a witness is a matter which you would be allowed on your own part to prove in evidence—if it has such a connection with the issues, that you would be allowed to give it in evidence—then it is a matter on which you may contradict him.
(at 99)

In short, one can safely conclude that if a party could have introduced the matter as part of its primary evidence, then that party may be allowed to produce evidence contradicting the answer given by the opposing side's witness in cross-examination.

4.44 *Exceptions to collateral-finality: Criminal Procedure Act 1865, ss 4 and 5.* Although detailed consideration of this topic is beyond the scope of an introductory work, under the Criminal Procedure Act 1865, if any witness, who has been asked about a previous inconsistent statement, denies making that statement, s 4 entitles the cross-examining party to prove that the witness did in fact make the statement. To take just one particular class of witnesses, defendants may be cross-examined on the contents of several types of previous statements that they are now routinely required to provide prior to trial, if those statements prove inconsistent with their testimony in court. Thus, 'alibi notices', with which the defence is required to supply the prosecution under the Criminal Procedure and Investigations Act 1996, s 5(7), and 'defence statements' giving prior notice of the principal elements of the accused's case in conformity with s 5(6) of that Act, may both provide material for cross-examination (eg *Terry* [2003] EWCA Crim 1800). In *Hayes* [2005] 1 Cr App R 33, by analogy, it was held permissible to have asked a defendant charged with wounding with intent about a letter, which had been written to the prosecution with his authority before commencement of his trial, indicating a willingness to plead guilty to a lesser charge but giving an account of matters inconsistent with the story he subsequently told at the trial. In Scott Baker LJ's opinion, such cross-examination involved no unfairness to the accused:

> [I]t was relevant to his credibility in just the same way that it may be relevant to a defendant's credibility to cross-examine him about details in his alibi notice when his evidence at the trial has turned out to be different. Likewise, there is no objection, in principle, to a defendant being cross-examined on what is contained in his defence statement when it becomes relevant to an issue at the trial. We cannot see that there was any unfairness to the defendant in the admission of this evidence...
>
> (at [23])

Section 4 of the Criminal Procedure Act 1865 lays down a procedure whereby, if he denies having made it, the witness's previous statement may be proved. Provided that the statement relates to the subject matter of the proceeding, the section requires that the witness must first be reminded of the circumstances in which the statement was made, and then can be asked whether he did in fact make it. If the witness does not 'distinctly admit that he has made such statement, proof may be given that he did in fact make it'. Because s 5 makes express provision for similar proof to be adduced (although the procedure is not identical) in the case of a witness's previous inconsistent *written* statements, it used to be assumed that s 4 related only to previous inconsistent *oral* statements. In *R v Derby Magistrates' Court, ex p*

B [1996] AC 487, however, the House of Lords held that s 4 is drafted more widely and may apply to both oral and written statements. These two sections, therefore, are concerned with contradicting a witness whose testimony is inconsistent with his earlier written or oral statement(s). When such a statement is admitted under ss 4 or 5 of the 1865 Act, once the statement has been proved 'to the satisfaction' of the tribunal of fact (*Zardad* [2007] EWCA Crim 279 at [39] *per* Keene LJ), the Criminal Justice Act, s 119(1) provides that the witness's 'statement is admissible as evidence of any matter stated of which oral evidence by him would be admissible'.

4.45 In contrast, cross-examination which is directed simply towards attacking the witness's credit—that is, towards asking questions which seek to discredit the witness in the eyes of the court, thereby inducing it to place less trust in that witness's testimony—is governed by common law. In criminal cases, such questioning has become less frequent following enactment of the Criminal Justice Act 2003, s 100. However, even in criminal cases it will continue to encompass questions that do not seek to introduce evidence of witnesses' bad character—that is to say, questions directed to 'evidence which has to do with the alleged facts of the offence with which the defendant is charged' (s 98(a); *ante*, para **4.36**), questions directed to 'evidence of misconduct in connection with the investigation or prosecution of [the] offence' (s 98 (b); *ante*, para **4.37**), and conceivably any questions which relate to improper behaviour that is held not to amount to 'reprehensible conduct' within the terms of ss 98 and 112 of the Criminal Justice Act 2003. The traditional underlying principle was clearly articulated by Lord Lane CJ in *Edwards* [1991] 1 WLR 207:

> Generally speaking questions may be put to a witness as to any improper conduct of which he may have been guilty for the purpose of testing his credit.

Subject to the above *caveat* concerning s 100 of the 2003 Act, with a view to avoiding the court having to pursue a multiplicity of issues, the general rule is that the witness's answers must be treated as final. Thus, in *Edwards* [1991] 1 WLR 207 answers given by police officers to questions respecting other trials in which they had testified but had not been believed, disciplinary hearings they had faced and so on could not be contradicted by further evidence (see *ante*, para **4.37**).

4.46 *Exception to collateral-finality: Criminal Procedure Act, s 6.* Another clear exception to collateral-finality relates to a witness's previous convictions. If a witness denies having a previous criminal conviction or refuses to answer questions concerning his criminal record, under the Criminal Procedure Act 1865, s 6 'it shall be lawful for the cross-examining party to prove such conviction.'

4.47 *Exception to collateral-finality: Bias.* Collateral-finality is subject to an important exception at common law: bias. At common law it is still the case that where a question is put imputing bias to a witness, that witness's denials may be contradicted. The classical example is *Thomas v David* (1836) 7 C & P 350, which held that where a witness denied being the mistress of the accused, evidence might be adduced by the cross-examining party rebutting her denial. The mistress's intimate relations with the defendant suggested that she might have been prepared to lie for him. The common law considers bias to go to the root of the case and therefore declines to treat answers given by witnesses challenged on grounds of bias as final. In more recent times the courts have occasionally adopted a generous interpretation of 'bias' in this context. In *Mendy* (1976) 64 Cr App R 4, for example, a police officer informed prosecuting counsel that he had noticed that a man, who had been making notes in the public gallery during M's trial, had subsequently spoken with M's husband. When he testified for the defence, the husband rejected the Crown's suggestion that he had been briefed. The Court of Appeal held that the trial judge had properly allowed the prosecution to call evidence showing that a briefing may have taken place, indicating as it did that the husband was prepared to cheat to deceive the jury in order to help his wife. (Of course, if the conduct of the individuals in these cases is held to amount to 'reprehensible behaviour' and hence 'bad character', the restrictions of the Criminal Justice Act 2003, s 100, as discussed *ante*, will also apply.)

4.47 Although it is sometimes given a broad interpretation, bias, it should be said, does not cover all cases of attempted corruption of witnesses. In *A-G v Hitchcock* itself, a prosecution witness was asked whether he had been offered a bribe. He said that he had not. Could the defence contradict his denial? The court held this was impermissible on the ground that, even it had been true that the witness had been offered a bribe, this would not have undermined his credit. There is nothing dishonourable in being offered a bribe, only in accepting one! The case, of course, is altered if the question is whether the witness has solicited a bribe, as this is undoubtedly discreditable to the witness (*Rasheed* (1994) 158 JP 941). In this context, too, it is sometimes hard to discern where exactly the limits of bias lie. In *Phillips* (1936) 26 Cr App R 17, for instance, two young girls were called to testify against their father on charges of incest. They denied having been schooled in their evidence by their mother. Lord Hewart CJ allowed the defence to rebut the girls' denials. It is generally accepted that where the court feels that the allegation made in cross-examination is sufficiently fundamental to the case, as it would have been in *Phillips*, the adduction of rebuttal evidence may be permitted. In *TM* [2004] EWCA Crim 2085 the court was again required to visit 'this notoriously difficult issue'. TM, who was charged with multiple sexual abuse charges relating to several complainants, had been denied leave to call a witness who would have testified that she had turned down an offer of money from an enquiry agent, employed by the person who had instigated the various complaints, in order to extract from her information adverse to TM. On the ground that this evidence suggested what technique the enquiry agent may equally have employed when he approached the other potential witnesses, Moses J concluded that this evidence ought to have been admitted to the extent that 'it went to an issue as to whether witnesses and complainants had been offered financial inducement and whether any such financial inducement had tainted their evidence' (at [38]).

4.48 *Issue and credit.* Although fundamental to the collateral-finality principle, it has to be acknowledged that the courts' attitude to the distinction between issue and credit is somewhat ambivalent. *Funderburk* (1990) 90 Cr App R 466, and a series of cases that have followed in its wake, have arguably blurred this distinction. In *Funderburk*, the Court of Appeal seemed to treat collateral-finality as almost a matter of instinct rather than simply the application of Pollock CB's test in *A-G v Hitchcock*. At one point, Henry J spoke of its being 'based on the prosecutor's and the Court's sense of fair play rather than any philosophic or analytic process' (at 476). Such an approach means that, sometimes, when confronted with situations such as arose in *Funderburk*, where the case pretty much boiled down to the complainant's word against that of the defendant, the courts will hesitate long before excluding evidence bearing upon whether or not there was fabrication (or collusion) in the case (see, eg, *R (David)* [1999] Crim LR 909). In *Nagrecha* [1997] 2 Cr App R 401, for instance, N was charged with indecent assault. N denied the charge. It was found that the trial judge had wrongly prevented N from calling the victim's works manager against whom, in cross-examination, she had denied making a previous false complaint of indecent assault. The Court of Appeal was persuaded that a new, more liberal attitude to collateral-finality was now discernible. Although, strictly speaking, the false complaint made against the works manager was a matter relating solely to credit, it also went to the heart of the matter and, besides, would not have involved the investigation of a host of peripheral issues. To take a further example, in *Tobin* [2003] EWCA Crim 190, [2003] Crim LR 408, evidence was admitted that tended to boost the credibility of the victim of an alleged indecent assault, by indicating that she was a polite and quiet girl, who got on well with her siblings and was respectful of other people. Pill LJ, recognising the force of Henry J's words in *Funderburk* that questions going to issue and questions going to credit may reduce to vanishing point, concluded that:

> ... in sexual cases, prosecution evidence of the complainant's background and characteristics is not inevitably excluded ... In the circumstances, our sense of fair play is not offended but rather affirmed by the admission of the very limited evidence about that complainant's characteristics and conduct which occurred.
>
> (at [16]–[17])

On the other hand, in contrast to cases like *Nagrecha* and *Tobin*, the courts occasionally revert to the more traditional approach to collateral-finality. In *Neale*

[1998] Crim LR 737 Evans LJ expressly declined to adopt the *Funderburk* analysis, although he then confusingly said that the collateral-finality principle is essentially pragmatic and there are no cast-iron definitions. One is dealing, of course, with a question that, on the one hand, is purportedly governed by principle but, on the other, is informed by a strong sense of what is practical. Woolf LJ captured the flavour perfectly in *S* [1992] Crim LR 307:

> There has to be a balance between keeping criminal trials within bounds and not distracting the jury from the principal issue by involving them in other issues which are unsuitable for determination in the forum of the trial taking place. The interests of justice are the final determinative factor.

4.49 *May defendants make unsubstantiated allegations against witnesses with impunity?* A defendant's strategy at trial will often rest on the contention that the prosecution witnesses are lying. This situation can be at its most acute in sexual cases in which the case often boils down very much to choosing between the defendant's word and that of the complainant. To what extent ought the defendant to be permitted to allege that his accusers are liars without having to justify these imputations? In *B* [2003] 1 WLR 2809, the accused stood trial for a number of very serious sexual offences committed on two of his four daughters. Appeal was subsequently taken on the ground that the trial judge ought not to have allowed the prosecution to ask B, when he came to testify, whether he knew of any reason why his daughters might have lied. On appeal, Rose LJ upheld the trial judge's ruling. Rose LJ noted that, in the experience of the court, such a question has been 'widely, if not invariably, permitted by trial judges' (at [40]). Adhering closely to the New Zealand Court of Appeal's reasoning in *T* [1998] NZLR 257 at 265–6, Rose LJ concluded that it was indeed right to allow this line of questioning. If B replied to such a question affirmatively, any answer he gave would tend to undermine the complainants' credibility, and could also reinforce his own case: B could hardly object to that. The mere fact that it was likely that a defendant would give a negative response to such a question could not be allowed to determine the question's admissibility. Indeed, more generally, the Crown was entitled to seek to close, 'with finality', an avenue which might otherwise be open to the defence. Of course, there must be no suggestion that the defendant bears any kind of burden of proving that the complainant had a motive to lie. But provided that this will have been made clear to the jury, there is no objection to such a question being put. Indeed, given that jurors will naturally wonder whether a complainant did have any motive to lie, this line of questioning accords with common sense and the promptings of human nature. As Eichelbaum CJ remarked in *T*:

> It would seem a strange legal system that allowed the accused to assert that complainants had fabricated their account but did not allow the prosecution to test the correctness of the proposition by inquiring what evidence supported it.
>
> (at 266)

Re-examination

4.50 A witness who has been cross-examined by the opposing party may then be re-examined by the party who called him. Re-examination ought to be confined to questions about matters that have been the subject of cross-examination. The purpose of re-examination is to afford the witness's side an opportunity to repair damage done during cross-examination. It allows the witness to explain inconsistencies that may have emerged in his testimony during cross-questioning or even to expand upon answers given in cross-examination, provided that no new matter is introduced. If some new matter does emerge during re-examination, or if the judge in discretion exceptionally allows counsel to explore some new issue, further cross-examination may then take place.

4.51 If it has been sought in cross-examination to undermine a witness's credibility—suggesting, for example, that the witness is untruthful—one might have expected that the collateral-finality principle would apply and that all applications to rehabilitate the witness's credibility would be refused (see *ante*, paras **4.42** ff). Although positive rebuttal evidence suggestive of a witness's good character is definitely held inadmissible (*Hamilton* (1998) Times, 25 July), courts do occasionally permit a witness whose character has been impugned in cross-examination to be asked in re-examination questions which bring out the fact that the witness does not have any criminal convictions (eg *O'Connor* (1996) 29 October). Such evidence of good character is obviously intended to re-establish the witness's impugned credibility. There is no particular explanation for such rulings, and the Court of Appeal simultaneously admits that in its experience counsel do not normally follow this practice, yet stresses that the judge has discretion whether or not to allow such questions in these cases (*Catherall* [2004] EWCA Crim 1732 at [30] *per* Buxton LJ).

4.52 Re-examination, it is frequently said, is far from easy. Maurice Healy's verdict on the respective levels of difficulty in performing effective examination, cross-examination and re-examination is worth quoting:

> All that can be learned about cross-examination is contained in a few principles; these must be applied to the particular circumstances of the case, but the fact remains that in nine cases out of ten a successful cross-examination depends upon the ammunition available. On the other hand, the examination-in-chief of a witness gives the artist full scope every time... Only one art is more difficult; that is the art of re-examination. Herein the object of the advocate is to overcome the effect of a destructive cross-examination. This object is attained by a miracle; if you can't perform them, you had much better allow your witness to go out of the box without further question.
>
> (*The Old Munster Circuit* (1939) 71–2)

Calling evidence relating to witnesses' veracity

4.53 *Oath-helping vs expert evidence that informs the tribunal of fact.* As a general principle, witnesses may not be called simply to endorse the credibility of another witness. As the Court of Appeal made clear in *Robinson* (1994) 98 Cr App R 370, the evidence of a witness is not to be supported by that of oath-helpers. R was charged with an array of sexual assaults committed on the 15-year-old daughter of the woman with whom he lived. Intellectually, the victim fell within the lowest 1 per cent of 15-year-olds. After the defence had suggested that the girl's evidence might have been influenced by her mother and by an educational psychologist, the trial judge allowed an educational psychologist to testify that the girl was neither suggestible nor prone to fantasise. Lord Taylor CJ stated that, in the absence of mental abnormality, such evidence ought not to have been admitted:

> In our view the Crown cannot call a witness of fact and then, without more, call a psychologist or psychiatrist to give reasons why the jury should regard the witness as reliable.

This traditional outlook, which holds that the tribunal of fact is normally well placed to assess a witness's credibility without expert assistance, has since been endorsed by Lord Hobhouse in *Pendleton* [2002] 1 WLR 72:

> The courts should be cautious about admitting evidence from psychologists, however eminent, as to the credibility of witnesses. The assessment of the truth of verbal evidence, save in a very small number of exceptional circumstances, is a matter for the jury. The suggestibility of some persons is well within the experience of ordinary members of the juries. To admit evidence from psychologists on such questions is not only contrary to the established rules of evidence, but is also contrary to the principle of trial by jury and risks substituting trial by expert.
>
> (at [45])

4.54 In the mind of the court, there is a clear line of demarcation separating evidence of opinion that may assist the tribunal in its task and mere comment on the credibility of a party. In *W* [2003] EWCA Crim 2490, a curious case in which a father was accused of having raped his young son, it was argued that an expert ought to have been permitted to testify to 'false memory syndrome' on behalf of the defence. As Judge LJ explained:

> Dealing with it broadly, evidence from expert witnesses is designed to inform a jury of what they might not know of their own collective experience of life. There is therefore...a distinction between evidence that a condition has been identified by experts in this particular field which may explain that the memory of an apparently truthful witness may, in fact, be false (which we describe as the syndrome), and evidence from an expert witness

based on a study of identical or virtually identical material to that available to the jury which directly (or much more likely, indirectly) informs the jury of the expert's opinion whether the witness in question was or was not to be believed (which we identify as credibility)... *The primacy of the jury on issues of credibility has to be maintained*. If, however, the trial judge is persuaded in a particular case that the jury would be better able to perform their duties on credibility issues by hearing evidence of the existence and nature of the syndrome, such evidence is in principle admissible. If admitted, trial judges have to be careful not to permit evidence about the syndrome to develop into comment, direct or indirect, on credibility. There will inevitably be grey areas, and questions whether and where in a particular case the appropriate line should be drawn.

(at [24], emphasis added)

Such a case arose in *JH and TG* (2005) 1 July, case no 04/5576/D3 and 04/5577/D3. Following an application to admit expert evidence in two sexual abuse appeals referred to it by the Criminal Cases Review Commission, the Court of Appeal declared admissible the evidence of a psychologist, who was an expert in memory formation and development, on the subject of 'childhood amnesia'. The victim had given two very similar, and unusually detailed and coherent, accounts of abuse inflicted on her by her father and by a music teacher on separate occasions when she was a very young girl. The father and the music teacher had been convicted by different juries at separate trials. The expert's testimony was to the effect that during the 'period of childhood amnesia', up to the age of about seven, memories of events tend to be fragmentary, disjointed and idiosyncratic: in short, quite unlike the testimony given by this particular victim. Smith LJ was of opinion that the psychologist 'provided information likely to be outside the knowledge and experience of the jury' which might have influenced a jury's view of the victim's credibility as a witness (at [36]). The court nevertheless sounded a strong note of caution, declaring:

[I]t will only be in the most unusual of circumstances that such evidence will be relevant and admissible at the trial of allegations of child abuse. The evidence would only be relevant in those rare cases in which the complainant provides a description of very early events which appears to contain an unrealistic amount of detail. That... does not happen often. The principles set out in *Turner* [1975] QB 834 [see *post*, paras **8.4** and **8.15–8.16**] should be kept firmly in mind...A witness's ability to remember events will, absent the special considerations arising from the period of early childhood amnesia, ordinarily be well within the experience of jurors.

(at [47]–[48])

4.55 *Witness support.* For some time there has been general concern that witnesses (and particularly victims of crime) fail to testify as effectively as they might simply because they feel uncomfortable or out of place when appearing for the first time in the unfamiliar surroundings of a courtroom. To combat this, witness support services are made available in courts. The importance accorded to witness support is evidenced by the fact that by December 2005 165 witness care units had been set up across England and Wales. These are designed to offer a single point of contact, providing those who are due to give evidence in court with information and practical help. Taking matters further, however, in November 2005 the government published a Consultation Paper, 'The Witness Charter', proposing a code of minimum standards of service witnesses can expect of the criminal justice system, brought into force in August 2007, which would operate alongside the Code of Practice for Victims of Crime. The Charter establishes 'core standards of service' for the 161,000 or so non-victim prosecution witnesses and the 60,000 or so defence witnesses who testify annually at trials in England and Wales. One elementary but useful function of witness support services is to familiarise witnesses with the layout of the court and to explain its procedures.

4.56 Witness support services, however, may introduce a problem if their otherwise well-intended efforts serve to interfere with witnesses' testimony. In *Catherall* [2004] EWCA Crim 1732, for example, it was reported that the relevant representative, who escorted the witness into court, had gone beyond this restricted role and had actually handed out to a crucial witness to a burglary the advice 'stick to your guns', if in cross-examination the witness's account was contradicted by the defence. Whilst agreeing that these exchanges were highly unsatisfactory, Buxton LJ considered that the witness's testimony in the case had not been contaminated to such a degree by this inappropriate advice that she ought not to have been permitted to testify at all. Moreover, it was felt that cross-examination of the witness on what had taken place was capable of curing the defect, at least in the context of this particular case. In another instance, *Salisbury* (2004) 19 May, T 2003/7200, a nursing sister stood trial at Chester Crown Court on four counts of attempting to murder elderly and sick patients. Pitchford J broke with tradition in ruling that the fact that as many as sixty potential prosecution witnesses had received tuition from a medico-legal training company prior to testifying did not amount to an abuse of process. The common understanding beforehand had been that coaching of witnesses was inappropriate. Pitchford J held that, although it was 'unfortunate' that the Crown had not disclosed to the defence from the outset what had occurred, since the witnesses had not discussed the specific case before the court:

> What they would have received was knowledge of the process involved... Acquisition of knowledge and understanding has probably prepared them better for the experience of giving evidence. They will be better able to give a sequential and coherent account. None of this gives them an unfair advantage over another witness.
>
> (at [29])

The training, which was said simply to have alerted witnesses to pitfalls in testifying and instructed them how best to prepare for the ordeal of the day in court, would not have been capable of converting a lying but incompetent witness into a lying but impressive witness. The training, however, might have aided them in giving a coherent, sequential account of events in the witness box. Despite Pitchford J's optimistic view that 'training' of Crown witnesses is not harmful to the interests of the defence, this departure aroused disquiet—not least because the activities of witness training companies had hitherto been completely unregulated. The process is self-evidently open to abuse. (The last thing that English lawyers would want is the sort of coaching of witnesses on the evidence that they will be called upon to give at trial that, say, the American advocate Louis Nizer crows about in his memoirs, *My Life in Court* (1961).)

4.57 The Court of Appeal subsequently considered pre-trial coaching of witnesses in *Momodou and Limani* [2005] 1 WLR 3442, a case arising out of the violent disorder that led to the partial destruction of the Yarl's Wood Immigration Detention Centre in February 2002. A number of potential prosecution witnesses, who had witnessed these traumatising events when detainees ran riot, either did receive or were said to have received training designed to familiarise them with the trial process in order to make testifying less intimidating; others received cognitive therapy, either in groups or individually. Judge LJ, obviously intent on allaying many of the fears that witness familiarisation programmes typically arouse, made clear:

> There is a dramatic distinction between witness training or coaching, and witness familiarisation. Training or coaching for witnesses in criminal proceedings (whether for prosecution or defence) is not permitted.
>
> (at [61])

Familiarising witnesses with the layout of the court and with legal procedure, if anything, is to be welcomed, as witnesses ought not to be disadvantaged by their ignorance of the trial process. The courts nevertheless must guard against such training contaminating witnesses' testimony:

> [T]he critical feature of training...is that it should not be arranged in the context nor related to any forthcoming trial, and it can therefore have no impact whatever on it.
>
> (at [62])

Judge LJ laid down guidance which was to be followed in future. In the case of prosecution witnesses, the Crown Prosecution Service was to be alerted and consulted in advance if witness familiarisation by outside agencies (ie not organised through the courts' witness service) was contemplated; in the case of defence witnesses, it was suggested that the defence should seek counsel's advice before embarking on witness familiarisation by outside agencies, and, in any event, that the trial judge and the prosecution should be informed if such training had actually taken place. The outside agency's course should be monitored—preferably by an accredited practitioner, none of those involved in training should have personal knowledge of the impending case, full written records of the content of the course should be retained, and none of the training material ought to resemble the case in which witnesses are eventually to testify or seek to trigger witness recollections. The principal concern, then, is that 'the evidence remains the witness's own uncontaminated evidence'.

4.58 *Impugning the opposing side's witnesses.* In contrast to the principle that a party may not normally adduce evidence to buttress his witnesses' credibility, there is an old common law rule that a witness may be called to impugn the opposing side's witness's reputation for veracity. This rule was reaffirmed in *Richardson* [1969] 1 QB 299, where Edmund Davies LJ set out the somewhat archaic principles that govern this form of evidence.

1. A witness may be asked whether he has knowledge of the impugned witness's general reputation for veracity and whether (from such knowledge) he would believe the impugned witness's sworn testimony.

2. The witness called to impeach the credibility of another witness may also express his personal opinion (based upon his personal knowledge) as to whether the latter is to be believed upon his oath, and is not confined to giving evidence merely on general reputation.

3. But whether his opinion as to the impugned witness's credibility be based simply upon the latter's general reputation for veracity or upon his personal knowledge, the witness cannot be permitted to indicate during his examination-in-chief the particular facts, circumstances or incidents which formed the basis of his opinion, although he may be cross-examined as to them.

It is said that because of the intrinsic weakness of this species of testimony, such witnesses are rarely called. In *Colwill* [2002] EWCA Crim 1320 at [12], Mantell LJ went so far as to say that the Court of Appeal felt 'bound to express [its] doubts whether a modern jury would be assisted by evidence of opinion by a witness the basis of which is not in any way particularised'. Such evidence, however, does continue to make an occasional appearance.

4.59 Sometimes a witness suffers from a medical or mental condition capable of rendering that person's evidence unreliable. The House of Lords in *Toohey v Metropolitan Police Commissioner* [1965] AC 595 held that evidence of mental abnormality that might affect the quality of a witness's evidence is admissible. In the words of Lord Pearce:

> Medical evidence is admissible to show that a witness suffers from some disease or defect or abnormality of mind that affects the reliability of his evidence. Such evidence is not confined to a general opinion of the unreliability of his evidence, but may give all the matters necessary to show not only the foundation of and the reasons for the diagnosis but also the extent to which the credibility of the witness is affected.
>
> (at 609)

However, as we shall see when we consider the opinion rule (see *post*, paras **8.15** ff), such evidence can only be called if the witness suffers from an abnormality of the mind. Thus, in *W* (2000) 20 December, transcript no 2000/04/374/X2), the accused was convicted of indecently assaulting M, who had stayed overnight at his home after consuming liberal quantities of liquor. On appeal, W sought to call a neuro-psychiatrist to testify that M may have dreamed the entire incident, which had its bizarre side, whilst in a state of 'confusional arousal' with sexual feelings brought on by deep sleep induced by her high alcohol intake. The Court of Appeal ruled that such evidence was inadmissible because vivid experiences and thoughts during sleep and when waking up were well within the normal experience of a jury. They did not derive from anything that could be designated an abnormality of the mind.

The Crown's right to reopen its case

4.60 The Crown may exceptionally, at the discretion of the court, obtain leave to present additional evidence after the close of the defence case. As Cassels J remarked in *Browne* (1943) 29 Cr App R 106:

> A little regularity about the conduct of criminal proceedings and trial by indictment is not unbecoming. It is not right to regard the procedure as being in the nature of a committee of inquiry, where one member of the committee after another gets up and makes various suggestions, and at various intervals people are called in to give evidence. There is a stage for the evidence of the prosecution. There is a stage for the evidence of the defence. Then there is a stage for the summing-up and it is wrong . . . for evidence to be called at the end of a case . . . unless it comes within certain well-recognised principles.

Similar remarks were made in *Munnery* (1990) 94 Cr App R 164, where Mustill LJ emphasised that the standard procedure is for prosecution and defence consecutively to present their entire cases. It would often be unfair if the defendant, having based his defence upon the evidence the prosecution initially produces, were to find that the Crown was then allowed to call further evidence which would possibly have dictated a quite different defence strategy. As Mustill LJ went on to explain:

> Tactics are a legitimate part of the adversarial process, but justice is what matters: justice to the public, represented by the prosecution, as well as to the defendant.
>
> (at 172)

4.61 The court in criminal cases nevertheless enjoys discretion to allow the prosecution to call additional evidence. This power is not clearly circumscribed and, it must be emphasised, the grant of leave to the Crown to reopen its case is entirely discretionary. As the Court of Appeal stressed in *Munnery*, in the final analysis 'justice is what matters; justice to the public, represented by the prosecution, as well as to the defendant'. Characteristically, the discretion centres upon three principal categories of situation.

- *Firstly*, if the prosecution has inadvertently omitted to prove some technical matter—not a matter of real substance, however—the court will commonly allow the Crown to prove such a thing after the close of the prosecution case. Similarly, the Crown may be allowed to introduce evidence that was previously omitted through pure oversight.

- *Secondly*, if evidence was not called during the Crown's case simply because it was unavailable at that time, if it is felt to be the just course the court may allow the prosecution to introduce it later in proceedings. Thus, in *Doran* (1972) 56 Cr App R 429 two members of the public, who had been attending the trial, came forward during the course of the trial only when they realised that they could give material testimony.

- *Thirdly*, the prosecution may apply to reopen its case under the so-called *ex improviso* principle. This Latin tag simply refers to cases where, through no fault of its own, the prosecution has been taken unawares by the direction that the defence has taken. In essence, if the prosecution ought reasonably to have foreseen that the issue could arise, discretion is most unlikely to be exercised in its favour (*Milliken* (1969) 53 Cr App R 330). In *O'Hadhmaill* [1996] Crim LR 509, however, in his closing speech to the jury, counsel acting for a university lecturer in sociology and self-confessed member of the IRA who was on trial for possession of bomb-making equipment, suddenly suggested that as peace talks were in progress between the British government and the IRA, it was unlikely that the IRA would be planning a mainland bombing campaign. The Court of Appeal held that the trial judge had properly allowed the Crown to call rebuttal evidence to show that the IRA bombing campaign was in fact still continuing.

4.62 Although these represent the principal situations in which the courts customarily may allow the prosecution to reopen the case, as Lloyd LJ observed in *Francis*

(1990) 91 Cr App R 271:

> There is a wider discretion. We refrain from defining precisely the limit of that discretion since we cannot foresee all the circumstances in which it might fall to be exercised. It is of the essence of any discretion that it should be kept flexible. But lest there be any misunderstanding and lest it be thought that we are opening the door too wide, we would echo what was said by Edmund-Davies LJ in the *Doran* case (1972) 56 Cr App R 429 at 437 that the discretion is one which should only be exercised outside the two established exceptions on the rarest of occasions.
>
> (at 275)

4.63　The court must be alert to the overall interests of justice, and particularly to the risk of prejudice to the defendant, operating by the rough rule of thumb that 'the later the stage in the proceedings when the application to call further evidence is made the more difficult the task of the prosecution becomes' to persuade the court to exercise discretion in its favour, bearing in mind also the nature of the evidence it is proposed to call and its likely effect upon the proceedings (*Khatibi v DPP* (2004) 168 JP 361 at [6] *per* Nelson J). Nevertheless, as Stanley Burnton J stressed in *Malcolm v DPP* [2007] 1 WLR 1230 at [31], an appeal from a decision of justices, one consequence of Criminal Procedure Rules, r 3.3, which requires parties to assist the court in active case management, is that: 'Criminal trials are no longer to be treated as a game, in which each move is final and any omission by the prosecution leads to its failure.' If the defence has not made clear the real issues in the case at latest before the close of the Crown case, this failure can provide the justices with grounds to allow the prosecution to lay more evidence before them, even when, after retirement, they have returned to court and begun to deliver their verdict.

4.64　In civil cases, too, even prior to the advent of CPR, r 32.1 (see *ante*, para **4.2**), the judge enjoyed discretion to allow a party to call evidence after it had closed its case. In *Neigut v Hanania* (1983) Times, 6 January, Stuart-Smith J held that this discretion was not confined to cases where a party had been taken by surprise or misled, but extended to any situation where the interests of justice dictated such a course of action. As Lord Atkin once aptly remarked, in a very different context, 'Finality is a good thing: but justice is better' (*Ras Behari Lal v King-Emperor* (1933) 50 TLR 1, 2).

Special protections extended to various classes of witness in criminal cases

4.65　During the latter portion of the twentieth century, it came to be accepted that certain categories of witness—notably, children and victims of sexual attacks—were deserving of particular solicitude when testifying before criminal courts. Although some of the rules detailed below straddle the law of evidence and the law of criminal procedure, they impinge so clearly upon the rules of evidence that it would be perverse to ignore them.

Restrictions on the cross-examination of sexual complainants on their previous sexual histories

4.66 It used to be commonplace in trials for sexual offences, and for rape in particular, for the victims to be cross-examined, sometimes aggressively, about their previous sexual history. The questioning was often designed simply to undermine the victim's credibility. Increasingly, however, the fairness and the relevance of such cross-examination came to be doubted. The victim's sexual history, it is now widely thought, will prove quite irrelevant in most sexual assault cases, especially in enabling the tribunal of fact to infer whether or not the victim consented to intercourse or sexual activity on the particular occasion charged.

4.67 Parliament first addressed this issue in the Sexual Offences (Amendment) Act 1976. This legislation set out to restrict the range of situations in which such cross-questioning would be permitted. However, research was to suggest that, despite the fact that the Act only allowed such questioning to take place with the leave of the court, cross-examination on previous sexual history was still being permitted quite routinely and rape complainants continued to suffer the indignity of having the intimate details of their personal lives raked over publicly in court—an ordeal which, it was strenuously argued, had little or no bearing on the issues in the case. Moved by these considerations, the legislature introduced far tougher restrictions on cross-examination in the Youth Justice and Criminal Evidence Act 1999, s 41. Some would now suggest that the rules are so restrictive of defence questioning that the pendulum has, if anything, swung too far in the opposite direction. Indeed, in July 2004 a study, sponsored by the Criminal Bar Association, investigated judicial views on the 1999 Act. This research revealed widespread disquiet amongst judges that the present, narrowly drawn rules, by excluding relevant evidence of the complainant's sexual history, might actually lead to miscarriages of justice ('Law' section, *The Times*, 20 July 2004, 5). The current rules are certainly convoluted and difficult of application, as the following exchange between judge and counsel in *Mukadi* [2004] Crim LR 373, [2003] EWCA Crim 3866 at [37]–[39] confirms:

> *Mantell LJ*: These are matters that trial judges grapple with on a daily basis.
>
> *Counsel*: My Lord, yes.
>
> *Mantell LJ*: They are not helped when sections are drafted in the terms of s 41, are they?

4.68 *The prohibition.* Section 41(1) of the 1999 Act contains the following explicit prohibition:

> If at a trial a person is charged with a sexual offence, then, except with the leave of the court—
>
> (a) no evidence may be adduced, and
>
> (b) no question may be asked in cross-examination,
>
> by or on behalf of any accused at the trial, about any sexual behaviour of the complainant.

As we shall see, the court's ability to allow such questioning or to allow such evidence to be led is tightly circumscribed. Indeed, s 41(4) expressly lays down that a court must not grant leave to the defence if it would be reasonable to assume that the purpose, or at least the main purpose, behind the questioning or the leading of sexual history evidence is to establish or to elicit material for impugning the credibility of the complainant as a witness. The potential breadth of this provision is brought home by the ruling in *C and B* [2003] EWCA Crim 29. The accused, who were charged with sexual offences against their two seven-year-old twins, had wished to bring out in cross-examination that the twins had made complaints of abuse against two other parties as well as against the parents. Mance LJ held that this line of questioning fell within s 41 and that the trial judge had been correct to consider that leave was required before such questions could be asked. They related to the complainants' sexual behaviour and experience. This was because it would not have been possible for the accused to introduce evidence suggesting that the complaints against third parties were in fact false, given that the only motive for the defendants seeking to ask about these other complaints would have been to discredit the twins:

> [I]f evidence is adduced about complaints that cannot be properly challenged as false, then the intention must be to elicit that other sexual behaviour or experience, the subject of such complaints, and so to deploy it in one way or another to the complainant's discredit, eg by arguing that it has been wrongly transposed and attributed to the present defendant in the complainant's account.
>
> (at [27])

4.69 *'Sexual behaviour'.* Significantly, the 'sexual behaviour' to which the Act refers is defined in s 42(1)(c) as:

> ... any sexual behaviour or other sexual experience, whether or not involving any accused or other person...

The prohibition is wide. It has been held to extend to general evidence of a victim's sexual orientation. In *B* [2007] EWCA Crim 23, [2007] Crim LR 910 the defendant, whose answer to a charge of homosexual rape was that it had been a casual, consensual encounter, was refused leave to adduce evidence that the victim was a practising homosexual who was accustomed to engage in ano-receptive intercourse. As in the case of female complainants, the court argued, s 41 was predicated upon the basis that previous consent was not normally any evidence of present consent. Although evidence of 'orientation' might not amount to exactly the same thing as evidence of 'any sexual behaviour' referred to in s 41(1)(c), such evidence would be suggestive of prior sexual experience and therefore fell within the prohibition put in place by s. 41 of the 1999 Act.

4.70 The virtual blanket prohibition on any reference being made, even to the accused's previous relations with the complainant, can actually jeopardise the fairness of some rape trials. This problem has already necessitated the intervention of the House of Lords, which in *A (No 2)* [2002] 1 AC 45 sought to reconcile the defendant's restricted right to cross-examine his accuser under the 1999 Act with the defendant's right of fair trial guaranteed under Article 6 of the European Convention on Human Rights. Even in this most emotive of contexts, Lord Bingham of Cornhill's general comments on the right of fair trial, made in *Brown v Stott* [2001] 2 WLR 817 at 825, need to be borne in mind:

> There is nothing to suggest that the fairness of the trial itself may be qualified, compromised or restricted in any way, whatever the circumstances and whatever the public interest in convicting the offender. If the trial as a whole is judged to be unfair, a conviction cannot stand.

4.71 *Matters unconnected with 'sexual behaviour'.* Although s 41 places severe restrictions on the accused's freedom of action, the section does not outlaw all cross-examination of sexual complainants touching upon what might be broadly described as sexual matters. It may be possible to hold that particular questioning relates to issues unconnected with the complainant's 'sexual behaviour'. In *RT* [2002] 1 WLR 632, for instance, a man charged with raping his niece was held to have been wrongly refused leave to ask her why she had not mentioned the assault earlier when other sexual allegations were being investigated: the question, the court pointed out, was not about the victim's sexual behaviour, but about why her accusation was slow in forthcoming. Again, in *PB* [2001] EWCA Crim 3042, it was held that B had been incorrectly prevented from asking a young complainant about an allegation, subsequently withdrawn, in which she had initially claimed that both B and another man had together indecently assaulted her. As Mance LJ explained, s 41 did not come into play in this situation:

> [T]he cross-examination proposed did not go to the complainant's sexual behaviour but to whether she had made a prior complaint and whether it was false. That is a critical distinction.
>
> (at [14])

In *MH* [2002] 1 WLR 632, too, a defendant was held to have been entitled to ask the complainant about lies she had told regarding sexual matters: the questions related to her lies, and not to her 'sexual behaviour'. The court, in *MH*, recognised that, because there is a danger that in her answers the complainant may advert to her past sexual behaviour, leave must be sought before such questions are put and, if the witness is accused of having lied, the defence must also have a proper evidential basis for asserting both that the statements were made and that they were untrue.

4.72 *Laying an evidential basis.* In *M(A)* [2009] EWCA Crim 618, [2010] Crim LR 792 Dyson LJ considered what constitutes a proper evidential basis for asserting that a previous complaint was false? He suggested that whilst it is something less than a strong factual foundation for concluding that the previous complaint was false, 'there must be some material from which it could properly be concluded that the complaint was false.' (at [22]). The enquiry is 'fact-sensitive', so there is no point in comparing facts in other cases:

> At one extreme will be cases where a previous complaint was obviously untrue, for example where the complainant admits that it was untrue and the withdrawal is manifestly reliable. It would be absurd if that evidence could not be adduced by the defendant or the subject of cross-examination on the grounds that it is about previous sexual behaviour. The other extreme is the case where the defendant suggests in cross-examination that a previous allegation by the complainant of a sexual offence against a third party is untrue where there is overwhelming evidence that it is true. Most cases are likely to fall between these two extremes. . . . It is not an exercise of discretion. Rather it is a matter for the judge to evaluate on the basis of all the relevant material. . . . [T]he relevant question is whether that material is capable of leading to a conclusion that the previous complaint was false.
>
> (at [23])

Subsequently, in *E(Stephen)* [2009] EWCA Crim 2668, Moore-Bick, LJ stated:

> The cases show that although a defendant has a right to cross-examine the complainant about the truth of a previous statement, the court must be vigilant to ensure that that right is not abused. . . . [I]n order to render such questioning legitimate the defendant must be able to point to material that is capable of supporting (though not which must *inevitably* support) the inference that the previous statement may be false. In the absence of such material any suggestion that it was false is merely a matter of speculation leading to the conclusion that the real purpose of cross-examination is to undermine the complainant's general credibility.
>
> (at [11])

As *E(Stephen)* shows, this enquiry may have to be quite detailed.

4.73 *Evidence of 'sexual behaviour' impugning the complainant's credibility.* Section 41(4) outlaws evidence or questions concerning a complainant's sexual behaviour which are primarily designed to impugn his or her credibility. This provision only applies 'if it appears to the court to be reasonable to assume the purpose (or main purpose) for which it would be adduced or asked is to establish or to elicit material for impugning the credibility of the complainant as a witness'. In *Martin* [2004] 2 Cr App R 22, M, who denied having raped the victim on Wednesday, at trial had been refused leave to ask her whether she had not pestered him for sex, and indeed performed a sex act upon him, on the previous Monday. His rejection of her advances on that occasion was said to have supplied the motive for her having invented her tale about what took place on the Wednesday. Crane J held that although the effect of M's cross-examination would indeed have been to impugn the credibility of the victim, thereby *prima facie* contravening s 41(4), M's questions ought to have been permitted to introduce this evidence:

> [Its] main purpose was to lay the basis for [M's] explanation of the falsity of her allegation... [I]t could be said that the proposed evidence went to his credibility rather than simply to hers. We conclude that, on ordinary principles of interpretation, it was one purpose but not "the purpose" or "the main purpose" of the questions to impugn the credibility of the complainant.

4.74 *Conditions of admissibility.* The court hears all applications for leave to introduce evidence relating to a complainant's sexual history in private, in the absence of the complainant (s 43). In a nutshell, the trial judge may only grant leave if two conditions, as follows, are both met.

- *Condition 1:* The judge may only grant the defence leave to address the victim's sexual history if 'satisfied... that a refusal of leave might have the result of rendering unsafe a conclusion of the jury or... the court on any relevant issue in the case' (s 41(2)(b)). This is an overriding condition which *must* be satisfied in every case.

- *Condition 2:* Additionally, the Act specifies four classes of situation in which leave may be granted. These are:

  - *The relevant issue in the case 'is not an issue of consent'* (s 41(3)(a))—The Act simply decrees that the complainant's sexual history, even with the defendant, is not relevant to determining pure issues of consent. 'Issue of consent', however, is defined in s 42(1)(b), which states that this expression refers only to cases where the question is whether the complainant in fact consented. Thus, it was held that the defence of mistaken belief in consent, recognised in *DPP v Morgan* [1976] AC 182 (admittedly, since superseded by the redefined requirement of an absence of reasonable belief in consent in the Sexual Offences Act 2003, s 1(1)(c)), still afforded grounds for questioning, provided that the questioning also satisfied the overriding condition of s 41(2)(b) and did not infringe s 41(4) (see *ante*, para **4.68**). In *Y* (2001) Times, 13 February, the Court of Appeal accepted that questioning of a complainant about a consensual sexual relationship with Y which had occurred between one and three weeks previous to the offence charged ought to have been permitted provided that it only went towards establishing Y's belief in the complainant's consent, not to consent itself. This was a nice distinction: as Rose LJ ruefully commented, if a judge is required in all seriousness to tell jurors that they may use the fact that Y and the complainant (V) have recently engaged in consensual sexual behaviour only to assist them in deciding whether Y believed that V consented but that they might not use it in determining whether V did actually consent to intercourse with Y on the relevant occasion, the summing-up would have more of a flavour of Lewis Carroll than of a rehearsal of matters of jurisprudence. It is perhaps worth making the point here that under the Sexual Offences Act 2003, s 1(2), although the defence of reasonable belief in consent is now required to be 'determined having regard to all the circumstances', when the Minister was asked during the Bill's passage through Parliament whether the victim's sexual history was relevant to those circumstances, he could only forlornly suggest that evidence of sexual history would be less relevant than before. In truth, it seems impossible to conceive that sexual history will not sometimes be relevant, given that the Act specifically enjoins the court to take into account 'all' the circumstances'.

– *The relevant issue 'is an issue of consent and the sexual behaviour of the complainant to which the evidence or question relates is alleged to have taken place at or about the same time as the event which is the subject matter of the charge against the accused'* (s 41(3)(b))—The idea is that the complainant's conduct at the time of the events may be relevant—for instance, that the complainant had indulged in consensual sexual activity with the defendant earlier the same evening. The evidence must be directly relevant to the issue of consent. Hence, in *Stephenson* [2002] EWCA Crim 1231 S was refused leave to ask the complainant whether she had kissed a number of other young men earlier on the evening when she was raped. Even if she had, it did not bear on the issue whether she would willingly have had intercourse with S. For similar reasons, in *Y* (2001) Times, 13 February, the Court of Appeal found it impossible to construe s 41(3)(b) as applying to events weeks or days or months prior to the alleged rape—a view later endorsed by all five members of the House of Lords on appeal, in *A (No 2)* [2002] 1 AC 45.

– The relevant issue—

is an issue of consent and the sexual behaviour of the complainant to which the evidence or question relates is alleged to have been, in any respect, so similar

   (i) to any sexual behaviour of the complainant which … took place as part of the event which is the subject matter of the charge against the accused, or

(ii) to any other sexual behaviour of the complainant which . . . took place at or about the same time as that event,

that the similarity cannot reasonably be explained as a coincidence.

(s 41(3)(c))

During the parliamentary debates preceding enactment of this bill, one member of the Lords suggested that this would allow admission of evidence that the complainant had indulged her propensity for reenacting the balcony scene from *Romeo and Juliet*. Another suggestion was that a defendant *might* be able to ask the complainant whether she had not been soliciting clients as a prostitute, if his contention is that that is what happened to him—although it has to be said that the words of the statute do not self-evidently predicate this interpretation. In *Wayne* [2009] EWCA Crim 434 V, [2010] Crim LR 54, a teacher, got drunk and took two men home with her, one of them being W, who was homeless. She had encountered them on the street. W, charged with rape, applied for leave to ask V about two letters referring to her earlier psychiatric history. They indicated that in the past she had engaged in risky, casual sex with strangers. The trial judge considered that there was no 'similarity' within the meaning of s 41(3)(c). To have allowed such cross-examination would have been tantamount to saying that the complainant was a person who had engaged in casual sex in the past and therefore would have been likely to do so on the occasion she was with W. Thomas, LJ agreed:

Judgements on what is similar for the purposes of s.41 are not always easy; some cases are easy—see, eg, *T* [2004] 2 Cr App R 552, where the similarity was so clear that it was not disputed—but some, such as this, are not. In this case . . . the judge adopted a view on similarity which was open to him within that margin of judgement open to a decision maker. . . . [H]e was entitled to conclude that what was set out in the letters was not sufficiently similar to what was alleged by the appellant to have happened on the night in issue. He was also entitled to conclude that cross-examination on the basis of what was set out in the two letters would have brought into play matters in relation to her general sexual behaviour and not the similarity of the two occasions.

(at [19])

– *The prosecution has adduced evidence relating to the complainant's previous sexual history (s 41(5))*. This provision has been held to refer only to:

evidence placed before the jury by prosecution witnesses in the course of their evidence in chief and by other witnesses in the course of cross-examination by prosecuting counsel. It does not naturally extend to evidence obtained from prosecution witnesses by the defence in the course of cross-examination.

(*Hamadi* [2007] EWCA Crim 3048 at [20] *per* Moore-Bick LJ)

Even in these cases, however, the defence may only probe such matters to the extent 'necessary to enable the evidence adduced by the prosecution to be rebutted or explained by or on behalf of the accused' (s 41(5)). Although the point proceeded on a concession made by Crown counsel, in *Rooney* [2001] EWCA Crim 2844 it was accepted that since this subsection, which is not to be read in conjunction with s 41(4), allows rebuttal of the complainant's evidence, *ex hypothesi* it must have been Parliament's intention also to permit the impugning of the complainant's credibility as a witness when her evidence falls within s 41(5).

4.75 It is further to be noted that in all of the circumstances enumerated in s 41(3) and (5), s 41(6) additionally requires that:

> The evidence or question must relate to a specific instance (or specific instances) of alleged sexual behaviour on the part of the complainant (and accordingly nothing in those subsections is capable of applying in relation to the evidence or question to the extent that it does not so relate).

For this reason, in *White* [2004] EWCA Crim 946, W was held to have been rightly prevented from asking his victim whether, at the time of the alleged rape, she was not still working as a prostitute. As Laws LJ pointed out, the argument that such evidence is admissible:

> is tantamount to the proposition that any sexual encounter of a complainant will satisfy s 41(6) if it happens to be possible to assign a date and place to that conduct. If that were all the subsection meant it would amount to very little indeed. In our judgment, the subsection only possesses intellectual coherence if it is taken to require that there must be something about the circumstances of a specific episode of alleged sexual conduct by a complainant which has potential probative force. That proposition is, we think, lent added strength by the terms of s 41(3)(c) by which it must be shown that the sexual behaviour sought to be adduced is so similar to the conduct complained of in the proceedings, or other contemporaneous conduct, as to be beyond a coincidence. Clearly that provision can only operate where the behaviour sought to be adduced consists in the specifics of a particular episode or episodes against which the possibility of coincidence can be measured.
>
> (at [16])

4.76 *Compatibility of rape-shield laws with requirements of human rights law.* It is obvious from the foregoing that only in highly exceptional circumstances does the 1999 Act contemplate that D will have need to make reference to the sexual history of the complainant. Tough 'rape-shield' laws have been introduced in other jurisdictions, not always with happy results. In Canada, for instance, in the case of *Seaboyer* (1991) 2 SCR 577, a majority of the Supreme Court held that a law which prevents the trier of fact from getting at the truth by excluding relevant evidence, in the absence of a clear ground of policy or law justifying the exclusion, runs foul of fundamental conceptions of justice and of what constitutes a fair trial. Significantly, the offending provision, s 276 of the Criminal Code, which provided for blanket exclusion of evidence of complainants' sexual history subject to three narrow exceptions, was held to offend against Canada's Charter of Rights and Freedoms. In essence, the Court concluded that although the provision addressed 'a pressing and substantial objective' (namely, the dispelling of the 'twin myths' that someone who engages in consensual sex is more likely to have consented to sexual activity with the defendant and is also less worthy of belief), a provision which excludes probative defence evidence that is not clearly outweighed by the prejudice it may cause to the trial strikes the wrong balance and unnecessarily impairs the rights of the defence. The Canadian provision has since been redrafted to take account of these strictures, and the new version has withstood scrutiny in the Canadian Supreme Court (see *Darrach* [2000] 2 SCR 443).

4.77 In England, too, the House of Lords, in *A (No 2)* [2002] 1 AC 45, has considered whether the rape-shield provisions of the Youth Justice and Criminal Evidence Act 1999 are compatible with human rights law, and more specifically with the right of fair trial guaranteed under Article 6 of the European Convention. The certified question for the House in *A (No 2)* was:

> May a sexual relationship between a defendant and a complainant be relevant to the issue of consent so as to render its exclusion under s 41 of the [1999 Act] a contravention of the defendant's right of fair trial?

As Lord Steyn pointed out, 'the genesis of the problem before the House' was that s 41 imposes identical exclusionary provisions in respect of a complainant's sexual experience with the accused as with other men, thereby posing 'an acute problem of proportionality' (at [29]–[30]). Whereas an accused's previous sexual relations with the complainant will not inevitably be relevant to the issue of whether the latter consented to intercourse on the occasion which led to the charge, in certain cases those previous relations may be relevant. Lord Hutton circumspectly observed:

> It does not follow…where there has been a recent affectionate relationship between a woman and a man, that one cannot say that the fact that she has consented previously is relevant in deciding whether she consented when there was intercourse with the same man a relatively short time later…Where there has been a recent close and affectionate relationship between the complainant and the defendant it is probable that the evidence will be relevant, not to advance the bare assertion that because she consented in the past she consented on the occasion in question, but (because) evidence of such a relationship will show the complainant's specific mindset towards the defendant, namely her affection for him.
>
> (at [151]–[152])

In *A (No 2)* the accused claimed to have had consensual intercourse with the complainant on a number of occasions during the three weeks preceding the offence charged. Lord Hutton, for one, doubted whether this particular evidence was strong enough to be relevant to the issue of consent (at [154]). The House of Lords nevertheless made clear that it will be for the trial judge in each case actually to determine whether or not the evidence is sufficiently probative to justify admission.

4.78 Once it was acknowledged that evidence of a defendant's prior relations with the complainant may be relevant to the issue of consent in a rape case, the question was whether such evidence could be admitted, applying conventional canons of statutory construction, under s 41 of the 1999 Act. The House concluded that it could not. In particular, even the words of s 41(3)(c), which allow the complainant's previous strongly similar behaviour to form the subject of cross-examination, cannot be stretched under conventional canons to encompass such questioning. In so far as it could therefore serve to prevent defendants in some situations from exploring matters that might be central to their defence, s 41 has the capacity to compromise the overall fairness of those criminal proceedings.

4.79 Since the provision does not adversely affect ' every case', (*per* Lord Hope at [104]) or 'make an excessive inroad into the guarantee of a fair trial' (*per* Lord Steyn at [38]), the House did not feel impelled to declare s 41 incompatible with human rights law *tout court*. Rather, it sought to interpret the section in a manner compatible with the demands of Article 6 of the Convention. Section 3 of the Human Rights Act 1998 provided the solution, to the extent that it requires that 'so far as it is possible to do so, primary legislation ... must be read and given effect in a way which is compatible with the Convention rights'. Although s 41(3)(c) only permits cross-examination to the issue of consent when the previous conduct is 'so similar to ... any other sexual behaviour of the complainant which ... took place *at or about the same time as the event*, that the similarity cannot be explained as a coincidence' (emphasis added), as Lord Steyn explained:

> Section 3 requires the court to subordinate the niceties of the language of s 41(3)(c), and in particular the touchstone of coincidence, to broader considerations of relevance judged by logical and common sense criteria of time and circumstances. After all, it is realistic to proceed on the basis that the legislature would not, if alerted to the problem, have wished to deny the right to an accused to put forward a full and complete defence by advancing truly probative material. It is therefore possible under s 3 to read s 41, and in particular s 41(3)(c), as subject to the implied provision that evidence or questioning that is required to ensure a fair trial under art 6 of the Convention should not be treated as inadmissible.
>
> (at [45])

The test of admissibility to be applied by the trial judge in every case will therefore be, due regard being paid to the importance of protecting complainants from unnecessary indignities:

> Is ... the evidence (and questioning in relation to it) ... nevertheless so relevant to the issue of consent that to exclude it would endanger the fairness of the trial under Art 6 of the Convention?
>
> (at [46] *per* Lord Steyn).

4.80 The principle elaborated in *A (No 2)* was applied in *R* [2003] EWCA Crim 2754. It was held that R, who was accused of raping C in August 2000, had been wrongly prevented from asking C about consensual intercourse that had taken place between the parties both previously to and subsequently to the date of the alleged offence. Although the strict wording of s 41 of the 1999 Act excluded the admission of evidence of events that had respectively taken place in April 2000 and around July 2001, as in *A (No 2)*, the Court of Appeal decided that in view of its relevance to the question of whether C had consented, the exclusion of this evidence had deprived R of a fair trial. It must nevertheless be stressed that the House of Lords decision in *A (No 2)* does not signify that all defendants will be accorded greater latitude in cross-examining victims of sexual assaults on their previous sexual experience. *A (No 2)* was not intended to signal a general return to the pre-1999, let alone the pre-1976, regime. This emerges clearly in *White* [2004] EWCA Crim 946 (see *ante*, para **4.75**). W, who stood charged with rape, had claimed that the victim had consented. The Court of Appeal unhesitatingly refused to allow W to question the complainant on the fact that she had for 19 years operated as a prostitute. As was made abundantly clear, whatever the position may once have been, a prostitute is as entitled as anyone else to say 'No' and the fact that a victim is a prostitute does not normally affect the issue of whether she consented to sexual relations. In the absence of special circumstances that had probative force and were so similar to the conduct complained of as to be beyond coincidence, even allowing for *A (No 2)*, such cross-examination was strictly outlawed.

4.81 In *A (No 2)* the House of Lords was concerned to render s 41(3)(c) compatible with human rights law. Although human rights law is most likely to be engaged when a defendant claims to have enjoyed a prior sexual relationship with the complainant, Moore-Bick LJ in *Hamadi* [2007] EWCA Crim 3048 made clear that s 3 of the Human Rights Act 1998 can play a role in the construction of other exceptions created by s 41—to wit, s 41(5):

> Their Lordships [in *A (No 2)*] were not, of course, concerned with the provisions of s 41(5), but they clearly attached the importance to the need to construe s 41(3)(c) in a way which will ensure a fair trial. That ... is the fundamental principle underlying their decision and accordingly we think that in order to ensure a fair trial there may be cases in which the

accused ought to be allowed to call evidence to explain or rebut something said by a prosecution witness in cross-examination about the complainant's sexual behaviour which was not deliberately elicited by defence counsel and is potentially damaging to the accused's case. For that reason we would accept that subs (5) has to be read in the somewhat broader sense that its language might otherwise suggest in order to accommodate such cases.

(at [21])

4.82 A further point should perhaps be mentioned. Whenever a defendant seeks to introduce evidence of a complainant's sexual behaviour or sexual experience under s 41 of the 1999 Act, the court may need to give a ruling not only on s 41 admissibility, but also under the Criminal Justice Act 2003, s 100 if the complainant's alleged sexual behaviour amounts to evidence of bad character within the meaning of ss 98 and 112(1) of the latter enactment (see, eg, *V* [2006] EWCA Crim 1901 at [25] *per* Crane J; see *ante*, paras **4.28** ff).

4.83 In June 2006 the Home Office published a gloomy report, reviewing the achievements of the 1999 legislation (Kelly, Temkin and Griffiths, *Section 41: An Evaluation of New Legislation Limiting Sexual History Evidence in Rape Trials*). Its authors noted that conviction rates in rape cases had continued to fall after 1999; that it would seem that sexual history continues to be employed quite regularly in rape trials to undermine complainants' credibility; that the judicial approach to the cross-examination of complainants under s 41 tends to be indulgent— particularly where defendants allege a previous relationship with the victim; that not infrequently sexual history evidence appears to be admitted regularly by agreement between the parties or without explicit reference to the Act; that 'the success of the reform ... has been undermined by *R v A (No 2)*'; and that there may be a correlation between the admission of sexual history evidence and the acquittal rate in rape cases. The report concludes by saying that 'the legislation has been evaded, circumvented and resisted, and ... the prosecution is reluctant to pursue cases which require grappling with these complex, contested areas'. A recent report (Thomas, *Are Juries Fair?* (February 2010, Ministry of Justice Research series 1/10) esp pp 31–2 gives a less dispiriting picture of rape prosecutions and conviction rates.

Protection of sexual complainants, child witnesses and others from cross-examination by the defendant in person

4.84 Traditionally, accused persons have had the right to conduct their own defence in court. They have also enjoyed what might be termed a right of confrontation: that is, the right to challenge in person the case put by their accuser. Some defendants have taken full advantage of this privilege. However, following some highly publicised rape trials in which defendants subjected their accusers to humiliating and unnecessarily prolonged cross-examination, and with a growing public feeling that the law ought to afford greater safeguards for the more vulnerable categories of witness, the legislature introduced major procedural changes in the Youth Justice and Criminal Evidence Act 1999, restricting the accused's right to cross-examine vulnerable witnesses in person. This 1999 Act legislates for three principal classes of case:

- Section 34 now provides that no one charged with a sexual offence, as defined in s 62 of the Act, may in any criminal proceedings cross-examine the complainant in person either in regard to the offence committed against the complainant or with regard to any other offence with which the defendant is charged;

- in similar vein, s 35 forbids the defendant from cross-examining in person either:

  - child complainants and other child witnesses under 17 years of age if he is charged with one of the sexual offences enumerated in s 35(3); or

  - child complainants and other child witnesses under the age of 14 if he is charged with kidnapping, false imprisonment, child abduction or 'any offence . . . which involves an assault on, or injury or a threat of injury to, any person' (on how this text might be interpreted, see *ante*, para **3.16**);

- additionally, under s 36 the prosecutor may apply to the court for an order preventing the accused from cross-examining any particular witness in person, or the court may raise the matter of its own motion. The court may only issue such an order, however, if three conditions are satisfied. It must appear to the court:

  (i) that the quality of that witness's evidence on cross-examination is likely to be diminished if the defendant cross-examines in person (taking into account a list of factors enumerated in s 36(3));

  (ii) that the quality is likely to be improved if the defendant were prohibited from cross-examining in person; and

  (iii) that it would not be contrary to the interests of justice to give such a direction.

If the court prevents an accused from cross-examining in person in any of these circumstances, the accused is given an opportunity to nominate a representative to act for him. In the event of his not doing so, if the court feels that this would be in the interests of justice, the court must nominate a legal representative to cross-examine the witness on his behalf. Additionally, in a trial on indictment the judge must warn the jury against drawing an adverse inference from the fact that the accused has been prevented from cross-examining the witness in person. (It has been suggested that a similar prohibition on defendants cross-examining victims of sexual abuse in person might be introduced in civil cases too: *H v L* [2007] FLR 162 at [25] *per* Roderick Evans J).

The provision made for protecting the welfare of children and young persons tried in the Crown Court

4.85 Following the judgment delivered by the ECtHR in Strasbourg in the case of *V v UK; T v UK* (1999) 30 EHRR 121, Lord Bingham CJ issued a practice direction governing trials of 'young defendants' in the Crown Court (*Practice Note (Trial of Children and Young Persons)* [2000] 2 All ER 285; see now *The Consolidated Criminal Practice Direction* [2002] 2 Cr App R 35, [Part III.30.3–17]). This followed in the aftermath of the trial of the two juveniles convicted of the murder of James Bulger, where the public was treated to the spectacle of young children, who appeared to understand very little of what was going on around them, standing trial on the most serious charge in the criminal calendar in Liverpool Crown Court. The direction's purpose was to extend to proceedings in relation to vulnerable persons (not just children) in the adult courts procedures analogous to those in use in youth courts, where children and young persons will normally be tried.

4.86 The practice direction ordained that the ordinary trial process was to be adapted so far as necessary to spare young defendants 'avoidable intimidation, humiliation or distress' and to assist them to understand and participate in the proceedings. Judges should, as far as possible, give their directions ahead of trial at the pleas and directions hearing. The Lord Chief Justice suggested a number of potential palliative measures. Young defendants, for instance, might be allowed to visit the courtroom where their trial was to take place out of court hours to familiarise themselves with the *locaux*. If the case was liable to attract strong public and/ or media interest (as occurred in the Bulger case), the police should be enlisted to take steps to avoid young defendants being exposed to intimidation, vilification or abuse. Trials should, if possible, be held in courtrooms where everyone was situated physically on the same level. Young defendants should, if they so desired, be allowed to sit with members of their families and always be able to have easy, informal communication with their legal representatives. The court should explain its procedures to them in terms they could understand, should remind their legal representatives of their continuing obligation to explain each step of the trial to them, and should ensure that the trial is conducted in language intelligible to young defendants. The trial timetable should take account of young defendants having shorter attention spans than adults. Robes and wigs should not be worn, unless young defendants requested this or the court for good reason ordered that they be worn. There should be no recognisable police presence in the courtroom, and those responsible for young defendants' security should not be in uniform.

Public access to the courtroom should be restricted to those with an immediate and direct interest in the case.

4.87 The foregoing measures were designed to promote the welfare of young defendants, recognising the fact that defendants appearing in the Crown Court are occasionally either very young or very immature. The steps the court orders must take into account in each case the age, maturity and development (both intellectual and emotional) of the young or vulnerable defendant concerned.

'Special measure directions' available to assist vulnerable and intimidated witnesses

4.88 Recognising that certain types of witness encounter especial difficulty when testifying in court in criminal cases, Part II of the Youth Justice and Criminal Evidence Act 1999 allows courts to issue 'special measure directions' in respect of three categories of witness. The relevant provisions (ss 16–32) descend into almost obsessive detail. A *précis*, therefore, cannot provide anything like a full account of these complex provisions. In outline, however, there are three categories of witness who are deemed deserving of special consideration:

- children under the age of 17 (s 16(1)(a), shortly to be raised to 18 by the Coroners and Justice Act 2009);
- witnesses, other than the accused, who suffer from a physical or mental disorder, or who have a disability or impairment of intelligence and social functioning that is likely to diminish the quality of their evidence (s 16(1)(b) and 16(2));
- witnesses whose evidence is likely to be affected by their fear or distress at having to testify in the proceedings (s 17(1)). The Act specifies factors to which the court must particularly attend when deciding whether or not a witness is eligible under s 17(1)—such matters as the nature of the offence; the witness's age; the witness's social, cultural, ethnic and domestic circumstances; and any behaviour towards the witness on the part of the accused, his family and associates, or any other person who is likely to be an accused or a witness in the proceedings (s 17(2)). The court must also take the witness's expressed views into account (s 17(3)). Complainants in sexual offences are automatically eligible under this provision unless the witness has informed the court that she does not wish to be so eligible (s 17(4)).

Apart from children and sexual complainants, in determining whether a witness is eligible for special measures directions the question for the court is whether or not the quality of that witness's evidence 'is likely to be diminished' if directions are not issued. Quality of evidence here refers to 'its quality in terms of completeness, coherence and accuracy' (s 16(5)).

4.89 Rule 29(1) of the Criminal Procedure Rules imposes time limits within which applications for special measures directions must be made. A party may apply for these limits to be extended (r. 29(2)) and applications may also be received out of time (r. 29(3)). A court that decides that a witness is eligible for a special measures direction has a number of special measures available to it. But in deciding whether to order them, s 19(2) says that it

> must then—
>
> (a) determine whether any of the special measures available in relation to the witness (or any combination of them) would, in its opinion, be likely to improve the quality of evidence given by the witness; and
>
> (b) if so—
>> (i) determine which of those measures (or combination of them) would, in its opinion, be likely to maximise so far as practicable the quality of such evidence; and
>> (ii) give a direction . . . providing for the measure or measures so determined to apply to evidence given by the witness.

In deciding whether to make special measures directions the court must take into account any views expressed by the witness and, more particularly, 'whether the measure or measures might tend to inhibit such evidence being effectively tested by a party to the proceedings' (s 19(3)). As can be seen, the legislature's aims are laudable. The court is to do what it feels appropriate to enhance the quality of evidence given by prosecution and defence witnesses of proven or assumed susceptibility, while at the same time ensuring that the rights of the opposing party are protected.

4.90 What special measures are available to the court? This depends in part upon the class of witness concerned. The law is especially solicitous of child witnesses. The degree of protection to which they are entitled under the 1999 Act varies according to whether or not they qualify as being 'in need of special protection'.

4.91 (1) *Child witnesses in general*—The legislation is especially sensitive to the needs of children. Section 21 imposes what it terms 'the primary rule' according to which the court:

- 'must provide for any relevant recording to be admitted' if the child's evidence-in-chief has been video recorded; *and*

- must also provide for any additional evidence given by that witness, whether in-chief or in cross-examination, to be given by means of a live link (s 21(3)).

The primary rule does not apply, however, if 'the court is satisfied that compliance with it would not be likely to maximise the quality of the witness's evidence so far as practicable' (s 21(4)(c)).

4.92 (2) *Child witnesses 'in need of special protection'*—If the proceedings relate to any offence specified in s 35 (notably, this includes sexual offences, kidnapping, false imprisonment, child abduction and assaults or threats of injury to any person), then the child witness is considered to be 'in need of special protection'. In such cases, if the court orders the admission of video-recorded examination-in-chief of the child, it must also make provision for video-recorded cross-examination ('otherwise than by the accused in person') and video-recorded re-examination of that witness.

4.93 (3) *Vulnerable witnesses*—The Act provides for a battery of protective measures which the court may order if satisfied that they are likely to maximise the quality of the witness's evidence. A number of these measures have been in use for years, but their ordering is now codified. The following special measures directions may be ordered by the court.

- *Screening of the witness*—Provided that the court, the legal representatives and the tribunal of fact can see the witness, a screen 'or other arrangement' may be erected shielding the witness from seeing the accused (s 23). As Jack J observed in *R (CPS) v Stoke-on-Trent Magistrates' Court* [2007] EWHC 3110 (Admin) at [5], 'The use of screens pursuant to the 1996 Act is now commonplace'. However, if it renders the witness anonymous, other issues arise (see further *post*, paras **9.104** ff).

The manner in which screens are deployed in the courtroom may be of importance. In *Att-Gen for the Sovereign Base Areas of Akrotiri and Dhekelia v Steinhoff* [2005] UKPC 31, although all five judges were agreed that a new trial was called for, this issue gave rise to a significant difference of opinions in the Judicial Committee. The case concerned the rape of a housemaid. The victim had been shielded in the courtroom in such a way that only one counsel at a time could see her. It was agreed that this had given rise to a breach of the Youth Justice and Criminal Evidence Act 1999, s 23(2) because the trial court, in its reasoning, had relied upon the way in which the victim had reacted at a time when defence counsel could not observe her. The question was whether this had led to a 'substantial miscarriage of justice' under the local Criminal Procedure Ordinance. The majority of the Privy Council determined that it had not. Baroness Hale, for example, rested her reasoning upon the following factors: (i) defence counsel had accepted the situation, and had not objected at the time to the arrangement of the screen (at [19]); (ii) the assertion that 'face-to-face confrontation is not an essential requirement of a fair trial in the law of England and Wales...' (at [16]); (iii) the consideration that, apparently, 'demeanour during examination-in-chief and re-examination is much less important than during cross-examination'; (iv) that the trial had been conducted by 'experienced professional judges...Had they been a jury, the defence would not have been able to complain' because no reasons for the verdict would have been given; and (v) because it was not right for an appellate court to retry a case since the original judges would have been in a better position to assess the credibility and demeanour of the witnesses. (One might just wonder: if it is so important for the original judges to view the witnesses, why is it not equally important for the defendant's counsel to have that opportunity also?) Lords Rodger of Earlsferry and Brown of Eaton-under-Heywood delivered a short but compelling dissenting opinion, concluding that S had not had a fair trial. The trial court's judgment showed that it had paid great heed to the victim's reaction, and that this reaction had not been visible either to S or to his counsel (at [31]: 'the long and the short of it is, therefore, that [S] was entirely unaware of what was judged to be a highly significant piece of evidence against him until it came to be mentioned in the court's reasons for convicting him'. It is suggested that para [32] of the dissenting opinion, which discusses the importance of all parties being able to view the witness, is crushing and exposes the serious weaknesses in the majority's arguments. Even if it could be said that S's counsel was partly to blame for this predicament by not lodging an objection, that surely does not justify an unfair trial (at [33]). *Steinhoff,* a Privy Council decision, is only of persuasive authority in an English court. It might be hoped that our domestic courts could adopt a more robust stance should this situation arise again.

- *Evidence by live link*—As s 24(8) explains, this means 'a live television link or other arrangement whereby a witness, while absent from the courtroom...is able to see and hear a person there and to be seen and heard by [the court, the jury, the legal representatives, any interpreter or other person appointed to assist the witness]'. Baroness Hale, in *R (D) v Camberwell Youth Court* [2005] 1 WLR 393, observed that the accused is omitted from this list, 'for the unfortunate reason that the list is taken from that referring to the use of screens'. Section 24(8), she suggested, 'is not an exclusive definition'. Therefore:

    > If the accused is in the courtroom, the court would and normally should, in the exercise of its power to ensure a fair trial, arrange matters so that he can see the witness too.
    >
    > (at [27])

- *Evidence given in private*—If the case involves a sexual offence or if 'it appears to the court that there are reasonable grounds for believing that any person other than the accused has sought, or will seek, to intimidate the witness', the court has wide powers to clear the courtroom. Basically, it may exclude any persons it chooses whilst the witness is giving evidence, other than the accused, the parties' legal representatives, interpreters, persons appointed to assist the witness and at least one member of the press corps. Interestingly, in *Richards* (1999)

163 JP 246 (*ante*, para **4.9**) the Court of Appeal has already gone further than this, holding that if a judge feels that clearing the courtroom is the only way of ensuring that justice is done, even if a witness is only saying that she would feel uncomfortable if she had to testify in public, he is entitled to take this action. Moreover, the Court also ruled that such an order will not infringe the right to a 'fair and *public* hearing' guaranteed by Article 6 of the ECHR since that Article allows the exclusion of the press and the public 'to the extent strictly necessary...in special circumstances where publicity would prejudice the interests of justice'. The courts will of course need to bear the 'strictly necessary' test in mind when issuing special measures directions under s 25.

• *Removal of wigs and gowns* (s 26).

• *Video-recorded evidence in-chief* (s 27)—Anxious to ensure that the admission of evidence-in-chief in the form of video recordings should not operate too prejudicially to the accused, a number of conditions attach to the admission of video-recorded evidence-in-chief.

  – First, there is a general condition that neither all nor part of such video recording may be admitted 'if the court is of opinion, having regard to all the circumstances of the case, that in the interests of justice the recording...should not be so admitted' (s 27(2)). Thus, the accused can make representations arguing for exclusion of the video recording. In determining whether to do so the court is to weigh the resulting prejudice to the accused if the video recording is admitted against 'the desirability of showing the whole, or substantially the whole, of the recorded interview' (s 27(3)). It is perhaps worth adding that if this latter phrase were given an unrestricted, literal interpretation, it might found a claim that Parliament's reference in s 27 to 'showing the whole...interview' was intended generally to override the conventional common law rules governing the admissibility of evidence in the case of video-recorded interviews, thereby allowing the prosecution to rely upon statements made by a witness at interview relating to matters adverse to the accused which in the normal run of events would have been excluded from evidence. In *R (CPS, Harrow) v Brentford Youth Court* (2003) 167 JP 614, appeal was taken against a trial judge's decision to exclude a videotape in which the victim had alleged a number of additional incidents against the accused, which did not fall within the restrictive rules governing the admissibility of bad character evidence (see generally, Chapter 7, *post*). The Divisional Court rightly dismissed this extravagant construction, holding that, even though it refers to 'the whole...of the recorded interview', s 27 did not set out to alter the general rules of evidence. Not only does s 31(5) of the 1999 Act actually state this, but as a matter of policy it is clear that the purposes pursued by s 27 are far narrower. On the one hand, it resolves the long-running debate on the comparative merits of video-recorded and live evidence. On the other, s 27(3) more specifically allows inadmissible material to be viewed by the court in exceptional cases in order to help it to determine whether a special measures direction needs to be issued; this provision was never meant to permit the subsequent admission of otherwise inadmissible evidence. It would, after all, be most bizarre if evidence which, if sought to be given orally, would be excluded by the court, became admissible by a side wind simply because it chanced to be presented in the form of an unedited video recording.

- There is so-called 'achieving best evidence' (ABE) guidance on how video recordings of children ought to be made. In *Powell* [2006] 1 Cr App R 31 the very young complainant was not interviewed until nine weeks after the alleged indecent assault. Because there is evidence that some children forget very quickly and that their memories can become contaminated more readily than those of adults, even though the nine-week delay could be explained, Scott Baker LJ was disturbed by this occurrence:

> [T]he plain fact is that where a case depends on the evidence of a very young child it is absolutely essential (a) that the ABE interview takes place very soon after the event and (b) that the trial (at which the child has to be cross-examined) takes place very soon thereafter...Looking at this case with hindsight, it was completely unacceptable that the appellant should have been tried for an offence proof of which relied on the evidence of a three-and-a-half year old when the trial did not take place until over nine months had passed from the date of the alleged offence. Special efforts must be made to fast-track cases of this kind and it is simply not an option to wait weeks for example for forensic evidence to become available.
>
> (at [41])

What is the status of a video recording that has not followed the ABE code of best practice? In *K* (2006) 170 JP 558, the trial judge admitted in evidence a child's video recording made in breach of ABE guidelines. In particular, the victim's mother had been present during the interviews and appeared to have coaxed her daughter into making her most serious allegations against the father. Having first noted that the Youth Justice and Criminal Evidence Act 1999, s 27 stipulates that there is a strong presumption in favour of the use of special measures, Hooper LJ held that in determining the admissibility of recordings made in breach of ABE guidance a court had to ask itself: were the breaches such that a reasonable jury properly directed could not be sure that the witness gave a credible and accurate account in the video interview? The prime consideration where breaches have occurred is the reliability of the videoed evidence. Its reliability will normally be assessed by reference to the interview itself, the conditions under which it was held, the age of the child, and the nature and extent of any breaches of the Code. Although other evidence in the case may occasionally demonstrate that the breaches have not had the effect of undermining the credibility or accuracy of the video interview, reference to such evidence should be undertaken with considerable caution since other evidence will rarely assist as to the credibility, accuracy and completeness of a video interview.

– If a special measures direction issues under s 27, the witness concerned *must* be called to be cross-examined in person unless:

   (a) an additional direction issues (under s 28) ordering that the cross-examination also take place *via* video recording; or

   (b) the parties have agreed that the witness need not be made available.

– Following cross-examination, the court may wish to alter its view as to a child witness's competence to testify at all (see *ante*, paras **3.3** ff). This matter may require to be reconsidered in some cases. In *Powell* [2006] 1 Cr App R 31, a child, three-and-a-half years of age, complained that she had been indecently assaulted by an uncle during the course of a party. The judge initially held that the child passed the competence threshold under s 53(1) of the 1999 Act, and her evidence-in-chief was duly admitted in the form of a video recording. During cross-examination, however, the complainant was reluctant to speak at all and even appeared to concede the truth of P's defence that she had spoken to her mother because P had earlier told her off and she thought that P might tell her mother. Scott Baker LJ felt that it was:

   ... unfortunate that the judge was not requested to revisit her decision on competence at the end of the complainant's evidence... What is relevant is the complainant's competence to give evidence at the time of the appellant's trial. It may be it was due to the lapse of time and lack of memory that the complainant was unable to understand the questions or give answers to them which could be understood. One simply does not know. The problem is that her answers simply were not intelligible in the context of the case. She was not... a sufficiently competent witness for the defence to be able to put its case. The onus of proof was on the Crown to establish competence and they failed to discharge it.
   (at [33])

– Where video-recorded evidence-in-chief has been admitted and the witness is available to testify, s 27 imposes restrictions on the witness giving additional evidence-in-chief in any other form. Thus the witness may not testify in-chief otherwise than by means of the recording:

   (i) as to any matter which, in the opinion of the court, has been dealt with adequately in the witness's recorded testimony, or

   (ii) without the permission of the court, as to any other matter which, in the opinion of
      the court, is dealt with in that testimony.

     (s 27(5))

- *Video-recorded cross-examination and re-examination*—If the court has ordered video-recorded examination-in-chief under s 27, it may also order the witness's cross-examination and re-examination to be admitted in video-recorded form (s 28). Such recordings must be made in the sight and hearing of the court, the legal representatives and the accused. Normally, the legislation anticipates that such recordings will constitute the witness's entire cross-examination and re-examination. However, the court may order that additional cross-examination be received under a further special measures direction:

if it appears to the court—

(a) that the proposed cross-examination is sought…as a result of that party having become aware, since the time when the original recording was made…, of a matter which that party could not with reasonable diligence have ascertained by then, or

(b) that for any other reason it is in the interests of justice to give further direction.
    (s 28(6))

- *Examination of witness through an intermediary*—Whether the witness's evidence is given in person, by live link or via video recording, the court may order that it be conducted through an interpreter or an intermediary, who must be approved by the court and have made a declaration 'that he will faithfully perform his function' (s 29(5)), which lays him open to perjury charges in the same way as a lawfully sworn interpreter (s 29(7)). The function of the intermediary, as defined in s 29(2), is:

to communicate—

(a) to the witness, questions put to the witness, and

(b) to any person asking such questions, the answers given by the witness in reply to them,

and to explain such questions and answers so far as necessary to enable them to be understood by the witness or person in question.

Any such examination of a witness must take place within the sight and hearing of the judge or justices, the legal representatives and, save in the case of video-recorded examination ordered under ss 27 and 28, the jury, if there is one.

- *Other aids to communication* (s 30)—The court may issue a special measures direction permitting a witness to be provided with 'such device as the court thinks appropriate with a view to enabling questions and answers to be communicated to or by the witness despite any disability or disorder or other impairment' from which the witness suffers. Thus, things like sign boards may be used, if the court so directs.

4.94 Evidence introduced by any of the above means 'shall be treated as if made by the witness in direct oral testimony in court' and is therefore 'admissible evidence of any fact of which such testimony from the witness would be admissible' (s 31(2)).

4.95 In trials on indictment, however, if evidence has been given in accordance with a special measures direction:

> . . . the judge must give the jury such warning (if any) as the judge considers necessary to ensure that the fact that the direction was given in relation to the witness does not prejudice the accused.
>
> (s 32)

This requirement will be most important in cases where a jury might be tempted to draw a prejudicial inference from the special measure directed—as, for example, where the court has ordered the erection of a screen to prevent the witness from seeing the accused. Although one might have assumed that these warnings would have formed part of the summing-up, it has been held that warnings may be delivered during the course of evidence. Indeed, Buxton LJ has suggested that a warning 'is much more likely to impress itself on the jury if it is given at the time that the witnesses give evidence than if it is repeated at a later date in the summing-up' (*Brown* [2004] EWCA Crim 1620 at [21]; [2004] Crim LR 1034).

4.96 The issue of how much solicitude the law ought to display towards those testifying in court, and indeed towards those charged with criminal offences, is under increasing scrutiny. There is, for example, even sporadic debate of the merit of reintroducing legislation granting anonymity to those charged with rape or child abuse—a privilege once granted to, and later withdrawn from, accused rapists. In any event, it emerges from a survey, published in 2004 by the Home Office, investigating the effect of special measures directions in trials involving vulnerable and intimidated witnesses, that they appear to have distinctly improved the lot of such witnesses.

> [T]he surveys have shown that the criminal justice system appears to be taking more effective action against either real or feared intimidation, and that anxiety levels are reduced. Moreover, satisfaction as measured by a number of indicators has increased among most categories of vulnerability, although improved satisfaction is particularly evident among witnesses affected by intimidation.
>
> (xv)

The Youth Justice and Criminal Evidence Act 1999 has increased the use of certain devices, such as live link. Many witnesses who have benefited from special measures now assert that, without them, they would not have been willing and able to give evidence. Meanwhile, many witnesses who testified in court without these measures recognised, after the event, that they would have found them helpful. The survey concludes that:

> [T]he provisions of the 1999 Act are not yet fully implemented, and it can be assumed that more widespread availability of special measures, including special measures not yet introduced such as video-recorded cross- or re-examination, will improve satisfaction further. Certainly the surveys show that there is more demand for use of measures.
>
> (*Are Special Measures Directions Working? Evidence from Surveys of Vulnerable and Intimidated Witnesses*, June 2004, Home Office Research Study 283, xv.)

4.97 What is clear is that thanks to less restrictive tests of witness competence, together with special measures directions, cases are now coming to trial which formerly would have been unthinkable. *Watts* [2010] EWCA Crim 1824 illustrates the point. W appealed against his convictions for sexual assaults committed on four inmates of the care home where he worked. All four patients were profoundly disabled and wheelchair-bound: three suffered from cerebral palsy, and one was tetraplegic with an acquired brain injury. As Lord Judge CJ remarked in this case, which was the first in which the evidence of complainants suffering from such profound levels of disability has been brought to the court's attention,

> less than half a generation ago the criminal courts would not have contemplated attempting to receive evidence from persons in the position of these complainants.
>
> (at [17])

One cannot read the judgment without some concerns about the evidence. The Court of Appeal, however, declared that, in the absence of any sort of irregularity in the trial process 'the primacy of the jury [had to] be respected (at [54]).'

4.98 *Special measures and human rights law.* The legality of provisions that deprive the accused of the right personally to confront witnesses against him was always likely to be contested on grounds of incompatibility with human rights law. Although evidence given by anonymous witnesses was declared contrary to traditional common-law principles by the House of Lords in *Davis* [2008] 3 WLR 125 and has since been regulated by the Coroners and Justice Act 2009 (see *post*, paras **9.104** ff), other forms of special measures have been held compatible with human rights law. In *R (D) v Camberwell Green Youth Court* [2005] 1 WLR 393 the courts were called upon to consider whether s 21(5) of the Youth Justice and Criminal Evidence Act 1999 was compatible with a defendant's right of fair trial under ECHR, Article 6. The crux of the problem is that the legislation requires that a special measures direction be given in respect of a child witness in need of special protection without consideration of whether the resultant restriction on the rights of the defendant is necessary or in the interests of justice (see *ante*, para **4.92**). For this reason, before the Divisional Court ([2003] EWHC 227 (Admin)), and subsequently before the House of Lords, it was urged that s 21(5) notably infringes Article 6(3)(d) of the ECHR, which embodies the defendant's right 'to examine or have examined witnesses against him' (see further *post*, paras **9.95** ff). In commenting upon the purpose underlying Article 6(3)(d), the ECtHR on one occasion did appear to say that this provision of the Convention means that 'all the evidence must in principle be produced in the presence of the accused at a public hearing with a view to adversarial argument' (*Barbera v Spain* (1989) 11 EHRR 360 at [78]). In the Divisional Court Rose LJ held that 'nothing in the fair trial provisions of art 6...prohibits a vulnerable witness from giving evidence in a room apart from the defendant', adding, 'neither live link, nor a video recording of evidence-in-chief...infringes that right, provided...the defendant's lawyers can see as well as hear the witness and can cross-examine' (at [48]). Moreover, other devices within the legislation can be employed to prevent injustice to an accused in such circumstances. After all, if, during the course of proceedings, it is perceived that those special measures directions, which the court must initially make under s 21(5), give rise to unforeseen difficulties or threaten to impair the fairness of the trial, the court still has powers under ss 20(2) and 24(3) variously to discharge or vary such directions. Additionally, the court retains its uninhibited powers at common law to prevent unfairness to the accused (at [47]). The applicant's right of fair trial, therefore, had not been infringed by the automatic issuing of the special measures directions. On further appeal, the House of Lords, too, rejected the claim that ECHR, Article 6(3)(d) confers upon defendants a general right to confront their accusers such that, if s 21(5) of the 1999 Act were to deprive them of a right to have their cases considered on an individual basis, it would be incompatible with the Convention. As Baroness Hale remarked, it would be 'irrational' for a law to require that the court must issue a special measures direction, which it was bound to make because of the rules applying to child witnesses, and then immediately to vary or discharge it in the interests of justice (at [33]). As the statute makes clear, 'the court must always start from the statutory presumption that there is nothing intrinsically unfair in children giving their evidence in this way (ie, by video recording and/or video link)' (at [46]). The case law of the ECtHR does not require that defendants be afforded an opportunity of face-to-face confrontation with their child accusers. It suffices that all the evidence is presented before the accused, some in pre-recorded form and some by contemporaneous transmission, and that the latter is afforded an opportunity to challenge such evidence. The 1999 Act allows for this. Indeed, the court also has an opportunity to scrutinise the pre-recorded interview at the outset and to exclude all or part of it, if necessary. In addition, it can order a child witness to give evidence in the courtroom or to expand upon the video recording if the interests of justice require it.

4.99 Likewise, the House of Lords in *Camberwell* rejected the argument that the 1999 Act's failure to confer upon defendants rights similar to other witnesses, which would permit defendants too to testify *via* video recording and/or video link, means that trials conducted under it may be in violation of the human rights principle of 'equality of arms'. This issue had previously arisen in *R (S) v Waltham Forest Youth Court* (2004) 168 JP 293. S, who was described by social services as 'vulnerable', was a 13-year-old girl, put on trial on two counts of robbery with three co-accused. S indicated that she would not be prepared to give physical evidence in the presence of her co-accused, some of whom, she alleged, had threatened both her and her mother. The trial judge held that he did not have the power to order special measures, and notably the facility of giving evidence by live link, in respect of a defendant. As Eady J freely acknowledged, Parliament appears deliberately to have excluded the defendant from the protection of the 'special measures directions'. Not only do some provisions refer explicitly to witnesses 'other than the accused' (eg s 16(1)(b)), but in some isolated situations the Act does recognise that a co-defendant might be vulnerable and in need of protection *vis-à-vis* his or her co-defendants (eg s 35, which lays down that no witness under the age of 17, charged with certain offences, may cross-examine in person a protected witness, the term 'protected witness' in this context including a co-accused). Nevertheless, whilst the courts cannot go against an explicit statutory prohibition, it was urged that they do retain inherent powers to make orders in respect of witnesses not eligible under the 1999 Act, of which *Richards* (1999) 163 JP 246 (*ante*, paras **4.9** and **4.93**) serves as a potent reminder. The categories of these inherent powers, which overlap with those enumerated in the 1999 Act, are said not to be closed and conduce to giving effect to the all-important principle according to which justice should be done. Nevertheless, Eady J upheld the trial judge's refusal to order special measures, or their equivalent under his common law powers, in respect of S. S, of course, retained her general right to a fair trial by virtue of ECHR, Article 6, and in accordance with 'equality of arms' in particular; but this simply requires the court to judge the fairness of the trial process as a whole. The 1999 Act does not derogate from a defendant's existing rights at common law, but is almost solely concerned to augment the protections afforded to other witnesses. In consequence, the Act is not incompatible with the Convention *per se*, and it would have been to cross the line between interpretation and legislation had the court availed itself of the Human Rights Act, s 3 and accepted the applicant's invitation to read s 16(1) of the 1999 Act as referring to 'a witness in criminal proceedings (other than the accused save where the accused intends to give evidence against any other person charged in the same proceedings).' More generally, Eady J also affirmed that courts do not possess any inherent power to permit a co-accused to give her evidence by live link, since video facilities were not a part of the courts' armoury of protective measures at common law prior to the relevant legislation. The statutory regime Parliament first created in 1988, and which it has since modified, has consistently provided exclusive guidance on when resort may be had to such facilities in criminal proceedings, and in his view that regime seemed 'incompatible with any inherent or common law jurisdiction existing in parallel' (at [29]). In *Camberwell*, the House of Lords adopted a similar analysis. As Lord Rodger of Earlsferry pointed out, a child defendant in an English court is not exactly without protection (at [16]). Alongside the right not to give evidence and the right to legal representation, which 'have hitherto been regarded as adequate arguments against the need to make such provision for child defendants in England and Wales', the court retains inherent jurisdiction to make orders or to give leave of any description in relation to testifying child defendants:

> Only if this power should prove to be inadequate in any given case might the defendant's trial be rendered unfair, with the result that there would be a breach of art 6(1).
>
> (at [17])

See further *SH* [2003] EWCA Crim 1208, especially at [23]–[24] *per* Kay LJ.

Baroness Hale also stressed the very real practical difficulties that would be posed were child defendants permitted to testify in-chief by means of a pre-recorded interview (at [58]), and further alluded to 'the environment and procedures in the Youth Court' and the altered procedures in the Crown Court (*ante*, paras **4.85–4.97**), adding vaguely that something more may yet need to be done in these areas (at [61]).

4.100 *Defendants and video links.* This is not to say, however, that at trial a defendant will never be permitted to have resort to video link or to some other similar device. The issue was considered in *Ukpabio* (2007) 171 JP 692. Whilst Latham LJ VP stressed that, as a matter of general principle, an accused's evidence has to be given in person in court, he also observed that the defendant's right to appear before a court, which is protected both by the common law and by Article 6 of the European Convention on Human Rights, is not absolute. It can be waived. Alternatively, to ensure an orderly trial, there may be circumstances in which it is necessary for the defendant to be absent for all or part of the proceedings. Conversely, circumstances may arise when it might be appropriate for a defendant, on his own application, to be absent from court for all or part of a trial, provided that his participation can be adequately secured by other means. If the relevant equipment is available and the court is persuaded that there exists sufficient justification for having recourse to such equipment, video link might be a sensible method of ensuring the participation of a defendant who otherwise would not be able to participate properly in all or some of the trial process.

4.101 *Vulnerable defendants and live video links.* The way in which an accused gives his testimony has been slightly modified by the Police and Justice Act 2006. Although the Act maintains the assumption that all adults ought to give evidence in person in court, s 47 has added a new s 33A to the Youth Justice and Criminal Evidence Act 1999 in order to safeguard the interests of vulnerable defendants. Section 33A now provides that a criminal court, on application by the accused, may direct that any evidence given by the accused should be given over a live video link. Before delivering a live link direction, however, the court must be satisfied that such a course is in the interests of justice (s 33A(2)(b)). In the case of an accused person over the age of 18, it must also be shown that the defendant suffers from a mental disorder or has a significant impairment of intelligence and social function, that he is therefore unable to participate effectively in the proceedings, and that a live link would enable him to do so more effectively (s 33(5)). In the case of a defendant under the age of 18, the conditions are less restrictive and it has only to be shown that his ability to participate effectively in the proceedings is compromised by his level of intellectual ability or social functioning, and that use of a live link would enable him to participate more effectively in the proceedings as a witness (s 33(4)).

Criminal trials of children

4.102 The general issue of criminal trials involving children has acquired prominence following ECtHR decisions in *V v UK* (2000) 30 EHRR 121 (the Bulger case) and, more recently, in *SC v UK* (2004) 40 EHRR 10. The key question is whether the forum in which they are tried allows young persons to participate adequately in the determination of the criminal charges levelled against them. In England and Wales the majority of such cases are tried before the Youth Court rather than before the Crown Court. Youth courts are specialised and adapted for hearing cases where children stand charged with crime. Judges in these courts will have received specialised training, and the lawyers too will have relevant expertise. There are no juries. Trying young defendants in the remote and confusing surroundings of a Crown Court poses the prosecution with risks. In *V v UK*, the ECtHR held that the two very young co-accused had not received a fair trial for murder before the Crown Court. Again, in *SC v UK* a majority of the ECtHR determined that an 11-year-old boy, who had been tried before the Crown Court on a charge of robbery, had been denied a fair trial. It was stressed that when trying children, it was vital that full account was taken of their age, their level of maturity and their intellectual and emotional capacities. Steps had to be taken to promote children's ability to understand and participate in the proceedings, and these would include conducting hearings so as to reduce to a minimum any feelings of intimidation or inhibition. More particularly, the ECtHR stated:

> The Court accepts…that Art. 6.1 does not require that a child on trial for a criminal offence should understand or be capable of understanding every point of law or evidential detail. Given the sophistication of modern legal systems, many adults of normal intelligence are unable fully to comprehend all the intricacies and exchanges which take place in the courtroom: this is why the Convention, in Art. 6.3(c), emphasises the importance of the right to legal representation. However, "effective participation" in this context presupposes that the accused has a broad understanding of the nature of the trial process and of what is at stake for him or her, including the significance of any penalty which may be imposed. It means that he or she, if necessary with the assistance of, eg, an interpreter, lawyer, social worker or friend, should be able to understand the general thrust of what is said in court. The defendant should be able to follow what is said by the prosecution witnesses and, if represented, to explain to his own lawyers his version of events, point out any statements with which he disagrees and make them aware of any facts which should be put forward in his defence.
>
> (at [29])

The ECtHR added that the type of court before which the young person was tried was of considerable importance:

> [W]hen the decision is taken to deal with a child, … who risks not being able to participate effectively because of his young age and limited intellectual capacity, by way of criminal proceedings rather than some other form of disposal directed primarily at determining the child's best interests and those of the community, it is essential that he be tried in a specialist tribunal which is able to give full consideration to and make proper allowance for the handicaps under which he labours, and adapts its procedure accordingly.
>
> (at [35])

4.103 It will be for the judge to decide in each given case whether a particular young defendant is capable of participating effectively in the case. If at any point it becomes clear that a particular defendant is incapable of so doing, the judge must stay the proceedings. To continue with proceedings in such circumstances would amount to an abuse of process. As Scott Baker LJ spelled out in *R (P) v West London Youth Court* [2006] 1 WLR 1219, the defendant has to establish on a balance of probabilities that he or she is not capable of participating effectively. By way of example, in the *West London* case there was evidence that a 15-year-old, who faced two charges of robbery and one of attempted robbery before a youth court, had significant mental impairment but was not mentally handicapped. Nevertheless, his low level of cognitive functioning required to be taken into account. In this case the following approach was proposed:

(i) to keep the claimant's level of cognitive functioning in mind;

(ii) to use concise and simple language;

(iii) to take regular breaks;

(iv) to allow additional time to explain court proceedings;

(v) to be proactive in ensuring the claimant had access to support;

(vi) to explain and ensure the claimant understood the ingredients of the charge;

(vii) to explain the possible outcomes and sentences;

(viii) to ensure that cross-examination was carefully controlled so that questions were short and clear and frustration was minimised. (at [26])

FURTHER READING

Police notebooks

Andrews, 'Re-opening the Case for the Prosecution' (1991) 107 LQR 577

Stephenson, 'Should Collaborative Testimony be Permitted in Courts of Law?' [1990] Crim LR 302

Cross-examination

Dein, 'Police Misconduct Revisited' [2000] Crim LR 801

Munday, 'The Quick and the Dead: Who Counts as a 'Person' under s 100 of the Criminal Justice Act 2003?' [2007] 71 J Crim Law 238

Redmayne, 'Confronting Confrontation' (LSE Law, Society and Economy Working Paper 10/2010: http://ssrn.com/abstract=1616200)

The course of the trial and evidence relating to witnesses' veracity

Blumenthal, 'A Wipe of the Hands, a Lick of the Lips: The Validity of Demeanour Evidence in Assessing Witness Credibility' (1993) 72 Nebraska L Rev 1157

Stuesser, 'Admitting Prior Inconsistent Statements for their Truth' (1992) 71 Can Bar Rev 48

Wolchover, 'Woeful Neglect' (2007) 157 NLJ 624 (arguing for generalised electronic recording of witnesses' statements)

Wolchover & Heaton-Armstrong, 'Unreliable Evidence' (July 2007) Counsel, p 10

Reluctant and hostile witnesses

Ellison, 'Cross-examination in Rape Trials' [1998] Crim LR 605

Munday, 'Calling a Hostile Witness' [1989] Crim LR 866

Witness familiarisation

Ellison and Wheatcroft, 'Could you ask me that in a different way, please?' [2010] Crim LR 823

Vulnerable and intimidated witnesses

Birch, 'A Better Deal for Vulnerable Witnesses' [2000] Crim LR 223

Hoyano, 'Variations on a Theme by Pigot: Special Measures Directions for Child Witnesses' [2000] Crim LR 250

Kelly, Temkin & Griffiths, *Section 41: An Evaluation of New Legislation Limiting Sexual History Evidence in Rape Trials* (Home Office, June 2006 rds online publication)

Kibble, 'The Sexual History Provisions' [2000] Crim LR 274

Kibble, 'Judicial Perspectives on the Operation of s 41 and the Relevance and Admissibility of Prior Sexual History Evidence: Four Scenarios' [2005] Crim LR 190

Kibble, 'Judicial Discretion and the Admission of Prior Sexual History under s 41 of the Youth Justice and Criminal Evidence 1999' [2005] Crim LR 263

SELF-TEST QUESTIONS

1. What is the difference between a 'hostile witness' and an 'unfavourable witness'? What steps may counsel take if his/her witness is declared hostile?

2. Although the point was not decided by the Court of Appeal, in *Llewellyn and Gray* [2001] EWCA Crim 1555 (not discussed in this book) the judge in this trial, which involved the supply of Class A drugs, ruled that the defence could ask a police officer, who testified for the Crown, whether at the time of the trial he himself was being investigated for having allegedly supplied drugs to a *News of the World* undercover reporter. The judge also ruled, however, that the defence could not call evidence in rebuttal to contradict any answers the officer might give. Would the trial judge's rulings be correct today, taking into account the provisions of the Criminal Justice Act 2003?

3. How do the courts distinguish between matters of issue and matters of credit? Is the distinction workable?

4. When may a party adduce evidence concerning the likely veracity of the opposing side's witness or witnesses?

5. What principal protections have been extended to the vulnerable or the intimidated or the young witness by the Youth Justice and Criminal Evidence Act 1999 (as amended)? What further reforms, if any, do you believe would be desirable?

6. In *A (No 2)* [2001] 2 WLR 1546 the House of Lords availed itself of s 3 of the Human Rights Act 1998 in order to 're-interpret' the rape-shield provisions in the Youth Justice and Criminal Evidence Act 1999. Do you consider that, had this decision not been taken and had s 41 been interpreted using traditional canons of statutory construction, s 41 would have made an excessive inroad into the guarantee of fair trial under Article 6 of the ECHR?

7. When, if ever, may those who stand accused of crime participate in their trials by live video link?

5

Witnesses' previous consistent statements and the remnants of the rule against narrative

SUMMARY

The rule excluding previous consistent statements

- Exception 1: Complaints by victims of crime (Criminal Justice Act 2003, s 120(4), (7) and (8))
  - Distress of the victim
- Exception 2: Rebutting suggestions of concoction or afterthought (Criminal Justice Act 2003, s 120(2))
- Exception 3: *Res gestae*
- Exception 4: Previous statements of a party identifying or describing a person, object or place (Criminal Justice Act 2003, s 120(5))
- Exception 5: Supplementing deficiencies in the memory of witnesses (Criminal Justice Act 2003, ss 139 and 120(6))

Evidence-in-chief delivered by video recording (Criminal Justice Act 2003, s 137)

Statements made by the accused when first taxed with incriminating facts

Statements made by the accused when incriminating articles are recovered

Well, in a legal inquiry...ten to one he won't be allowed to read [his documents]. He'll be tripped up every two or three minutes with some tangle of old rules. A man can't tell the truth in public nowadays.

GK Chesterton, *Manalive* (1912)

The rule excluding previous consistent statements

5.1 In criminal cases a witness was normally forbidden from referring to self-serving statements, that is from corroborating or reinforcing his testimony by invoking his previous consistent statements. To take a classical example, in *Roberts* (1942) 28 Cr App R 102 R's defence to a charge of murder was accident. R was not allowed to call his father to tell the court that two days after the shooting he had told his father that the gun had gone off by accident. As Humphreys J explained:

> [A] party is not permitted to make evidence for himself... [I]n a criminal case an accused person is not permitted to call evidence to show that, after he has been charged with an offence, he told a number of persons what his defence was going to be.
>
> (p 105)

A similar rule used to obtain in civil cases, too. However, the provisions of the Civil Evidence Act 1995 now render such statements admissible in the same way that hearsay statements are made admissible under that legislation (the Civil Evidence Act 1995 is considered in the chapter on the rule against hearsay: see *post*, paras **9.115–9.122**). 'The rule against narrative' prohibiting previous consistent statements, however, still operates in criminal cases, although its force is considerably diminished by the fact that it is subject to three common law exceptions, to which the Criminal Justice Act 2003 has made enlargements and additions.

5.2 Like its cousin germane, the rule against hearsay, the rule against previous consistent statements could prove highly inconvenient, excluding evidence that laypersons would unhesitatingly consider relevant. In consequence, the courts sometimes turned a blind eye to the rule against narrative. Take the case of *Cook* [1987] QB 417, where the rule was bypassed in order to achieve a result that accorded with dictates of common sense. In *Cook* the victim of an indecent assault and robbery had failed to pick C out at a staged identification in a shopping centre, but eventually identified C as he was leaving the centre. The prosecution sought to reinforce the victim's hesitant identification of C by putting in evidence a photofit portrait made under her direction fairly soon after the assault. As Watkins LJ acknowledged, two rules of evidence were potentially infringed by the admission of this evidence: the rule against hearsay and the rule against narrative. Since there was evidence that the victim had identified C, the photofit evidence was intended to corroborate this testimony and therefore offended against the rule against narrative. The judge sought to side step this difficulty by arguing that the composition of a photofit picture was 'akin to a camera'. Just as records made by a camera or any other machine operating normally can provide admissible real evidence (see, eg,

The Statue of Liberty [1968] 1 WLR 739), so too the police artist or photofit technician is to be likened to 'another form of... camera, albeit imperfectly and not produced contemporaneously with the material incident but soon or fairly soon afterwards'. This analogy is problematical. The simple truth is that, in the same way that a witness's previous identification of the accused has for long been treated as an exception to the rule against previous consistent statements, in the case of police artists' portraits (see *Smith* [1976] Crim LR 511) and photofits the courts would discreetly close their eyes to the technical inadmissibility of the evidence. The outcome in *Cook* made perfect sense, but the price was the creation of an untidy exception to the legal principle. It should be noted that the distortion of the law performed in *Cook* will no longer be necessary today. In so far as s 115(2) of the Criminal Justice Act 2003 declares that photofits, like sketches and 'other pictorial forms', are henceforth to be considered 'statements', a previous statement of a witness is now admissible under s 120(5) of that Act provided that 'the statement identifies or describes a person'.

5.3 The law recognises three traditional exceptions to the rule against previous consistent statements. Each of these common law exceptions has been modified by the Criminal Justice Act 2003, which has also added further exceptions.

Exception 1: Complaints by victims of crime (Criminal Justice Act 2003, s 120(4), (7) and (8))

5.4 Under the old common law, complaints made by victims of sexual offences, whether male or female, comprised a significant exception to the general rule against the admission of previous consistent statements. Provided that a complaint had been made at the first reasonable opportunity and was voluntary, the person to whom the complaint had been made might recount its terms to the court. The purpose of admitting such evidence was to demonstrate the credibility of the complainant by showing that he/she had told a consistent story from the earliest opportunity or, in appropriate cases, to negative an allegation of consent. As Evans LJ explained in *Churchill* [1999] Crim LR 664, very loosely speaking, such evidence was 'relevant as a matter of common sense to the issue whether the complainant was... a victim or not'.

5.5 The admission of complaints at common law proceeded upon the basis that from an early point a victim had told a consistent story. More specifically, statements received as recent complaints were not treated by the court as evidence of the facts, but were only considered relevant to the victim's credibility. Additionally, the recent complaint rule applied exclusively in cases of sexual offending. Until the nineteenth century complaints had been admissible in cases of violent offending, thefts, and even in some divorce cases. However, the justification most frequently advanced to explain the modern restriction was that since sexual cases often boil down to disputes between the word of the defendant and that of the victim, questions of credibility can assume particularly high importance. Indeed, in an oft-quoted passage in his judgment in *Funderburk* [1990] 2 All ER 482, 491, Henry J noted that 'where the disputed issue is a sexual one between two persons in private the difference between questions going to credit and questions going to the issue is reduced to vanishing point' (see *ante*, para **4.48**). Evidence of a recent complaint, it was thought, could therefore materially assist a tribunal of fact called upon to resolve such fraught issues.

5.6 The Criminal Justice Act 2003 considerably altered the law governing recent complaints. The relevant provisions, s 120(4), (7) and (8)—which are not simply re-enactments of the common law rules but are 'freestanding and provide their own criteria' (*O* [2006] 2 Cr App R 27 at [24] *per* McCombe J)—now lay down:

> (4) A previous statement by the witness is admissible as evidence of any matter stated of which oral evidence by him would be admissible, if—
>
> > (a) any of the following three conditions is satisfied, and
> >
> > (b) while giving evidence the witness indicates that to the best of his belief he made the statement, and that to the best of his belief it states the truth.
>
> (7) The third condition is that—
>
> > (a) the witness claims to be a person against whom an offence has been committed,
> >
> > (b) the offence is one to which the proceedings relate,
> >
> > (c) the statement consists of a complaint made by the witness (whether to a person in authority or not) about conduct which would, if proved, constitute the offence or part of the offence,
> >
> > (d) ... [*Paragraph repealed by the Coroners and Justice Act 20093, s 112*]
> >
> > (e) the complaint was not made as a result of a threat or a promise, and
> >
> > (f) before the statement is adduced the witness gives oral evidence in connection with its subject matter.
>
> (8) For the purposes of subsection (7) the fact that the complaint was elicited (for example, by a leading question) is irrelevant unless a threat or a promise was involved.

As with many of the evidence provisions of the Criminal Justice Act 2003, the statutory rule is a blend of the old and the new.

5.7 The provision has retained both the old nomenclature, 'complaints' (s 120(7) (c)), and elements of the old common law relating to complaints. As was the case before the 2003 Act, in the paradigm situation the law tends to assume that the victim/complainant will have confided in another person after the commission of an offence, and will have told that other person that he/she has been the victim of a crime. When presented in court, it is the recipient of the complaint who must testify to the complaint having been made; the complaint cannot simply be related by the complainant. Section 120(7)(c) indicates that a complaint may have been made to 'a person in authority'. This expression is not actually defined in the statute, but is of course used in PACE, s 82(1) (see *post*, para **10.5**), where it retains its old common law meaning of a person who can influence the course of proceedings. This, in the main, would signify police officers and others responsible for the investigation of crime. The subsection therefore makes clear that a victim's account of a crime, as related to a police officer, may qualify as a complaint, provided that the other conditions of admissibility are met.

5.8 *The complaint must relate to an offence which is the subject of the proceedings.* Under the old law this entailed that complaints would only be admitted if they had been made by victims of offences actually charged in the indictment. Although not authoritatively settled, there is every likelihood that that this limitation will continue to apply under the 2003 Act. As David Clarke J remarked in *Trewin* [2008] EWCA Crim 484 at [17], the Act's 'provisions were not intended to open the door to . . . complaints by those who are not complainants on the indictment.'

5.9 *The complaint must relate to 'conduct which would, if proved, constitute the offence or part of the offence'* (s 120(7)(c)). What is meant by 'part of the offence' is not clear. Given that the object is to buttress the victim's testimony, one would assume that the complaint has to refer to a significant element of the offence. Thus, if in a case of a robbery, the witness relates that the victim only mentioned to him that she had had an unpleasant encounter on the night in question with someone who was wearing a Halloween mask and who smelled of petrol, such an account could not constitute a complaint because, if proved, it would not constitute 'part of the offence'. In contrast, if the victim were to add that the masked man brandished a knife in her direction, the case would presumably be altered.

5.10 *The complainant must testify.* At common law there was a general requirement that a complaint could only be admitted if the victim also testified (eg *White v R* [1999] 1 AC 210, where the Privy Council emphasised that in order for complaint evidence to be admissible it was necessary both that the complainant should testify to the making of the complaint and that its terms should be proved by the person to whom it was made). Section 120(7)(f) retains this condition, insisting that 'before the statement is adduced the [victim] gives oral evidence in connection with its subject matter'. The expression 'in connection with its subject matter' is imprecise. It may be designed to take account of cases like *ES* [2004] 1

WLR 2940. In *ES* the court had to decide whether, before it can be admitted in evidence, the complaint must be shown to be consistent with the witness's actual testimony; and, if so, how consistent it needs to be. Even though the content of the victim's story was significantly at variance with the evidence she gave in court, the trial judge had admitted evidence of what the victim, who complained of a catalogue of sexual attacks by her stepfather, had told a school friend shortly after some of the incidents. Thomas LJ, adopting the reasoning of Australian and New Zealand courts, concluded:

> It is... a matter of common experience that the terms of the evidence of a complainant given at trial and the evidence of the complaint may differ, but it would be contrary to good sense to exclude the latter if it is capable of supporting the credibility of the complainant. Provided that the evidence as to the terms of the complaint is sufficiently consistent that it can, depending on the view the jury takes, support the credibility of the complainant, it is... both fair to the defendant and in accordance with the long established principles to permit such evidence to be given and to leave it to the jury to assess its weight. We accept that such evidence may be prejudicial, but... it can be highly probative of the veracity of the complainant in putting before the jury what complaint was being made after the occurrence of the conduct complained of... Reason and good sense and principle are against us excluding what may be very important evidence from the jury, just as [they] laid the foundation in 1896 [referring to *Lillyman* [1896] 2 QB 167] of the modern law relating to the admissibility of the terms of the complaint.
>
> (at [32])

Clearly, if a complainant's evidence is at wide variance with his or her complaint, a judge would need to deliver a clear warning to the jury on the extent and potential significance of the discrepancies, to draw to the jury's attention any reasons for the inconsistencies, and to tell them to take all these matters into account in determining whether they considered the complainant to have been telling the truth. Has this ruling survived the Criminal Justice Act 2003? The only provision that obliquely addresses the issue is s 120(7)(f), which requires that 'before the statement is adduced the witness gives oral evidence in connection with its subject matter'. The loose expression, 'in connection with', does not seem calculated to demand an exact correlation between the victim's testimony and the terms of the reported complaint. This, coupled with the knowledge that the statute's policy is to maximise the admissibility of what hitherto have been treated as inadmissible hearsay statements, would suggest that Thomas LJ's approach in *ES* will continue to hold good under the new statutory regime.

5.11 *Must the complaint have been received by another party?* The complaints rule was normally stated in such a way as to suggest that the victim would have spoken to another person about the offence fairly soon after its commission. This, however, was not always the case. Prior to the 2003 Act, in *M* (2000) 9 August, case no 99/07320/Z2, a rather unusual case, a daughter, who alleged that she had been sexually abused by her father between 1983 and 1987, after viewing a Childline programme on the television in 1988, typed a long letter detailing her experiences with the intention of sending it to Childline. The letter was never sent. Nevertheless, at M's trial the letter was admitted as evidence under the complaints rule. The Court of Appeal ruled that what mattered was whether the document amounted to more than mere narrative and was in fact composed in the form of a complaint. Actual communication, it was said, was not an essential element. The form and content of the document, however, were telling. In this particular case it was plain that the writer's intention was to communicate the information to Childline. Whereas the daughter's failure to send the letter might affect the weight of the evidence, the form and content of the document so clearly showed that the girl intended to make a complaint that her omission to send it did not affect the letter's admissibility as a complaint. Nothing in s 120(4), (7) and (8) prevents the courts from continuing to adopt this interpretation.

5.12 *When must the complaint have been made?* Prior to the entry into force of s 112 of the Coroners and Justice Act 2009, s 120(7)(d) of the Criminal Justice Act 2003 required that the complaint had to have been 'made as soon as could reasonably be expected after the alleged conduct.' This meant that the court needed to examine the surrounding circumstances, and notably the character of the victim and the victim's relationship with the parties to whom he or she could potentially have made complaint, in order to determine whether this requirement was satisfied (eg, *O* [2006] 2 Cr App R 27, esp at [20] *per* McCombe J). It was then for the tribunal of fact to decide whether they considered that in fact this was the case (*Spencer* [2008] EWCA Crim 544 at [27] *per* Dyson LJ).

5.13 The requirement that a complaint has to have been made as soon as could reasonably be expected was repealed by the Coroners and Justice Act 2009. It is now widely accepted that prompt complaint by sexual complainants, for example, is far from being the norm (see Thomas J's powerful judgment in *H* [1997] 1 NZLR 673). It is not necessarily the natural reaction in children who have been abused by members of their household. Similarly, many adults prove reluctant to tell others of sexual or physical indignities they may have undergone. As the New Zealand Court of Appeal observed in *M* (1998) 26 June, unreported, it is 'now well accepted, a complaint in the sense of creating a hue and cry immediately after a shocking incident is simply not relevant to most instances of intra-family sexual assault'. Whereas under the 2003 Act, as originally worded, in a case like *PK and TK* [2008] EWCA Crim 434 complaints made years after the incidents that led to charges of indecent assault and indecency with a child were admitted because the court accepted that the respectable and tight-knit families to which the complainants belonged had put pressure on them to keep events to themselves (at [55]), under the amended provision the complaints would now be admissible without the prosecution first needing to persuade the trial judge that some special feature of the offending or some unusual feature of the victim made it reasonable in that particular case to allow in a delayed complaint. The original intention of the amendment introduced by the Coroners and Justice Act 2009 was 'to help improve successful prosecution of sexual offences while ensuring that a defendant's right to a fair trial is not undermined', as recommended in *Convicting Rapists and Protecting Victims – Justice for Victims of Rape: Response to Consultation* (November 2007) § 15. It was decided, however, that the repeal ought to extend to all offences, principally owing to concerns over domestic violence cases and suchlike where often victims do not complain promptly (§ 16).

5.14 Under the amended provision a complainant must still give evidence so that he or she can be cross-examined on the complaint (Ministry of Justice Circular no 2010/02). The fact that the complaint was not delivered promptly after the alleged offence will be one matter that can then be explored before the court. However, it will be for the tribunal of fact to decide what weight it wishes to attribute to the complaint. The length of time that has elapsed between an offence and the victim's complaint will not affect its admissibility; it may merely detract from its persuasive force.

5.15 *Multiple complaints.* In *Valentine* [1996] 2 Cr App R 213, a decision under the old law, a victim had told her brother in the morning that she had been raped the previous night, and subsequently that evening she had also recounted the incident to a friend from work. The court admitted both complaints as each satisfied the criteria of s 120(7). Although the court admitted multiple complaints by the victim, Roch LJ cautioned that a court should be careful about admitting multiple complaints as this might prejudice the jury by inducing them to think that by dint of repetition the complaints were evidence of the facts, not just evidence that could buttress the victim's credibility. Given that under s 120(4) of the 2003 Act a complaint is now 'evidence of any matter stated of which oral evidence by him would be admissible', this qualification no longer holds. *O* [2006] 2 Cr App R 27 subsequently suggested what the position was likely to be under the 2003 Act. Having observed that the wording of s 120 does not preclude the admission in evidence of multiple complaints (at [21]), in *O* the trial judge had formed the view that the two complaints had been made in such different circumstances—one when the victim was still living under the same roof as the abuser, and the second when she had moved out—that they both constituted relevant evidence and that it was fair to admit both complaints. McCombe J agreed:

> We see the force of the learned judge's conclusion...It has to be remembered that a statement admitted under the new statutory provisions is admissible to prove the truth of the matter stated and not merely to demonstrate consistency of the complainant's account as was the case under the old law. There is obviously a need in fairness to restrict evidence of "complaint upon complaint" which may merely be self-serving. But broadly for the reasons given by [the judge], we agree that the evidence in this case had a relevance over and above that of the complaint to L and her mother some months earlier.
>
> (at [23])

This view has since been resoundingly endorsed by the Court of Appeal in *PK and TK* [2008] EWCA Crim 434, where it was held that evidence had been properly admitted of multiple complaints, made by as many as thirteen witnesses (including the complainants) years after PK and TK were alleged to have committed their various acts of child sexual abuse.

5.16 *A complaint must not have been elicited by threats or inducements.* At common law, it used to be the case that an admissible complaint had to have been made voluntarily. This meant that it had neither been extracted by means of leading questions nor coerced. In short, it must have been freely made. The Criminal Justice Act 2003 has relaxed these requirements somewhat. First, it has retained the idea that a complaint cannot be admitted if it was elicited by threats or inducements. Thus, s 120(7)(e) expressly stipulates that 'the complaint was not made as a result of a threat or a promise'.

5.17 The old requirement, however, that the complaint must not have been extracted by leading questions has been dispensed with. An oddly worded s 120(8) lays down that:

> For the purposes of subsection (7) the fact that the complaint was elicited (for example, by a leading question) is irrelevant unless a threat or a promise was involved.

If the complaint was the result of a leading question, this factor can of course still be brought out in cross-examination; only the admissibility of the complaint is unaffected. Whether one really wants to admit 'complaints' that are the product of persistent leading questioning or which have been fed to the complainant is another matter. Let us imagine a police officer interviewing a putative robbery victim and asking: 'Did Tony hold you up at gun-point and run off with the contents of your handbag?' The witness replies, 'Yes', and then becomes hysterical and has to be sedated. Would the witness's response be admissible as a 'complaint' under the

2003 Act? Since s 120(7)(c) employs the word 'statement', the definition of this term in s 115 applies:

(1) In this Chapter references to a statement . . . are to be read as follows.

(2) A statement is any representation of fact or opinion made by a person by whatever means . . .

If the court is satisfied that the witness's bald assent constitutes a 'representation of fact', and given that a leading question is 'irrelevant', presumably the answer is in the affirmative. The admissibility of such evidence would presumably remain subject to the court's general right to exclude evidence under PACE, s 78 (which is specifically preserved in s 126(2)(a)), and even to an additional discretion to exclude evidence that would be wasteful of the court's time, introduced for the first time in s 126(1)(b), which provides:

In criminal proceedings the court may refuse to admit a statement as evidence of a matter stated if . . .

(b) the court is satisfied that the case for excluding the statement, taking account of the danger that to admit it would result in undue waste of time, substantially outweighs the case for admitting it, taking account of the value of the evidence.

It might be noted that the statute uses a sloppy expression, which is becoming more common in legislation: 'for example'. To what other means of coaxing complaints from victims, other than leading questions, does the legislature wish the court to turn a blind eye? Was s 120(8) meant to cover statements made under hypnosis or narco-hypnosis, in the course of a spiritualist séance, in exchange for money or a gift, or under the effects of truth serums like scopolamine or sodium amytal?

5.18 *The complaints rules apply only to Crown evidence.* Not every 'complaint' that may have been elicited in evidence need be treated as a 'complaint' under the statute. In *Leach* [2006] EWCA Crim 58 L had been convicted of indecently assaulting a 14-year-old supporter of his skittles team. During the trial the defence got wind of a talk which the victim had had with her mother on the day after the incident, and in cross-examination questioned the mother about its contents. In their conversation it turned out that the girl had omitted to mention significant details of the assault which had been central to her testimony. The defence sought to exploit these inconsistencies. Following his conviction, L appealed on the ground that the judge had failed to deliver a complaint direction in respect of that part of the mother's evidence. Moses LJ, however, held that in this case the judge was only required to explain to the jury why they had heard the evidence of what was, arguably, an inconsistency, adding:

[W]e reject the suggestion that this was a recent complaint in respect of which the full panoply of the directions, as identified in Judicial Studies Board Vol I [*scilicet* specimen direction no 31], should have been given. This was not relied upon by the Crown as a recent complaint. The Crown never adduced this evidence at all. The jury only heard it as a result of the decision of the defence...That...does mean that it would not have been appropriate, either under the old or new law to give the jury directions relevant to the issue of recent complaint.

(at [16])

Only if a complaint is adduced as such by the Crown is there need to treat it as a complaint and to deliver the appropriate direction.

5.19 By way of an example of s 120(7) in action, in *Xhabri* [2006] 1 Cr App R 26, L, who had been imprisoned, raped and forced into prostitution by X, had managed to speak to her mother a few times on a borrowed mobile telephone and to tell her that she had been kidnapped by Albanians, had had a face-to-face conversation with a neighbour in which she had related what had befallen her, and via that neighbour had got a message to her father. The question, on appeal, was whether the evidence of these three witnesses—the parents and the neighbour—as to what she had said was admissible. Lord Phillips of Worth Matravers CJ held that these statements, made by L at various points during her captivity, were indeed admissible under s 120(7) because the six conditions then laid down in that provision 'were, or were likely to be, satisfied' (at [35]):

(i) L claimed to be a person against whom an offence had been committed.

(ii) The offence was one to which the proceedings related.

(iii) The complaint concerned conduct which would, if proved, constitute part of the offence.

(iv) The complaint was made as soon as could reasonably be expected after the alleged conduct. The complaints were, in fact, made while the alleged conduct was continuing. (*This would of course no longer be a relevant consideration: Coroners and Justice Act 2009, s 112*).

(v) The complaint was not made as a result of a threat or promise.

(vi) L was expected to give evidence before the material evidence relating to her previous statements was adduced.

(Even if this analysis was mistaken, the court indicated that it would have exercised its general inclusionary discretion to admit this evidence under the Criminal Justice Act 2003, s 114(1)(d): see *post*, paras **9.70–9.80**.)

Explaining a victim's failure to complain. A final point: because the common law rule allowing a complaint to be admitted provided that it was made soon after the commission of the offence might have suggested that a failure to complain promptly diminished the credibility of the witness's testimony, the courts responded by allowing the Crown to adduce evidence in order to explain why a complaint had not been forthcoming at an early stage (eg *Greenwood* [1993] Crim LR 770). Thus, in *DS* [1999] Crim LR 911, the Court of Appeal admitted evidence of the harsh regime operating at a residential home for disturbed children in order to explain why boys had not made prompt complaints of sexual assaults committed upon them by members of staff. In some jurisdictions, attempts have even been made to introduce expert evidence to this end. The Canadian Supreme Court, for example, in *DD* [2000] 2 SCR 275 found itself profoundly divided over whether a judge, trying an indecent assault case, had properly allowed the Crown to introduce expert psychological evidence to explain away a complaint made by a child two and a half years after the alleged assaults. A narrow majority of the judges (4–3) ruled inadmissible a psychologist's testimony to the effect that a late complaint does not necessarily support an inference of falsehood. Since the 2003 Act no longer requires that a complaint must have been 'made as soon as could reasonably be expected after the alleged conduct', the sort of evidence admitted in *DS* will no longer be required in order to justify admission of the complaint. However, paradoxically, it looks likely that with the widespread admission of complaints made by victims at any time after the event, such evidence will remain just a relevant in informing juries of the reason why a particular complainant took so long to speak out. Popular misconceptions still fuel the idea that real victims of crime will make complaint promptly; delay in so doing in likelihood indicates recent concoction. If such evidence does continues to serve a purpose, the relaxation in the rules governing the admissibility of hearsay statements will render its adduction easier than in cases like *Greenwood* (*supra*), where, as it happened, the evidence which explained the delay in complaining was also tainted by hearsay (see *post*, Chapter 9).

Distress of the victim

5.21 Signs of distress will often accompany complaints, especially those made by victims of sexual attacks. Evidence of a complainant's distress at the time of, or shortly after, the assault is admissible to show that the victim has acted consistently, thereby reinforcing the victim's credibility. Such evidence, however, can be easily simulated. Judges, therefore, frequently warn juries against attaching too much weight to such evidence, in the absence of circumstances that make it more convincing—for example, if the complainant had no reason to imagine that s/he was being observed. As Lord Lane CJ pointed out in *Chauhun* (1981) 73 Cr App R 232,

> the weight to be given to distress varies infinitely, and juries should be warned that . . . they must be fully satisfied that there is no question of it having been feigned.
>
> (at 235)

This does not mean that such a warning should be delivered routinely in every case in which distress figures. As Scott Baker LJ explained in *Romeo* [2004] 1 Cr App R 417 at [13]: 'what is necessary is that in appropriate cases the judge should alert the jury to the sometimes very real risk that the distress may have been feigned.' In *Keast* [1998] Crim LR 748, the Court of Appeal did observe that evidence of distress, which is somewhat problematical anyway, becomes even more so when offences have been committed over a long period and the victim has not complained from the outset. Evidence of distress, it was therefore suggested, ought only to be admitted if there is 'some concrete basis for regarding the demeanour... described by the witnesses as confirming... that sexual abuse has occurred'. Evidence of a witness's demeanour, of course, is not relevant only to sexual offences. In *Townsend* [2003] EWCA Crim 3173, for instance, T was charged with doing an act intended to pervert the course of justice, in that he had offered money to V to induce her to withdraw a rape allegation she had made against her partner. T admitted offering V money, but claimed that it was only to help her out financially. V's friend testified that shortly after T's visit V had seemed angry and distressed, but at the time would not explain why. The Court of Appeal said that a person's reaction shortly after an incident was not dissimilar to *res gestae* (see *post*, paras **9.45–9.62**). A witness's demeanour, if close in time to the relevant event, might therefore have probative value, in which case it constituted evidence that the jury could take into account.

Exception 2: Rebutting suggestions of concoction or afterthought (Criminal Justice Act 2003, s 120(2))

5.22 Sometimes it may be suggested to a witness in cross-examination that his or her testimony is an invention—something that the witness has concocted. When this occurs, as another exception to the rule prohibiting self-serving statements, evidence may be adduced to show that the witness has not lately concocted that testimony but has consistently told the same tale from an early juncture. In *Benjamin* (1913) 8 Cr App R 146, for instance, the defence suggested that a police officer's testimony, to the effect that he had kept a suspected gaming house under surveillance from a perilous perch on a neighbouring chimney-stack, was a recent fabrication and that he had made no mention of this in his original depositions before the magistrate. The prosecution was allowed to introduce into evidence the notebook the police officer had used during the period of surveillance recording his observations in order to rebut the suggestion that his testimony was a recent invention. Similarly, in *Oyesiku* (1971) 56 Cr App R 240, a case involving an assault on a police officer, doubt was cast on the evidence of O's wife, who had testified that her husband had not been the aggressor but had merely been defending himself against an assault made upon him by the victim, whom O did not realise was a policeman.

Since Crown counsel had alleged that this version of events was a late invention, the Court of Appeal held that the defence ought to have been allowed to adduce the statement O's wife had made to a solicitor two days after the event to identical effect.

5.23 In *Oyesiku*, Karminski LJ expressly approved a passage from the judgment of Dixon CJ in the Australian High Court in *Nominal Defendant v Clements* (1960) 104 CLR 476, in which the latter said:

> The rule of evidence under which [a previous consistent statement] was let in is well rec-
> ognized and of long standing. If the credit of a witness is impugned as to some material
> fact to which he deposes upon the ground that his account is a late invention or has been
> lately devised or reconstructed, even though not with conscious dishonesty, that makes
> admissible a statement to the same effect as the account he gave as a witness if it was
> made by the witness contemporaneously with the event or at a time sufficiently early to
> be inconsistent with the suggestion that his account is a late invention or reconstruction.
> But, inasmuch as the rule forms a definite exception to the general principle excluding
> statements made out of court and admits a possibly self-serving statement made by
> the witness, great care is called for in applying it . . . [T]he judge at the trial must exercise
> care in assuring himself not only that the account given by the witness in his testimony
> is attacked on the ground of recent invention or reconstruction or that a foundation for
> such an attack has been laid by the party but also that the contents of the statement are
> in fact to the like effect as his account given in his evidence and that having regard to the
> time and circumstances in which it was made it rationally tends to answer the attack. It is
> obvious that it may not be easy sometimes to be sure that counsel is laying a foundation
> for impugning the witness's account of a material incident or fact as a recently invented,
> devised or reconstructed story. Counsel himself may proceed with a subtlety which is the
> outcome of caution in pursuing what may prove a dangerous course. That is one reason
> why the trial judge's opinion has a peculiar importance.
>
> (at 479)

5.24 *Does the accusation need to refer to 'recent' concoction?* It was often assumed that in order to trigger this exception to the rule against narrative the asccusation had to be that the invention was *recent*. However, in *Athwal* [2009] 1 WLR 2430 Maurice Kay LJ pointed out that s 120(2) only states: 'If a previous statement by the witness is admitted as evidence to rebut a suggestion that his oral evidence has been fabricated . . .':

> "[R]ecent" is an elastic description, the purpose of which is to assist in the identification of
> circumstances in which the traditional rule against self-corroboration, sometimes referred
> to as the rule against narrative, should not extend to the exclusion of a previous consistent
> statement where there is a rational and potentially cogent basis for its use as a tool for

deciding where the truth lies. . . . There is no margin in the length of time. The touchstone is whether the evidence may fairly assist the jury in ascertaining where the truth lies. It is for the trial judge to preserve the balance of fairness and to ensure that unjustified excursions into self-corroboration are not permitted, whether the witness was called by the prosecution or the defence.

(at [58])

There is no statutory requirement that the invention must have been recent. As a matter of fact, although the cases have variously spoken of the exception as involving 'recent concoction', 'recent fabrication', 'late invention' and so on, the Law Commission simply referred to it as 'afterthought' and in practice recency seems never to have been a strict requirement (eg, *Benjamin*). In the influential Irish case, *Flanagan v Fahy* [1918] 2 IR 361, esp at p 389 *per* Ronan, LJ, members of the court strongly implied that the exception only came into play if a cross-examiner was effectively asking the question: 'When did you first invent this story?' I would contend that s 120(2) has made no substantive alteration to the exception to the rule against narrative allowing the adduction of evidence to rebut the suggestion that a witness's evidence is fabricated (see further Munday, *Athwal and All That*... [2010] J Crim Law 415).

5.25 Prior to the Criminal Justice Act 2003, evidence of a witness's prior consistent statement admitted under this exception was admissible only to reinstate that party's credibility: that is, to show that the witness had indeed told a consistent tale from the outset. Section 120(2) of the 2003 Act, however, has altered the status of such prior statements, when admitted, by enacting that:

If a previous statement by the witness is admitted as evidence to rebut a suggestion that his oral evidence has been fabricated, that statement is admissible as evidence of any matter stated of which oral evidence by the witness would be admissible.

Therefore, such statements may be treated henceforth by the tribunal of fact as evidence of the facts... unless, of course, one subscribes to the view that, contrary to the Court of Appeal's claim in *Athwal*, the Act, as drafted, does not successfully integrate this former common law exception into the broader fabric of the new hearsay regime (see wording of s 114(1)(a) of the Criminal Justice Act 2003 and Munday, *Athwal and All That*).

Exception 3: *Res gestae*

5.26 This third category of case, which, as we shall see, also constitutes a significant exception to the hearsay rule (see *post*, paras **9.45–9.62**), allows previous consistent statements made by a party which form part of what is called the *res gestae* to be admitted as evidence of the facts as an exception to the rule against narrative. The expression *res gestae* refers to words that are part and parcel of the transaction and that are uttered in circumstances where the mind is so dominated by the event as to eliminate the risk of fabrication. This exception to the hearsay rule was expressly retained by the Criminal Justice Act 2003, s 118, r 4, which now provides:

> Any rule of law under which in criminal proceedings a statement is admissible as evidence of any matter stated if—
>
> (a) the statement was made by a person so emotionally overpowered by an event that the possibility of concoction or distortion can be disregarded,
>
> (b) the statement accompanied an act which can be properly evaluated as evidence only if considered in conjunction with the statement, or
>
> (c) the statement relates to a physical sensation or a mental state (such as intention or emotion).

The classical example of *res gestae* in the context of the rule against narrative is *Fowkes* (1856) Times, 8 March. At a trial that took place at Leicester Spring Assizes, the deceased's son testified that he and a police officer had been sitting in a room with his father. As a shot rang out, the son looked towards the window, saw a man with a gun 'and hooted, "There's Butcher!"' ('The Butcher' was the name by which the defendant was known.) Lord Campbell CJ ruled that this exclamation might be proved. The son related what he had called out, and the police officer too was allowed to report the son's exclamation. This was in effect an assertion that 'The Butcher' was the assassin and corroborated the witness's account in court of who shot his father. However, the statement also formed an obvious part of the *res gestae*, in the sense that it 'was made by a person so emotionally overpowered by an event that the possibility of concoction or distortion can be disregarded' (r 4(a)). The son's exclamation was, and would therefore still be, held admissible.

Exception 4: Previous statements of a party identifying or describing a person, object or place (Criminal Justice Act 2003, s 120(5))

5.27   The Criminal Justice Act 2003 has carved out a further exception to the rule against narrative, permitting the previous statements of a witness to be proved where the purpose is to identify or describe a person, object or place. Prior to the Act, problems quite frequently arose when a witness, who had perhaps previously identified a suspect at an identification parade, was no longer able to recollect all the details—or, conceivably, could recollect nothing at all—by the time of trial. Take the case of *Osborne and Virtue* [1973] QB 678. One witness, Mrs B, had picked O and V out at an identification parade but by the time of trial could not actually recall having picked anyone out. Another witness, Mrs H, somewhat less forgetful, did not believe that the person she had picked out at the parade was present in court. To supplement these deficiencies in the Crown case, in this instance the police officer responsible for the parade was permitted to give evidence of the relevant identifications made by the witnesses. The Court of Appeal, overlooking the uncomfortable fact that strictly speaking this evidence was inadmissible hearsay, held that the police officer's testimony had been properly admitted because 'all the prosecution were seeking to do was to establish the fact of identification'. Even if the courts were often able to arrive at a commonsensical solution by slightly distorting the law, the position was far from satisfactory.

5.28 This type of situation is now covered by s 120. Section 120(4) provides that:

> A previous statement by the witness is admissible as evidence of any matter stated of which oral evidence by him would be admissible, if—
>
> (a) any of the following three conditions is satisfied, and
>
> (b) while giving evidence the witness indicates that to the best of his belief he made the statement, and that to the best of his belief it states the truth.

The first condition referred to in s 120(5) is that:

> . . . the statement identifies or describes a person, object or place.

Henceforth, whenever a witness wishes to refer to any such previous statement, presumably made at a time when matters were fresh—or fresher—in his mind, provided that the witness declares that, to the best of his belief, he both made the statement and it states the truth, that previous statement will be admissible as evidence of the facts. The admissibility of the statement will of course be subject to the discretion of the court under PACE, s 78 (preserved by the Criminal Justice Act 2003, s 116(2)(a)) and, conceivably, the court's additional discretion to exclude statements if their admission would unduly waste court time (s 126(1)(b): see *ante*, para **5.17**).

Exception 5: Supplementing deficiencies in the memory of witnesses (Criminal Justice Act, ss 139 and 120(6))

5.29 English law traditionally placed a premium on testimony being given in court by the witnesses in person. Such testimony had to be, to a high degree, self-sufficient. This used to come across in two ways. On the one hand, 'self-sufficiency' signified—and, to a great extent, still signifies—that, unlike the practice followed in some legal systems, witnesses appearing in English courts ought not to have been coached in what they are going to say and how to say it. As the Court of Appeal said in *Arif* (1993) 26 May, unreported:

> It is right to emphasise that nothing in this judgment should be taken as affording the slightest encouragement to rehearsals of the evidence of witnesses either for the Crown or defence in a criminal trial, much less to the coaching of witnesses. Such practices are to be strongly discouraged because the risk of abuse is so very great. Any practice which raises the risk of fabrication of evidence must be avoided. Even in the absence of such fabrication the dangers of abuse of the practice are likely to give rise to substantial investigations both before and during the trial which in many cases may well impede and complicate the conduct of the trial.

Rather like a bullfight, the bull ought not to know too much about what awaits him in the arena. In the same way, pre-trial conferences, where the prosecution's police witnesses get together to compare notes and to agree on their evidence, have been strongly discouraged. As Farquharson LJ said in *Skinner* (1993) 158 JP 931:

> It is one thing to have a conference to plan the presentation of the case well ahead of the hearing, but a quite different thing where witnesses are drawn together immediately before the trial at the courthouse, and take part in the kind of discussions we have been referring to here.
>
> (at 937)

'Self-sufficiency' also used to manifest itself in another way. The common law imposed considerable restrictions on the ability of witnesses to remind themselves of the facts to which they were called to testify. It was far from a foregone conclusion that a witness, who was unable any longer to recall events clearly by the time he stood in the witness box and who wished to refresh his faltering memory from the text of an earlier statement he had made, would be permitted to do so. The courts clung to the notion that witnesses come into court to testify to what they can actually recollect rather than to what they may once have known of a particular incident. Testimony, it was sometimes said, constituted more of a memory test than a search for accurate information.

5.30 In latter years, the common law courts' restrictive attitude began to alter, and the giving of evidence came to be viewed less as simply a test of a witness's memory and more as a realistic attempt to provide the tribunal of fact with the most reliable account of what may have taken place. Lloyd LJ, for example, in *Sutton* (1991) 94 Cr App R 70 cited with approval a passage from *Richardson* [1971] 2 QB 484 to the effect that:

> The courts . . . must take care not to deprive themselves by new, artificial rules of practice of the best chances of learning the truth.

Nevertheless, despite the progress made, the Criminal Justice Act 2003 had to intervene in order to liberalise the rules regulating the refreshing of witnesses' memories.

5.31 Witnesses will very frequently have made a statement at a time when events were fresh, or were at least fresher, in their minds than they are by the time of trial. The statement will often be a witness statement made to the police. But occasionally, a witness may have composed a personal *aide-mémoire*, contemporaneous with events, with a view to preserving a reliable account of matters. In *Britton* [1987] 1 WLR 539, for example, B, who had been arrested for assaulting a police constable, when released, went straight home and typed an account of events, from which he was subsequently allowed to refresh his memory at trial. The courts, it might be noted, have not restricted refreshing of memory exclusively to written documents. As Judge LJ remarked in *Bailey* [2001] EWCA Crim 733, echoing the Court of Appeal's rather less robust remarks in *Maqsud Ali* [1966] 1 QB 688 that it would be wrong to deny the law of evidence the advantages to be gained from new techniques and devices,

> We can see no reason why the principle by which a witness is permitted to refresh his memory to the fullest permissible extent should be confined to him looking at a piece of paper with writing on it. Common sense suggests that if modern technology provides a better or different means for the same purpose, it should be available for use in court.
> (at [10])

It would therefore have been perfectly acceptable in *Bailey* for undercover police officers to have refreshed their memories from the tape recordings they had secretly made of conversations with drug dealers, to have compiled their notebooks from the tapes, and then to have given their evidence accordingly. This species of eventuality is now covered by s 139(2) of the 2003 Act (see *post*, para **5.33**).

5.32 Witnesses, prior to going into court to give evidence, have also regularly had access to their witness statements. It has for long been accepted practice that, in order to improve their recall, witnesses are allowed to read through their statements outside the courtroom prior to giving evidence. This is permitted subject to the opposing party, as a matter of courtesy, being informed that the statements have been so used. The concession not only recognises the futility of attempting to ban witnesses from referring to these statements, but also affords some recognition by the courts that over time memory fades and that earlier statements a witness may have made are more likely to contain reliable accounts of events. Indeed, as the court frankly acknowledged in *Richardson* [1971] 2 QB 484:

> Testimony in the witness box becomes more a test of memory than of truthfulness if witnesses are deprived of the opportunity of checking their recollection beforehand by

reference to statements or notes made at a time closer to the events in question (at p 489, quoting from the judgment of the Supreme Court of Hong Kong in *Lau Pak Ngam v R* [1966] Crim LR 443).

5.33 Witnesses may also refer to documents to refresh their memories in the course of giving evidence. Section 139(1) of the Criminal Justice Act 2003 now sets out the circumstances in which a witness may use documents to refresh his memory:

> A person giving oral evidence in criminal proceedings about any matter may, at any stage in the course of doing so, refresh his memory of it from a document made or verified by him at an earlier time if—
>
> (a) he states in his oral evidence that the document records his recollection of the matter at that earlier time, and
>
> (b) his recollection of the matter is likely to have been significantly better at that time than it is at the time of his oral evidence.

Section 139(2) makes similar provision for any witness whose earlier statement is retained in a sound recording provided that a transcript has been made of the sound recording.

5.34 A contemporaneous document typically used for refreshing memory is the police officer's notebook. As with any other witness who refreshes his memory from a document, the opposing side may ask to view the officer's notebook and may cross-examine him on its contents. If counsel did this, under the old common law care had to be taken not to cross-examine on matters in the notebook to which the police officer had not actually referred when refreshing his memory; otherwise, the entire contents of the notebook might become evidence in the case. Section 120(3) lays down:

> A statement made by the witness in a document—
>
> (a) which is used by him to refresh his memory while giving evidence,
>
> (b) on which he is cross-examined, and
>
> (c) which as a consequence is received in evidence in the proceedings,
>
> is admissible as evidence of any matter stated of which oral evidence by him would be admissible.

In *Pashmfouroush* [2006] EWCA Crim 2330 Richards LJ took the wording of para (c), 'which as a consequence is received in evidence in the proceedings', to signify that the old common law principle endures:

> Even if it could be said that the document had been used by the witness to refresh her memory while giving evidence, it still does not seem to us that the matter falls within

s.120(3) so as to render the witness statement as a whole admissible in evidence. Section 120(3) does not provide for the circumstances in which a documentary statement may be received in evidence, but provides for the evidential status of a document where it is received in evidence. Whether it should be received in evidence in the first place is subject to the former common-law rules. . . . [W]here a document is used to refresh a witness's memory and cross-examination is confined to those parts of the document which have already been used by the witnesses to refresh his memory, then the document does not become evidence in the case. If, however, the cross-examination strays beyond that part of the document which has been used to refresh the witness's memory, then the party calling the witness can insist on it being treated as evidence in the case and it will thereupon become an exhibit. . . . [Section] 120 does not purport to alter the common law rule as to the circumstances in which a memory-refreshing document may be exhibited, but provides that the effect of exhibiting such a document is that it becomes evidence as to the truth of its contents.

(at [25])

5.35 Under the old common law if more than one police officer had attended an incident, the Court of Appeal held that the officers might make up their notebooks jointly (*Bass* [1953] 1 QB 680). There is some force in the Court's argument that, basically, two heads are better than one and that a pooling of memories ought to achieve a fuller and more accurate account. However, it could also be argued that a procedure that produces a uniform police version of events serves to deprive the defence of an opportunity of exploiting inconsistencies in the various police officers' accounts. This is not necessarily desirable. Section 139 is silent on this point, but one might assume that the law remains as stated by the Court in *Bass*.

5.36 Before the intervention of the Criminal Justice Act 2003 witnesses' previous statements already played some role in proceedings, and the rules governing the refreshing of memory were being progressively relaxed. However, under the common law, even when witnesses were allowed to make use of their previous statements, these statements did not constitute actual evidence of the facts but were only employed as *aide-mémoires*. Section 120 of the 2003 Act, however, has swept aside many of the remaining obstacles to the admission of previous statements made by witnesses as evidence of the facts in criminal cases. Section 120(4), it will be recalled, provides:

A previous statement by the witness is admissible as evidence of any matter stated of which oral evidence by him would be admissible, if—

(a) any of the following three conditions is satisfied, and

(b) while giving evidence the witness indicates that to the best of his belief he made the statement, and that to the best of his belief it states the truth.

The second condition, set forth in s 120(6), requires:

> ...that the statement was made by the witness when the matters stated were fresh in his memory but he does not remember them, and cannot reasonably be expected to remember them, well enough to give oral evidence of them in the proceedings.

Therefore, provided that a witness:

(i) can vouch that, to the best of his belief, he actually made the statement in question,

(ii) is prepared to indicate that, to the best of his belief, it states the truth, and

(iii) possessed the requisite legal capability at the time the statement was made (s 123(1)),

the court may receive a statement that meets the conditions set out in s 120(6). The statement will then be treated as evidence of any matter stated of which oral evidence by the witness would have been admissible. (According to s 115(2), it bears repeating: 'A statement is any representation of fact or opinion made by a person by whatever means; and it includes a representation made in a sketch, photofit or other pictorial form.')

5.37 The old common law rules prescribed that the statement from which a witness might refresh his memory:

(i) must have been made by him personally or under his personal direction; and

(ii) must also have been made contemporaneously with the events recorded.

Each of these restrictions posed its problems: the first condition interacted with the hearsay rule to produce a case law of some intricacy (see second edition of this work, para **5.18**), whilst the contemporaneity requirement was somewhat vague: how soon after events did a witness need to have made his statement? True, in *Richardson* [1971] 2 QB 484 Sachs LJ did state that contemporaneity should not refer to 'an over-short period' but that the account 'must have been written down either at the time of the transaction or so shortly afterwards that the events were fresh in his memory'. Sometimes, this meant that several weeks would have elapsed before the witness made a note of events, although in *da Silva* [1990] 1 All ER 29 Stuart-Smith LJ did doubt whether a statement made a month after the relevant events could be treated as contemporaneous. The Criminal Justice Act 2003 side-steps some of these problems. The Act still requires that the statement was 'made' by the witness, but relaxation of the hearsay rule (see *post*, Chapter 9) will avoid the problems encountered under the old law.

5.38 Under the 2003 Act it only has to be shown:

(i) that the statement was made whilst matters were still fresh in the witness's mind. Strict contemporaneity is no longer a requirement. As Tuckey LJ explained in *McAfee* [2006] EWCA Crim 2914,

> [It is] for the judge to decide, having heard what the witness had to say, whether it was likely that her memory would have been significantly better or not. The statute contains no requirement of contemporaneity. This is just the sort of decision which a trial judge is in the best position to make...Judges' decisions should be accepted unless they are obviously wrong, unreasonable or perverse....A judge must have a residual discretion to refuse a s.139 application even if the statutory conditions are met. But there were no good reasons for doing so in this case. The prosecution were entitled to present their best case to the jury. That is the object of many of the provisions in the 2003 Act. The defence of course were free to make, and in this case did make, forensic capital out of how this evidence emerged and of course the other inconsistencies in this witness's evidence.
>
> (at [33])

(ii) that the witness does not now remember the matters related in the statement. Given that s 120(6) goes on to refer to the witness not recalling the matters recorded in the statement well enough to give oral evidence of them, it seems clear that imperfect recall will be sufficient to activate this provision. The subsection, however, may not cover cases where a witness simply cannot recall the odd fact. It appears rather directed at the witness who has suffered a more generalised failure of recollection;

(iii) that the witness could not reasonably be expected to remember the matters treated in his earlier statement well enough to give oral evidence of them. Again, it will be for the court to determine in individual cases what it would and would not be reasonable for a particular witness to remember. The more detailed and complicated the data, presumably the more likely it would be that the witness might have forgotten them.

5.39 Statements can be proved by producing either the original document or a copy of all or the material part of the statement 'authenticated in whatever way the court may approve' (s 133). Under the old common law, too, it was permissible for a witness to refresh his memory from derivative documents. Thus, in *Mills* [1962] 1 WLR 1152 a policeman was allowed to refresh his memory from notes made from a tape-recorded conversation between two suspects. In *Cheng* (1976) 63 Cr App R 20 the court went further. A policeman had made notes in 1972 on observation he had kept on C. Before he could be tried, C absconded. By the time that C had been recaptured in 1975, the police officer had been affected to another force and his notebook was lost. He was allowed to refresh his memory from a document prepared from those notes, which he had intended to use at C's original committal proceedings. Since, under s 115(2), 'a statement is any representation of fact or opinion made by a person by whatever means', such documents will continue to be admissible provided that they comply with s 120(4) and (6).

5.40 Although the 2003 Act makes witness statements widely utilisable as evidence of the facts, in jury trials the statements themselves will not normally be placed in the jurors' hands during their deliberations. Section 122 provides that when such a 'document'—which, according to s 134, includes 'anything in which information of any description is recorded'—or a copy thereof is produced as an exhibit:

> The exhibit must not accompany the jury when they retire to consider their verdict unless—
>
> (a) the court considers it appropriate, or
>
> (b) all the parties to the proceedings agree that it should accompany the jury.

Although para (a) supplies no further guidance on how a court is expected to exercise its discretion, in *Hulme* [2007] 1 Cr App R 26 at [25] Richards LJ warned that the discretion was not to be exercised lightly as there is 'the undoubted risk that the jury would place disproportionate weight on the contents of the document, as compared with the oral evidence, for the reason that they had the document there in front of them.'

5.41 Additionally, under the 2003 Act a court retains further discretion to exclude statements made otherwise than in oral evidence in the proceedings. As well as the customary discretion to exclude statements whose admission would reflect adversely on the fairness of the proceedings (PACE, s 78), as we have already seen (*ante*, para **5.17**), the Criminal Justice Act 2003, s 126(1) additionally allows the court to exclude statements made otherwise than in oral evidence if it is satisfied that the case for excluding the statement, taking account of the danger that to admit it would result in undue waste of time, substantially outweighs the case for admitting it, taking account of the value of the evidence.

5.42 *Taxonomy.* A question of classification perhaps deserves brief mention. In *Athwal* [2009] 1 WLR 2430 Maurice Kay LJ concluded that since statements rebutting suggestions of afterthought, and indeed statements admitted under the other exceptions to the rule against narrative by virtue of s 120 of the Criminal Justice Act 2003, are 'admitted as admissible *hearsay* under the regime of the 2003 Act', '*it would be helpful if the leading practitioners' textbooks were now to reflect this*' (at [53] and [61]). As I have argued elsewhere, in this respect it is not clear that the 2003 Act has succeeded in its goal. However, leaving questions of statutory construction to one side, it should be remembered that historically the rule against narrative and the rule against hearsay developed separately, and served rather different ends. Furthermore, save in those situations where, exceptionally, such evidence is now admitted via s 120, the independent rule against narrative continues to apply. With respect, I am not persuaded that it is necessary to transpose this entire topic into the already bulging chapter on hearsay evidence. Nevertheless, I would point out that once a witness's statement falls within any of the exceptions enumerated in s 120, since it becomes 'admissible as evidence of any matter stated of which oral evidence by him would be admissible', it behaves in many ways like other items of admissible hearsay, whose principles are set out in Chapter 9 of this book. (See further Munday, *Athwal and All That*... [2010] J Crim Law 415.)

Evidence-in-chief delivered by video recording (Criminal Justice Act 2003, s 137)

5.43 Although this provision may not be brought into force in the immediate future, one further reform contained in the Criminal Justice Act 2003 looks set to exert considerable impact on the way in which witnesses give their evidence, at least in the more serious criminal cases. Section 137 provides that if a person claims to have witnessed, 'visually or in any other way', an indictable offence or a prescribed offence triable either way, or has even just witnessed events closely connected with such an offence, and that witness has made a video-recorded statement when events were fresh in his or her mind, the court may direct that the video recording be played as the witness's evidence-in-chief in the proceedings. Such a witness will not need to have been on oath at the time the recording was made (s 137(5)). The court's order may be to the effect that either the entire recording, or merely a part of the recording, be so admitted (s 138(2)). If the judge is minded to admit all or part of the video recording, s 138(3) requires him to consider whether such an order would carry a risk of prejudice to the defendant and, if so, whether that risk is outweighed by the desirability of showing the whole or part of the recording. Provided that the witness asserts in his oral testimony that the statements made in the video recording are true, 'they shall be treated as if made by him in that evidence' (s 137 (2)).

5.44 These provisions only apply to the witnesses in the case, not to the defendant. Moreover, a court may only direct that a video recording be used in this way if it appears that:

(i) the witness's recollection of the events in question is likely to have been significantly better when he gave the recorded account than it will be when he gives oral evidence in the proceedings, and

(ii) it is in the interests of justice for the recording to be admitted...(s 137(3)(b))

In determining what is in the interests of justice for this purpose, as is now routine statutory practice, Parliament instructs the courts as to what matters they must have 'regard in particular' in coming to their decision. Thus, they are told that they must consider:

(a) the interval between the time of the events in question and the time when the recorded account was made;

(b) any other factors that might affect the reliability of what the witness said in that account;

(c) the quality of the recording;

(d) any views of the witness as to whether his evidence in chief should be given orally or by means of the recording. (s 137(4))

Whenever this procedure is followed, s 138 stipulates that 'the witness may not give evidence in chief otherwise than by means of the recording as to any matter which, in the opinion of the court, has been dealt with adequately in the recorded account'.

5.45 It will be seen that, when brought into force, this provision, which emerged from the *Auld Review* but which, disturbingly, has not been the subject of widespread discussion, could mean that in the fullness of time the evidence-in-chief of the principal witnesses in the most serious criminal cases could be given predominantly in the form of video-recorded statements. These statements would then be supplemented, if need be, by oral evidence-in-chief in relation to matters not adequately covered by the witness's video recording. Such a procedure will make further inroads into the principle of orality that hitherto has dominated thinking about the common law form of trial. Given the substantial investment that these provisions will require, it is not anticipated that they will be brought into force in the immediate future. This may even afford time properly to consider their merits.

Statements made by the accused when first taxed with incriminating facts

5.46 A suspect, when first questioned, may make incriminating replies. Such replies may be admissible evidence against him as a confession, because, as we shall see, provided that they comply with the legal requirements imposed by PACE, s 76, confessions made by the accused constitute an exception to the hearsay rule (see *post,* Chapter 10). Alternatively, the suspect may make replies that include both admissions and denials. Such statements, which are known as 'mixed statements', are more fully considered in the context of the law relating to confessions. As we shall see, the House of Lords has determined that, when adduced by the Crown, the entire contents of such mixed statements are admissible as evidence of the facts, although the judge can direct the jurors that they may wish to attribute greater weight to the incriminating portions of the statement than they do to the exculpatory parts (*Sharp* [1988] 1 All ER 65; *Aziz* [1996] AC 41: see *post,* paras **10.50** ff). On other occasions the suspect may make replies which are wholly exonerating. Under the rule against narrative, these self-serving replies are inadmissible and do not constitute evidence that the defendant may use to establish his innocence. However, the courts do hold that the accused's reaction on first being taxed with incriminating facts is admissible evidence. As the Court of Appeal explained in *Storey* (1968) 52 Cr App Rep 334:

> A statement made voluntarily by an accused person to the police is evidence in the trial because of its vital relevance as showing the reaction of the accused when first taxed with incriminating facts.
>
> (at 337–8)

As this passage indicates, the defendant's exculpatory statement is not evidence of the facts but merely evidence of his reaction when first taxed. It could also be noted that the expression 'first taxed' is not to be taken too literally. As the Court of Appeal explained in *Pearce* (1979) 69 Cr App R 365, it is simply that the more time that has elapsed after the first encounter the less weight that can be attributed to the statement.

5.47 Since the statement affords evidence of the accused's reaction, a degree of spontaneity is demanded. If the accused tenders a statement prepared with the assistance of his lawyer, for example, a court is entitled not to admit it as evidence of the accused's reaction since a statement drafted with legal advice may reveal nothing of the accused's true state of mind at the relevant time. In *Newsome* (1980) 71 Cr App R 325, N was charged with rape. After two police interviews, N conferred with his solicitor and, finally, at a third interview wrote down a statement in which he related that the complainant had been a willing party. The Court of Appeal upheld the trial judge's decision to exclude N's self-serving statement. The function of what one might term reaction evidence is broadly similar to that of recent complaint evidence under the old common law (see *ante,* paras **5.4–5.5**) in the sense that it may show that the defendant has maintained a consistent stance, denying the offence from the outset. Like recent complaint evidence, which is not admitted if the complainant fails to testify (*ante,* para **5.10**; Criminal Justice Act 2003, s 120(4)(b)), evidence of exculpatory statements by the accused need not be left to the jury if the defendant elects not to testify—unless admitted in order to rebut a suggestion of concoction or afterthought (*ante,* paras **5.22–5.25**) or, possibly, to refresh memory under the exception discussed above (*ante,* paras **5.29** ff). In *Barbery* (1975) 62 Cr App R 248,

B, who had made a voluntary statement to the police that he had not been involved in an affray, was not allowed to adduce this statement in evidence precisely because he had chosen not to give evidence; such statements are not admitted as to the truth of their contents, only to afford evidence of the accused's attitude at the time they were made. Although it might have presented a more harmonious picture had it reformed this rule, the Criminal Justice Act 2003 has left this situation unchanged: an accused's exculpatory statements continue to be evidence only of his reaction when first taxed and are still not admissible as evidence of the facts.

Statements made by the accused when incriminating articles are recovered

5.48 When a defendant is charged with theft or with handling stolen goods, if the prosecution can show that he was found in possession of *recently* stolen goods, a presumption of fact comes into play. In the absence of an innocent explanation, the jury is entitled, if it so wishes, to draw the inference that because the goods were recently stolen the defendant knew or believed those goods to be stolen and—provided, of course, that the jury is sure that the prosecution has established the other elements of the offence charged—may go on to hold that the accused is therefore the thief or the handler. Because the inference of guilty knowledge may be drawn if the defendant has no explanation for his possession of the goods, what the defendant says when found in possession of recently stolen goods is treated as admissible. Although the presumption was not invoked in the case, in a separate concurring judgment in the Canadian Supreme Court case of *Graham* (1972) 26 DLR (3d) 579 Laskin J explained how such statements operate. In essence, 'if the accused has made a pre-trial statement in explanation of his recent possession, it is for the trial judge to decide as a question of law whether that statement has contemporaneity; and if so, no adverse inference of guilty knowledge is open if the trier of fact...should...find that the defendant's explanation is one that may reasonably be true'.

FURTHER READING

Sir Robin Auld, *Review of the Criminal Courts of England and Wales* (2001) especially paras 11.81–11.94

Munday, '*Athwal* and All That: Previous Statements, Narrative, and the Taxonomy of Hearsay' [2010] J Crim Law 415

SELF-TEST QUESTIONS

1. Grope is on trial for having indecently assaulted his stepdaughter, Laetitia, on 1 May. On 2 May Laetitia's mother found Laetitia in floods of tears. The mother demanded to know what was the matter, and Laetitia told her that Grope had done something terrible to her. Their conversation, however, was interrupted by an incoming call on her mother's mobile telephone. At this point Laetitia stormed out of the house and the matter was never mentioned again. On 15 June, having consumed a couple of 'Alabama slammers' at the gym, Laetitia gave her personal trainer, Aerobia, a detailed account of how Grope had molested her on 1 May. At his trial, Grope denies the offence. He also suggests that Laetitia has concocted this story because in July Grope threw her boyfriend, Lout, out of the house for violently breaking wind during Sunday lunch. The trial judge has refused the prosecution leave to call Aerobia as a witness. Discuss.

2. When and how may a witness refresh his/her memory?

3. Under what circumstances can a witness's previous statement be treated as evidence of the facts?

4. In cases like *Storey* (1968) 52 Cr App R 334, the courts hold that a defendant's response when first taxed with an offence may be given in evidence in order to show his reaction but, if the defendant makes an exculpatory statement, such statement may not be used by the defence as evidence of the truth of its contents. Does this distinction, which has been retained by the Criminal Justice Act 2003, make sense?

5. Miss Coelha, who was the victim of a street robbery, attended an identification procedure (a video parade) at which she formally identified Mme Vulpina as the culprit. At Mme Vulpina's trial Miss Coelha cannot even recall ever having attended a procedure, and she is quite unable to identify Mme Vulpina as the person she picked out at any procedure. Can the prosecution call PC Raffles to testify that he was present during the identification procedure and that on that occasion Miss Coelha picked out Mme Vulpina?

6. Under what circumstances may a witness's testimony eventually be given in the form of a video recording under s 137 of the Criminal Justice Act 2003? Why might this be thought a welcome reform?

6

Character and credibility

SUMMARY

Issue and credit

The concept of 'credibility'

Bringing out the character of the parties and their witnesses

- Evidence relating to the character of one's own witness
- Evidence relating to the character of one's opponent's witness

Evidence of the defendant's good character

- What constitutes admissible character evidence?
- When will a defendant be considered of good character?
- The form of the good character direction
- Consequences of a defendant adducing evidence of good character

The law is no stranger to the philosophy of "As if". It has built up many of its doctrines by a make-believe that things are other than they are.

Benjamin Cardozo, *The Paradoxes of Legal Science* (1928)

Issue and credit

6.1 Evidence introduced to illuminate someone's character is a fairly common feature in both civil and criminal trials. According to the context, however, it may fulfil different purposes. On the one hand, it may serve as an indicator of whether or not someone is likely to be a truthful witness. If it can be shown, for example, that a witness has a clutch of previous convictions for deception and perjury, the court is liable to hesitate before placing too great a faith in that witness's testimony. In such cases, it is said that the party's revealed character reflects adversely on his or her 'credit' or 'credibility'. In contrast, in other circumstances—which, in the main, will arise in criminal cases—evidence which shows that a defendant is of bad character because he has committed similar acts on other occasions, may reveal that defendant's propensity to commit acts of the type charged (ss 101(1)(d) and 103, Criminal Justice Act 2003). We have already seen that such evidence may also be admissible against other persons, where, for instance, a defendant is endeavouring to show that a third party is in fact responsible for the crime with which the defendant stands charged: *H* (2010) 174 JP 203 (see *ante*, para **4.30**). Such evidence is admitted on account of its relevance to the principal 'issues' in the case. Although we shall see that the current rules do not by any means routinely demand evidence as strong as this, the colourful examples given in Lord Hailsham's speech in *DPP v Boardman* [1975] AC 421, 454 perhaps illustrate the point:

> While it would certainly not be enough to identify the culprit in a series of burglaries that he climbed in through a ground floor window, the fact that he left the same humorous limerick on the walls of the sitting room, or an esoteric symbol written in lipstick on the mirror, might well be enough. In a sex case . . . while a repeated homosexual act by itself might be quite insufficient to admit the evidence as confirmatory of identity or design, the fact that it was alleged to have been performed wearing the ceremonial head-dress of an Indian chief or other eccentric garb might well in appropriate circumstances suffice.

In these situations, the prosecution can point to a distinguishing feature in the conduct of the defendant. Evidence of this type will be directed towards the issue of whether the defendant has a propensity to commit the offence charged rather than simply the question of the defendant's credibility. In Lord Hailsham's examples, the character evidence will actually contribute to identifying the defendant as the culprit and to proving that he committed the offence charged. (As we shall see, defendants in criminal cases follow some special rules. Under s 103(1)(b) of the Criminal Justice Act 2003, in cases where an accused person's credit is in issue to the extent that it constitutes 'an important matter in issue between the defendant and the prosecution' (s 101(1)(d)), evidence of bad character will only be admitted if it relates to what is termed the accused's 'propensity to be untruthful'. This concept, which is more restrictive than 'dishonesty' and 'credibility', was first explained by Rose LJ in *Hanson* [2005] 2 Cr App R 21 at [13]: see *post*, paras **7.77–7.79**.)

6.2 When considering the character both of the accused and of the witnesses at the trial, the law of evidence draws a sharp distinction between matters affecting issue, on the one hand, and matters affecting credibility (or credit, as it is also known), on the other. The distinction comes into play in a variety of contexts. We have already noted that, in relation to the examination of witnesses, this distinction has an impact on a party's right to call evidence in rebuttal of his opponent's claims (see *ante*, paras **4.42–4.49**). The division between issue and credit, however, also runs through the rules that govern those exceptional situations, primarily in criminal cases, when an accused's bad character is brought to the attention of the tribunal of fact (*post*, Chapter 7). Additionally, the distinction is important in a sizeable class of criminal cases where, as we shall see presently, a judge is obliged to deliver a direction if, in the eyes of the law, an accused is of good character (see *post*, paras **6.16** ff). Finally, a party may be entitled to probe the character of the opposing party's witnesses with a view to suggesting that, owing to their dubious pasts, their testimony is more likely to be unworthy of belief than if they had been of unblemished pedigree (see *ante* paras **4.22–4.36**).

The concept of 'credibility'

6.3   *Character and credibility*. From the above, it will be apparent that the law frequently employs a concept of 'credibility'. Moreover, the law assumes that there is a direct relationship between 'character' (and more often than not, bad character in the form of past criminality) and 'credibility'. This assumption may be somewhat tendentious. In part, it is founded upon postulates that seem not to be fully borne out by the findings of applied psychology. It also rests upon a possible linguistic misapprehension. The linguistic point is that there is a tendency to refer to persons of bad character (and notably, to those with previous criminal records) as 'dishonest'. Similarly, those who are untruthful are also designated 'dishonest'. In short, the language we employ may induce us to regard 'truthfulness' and 'honesty' as a single unity. No clear line is drawn between dishonesty, in the sense of general criminality, and testimonial dishonesty. This would not especially matter if there were any evidence to suggest that these are in fact related and unified character traits. Unfortunately, the truth is that the 'Character Education Inquiry', a monumental piece of research conducted in the United States in the 1920s by Hartshorne and May, did much to dispel any such ideas. Their 'theory of specificity' found 'that neither deceit nor its opposite, "honesty", are unified character traits, but rather specific functions of life situations'. More particularly, they concluded:

> When situations involving the possibility of deception were almost identical, the behaviour of individuals did not greatly vary from occasion to occasion. But when the situations permitting dishonesty were altered...then there was found greater and greater diversity

of behaviour. So that one could not predict from what a person did in one situation what he would do in a different situation.

Hartshorne, May & Shuttleworth '3 Studies in the Organization of Character' (1930, New York) p 1)

As one leading commentator has remarked, 'the data on moral behaviour provide no support for the widespread psychodynamic belief in...a unitary entity of conscience or honesty' (Mischel, *Personality and Assessment* (1968, New York)). In fact, one could argue that the law adheres to psychological notions that, broadly speaking, were abandoned by the psychological community almost a century ago. The current situation in applied psychological circles in fact is more nuanced than this (see Redmayne, 'The Relevance of Bad Character' [2002] CLJ esp at 688 ff). Nevertheless, were the law to take the views of applied psychology seriously, there would appear to be less grounds than might be commonly assumed for inferring truthfulness in witnesses from their 'honesty' or from an absence of bad character. Similarly, it might be unwise too readily to infer untruthfulness specifically from the presence of a previous criminal record. This, however, is what the law does. Indeed, this putative rift between the psychological realities and the legal principles may even help to explain why many of the rules relating to character evidence—and especially those relating to credibility—prove so complex to operate in practice. This is not to say that the courts are totally unaware of the conceptual difficulties: as Buxton LJ noted in *Phillips* [2002] EWCA Crim 1198, 'an individual's credibility is not a seamless robe any more than is their reliability' (at [4]).

6.4 In the ensuing sections we shall examine some of the character rules relating to both witnesses and criminal defendants, where these elements come into play. Further aspects of these rules were dealt with in Chapter 4, which treats of 'The course of the trial'.

Bringing out the character of the parties and their witnesses

Evidence relating to the character of one's own witness

6.5 When deciding whether or not to believe a particular witness's testimony, the tribunal could find it extremely helpful to know something of that witness's character and general make-up. Nevertheless, as a general rule a party is not permitted to call evidence in order to reinforce the credibility of its own witnesses. Thus, as has already been mentioned, in *Robinson* (1994) 98 Cr App R 370 (*ante*, para **4.53**), the Crown was held to have been wrongly allowed to call an educational psychologist at R's trial for rape and indecent assault committed upon a mentally retarded 15-year-old. The psychologist had testified, *inter alia*, that, although seriously retarded, the complainant was not suggestible and had only a limited imagination. In short, the psychologist's testimony had been designed to enhance the reliability of the complainant's evidence by ruling out the likelihood of her being unable to remember events and by doubting her vulnerability to suggestion. Lord Taylor CJ observed:

> [A party] cannot call a witness of fact and then, without more, call a psychologist or psychiatrist to give reasons why the jury should regard the witness as reliable.
>
> (at 374)

Having referred to *Turner* [1975] QB 834, a case in which English law resolutely set its face against the admission of evidence which normally falls within 'the experience and knowledge of a judge or jury' (see *post*, paras **8.15** ff), Lord Taylor went on to hold that evidence demonstrating a witness's mental *normality* would only be admissible in restricted circumstances: for example, it might have been permissible if in *Robinson* the Crown had sought thereby to rebut evidence called by the defence suggesting that the complainant was suffering from some mental abnormality that rendered her evidence suspect. Even then, Lord Taylor added, as a rider, that 'great care would need to be taken to restrict the expert opinion to meeting the specific challenge and not to allow it to extend to "oath-helping"' (at 352).

6.6 Of course, evidence implying that a party's witness is likely to be trustworthy can insinuate itself into the case in other and subtler ways. In *DS* [1999] Crim LR 911, for instance, the accused was convicted of acts of buggery, dating back to the 1970s, committed while he was working with disturbed children, Boy Scouts and young offenders. The jury became aware that one of the complainants had since become a senior Church of England clergyman. DS argued that this information was wrongly allowed to come to the jury's attention. The Court of Appeal, however, pointed out that it was normal practice to elicit the profession of one's own witness and that this was a 'far cry' from calling evidence to bolster the witness's testimony. Moreover, the Court approved the judge's direction to the jury instructing them that while they might take into account the witness's calling, they should primarily concern themselves with the impression he made on them in the witness box.

6.7 *Disclosure of witnesses' bad character.* In criminal cases, the Crown will not infrequently call witnesses with bad characters, and more specifically with criminal convictions. The prosecution is under an obligation to reveal such information to the defence. What happens if it can be shown that the credibility of prosecution witnesses was a key issue in the case and that the Crown failed to make disclosure? Although Lord Bingham CJ acknowledged in *Farrell* (2000) March 20, unreported, 'There is no simple and straightforward answer to that question,' it may lead to the quashing of a conviction. In *Vasilou* [2000] Crim LR 845, V was not informed that three of the prosecution witnesses had bad characters, one of them possessing a record for serious offences. Because the case turned upon whether the jury believed V's account or that of the prosecution witnesses, Mance LJ quashed V's conviction since there was a realistic prospect that matters would have proceeded differently had the jury known of the latter's convictions. Even taking into account the more restrictive policy affecting non-defendants' bad character implemented in the Criminal Justice Act 2003, s 100, the appellate court would still be likely to treat a case like *Vasilou* in the same manner (see *ante*, paras **4.22** ff). Even factoring in the more restrictive policy affecting the admissibility of non-defendants' bad character, an appellate court may still take a dim view if the prosecution fails to reveal its witnesses' bad character if it might amount to either 'important explanatory evidence' or even to evidence having 'substantial probative value' under that section. In *S v DPP* (2006) 170 JP 707, S appealed by way of case stated from the refusal of justices to adjourn his trial. S had pleaded not guilty to a charge of committing a common assault upon his 16-year-old son, N, claiming that he had only acted in self-defence. N's credibility was critical. At the time of trial N had no previous convictions, but was awaiting trial at the Crown Court on a serious allegation of affray. Recognising the potential significance of this pending charge, at the pre-trial review S had asked the prosecution to supply details of the outstanding case so that he might consider whether to make an application under s 100 of the Criminal Justice Act 2003 to put these matters in evidence during S's trial, or at least to put the allegations to N in cross-examination. The prosecution failed to provide those details. At trial, S applied for an adjournment to enable that further information relating to N's outstanding court appearance to be obtained. Although the prosecution did not oppose S's application, the justices refused an adjournment. On appeal it was held that whenever it is necessary to adjourn a case to enable justice to be done following a failure by the Crown properly to disclose matters which ought to be disclosed, the adjournment must be granted, unless the court is satisfied that no prejudice would be caused to the defendant by proceeding. In this case everything depended on the credibility and reliability of N. Therefore, the detail of the case pending against him in the Crown Court may well have both damaged his credibility and borne upon his propensity for violence. In this sense, because it may have undermined the prosecution or assisted the defence, it ought to have been disclosed, and if it had been, the defence would have almost certainly have been able to argue successfully that the criteria for admissibility under the 2003 Act were fulfilled. By wrongly ordering the trial to proceed, the justices deprived the defence of the opportunity of investigating these matters.

6.8 *S v DPP* might be contrasted with *Underwood* [2003] EWCA Crim 1500, where the defence remained ignorant of a prosecution witness's 54 previous convictions, 39 of them for dishonesty. The witness had deliberately concealed his identity from the police and might have had a motive to fabricate important evidence against U.

Because the tainted witness's evidence did not relate to 'the main facts in issue' and the prosecution's other evidence made a strong case against U, the Court of Appeal declined to hold that U's conviction was unsafe (esp at [30]). As Lord Bingham explained in *Farrell*,

> The answer will depend on the weight of evidence in the case, apart from the evidence of the witness whose convictions have not been disclosed. The greater the weight of the other evidence the less significance, other things being equal, the non-disclosure is likely to have had. The answer will also depend on the extent to which the credibility and honesty of the prosecution witness whose convictions have not been disclosed is at the heart of the case.
>
> (at [7])

For this reason, in *McCallan* [2004] EWCA Crim 463, M, who had held a pistol to F's head in the toilets of a nightclub, unsuccessfully appealed his conviction for possessing a firearm with intent to cause fear of violence. Even though the victim's recent conviction for assault had not been disclosed, M's failure to give evidence at trial, another witness's testimony confirming F's distressed state after the event, the fact that the starting pistol was found loaded and cocked accorded with F's rather than M's account, and the fact that F's propensity for violence was not an issue in the case, cumulatively led the Court to the conclusion that M's conviction was safe.

6.9 Although the defendant must be informed of the Crown witnesses' bad characters, the prosecution is not obliged in all cases to reveal this to the court. As we shall see, this can pose problems for the defence given that any defendant who is also of bad character may pay a heavy price under the terms of the Criminal Justice Act 2003, s 100(1)(g), should he seek to 'make an attack on another person's character' (see *post*, paras **7.117** ff). The Court of Appeal, however, has slightly improved the accused's predicament by declaring that good practice requires that, at least if the Crown witnesses are the accomplices of the defendant, 'normally counsel for the prosecution should offer to...tell the jury about them from the outset' (*Taylor and Goodman* [1999] 2 Cr App R 163). One might even hope that good prosecution practice will extend beyond this minimum courtesy.

Evidence relating to the character of one's opponent's witness

6.10 It is not generally permissible to impeach the character of one's own witness. However, as we have seen, a party may legitimately impugn the credibility of his opponent's witness. Apart from eliciting contradictions and revealing *lacunae* in that witness's testimony, subject to the Criminal Justice Act 2003, s 100—which will apply in criminal cases, and which may permit evidence of non-defendants' bad character to be adduced—this may be achieved by questions put in cross-examination directed to bringing out the witness's previous convictions, disreputable behaviour, corruption, bias or general lack of veracity. (These matters were considered in Chapter 4, *ante*.) Such questioning will be allowed, provided that the court considers that it is relevant to the witness's credibility and provided that the cross-examination is not conducted in a manner that the court deems 'unfair or oppressive' (*Wong Kam-ming v R* [1979] 1 All ER 939, 946 *per* Lord Edmund-Davies).

6.11 As regards previous convictions, the literal wording of the Criminal Procedure Act 1865, s 6 permits a witness to be asked about 'any...misdemeanour'. Indeed, Cairns J went so far as to claim in *Clifford v Clifford* [1961] 1 WLR 1274, 1276 that 'it has never...been doubted that a conviction for any offence could be put to a witness by way of cross-examination as to credit, even though the offence was not one of dishonesty'. Cairns J's view, which proceeds on the improbably simplistic basis that all criminality is relevant to a witness's credibility, does however seem to conflict with Lawton LJ's oft-quoted *dictum* in *Sweet-Escott* (1971) 55 Cr App R 316, 320, which runs:

> Since the purpose of cross-examination as to credit is to show that the witness ought not to be believed on oath, the matters about which he is questioned must relate to his likely standing after cross-examination with the tribunal which is trying him or listening to his evidence.

6.12 *Rehabilitation of Offenders Act 1974*. In fact, Cairns J's statement can be further qualified. The Rehabilitation of Offenders Act 1974 has imposed limitations on the range of previous convictions that may form the subject of cross-examination. Although the 1974 Act, strictly speaking, is restricted in its terms to civil cases, it also now applies in criminal cases to the extent that the Consolidated Criminal Practice Direction, paras I.6.4 and I.6.6 require criminal courts to respect the policy underlying this legislation. The practice direction recommends 'that both court and advocates should give effect to the general intention of Parliament by never referring to a spent conviction when such reference can reasonably be avoided' (para I.6.4). It further stipulates that 'no one should refer in open court to a spent conviction without the authority of the judge, which authority should not be given unless the interests of justice so require' (para I.6.6).

6.13 In civil cases, too, it should be noted that the ambit of the Rehabilitation of Offenders Act is subject to significant limitations. Although s 4(1) of the Act provides that a person who has become a rehabilitated person for the purpose of the Act in respect of a conviction (known as a 'spent' conviction) shall be treated for all purposes in law as a person who has not committed or been charged with or prosecuted for or convicted of or sentenced for the offence or offences which were the subject of that conviction, in *Thomas v Metropolitan Police Commissioner* [1997] QB 813 the Court of Appeal held that judges enjoy discretion to allow reference to be made to spent convictions, provided that they are satisfied that justice cannot otherwise be done. Such discretion may be exercised not only when the spent convictions are relevant to an issue in the case, but also if they are demonstrated to be relevant to credit.

6.14 Regarding questions put to a witness in cross-examination alleging other forms of misconduct, Lawrence J in *Harris v Tippett* (1811) 2 Camp 637 declared that it is permissible to put questions to a witness relating to any improper conduct of which he may have been guilty for the purpose of trying his credit. Such questioning, however, is only proper if it refers to matters that could seriously impair the credibility of the witness. If the questions relate to matters so distant in time or so remote in character that, even if true, they would not seriously impair the witness's credibility, they cannot be asked. Again, if the gravity of the imputation that lies behind the question is in disproportion to the importance of the issue being tried, the questioning should be disallowed (see generally *Hobbs v Tinling & Co Ltd* [1929] 2 KB 1).

6.15 One further method of discrediting the opposing side's witnesses has already been discussed in a previous chapter (*ante*, para **4.58**). Although Edmund Davies LJ claimed in *Richardson* [1969] 1 QB 299 that the procedure was 'little known', 'ancient' and 'used with exceeding rarity', and Mantell LJ in *Colwill* [2002] EWCA Crim 1320 at [12] doubted its effectiveness, a party is permitted to call someone to testify to the veracity of the other side's witness. Such evidence may either relate to the impugned witness's reputation for untruthfulness or to someone's opinion of that witness's ability to tell the truth or may take the form of medical evidence indicating the unlikelihood of the witness giving a true account in the witness box.

Evidence of the defendant's good character

Everyone who spoke on my behalf was asked by the magistrates' clerk if he knew that I was homosexual and replied that he did. This question was in each case followed by the words, uttered in a voice hoarse with incredulity, "and yet you describe him as respectable?" All said, "Yes".

Quentin Crisp, *The Naked Civil Servant* (1968)

6.16 In criminal trials a defendant's character can become a relevant feature in a variety of ways. In the ensuing chapter, we will be considering the defendant's bad character. More particularly, we will explore the circumstances, delimited by statute, in which the prosecution may bring such evidence to the notice of the tribunal of fact. In the present chapter, we will examine the very different situation where a defendant is able to present himself before the court as someone possessed of a good character.

6.17 Self-evidently, it is to a defendant's advantage if he can establish that he is a person of previous good character. In this situation the law presses into service the two forms of character evidence, character evidence relating to issue and character evidence relating to credit, which were outlined at the beginning of this chapter. Although we shall see that this is not always necessary, a defendant may adduce evidence showing that he is of good character, notably by calling witnesses who will testify to such effect. Alternatively, the defendant may extract this evidence during cross-examination of the Crown's witnesses. If the issue of good character is raised, the judge then falls under a duty to give a direction to the jury, known as a '*Vye* direction', indicating how they should use this information (see *Vye* [1993] 3 All ER 241). Good character directions have come to the fore in comparatively recent times, but now figure prominently in criminal trials. Owing to their complexity, good character directions also provide a fertile source of grounds of appeal. Just how much difficulty this direction can generate may be gauged from the fact that the Judicial Studies Board prefaced its suggested specimen direction no 23 on good character with an explicit warning that, wherever it is thought that there may be need in the particular circumstances of the case to 'modify' the direction, it is 'desirable' that the judge canvass his proposed direction with counsel before their closing speeches.

What constitutes admissible character evidence?

6.18 Strictly speaking, at common law, evidence of character, whether it is adduced by the defence or by the prosecution, ought to be given in the form of evidence of reputation. In the leading case, *Rowton* (1865) Le & Ca 520, the Court of Crown Cases Reserved held that at trial evidence had been wrongly received from a prosecution witness, who had said that in his opinion—and that of his brothers—R, who was indicted for indecent assault, was capable of the grossest indecency and the most flagrant immorality. The majority of the court so held because the evidence was of the witness's opinion, and not evidence of general reputation. This principle has an antiquated air, and evokes Abraham Lincoln's words: 'Character is like a tree and reputation like its shadow. The shadow is what we think of, the tree is the real thing.' Yet the principle still applies today—and has even been specifically retained in a would-be modernising statute, the Criminal Justice Act 2003, s 99(2)—even though it is widely recognised that evidence of general reputation can very easily prove unreliable.

6.19 Character witnesses still may not give their personal opinion of the defendant. Nor should they make reference in their evidence-in-chief to specific incidents with a view to establishing the defendant's character. Hence, in *Redgrave* (1981) 74 Cr App R 10, in order to repel a charge of persistently importuning for immoral purposes, R sought to adduce evidence of love letters and Valentine cards he had received, along with photographs, which, he claimed, showed a disposition towards heterosexual rather than homosexual relationships. The Court of Appeal ruled this evidence inadmissible. Whilst acknowledging that in practice judges allow some relaxation of the prohibition—routinely permitting defendants to be asked if they are happily married, for example—Lawton LJ upheld the old common law restriction which forbids the defence, just like the prosecution, from adducing evidence of disposition. Despite the decision in *Redgrave*, which applied the strict letter of the law, the rule restricting character evidence to evidence of general reputation is probably more often honoured in its breach than in its observance.

When will a defendant be considered of good character?

6.20 Clearly, if a defendant calls witnesses to testify to his good name and reputation in the community, or if he testifies personally to like effect, he thereby lays claim to a good character. However, the courts go considerably further in attributing good character to defendants.

- *First*, if the accused merely happens to have no criminal record, this tends to be taken without more ado in English law to amount to a good character. (It may be noteworthy that in New Zealand the courts will only consider that an accused is of good character if he can adduce positive evidence to that effect; the mere absence of previous convictions will not normally suffice: *Falealili* [1996] 3 NZLR 664.)

- *Second*, the courts have discretion to overlook discreditable conduct on the defendant's part in determining whether he merits a good character. In *Anderson* [1990] Crim LR 862, for example, despite the plain impropriety, the Court of Appeal held that a police officer, who admitted having had consensual intercourse with a woman in his Panda car while he was on duty but denied raping her, had wrongly been denied a good character direction by the trial judge. In *Maye* [2008] UKPC 36 the Privy Council held that a good character direction ought to have been given even though M, who was indicted for the murder of his sister's boyfriend, had been carrying a knife. M proffered no explanation whatever for having a knife, but Lord Brown of Eaton-under-Heywood considered that, had it been delivered, such a direction could have 'materially advantaged' M in his defence of provocation or self-defence (at [19]).

- *Third*, even if the defendant has a criminal record, provided that his convictions are for minor offences or for offences remote from the offence charged, or are elderly or even spent under the Rehabilitation of Offenders Act 1974, the court may ignore them. As Maurice Kay LJ noted in *Remice* [2010] EWCA Crim 1952:

> [T]the weight of modern authority recognises that in a clear case the judge ought to direct the jury to treat a defendant with only an old and irrelevant conviction as being a person of good character entitled to both limbs of the conventional good character direction.
>
> (at [11])

6.21 *Durbin* [1995] 2 Cr App R 84, supplies a telling illustration of some of these principles in operation. D, a long-distance lorry driver, successfully appealed against his conviction for importing £2.5m of cannabis into the UK in the back of his rig. D had two previous convictions for offences of dishonesty, both of them spent— although one of them only became spent a few days before the trial opened. D admitted to having told Customs officers elaborate lies when first questioned by them. Finally, D acknowledged that, while driving his lorry around Europe, he had been engaged in smuggling computer parts, not drugs, from Holland into France, via Belgium. Despite having racked up this catalogue of discreditable actions, the Court of Appeal still held that the trial judge had been wrong not to treat D as of good character and to fail to deliver a suitable direction to the jury in D's favour.

6.22 In many ways the House of Lords case of *Aziz* [1996] AC 41 looks similar. A, T and Y were jointly charged with income tax and VAT fraud. A had no criminal record. Y likewise relied upon the fact that he had no criminal record, but admitted to having knowingly made a false mortgage application and to having lied to Customs officers during interview. T also relied upon an absence of previous convictions, but acknowledged that he had not declared his full income to the Inland Revenue and had also allowed his employees to declare less income than they were actually earning. Lord Steyn first conceded that a court possesses a 'residual discretion' to refuse to treat even a defendant with no previous convictions as of good character where it would be 'an insult to common sense' to do so, adding that 'a judge should never be compelled to give meaningless or absurd directions'. In *Aziz* itself, however, he held that, even taking into account their various peccadilloes, A, T and Y ought each to have been treated by the trial judge as persons of good character and thus entitled to good character directions. The ruling recalls the straight-talking Judge Alex Kozinski's paradoxical thumbnail sketch of one witness's character in *US v Simpson*, of whom he famously said: 'Miller was a prostitute, heroin user and fugitive from Canadian justice; but otherwise she was okay' (927 F 2d 1088, 1089 (9th cir, 1991)).

6.23 The decision in *Aziz* almost causes one to wonder when, if ever, a court will be prepared to refuse a defendant a good character. Lord Steyn suggested that a defendant would not merit a good character if, for instance, he had committed 'serious criminal behaviour similar to the offence charged in the indictment'. In view of *Durbin*, where a drug smuggler's admission to having been engaged in smuggling computer parts seems not to have deprived him of a good character, it may well be that the behaviour to which Lord Steyn refers has either to be very serious indeed, or very similar indeed, to the offence charged. However, Lord Steyn's words concerning 'serious criminal behaviour similar to the offence charged' have not always been followed too literally. In *Shaw v R* [2001] 1 WLR 1519 at [30]–[31], for instance, the Privy Council held that S, who was charged with two murders, had not been wrongly deprived of a good character direction even though he had no criminal record. The jury knew that S had dealt in a substantial quantity of cocaine and had also been a member of an armed posse that had set out to seek reparation from the deceased. In these circumstances, Lord Bingham noted, 'Had the judge given the jury a full direction, it could properly have been so qualified as to do the appellant more harm than good'.

6.24 Although, taken together, the cases concerned with *Vye* directions would seem to treat 'good character' as an elastic concept, there are certain recognised limits. In *Lawson* [2007] 1 WLR 1191, for instance, Hughes LJ refused to accept that in every case in which a judge rules that a defendant's bad character is inadmissible that defendant is automatically entitled to a good character direction:

> The good character direction is appropriate to those who are, or who the judge rules may be treated as if they are, … without known bad character of any kind. It does not extend automatically also to those whose bad character exists, but is not of sufficient probative value or relevance to be admitted against them. Still less does it extend to those whose bad character is excluded as a matter of discretion.
>
> (at [40])

The form of the good character direction

6.25 It is for the defendant, not for the judge, to raise the issue of good character 'distinctly', by giving or calling evidence of good character or by eliciting it from prosecution witnesses in cross-examination. It is also a necessary part of defence counsel's duty to ensure that the direction is delivered whenever a defendant is so entitled (*Thompson v R* [1998] AC 811; *Teeluck v Trinidad and Tobago* [2005] 1

WLR 2421 at [33] *per* Lord Carswell). If this rule is not adhered to, Lord Woolf has suggested that 'there is a danger that an unscrupulous defendant will be able to manufacture a ground of appeal based upon the failure of the judge to give the proper character direction' (*Gilbert v R* [2006] 1 WLR 2108 at [21]). Just occasionally, there may be circumstances where, despite counsel's failure to raise the matter, an appellate court will have to declare a conviction unsafe (*Sealey and Headley v The State* [2002] UKPC 52 at [30]; *Maye* [2008] UKPC 36 at [19]). One such situation, suggested by Lord Carswell in *Teeluck*, is that of 'cases in which counsel's misbehaviour or ineptitude is so extreme that it constitutes a denial of due process to the client' (at [39]. Cp *Campbell v R* [2010] UKPC 26 at [39]–[423] *per* Lord Mance).

6.26 If the defendant has a good character and the defence raises the matter, it then becomes obligatory for the judge to deliver a direction to the jury instructing them on the evidentiary significance of that good character. Following the decisions of the Court of Appeal in *Vye* [1993] 3 All ER 241, and of the House of Lords in *Aziz* [1996] AC 41, the Judicial Studies Board issued a specimen direction (no 23) reminding judges that, whilst warning the jurors that good character on its own is no defence to a criminal charge, they must also be told the two following things.

- *Direction on good character and credibility.* In cases where *either* the defendant has given evidence *or* the defendant has not testified but the prosecution has put in evidence a 'mixed statement' made by him or his police interview, containing exculpatory as well as inculpatory elements (see *Aziz, ante* para **6.22**; 'mixed statements' are discussed *post*, paras **10.50–10.53**), they may take account of his good character when deciding whether they believe his evidence or statement. In short, the judge must tell the jury that the defendant's good character is relevant when they come to assess his credibility. Moreover, given that it extends not only to whether what the accused says in the witness box should be believed but may also sometimes comprehend the likelihood of his being truthful when responding to police questions at the investigative stage, it will be noted that the concept of 'credibility' in the context of the good character direction bears a more extended meaning than it customarily does in other contexts (see *ante*, Chapter 4).

- *Direction on good character and propensity.* In *almost all* cases, the jury must be told that by virtue of his good character the accused may be less likely than otherwise to have committed the offence charged. In other words, his good character has a bearing on his propensity to offend and, hence, on the likelihood that he is guilty of the offence charged.

6.27 The rules laid down in *Vye* and *Aziz* are not without their difficulties. In particular, in joint trials if D1 possesses a good character but D2 has a relevant criminal record, the rules ordain that the judge must still direct the jury that D1's good character counts to his advantage in the two ways mentioned above while saying nothing concerning D2. It has been argued that this operates unfairly to D2, given that jurors may legitimately wonder why, after receiving full instruction on how to approach D1's character, they have heard nothing respecting that of D2. Although this situation may well prove prejudicial to D2, in *Vye* it was held that the judge must nevertheless give the direction to which D1 is entitled, even if there is a risk that indulging D1 may operate to the detriment of D2. As is very often the case, one sees that rules of evidence which operate quite satisfactorily when only one defendant is on trial work markedly less well when co-accused are jointly tried.

6.28 *Qualified judicial directions.* As was mentioned earlier 'good character' may essentially mean that the accused does not have any relevant previous convictions or known bad character. Indeed, Lord Steyn made clear in *Aziz* that if the defendant is not of absolutely good character but still qualifies in the judge's view for the good character direction, the judge should convey a fair and balanced picture by adding words of qualification concerning any other proved or possible criminal conduct of the accused which may have emerged at trial. As Evans LJ put it in *Durbin*, what matters most is that 'the jury should not be directed to approach the case on a basis which, to their knowledge, is artificial or untrue'. Tempering the direction to take account of blemishes on the defendant's good character will not always be an easy matter.

6.29 *Defendants of good and bad character.* Owing to the generous reading the courts give to the notion of 'good character' and the increasing number of cases in which a defendant's 'bad character', too, may become admissible (see further Chapter 7, *post*), it can happen that technically an accused is entitled to directions on both forms of character. Clearly, judges will find it difficult simultaneously to tell juries (i) that a defendant's good character may speak in his favour both in regard to his propensity to commit offences and to his credibility and (ii) that his bad character may do exactly the opposite. In *Doncaster* (2008) 172 JP 202 (for the facts, see para **7.143**, *post*) the Court of Appeal suggested how a trial judge might cater for a defendant, who is of good character in the sense of having no relevant criminal convictions, but whose bad character has been admitted as part of the Crown's case. Where, as in *Doncaster*, evidence of bad character had been admitted under the 2003 Act on the grounds of its relevance to both D's propensity and credibility, it would have made no sense for the judge to deliver a standard direction, stating the relevance of D's good character to propensity and credibility in direct contradiction to the bad character direction. In *Doncaster* a full good character direction would have been but a charade (cf *Aziz* [1996] 1 AC 41, 53 *per* Lord Steyn). In such cases Rix LJ suggested that, rather than invoke the good character direction, the right approach might be to adjust the bad character direction to take some account of the defendant's lack of criminal record:

> [O]ne way to deal with the difficulties presented in the aftermath of the 2003 Act by a defendant without previous convictions but with evidence of bad character admitted under s 101 is by modifying the bad character direction. . . . [I]n the post-2003 Act world, where bad character directions as to propensity have more frequently become necessary, even in the absence of previous convictions, it may be possible similarly to tailor a modified bad character direction, along the following lines. Thus when a judge is directing the jury about the relevance of bad character to propensity or propensities, he could remind them that the defendant had no previous convictions and say that, in the ordinary case, where there was no evidence of bad character, a defendant of no previous convictions would have been entitled to a direction that the jury should consider that that counted in his favour on the questions of both propensity and credibility; as it was, it was for the jury to consider which counted with them more—the absence of previous convictions or the evidence of bad character; and if the former, then they should take that into account in favour of the defendant, and if the latter, then they would be entitled to take that into account against him.
>
> (at [43])

6.30 *The importance of the good character direction.* Although, on its own, the failure to give an appropriately worded direction will not inevitably render a conviction unsafe, an appellate court will take any such omission into account when deciding whether a verdict is in fact safe (eg *Miller* [2000] 1 WLR 661). Sometimes, however, the failure to deliver the good character direction in due and proper form may assume such importance within the context of a case that, in the event of the direction not being correctly delivered, a conviction has to be quashed. In *Lloyd* [2000] 2 Cr App R 355, a trial judge chose to deliver the *Vye* direction in the form of a series of rhetorical questions. The Court of Appeal held that because the credibility of both L and his alleged sexual victim was central to the case, because the complainant was himself of bad character, and because the complaint concerned an incident which had occurred 24 years before the trial, it was imperative that the trial judge should have adhered closely to the Judicial Studies Board's specimen direction. Although no other complaint could be made of the judge's handling of the case, L's conviction could not be regarded as safe. The Court of Appeal's ruling in *Lloyd* is perhaps unusually *dirigiste*, but the decision was later followed at least once (see *Scranage* [2001] EWCA Crim 1171).

6.31 As one Privy Council case demonstrates, there is scope for strong disagreement concerning the importance of good character directions in the context of individual trials. In *Sealey and Headley v State* [2002] UKPC 52 S and H had been sentenced for the murder of a bodyguard in the course of an armed robbery in Trinidad. Given that both defendants had put forward alibis, the case turned on whether a particular police witness's evidence that he had recognised the pair at the scene of crime was to be believed. One ground of appeal was that counsel at the trial had failed to raise the issue of the appellants' good characters. Speaking for the majority, Lord Hutton considered this omission of critical importance; Lord Hope of Craighead and Sir Philip Otton, however, treated it as of considerably less significance. All five judges agreed that, even though case law establishes that it is counsel's responsibility to raise the issue of good character, the question on appeal was simply whether or not the court felt that the jury would inevitably have reached the same verdict had a full good character direction been given. Lord Hutton pointed out that courts have several times quashed convictions when a trial judge has failed to deliver the good character direction. In particular, he referred to Kennedy LJ's sweeping declaration in *Fulcher* [1995] 2 Cr App R 251 that:

> In the light of the authorities, we must accept that a proper direction as to character has some value, and therefore is capable of having some effect in every case in which it is appropriate for such a direction to be given.
>
> (at 260)

In contrast, Lord Hope concluded that in this case 'it is stretching imagination too far to suppose that a good character direction would have made any difference to the result'. What the majority seems to have extrapolated from the case law is that, whenever credibility is a critical issue in the case, the failure to deliver the direction is likely to render a conviction unsafe (see, eg, *Kamar* [1999] 31 March, case no 98/00130/X3). The majority founded on the premise that 'the crucial question before the jury was whether they could accept the evidence of [the police officer] and reject as untrue the evidence of the two appellants' (at [32]). On this basis, they concluded that the verdicts were unsafe:

> [W]here the issue in dispute is fundamental to the question of guilt or innocence of the accused, then whether it relates to non-participation in the crime charged or to consent or to some other defence, . . . the good character direction is an important safeguard to the accused.
>
> (at [34])

The minority, in contrast, interpreted the earlier cases more restrictively—and, I venture to suggest, more realistically. Lord Hope, having taken due note of Lord Lloyd's observation in *Barrow v State* [1998] AC 846, at 852, that not every omission will lead to the quashing of a conviction, proceeded to examine the special factors that played a role in cases like *Fulcher* and *Kamar*. Lord Hope concluded that what differentiated *Sealey and Headley* was that neither of the above-mentioned cases involved convictions 'where the issues of credibility and propensity were directed solely to a defence of alibi' (at [44]). Here, a police officer had testified that he had recognised two of four robbers. They both lived near him, he encountered them regularly, and indeed had seen them earlier that very morning. Moreover, both S and H, whose alibis were 'very weak', admitted in evidence that the policeman knew them. Not only was 'this...as clear a case of recognition as could be imagined' (*per* Lord Hope at [47]), but additionally the police witness neither nursed any sort of grudge against the co-accused nor sought to embellish his account of the incident. What *Sealey and Headley* graphically illustrates is the difficulty our senior judges encounter when trying to attribute an exact value to good character and to settle the situations in which such evidence will weigh with the court.

6.32 The law on good character directions at present is distinctly tilted in the defendant's favour. Not that this means that convictions are likely to be quashed in every instance where a trial judge fails to deliver a good character direction. As Lord Bingham explained in *Jagdeo Singh v Trinidad & Tobago* [2006] 1 WLR 146 at [14]:

> The significance of what is not said in a summing-up should be judged in the light of what is said. The omission of a good character direction on credibility is not necessarily fatal to the fairness of the trial or to the safety of a conviction. Much may turn on the nature of and issues in a case, and on the other available evidence. The ends of justice are not on the whole well served by the laying down of hard, inflexible rules from which no departure may ever be tolerated.

Lord Brown of Eaton-under-Heywood was even more explicit in *Bhola v Trinidad and Tobago* [2006] UKPC 9 in declaring:

> The cases where plainly the outcome of the trial would not have been affected by a good character direction may not after all be so "rare".
>
> (at [17])

6.33 Although the rules are well established, some judges have expressed misgivings. Kennedy LJ, for example, in *Fulcher*, seemed only grudgingly to concede that the cases firmly establish that 'a proper direction as to character has some value, and therefore is capable of having some effect in every case in which it is appropriate for such a direction to be given'. More obviously, Staughton LJ, in *Wood* [1996] 1 Cr App R 207, asked:

> Ever since the law started to lay down what a jury must be told as to the effect of good character nearly thirty years ago...there has been trouble. Could the jury perhaps be allowed to work it out for themselves?
>
> (at 218)

Arguably, the judicial directions do little more than make explicit what average jurors, applying common sense, would appreciate on their own initiative. There is, then, an argument that the law could, without risk of damage to the interests of those accused of crime, dispense with this unnecessarily complicated apparatus of rules. However, there is now a counter-argument to be considered. As we shall see in the next chapter, Part 11 of the Criminal Justice Act 2003 has expanded both the range of situations in which a defendant's bad character becomes admissible in evidence and the extent of the bad character that may thereby come to be revealed to the tribunal of fact. Against this increasingly illiberal backdrop, one might feel less concern at a single rule that does perhaps tilt the scales ever so slightly in the defendant's favour.

Consequences of a defendant adducing evidence of good character

6.34 Several consequences may flow from a defendant adducing evidence of his good character. Notably, if he calls witnesses to testify to his good character, the Crown may be given leave to cross-examine them to elicit evidence of the defendant's bad character (*Waldman* (1934) 24 Cr App Rep 204). Moreover, if the defendant introduces evidence of good character, the prosecution may be permitted to call evidence in rebuttal to contradict him. The evidence to which exception was taken in *Rowton* (*ante*, para **6.18**), it might be noted, was in fact prosecution evidence admitted to rebut that of a number of R's witnesses, who had been called to testify to R's supposed good character. This principle is also illustrated by *de Vere* [1982] QB 75, where D did not give evidence on oath but only made an unsworn statement from the dock (a procedure which has since been abolished). In his dock statement D had claimed to be a man of substance and of good repute. Lord Lane CJ held that the trial judge had been entitled to exercise his discretion so as to permit the prosecution to call witnesses in rebuttal showing that in fact D was not a man of substance and, indeed, had previous convictions for fraud. Finally, if the court considers that by calling the evidence, the defendant is responsible for making an assertion that creates a false impression contrary to ss 101(1)(f) and 105 of the Criminal Justice Act 2003, then, as we shall see in the ensuing chapter, this may mean that the defendant's bad character in turn becomes admissible to the extent that 'it goes no further than is necessary to correct the false impression' (s 105(6): see paras **7.105** ff).

FURTHER READING

Munday, 'What Constitutes a Good Character?' [1997] Crim LR 247

Munday, 'Judicial Studies Board Specimen Directions and the Enforcement of Orthodoxy: A Modest Case Study' [2002] J Crim Law 158

Redmayne, 'The Relevance of Bad Character' [2002] CLJ 684

Ross, ' "He Looks Guilty": Reforming Good Character Evidence to Undercut the Presumption of Guilt', 65 Univ Pittsburgh L Rev 227 (2003)

Sankoff, '*Corbett*, Crimes of Dishonesty and the Credibility Contest: Challenging the Accepted Wisdom on what makes a Prior Conviction Probative' [2006] 10 Can Crim LR 215

SELF-TEST QUESTIONS

1. What do you understand by 'credibility' (i) generally in the law of evidence, and (ii) in the specific context of a defendant who can lay claim to a good character?

2. Why is a party normally forbidden from introducing evidence to bolster the credibility of its own witnesses?

3. What effect has the Rehabilitation of Offenders Act 1974 had on the extent to which evidence of witnesses' previous convictions may be introduced in evidence in both civil and criminal cases?

4. Trash was tried in 2000 for robbery. During the case it emerges that until 1993 Trash was a university lecturer in criminal law, but was dismissed from this post for persistent absenteeism, drunkenness and solvent abuse. Trash was once fined for assaulting a policewoman in the execution of her duty on New Year's Eve, but this conviction is now spent. In his evidence, Trash has chosen to disclose that he did once plan to rob a bank in Brazil, but having contracted an acute bout of malaria was compelled to abandon this plan. Trash has also called Dribble, the dean of his former Law faculty, who testifies that Trash basically had a reputation for being a nice chap who just had a lot of personal problems, many of which were brought on by the stress of having to lecture on a subject he did not fully understand. Trash's counsel has requested that the trial judge deliver a good character direction. Ought the judge to do so, and if so, what exactly should she tell the jury?

5. 'Here was a man who admitted buggery with his stepdaughter when she was aged 17—which is a criminal offence although not the one with which the appellant was charged. His admissions also disclosed a serious breach of trust towards his step-daughter and adultery so far as his wife was concerned. In those circumstances we think the judge was entitled to take the view that the appellant's claim to good character was so spurious that he was not obliged to give any good character direction. One asks rhetorically: "How could such a direction be tailored in a way which would be in any way meaningful for this appellant in the circumstances of this case?" ': *H (William)* (2000) 14 December, case no 2000/1091/Z4 at [19], *per* Tuckey LJ. Discuss.

6. 'Particularly when there are a number of co-accused, character represents a difficult area': *Louden-Barratnew* [2004] EWCA Crim 1753 at [7] *per* Kay LJ. Why should it do so?

7

Evidence of the defendant's bad character

SUMMARY

Whether or not to admit evidence of a defendant's misconduct on other occasions

I. The admission of evidence of a defendant's bad character in criminal cases: Part 11 of the Criminal Justice Act 2003

- Two classes of situation that fall outside the bad character provisions
- Discretion
- What actually constitutes evidence of 'bad character'?
- Acquittals may be admissible as 'evidence of bad character'
- When is evidence of a defendant's bad character admissible under the 2003 Act?
- Situations in which bad character evidence becomes admissible under s 101: the seven gateways
  - Gateway (a): When 'all parties to the proceedings agree to the evidence being admissible' (s 101(1)(a))
  - Gateway (b): When 'the evidence is adduced by the defendant himself or is given in answer to a question asked by him in cross-examination and intended to elicit it' (s 101(1)(b))
  - Gateway (c): When 'it is important explanatory evidence' (s 101(1)(c))
  - Gateway (d): When 'it is relevant to an important matter in issue between the defendant and the prosecution' (s 101(1)(d))
    - The defendant's 'propensity to commit offences' (s 103(1)(a))
    - The defendant's 'propensity to be untruthful' (s 103(1)(b))

- Gateway (e): When 'it has substantial probative value in relation to an important matter in issue between the defendant and a co-defendant' (s 101(1)(e))

  (i) When a co-accused's 'propensity' has 'substantial probative value in relation to an important matter in issue between the defendant and a co-defendant'

  (ii) When a co-accused's 'propensity to be untruthful' has 'substantial probative value in relation to an important matter in issue between the defendant and a co-defendant'

- Gateway (f): When 'it is evidence to correct a false impression given by the defendant' (s 101(1)(f))

- Gateway (g): When 'the defendant has made an attack on another person's character' (s 101(1)(g))

• Contaminated evidence (s 107)

• The court's duty to give reasons for rulings on matters affecting bad character (s 110)

• Rules of court (s 111)

• Jointly charged offences treated as separate proceedings (s 112(2))

• Appealing against trial court rulings and directions on bad character

• Surviving legislation allowing the Crown to adduce evidence of a defendant's wrongdoing and bad character

  (i) The Official Secrets Act 1911, s 1(2)

  (ii) The Theft Act 1968, s 27(3)

• Envoi

• How does one prove previous convictions?

  II. Similar fact evidence in civil cases

The trial took a day and a half, the jury made up its mind this morning in about an hour. The way they saw it, Jack's a bank robber, wasn't he? Hell, send him to prison.

Elmore Leonard, *The Hot Kid* (2005)[1]

---

[1] COPYRIGHT © 2005 BY ELMORE LEONARD. Reprinted by permission of Harper Collins Publishers.

Whether or not to admit evidence of a defendant's misconduct on other occasions

7.1 Human behaviour tends to follow patterns. It is known that those who have previously been convicted of crime or who can be shown to have committed other offences or to have behaved disreputably either have a tendency to reoffend or are more likely to commit offences than those without such attributes. Offending may even fit a recognisable social template, and earlier acts may prove a reasonable predictor of a person's subsequent behaviour. To take an example, which is gaining acceptance, American research is establishing a link between animal abuse and violent crime. A study in 1997 conducted by Northeastern University and the MSPCA found that approximately 70 per cent of animal abusers had committed at least one other criminal offence and, more significantly, that just under 40 per cent had committed violent crimes against people. In 1998 the Buffalo police department and the Erie County SPCA found that one third of the houses about which animal abuse complaints had been made had also been the origin of domestic violence complaints. A New Jersey survey in 1983 found that 88 per cent of families reported for incidents of child abuse also had animal abuse to their credit. More recently, an extensive study conducted by the US National Juvenile Online Victimization Study revealed a close link between possession of child pornography and actual victimisation of children. No less than 40 per cent of cases studied involved 'dual offending'—that is, both possession of child pornography and actual child victimisation (J Wolak, D Finkelhor and KJ Mitchell, 'Child-Pornography Possessors Arrested in Internet-Related Crimes: Findings from the National Juvenile Victimization Study' (2005)). In everyday life, we regularly use what we know of someone's history and past character to calculate how they are likely to conduct themselves in the future. The prosecution in criminal cases, however, was not traditionally permitted to establish a defendant's guilt by adducing evidence of his past misconduct; and such background information, which in other circumstances would not normally be discounted, has been kept from the tribunal of fact.

7.2 *Offender profiling.* This refusal to admit evidence of a defendant's other misconduct as a matter of course largely explains why criminal courts have until now proven hostile to that branch of investigative psychology, popular with the police and writers of fiction, generally known as 'offender profiling'. On one occasion an English court has had occasion to pronounce on the matter. At the trial of Colin Stagg in 1994, Ognall J conceded that 'in certain cases the assistance of a psychologist of that kind can prove a very useful investigative tool' and also that 'public policy is in favour of the proposition that the more serious the offence, the more unusual form of investigation may be justified'. The judge, however, was clear that 'the notion that a psychological profile is in any circumstances admissible in proof of identity is to my mind redolent with considerable danger'. In the *Stagg* case the police, who were investigating the brutal murder of Rachel Nickell on Wimbledon Common, had used a psychologist to guide an undercover policewoman in her attempts to win the suspect's confidence. They had employed the expert's portrayal of the likely character traits of a person who would typically have committed a frenzied attack on a young woman. The case, which would have sought to show that Stagg conformed to the psychologist's profile, was utterly misconceived, and Ognall J cannot be faulted for having ruled the 'profiling' evidence inadmissible under s 78 of PACE (see *ante*, para **1.52**)—and, indeed, for describing the police operation in that case as 'wholly reprehensible'. One criminal practitioner, writing in the quality press, was to remark that the case against *Stagg* was so flawed that 'even a moron in a hurry could see that it could never stand up'. In the event, in December 2008, thanks to advances in DNA profiling, a paranoid schizophrenic inmate of Broadmoor was eventually convicted of Rachel Nickell's manslaughter by reason of diminished responsibility.

7.3 Although profiling evidence raises a constellation of legal issues, thankfully, the principal obstacle to its admission has been that whereas it may well show that the defendant falls into a likely class of suspects by reason of his psychological profile, the law of evidence has decreed: 'There is all the difference in the world between evidence proving that the accused is a bad man and evidence proving that he is the man' (*Thompson* [1918] AC 221, 234 *per* Lord Sumner).

7.4 *The views of applied psychology.* Lord Griffiths remarked in *Scott v R* [1989] 2 All ER 305, 311: 'English law does not regard a propensity to commit crime as probative of the particular crime with which the accused is charged'. This used to be because it was feared—and with some justification— that, were a jury to learn that the accused had previous convictions or had other discreditable conduct to his name extraneous to the case they were trying, the knowledge might prejudice them and they might convict him on account of his past rather than upon the evidence before the court which bore directly on his guilt. The Law Commission, in its review of evidence of defendants' previous misconduct reviewed the findings of two principal studies, the LSE Jury Project 1968–73 (see Cornish and Sealy [1973] Crim LR 208) and an Oxford Study conducted in 1995. The studies had their distinct limitations and, as so often with applied psychological experiments, one could legitimately doubt to what degree their results would be replicated in the real world. But both investigations suggested that, when told of his recent similar convictions, jurors were markedly more likely to convict an accused. However, with the exception of scandalous convictions, like indecent assault on a child, dissimilar previous convictions in many circumstances were said actually to have served to reduce the likelihood of conviction. Although the psychological data is a long way from establishing that awareness of an accused's bad character will generally prejudice jurors against him, the law has hitherto proceeded upon the benevolent, commonsensical assumption that it could do so. Those in criminal practice, too, are more than aware of the likely effect once a defendant's prior criminal convictions and other bad character have been revealed, whether to jurors, judges or magistrates. The law's traditional refusal to make such evidence generally available to tribunals of fact could therefore be said to recognise a fact that the statistically inclined all too readily overlook, namely that even the above-mentioned studies do actually establish that in a substantial minority of cases knowledge of the accused's bad character will in likelihood prejudice the tribunal of fact.

7.5 *Risk of prejudice.* It is commonly said that the prejudice knowledge of a defendant's bad character engenders can assume two forms. On the one hand, it may adopt the guise of 'reasoning prejudice'. This means that jurors might be tempted to conclude that because they know that the accused was convicted in 2008 for occasioning actual bodily harm, they can infer from this that he is guilty of the murder with which he is charged in 2011. The knowledge of his violent past encourages a forbidden reasoning by which verdicts are dictated by the sort of person the accused appears to be according to his criminal record and/or other misdeeds. On the other hand, there may be 'moral prejudice'. Because an accused has previous convictions or is known to have done things that emphatically do not redound to his credit, the jurors may think that he has less to lose than an accused with an unblemished record: jurors may therefore treat the burden of proof more lightly, and may even feel that in reaching their verdict they are meting out punishment for the earlier lapses as well as for the offence charged. English law's refusal routinely to admit evidence of an accused's misconduct on other occasions frequently excites comment. Only following the conviction of Roy Whiting in December 2001 for the abduction and murder of Sarah Payne was the jury told of W's previous conviction for kidnapping and indecently assaulting another young child. Predictably, some—and, most notably, the Home Office—argued that this information ought to have been revealed to the jury from the outset. Whereas once wiser heads might have perceived the risks such a course would introduce into such delicately balanced cases, the government elected to take another course and Part 11 of the Criminal Justice Act 2003, along with its accompanying orders, was designed greatly to enlarge the category of situations in which evidence of a defendant's bad character may henceforth be laid before the tribunal of fact. As Lord Phillips of Worth Matravers put it in *Campbell* [2006] EWCA Crim 1305 at [12]:

> [T]he 2003 Act altered the criminal law by restricting the circumstances in which the prosecution were precluded from placing before the jury prejudicial material that was relevant to the jury's task.

7.6 *Preventative measures.* Hitherto, the exclusion of evidence of a defendant's bad character has been a prominent article of faith in English criminal procedure. If such evidence were inadvertently revealed during the course of the trial, the judge would have to consider whether the risk of prejudice to the accused was such that proceedings had to be stayed and a new trial ordered before a fresh jury. The Court of Appeal was also quite likely to quash as unsafe any conviction obtained in a case where the jury has wrongly been allowed to learn of the accused's previous convictions or misconduct. Moreover, this general exclusionary principle is buttressed by criminal sanctions for contempt of court, which can be taken against those who reveal such information prior to the accused's conviction.

7.7 Although the exclusionary principle characteristically operated to protect the accused, the principle has proven open to a very different form of exploitation when accused are tried jointly. We see elsewhere that the standard rules of evidence often take on a different character in joint trials (see *ante*, para **6.27**). The fact that the judge will stop a case when a defendant's previous misconduct is revealed may actually be used by a co-accused as a spoiling tactic. In *Pearce* (1999) 163 JP Jo 982, for example, one of a number of co-accused, J, who was conducting his own defence, appeared deliberately to ask a police officer if he knew that DW and P (two other co-accused) were serving prisoners, whereupon JS and P, in what could have been a staged move designed to indicate that this was true, got up and went to the dock door. The Crown contended that this was just an attempt to disrupt the trial (and not the first attempt at that). Thereupon, the judge, whose decision was upheld on appeal, refused to discharge the jury and order a new trial, emphasising the desirability of trying all the defendants together and the fact that there was no guarantee that J's conduct would not be repeated at any eventual retrial. The judge, whose ruling was approved by Tuckey LJ in the Court of Appeal (case no 98/06726/Y5, esp at [30]) simply gave the jury a direction that they should disregard the reference to DW's and P's bad character, along with their reaction to it.

7.8 *'Similar fact evidence' in civil* cases. In civil cases, too, as we shall see, a claimant does not enjoy anything like *carte blanche* to introduce evidence of incidents other than the one to which his claim relates in order to reinforce his case. In civil claims the court would seek to avoid oppression and unfairness, whilst also having proper regard for the need for advance notice of evidence. In more recent times, the court must also further the fundamental procedural desiderata enumerated in 'the overriding objective' of the Civil Procedure Rules (CPR). This overriding objective is defined in CPR, Part 1: 'active case management' lies at its heart. The overriding objective incorporates a number of elements: those of 'saving expense', dealing with cases in ways that are 'proportionate to the amount of money involved, to the importance of the case, to the complexity of the issues and to the financial position of each party', 'ensuring that [cases are] dealt with expeditiously and fairly', as well as 'allotting to [cases] an appropriate share of the court's resources, while taking into account the need to allot resources to other cases' (CPR, Part 1.1) The parties have an obligation under the CPR to assist the court in attaining its overriding objective (CPR, Part 1.3). 'Active case management', which is extensively but not exhaustively defined in the CPR, includes the court's power to deliver 'directions to ensure that the trial of a case proceeds quickly and efficiently' (CPR, Part 1.4). 'Case management' may well be the watchword today. However, as Eady J reminded us in a libel case, *Lowe v Associated Newspapers* [2007] 2 WLR 595 at [2], 'questions of principle need to be given priority over case management, and arguments based on the "'real issues" between the parties sometimes beg the question of what those issues are.'

7.9 The exceptional circumstances in which the prosecution in criminal cases and the claimant in civil cases were permitted to adduce evidence of the defendant's misconduct on other occasions both used to go under the common generic title, 'similar fact evidence'. Since the entry into force of Part 11 of the Criminal Justice Act 2003, the term 'similar fact evidence' is only now properly applicable in civil cases. The evidence of other misconduct admissible in civil and criminal cases will be treated separately.

I. The admission of evidence of a defendant's bad character in criminal cases: Part 11 of the Criminal Justice Act 2003

7.10 Prior to the entry into force of the Criminal Justice Act 2003, the situations in which the prosecution or a co-accused were entitled to adduce evidence of a defendant's bad character used to be regulated by a small number of statutes—notably, the Criminal Evidence Act 1898—and by an assortment of rules of common law. The old rules were complicated and restrictive; but they had the merit of being generally understood by the profession, and many felt that they operated in a more or less serviceable manner. Nevertheless, both the Law Commission, which reported on 'Evidence of Bad Character in Criminal Proceedings' in 2001, and Sir Robin Auld's *Review of the Criminal Courts in England and Wales*, published later the same year, strongly criticised the bad character rules. Their strictures set the tone for what was to become Chapter 11 of the Criminal Justice Act 2003. First, the Law Commission generally concluded that:

> The present law suffers from a number of defects...In summary,...they constitute a haphazard mixture of statute and common law rules which produce inconsistent and

> unpredictable results, in crucial respects distort the trial process, make tactical consid-
> erations paramount and inhibit the defence in presenting its true case to the fact-finders
> whilst often exposing witnesses to gratuitous and humiliating exposure of long forgotten
> misconduct.
>
> ((2001) Law Com No 273, para 1.7)

This may have rather exaggerated the position. However, Sir Robin Auld, too, noted that:

> It has long been acknowledged that the law in this area is highly unsatisfactory in its
> complexity and uncertainty... it is not an honest system in that it does not do what it is
> claimed to do.
>
> ((Oct 2001) Ch 11, paras 113–14)

Seizing upon these comments, the government adopted the Law Commission's proposals as the foundation for change, but then consciously extended their scope in its own proposals (Standing Committee B, col 543 (23 January 2003)). The bill had a turbulent passage through Parliament. At one point, the House of Lords actually rejected the bill's bad character provisions in their entirety, but then relented almost immediately. What we now have is an intricate legislation, which undoubtedly succeeds in producing a more repressive regime than the amalgam of statute and common law that preceded it. By failing to make a clean sweep and by retaining two of the old statutes, however, the new bad character rules arguably lack overall coherence. As we shall see, the new statute left several important issues unresolved and has spawned a case law, if anything, more profuse than the one from which we sought to escape.

7.11 The Criminal Justice Act 2003 has effected a virtual *tabula rasa*. With one exception, s 99 abolishes all common law rules that formerly governed the admissibility of evidence of bad character. The sole exception, specifically retained in s 118(1) of the Act, is the rule which holds that in criminal proceedings a person's reputation is admissible for the purposes of proving his good or bad character (see *Rowton* (1865) Le & Ca 520: *ante*, para **6.18**). In view of the curious origins of this rule, it is odd that it should have been retained in what affects to be a modernising statute: see further, Wigmore, *A Treatise on the Anglo-American System of Evidence in Trials at Common Law* (2nd edn, 1923, §1981). Additionally, the 2003 Act repeals the principal statute that previously regulated the cross-examination of defendants on their bad character, the Criminal Evidence Act 1898. Nevertheless, although the old law has been virtually swept away in its entirety, the overall scheme adopted in the new legislation is not too dissimilar in general shape to what went before. In some cases (eg 'important explanatory evidence' admitted under ss 101(1)(a) and 102) the legislature has effectively reintroduced the previous law (what used to be called 'background evidence':

post, paras **7.41–7.46**). Elsewhere, although their ambit may have been widened, old mechanisms (such as the old 'tit for tat' exception, that allowed the Crown to introduce an accused's bad character if the latter made an attack on various categories of persons' character) have been broadly retained (see ss 101(1)(g) and 106: *post*, paras **7.117–7.132**). Additionally, two statutes, which permitted a defendant's bad character to be adduced in cases involving charges of handling stolen goods or breaches of the Official Secrets Act, have escaped repeal (see *post*, paras **7.144–7.155**). The Act, then, presents a face that is half-recognisable to those familiar with the old law and that yet will appear unfamiliar to them in its detail. Despite appearances, the new provisions represent a veritable 'sea change' (*Chopra* [2007] 1 Cr App R 16 at [12] *per* Hughes LJ), and normally fall to be interpreted without reference to the former law whose general outline they may appear to follow.

Two classes of situation that fall outside the bad character provisions

7.12 Not all evidence that might technically qualify as evidence of 'bad character', as defined in the 2003 Act, is subject to the regime of admissibility set out in s 101. Section 98, which opens Part 11 of the Criminal Justice Act 2003, provides for two situations in which the bad character rules described below will not apply. Section 98 reads:

> References in this Chapter to evidence of a person's "bad character" are to evidence of, or of a disposition towards, misconduct on his part, *other than* evidence which—
>
> (a) has to do with the alleged facts of the offence with which the defendant is charged, or
>
> (b) is evidence of misconduct in connection with the investigation or prosecution of that offence.

This means that the restrictions on the admissibility of bad character evidence imposed by the 2003 Act have no application in the two classes of situation mentioned. Even if it reflects adversely on the defendant, the proffered evidence is subject only to conventional principles of evidence—and, more particularly, to the general test of relevance to which all evidence is normally subject.

7.13 '*(a) Evidence which…has to do with the alleged facts of the offence with which the defendant is charged.*' The expression 'has to do with the alleged facts of the offence' is not especially clear. The idea behind the exception, as explained by the Law Commission, was that it would allow the Crown to introduce as part of its case a defendant's misdoings, other than those charged, provided that they formed part of the general narrative of the offence charged. Thus, if X is charged with murder by slitting someone's throat with a bayonet, the fact that X is not also charged with possession of an offensive weapon will not prevent the Crown from adducing evidence relating to possession of the weapon. Similarly, if A is charged with driving whilst disqualified, s 98(a) permits the Crown to adduce evidence of A's prior disqualification without having to pass through the gateways of s 101 as very clearly it 'has to do with the alleged facts of the offence' (*DPP v Agyemang* (2009) 173 JP 487). Section 98(a), therefore, is potentially of great significance. As Scott Baker LJ noted at the beginning of his judgment in *Edwards* [2006] 1 WLR 1524:

> Often the first inquiry is whether it is necessary to go through the "bad character" gateways at all. In this regard, s 98 is not to be overlooked. It excludes from the definition of bad character evidence which "has to do with the alleged facts of the offence" or evidence "of misconduct in connection with the investigation or prosecution of that offence". While difficult questions can arise as to whether evidence of background or motive falls to be admitted under those exclusions in s 98 or requires consideration under s 101(1)(c), it does not follow that merely because the evidence fails to come within the s 101 gateways it will be inadmissible. Where the exclusions in s 98 are applicable the evidence will be admissible without more ado.
>
> (at [1])

Scott Baker LJ later amended this statement, pointing out in *W* [2006] EWCA Crim 2308 at [19] that the final sentence ought to have read, 'the evidence *may* be admissible without more ado'.

7.14 We examined the way in which the court, in *Machado* (2006) 170 JP 400, applied s 98(a) in relation to s 100 of the Criminal Justice Act 2003, which restricts the extent to which the bad character of non-defendants may be admitted in criminal trials (see *ante*, para **4.36**). Similar questions have arisen in relation to the admission of a defendant's bad character. In *Malone* [2006] EWCA Crim 1860, where M was convicted of murdering his wife, the Crown had been allowed to put in evidence a forged report purportedly drafted by an enquiry agent employed by M to watch his wife. M, who said that he had put the report to his wife shortly after the genuine surveillance by the enquiry agent had ended, at a time when he and his wife were experiencing marital difficulties, admitted that the report was a forgery. The Crown had successfully argued that this reprehensible conduct was admissible pursuant to s 98(a) of the 2003 Act as evidence of bad character 'to do with the alleged facts of the offence'. On appeal, the defence contested this ruling. Gage LJ dealt with the s 98(a) point in the following way:

> There is no dispute that the document constituted evidence of bad character. It was, at the least, reprehensible behaviour (see s 112(1)). In our judgment, evidence of this sort was capable of being admitted under section 98(a). The prosecution case was based on circumstantial evidence. Its case was that the matrimonial difficulties between the

appellant and his wife caused him to flare up and kill her. The evidence of his actions before her disappearance showed a build-up to a situation which led to him killing her. As such evidence of matrimonial difficulties, the intensity of the effect of these difficulties on the appellant and how he dealt with them before she disappeared could...have been admissible as evidence going directly to show with other circumstantial evidence that he had committed the offence. As such it was capable of being evidence "to do with the alleged facts of the case" in the same way as evidence to show a conspiracy or a joint venture would be admissible under section 98(a).

(at [48])

7.15 There is broad consensus that what has to do with the alleged facts of the offence charged must be judged temporally. In *Tirnaveanu* [2007] 1 WLR 3049 at [23], for instance, Thomas LJ expressed the view that 'the exclusion [in s 98(a)] must be related to evidence where there is some *nexus* in time between the offence with which the defendant is charged and the evidence of misconduct which the prosecution seek to adduce', adding that 'the application of s 98 is a fact-specific exercise involving the interpretation of ordinary words.' Courts, however, sometimes interpret the expression, 'evidence which...has to do with the alleged facts of the offence with which the defendant is charged', more laxly. In *McNeill* (2008) 172 JP 50, M contested her conviction for making threats to kill. Believing that her neighbour, C, had made off with a half-bottle of her brandy, the Crown alleged that M had gone to C's flat, smashed a hole in the door with a mallet and threatened to stab C and cut him into little pieces. Following her arrest, M was released on conditional bail, the condition being that she should reside at a certain address. M later found that she could not reside there, and therefore had nowhere to stay. The Crown was permitted to call a local council housing officer, MC, who testified that two days after the original incident, M had come to the housing office seeking temporary accommodation. Upon learning that the housing office could not help her, M had threatened to go and burn the neighbour's flat down, declaring: 'They'll come out in body bags'. In evidence M admitted having occasioned damage to C's door but broadly denied that she had made threats to kill, and even called B, who had been present at the relevant time, as a witness to confirm that she had heard no such threats. M also claimed that what she had actually said to the housing officer was: 'What do you want me to f***ing do? Do you want me to burn it down? Do you want them to come out in body bags?' The Crown had originally contemplated applying for MC's evidence to be admitted as evidence of propensity under s 101(1)(d) of the 2003 Act. In the event, however, the trial judge ruled that MC's evidence '[had] to do with the alleged facts of the offence with which the defendant is charged' within the meaning of s 98(a) and therefore fell outside the statutory definition of evidence of bad character. On appeal, M argued that MC's evidence was evidence of 'bad character' within the meaning of the 2003 Act—being evidence of words spoken on a quite separate occasion—and, more specifically, ought to have been excluded by the trial judge either under s 101(3) of that Act or under s 78 of PACE. Rix LJ upheld the trial judge's ruling on s 98(a). Leaving aside that Rix LJ actually misquotes the statute as saying 'has to deal with' rather than 'has to do with' the alleged facts of the offence charged, the court's reasoning is questionable notably because (i) it admits evidence of other misconduct that looks suspiciously like evidence of propensity and (ii) also stretches the test set out in *Machado* (2006) 170 JP 400 (see *ante*, para **4.36**) from events *'contemporaneous with*...the alleged facts of the offence' to matters *'reasonably contemporaneous with'* the alleged facts of the offence. (See further Munday [2008] J Crim Law 21.)

7.16 Where the offence with which a defendant is charged is of a continuing nature—eg, when an employer is accused of permitting his driver to fail, without reasonable excuse, to keep proper records contrary to the Transport Act 1968—since the *actus reus* of the offence may be proved by evidence of the employer's systematic failure to perform his duty, it has been held that s 98(a) applies in regard to the employer's prior contraventions: *VOSA v Ace Crane & Transport Ltd* (2010) 174 JP 329.

7.17 Even if the courts are sometimes minded to give the words of s 98(a) a broad interpretation, there are limits. Thus, s 98(a) does not normally entitle the Crown to introduce evidence showing that an accused has a particular bad character propensity: such evidence, we shall see, is properly admissible via gateway (d) of s 101. In *Benguit* [2005] EWCA Crim 1953, because B denied ever having carried a knife, two witnesses were permitted to testify to the contrary. Latham LJ considered that such evidence could not be admitted under s 98(a):

> ...although the prosecution...sought to persuade us to the contrary,...this evidence was indeed evidence of bad character. It was not evidence which under s 98 of the 2003 Act could be admitted because it "has to do with the alleged facts of the offence with which the defendant is charged." The basis upon which [it was sought] to admit the evidence was not to establish so much that the appellant had the knife on him that day, but to establish that he was the sort of person who carried a knife. That seems to us to mean that it was evidence of bad character in a general sense and was insufficiently related to the actual offence itself as to be evidence admissible under s 98.
>
> (at [31])

7.18 *'(b) Evidence of misconduct in connection with the investigation or prosecution of that offence'*. Section 98(b) serves a similar purpose to s 98(a). Therefore, if an accused has sought to intimidate prosecution witnesses or has offered bribes to police officers investigating the case, such evidence will be admissible without needing to satisfy the requirements of the bad character provisions, detailed below.

Discretion

7.19 Traditionally, at common law criminal courts enjoyed discretion to exclude technically admissible evidence if its prejudicial effect exceeded its probative value (see *ante*, paras **1.48–1.51**). PACE, s 78 later conferred on courts a further power to exclude evidence if its admission would reflect adversely on the fairness of proceedings (see *ante*, paras **1.52–1.54**). The interrelationship between these two discretions is difficult to untangle in criminal evidence generally. The bad character provisions of the Criminal Justice Act 2003 have introduced further provisions dealing with judicial discretion but still leaving question marks hanging over the exact status of existing evidentiary discretions at common law and under PACE, s 78.

7.20 Section 99 declares that:

> . . . the common law rules governing the admissibility of evidence of bad character in criminal proceedings are abolished.

Since s 99 refers only to the abolition of 'the common law rules governing the admissibility of evidence of bad character', the statute was not intended to do away with the discretion courts generally enjoy at common law to exclude prejudicial evidence (preserved explicitly by PACE, s 82(3)) and that the courts therefore retain the power to exclude bad character evidence if it is deemed more prejudicial than probative. This reading of the Act is reinforced by s 112(3)(c) which provides:

> Nothing in this Chapter affects the exclusion of evidence. . .
>
> (a) on grounds other than the fact that it is evidence of a person's bad character.

Part 11 says nothing explicitly about the statutory discretion created by PACE, s 78. Section 101, however, does make glancing reference to this issue. Having enumerated in lettered paragraphs (a)–(g) the situations in which, under the Act, a defendant's bad character may become admissible, s 101(3) states:

> The court must not admit evidence under subsection (1)(d) or (g) if, on an application by the defendant to exclude it, it appears to the court that the admission of the evidence would have such an adverse effect on the fairness of the proceedings that the court ought not to admit it.

It is just about arguable that this deliberate, restricted restatement of the principle laid down in PACE, s 78 was meant to override the general exclusionary discretion courts customarily enjoy under the latter provision. Therefore, by implication, s 101(3) ought to exclude exercise of s 78 discretion in all other circumstances in which bad character can become admissible under the Act—namely, under s 101(1)(a)–(c) and (e)–(f). Were this correct, one would have to say that the method Parliament selected to achieve its purpose is most unconventional. Section 101(3) might be regarded as a partial derogation from PACE, s 78: unlike s 78, s 101(3) requires that the defendant makes an application to have evidence that is otherwise admissible under paras (d) or (g) excluded on grounds of its potential unfairness; in all other cases, the court retains its duty of vigilance to oversee the fairness of the proceedings. Moreover, as Rose LJ pointed out in *Hanson* [2005] 1 WLR 3169 at [10], 'must not admit' in s 101(3) is stronger wording than 'may' in PACE, s 78 (but cf *Hasan* [2005] 2 WLR 709 at [53] *per* Lord Steyn).

7.21 Courts, however, have been loath to conclude that PACE, s 78, a provision that was passed to ensure that trial judges can control the overall fairness of the trial over which they are presiding, has been overturned by a side wind. Thus far, the courts have shied from explaining the precise position of the established discretions courts possess either under PACE, s 78 or at common law in the greater scheme of things. Nevertheless, they have suggested that, as a counsel of prudence, judges at least should continue to apply PACE, s 78 to bad character evidence in addition to any other relevant discretions created by the 2003 statute. As Lord Woolf CJ put it in *Highton* [2005] 1 WLR 3472:

> . . . our inclination is to say that s 78 provides an additional protection to a defendant. In light of this preliminary view . . . , judges may consider that it is a sensible precaution, when making rulings as to the use of evidence of bad character, to apply the provisions of s 78 and exclude evidence where it would be appropriate to do so under section s 78, pending a definitive ruling to the contrary.
>
> (at [13])

Similarly, in *Amponsah* [2005] EWCA Crim 2993 Sir Igor Judge P noted that:

> Section 101(3) itself makes express provision granting a discretion to the court to deny an application to allow bad character evidence to be given in relation to two of the particular gateways provided by s101(1). It could therefore be argued that by dealing with the matter expressly, Parliament had concluded that no discretion should exist in respect of the other gateways. On the other hand, there is the overriding provision in s 78 of the Police and Criminal Evidence Act 1984 and at common law giving a judge what would reasonably be described as the widest possible discretion to decide that the admission of material would so adversely affect the fairness of the proceedings that it should not be admitted. As I say, we do not need to resolve that issue today.
>
> (at [20])

The tone of these judgments is understandably tentative. The Act gives no clear clue as to the legislature's true intention in the matter.

What actually constitutes evidence of 'bad character'?

7.22 The expression 'bad character' has already been employed several times in this chapter. What exactly does it mean? Prior to the 2003 Act, although the expression 'bad character' was actually employed in one evidence statute (the Criminal Evidence Act 1898), the notion was left without precise definition. Whilst it was generally agreed that a person's previous convictions, if judged relevant, would certainly fall within 'bad character', the definition's outer bounds were not crisply delineated. Indeed, on a rare occasion when the Court of Appeal did give passing attention to the question, in *Carter* (1997) 161 JP 207, 'bad character' was said simply to mean something discreditable that was relevant to the defendant's credibility—evidence whose 'purpose was to show that [the accused] was of a dishonest disposition'. The position is quite altered today. The Act specifies what English law understands by 'bad character'.

7.23 Section 98 states that:

> References in this Chapter to evidence of a person's "bad character" are to evidence of, or of a disposition towards, misconduct on his part...

'Misconduct' is further defined in s 112, which reads:

> "misconduct" means the commission of an offence or other reprehensible behaviour.

In addition to any offences that have been committed, the courts will therefore be required to consider what amounts to 'evidence of, or a disposition towards... other reprehensible behaviour'. It is not easy to ascribe a precise meaning to this expression. The word 'reprehensible', which was added to the bill at a very late stage and with minimal explanation, is a strangely antiquated word to come upon in what affects to be a modernising statute. A moment's reflection, or even a glance in any leading dictionary—something courts are prone to do when confronted with unfamiliar words in a statute (eg *Sheldrake v DPP* [2004] 1 AC 264 at [48] *per* Lord Bingham of Cornhill)—and it will be apparent that behaviour that is 'reprehensible' can either signify serious misdoings or encompass minor peccadilloes. Which meaning was intended in this legislation? And does it particularly matter?

7.24 Prior to the 2003 Act, the outer bounds of 'bad character' excited little interest. Unless easily established, the Crown rarely sought to introduce as evidence of bad character more than an accused's previous convictions. In *Marsh* [1994] Crim LR 52, however, a case involving a serious off-the-ball assault during a game of rugby, the defendant's 'bad character' did include a survey of his disciplinary record for violence on the field of play. Admittedly, general bad character evidence can pose problems. For whereas previous convictions can be easily proven, if denied, less well-defined allegations can be more readily contested. (This, of course, is not a universal truth.) The presence of a statutory definition in the 2003 Act, together with the knowledge that the government's intention was that evidence of bad character would be placed before juries more frequently than in the past (*Edwards* [2006] 1 WLR 1524 at [1(iii)] *per* Scott Baker LJ), alters matters. Some prosecutors will be eager to exploit in full the possibilities offered by this legislation. The question of what constitutes 'other reprehensible behaviour', therefore, assumes a certain importance—an importance which is increased by the fact that under the Act judges are required to give reasoned rulings for admitting or refusing to admit evidence of bad character (s 110).

7.25 Reverting to the definition of 'bad character' under the 2003 Act, if one conflates the relevant provisions, evidence of bad character constitutes:

> evidence of, or of a disposition towards...the commission of an offence or other reprehensible behaviour.

The meaning of 'evidence of, or of a disposition towards the commission of an offence' is tolerably clear—although it is true that s 108 has slightly expanded the range of offences to which reference may be made to the extent that where a defendant is alleged to have committed an offence when over the age of 21, evidence that he has a conviction for an offence committed when he was under the age of 14 may now be admissible provided that both offences are indictable and 'the court is satisfied that the interests of justice require the evidence to be admissible' (s 108(2)). One senses that this open-ended discretion will rarely be invoked.

7.26 *Evidence of the 'commission of an offence'.* Apart from convictions figuring on a defendant's criminal record or independent evidence adduced to show that he has committed offences, what other penalties will qualify under this head? In *S (Stephen Paul)* [2006] 2 Cr App R 23 at [12], not surprisingly, Rose, LJ held that a formal caution was properly characterised as evidence of 'bad character' within the meaning of the 2003 Act: cautions, after all, are administered by the police to persons, normally young, who have fully acknowledged their guilt of offences which otherwise would be the subject of criminal proceedings. In contrast, in *Hamer* (2011) 175 JP 19 fixed penalty notices issued under the Criminal Justice and Police Act 2001 in respect of specified offences were held not to equate with cautions: penalty notices do not amount to admissions of guilt, are not even proof that a crime has been committed, and do not impute any stain on an accused's character. On the other hand, in *Edwards* [2006] 1 WLR 1524 at [78] Scott Baker LJ could not see why allegations that had never been tried, on the ground that the proceedings would have amounted to an abuse of process, might not also be admissible as evidence of bad character in appropriate circumstances.

7.27 In *Ali* [2010] EWCA Crim 1619 the Court of Appeal judged the criminality of A's other misconduct according to the rules of English law. At A's trial on one count of murder and two of attempted murder it was held that the Crown had been properly allowed to introduce two photographs of A holding firearms, evidence that he had been found in possession of two sets of body armour, and a witness's statement that he had seen A stroking his beard with a gun. The photographs had been taken in Pakistan, where handling guns, which in any case were photographic props, was not illegal. A, therefore, had committed no offence; nor could this conduct in Pakistan be characterised as reprehensible. *Item* the possession of body armour, which was nevertheless relevant to establishing whether A had been correctly identified as the gunman. ('[I]t would have been another unfortunate coincidence that the man identified as the gunman showed an attraction to guns, and had body armour at home' (at [50]) *per* Stanley Burnton LJ.) On the other hand, had the photographs and the witness statement related to the possession in this country of unlicensed weapons, that would have amounted to bad character evidence, which could only have become admissible via one of the gateways set out in s 101 of the 2003 Act.

7.28 *Evidence of 'reprehensible behaviour'.* Generally speaking, the courts are not inclined to treat minor peccadilloes and general misbehaving as evidence of bad character. In *V* [2006] EWCA Crim 1901 at [41], for instance, Crane J doubted whether 'a piece of exaggeration to fellow pupils after some everyday classroom behaviour attains the level of "reprehensible" behaviour envisaged in ss 98 and 112(1)...of the Criminal Justice Act 2003'. Similarly, in *Weir* [2006] 1 WLR 1885 the fact that appellants were known to the police from previous incidents in which they had variously been the victims of an attack but had declined to give witness statements, and the further fact that they had been arrested on suspicion of having committed a serious assault but had subsequently been released without charge could not be counted 'reprehensible behaviour'.

7.29 In *Weir*, the court also declined to treat W's relationship with a much younger female *per se* as evidence of reprehensible behaviour. As Kennedy LJ explained:

> In our combined view, the judge was wrong to conclude that the sexual relationship between the appellant [a 39 year-old, convicted of three indecent assaults on A] and B [aged 16 years at the time], without more, amounted to 'evidence of, or of a disposition towards, misconduct on his part' and therefore evidence of bad character...The definition of 'misconduct' in s 112(1) is very wide. It makes clear that behaviour may be reprehensible, and therefore misconduct, though not amounting to the commission of

an offence. The appellant was significantly older than B. But there was no evidence, or none that the Crown put forward and the judge ruled admissible, of grooming of B by the appellant before she was sixteen, or that her parents disapproved and communicated their disapproval to the appellant, or that B was intellectually, emotionally or physically immature for her age, or that there was some other feature of the lawful relationship which might make it 'reprehensible'.

(at [94])

This ruling did not mean that the evidence was inadmissible. On the contrary, because it fell outside the bad character provisions the evidence was admissible at common law simply because it was relevant in showing M's interest in younger girls—as, indeed, was an 'unattractive' (at [97]) alleged conversation with C, A's 15-year-old sister, suggesting that if she were a bit older and he were a bit younger... (cf *ante*, para **7.13**).

7.30 A court will assess whether something does or does not constitute 'reprehensible behaviour' within the meaning of the Act in the context of the charges weighing against a defendant. In *Osbourne* [2007] EWCA Crim 481 ([2007] Crim LR 712), for example, it was held that evidence that O, who had fatally stabbed his friend, had been prone to snap and shout at a former partner if he had not taken his medication did not amount to 'reprehensible conduct'. Significantly, Pill LJ stated:

In the context of this charge of murder, we do not accept that shouting at a partner in the manner described can amount to 'reprehensible behaviour' within the meaning of... the 2003 Act. Shouting between partners over the care of a very young child is not of course to be commended but in the context of a charge of murdering a close friend, it does not cross the threshold contemplated by the words of the statute.

(at [34])

In contrast, in *Saint* [2010] EWCA Crim 1924 esp at [19], evidence that S, who was charged with various sexual assaults, had an interest in 'swinging parties' and in 'dogging' in camouflage with a night sight was treated as reprehensible behaviour. Sometimes the judges admit to uncertainty as to whether or not particular evidence ought to be treated as evidence of bad character. In *Kiernan* [2008] EWCA Crim 972 at [81], for instance, Laws LJ confessed to experiencing such difficulty. B had been charged with offences arising out of mortgage frauds. The Court of Appeal said that B's ex-wife 'was describing things done in an entirely domestic setting, and it must be questionable whether evidence of a husband giving his wife blank forms to sign can realistically be said to show misconduct on his part, at least in the absence of a telling and specific context. But even if this was bad character evidence, ...'

7.31 It also bears mentioning that ss 98 and 112(1) are concerned only with evidence of bad character. Thus, a simple *belief* that someone is of bad character is not, as such, *evidence* of bad character. In *Hussain* [2008] EWCA 1117 H and M were jointly indicted for attempted robbery. H claimed that he had acted under duress exerted by M, but was not allowed to introduce evidence that he believed that M had been convicted of murder. In fact, M had been once been tried for murder arising out of a road rage incident, but at a re-trial the Crown had accepted a plea of guilty to assault occasioning abh. The Court of Appeal emphasised that, at least in cases where a defendant is advancing a defence of duress, whilst an allegation of actual 'misconduct' will fall within the bad character provisions of the 2003 Act, a defendant's claim that he believed that his co-accused had been convicted of murder would be a different matter:

> If [the judge] had been asked to admit the evidence of what H believed about M, however mistaken it might have been, and together with that to admit evidence that M had in the past been tried for murder, on the different basis that this might help to show that there was some foundation for H's asserted belief, then ... it would have been relevant evidence which ought to have been admitted.
>
> (at [14])

Acquittals may be admissible as 'evidence of bad character'

7.32 Section 98 is so widely drafted that 'evidence of bad character' is not restricted to evidence of previous convictions or of more general reprehensible behaviour. In cases where a defendant has one or more previous acquittals to his credit, such evidence may also be admissible, provided of course that it reveals 'evidence ... of a disposition towards the commission of an offence or other reprehensible behaviour'.

7.33 In what context might a defendant's previous acquittals furnish evidence of his bad character? Prior to the 2003 Act, the House of Lords considered this question in *Z* [2000] 2 AC 483. Although the old rules of common law have now been abolished by s 99(1), *Z*'s case is still relevant both by way of illustration and in its approach to the question of double jeopardy—an approach that courts continue to adopt towards this issue. Z was charged with a single rape, alleged to have been committed in 1998. The Crown sought leave to introduce evidence that on four prior occasions—in 1984, 1985, 1989 and 1993—Z had been charged with other rapes. On only one of those occasions had Z actually been convicted. Thrice, therefore, he had been acquitted. It was accepted that, taken together, had they all resulted in convictions the four earlier incidents would have constituted admissible evidence tending to show that Z was guilty of the fifth rape. The sole disputed question was whether the Crown was entitled to lead evidence of three previous acquittals.

It obviously arouses profound suspicion that someone with three acquittals and one conviction for rape to his name, where at each trial the central issue had been whether the complainant had consented, should once more be facing a rape charge. Two arguments might be deployed.

- *Firstly*, it is legitimate to ask, what does an acquittal actually signify? It could be said that since the law demands proof beyond reasonable doubt before a defendant can be convicted, an acquittal cannot be taken to signify that a jury has decided that the defendant is innocent. Juries may not have considered that Z was innocent of the three rapes for which he had stood trial but been acquitted, only that they could not be sure of his guilt. That being so, is there any compelling justification for treating the three acquittals in all circumstances as incontestable evidence of Z's innocence?

- *Secondly*, the coincidence of Z's similar misconduct, even if in the form of previous acquittal evidence, may enjoy an evidential force not possessed by the facts of any one case alone. The pattern of previous charges immediately places a serious question mark over Z's behaviour in the case of the 1998 incident. In the Court of Appeal Mance LJ, in Z (2000) 164 JP 240, thought that this point was, in legal logic, 'unanswerable'.

The Court of Appeal, in Z, nevertheless concluded 'with regret' that evidence of the previous acquittals was inadmissible. Decided authority clearly established that the prosecution was precluded from asserting, or adducing evidence to show, that a defendant had actually been guilty of offences for which he had been acquitted. Notably, *dicta* in Lord Macdermott's speech in *Sambasivam v Public Prosecutor Federation of Malaya* [1950] AC 458 appeared to exclude this possibility:

> The effect of a verdict of acquittal pronounced by a competent court on a lawful charge and after a lawful trial is not completely stated by saying that the person acquitted cannot be tried again for the same offence. To that it must be added that the verdict is binding and conclusive in all subsequent proceedings between the parties to the adjudication.
>
> (at 479)

In the case in hand, the significance of adducing evidence of Z's previous brushes with the law would have been to show that he had persistently assaulted women in a particular way, later claiming—more often than not, successfully—that they had consented to intercourse with him. The clear import was that, although acquitted, in those three cases, too, he had in fact been guilty of rape.

7.34 On appeal, the House of Lords held that acquittal evidence could become admissible, provided that it was sufficiently relevant in the context of the case. As Lord Hobhouse observed:

[The accused] may be acquitted a number of times. But after a time it may become implausible and the case become overwhelming that he must have realised that the woman concerned did not consent.

(at 509)

Acquittal evidence, prior to the 2003 Act, was only to be excluded if its admission would compromise the fairness of the trial, taking into account the interests both of the prosecution and of the accused. Whereas *Sambasivam* may have suggested that a previous acquittal conclusively militated against the admissibility of such evidence, following *Z*, when a court had to determine whether to admit such evidence, the fact that a previous trial had ended in an acquittal was 'simply another factor to be put in the balance'—as is the fact that the accused may have to deal a second time with evidence proving facts that were in issue in an earlier trial. [And so it came to pass that in October 2000 'Z', aka Nicholas Edwards, was eventually tried and convicted of rape, the testimony of all four other complainants having been admitted in evidence.]

7.35　Given that acquittals result whenever a tribunal is left with a reasonable doubt as to the accused's guilt, it is not illogical that the House of Lords in *Z* should have recognised that evidence of a series of previous acquittals involving broadly similar circumstances might be treated as sufficiently suggestive to be left to the jury as probative of the defendant's guilt on another charge. However, there is one possible danger in admitting acquittal evidence. The tribunal of fact can all too easily be misled into assuming that there is no smoke without fire. In 1956 Lt-Commander Swabey was convicted by court martial of indecently assaulting a sub-lieutenant. A mere 17 years later, following a catalogue of appeals and petitions, the Ministry of Defence acknowledged that he had unquestionably been the victim of a miscarriage of justice. The members of the court that had tried him, quite improperly, had been aware that, by coincidence, in 1950 Swabey had been acquitted by court martial on another charge of committing indecency with a naval rating. Plainly, such information would have weighed heavily in the deliberations of the court in 1956. After all, there is no smoke without fire. Under the 2003 Act, in cases where it is permissible to do so, the prejudicial effect of the other 'misconduct' will need to be weighed carefully against its probative force and a court is likely to hesitate before admitting prosecution acquittal evidence.

7.36　A word of caution: it might be tempting to overestimate the frequency with which evidence of previous acquittals will become admissible. Had *Z*, who was charged with having committed one rape, only once before been acquitted of a rape, it is most doubtful that that previous acquittal would have been admissible under the old law. What made the evidence especially compelling in *Z* was the fact that there had been a particularly sinister sequence of no less than three earlier acquittals and a conviction, all arising out of factually similar rapes. Indeed, it is noteworthy that in one of the very few cases where acquittal evidence was subsequently held to have been properly admitted, *Harrison* [2004] EWCA Crim 1792, in addition to the strangling with which H was charged, on no less than four previous occasions witnesses alleged that H had made attempts to strangle them. Criminal charges had resulted from two of these incidents—on one occasion, H had been convicted of common assault, whereas on the other H had been acquitted by the justices. Regarding the other two occasions, the court had heard witnesses' accounts of the strangulations. As in *Z*, in *Harrison* it was the persistent pattern of previous conduct that lent the acquittal evidence its particular weight in the context of the case. So, too, under the Criminal Justice Act 2003, the defendant's acquittals ought not too readily to be assumed to furnish, in the words of that statute, 'evidence...of a disposition towards the commission of an offence or other reprehensible behaviour'. Nevertheless, *e contra*, in *Barney* [2005] EWCA Crim 1385, a decision under the old law, Dyson LJ upheld a trial judge's decision in a homosexual rape case to admit evidence of a single previous acquittal for homosexual rape committed in broadly similar circumstances. As the court observed, 'the issue is not one of arithmetic...The nature of the allegations is always important' (at [11]), and it is a matter of gauging the probative value of the particular misconduct evidence proffered by the Crown in any given case.

When is evidence of a defendant's bad character admissible under the 2003 Act?

7.37　The general principle, embodied in the 2003 Act, is that evidence of a defendant's bad character is inadmissible unless it falls within one of the categories (referred to as 'gateways') specified in the statute. Section 101(1) enumerates the seven exceptional situations—these are known as 'gateways'—in which such evidence may be admitted:

> In criminal proceedings evidence of the defendant's bad character is admissible if, but only if—
>
> (a) all parties to the proceedings agree to the evidence being admissible,
>
> (b) the evidence is adduced by the defendant himself or is given in answer to a question asked by him in cross-examination and intended to elicit it,
>
> (c) it is important explanatory evidence,
>
> (d) it is relevant to an important matter in issue between the defendant and the prosecution,

(e) it has substantial probative value in relation to an important matter in issue between the defendant and a co-defendant,

(f) it is evidence to correct a false impression given by the defendant, or

(g) the defendant has made an attack on another person's character.

Subsequent accompanying provisions in Part 11 set out in greater detail how the courts are to approach some of the gateways, each of which we shall consider separately.

7.38 Before doing so, it is to be noted that s 101 imposes restrictions on the admissibility of bad character evidence sought to be admitted via two of these gateways. First, s 101(3) provides that evidence is not to be admitted via gateways (d) or (g):

if, on an application by the defendant to exclude it, it appears to the court that the admission of the evidence would have such an adverse effect on the fairness of the proceedings that the court ought not to admit it.

Second, in cases where the defence takes objection to the admission of bad character evidence under these selfsame paragraphs (d) and (g), s 101(4) directs the manner in which the court is to exercise this discretion to the extent of stating that:

...the court must have regard, in particular, to the length of time between the matters to which that evidence relates and the matters which form the subject of the offence charged.

Section 101(4) has chosen to emphasise the staleness of convictions as a reason for excluding potentially admissible bad character evidence; and, in *Hanson* [2005] 1 WLR 3169 at [11], the Court of Appeal underlined that s 101(4) stipulates that staleness is to be measured by the dates of commission of offences, not by their date of conviction. Previous convictions, however, will not necessarily be excluded simply because they are relatively elderly. The elapse of time may be perfectly explicable on grounds other than that the leopard might have changed its spots. Thus, in *Campbell* [2006] EWCA Crim 1305 Lord Phillips of Worth Matravers, CJ noted that although eight and six years had passed between the earlier misconduct and the offence charged, 'part of the time interval between the latter offence and the current offence was the time that the applicant spent in prison pursuant to the sentence of four years' imprisonment imposed upon him' (at [14]). Again, as Hallett LJ pointed out in *Jordan* [2009] EWCA Crim 953:

We take [counsel's] point that the...convictions were relatively old, but we also note that in the meantime [J] had spent some years in prison. Far from turning over a new leaf, as he claimed he had continued to commit offences.

(at [21])

Nor does s 101(4) prevent a court from considering other issues, such as the triviality of the other previous misconduct or its highly prejudicial character in the context of the case. These features may prove just as important.

Situations in which bad character evidence becomes admissible under s 101: the seven gateways

Gateway (a): When 'all parties to the proceedings agree to the evidence being admissible' (s 101(1)(a))

7.39   Defendants will rarely agree to their bad character being introduced in evidence. The normal tactic is to resist this revelation, if at all possible. However, the Act caters for the eventuality, and the Court of Appeal in *Hanson* [2005] 1 WLR 3169 expressed the hope, in cases where defendants might be tempted to contest the details of previous convictions:

> We would expect the relevant circumstances of previous convictions generally to be capable of agreement, and that, subject to the trial judge's ruling as to admissibility, they will be put before the jury by way of admission.
>
> (at [17])

As regards what exactly is meant by 'agree' in s 101(1)(a), we shall see that in *Williams v VOSA* (2008) 172 JP 328 the notion was given a broad interpretation in relation to hearsay evidence (see *infra*, paras **9.68–9.69**) and that, depending upon the circumstances, agreement might be inferred simply from a party's acquiescence to the evidence being led. A similar construction applies to s 101(1)(a). Thus, in *Marsh* [2009] EWCA Crim 2696 at [46] M's bad character, which had been adduced at trial 'without demur', was held rightly to have been admitted 'because there was tacit agreement between all parties to the proceedings that the evidence was relevant, admissible and should be admitted.'

Gateway (b): When 'the evidence is adduced by the defendant himself or is given in answer to a question asked by him in cross-examination and intended to elicit it' (s 101(1)(b))

7.40   Once again, in the great majority of cases an accused is unlikely to wish to introduce evidence of his bad character voluntarily. However, s 101(1)(b) may cater for one class of case. Experience prior to the 2003 Act taught that if an accused appreciates that his bad character will inevitably emerge at trial, there may be something to be said for the defence volunteering the information rather than allowing the prosecution or a co-accused dramatically to introduce the evidence like a conjuror yanking rabbits, with a flourish, out of a top hat. Tactically, it may suit the defendant to introduce the evidence himself, simply to convey the impression that he is being perfectly candid about himself and has nothing to fear from the court's being made aware of his murky past. This tactic is sometimes referred to in the literature as 'stealing sunshine' (see Perry & Weimann-Saks (2011) *infra*).

Gateway (c): When 'it is important explanatory evidence' (s 101(1)(c))

7.41 In this provision, the Criminal Justice Act 2003 has incorporated into the statute what, prior to the Act, used to be called 'background evidence'. The meaning of 'important explanatory evidence' is further defined in s 102, which provides:

> For the purposes of s 101(1)(c) evidence is important explanatory evidence if—
>
> (a) without it, the court or jury would find it impossible or difficult properly to understand other evidence in the case, and
>
> (b) its value for understanding the case as a whole is substantial.

Although the rules of common law have been abolished by s 99(1)—and, admittedly, today it has to be borne in mind that 'the gateway is now governed by the new statutory language [which] has to be seen in its overall setting' (*Davis* (2008) 172 JP 358 at [33] *per* Hughes LJ)—the close match between this provision and the manner in which the courts defined 'background evidence' make it worthwhile, if only by way of illustration, to refer to some of the pre-2003 cases, which would in all likelihood be decided similarly under s 101(1)(c). 'Background evidence', of course, is a wide concept, encompassing not only what amounts to evidence of bad character but also much other relevant evidence.

7.42 *Some illustrations.* Under the old law the Court of Appeal authoritatively defined 'background evidence' in *Pettmann* (1985) 2 May, unreported, as follows:

> Where it is necessary to place before the jury evidence of part of a continual background of history relevant to the offence charged in the indictment and without the totality of which the account placed before the jury would be incomplete or incomprehensible, then the fact that the whole account involves including evidence establishing the commission of an offence with which the accused is not charged is not of itself a ground for excluding the evidence.

The similarity between the common law concept and ss 101(1)(c) and 102 is obvious. Immediately prior to the entry into force of the 2003 Act, cases in which this species of evidence was admitted were becoming increasingly common. In *TM* [2000] 2 Cr App R 266, for instance, a horrifying sexual abuse case involving 43 counts brought against nine defendants in two separate trials, Kennedy LJ upheld a trial judge's decision to admit background evidence explaining how the parents gradually introduced their elder son to sexually abusing his sister as a spectator and later as a participant. Without this information concerning the way in which the children were groomed, it was said, the jury could not have properly appreciated the significance of the other evidence in the case. In *Phillips* [2003] 2 Cr App R 35, where P was accused of having murdered his wife, the trial judge was held rightly to have admitted evidence of the parties' recent stormy matrimonial relationship. As Dyson, LJ noted:

> ...where one spouse is charged with the murder of the other, it will often be relevant for the jury to know about the matrimonial relationship in order to make a properly informed assessment of the entire evidence...Also relevant was any safe and reliable evidence that the appellant had previously thought of murder, either as revenge (she had had a brief affair with another man), or as his way out of the marriage.
>
> (at [32]–[33])

Again, in *West* [2003] EWCA Crim 3024, Pill LJ upheld a trial judge's decision to admit evidence of two boys' previous sexual relationship in order to explain how the victim had been manipulatively conditioned from an early age to submit to the infliction of assorted sexual indignities by W.

7.43 The best-known example of 'background evidence', however, was *Sawoniuk* [2000] 2 Cr App R 220. S, a former policeman, was charged on two counts of murdering Jewish civilians in Belorussia during World War II, contrary to the War Crimes Act 1991. Two witnesses, B and Z, gave evidence relating to the two counts in the indictment. However, two further witnesses, I and E, testified to other incidents in which they had seen S rounding up and maltreating Jews. S was not charged with these murders. On appeal, the evidence relating to uncharged murders in which S was implicated was ruled admissible on what the court termed a broad basis. In the words of Lord Bingham CJ: 'Criminal charges cannot be fairly judged in a factual vacuum.' The evidence was relevant because it established S's relative role in Nazi search and kill operations. Moreover, 'in order to make a rational assessment of evidence directly relating to a charge it may often be necessary for a jury to receive evidence describing, perhaps in some detail, the context and circumstances in which offences are said to have been committed'. Here, to comprehend the extraordinary conditions that prevailed in a foreign country in wartime in the 1940s it had been necessary and appropriate for the Crown to prove the policy of Nazi Germany, the extent of the local police's active participation in that policy, and the fact that S participated in the search-and-kill missions to mop up survivors of an earlier massacre. Whilst the judge did not direct the jury in terms not to use this information as evidence of S's propensity, he had made sufficiently clear that the jury should not fall into the trap of inferring that because S had been implicated in other acts of violence against Jews he was that much more likely to have committed these two specific offences. The background evidence was relevant, probative and admissible, even if it did incidentally disclose the commission of other offences not charged on the indictment. The evidence of other misconduct admitted in this quartet of cases, it is suggested, would similarly pass muster under ss 101(1)(c) and 102. In the words of s 102, in each of the four cases 'without it, the…jury would [have found] it impossible or difficult properly to understand other evidence in the case' and 'its value for understanding the case as a whole [was] substantial'.

7.44 The Court of Appeal has had several opportunities to consider the application of s 101(1)(c). In *Pronick* [2006] EWCA Crim 2517, P had been convicted for the attempted rape of his partner. Even though P had admitted that their relationship had been volatile, the trial judge admitted evidence of P's conviction for assault as well as the complainant's evidence relating to seven previous incidents when, she alleged, P had either assaulted her or, in one case, actually raped her. Latham LJ concluded:

> Unless the complainant was allowed to give her account of the nature of the relationship, the jury would not be able to make a proper assessment of the respective evidence of the two protagonists. It was accordingly necessary material for the jury's consideration, and its importance for the jury was likely to be substantial.
>
> (at [8])

In contrast, in *Beverley* [2006] Crim LR 1064, the trial judge was held to have been mistaken in allowing the Crown to introduce via gateway (c) B's two previous convictions for possession of cannabis with intent to supply and for simple possession of cannabis at his trial for conspiracy to import more than 1 kg of cocaine from Jamaica. B had been stopped whilst conveying in his car two individuals who later pleaded guilty to the offence. B, however, claimed that he had been unaware that his passengers had been carrying cocaine. Laws LJ made clear that this was a seriously mistaken application of ss 101(1)(c) and 102:

> [The Crown's] submission ignores the provisions of s 102, whose two parts at (a) and (b) are cumulative. We are entirely unable to see how the jury would have been disabled or disadvantaged in understanding any of the evidence allegedly connecting the appellant with the crime without having these convictions before them. The evidence was perfectly clear. It required no footnote or lexicon…There should never have been an application under s 101(1)(c) in this case nor should it have been supported here. The gateway at s 101(1)(c) was entirely unavailable.
>
> ([2006] EWCA Crim 1287 at [7])

Similarly, in *Saint* [2010] EWCA Crim 1924, where S *inter alia* was charged with raping V in a car park at night, the Court of Appeal held that evidence showing that in the 1990s S used to put on camouflage clothing, black his face at night and observe couples in a country park and that he was interested in swinging and dogging, had been wrongly admitted:

> It simply did not satisfy the test of evidence without which the jury would find it impossible or difficult properly to understand other evidence in the case, nor was its value for understanding the case as a whole "substantial": s.102. The evidence it was said to explain was the evidence, mainly from [J], about footsteps. That evidence was not impossible or difficult to understand. On the contrary, it was readily intelligible. Its deficiency was that the Crown could not identify the footsteps with the appellant. Nor...could they readily do so by resort to the bad character evidence,...
>
> (at [16])

Beverley and *Saint*, then, provide salutary reminders that the statutory provisions regulating gateway (c) are restrictive and only allow the prosecution to adduce bad character evidence when it is genuinely vital to the tribunal's understanding of the case *and* it is of substantial value in that context.

7.45 *The judicial discretion to exclude technically admissible important explanatory evidence.* Consideration of the cases brings out the restricted use to which evidence admitted via gateway (c) may be put, as well as the importance of the courts' discretion to exclude unfair evidence which may be technically admissible under s 101(1)(c). Under the previous legal regime, it was widely recognised that the admission of 'background evidence' could be fraught with danger: a jury might become prejudiced once it became apprised of a 'tide of filth' involving the defendant. Therefore, if 'background evidence' was admitted, judges used to have to give the jury a careful direction explaining the limited purpose for which it was being admitted (to facilitate their general understanding of the case) and, preferably instructing them not to treat background evidence as proof of the defendant's guilt. Indeed, recognising the need to control the admission of this potentially prejudicial species of evidence, the Court of Appeal in *Butler* [1999] Crim LR 835 actually recommended the expedient of requiring counsel jointly to suggest or to present an agreed statement of those facts which were strictly necessary to enable to jury to understand the background to the case without being distracted from consideration of the central events. The wording of s 101(1)(c) strongly suggests that a similar practice is required under the 2003 Act. But more generally, despite the statutory tabulation of what is meant by 'important explanatory evidence', the old cases are a reminder that the notion that, without this bad character evidence 'the court or jury would find it...difficult properly to understand other evidence in the case' is quite an elastic concept. Tuckey LJ wisely observed in *Dolan* [2003] 1 Cr App R 18 at [23]:

> [I]t is important to bear in mind...that the label "background evidence" may be a vehicle for smuggling in otherwise inadmissible evidence for less than adequate reasons.

For this reason, in *Dolan* the Court of Appeal concluded that evidence that D had in the past vented his fury on inanimate objects had been wrongly admitted in a murder case in which the jury had to decide which of two parents had killed the baby. As Tuckey LJ pointed out:

> The fact that a man who is not shown to have any tendency to lose his temper and react violently towards human beings becomes frustrated with and violent towards inanimate objects is...irrelevant. Those of us who are ham-fisted or over-ambitious DIY enthusiasts would be horrified to learn that frustration in this difficult field of endeavour could be used against us. By the same token it was not necessary for the jury to know about this. It was prejudicial and could only have diverted their attention from the very serious issue which they had to try.

For the same reason, in *Osbourne* [2007] EWCA Crim 481, a decision under the 2003 Act in which the court referred to pre-2003 case law, Pill LJ observed that, in the context of his trial for murdering a friend, evidence that O had shouted at a former partner was probably of even less relevance as 'important explanatory evidence' than D's flying off the handle at inanimate objects had been in *Dolan*.

7.46 It is important that gateway (c) is not employed as a means of admitting bad character evidence properly admitted through other gateways. In *Davis* (2008) 172 JP 358, D pleaded provocation to a charge of murdering his partner of 14 years' standing who had admitted to him that she had been having an affair and intended leaving him. The Crown was allowed to adduce, under the guise of important explanatory evidence, a former girlfriend's evidence that twenty years earlier D had been jealous and controlling, had accused her of having an affair and had threatened to kill her. In his summing-up the judge referred to this as evidence showing a propensity to jealousy and aggression. The Court of Appeal held that this evidence had been wrongly admitted through gateway (c). First, one could not say that without the girlfriend's evidence the jury would have found it impossible or difficult properly to understand other evidence in the case, nor that the value of the evidence for understanding the case as a whole was substantial, as required by s 102(a) and (b). Before admitting bad character evidence through gateway (c) it is essential that the statutory criteria for admissibility should have been satisfied. Secondly, and just as importantly, by admitting what was essentially propensity evidence through gateway (c), as we shall see, the judge had deprived D of protections afforded to an accused when propensity evidence is admitted via gateway (d)—namely, the discretions provided for in s 101(3) and (4) and, where appropriate, in s 103(3). Hughes LJ pointed out, there had to be a danger in admitting evidence merely as 'important explanatory evidence' if the use to which it was really intended to be put was as evidence of propensity, where the statutory tests and safeguards were different. Maurice Kay LJ reiterated this warning in *Saint* [2010] EWCA Crim 1924:

> [E]vidence of propensity should not readily slide in under the guise of important background evidence and…evidence which is admitted under gateway (c) should not readily be used, once admitted, for a purpose, such as propensity, for which additional safeguards on different tests have first to be met.
>
> (at [14])

Gateway (d): When 'it is relevant to an important matter in issue between the defendant and the prosecution' (s 101(1)(d))

7.47 *Matters in issue between defendant and prosecution.* 'Gateway' (d) is likely to prove the most frequently travelled route whereby a defendant's bad character becomes admissible under the Criminal Justice Act 2003. Only the prosecution may avail itself of this gateway (s 103(6)). Emphasising that bad character evidence is not to be admitted lightly, s 112 stresses that in this context when s 101(1)(d) refers to bad character 'relevant to an important matter in issue between the defendant and the prosecution'

> …"important matter" means a matter of substantial importance in the context of the case as a whole.

Section 103 details what is to be treated as a 'matter in issue between the defendant and the prosecution'. Matters in issue, according to s 103(1), fall into two principal (but not exclusive) types:

> (1) For the purposes of s 101(1)(d) the matters in issue between the defendant and the prosecution include—
>
> (a) the question whether the defendant has a propensity to commit offences of the kind with which he is charged, except where his having such a propensity makes it no more likely that he is guilty of the offence;
>
> (b) the question whether the defendant has a propensity to be untruthful, except where it is not suggested that the defendant's case is untruthful in any respect.

7.48 *Propensity to commit offences of the kind with which he is charged.* The first form of 'matter in issue' comprises evidence of bad character which shows that the defendant has a propensity to commit offences of the kind with which he is charged *and* that it is thus more likely that he has done so. Obviously, before gateway (d) can apply, there must actually be a live 'important matter in issue' between the parties. In *Whitehead* [2007] EWCA Crim 2078, for example, W was charged with causing death by dangerous driving. At trial there was no dispute as to W's speed at the time when he collided with a motorcyclist. The Crown, nevertheless, was permitted to adduce evidence of W's previous conviction for speeding in mid-2004 as showing a relevant propensity. As Laws LJ remarked on appeal,

> We regard this ruling as extremely surprising and entirely misconceived. There was no issue between the parties as to the speed at which the appellant was driving; it was admitted. There was no basis for admitting this evidence on propensity grounds; again, the relevant facts were admitted.
>
> (at [5])

7.49 *Propensity to be untruthful.* The other species of 'matter in issue', which is potentially of wide application, arises in cases where a central question in the case is whether or not the defendant is telling the truth. In this category of situation it is particularly to be noted that a defendant's bad character may only be adduced in order to illuminate his likely truthfulness if, in the words of a 101(1)(d), this is 'relevant to an *important* matter in issue between the defendant and the prosecution'—ie the matter in issue is 'of substantial importance in the context of the case as a whole' (s 112). These two forms of 'important matter in issue' will be considered separately.

7.50 When assessing the 'relevance' of bad character evidence, s 109 requires the court to assume that the evidence to be tendered is true, unless 'it appears, on the basis of any material before the court... that no court or jury could reasonably find it to be true'.

7.51 *Other matters that may be in issue as between defendant and Crown.* It should also be noted that s 103 states that 'the matters in issue between the defendant and the prosecution *include* ...', plainly signalling that important matters in issue may take forms other than those set out in s 103(1)(a) and (b). To what is this meant to allude? One category of case, where evidence that incorporated an element of bad character used to be admissible under the old law, arose where the prosecution's purpose in adducing the evidence was restricted to proving the defendant's knowledge of some fact. In the classical example, *Francis* (1874) LR 2 CCR 278, F was charged with false pretences, having tried to persuade a pawnbroker that a crystal ring was in fact a diamond ring. It was held that the Crown had properly been permitted to adduce evidence that F on an earlier occasion had tried to pass off the selfsame ring as a diamond ring. The evidence was admitted not to show that F had committed an offence on the previous occasion, but simply to show his state of knowledge: given that he had already been put right once, he could have been under few illusions concerning the composition of the ring when he approached the pawnbroker in the incident that gave rise to the charge. (For a broadly analogous case, where the court admitted evidence of an acquittal, see *Deighton and Thornton* [1954] Crim LR 208.) In likelihood, in a case like *Francis* (where, it might be noted, under the new statutory definition F's earlier 'misconduct' might not now qualify as evidence of bad character), evidence of the earlier incident would be admissible under s 101(1)(d) because 'relevant to an important matter in issue between the defendant and the prosecution'—namely, F's *mens rea* (see, eg, *Jordan* (2009) 173 JP 616 *per* Hallett LJ).

7.52 *Bad character evidence where the issue is to 'identify' the culprit.* One context in which evidence of bad character has been regularly utilised, thanks to insertion of the word 'include' in 103(1), is where such evidence serves to identify the defendant as the author of the offence. In *Isichei* (2006) 170 JP 753, the Crown wished to confirm the accuracy of F's video identification of I as the man who had mugged her. F, and her companion M, related that before robbing her I had leaned out of a taxi and called out that he wanted his 'coke' back. (This was taken to be a reference to cocaine.) The Crown was permitted to introduce, via gateway (d), evidence of I's previous conviction, six and a half years earlier, for being concerned in the importation of cocaine. The trial judge carefully instructed the jury that I's conviction was not evidence of a general propensity to commit drugs offences but was being admitted solely to show that I, who contested identification, had previously had an interest in cocaine, thereby strengthening F's identification. On appeal, I contested this use of his previous bad character. The Court of Appeal held that evidence of the previous conviction had been rightly admitted since the judge had not delivered a direction as to propensity, but an express direction as to identification through the medium of a connecting factor so as to place I in a discrete category of person interested in cocaine, tying it to the girls' evidence as to the mention of cocaine by one of their assailants. The connecting factor was one in which the prosecution sought to find a way to support the evidence of identification; not a propensity to commit robbery or assault. One might like to think that, in view of the prejudicial nature of the conviction, its relative antiquity and its limited relevance, this case was near the outer limits of admissibility. Certainly, in such circumstances a judge will need to deliver the clearest direction of the limited use to which the jury may put such evidence.

7.53 In *Brima* [2007] 1 Cr App R 248, where B, who was charged with stabbing V in October 2004, claimed mistaken identity, the Court of Appeal upheld the trial judge's decision to admit evidence that B, in November 2002, had been convicted of assault occasioning abh during the course of which he had stabbed someone in the leg and, in April 2003, had also been convicted of a robbery committed in September 2002 during which he had held a knife to someone's throat. These convictions showed a relevant propensity to commit offences of violence using knives either by inflicting or threatening injury, thereby serving to identify B as the perpetrator. Again, in *Saleem* [2007] EWCA Crim 1923 the trial judge rightly admitted evidence of bad character in order to counter S's claim that his presence at an assault had been perfectly innocent. The victim's face had been carved up with a Stanley knife by three young men, one of whom was said to be S. Evidence was admitted (i) that violent images and films had been found on S's computer showing people with facial injuries inflicted by assaults and that these images had last been accessed just a few days before the attack, and (ii) that violent rap lyrics had been downloaded from the Internet, and that they had been amended to include a reference to S's birthday and the fact that an assault resulting in significant injuries was planned for that day ('February 24th my birth day, im gon make it ur worst day, do I have 2 have u layin in emergency 2 have dem stitch ya?'). Rejecting the argument that the rap lyrics 'had to do with the alleged facts of the offence' under s 98(a) (*ante*, paras **7.13–7.17**), Thomas LJ concluded that 'the evidence was relevant to rebutting the case of innocent presence put forward by [S]' (at 27]). See further Andrea Dennis, 'Poetic (In)Justice? Rap Music Lyrics as Art, Life and Criminal Evidence', 31 Columbia J of Law and the Arts 1 (2007). Finally, in *Spittle* [2009] RTR 14, where S was convicted of dangerous driving, driving whilst disqualified and breach of an ASBO, it was held that S's three convictions for driving whilst disqualified had been correctly admitted to show that S was correctly identified as the perpetrator.

The defendant's 'propensity to commit offences' (s 103(1)(a))

7.54 The most significant reform the 2003 Act introduced into the realm of bad character evidence was that a defendant's 'propensity' to commit offences might become admissible evidence. As Hughes LJ remarked in *Chopra* [2007] 1 Cr App R 16:

> [T]he important change is that whereas previously evidence of the defendant's propensity to offend in the manner now charged was *prima facie* inadmissible, now it is *prima facie* admissible.
>
> (at [12])

Although the term 'propensity' is nowhere defined in the statute, the Act does give guidance on what 'may' constitute evidence indicative of a defendant's 'propensity to commit offences of the kind with which he is charged' under s 103(1)(a). The methods enumerated in the Act do not make up an exclusive list. Section 103(2) nevertheless prescribes two principal types of offence that may be treated as admissible for this purpose:

> . . . a defendant's propensity to commit offences of the kind with which he is charged may (without prejudice to any other way of doing so) be established by evidence that he has been convicted of—
>
> (a) an offence of the same description as the one with which he is charged, or
> (b) an offence of the same category as the one with which he is charged.

7.55 'Offences of the same description' and 'offences of the same category' are further defined. Regarding 'offences of the same description', s 103(4)(a) stipulates that:

> Two offences are of the same description as each other if the statement of the offence in a written charge or indictment would, in each case, be in the same terms.

So, if D is charged with rape, *prima facie* evidence that he has been previously convicted of rape may be admissible under s 103(2)(a) as showing his propensity to commit offences of the kind with which he is charged, which also will surely qualify as 'a matter of substantial importance in the context of the case as a whole' (s 112). In a similar manner, as regards 'offences of the same category', s 103(4)(b) states that:

> Two offences are of the same category as each other if they belong to the same category of offences prescribed for the purposes of this section by an order made by the Secretary of State.

The Secretary of State, whose responsibility it is to prescribe what offences will be admissible under s 103(2)(b), is specifically enjoined in his order only to nominate 'offences of the same type' (s 103(5)). It is not clear what a 'type' of offence means. The Act gives no further guidance. 'Types' could signify something as generalised as, say, 'offences of dishonesty', 'offences of violence', 'road traffic offences', 'public order offences', 'sexual offences', etc. But such 'types' overlap, and many offences could fall into more than one 'type'. Other types, such as 'sexual offences' subdivide into a number of sexual specialities, some of which are almost mutually exclusive—eg homosexual and heterosexual offenders.

7.56 In October 2004 the then Home Secretary laid an order before Parliament setting out two categories of offences for the purposes of s 103(4)(b) (see Criminal Justice Act 2003 (Categories of Offences) Order 2004, SI 2004/3346). These particular categories were responses to public concern at the prevalence of certain types of offences. The first, the so-called 'Theft Category', prescribed previous convictions that could in future be treated as mutually admissible in the realm of offences of dishonesty. These comprised convictions for theft, robbery, burglary, aggravated burglary, taking conveyances without consent, handling stolen goods, going equipped for theft, making off without payment and inchoate offences (but not conspiracies) respecting any of the above. In similar fashion, the second category, entitled 'Sexual Offences (Persons under the age of 16) Category', listed no less than 36 different offences of a sexual character that included rape (of a victim under the age of 16), intercourse with girls under 13 and 16 years of age, intercourse with a defective or a patient, incest, buggery, indecency between men, indecent assault and offences under ss 1–10, 14–17, 25–26, 30–31, 34–35, and 38–39 of the Sexual Offences Act 2003, together with all inchoate variants save conspiracy. In both these prescribed categories, it will be recalled that under s 103(2)(b), '...a defendant's propensity to commit offences of the kind with which he is charged may...be established by evidence that he has been convicted of...an offence of the same category as the one with which he is charged'. Although conspiracy is not included amongst the inchoate offences covered by the ministerial orders, this does not mean that convictions for conspiracy may not be admissible under s 103(2). In *Johnson* [2009] 2 Cr App R 7, where six co-defendants were jointly charged with conspiring to burgle large country houses and commercial premises over a period of about a year, whilst defendants' convictions for conspiracy to burgle were inadmissible under SI 2004/3346, they would nevertheless have been admissible ('without prejudice to any other way of doing so') as they were still relevant to the central question in the case, 'whether a defendant would participate in a conspiracy to burgle.'

7.57 *Bad character evidence not to be used to bolster weak cases.* Not surprisingly, some commentators have warned of the heightened risk of miscarriages of justice as a result of the ease with which seemingly damning propensity evidence might now be placed before juries (and judges for that matter) to condemn the usual suspects. In *Hanson* [2005] 1 WLR 3169, the first case in which the Court of Appeal sought to interpret this Part of the 2003 Act, the Court of Appeal showed itself alert to this possibility, and was at pains to stress that the purpose of the 2003 Act was 'to assist in the evidence-based conviction of the guilty' (at [4]), that 'evidence of bad character cannot be used simply to bolster a weak case, or to prejudice the minds of a jury against a defendant' (at [18]), and that the previous convictions must genuinely show a propensity in the defendant to commit the offence(s) charged. It noticeable that appellants frequently plead that their bad character has been wrongfully introduced by the Crown to bolster a weak case; such grounds seldom succeed.

7. 58 One consequence of this principle that bad character evidence ought only to be admitted to support evidence-based convictions, is that the appropriate time at which a judge ought to rule on its admissibility will vary from case to case. Many applications can properly be heard before the case begins; others will be more properly dealt with at the close of the Crown case. If, for example, the strength of prosecution evidence is in doubt, the right course may be to delay this decision. Although the Court of Appeal in *HSD* [2006] EWCA Crim 1703 declined to deliver more specific guidance on this matter, in *Gyima* [2007] EWCA Crim 429, [2007] Crim LR 890, where the victim of a mugging failed to come up to proof at trial and the only other evidence implicating the defendants derived from a video interview conducted with an absent 14-year-old witness, it was held that the judge had been in error in ruling on the admissibility of G's previous convictions for robbery at the outset of the trial without waiting to assess the true strength of the Crown's case. Again, in *Hewlett* [2008] EWCA Crim 270 the victim of two alleged

Evidence of the defendant's bad character

robberies had a history of mental problems. Partly owing to his confused accounts and partly thanks to police insouciance, there was serious doubt as to whether any robberies had actually occurred. In addition, the identification evidence was less than convincing. H, however, had a serious criminal record that included convictions for entering the accommodation of the vulnerable in order to demand money. Quashing H's convictions, Hooper LJ declared that this was 'one of those cases where the judge ought to have delayed any ruling on the admissibility of the previous convictions until he had heard the evidence in-chief and cross-examination of the witnesses' (at [23]). Had he done so, he would have seen how threadbare the prosecution's case was and it would have been 'unlikely' that he would have admitted evidence of H's bad character. (See also *Harding* [2010] EWCA Crim 2145.)

7. 59 *The minimum number of other events.* The Court in *Hanson* additionally warned that whilst there is no minimum number of events necessary to establish a propensity, the fewer the number of convictions the weaker is likely to be the evidence of propensity. Single events, nevertheless, may establish propensity if they show a tendency to unusual behaviour:

> Child sexual abuse or fire setting are comparatively clear examples of such unusual behaviour but we attempt no exhaustive list. So, a single conviction for shoplifting, will not, without more, be admissible to show propensity to steal. But if the *modus operandi* has significant features shared by the offence charged it may show propensity.
>
> (at [9])

It is accepted that:

> There is no rule of law . . . that a single previous conviction cannot be sufficient for propensity, but it is clear that great care must be exercised before admitting a single offence in that way
>
> (*McDonald* [2007] EWCA Crim 1194 at [16] *per* David Clarke J)

Thus, in *Woodhouse* (2009) 173 JP 337 a farmworker's conviction for sexual activity with a child was upheld in a case where the prosecution had been allowed to adduce evidence of a similar incident ten years earlier for which the offender had received a caution. The earlier case displayed close similarities to the offence charged—the children were roughly the same age, and the two offences had taken a very similar form. Nevertheless, in such cases the courts must be properly mindful of their discretion, variously under s 101(3) and (4) and under s 103(3), to exclude such evidence were it either unfair or unjust to admit it as evidence of a 'propensity to commit offences of the kind with which he is charged'. (See further Munday [2010] J Crim Law 128.)

7.60 *Identifying evidence showing a relevant 'propensity'.* Although the Act does not seek to define what is meant by 'propensity', obviously there are limits to what a court ought to consider amounts to evidence of propensity. In *Tully and Wood* (2007) 171 JP 25, for example, T and W had been convicted of robbing a taxi driver. T and W each had a number of relatively stale convictions for robbery. However, both defendants also had numerous other convictions, notably for offences of dishonesty. Although not originally part of the Crown's game plan, with a certain amount of encouragement from the judge, the prosecution successfully applied to have all T's and W's previous records for dishonesty admitted, the judge stating that they could be adduced because 'the number of convictions...[is] evidence of a propensity to acquire other people's property by unlawful means, by robbery if necessary'. On appeal, it was held that in so determining the trial judge had adopted too expansive a view of 'propensity':

> [T]he judge was wrong to hold, in effect, that a propensity to obtain other people's property by one means or another made it more likely that these appellants would have committed this offence...To allow the Crown to prove a propensity to obtain other people's property by some means or another is...to allow them to cast far too wide a net. Such evidence has limited probative value and has a potentially prejudicial and harmful effect. In *Hanson* the court said that the judge should look for similarities between what the defendant had done in the past and what he was now charged with. Those similarities did not have to be striking in the way that similar fact evidence has to be, but there must be a degree of similarity. The fact that the convictions are for offences of the same description or category does not automatically mean that they should be admitted. It is not possible to define the degree of similarity which must be shown. That must be for the judge's discretion and judgment to be exercised on the facts and circumstances of the individual case. But the judge must strike a balance and in doing so must remember the words of s 101(3).
>
> (at [26])

Smith LJ added that the judge appeared to have apprehended that s 103(2) gave him complete freedom to admit all convictions of the same category as the offence of robbery regardless of their probative effect. He seemed to have assumed that:

> Robbery being a theft offence, all convictions for other theft offences could go in to prove a general propensity to acquire other people's property by one means or another. The judge did not consider whether evidence of those convictions would make it more likely that each appellant had committed this offence...[H]ad he done so, he would have concluded that such evidence had little probative force. There are a great many people who have a propensity to acquire other people's property by one means or another. On the other hand, previous convictions for robbery would be much more probative and a conviction for robbing somebody using a knife to reinforce a threat of violence would increase the probative effect. In short, the more similar the circumstances of the past offences to the present allegation, the greater the probative force.
>
> (at [27])

Tully and Wood is important in making clear that a trial judge does not enjoy an unrestricted discretion to admit previous convictions and other general bad character under s 103(2), but must focus on the particular case to determine whether or not a defendant's bad character truly demonstrates a propensity to commit the specific offence(s) charged. (See also *Urushadze* [2008] EWCA Crim 2498, where six shoplifting convictions were held to have been wrongly admitted to show that U would have appreciated that a robbery was unfolding before his eyes and that U had a propensity to commit the theft-element of the robbery with which he was charged.)

7.61 *Bullen* [2008] 2 Cr App R 25 affords another timely reminder that, if it is to be admitted, the accused's bad character must be directed at the specific issues raised by the case in hand and not simply address a general propensity of the accused which is not an issue in the case. B was charged with murdering S, having severed his jugular with a broken bottle in the course of a drunken fight. At trial B pleaded guilty to manslaughter. In consequence, the sole issue for the jury was whether or not B had had the necessary intention to be convicted of murder. In holding that the trial judge had misdirected the jury on, and possibly wrongly admitted, evidence of B's seven previous convictions, which the Crown claimed showed a propensity to commit acts of violence, Rix LJ stressed that 'for all the change in the law, the test is still relevance ... The fact that s 103(1) seems also to have the effect of always potentially including the "question of" propensity among "the matters in issue" should not be overstated to the extent that sight is lost of the need for relevance: the bad character must still be relevant to an "important issue"' (at [29]). More specifically, in B's case the Court warned:

> Given that the issue was not whether [B] had committed a violent unlawful act caus-ing death, but whether he had the specific intent necessary to murder, the judge should...have been reminding himself, even while accepting that B's career had cer-tainly showed a propensity for violence, that "a propensity to commit offences of the kind charged" was a deliberately broad concept, properly designed for the generality of cases, but to be handled with care when the sole issue was specific intent.
>
> (at [33])

7.62 Not only must any evidence of bad character genuinely relate to a relevant criminal tendency on the part of the defendant, the judge must also direct the jury clearly on how they may use that evidence. In *L* [2006] EWCA Crim 2988, for example, the Court of Appeal, with regret, quashed L's convictions because in a two-count trial the judge had omitted to make clear to the jury that L's previous conviction for indecent exposure was relevant to the rape charge, showing that L was the sort of person who was prepared to insult and degrade a woman for his own sexual gratification, but had no bearing on the other charge on the indictment of causing gbh with intent.

7.63 In order to determine the admissibility of bad character evidence, a trial judge will often be obliged to enquire quite closely into details of earlier convictions in order to determine whether they genuinely display evidence of a relevant propensity. Thus in *Long* [2006] EWCA Crim 578, where a single previous conviction for a dissimilar type of robbery was admitted at L's trial for robbery, Rafferty J found that the recorder had failed to delve sufficiently into the detail of L's earlier offending. The recorder had mistakenly relied upon the fact that gateway (d) does not explicitly require that there exist any particular similarity between a defendant's past misconduct and the offence charged.

7.64 Although in *Hanson* [2005] 1 WLR 3169, the Court of Appeal's first foray into interpretation of this part of the Act, Rose LJ did acknowledge that 'circumstances demonstrating probative force are not confined to those sharing striking similarities', his Lordship also pointed out that 'the fewer the number of convictions the weaker is likely to be the evidence of propensity' and that 'if the *modus operandi* has significant features shared by the offence charged it may show propensity' (at [9]). More generally, Rose LJ cautioned that in cases where the Crown applied to adduce evidence of an accused's bad character:

> It will often be necessary, before determining admissibility and even when considering offences of the same description or category, to examine each individual conviction rather than merely to look at the name of the offence or at the defendant's record as a whole.
> (at [12])

7.65 Courts, therefore, have to take real care over their decisions whether or not to admit bad character evidence and to explain clearly in their rulings why they have decided as they have. In *Sully* (2007) November 27, for instance, at S's trial for sexual assault committed on a six-year-old child, the Court of Appeal upheld a judge's decision to admit, via gateway (d), evidence of S's two previous convictions for offences committed against pre-pubescent girls in 1968 and 1974. Although the earlier misconduct was stale, there were two previous incidents rather than just one, and the form the previous offending had taken was analogous if not identical to the offence charged. At the same time, it is desirable that courts should be vigilant not to become distracted by over-complicated and protracted enquiries into the details of defendants' previous offending. To quote from Rose LJ's judgment in *Hanson* once more:

> Where past events are disputed the judge must take care not to permit the trial unreasonably to be diverted into an investigation of matters not charged on the indictment.
> (*ibid*)

7.66 *The logical process the court must follow.* To be admissible the bad character evidence must plainly show that the defendant possesses the required propensity that makes it more likely that he committed the offence(s) charged. Therefore, before admitting bad character evidence *Hanson* laid down that the judge must in every case follow a three-stage reasoning process, asking himself the following questions:

1. Does the history of conviction(s) establish a propensity to commit offences of the kind charged?

2. Does that propensity make it more likely that the defendant committed the offence charged?

3. Is it unjust to rely on the conviction(s) of the same description or category; and, in any event, will the proceedings be unfair if they are admitted?

(at [7])

7.67 *The introduction of unpleasant details by way of evidence of bad character.* The great difference between the provisions of the 2003 Act and the old law relating to bad character is that the purpose of admitting such evidence is now to establish propensity, and to adduce probative material on that issue. In *Smith* [2006] EWCA Crim 1355, S was charged with burglary, having tricked an elderly woman into letting him into her home by telling her that he was from the water company. S's fingerprint was found on a bowl inside the victim's house. At trial, the Crown successfully applied for S's previous convictions for attempted burglary to be admitted, via gateway (d): the question was whether the similarity of the antecedent offending was such as to be admissible evidence of S's propensity to commit the type of offence with which he was charged, pursuant to s 103. The previous convictions had involved entering houses of elderly people by trick, and then stealing or attempting to steal from them. In cross-examination, Crown counsel put to S the similarities between the circumstances of his previous convictions and the instant offence, emphasising that he had preyed on the elderly. On appeal, S unsuccessfully argued that, whilst the judge had been entitled to admit the fact of his previous convictions for attempted burglary, he had wrongly permitted explicit and prejudicial details of the facts of the previous convictions to be admitted, thereby diverting attention away from the principal issue in the case. In upholding the conviction, the Court of Appeal held that whilst a balance must be struck, it could never be a rule that, because the previous offences were unpleasant, the detail of those offences could not be admitted. The very circumstances of S's previous offences provided their probative value, and the whole basis for the prosecution application to adduce the evidence was the similarity between the circumstances of the previous offences and the one with which the defendant was charged in the instant case, and cross-examination as to the details of the previous offending had been in order to persuade the jury of the defendant's propensity to commit such offences.

7.68 *Propensity may be established by other incidents prior to and, in suitable cases, by events subsequent to the offence charged.* Although evidence of bad character will normally relate to incidents prior to the offence charged, it may also take in events posterior to that date. As the court observed in *Adenusi* (2006) 170 JP 169, in deciding whether the accused had the relevant propensity at the time of the offence charged nothing predicated, as a matter of law, that a jury could not determine propensity at the time of the alleged instant offence by considering offences committed afterwards. Whether or not the later offences help in determining propensity is quintessentially a matter for the jury. In *A* [2009] EWCA Crim 513, where A was charged with serious sexual offences against his daughter between 1981 and 1992, the prosecution was allowed to adduce evidence that A possessed many incest-related, indecent images on his computer between 2005 and 2008 as well as evidence of visits to incest-related websites. The jury was not shown the images themselves. Maurice Kay LJ upheld the judge's ruling:

> An allegation of incestuous rape is more likely to be true when made against a man with an obvious interest in deriving sexual gratification from material depicting incestuous rape, even many years later, than made against a man with no such provable interest.
>
> (at [20])

7.69 *Bad character established by foreign convictions.* Whilst a defendant's convictions, introduced as evidence of bad character, will normally be convictions handed down in this country, it has been held in *Kordansinki* [2007] 1 Cr App R 17 that where they have been duly authenticated in accordance with the Crime (International Co-operation) Act 2003, evidence of foreign convictions too may be admitted under Part 11 of the Criminal Justice Act 2003.

7.70 *Evidence of propensity not admitted if it 'makes it no more likely that [the defendant] is guilty of the offence'.* Section 103(1)(a) states that evidence of offences admitted to show the defendant's 'propensity to commit offences of the kind with which he is charged' is subject to a qualification. Such evidence is not to be admitted in any case where 'his having such a propensity makes it no more likely that he is guilty of the offence'. On its face, this would appear to signify that such evidence is only admitted if it makes the defendant's guilt more likely. In other words, it might suggest that if the prosecution sought to introduce evidence that someone accused of making off without payment had a previous conviction for aggravating vehicle-taking (using SI 2004/3346, paras 7 and 10), it is open to the defence to argue that those who have once before been convicted of aggravated vehicle-taking are no more likely, statistically speaking, to make off without payment than anyone else. However, this is in any case a matter that a judge must always consider in determining whether previous offending upon which the Crown wishes to rely actually does demonstrate a propensity to commit offences of the kind charged. As Rose LJ made clear in *Hanson*, by no means is it 'necessarily sufficient, in order to show...propensity, that a conviction should be of the same description or category as that charged' (at [8]).

7.71 However, if the Explanatory Notes that accompanied the original bill are consulted, it emerges that this particular qualification had a quite different purpose: it was supposedly designed to stop character evidence being admitted in cases 'where there is no dispute about the facts of the case and the question is whether those facts constitute the offence (for example, in a homicide case, whether the defendant's actions caused death)'. In other words, the concession was meant to exclude from the bad character provisions cases where there is no dispute between prosecution and defence concerning the facts, only over the legal significance of what occurred. (Although widely practised, the use of explanatory notes as an aid to the interpretation of legislation is highly problematical: see Munday, 'Explanatory Notes and Statutory Interpretation' (2006) 170 JP J 124).

7.72 *Proving a defendant's propensity other than by adducing evidence of convictions.* Although propensity will most frequently be established by introducing evidence of a defendant's previous convictions, other means are available to the prosecution to show relevant bad character. Section 103(2) states explicitly that:

> ...a defendant's propensity to commit offences of the kind with which he is charged may (*without prejudice to any other way of doing so*) be established by evidence that he has been convicted of...

offences of the two types discussed above (convictions of the same description and convictions of the same category: see *ante*, para **7.54** ff). As the Court pointed out in *Hanson*, 'section 103(2) is not exhaustive of the types of conviction which might be relied upon to show evidence of propensity to commit offences of the kind charged' (at [8]). By way of example, in *Weir* [2006] 1 Cr App R 19 it was held that the trial judge had rightly admitted evidence that W, who was charged with having sexually assaulted a girl under the age of 13, had previously been cautioned for taking an indecent photograph of a child contrary to the Protection of Children Act 1978. Although the judge had mistakenly believed that the caution was admissible as an offence of the same 'category' as that charged under s 103(2)(b), the evidence in this case simply constituted another way of proving W's propensity to commit offences of the kind with which he was charged under s 103(2). The italicised qualification in s 103(2) will also, occasionally, permit the Crown to adduce propensity evidence in the form of acquittals (*ante*, paras **7.32–7.36**. See *Boulton* [2007] EWCA Crim 942 at [38]).

7.73 *Cross-admissible counts in the indictment.* Another way in which a defendant's propensity may be demonstrated, in a multi-count indictment involving similar offending, is by treating the various offences as cross-admissible and by inviting the jury to use the defendant's established guilt in respect of one offence as evidence of guilt in respect of other offences, etc. In *Tangang* [2007] EWCA Crim 469, for example, where almost identical email lottery frauds had been perpetrated within a fortnight of one another, jurors were properly told that if they convicted on one count that might serve as evidence of propensity in respect of the remaining counts. The Court of Appeal endorsed this approach in *Chopra* [2007] 1 Cr App R 16. In *Freeman and Crawford* [2009] 1 WLR 27, (2008) 172 JP 529, however, it was observed that it may not always be helpful to concentrate on the concept of propensity when the nature of the evidence is such that, in itself, it is capable of being probative in relation to another count, in the sense that it makes it more likely either that the offence was committed (*Chopra*, *ante*) or that this defendant committed the offence (*Wallace* [2008] 1 WLR 572). Although the impression may sometimes have been given that the tribunal of fact, in its decision-making process in cross-admissibility cases, should first determine whether it is satisfied on the evidence in relation to one of the counts of the defendant's guilt before it can move on to using the evidence in relation to that count in dealing with any other count in the indictment, such an approach is too restrictive. Whilst the tribunal must be reminded that it has to reach a verdict on each count separately, in determining guilt in respect of any count it is entitled to have regard to the evidence in regard to any other count, or any other bad character evidence if that evidence is admissible and relevant. Sometimes the tribunal will find it easier to decide the guilt of a defendant on the evidence relating to that count alone. That does not mean that in other cases it cannot use the evidence in relation to the other count, or counts, to help it decide on the defendant's guilt in respect of the count that it is considering. To do otherwise would fail to give proper effect to the decision on admissibility.

7.74 *Uncharged misconduct.* Is there any requirement that the bad character evidence the prosecution adduces ought to consist of charged misconduct? On several occasions the courts have held that the law imposes no such requirement. Provided that the tribunal of fact is persuaded beyond reasonable doubt that the misconduct, which has not been charged and for which the accused has never stood trial, took place, it is entitled to use that evidence, for example, as evidence of propensity under gateway (d). In *Ngyuen* [2008] EWCA Crim 585 N was convicted of murder, having glassed his victim in a fight, following an argument in a public house. The Crown was permitted to adduce evidence that 18 days earlier N had glassed another man with intent to cause serious bodily harm in broadly similar circumstances in another public house. The earlier incident had not led to any charge being brought against N as the CPS considered that it had insufficient evidence owing to the victim's unwillingness to tell his story. On appeal, N unsuccessfully contended that the admission of the bad character evidence in these circumstances was unfair, and therefore contrary to s 101(3) and PACE s 78, because N was necessarily worse off when evidence admitted under s 101(1)(d) was not made the subject of a prosecution and trial. In *Smith* [2006] 2 Cr App R 4, the Court of Appeal had already considered a case where a defendant had been informed that no further action would be taken against him in relation to certain alleged sexual offences. The Crown later started proceedings against the defendant, which included the offences in respect of which they had said that no further action would be taken. The counts in respect of those offences were stayed as an abuse of process. The Crown then applied to adduce the evidence which would have supported the stayed counts. The judge granted the application under s 101(1)(d) of the 2003 Act. An appeal against the judge's ruling was dismissed. In *Ngyuen* Dyson LJ declared that the reasoning in *Smith* applied with equal force to situations where the Crown itself decided not to prosecute:

> On the assumption that in both cases the bad character evidence is relevant, we can see no difference in principle between the two cases. We do not accept that the mere fact that the Crown chooses to rely on relevant bad character evidence which it decides not to make the subject of a criminal charge can of itself have such an adverse effect on the fairness of the proceedings that the court ought not to admit it. Something more is needed.
>
> (at [37])

7.75 Section 103(2) permits the Crown to establish the relevant propensity not only by means of evidence that the defendant has committed other offences, but also by means of that other form of 'bad character' under the Act, the defendant's other 'reprehensible behaviour'. If this is sufficiently directed, it too may serve to establish the defendant's propensity to commit offences. What sorts of misbehaviour might the courts deem 'reprehensible behaviour' and, hence, 'misconduct' under the 2003 Act? Let us contemplate some examples, of diminishing intensity. First, take the pre-Act case of *Lewis* (1982) 76 Cr App R 33. L was charged with having committed indecent assaults on his landlady's children. Upon arrest, there was evidence—in the form of literature, admissions, and membership of a paedophile organisation—indicating that L had distinct paedophile leanings. Although the Court of Appeal, held that this evidence was relevant to only certain of the charges on the indictment, under the 2003 Act it can be seen that this 'evidence...of a disposition towards...the commission of an offence or other reprehensible behaviour' could quite readily satisfy the test of admissibility under ss 101(1)(d) and 103(1)(a). Another case that merits mention is *Wright* (1990) 90 Cr App R 325, where a headmaster was accused of having committed homosexual offences by a number of boys whom he had led on a school trip to France. In a drawer of the desk in the headmaster's study the police found *The Incognito Guide to Paris* (a *vade mecum* to that capital's homosexual meat racks), whilst at the headmaster's home, police found a video recording of two or more men performing acts of buggery. Under the 2003 Act, provided that the court first concluded that this was indeed evidence of misconduct indicative of 'a disposition towards...reprehensible behaviour'—something of a borderline decision—its task would then be to determine whether that 'misconduct' was also evidence of a 'propensity to commit offences' under s 103(1)(a)—a possible, but by no means foregone, conclusion. Finally, let us consider the case of *Butler* (1987) 84 Cr App R 12, where B was charged with the rapes of two women. On each occasion, the rapist had first inflicted a particular series of indignities on the victims. In order to identify B as the rapist, the prosecution called his former girlfriend to testify that B had performed similar acts upon her, but with her consent, prior to intercourse. Today, the big question in such a case would be whether the consensual behaviour with the girlfriend amounted to 'misconduct' under the Act at all. If it did not—which is more than likely in today's moral climate—then its admissibility would be determined by ordinary principles of relevance and its admission would fall outside the 2003 Act.

7.76 The use by the prosecution of uncharged misconduct under s 103(2) carries with it certain risks. As the Court of Appeal made clear in *McKenzie* (2008) 172 JP 377, whereas convictions admitted under s 103(2) operate as a launch pad for establishing a defendant's propensity, uncharged misconduct admitted under that provision will first require the determination of a collateral or satellite issue—namely, whether the misconduct actually occurred as alleged. The introduction of collateral issues can not only add to the length and cost of the trial, but can also complicate the issues before the court and distract attention away from the most important issue or issues. Additionally, if allegations of misconduct have not given rise to any previous investigation, the evidence relating to them is liable to be stale and incomplete. A defendant may be prejudiced in trying to meet it, for lapse of time and inability to pinpoint details may make such allegations hard to repel. The court may be left thinking that there is no smoke without fire. Courts must therefore approach such prosecution applications with considerable caution. Moreover, if a judge decides to admit such evidence, he must also consider how to deal with it in his summing-up in a way that is fair and does not give undue prominence to the bad character evidence.

The defendant's 'propensity to be untruthful' (s 103(1)(b))

7.77 Section 103(1)(b) makes clear that evidence of bad character is not to be admitted under this head if there is no dispute between the Crown and the defendant as to whether the latter has been truthful. Also, in those cases where such a dispute does arise, it can only lead to the admission of bad character provided that the propensity to be untruthful is 'an important matter in issue between the defendant and the prosecution' (s 101(1)(d)), in the sense that the defendant's truthfulness on a particular matter is 'a matter of substantial importance in the context of the case as a whole' (s 112). Minor discrepancies between the Crown's and the defendant's respective accounts of events, therefore, cannot trigger this provision. The bad character only becomes admissible under s 103(1)(b) in situations where disagreement between prosecution and defence is a key element in the case.

7.78 *What furnishes evidence of a propensity to be untruthful?* Section 101(1)(d) requires more than the simple fact that prosecution and defence differ on a matter in issue in the case. Section 101 renders evidence of bad character admissible 'if, but only if ... it is relevant to an important matter in issue'. The court will therefore be required to determine whether the particular bad character evidence proffered by the Crown is 'relevant' in this heightened sense. The relevance of evidence of previous convictions and other misbehaviour, now designated reprehensible, has always been problematical. The 2003 Act does little to resolve such imponderables. How then is a court to interpret 'relevance' in this context? The Explanatory Notes accompanying the Act (see *ante*, para **7.71**) give some indication of what this provision was meant to address. The intention is:

> ... to enable the admission of a limited range of evidence *such as* convictions for perjury or other offences involving deception (for example, obtaining property by deception), as opposed to the wider range of evidence that will be admissible where the defendant puts his character in issue by for example, attacking the character of another person [see *post*, paras **7.117–7.132**].
>
> (para 374)

As in the case of s 103(1)(a), the Explanatory Notes do not exactly replicate the text of the statute—and, on closer examination, are actually quite imprecise (see italicised words). By coincidence, without overtly referring to the Explanatory Notes, the Court's judgment in *Hanson* [2005] 1 WLR 3169 approximates to the Home Office's suggested meaning of 'propensity to be untruthful':

> As to propensity to untruthfulness, this ... is not the same as propensity to dishonesty. It is to be assumed, bearing in mind the frequency with which the words honest and dishonest appear in the criminal law, that Parliament deliberately chose the word " untruthful" to convey a different meaning, reflecting a defendant's account of his behaviour, or lies told when committing an offence. Previous convictions, whether for offences of dishonesty or otherwise, are therefore only likely to be capable of showing a propensity to be untruthful where, in the present case, truthfulness is an issue and, in the earlier case, either there was a plea of not guilty and the defendant gave an account, on arrest, in interview, or in evidence, which the jury must have disbelieved, or the way in which the offence was committed shows a propensity for untruthfulness, for example, by the making of false representations. The observations made above in para 9 as to the number of convictions apply equally here [(see *ante*, para **7.59**].
>
> (at [13]. See eg, Ellis [2010] EWCA Crim 163.)

7.79 At one end of the scale, when seeking to cast light on an accused's propensity to be untruthful an obviously relevant conviction would be a conviction for perjury (*Blake* [2006] EWCA Crim 871 at [26] *per* Collins J). However, as with convictions admitted under s 103(1)(a), the court must consider the individual convictions carefully to determine which in reality reflect on the defendant's propensity to be untruthful. As Scott Baker LJ explained in *Edwards* [2006] 1 WLR 1524:

> [D]ishonesty does not necessarily equate with a propensity to be untruthful. It may be that the offences of theft by shoplifting, had the appeal centred on that aspect of the matter alone, could properly be regarded as not showing a propensity to be untruthful, rather than merely dishonesty. That cannot, however, be said in relation to the offences of benefit fraud, committed on four occasions.
>
> (at [33])

7.80 *The purpose and scope of bad character admitted to establish a propensity to be untruthful.* Because the defendant's bad character is admitted for a limited purpose only, the jury must be told explicitly that they are not to conclude that the accused is guilty merely because they have learned that he has previous convictions. They must also be instructed that they may use the accused's record only 'to judge the truthfulness of his evidence', or words to that effect.

7.81 The fact that previous convictions and bad character revealed in a particular case were only meant to be relevant to the defendant's 'propensity to be untruthful' has posed certain problems in the past, particularly if the defendant had a record of offending similar to the offence charged. As the Court of Criminal Appeal remarked in *Samuel* (1956) 40 Cr App R 8, 12, it is hard to see:

> ...how, if it is permissible to cross-examine a prisoner with regard to convictions...if he is a thief and he is cross-examined on previous convictions for larceny, the jury is not, in effect, being asked to say: "The prisoner is just the sort of man who will commit those crimes and therefore it is highly probable he did".

Such problems, however, are eased by the fact that previous convictions for 'offences of the same description' and, for certain types of offence, 'offences of the same category', may often be admissible as evidence of propensity under s 103(2). Nevertheless, cases may still arise where the previous convictions are too close for comfort, when the Crown is seeking only to show the defendant's propensity to be untruthful. Under the Criminal Justice Act 2003, in any such case it will be for the trial judge to decide whether, in the particular circumstances of the case, taking into account all relevant factors, admission of bad character evidence of this nature is relevant to the defendant's 'propensity to be truthful' and also that its admission in evidence will not prove unduly prejudicial under s 101(3) (s 103(3)) having no application to evidence admitted under s 103(1)(b)—and under PACE, s 78.

7.82 *'Untruthfulness' does not equate with general dishonesty or general criminality.* What is clear under the 2003 Act is that what could be loosely termed 'offences of dishonesty' are not automatically relevant to a defendant's propensity to be untruthful. In *Blake* [2006] EWCA Crim 871 B was charged with having burgled a dwelling house. The occupier subsequently identified B in a video identification procedure. At trial, the judge admitted this evidence, despite B's complaints concerning serious defects in identification procedure. The Crown successfully applied, pursuant to s 101(1)(d), for B's 15 previous convictions for burglary to be admitted. Ten of them were domestic burglaries. The judge told the jury that B's previous convictions were relevant to whether they could be sure that the identification made by the occupier was correct, and that they were also relevant to B's truthfulness. Although the Court of Appeal dismissed B's appeal on the ground that the trial judge had properly admitted B's previous convictions to establish B's propensity to commit such offences and the correctness of the identification, Collins J added:

> We are bound to say that if matters stood without more we would be somewhat concerned about those directions. The Recorder clearly should have made it clear that he was tieing [sic] the previous convictions to the reliability of the identification evidence, but he went further and also dealt with the question of credibility. This...he should not have done.
> (at [25])

A similar course had been taken by the trial judge in *Leaver* [2006] EWCA Crim 2988. The Court of Appeal held that in a rape case evidence of L's previous conviction some years before for indecent exposure with intent to insult a female, to which L had pleaded guilty, had no relevance to his credibility, and it was impossible to see how the fact that, some years earlier, he had exposed himself bore on the question as to whether his account in relation to the rape was truthful.

7.83 *When will bad character showing a propensity to be untruthful be relevant?* It was suggested in one influential case, *Campbell* [2007] 1 WLR 2798, that evidence of a propensity to be untruthful ought to be admitted only in a very limited range of situations. The import of this judgment remains unclear. In *Campbell*, where C was charged with falsely imprisoning a lover, Lord Phillips of Worth Matravers took a highly restrictive line on when evidence of untruthfulness may be admitted under s 103((1)(b). C's previous convictions for assaults committed on other women had been admitted under gateway (d) as evidence of his propensity for violence towards women. The trial judge was held to have wrongly told the jury that this evidence might also be treated as evidence of C's propensity to be untruthful. This led Lord Phillips to reflect generally on when evidence of a propensity of untruthfulness will be relevant in a criminal case:

> The question of whether a defendant has a propensity for being untruthful will not normally be capable of being described as an important matter in issue between the defendant

and the prosecution. A propensity for untruthfulness will not, of itself, go very far to establishing the commission of a criminal offence. To suggest that a propensity for untruthfulness makes it more likely that a defendant has lied to the jury is not likely to help them. If they apply common sense they will conclude that a defendant who has committed a criminal offence may well be prepared to lie about it, even if he has not shown a propensity for lying whereas a defendant who has not committed the offence charged will be likely to tell the truth, even if he has shown a propensity for telling lies. *In short, whether or not a defendant is telling the truth to the jury is likely to depend simply on whether or not he committed the offence charged.* The jury should focus on the latter question rather than on whether or not he has a propensity for telling lies.

(at [30]. Emphasis added)

Lord Phillips continued:

For these reasons, *the only circumstance in which there is likely to be an important issue as to whether a defendant has a propensity to tell lies is where telling lies is an element of the offence charged.* Even then, the propensity to tell lies is only likely to be significant if the lying is in the context of committing criminal offences, in which case the evidence is likely to be admissible under section 103(1)(a).

(at [31]. Emphasis added)

This reading of s 103(1)(b) is far narrower than was previously thought appropriate. Indeed, it raises serious questions as to the relevance of evidence relating to truthfulness and credibility in other contexts, whether the evidence of bad character is admitted under gateways (d), (g) or (e), or even under s 100 of the 2003 Act (see further Mirfield [2008] 124 LQR 1).

7.84 *Discretion to exclude propensity evidence* CJA 2003, s 101(3). We have seen that a judge possesses a number of discretions to exclude evidence of an accused's propensity. Under s 101(3), provided that the defendant makes application to the judge, the latter must not admit bad character evidence via gateway (d):

... if it appears to the court that the admission of the evidence would have such an adverse effect on the fairness of the proceedings that the court ought not to admit it.

In applying this 'fairness' test, under s 101(4) the court:

... must have regard, in particular, to the length of time between the matters to which that evidence relates and the matters which form the subject of the offence charged.

Although s 101(3) requires a defendant to make application in order to compel the judge to consider exercising the 'fairness' discretion, Kennedy LJ handed down the following advice in *Weir* [2006] 1 WLR 1885 at [38]:

> [B]earing in mind the provisions of Art. 6 of the European Convention, we consider it important that a judge should if necessary encourage the making of such an application (under s 101(3)) whenever it appears that the admission of the evidence may have such an adverse effect on the fairness of the proceedings that the court ought not to admit it. [S]ection 101(3) does require the judge to perform a balancing exercise, and that exercise does require the judge to look carefully at the evidence sought to be adduced.

7. 85 *CJA 2003, s 103(3).* Additionally, the prosecution's entitlement to adduce evidence of bad character in order to establish the defendant's propensity to commit offences of the type charged is circumscribed by s 103(3). Section 103(3) imposes a 'justness' test:

> [Section 103(2)] does not apply in the case of a particular defendant if the court is satisfied, by reason of the length of time since the conviction or for any other reason, that it would be unjust for it to apply in his case.

Since the criteria of ss 101(3) and 103(3) are stated differently, one must conclude that these are intended to be subtly different tests. As Rose LJ noted in *Hanson* [2006] 1 WLR 3169, alongside the matters explicitly mentioned in ss 101(4) and 103(3), the judge must consider the cogency of the bad character evidence:

> When considering what is just under s 103(3), and the fairness of the proceedings under s 101(3), the judge may, among other factors, take into consideration the degree of similarity between the previous conviction and the offence charged, albeit they are both within the same description or prescribed category. For example, theft and assault occasioning actual bodily harm may each embrace a wide spectrum of conduct. This does not however mean that what used to be referred as striking similarity must be shown before convictions become admissible.
>
> (at [10])

7. 86 *PACE, s 78.* In addition to the discretions under s 101(3) and (4) and s 103(3), as has already been noted, a trial judge is well advised to refer also to PACE, s 78 when pronouncing upon the admissibility of evidence of bad character (see *Highton* [2005] 1 WLR 3472 at [13] *per* Lord Woolf CJ: *ante* para **7.21**).

7.87 *Case management under CPR.* Finally, judges must not forget their case management obligations under the Criminal Procedure Rules 2010. As Beatson J recalled in *O'Dowd* (2009) 173 JP 640 at [61], 'A judge has wide case management powers under the Criminal Procedure Rules'. Here, the trial judge had exercised discretion under s 101(3) without considering the cumulative effect of introducing three separate contested issues into the trial on its overall length and on the jury, or how the evidence might be timetabled or truncated:

> The . . . most serious difficulty with the Crown's application to adduce evidence of all three allegations and to call all three complainants is that so much of what the Crown wished to adduce was disputed. It was known at the time the Crown's application to adduce the bad character evidence was first considered that all the facts of the allegations by the three women were contested. Accordingly, particularly in the case of the allegations that did not result in a conviction, proof of the previous alleged misconduct would require the trial of three collateral or satellite issues as part of the trial of the applicant for the offences with which he was charged.
>
> (at [55])

Gateway (e): When 'it has substantial probative value in relation to an important matter in issue between the defendant and a co-defendant' (s 101(1)(e))

7.88 Paragraph (e) regulates the admission of evidence of bad character in cases where a serious dispute arises between those jointly accused of crime in the same proceedings. The term 'co-defendant' is in fact defined in s 112 as follows:

> "co-defendant", in relation to a defendant, means a person charged with an offence in the same proceedings.

As in the case of s 101(1)(d), s 112 stresses that in this context:

> . . . "important matter [in issue between the defendant and a co-defendant]" means a matter of substantial importance in the context of the case as a whole.

Thus, where a defendant is allowed to adduce evidence of a co-defendant's bad character, the purpose must be to resolve a matter of genuine significance in the context of the case; not simply some minor disagreement between the co-accused, or a trifling discrepancy between the cases being advanced by the two co-defendants. In fact, if one conflates ss 101(1)(e) and 112, what is required is that the evidence has:

> . . . *substantial probative value* in relation to a matter of *substantial importance* in the context of the case as a whole.

Section 101(1)(e) is not to be lightly invoked.

7.89 As is the case under s 101(1)(d), for the purpose of weighing the 'probative value' of any item of evidence proffered under para (e), s 109 demands that the court assumes that the evidence tendered is true, unless 'it appears, on the basis of any material before the court (including any evidence it decides to hear on the matter), that no court or jury could reasonably find it to be true'.

7.90 What sorts of issue, then, will trigger s 101(1)(e)? Broadly speaking, they will fall into two types: one of these is not explicitly mentioned in paragraph (e), whilst s 104 makes specific provision for the other.

(i) When a co-accused's 'propensity' has 'substantial probative value in relation to an important matter in issue between the defendant and a co-defendant'

7.91 The first type of 'important matter in issue' affecting co-accused occurs where there are cut-throat defences, with each defendant casting the blame on the other. Under pre-2003 law, the circumstances in which evidence of bad character would be treated as admissible to assist the court in resolving a dispute as to which of two co-accused was more likely to have committed an offence, for which each contended that the other was responsible, were somewhat uncertain. *Lowery and King v R* [1974] AC 85, the leading case under the old common law, illustrates this type of situation—which, it should immediately be said, the Criminal Justice Act 2003 too would treat as a case where there exists 'an important matter in issue between the defendant and a co-defendant'. In *Lowery*, L and K were jointly charged with a particularly sadistic murder, whose motive was said to have been that the two men wanted to see what it was like to 'kill a chick'. L and K each blamed the other for the crime. L testified that he was not the sort of person to commit such a brutal offence. Indeed, L claimed that he had done what he could to prevent K from doing the deed. K denied the offence, maintaining that at the relevant time he was under the influence of drugs and therefore in no position to prevent L from killing the girl. The Privy Council held that K had been properly allowed to call a psychologist to testify that while K was immature and easily led, L was callous, aggressive and sadistically inclined, thereby opining that by reason of his personality K was the less likely of the two men to have committed a vicious killing. The psychologist, who had examined both co-accused, was well placed to offer such evidence to assist the jury and, more importantly, the case involved co-defendants, one of whom, K, was being permitted directly to rebut evidence given by his co-accused, L, that by reason of his personality K was more likely than L to have killed the girl. At one point in his opinion Lord Morris, however, had gone further and suggested that this type of evidence would generally be relevant and admissible whenever it tended to show that the version of events put forward by one co-defendant was more likely than that put forward by his co-accused. This broad proposition did not find favour in English courts. The broad wording of s 101(1)(e), however, enables courts to permit defendants to call bad character evidence— evidence of relevant convictions and reprehensible behaviour—in precisely such circumstances, provided that the bad character evidence has 'substantial probative value'.

7.92 Not surprisingly, English courts extended the *Lowery* principle to other analogous contexts. In joint trials, where it could be shown that evidence of one co-defendant's bad character was especially relevant, English courts would occasionally admit such matter—normally to rebut a claim put forward by one accused that he was not the sort of person to have committed offences or the offence charged. Some of these decisions raised the kind of issues that will arise under s 101(1)(e) of the 2003 Act. In *Bracewell* (1978) 68 Cr App R 44, for example, B and L were charged with having committed a murder in the course of a burglary. L denied guilt and contended that, whereas B was a jumpy, inexperienced burglar who had possibly been under the influence of alcohol at the relevant time, L was cool-headed and professional, and therefore less likely to have panicked and killed someone. The Court of Appeal held that, in view of L's claims, B ought to have been allowed to call L's mistress to testify that in the past L had attacked her ferociously on several occasions, in an uncontrollable frenzy. One can see that under s 101(1)(e) it is highly likely that a court today would hold that, as between B and L, there existed 'an important matter in issue' and that, under the terms of that paragraph, evidence of L's attacks on his mistress had 'substantial probative value'. In *Douglass* (1989) 89 Cr App R 264 D and P, who did not previously know one another, were jointly charged with causing death by reckless driving, having engaged in a race on a public road which led to the death of a driver in an oncoming vehicle. The Crown called evidence suggesting that D had been drinking, and P made much of this. During cross-examination of his girlfriend, who appeared as a prosecution witness, P elicited that he (P) had not drunk alcohol in the two years she had known him, implying thereby that P was unlikely to have been affected by drink and therefore to have driven badly or aggressively. Because P's propensity thereby became relevant to the issue of D's guilt (which of the two men was more likely to have driven recklessly), Auld J held that the trial judge ought to have allowed D to adduce evidence of P's extensive criminal record, which comprised convictions for bad driving, drink-related crime, dishonesty and violence, in order 'to counter the responsible impression of him that his counsel had sought to place before the jury through the mouth of the [girlfriend]'. In certain ways the decision went further than *Lowery*. Notably, Auld J considered the convictions for being drunk and disorderly and for driving with excess blood alcohol should have been admitted even though, in a sense, they confirmed the testimony of the girlfriend, in as much as they antedated the trial by at least six years. *Douglass* therefore appeared to establish that evidence of disposition might still be relevant under the *Lowery* principle even if did not directly rebut claims advanced by the other party. The relevance of P's convictions for dishonesty and violence, it could be added, was even more questionable as these merely showed P's bad character in the most general sense and furnished little helpful information on the likelihood on his having driven recklessly.

7.93 Today, mindful of the language of the Act, a court might be less disposed to admit as much of P's criminal record. A co-accused's previous convictions are only admissible via gateway (e) to the extent that they had '*substantial probative value in relation to* a matter of substantial importance in the context of the case as a whole'. Thus, in *Passos-Carr* [2009] EWCA Crim 2018, where D1 and D2's disagreement as to whether theirs had been a joint venture was undoubtedly 'an important matter in issue' between them, in the context of the case the offences of violence adduced via gateway (e) simply did not have the required probative value.

7.94 *De Vos* [2006] EWCA Crim 1688 provides an example of gateway (e) at work. Having been seen by Customs officers fixing a rendezvous in a lorry park with A-D, a co-defendant, DV was later seen to take from his cab and hand over to A-D a sizeable box, subsequently found to contain heroin. DV was duly charged, along with three co-defendants, with being concerned in the importation of 20 kilos of heroin. DV eventually admitted that he had given A-D a box at the request of a Frenchman with whom he had earlier had a chance meeting, but denied knowing that the box contained drugs. A-D also claimed to have been duped and to have had no knowledge that the box contained drugs. Rather surprisingly, the Crown's application to adduce evidence of DV's two previous convictions in Holland for smuggling 33 kilos and 4.5 kilos respectively of cocaine in 1996 via gateway (d) was rejected, under s 101(3), on grounds of unfairness. During cross-examination of A-D, and in DV's own testimony, it was suggested that A-D had altered the venue of the rendezvous saying, 'It is too dangerous here', such an assertion being consistent with DV's defence that he had been used by others, including A-D. A-D thereupon applied to have DV's convictions admitted via gateway (e): DV's defence involved an attack on A-D. The judge admitted full details of the convictions under s 101(1) (e). On appeal, DV argued that the bad character evidence was relevant only to his propensity to be untruthful, rather than to his propensity to commit an offence of the kind charged. The court reviewed the operation of gateway (e). As Hughes LJ explained, under the 2003 Act evidence of bad character in some cases may demonstrate a propensity in the accused to be untruthful; in others bad character evidence goes directly to establish a propensity to commit the kind of offence charged. The reality of this case was that the evidence of DV's previous convictions did not go simply to his untruthfulness; they went to whether DV was implicated in the drug smuggling. DV claimed to have been duped by A-D. It was more likely that A-D was innocent if DV was guilty. DV's truthfulness was in this case in issue only as an ancillary matter to whether he was telling the truth when he said, in effect, that it was A-D who was the drug smuggler rather than him. For the purposes of s 101(1)(e), therefore, the issue between these co-defendants was, which was the dupe? DV's two previous convictions for drug smuggling were clearly admissible on that issue—and, indeed, might well have been admissible had the application been made by A-D irrespective of whether A-D had been cross-examined in the way that he was on the behalf of DV. Once the statutory gateway is passed, a co-defendant is entitled to call the evidence which he needs in order to present his case. In this case the overall fairness of the trial required the jury to know that DV had done this before.

(ii) When a co-accused's 'propensity to be untruthful' has 'substantial probative value in relation to an important matter in issue between the defendant and a co-defendant'

7.95 A second species of 'important matter in issue' under s 101(1)(e), which is further regulated by s 104, arises in cases where one co-accused is permitted to introduce the other co-defendant's bad character in order to show that he is unlikely to be truthful. Section 104(1) sets out when such evidence will be admitted:

> Evidence which is relevant to the question whether the defendant has a propensity to be untruthful is admissible on that basis under s 101(1)(e) only if the nature or conduct of his defence is such as to undermine the co-defendant's defence.

The phraseology may be inverted, but it is plain that what the subsection is laying down is that only if D2, in the course of his defence, has undermined D1's defence, is D1 entitled to introduce evidence of D2's bad character. Surprisingly perhaps, the wording of s 104(1) is more restrictive than that which was found in the previous statute, the Criminal Evidence Act 1898, s 1(3)(iii). The 1898 Act allowed such cross-examination to occur if D2 'gave evidence against' D1. Since evidence given against another co-accused under that Act was taken to mean either evidence that reinforced the prosecution case against D1 or evidence that undermined D1's defence (*Murdoch v Taylor* [1965] AC 574)—and in some cases the courts succeeded in distinguishing between these two notions—there is a case for saying that s 104(1) is restricted to cases where D2 saps D1's defence to a significant degree.

7.96 As in the case of evidence of propensity relevant to issue (discussed *ante*), s 101(1)(e) requires that the extent to which D1's defence is undermined must constitute 'an *important* matter in issue between the defendant and a co-defendant', in the sense of amounting to 'a matter of substantial importance in the context of the case as a whole' (s 112). In short, mere discrepancies between the stories told by two co-accused will not suffice to trigger this provision. There is no requirement of hostile intent: whatever D2's feelings, the law's concern is simply whether the effect of D2's case is to undermine D1's defence. Thus, one would assume that in a situation such as arose in *Davis* (1974) 60 Cr App R 157, s 101(1)(e) would be activated. In *Davis*, D2 deliberately omitted to give evidence accusing D1 of the theft of a gold cross which D1 had alleged he had seen in D2's possession. D2 simply denied D1's story, adding: 'I am not suggesting D1 took the cross and chain. As I never, and it is missing, he must have done, but I am not saying he did.' Because, on the facts of the case, one or other of these co-defendants must have stolen the cross, the Court of Appeal held that D2's denial rendered D1's acquittal less likely and thereby undermined D1's defence.

7.97 *What furnishes evidence of a propensity to be untruthful?* What sort of bad character evidence is admissible if a co-defendant activates ss 101(1)(e) and 104? Given that s 104 refers to a co-defendant's 'propensity to be untruthful', it could plausibly be argued that the bad character evidence admissible under this section ought to equate with that admitted where a defendant's propensity to be untruthful is in question under s 101(1)(d) (see *ante*, paras **7.78–7.79**). Significantly, the Law Commission put forward a vaguely similar, but highly cumbrous, proposal in its Final Report. The courts have not chosen to follow this line.

7.98 In *Lawson* [2007] 1 Cr App R 11, L was one of three co-defendants charged with the manslaughter of W, who was mentally handicapped. W had been pushed into a lake after telling them that he could not swim. Q, who pleaded guilty, did the pushing, but CCTV footage showed L making a mock pushing action behind W, immediately followed by Q's actual pushing of W into the water. L and K each denied that they were secondary offenders, encouraging Q to push W into the water, and each sought to incriminate the other as to his true intentions regarding W. At trial, K, who was acquitted, adduced evidence of L's conviction for assault and cross-examined L upon it. On appeal, L submitted that the judge had been wrong to admit the conviction under s 101(1)(e) because the conviction did not have substantial probative value regarding an important matter in issue between L and K, as required by ss 101(1)(e) and 112 of the 2003 Act. Nor had L's evidence undermined the case against K, as is necessary under s 104 of the Act. Hughes LJ held that the issue in this case was whether, at or about the time that he returned with Q and L to the end of the pontoon, K had said that he had intended to push W into the lake. With it went the issues whether K was now lying or truthful when he said that he had not uttered any such remark, and whether L was truthful when he said it had been said. L's evidence, if accepted by the jury, was likely to reinforce the Crown's case against K, which was that he had resumed the intention to push W into the water when he returned to the pontoon with the other two men. Once L had given evidence of what K had said, L's truthfulness in saying so became an important matter in issue in the case. Because L's truthfulness constituted an important matter in issue in the case, under s 104(1), the bad character evidence could be adduced only if (i) the nature or conduct of L's defence was such as to undermine the defence of K, and (ii) the bad character evidence had substantial probative value in relation to the issue of L's truthfulness. A court had to address these issues *seriatim*. Here, L's evidence had undermined K's defence. Although a judge has no discretion to exclude evidence admissible via gateway (e), an exercise of judgement was nevertheless called for. More specifically, if objection is taken to the introduction of the evidence, the judge has to determine whether it has substantial probative value in relation to the important matter in issue which has arisen, whether such evidence of bad character is adduced by cross-examination of the defendant or otherwise. Hughes LJ went on to say that regarding the evidence that may become admissible, it does not follow that previous convictions, which do not involve the making of false statements or the giving of false evidence are incapable of having substantial probative value in relation to credibility of a defendant, when he has given evidence which undermines the defence of a co-accused. A defendant who is defending himself against the evidence of a person whose history of criminal behaviour or other misconduct is such as to be capable of showing him to be unscrupulous and/or otherwise unreliable should be enabled to present that history before the jury for its evaluation of the evidence of the witness. Such suggested unreliability, it was said, may be capable of being shown by conduct which does not involve an offence of untruthfulness; it may be capable of being shown by widely differing conduct, ranging from large-scale drug or people trafficking via housebreaking to criminal violence. Whether in a particular case it is in fact capable of having substantive probative value in relation to the witness' reliability is for the trial judge to determine on all the facts of the case. An appellate court, however, is unlikely to interfere with a trial judge's determination unless it is demonstrated to be plainly wrong or *Wednesbury* unreasonable. (See also, *Rosato* [2008] EWCA Crim 1243.)

7.99 *Jury direction.* When bad character evidence is admitted on account of its relevance to a co-defendant's 'propensity to be untruthful', the judge must deliver a clear direction to the jury explaining that this evidence is only to be used for this purpose and that it does not constitute evidence of the co-defendant's propensity to commit offences or the offence charged.

7.100 *The prosecution may not make use of gateway (e).* Section 104(2) makes clear that it was not Parliament's intention that the prosecution might make use of gateway (e):

> Only evidence—
>
> (a) which is to be (or has been) adduced by the co-defendant, or
>
> (b) which a witness is to be invited to give (or has given) in cross-examination by the co-defendant,
>
> is admissible under s 101(1)(e).

E contra, D1 may not adduce evidence of a D2's bad character under gateways (f) and (g) (discussed *infra*). Unlike gateway (e), these are the exclusive preserve of the prosecution: *Assani* [2008] EWCA Crim 2563, [2009] Crim LR 514.

7.101 *Methods of proving bad character.* As elsewhere under the 2003 Act's bad character provisions, s 104(2) makes clear that once evidence has been ruled admissible via gateway (e), D1 may adduce evidence of D2's bad character either in the course of D2's cross-examination or by calling evidence as part of his own case (*Jarvis* [2008] EWCA Crim 488, [2008] Crim LR 632 at [39] *per* Hughes LJ).

7.102 *No judicial discretion to exclude relevant bad character evidence.* If evidence of bad character possesses 'substantial probative value in relation to an important matter in issue between the defendant and a co-defendant', the judge possesses no discretion to exclude any part of that evidence. This is because s 112(3)(c) only retains that discretion which judges exercised prior to the entry into force of the Criminal Justice Act 2003. No question of discretion can therefore arise under s 101(1)(e) because, traditionally, where disputes arose between co-accused the judge enjoyed no discretion to exclude bad character evidence. In the words of Lord Steyn in *Randall v R* [2004] 1 Cr App R 375:

> [T]he discretionary power to exclude relevant evidence which is tendered by the prosecution, if its prejudicial effect outweighs its probative value, does not apply to the position as between co-accused. In a joint criminal trial a judge has no discretionary power at the request of one accused to exclude relevant evidence tending to support the defence of another.
>
> (at [18])

The reasons for this absence of discretion at common law are fairly obvious. Most commonly, it was said that it was not the judge's role, even in the slightest degree, to obstruct a co-accused from defending himself. If it was relevant for D1 to show that D2 had bad character, the court ought not to impede the admission of such evidence, no matter how damaging that might prove to D2. There is another reason perhaps for striking this posture. If the role of the judge, in essence, is to stand impartially above the battle and primarily to ensure that the various combatants comply with all due procedural requirements, one can see that a judge who intervenes to restrain D1 from bringing out the full bad character of D2, whilst in a sense being fair to D2, may in fact be all too easily perceived as acting unfairly to D1. Any exercise of discretion, then, would risk compromising judicial neutrality.

7.103 Nevertheless, the judge does enjoy some control over what evidence of bad character is admitted under s 101(1)(e). The Act explicitly requires that the bad character evidence must have 'substantial probative value'. The judge must therefore identify with precision the 'important matter in issue between the defendant and a co-defendant' which has arisen in the particular case and must equally settle those items of bad character evidence that are especially relevant thereto. If, in a case like

Douglass, the important matter is whether or not, by reason of his recent conversion to teetotalism, D was likely to have driven his motor car in a responsible rather than a furious fashion, clearly the Act demands even more clearly than the old common law that any evidence of bad character adduced under s 101(1)(e) be restricted to evidence that tends to refute this specific issue. Section 101(1)(e) does not give D1 *carte blanche* automatically to reveal D2's entire bad character. Moreover, the reasoned ruling, which the judge is required to provide under s 110, will need to make these matters clear.

7. 104　With the advent of the Criminal Procedure Rules 2005 there exists another way in which the trial judge can control the admission of bad character evidence through gateway (e). It will be obvious that in many instances when D2 undermines the defence of D1, D1 cannot be expected to have complied with the requirement to give advance notice of an intention to adduce evidence of D2's bad character ahead of trial. In *Jarvis* [2008] EWCA Crim 488, for example, before J testified it was not apparent from his police interviews that, in answer to various charges of theft, J, a jeweller, would allege that the owner of the jewellery he was said to have stolen had induced him to make a bogus insurance claim based upon a fictitious theft in Germany. As Hughes LJ remarked, 'applications which are based on the evidence given by one defendant will very often not arise until that evidence is given' (at [22]). Part 35, r 8 of the Criminal Procedure Rules confers a broad discretion on the trial judge to dispense with the customary notice requirements. Nevertheless, the Court cautioned,

> That does not mean that the judge could not remain in control of proceedings. . . . [I]f the application were to be made so late that the judge took the view that the target of the application would . . . simply be unable to deal with the evidence, he has ample power under the Rules to refuse to admit it. Whether such unfairness will arise will, of course, be a question of fact in each individual case.
>
> (at [34]. See also, *Musone* [2007] 1 WLR 2467, *ante* p16; *Ramirez* [2009] EWCA Crim 1721, [2010] Crim LR 235)

Gateway (f): When 'it is evidence to correct a false impression given by the defendant' (s 101(1)(f))

7.105　Broadly speaking, portal (f) widens a 'gateway' for the admission of evidence of bad character that existed under the old law. The simple idea that lies at its root is that if a defendant does something to create a false impression about his good character in the eyes of the tribunal of fact, the prosecution may be permitted in turn to adduce evidence to correct that false impression. It is simply not appropriate to allow a defendant to gain an unfair advantage by deceiving the tribunal as to his true character. Only the prosecution is entitled to avail itself of s 101(1) (f) and to dispel any false impression that may have been created by the defendant (s 105(7)). Therefore, in trials involving co-accused, if D1 creates a false or misleading impression of his good character, D2 may only intervene under s 101(1) e) provided that the issue raised thereby 'has substantial probative value in relation to an important matter in issue between the defendant and a co-defendant'. Section 105 supplements in a number of important details the terse provision laid out in s 101(1)(f).

7.106 *How may a defendant create a 'false' or a 'misleading' impression?* According to s 105(1) (a), a defendant may do so either expressly or by implication:

> [T]he defendant gives a false impression if he is responsible for the making of an express or implied assertion which is apt to give the court or jury a false or misleading impression about the defendant.

A defendant who simply denies guilt will not activate the gateway (*Weir* [2006] 1 WLR 1885 at [43] *per* Kennedy LJ). An accused might create the 'false impression' expressly, however, by claiming untruthfully that he had always led 'a good, clean life', as occurred in the old case of *Maxwell v DPP* [1935] AC 309, or by asserting falsely that he had no criminal record, as happened in *Marsh* [1994] Crim LR 52. In *Ullah* [2006] EWCA Crim 2003, U, who was charged with conspiracy to defraud, said in interview: 'I will say again that both in my capacity as an individual and as a director of a reputable solvent company I have never acted dishonestly and have been meticulous in respect of my business dealings. This is what I have told the police from the first question and this is what I say today.' The Crown successfully applied to adduce evidence of U's previous conviction for obtaining property by deception to correct this false impression. Similarly, in *Kiernan* [2008] EWCA Crim 972 the prosecution wished to introduce via gateway (f) the fact that one co-defendant, G, had absconded following a previous conviction and had remained unlawfully at large for thirteen years, until arrested on the present charges. Laws, LJ held,

> In the witness-box [G] was purveying the impression that he was a reformed character, having "learned his lesson" by serving his time for previous crimes. He was nothing of the sort. He had by no means served his time. He had been on the run and (plainly) would have remained so had he not been arrested for these fresh crimes.... The judge was quite right to allow cross-examination of G's absconding as "evidence to correct a false impression given by the defendant" within the meaning of s 101(1)(f) of the Criminal Justice Act 2003.
> (at [84]–[85])

7.107 As regards an accused impliedly giving a 'misleading', as opposed to a 'false', impression, let us consider the facts in *Lee* (1976) 62 Cr App R 33. L, who was charged with theft, had confined himself to giving evidence that other persons who had had the opportunity to commit the theft with which he was charged had convictions for dishonesty. L refrained from explicitly claiming a good character for himself. Nevertheless, by implication it seemed obvious to the trial judge that L was trying to suggest that, in contrast to those other persons, he was of good character and therefore less likely to have committed the offence. Although under the old law this strategy avoided L's bad character being introduced in evidence, unless a court followed Orr LJ's ruling in *Lee* to the effect that 'it is not implicit in an accusation of dishonesty that the accuser himself is an honest man', under s 105(1)(a) it would in all likelihood now lead to L's bad character becoming admissible via gateway (f). The wording is even wide enough to cover the case where the defendant reveals only part of his bad character—for example, D is charged with rape and only acknowledges his convictions for traffic offences, not for serious violence. Here, the impression created could very well be considered 'misleading'.

7.108   The legislature has chosen one unusual expression in s 105(1)(a): namely, that an assertion may be 'apt to' give the tribunal a false or misleading impression. The draftsman will have employed the expression because whilst under s 105(1)(a) the defendant is 'responsible for the making of an express or implied assertion' as to his character, it was presumably necessary to distinguish this from the more specific situation covered by s 105(2)(d) where the defendant would be held responsible, in the first instance, for 'a question asked...that is intended to elicit, or is likely to [elicit an assertion apt to create a false impression]'. Given the general width and repressive character of both s 101(1)(f) and Part 11 as a whole, this expression may merit a wide construction, thereby facilitating the admission of bad character evidence. Let us imagine a defendant, charged with murdering a victim by strangulation, who denies the offence but, in the course of his testimony, imprudently remarks: 'Goodness gracious me! Having served for 11 years as a pack leader in the Scouts, I would certainly have been able to tie a far neater ligature around that poor blighter's neck.' If the defendant, who has now left the Scout movement, in fact has a relevant criminal record, this might well be a case where a casual glancing reference to his earlier career doing good works amongst Britain's youth might have a tendency/be 'apt to' create a misleading impression within the terms of the Act.

7.109   *When is the defendant responsible for an express or implied assertion?* Section 105(1) refers to the defendant being 'responsible' for the making of an assertion. The circumstances in which a defendant will be treated as responsible are enumerated in s 105(2):

A defendant is treated as being responsible for the making of an assertion if—

(a) the assertion is made by the defendant in the proceedings (whether or not in evidence given by him),

(b) the assertion was made by the defendant—

    (i) on being questioned under caution, before charge, about the offence with which he is charged, or

    (ii) on being charged with the offence or officially informed that he might be prosecuted for it, and evidence of the assertion is given in the proceedings,

(c) the assertion is made by a witness called by the defendant,

(d) the assertion is made by any witness in cross-examination in response to a question asked by the defendant that is intended to elicit it, or is likely to do so, or

(e) the assertion was made by any person out of court, and the defendant adduces evidence of it in the proceedings.

7.110 Essentially, an assertion of which the court learns is attributable to the defendant, whenever made, from the moment he is being questioned under caution to the moment he presents his case, gives testimony or cross-examines the other side's witnesses. In particular, the defendant, by s 105(2)(c), is *prima facie* rendered responsible for the content of the testimony of the witnesses called by him. He is similarly rendered *prima facie* responsible for answers given in cross-examination by opposing witnesses in response to questions put by him, provided that his questions were designed to elicit those responses or were 'likely to do so'.

7.111 *Withdrawal or disassociation.* It is obviously excessive to presume that a defendant ought to be held responsible for the making of all these possible types of assertion in all eventualities. Therefore, s 105(3) offers the defendant an escape route:

> A defendant who would otherwise be treated as responsible for the making of an assertion shall not be so treated if, or to the extent that, he withdraws it or disassociates himself from it.

The statute prescribes no methods for signifying that the defendant wishes to withdraw an assertion or to dissociate himself from an assertion made by someone else, but for which s 105(2) holds him responsible. Whether the court will require a formal declaration from the defendant to this effect, or whether a statement by his legal representative will suffice, remains to be seen. Is it enough for the defendant's counsel to indicate a retraction in the course of his closing address to the jury? Section 105(3), of course, also makes provision for a partial retraction. In these circumstances, it is even more important to be clear about what is still asserted and what has been retracted. What seems clear is that the correction of a false impression ought to be a conscious act and not simply a concession wrung from a defendant in the course of cross-examination:

> There is a significant difference between the defendant who makes a specific and positive decision to correct a false impression for which he is responsible, or to dissociate himself

from false impressions conveyed by the assertions of others, and the defendant who in the process of cross-examination is obliged to concede that he has been misleading the jury. A concession extracted in cross-examination that the defendant was not telling the truth in part of his examination-in-chief will not normally amount to a withdrawal or dissociation from the original assertion for the purposes of section 105(3).

(*Renda* [2006] 1 WLR 2948 at [21] *per* Sir Igor Judge P)

7.112 *Conduct creating a false or misleading impression.* Prior to the enactment of the 2003 Act, the courts encountered difficulty in determining what to do in cases where the defendant had sought to create a favourable impression by his conduct or by his garb. In *Hamilton* [1969] Crim LR 486, for example, a trial judge instructed H not to wear his regimental blazer in court (a ruling which was subsequently criticised by the Court of Appeal). In contrast, in *Robinson* [2001] EWCA Crim 214 R, who was charged with burglary, throughout his testimony had held a small Bible in his hand, waving it around at shoulder height from time to time. The Court of Appeal determined that allowing the Crown to introduce evidence of R's bad character was not the proper way to discourage disruptive or exhibitionist behaviour. Although the Court accepted that brandishing the Bible was a cynical, manipulative action on R's part, intended to imply that he was a devout fellow whose word could be believed, it concluded that R had not asserted his good character within the meaning of the 1898 Act merely by taking the oath, by reminding the Court that he had sworn on the Bible to tell the truth or, more particularly, by clasping a Bible in his hand whilst testifying. The old law, then, required some positive and deliberate assertion of good character on behalf of or on the part of the accused. (Indeed, Henry LJ took note in *Robinson* that all remand prisoners are given a Bible, and it appears that R had simply brought his copy into court with him. It was subsequently reported that Barry George, prosecuted for and subsequently acquitted of the murder of Jill Dando, also held a Bible in his hand from the commencement of proceedings: see [2003] Crim LR 282.)

7.113 Whilst such conduct did not trigger the admission of bad character evidence under the old law, the case is altered under the Criminal Justice Act 2003. Section 105 (4) provides:

Where it appears to the court that a defendant, by means of his conduct (other than the giving of evidence) in the proceedings, is seeking to give the court or jury an impression about himself that is false or misleading, the court may if it appears just to do so treat the defendant as being responsible for the making of an assertion which is apt to give that impression.

For good measure, s 105(5) adds that in the above subsection 'conduct' includes appearance or dress. The court, then, enjoys discretion whether or not to treat the defendant as responsible for making an assertion in these circumstances. Defendants, after all, do tend to spruce themselves up for their trial. Given how uncomfortable some of them look, wearing an unaccustomed suit, cleanly shaven and sporting a metaphorical rosebud in their buttonhole, it would seem unnecessarily vindictive to insist on introducing their bad character as well in every case. Subsections (4) and (5), however, still do not really tell us what to do in such cases. How ought the court to treat the old soldier, accused of shoplifting, who turns up to court in his regimental blazer and tie; with the cat burglar who arrives in court pushing a Zimmer frame; with the undergraduate, up for assaulting one of his lecturers, who rolls up in a Crown Court situate in a university town in cap and gown; with the corporate fraudster who attends court unshaven and looking palpably dress-down Friday; or with the defendant in a rape case who appears wearing women's clothes, reeking of Chanel No 5, and sporting dazzling make-up? The point of these examples is to draw attention to the fact that the focus of ss 101(1)(f) and 105 is actually different to the antecedent law. Whereas the old law was concerned with the defendant who proffered evidence of his good character, the 2003 Act is equally interested in the defendant who creates a false or misleading impression of good character.

7.114 *Bad character evidence correcting the false or misleading impression.* What sort of evidence can the prosecution lead if the defendant creates a false or misleading impression? Section 105(1)(b) stipulates that:

> . . . evidence to correct such an impression is evidence which has probative value in correcting it.

This provision is supplemented by s 105(6), which adds:

> Evidence is admissible under section 101(1)(f) only if it goes no further than is necessary to correct the false impression.

This pair of provisions brings us back to an issue raised earlier (*ante*, paras **7.19–7.21**) in that, by implication, they might suggest that a court does not enjoy discretion under s 101(3) to exclude evidence of bad character under s 101(1)(f) if it appears that the admission of the bad character evidence 'would have such an adverse effect on the fairness of the proceedings' that the court feels that it ought not to admit it. However, there seems no reason why PACE, s 78 should not apply, under the terms of s 112(3)(c). Under s 101(5) and (6), the evidence adduced by the prosecution has to be confined strictly to items of bad character that specifically go towards refuting the precise assertions for which the law holds the defendant responsible.

7.115 To review an old case, in *Winfield* [1939] 4 All ER 164, W was charged with indecent assault. W called two female witnesses, who affirmed that he had always behaved impeccably towards them. Just as under the old law this would have amounted to an attempt to establish his good character, so too under the 2003 Act W would be held responsible for this assertion that he deliberately elicited from his own witnesses under s 105(2)(c). W, it turned out, had some previous convictions for offences of dishonesty. Under the old law, there was considerable debate as to whether, in these circumstances, the Crown ought to have been allowed to introduce evidence of W's convictions for dishonesty. Today, the case is altered. It would be difficult to maintain that convictions for offences of dishonesty were, in the words of s 105(6), 'necessary to correct the false impression'. *Winfield* is a salutary reminder, if such were needed, that decisions on admissibiloity of bad character evidence reached under the old law are now of doubtful utility. (See comments of Kennedy LJ in *Weir* [2006] 1 WLR 1885 at [43].)

7.116 *Manipulation of gateway (f).* The courts must be vigilant to ensure that the prosecution does not unfairly manipulate gateway (f) by trapping a defendant into making an assertion which will engage the gateway. In *RB* [2008] EWCA Crim 1850, for example, where B was convicted of raping his 13-year-old daughter and of indulging in sexual activity with his stepson, Hooper LJ disapproved of the Crown deliberately seeking to get a broad exculpatory statement made by RB in interrogation, to the effect that he was not interested in young girls and that it was 'disgusting even to think about', into evidence in order to trigger gateway (f):

> [T]o use an answer of this kind in response to a direct question, "Are you interested in young girls?", to trigger gateway (f) is unfair.
>
> (at [35])

Gateway (g): When 'the defendant has made an attack on another person's character' (s 101(1)(g))

7.117 The final 'gateway' offered by the Criminal Justice Act 2003 is an expanded version of the old 'tit for tat' provision that used to be found in the Criminal Evidence Act 1898. Broadly speaking, the new provision could still be said to embody in part the following philosophy: if the defendant chooses to attack the character of the victim of the offence, the prosecution witnesses, parties whose testimony is reported to the court, those involved in the investigation of the offence, or indeed anyone else, it may only be fair that the accused's true colours should in turn be revealed to the tribunal of fact. When the accused invites it to discount or question the integrity of other individuals, the tribunal of fact deserves to have placed before it the material with which to assess the defendant's own character and trustworthiness. Although, as we shall see, the attacks on another person's character are not limited to attacks made upon those who actually testify in the case, this provision could also be argued at the same time to provide prosecution witnesses with some protection against attacks on their characters by unscrupulous or desperate defendants. As Lord Pearce remarked of the old law, in *Selvey v DPP* [1970] AC 304, at 355, without such a deterrent provision 'there would be no limit to the amount of mud which could be thrown against an unshielded prosecutor while the accused could still crouch behind his own shield'.

7.118 *Making an attack on another person's character.* How is one to tell when the accused has 'made an attack on another person's character'? Section 106(1) puts some flesh on the bones by specifying when a defendant will be considered to have done this:

> (1) For the purposes of s 101(1)(g) a defendant makes an attack on another person's character if—
>
> (a) he adduces evidence attacking the other person's character,
>
> (b) he (or any legal representative appointed under s. 38(4) of the Youth Justice and Criminal Evidence Act 1999 to cross-examine a witness in his interests) asks questions in cross-examination that are intended to elicit such evidence, or are likely to do so, or
>
> (c) evidence is given of an imputation about the other person made by the defendant—
>
> (i) on being questioned under caution, before charge, about the offence with which he is charged, or
>
> (ii) on being charged with the offence or officially informed that he might be prosecuted for it.

It will first be noted that the section places no restriction on which persons, whose character the defendant has attacked, will justify the court in allowing the defendant in turn to have his bad character revealed. This means that any defendant with a criminal record, or other admissible bad character, will have to think carefully before launching any sort of attack on whomsoever. He will no longer be able, with impunity, to refer to the judge as 'a biased old codger', to call prosecuting counsel 'a drunken bullying oaf', to describe a police officer who is not called to testify as being 'bent as a corkscrew', or to impute criminal offences to all and sundry. In fact, according to *Hanson* [2005] 1 WLR 3169 at [5], the protection extends to any person, 'whether alive or dead'. Although the 1898 Act was deliberately amended to include 'the deceased victim of crime', the 2003 Act has pointedly abandoned this language. I would argue that the Court of Appeal's eagerness to assume that, when used in a statute, the expression 'another person' obviously covers both the living and the dead is probably unwarranted. This is not the normal sense in which the word 'person' is understood, and nothing in the Act predicates such a generous meaning (at least from a prosecutor's point of view. See further, Munday [2007] 71 J Crim Law 238).

7.119 The reference to adducing evidence in s 106(1)(a) and the reference to cross-examination in s 106(1)(b) mean that this provision covers both cases where the defendant in person makes such an attack, cases where the defendant calls witnesses who make similar allegations, and cases where the defence extracts such allegations from cross-examining another party's witnesses. In view of the drafting of s 106(1)(b), it is obvious that a defendant ought not to take risks when cross-examining: even questions that are 'likely to' elicit an attack on another person's character will fall foul of s 101(1)(g). The use of the word 'adduces' in s 106(1)(a), however, does suggest one limitation: where one of the defendant's witnesses gratuitously volunteers evidence attacking another party, it would be a perversion of language to say that the defendant had 'adduced' that evidence, and just as artificial to say that 'the defendant [had] made an attack on another person's character', as demanded by s 101(1)(g). Unlike s 101(1)(f), there is no notion of a defendant being held *prima facie* 'responsible' for his witnesses' testimony under s 101(1)(g). Nevertheless, it is obvious that s 101(1)(g), in the first instance, is designed to exact a price whenever a defendant elicits or presents evidence denigrating another person. Indeed, s 106(1)(c) brings home just how extensive this provision is intended to be. Provided that the defendant has been duly cautioned, attacks he makes on other persons in the course of interrogation may also trigger s 101(1)(g) and lead to the admission of his bad character. Like the failures provisions introduced by the Criminal Justice and Public Order Act 1994 (*post*, Chapter 11), this means that the right to legal advice at the interrogation stage becomes all the more important, precisely to ensure that under pressure during police interview a suspect does not make rash allegations which will subsequently lead to his bad character becoming admissible at any eventual trial.

7.120 One curious point of interpretation may arise under this 'gateway'. Since s 106(1) refers *simpliciter* to an attack made on 'another person', this other person might conceivably include a co-accused. It is true that s 106(3) is careful to state that:

> Only prosecution evidence is admissible under section 101(1)(g).

Also, as we have seen, it is the case that the ordained vehicle that permits a co-defendant (D2) to retaliate, if attacked by the defendant (D1), is s 101(1)(e), qualified by s 104(1), which additionally requires that 'the nature or conduct of [D1's] defence is such as to undermine [D2's] defence'. However, it is possible to read s 106 in such a way that wherever the court finds that D1 has made an attack on D2, the prosecution is permitted to adduce evidence of D1's bad character. This is reinforced by the fact that s 106(2)(a) contemplates that 'evidence attacking the other person's character' can include:

> ...evidence to the effect that the other person has committed an offence (whether a different offence from the one with which the defendant is charged *or the same one*).

Whether such a solution really makes sense, and whether the statute requires to be read in quite such a literal-minded way, is most unlikely. One would like to imagine that the fundamental question was whether it is possible to discern any legitimate interest in the prosecution's introducing evidence of D1's bad character in such circumstances (for instance, if D2 chooses not to take advantage of s 101(1) (e); or if the court considers that the attack on D2's character is not such as to undermine D2's defence because it does not amount to 'an important matter in issue between' D1 and D2, as required under s 101(1)(e)). Lurking in the background, of course, is awareness that this legislation was largely intended to make a defendant's criminal record and other reprehensible behaviour more widely available than in the past (see *Edwards* [2006] 1 WLR 1524 at [1(iii)]). In such a context, there may not be much room for arguments founded on principle and logical coherence.

7.121 *'Evidence attacking the other person's character'*. It is obviously important to be able to identify when an attack has occurred. Section 106(2), therefore, explains:

> In subsection (1) "evidence attacking the other person's character" means evidence to the effect that the other person—
>
> (a) has committed an offence (whether a different offence from the one with which the defendant is charged or the same one), or
>
> (b) has behaved, or is disposed to behave, in a reprehensible way;
> and "imputation about the other person" means an assertion to that effect.

Section 106(2)(a) is unproblematic. It will not be difficult for a court to determine whether or not the defendant has alleged that some other person has committed an offence. However, s 106(2)(b) raises the question: what is meant by 'reprehensible behaviour'? By way of illustration, let us consider a case that arose under the old law. Although the solution might not have commended itself to a court so readily thirty-five years later, in *Bishop* [1975] QB 274, B's claim, that his fingerprints were found all over his landlord's burgled premises merely because the latter was a homosexual with predatory designs on B, was held to amount to an 'imputation' under the old law. Under present law, the question would be whether B's contention that his landlord had sexual designs on him amounted to an imputation such as to suggest that he had behaved, or was disposed to behave, in a reprehensible way. Judged by contemporary *mores*, a court is very unlikely to hold that homosexuality *per se* would amount to evidence such as to trigger s 101(1)(g). Whether the allegation that B was a homosexual who would give unfettered rein to his desires might qualify is a more difficult question. To take another example, one would anticipate that s 101(1)(g) would not be activated by the sort of facts that arose in *McLean* [1978] Crim LR 430, an assault case arising out of a drunken fracas where the Court of Appeal decided that M had not made imputations on the prosecution witness's character merely by suggesting that the victim was intoxicated and swearing. Courts will not treat every footling peccadillo laid at the door of some other person as amounting to an imputation of reprehensible behaviour within the meaning of the 2003 Act, thereby leading to introduction of the defendant's bad character. Only the grosser allegations of immorality ought to qualify.

7.122 Uncertainty as to the meaning the courts might attribute to 'reprehensible behaviour' may prove troublesome in a respect familiar to those conversant with the law prior to the 2003 Act. The adversarial nature of English criminal procedure generated a problem under the old law: when did an allegation that a prosecution witness was lying amount to an imputation? A similar question will arise under the 2003 Act as to whether an allegation that another person was lying will amount to 'evidence to the effect that the other person... has behaved, or is disposed to behave, in a reprehensible way'? Because the aim of our procedure is to confront two adversaries' competing versions of events, an accused's simple denial of guilt will be tantamount to an allegation that the prosecution's witnesses are lying. If that is treated as 'reprehensible behaviour', then there will be precious few cases in which the accused's bad character will not come out.

7.123 In ordinary parlance, calling someone a liar might readily be considered an 'imputation', even a serious imputation, and hence, 'reprehensible'. Had the 1898 Act been so construed, whenever he contested the prosecution case the defendant would have risked disclosure of his bad character. This would have proved excessive. Interpretation of the term 'imputation' therefore took into account this procedural context. Darling J's ruling in *Rouse* [1904] 1 KB 184, 187 still broadly states the position:

> Merely to deny a fact alleged by the prosecution is not necessarily to make an attack on the character of the prosecutor or his witnesses. Such a denial is necessary and inevitable in every case where a prisoner goes into the witness box, and nothing is more than a traverse of the truth of an allegation made against him; to add in cross-examination that the prosecutor is a liar is merely an emphatic mode of denial, and does not affect its essential quality.

As the courts repeatedly held (eg *Desmond* [1999] Crim LR 313), even though it carried the implication that the witnesses were lying, an accused's merely contesting the prosecution's account was not to be deemed an 'imputation' under the Act, provided that it went no further than an emphatic denial. It was not to amount to deliberate disparagement beyond what was necessarily incidental to vigorously contesting the prosecution's case. Such an approach, however, still allowed the courts considerable leeway. Thus, in *Barrett* [2000] Crim LR 847 the Court of Appeal passed over without comment the fact that the trial judge had treated B's forceful suggestion that the prosecution witnesses had grossly exaggerated their stories to avoid responsibility for having sold B a dodgy motor car as an imputation under the 1898 Act.

7.124 A defendant's denials can of course be intemperate to the point of not just contradicting the Crown's case but, additionally, of suggesting that the prosecution's evidence is fabricated. After all, it is not exactly unknown for an accused to allege that policemen have planted or massaged evidence. How ought such cases to be treated? They contain within them both the elements of (a) a powerful denial and (b) a potential allegation of reprehensible behaviour, necessarily incidental to the conduct of the defence. Under the old law, in *Britzmann* [1983] 1 All ER 369 the Court of Appeal adopted the line that any denial by the accused that went beyond a pure rejection of the opposing case and actually amounted to a claim that prosecution witnesses (in this instance, policemen) had fabricated evidence ought to be considered an imputation under that Act. The courts have adopted a similar approach under the 2003 Act. In *Williams* [2007] EWCA Crim 1951 W contested his convictions on six counts of doing acts prohibited by a sexual offences prevention order [SOPO] contrary to s 113 of the Sexual Offences Act 2003. The SOPO forbade W, a convicted sex offender, from carrying out lengthy and sustained observations on children outside of his home address. At trial, W's case was that the police had been determined to stitch him up and, to this end, had fabricated their observation evidence. As Dyson LJ observed,

> It is one thing to say that the prosecution witnesses misinterpreted what they saw. Even that they were lying in their account as to what they saw. It is a criticism of a different order to say that the prosecution witnesses had put their heads together to produce a jointly fabricated statement, even more so if the allegation is that the prosecution "stitched him up" by encouraging him to do acts which would amount to breaches of the SOPO.
> (at [26])

The court's discretion to exclude evidence of bad character

7.125 Despite this, the court may nevertheless exercise discretion in the defendant's favour and disallow cross-examination if it felt the justice of the case demanded it. In *Britzmann*, under the old law, the court suggested that, in exercising this discretion, judges ought to take the three following factors into account:

- it may be appropriate to exercise discretion in an accused's favour if his denial, even when offensively made, refers to a single incident rather than to evidence deriving from long periods of observation or denials of long conversations;

- the judge should take account of the strain accused persons are under in the witness box, and only allow cross-examination if sure that the denial will inevitably leave the jury having to decide whether or not the evidence was in fact fabricated;

- finally, it would seem that, rather like a boxing referee stepping in to prevent a pugilist from soaking up unnecessary punishment, 'there is no need for the prosecution to rely upon [bad character evidence] if the evidence against the defendant is overwhelming'. This does seem an odd principle in a criminal trial.

The courts can still accommodate these general principles (perhaps, disregarding the last one) within the broad discretion which they have been accorded under s 101(3) and s 101(4). It seems appropriate that they should.

7.126 It will be recalled that s 101(3) provides:

> The court must not admit evidence under subs ... (1)(g) if, on an application by the defendant to exclude it, it appears to the court that the admission of the evidence would have such an adverse effect on the fairness of the proceedings that the court ought not to admit it.

This modified version of the general discretion that operates under PACE, s 78 will mean that a court ought not automatically to permit the introduction of a defendant's entire bad character whenever the latter attacks the character of another person. If the defendant applies for its exclusion and the court is of the view that it would be unfair in the sense prescribed by s 101(3) to admit it, the defendant's bad character 'must' be excluded. The court's discretion is further guided by s 101(4), which states:

> On an application to exclude evidence under subs (3) the court must have regard, in particular, to the length of time between the matters to which that evidence relates and the matters which form the subject of the offence charged.

The more elderly the evidence of bad character is, the more predisposed the court should be to refuse to admit it. However, s 101(4) does not exclude other factors from playing a role in the exercise of this judicial discretion. As we saw, when discussing s 101(1)(d) (evidence 'relevant to an important matter in issue between the defendant and the prosecution'), the discretion operates as a civilising factor restricting the extent to which the bad character evidence will simply serve to prejudice the tribunal of fact. For example, previous misdeeds that would be apt to scandalise the tribunal unduly could be winnowed out, just as minor offending or evidence of offences that shed little light on the moral make-up of the convicted party might figure in this context. In *Nelson* [2006] EWCA Crim 3412; [2007] Crim LR 709 the Court of Appeal has handed down further guidance on how judicial discretion ought to apply in this context. It suggested, for example, that the fairness of proceedings would normally be damaged were a defendant's bad character admitted when the latter had attacked the character of a non-witness who was not the victim of the offence charged. Additionally, the court made the ethical point that it would be improper for the Crown to seek to admit comments made in interview which had no relevance to the issues in the case merely with a view to engineering the admission of a defendant's bad character via gateway (g) (cp *RB* [2008] EWCA Crim 1850, *ante*, para **7.116**).

7.127   *Where the imputation is an inevitable element of the accused's defence.* Under the old law, one particular issue arose with some regularity. In cases where it was essential for the defendant to launch an attack on someone else's character in order to make out his defence, was the court automatically supposed to exercise its discretion in the defendant's favour? In rape cases the courts, exceptionally, held that, even though such a defence might incidentally convey a slur on the victim's character, merely to allege consent on the part of the victim did not constitute an imputation, and it did not render the defendant's previous bad character admissible in evidence (*Turner* [1944] KB 463). Again, in *Selvey v DPP* [1970] AC 304, a contested case of buggery, S's assertion that the complainant was a male prostitute who had both offered to allow himself to be buggered by S for £1 and told S that he had already been buggered at that price by someone else earlier that day, amounted to an indisputable imputation on the character of the complainant. It was argued that since these allegations formed an indispensable component of S's defence, the trial judge ought to have excluded the defendant's terrible previous record for homosexual offences. The House of Lords held that, the case of rape apart, even where an imputation on someone's character was an inevitable consequence of the line taken by the accused, this did not mean that trial judges had routinely to exercise discretion in the accused's favour and turn down prosecution applications to introduce evidence of his bad character. In each case judges were free to exercise discretion, allowing or refusing cross-examination as they saw fit. Contrary to what had been proposed by the Law Commission, under s 106 the defendant enjoys no immunity from his character becoming admissible merely because imputations he makes relate either to the alleged facts of the offence or to its manner of investigation or prosecution (cf s 98, discussed *ante*, paras **7.12–7.18**). In *Lamaletie and Royce* (2008) 172 JP 249 the Court of Appeal resolved that a claim made during police interrogation under caution that the victim of L, who was charged with inflicting gbh, 'was attacking [him] everywhere' plainly constituted an attack on the victim's character within the meaning of s 101(1)(g) as it indicated that the victim had behaved in a reprehensible way. The fact that this allegation was made in the context of L's raising a defence of self-defence, and was therefore an inevitable feature of his defence, was just one of the considerations relevant to the exercise of judicial discretion under s 101(3). In the event, the judge's decision nonetheless to admit L's previous convictions was upheld.

7.128 Where attacks range beyond 'the alleged facts of the offence', and the introduction of third parties' 'bad character' is permitted under s 100, a defendant may still be placed in a serious dilemma if he happens to have bad character. Revealing to the jury that a particular party is an out-and-out knave or that particular police officers have persistently set defendants up may form an essential part of the defence strategy. Yet, the accused has also to be aware that if he triggers s 101(1)(g) by making attacks on such persons, the jury's view of him may be seriously prejudiced when, in turn, they learn of his bad character. Under the old law, the consequence was a chilling effect, with some defendants choosing not to testify rather than incur the risk of disclosing their own unsavoury pasts. Prior to the 2003 Act, however, matters were slightly ameliorated by the Court of Appeal's decision in *Taylor and Goodman* [1999] 2 Cr App R 163. In that case, Judge LJ declared that it ought to be the universal practice of prosecuting counsel to offer to disclose to the jury the convictions of any accomplices who testified for the Crown, thereby removing some defendants from the horns of this particular dilemma. Nevertheless, in other cases the dilemma will remain. Prior to the 2003 Act, in *Dempster* [2001] EWCA Crim 571, [2001] Crim LR 567 counsel sought to take matters further, actually requesting an advance ruling from the judge on whether he was likely to allow the prosecution to adduce evidence of D's bad character before D actually decided whether or not to give evidence. D had been convicted of choking a prostitute with intent to commit indecent assault. D claimed that the woman had taken his money and then run off. He admitted that he had had his hands at her throat but denied that he had had any indecent intent. D's counsel sought a ruling from the judge at the close of the Crown case as to whether, in light of these imputations (which, under the 2003 Act, would surely be considered reprehensible behaviour on her part), he proposed allowing the Crown to cross-examine D on his previous convictions (some elderly convictions for dishonesty, and two convictions for rape). This, the trial judge declined to do. In consequence, D did not elect to give evidence. Mance LJ upheld the judge's ruling, noting that a judge was fully entitled to conclude that any exercise of discretion whether or not to allow cross-examination should be made only as and if it became necessary after having heard D give his evidence. To deliver such a ruling ahead of D's giving evidence would confer upon D considerable latitude as to what evidence he might give, as well as constituting an exercise of discretion before the judge was in possession of the full facts (esp at [51]). The notice provisions prescribed under the Criminal Procedure Rules 2010 (*post*, paras **7.137–7.138**), if strictly enforced, could answer many of the defence's questions.

7.129 *What bad character evidence is admissible via gateway (g), and for what purpose or purposes may it be used?* Under the old law, evidence of bad character admitted under analogous circumstances redounded only to the defendant's credit—ie, related only to his likely truthfulness. Section 101(1)(g) gives no indication of the purpose bad character evidence admitted via this gateway is now meant to serve. It would seem, however, that all manner of convictions may become admissible once a defendant has tripped gateway (g). It will be for the judge to determine how much of a defendant's bad character it is appropriate to admit in the circumstances of the case. Thus, in *Williams* (*ante*, para **7.124**), having once settled that W had launched an attack on other persons within the meaning of s 101(1)(g), the Court of Appeal had to decide whether the judge had been entitled to leave to the jury W's convictions for offences of dishonesty, dating from 1984. On behalf of W it was argued that, in light of Rose LJ's remarks in *Hanson* [2005] 1 WLR 3169 at [13]—to the effect that convictions, whether for offences of dishonesty or otherwise, were only likely to show a propensity to be untruthful either if there had been a plea of not guilty and the defendant had given an account on arrest, in interview or at trial which the jury must have disbelieved or if the offences themselves involved false representations and suchlike—offences of dishonesty *simpliciter* ought not to be admitted via gateway (g). Dyson LJ rejected this argument. A 'propensity to be untruthful', he observed, was a concept specific to s 103(1)(b) and concerned only bad character admissible via gateway (d). Gateway (g) made no mention of any such restriction. Therefore, in *Williams*, since W had made an attack on other persons within the terms of s 101(1)(g), the judge had been entitled to admit the evidence of W's convictions for dishonesty:

> In a case where the defence had launched an attack on the character of the prosecution witnesses the jury were entitled to know about the character of the defendant and in particular that he had offences of dishonesty in deciding whether or not to believe his evidence rather than that of the prosecution witnesses.
> (at [28])

The Court, however, did not dispute the trial judge's decision not to admit convictions registered against W in 1991 for taking a child without lawful authority and for false imprisonment. The Court of Appeal adopted a similar line in *Lewis* [2007] EWCA Crim 3030 where L's single conviction 21 years earlier for gross indecency, to which he had pleaded guilty, was admitted via gateway (g) at L's trial on a charge of sexual activity with a child contrary to the Sexual Offences Act 2003, s 9. Keene LJ observed:

> We are not aware of any authority which suggests that a previous conviction arising from a plea of guilty cannot have relevance to whether the defendant is telling the truth at a subsequent trial.... [T]the existence of a criminal conviction in the past may well be

relevant to a defendant's credibility, even if that conviction resulted from a plea of guilty. Such a defendant is not a person of previous good character. In any event, when the jury are having to assess the credibility of two conflicting witnesses, it will often not be right or fair that a defendant can blacken the name of the prosecution witness while presenting himself as having an unsullied character, at least by implication.

(at [14])

7.130 In *Highton* [2006] 1 Cr App R 7 Lord Woolf CJ indicated that there were no limits on the use to which bad character evidence, once admitted via gateway (g), might be put. More particularly, his Lordship stated:

[O]nce the evidence is admitted, it may, depending on the particular facts, be relevant not only to credibility but also to propensity to commit offences of the kind with which the defendant is charged.

(at [10])

As has been argued elsewhere (see Munday [2006] Crim LR 300), the arguments the Court of Appeal advanced in *Highton* in favour of the interchangeability of the various gateways are not overwhelming. Nevertheless, as Hughes LJ remarked in *Pittard* [2006] EWCA Crim 2028, a case in which P had volunteered information evidence of bad character via gateway (b):

[O]nce evidence of bad character is admissible through one of the new statutory gateways, then, whatever the occasion of the opening of the gateway, the evidence becomes material and relevant for any purpose to which it is relevant.

(at [10]. See also *Weir* [2006] 1 WLR 1885 at [45].)

7.131 In *Lamaletie and Royce* (2008) 172 JP 249 the Court of Appeal indicated how gateway (g) might function. L and R had jointly inflicted gbh on a minicab driver but claimed that the victim had been the aggressor throughout and that they had merely been defending themselves. Principally owing to difficulty in proving the details of those offences, the Crown had indicated that it did not intend employing L's six previous convictions for violence as propensity evidence under gateway (d). At trial, however, prosecuting counsel applied for leave to adduce L's bad character under gateway (g) on the basis that L had 'made an attack on another person's character' during his answers in interview, when he had accused the victim of having initiated an unprovoked attack on himself. The judge allowed the prosecution to put in evidence L's six convictions for violence, but on the express basis that he would direct the jury that they should take them into account only for the purpose of assessing L's credibility. One point raised by L on appeal was that because the six previous convictions related to offences of violence and he was charged with an offence of violence, even though the judge had addressed the jury in terms of general credibility he had effectively admitted propensity evidence through the back-door and therefore ought to have excluded evidence of L's criminal record under the discretion conferred on him by s 101(3) of the 2003 Act. Having acknowledged at one point in his judgment that in the particular case of gateway (g) pre-2003 Act authorities may continue to be helpful, Underhill J explained that the conception underlying s 101(1)(g) continues to be that where a defendant has impugned the character of a prosecution witness the jury will be assisted in deciding who to believe by knowing of the defendant's character. What is relevant in this regard is the defendant's 'character' in a broad general sense. As under the pre-2003 Act law, where details of a defendant's offences were considered unnecessary and potentially distracting, under s 101(1)(g) too it is not necessary to consider the details of the evidence of bad character sought to be adduced. Thus, in this case what, in essence, the jury was being invited to put into the balance, when considering whether to believe L's or the victim's account of how the fight started, was simply the fact that L was a man with a significant record of offences of violence. In deciding whether to accept L's account that the victim was the initial aggressor who, as L claimed, had 'attacked him everywhere', the jurors were entitled to take into account that significant record. Whilst L's antecedent history, as presented to the jury, was capable of being regarded as evidence of a propensity to commit offences of violence and therefore as making it more likely that he was the aggressor in the confrontation with the minicab driver—indeed, even in the absence of details of those offences, the Court indicated that, contrary to the judge's ruling, the six convictions for violence may have been technically admissible as evidence of propensity under s 101(1)(d)—the fact that the direction to the jury might not have been 100 per cent effective in guarding against the jurors so using L's criminal record gave L no cause for complaint. The mere fact that the offences were of a similar type to that charged and had the incidental effect of suggesting a disposition to commit the offence charged did not make their admission in evidence improper.

7.132 It is clear that, from time to time, courts do admit evidence of propensity, more naturally admissible via gateway (d), through gateway (g). Thus, in *O* (2009) 173 JP 616 it was held that at his trial on charges of unlawful wounding with scissors and wounding with intent to do grievous bodily harm with a Stanley knife, following strong attacks made by O on the characters of the two complainants, evidence of O's single conviction for possession of a Stanley knife had properly been admitted via gateway (g). Moreover, it had been open to the judge to rule that, in a case where there was a straight conflict of evidence as to who had started the violence, the jury was entitled to know whether O or the complainant was more likely to have reached for a bladed article for the purposes of attack rather than defence. The knowledge that O, only a few months previously, had been carrying a Stanley knife at school was strongly relevant. The fact that this bad character evidence served as evidence of propensity did not render it inadmissible:

> The question of who started the violence (in the case of the Stanley knife) and who picked up the weapon were important matters in issue between the appellant and the prosecution. The previous conviction was in the circumstances of this case relevant for those purposes too. However, the essence of the matter... is that the judge was entitled to say that this was a case within gateway (g). She was also entitled to say that this was not a case where it would be unfair to admit the character of the appellant under that gateway in the light of the allegations that the appellant was making in respect of each of the complainants.
>
> (at [22])

Contaminated evidence (s 107)

7.133 The Criminal Justice Act 2003 contains a provision setting out when a judge must stop a case from proceeding where evidence of bad character has been admitted under s 101(1)(c)–(g) and it is subsequently realised that this evidence is contaminated. Section 107(5) explains that a person's evidence is 'contaminated' for the purposes of the Act where such evidence is 'false or misleading in any respect, or is different from what it would otherwise have been', either:

(a) as a result of an agreement or understanding between the person and one or more others, or

(b) as a result of the person being aware of anything alleged by one or more others whose evidence may be, or has been, given in the proceedings.

Thus, if there is evidence of concoction, collaboration, that a witness's evidence has been trimmed to fit in with that of others who are testifying, or that a witness's evidence has been contaminated inadvertently, and this has led either to alterations in the evidence or to its becoming false or misleading, the court must consider whether to stop the case. The decision to stop the case turns upon the court being satisfied, after the close of the prosecution case, of two things—namely, that:

(i) the evidence is contaminated, and

(ii) the contamination is such that, considering the importance of the evidence to the case against the defendant, [the defendant's] conviction of the offence would be unsafe.

If the court is satisfied that these two conditions are satisfied, then s 107 states that 'the court must either direct the jury to acquit the defendant of the offence or, if it considers that there ought to be a retrial, discharge the jury'. The section is clearly directed towards combating the risk of wrongful conviction, but will only come into play in those rare cases where the evidence of bad character plays a predominant role in the case and the contamination is of a serious nature.

7.134　The courts are anxious to ensure that s 107 is not misused:

> Section 107 deals with a particular situation where the evidence of 'bad character' has been admitted and proves to be false or misleading in the circumstances described in s 107(5). Unless the case falls squarely within that statutory provision, the Court of Appeal, Criminal Division is the appropriate court in which the correctness of the judge's decision should be questioned.
>
> (*Renda* [2006] 1 WLR 2948 at [27] *per* Judge LJ)

To illustrate a proper application of s 107, in *C* [2006] 1 WLR 2994 C was convicted of sexual assault on a child aged under 13 years. There was evidence that the complainant had sat with his mother at home and that she had told him what to say, and also that the child had been given information about sexual abuse that his mother claimed to have suffered, strongly suggesting that somewhere in the process the child had acquired more 'information' than he possessed before the family discussion at which he had originally made a complaint, and before the arrival of the police. The Court of Appeal held that in this case the conditions of s 107 had been established and that evidence of C's previous convictions for sexual offences with children ought to have been excluded. The direct concern of s 107 is not the admissibility of bad character evidence, but rather the consequences of its admission. Unusually, s 107 imposes a duty on the judge to make a finding of fact: his enquiry into whether the evidence of a witness is false, or misleading, or different from what it would have been had it not been contaminated, requires that the judge should form his own assessment of matters traditionally regarded as questions of fact for the exclusive decision of the jury. Section 107 is meant to reduce the risk of a conviction based on over-reliance on evidence of previous misconduct, and the section acknowledges the potential danger that, where the evidence is contaminated, evidence of bad character may have a disproportionate impact on the evaluation of the case by the jury. Evidence of a defendant's bad character may obscure the dangers inherent in contamination. The duty to act under s 107 does not arise unless the judge is satisfied that there has been important contamination of the evidence. If so satisfied, however, the judge has no choice but to stop the trial and either direct an acquittal or order a retrial.

7.135　In the standard run of cases in which witnesses' evidence may have become innocently contaminated, but not to such a degree as to threaten the safety of any eventual conviction, the judge will be expected to deliver a suitable direction to the jury urging them to show caution. (Eg, *Lamb* [2007] EWCA Crim 1766, a case concerning cross-admissible allegations made against a religious studies teacher at successive school Leavers' Balls, where there had been considerable interaction between the two complainants prior to complaints being lodged.)

The court's duty to give reasons for rulings on matters affecting bad character (s 110)

7.136 Section 110 provides that whenever a court delivers a ruling:

- *either* on whether or not a particular item of evidence amounts to evidence of bad character, and thus subject to the 2003 Act;
- *or* whether or not to admit evidence of bad character;
- *or* whether the evidence is contaminated within the terms of s 107,

in indictable cases, 'it must state in open court ... its reasons for the ruling'. For obvious reasons, such a ruling is delivered in the absence of the jury. Even if a judge's compliance with this requirement is considered 'over-parsimonious', his decision is likely to be upheld by the Court of Appeal, provided that it was correct (*Renda* [2006] 1 WLR 2948 at [60] *per* Sir Igor Judge P).

Rules of court (s 111)

7.137 Although most of it is expressed facultatively, s 111 provides for the making of certain rules of court (see now Criminal Procedure Rules 2010, Part 35). One rule, which must be included in any eventual rules, imposes an obligation on the prosecution to give advance notice to the defendant if it intends adducing bad character evidence:

> The rules may, and, where the party in question is the prosecution, *must*, contain provision requiring a party who—
>
> (a) proposes to adduce evidence of a defendant's bad character, or
>
> (b) proposes to cross-examine a witness with a view to eliciting such evidence,
>
> to serve on the defendant such notice, and such particulars of or relating to the evidence, as may be prescribed.
>
> (s 111(2): emphasis added)

The section nevertheless goes on to add that this requirement can be dispensed with in circumstances prescribed in those rules and suggests that deductions may be made from costs due in case of failures to give proper notice:

> In considering the exercise of its powers with respect to costs, the court may take into account any failure by a party to comply with a requirement imposed by virtue of subs (2) and not dispensed with by virtue of subs (3).
>
> (s 111(4))

The time limits prescribed by the relevant Rule Committees are tight. Broadly speaking, the Crown Court Rules typically provide that if the prosecution intends to introduce evidence of a defendant's bad character under s 101, notice 'must be received by the appropriate officer of the Crown Court and all other parties to the proceedings' not more than 14 days after committal' (r 23E(3)). Defendants receiving such notice then have 14 days from receipt to lodge any objections. Defendants and co-defendants wishing to introduce such evidence are normally required to do so within 14 days of the prosecutor's complying with his disclosure obligations under the Criminal Procedure and Investigations Act, s 3. Part 35(8) states that the Crown Court may shorten or extend such time limits.

7.138   The courts sometimes convey the impression that it is vital that parties comply with the notice requirements. To this end, in *Edwards* [2005] EWCA Crim 1813 Rose VP said:

> As this Court has previously pointed out, (see *Bovell and Dowds* [2005] 2 Cr App R 401 at [2]) it is important that provisions in relation to notice are observed so that adequate enquiries can be made on both sides as to the circumstances of offences, in so far as those circumstances may be relevant when the question of the admissibility of previous convictions arises.
>
> (at [32])

Similarly, in *Lawson* [2007] 1 Cr App R 11 the Court of Appeal characterised one co-defendant's counsel's decision to adduce bad character evidence at trial, without notice to the other co-accused, as reprehensible and contrary to established rules and principles of advocacy. Yet, on other occasions the courts have displayed indulgence towards courts that have exercised discretion allowing parties to make late application to adduce evidence of bad character (eg *Delay* (2006) 170 JP 581; *R (Robinson) v Sutton Coldfield Magistrates' Court* [2006] 2 Cr App R 13). In *Malone* [2006] EWCA Crim 1860, Gage LJ responded as follows to the objection that the Crown had failed to comply with the notice requirements:

> Finally, the Criminal Procedure Rules provide for notice to be given orally and time limits to be abridged. Whilst we would not wish to say anything which might encourage prosecuting authorities not to comply with these rules, we do not see the fact that in this case

no notice had been served under Rule 35 as an insuperable obstacle to this document being admitted under s 101(1)(d).

(at [53])

It could be added that in *Hanson* [2005] 1 WLR 3169 at [15] the Court of Appeal signified that it would be 'very slow to interfere' with rulings delivered by trial judges on failures to comply with the notice requirements, provided the judges have directed themselves correctly.

Jointly charged offences treated as separate proceedings (s 112(2))

7.139 Section 112(2) provides:

where a defendant is charged with two or more offences in the same criminal proceedings, [the bad character provisions have] effect as if each offence were charged in separate proceedings; and references to the offence with which the defendant is charged are to be read accordingly.

This provision has had unlooked-for consequences. In *Wallace* [2008] 1 WLR 572 the Court of Appeal decided that s 112(2) dictates that whenever a defendant faces multiple counts in an indictment, technically, for the purposes of s 98, when considering each of the other offences the court must approach the matter on the basis that, when considering offence 1 it has to pretend that offences 2, 3 and 4 are charged in separate proceedings, and so on. All the evidence other than that which bears directly on offence 1 will fall within the description of evidence of or a disposition towards, misconduct on the defendant's part (cf s 112(1)). Moreover, because such evidence has to do with offences 2, 3 and 4 rather than offence 1, it will not fall within the exception of 'evidence which has to do with the alleged facts of the offence with which the defendant is charged' created by s 98(a). Evidence relating to counts other than count 1 will therefore trigger the bad character provisions, and will only be admissible provided that it passes through one of the gateways of s 101. In *Wallace* W appealed against his conviction on three counts of robbery and one count of attempted robbery. The case against W depended on circumstantial evidence, the Crown contending that there were common features to the robberies and that the appellant was a party to each of them, although not necessarily present when the various robberies were committed. W, it was claimed, was involved in their organisation. W did not give evidence. His case was that, viewed individually, there was insufficient evidence to convict him of any of the robberies. On appeal it was submitted that the definition of 'bad character' in s 98 of the 2003 Act is such that the prosecution ought to have made an application under s 101 of the 2003 Act to adduce the evidence and the judge ought to have ruled upon it. As Scott Baker LJ observed, conceding the point,

> We doubt whether the draftsman of the 2003 Act intended to bring a case such as the present within the bad character provisions of the Act. But we think it is difficult to escape the conclusion that he has done so.
>
> (at [41])

In the event, the convictions were upheld. However, the Court did suggest how the problem might be avoided:

> It would of course always be possible in a case such as the present where evidence falls technically within the definition of bad character, albeit its admission is received for some quite different purpose, for the parties to agree to its admission under s.101(1)(a). That, in our view, would be the simplest course.
>
> (at [44])

It is unclear how realistic this proposal is, even in a post-Criminal Procedure Rules world.

Appealing against trial court rulings and directions on bad character

7.140 The bad character rules in Part 11 of the Criminal Justice Act 2003 are complex. From the outset, however, the Court of Appeal has made abundantly clear that it does not wish to be confronted by large numbers of appeals against trial court rulings on the admission of bad character. In *Hanson* [2005] 1 WLR 3169 Rose LJ declared:

> If a judge has directed himself or herself correctly, this Court will be very slow to interfere with a ruling either as to admissibility or as to the consequences of non-compliance with the regulations for the giving of notice of intention to rely on bad character evidence. It will not interfere unless the judge's judgment as to the capacity of prior events to establish propensity is plainly wrong, or discretion has been exercised unreasonably in the *Wednesbury* sense (cf *Makanjuola* [1995] 2 Cr App R 469, 473E).
>
> (at [15])

In *Renda* [2006] 1 WLR 2948 Sir Igor Judge P, too, indicated that 'the circumstances in which this court would interfere with the exercise of a judicial discretion are limited' and that 'the trial judge's "feel" for the case is usually the critical ingredient of the decision at first instance which this court lacks. Context therefore is vital'. Responsibility for the application of the relevant principles 'is...for the trial judge' (at [3]). In *M* [2006] EWCA Crim 3408 at [14] Keene LJ actually noted that the Court was 'unaware of any reported case on propensity and gateway (d) where this Court has overturned the judge's ruling.' Appellate courts are equally reluctant to overturn lower court acquittals where the latter have adjudged that the Crown was adducing evidence of bad character simply to bolster a weak case: *DPP v Chand* (2007) 171 JP 285.

7.141 *Reducing complexity.* The Court of Appeal has also denounced the introduction of unnecessary complexity into bad character directions under the 2003 Act. In *Campbell* [2007] 1 WLR 2798, Lord Phillips of Worth Matravers CJ, observed that

> The change in the law relating to character evidence introduced by the 2003 Act should be the occasion for simplifying the directions to juries in relation to such evidence. . . . Where evidence of bad character is introduced the jury should be given assistance as to its relevance that is tailored to the facts of the individual case. Relevance can normally be deduced by the application of common sense. The summing-up that assists the jury with the relevance of bad character evidence will accord with common sense and assist them to avoid prejudice that is at odds with this.
>
> (at [24])

Lord Phillips explained how this situation comes about:

> The Court of Appeal criticises an aspect of a judge's summing-up and suggests an alternative direction that would have been appropriate. The Judicial Studies Board then incorporates this suggestion in a specimen direction. Thereafter, if the specimen direction is not given, this is treated as a defect in the summing up that warrants permission to appeal and has, on occasion, been treated in this court as rendering the conviction unsafe without considering whether the jury would have reached the same conclusion by the application of common sense to the evidence, whether or not the specimen direction was given. Failure to give a direction that is no more than assistance in applying common sense to the evidence should not automatically be treated as a ground of appeal, let alone as a reason to allow an appeal.
>
> (at [23])

[See further Munday, '*Exemplum habemus*: Reflections on the Judicial Studies Board's Specimen Directions' [2006] J Crim Law 27, and Pitchford LJ's preface to the 2010 edition of the Crown Court Bench Book.]

7.142 *Jury direction essential.* It is essential that a trial judge delivers a direction to the jury on how they may employ the defendant's bad character evidence. And this applies not only when the evidence is admitted under the 2003 Act, but even if for tactical reasons an accused decides to admit his previous record. Thus, in *Harper* [2007] EWCA Crim 1746, in order to alleviate the risk of the jury speculating, H's counsel decided to put H's previous convictions in evidence. No significant play was made of H's convictions either by the Crown or by his co-accused. The judge, however, gave the jury no direction on how this evidence was to be used. Latham VP acknowledged:

> The fact that these convictions were not put before the jury strictly under the provisions of the Criminal Justice Act 2003 does not mean that the jury should not have been given some appropriate direction as to the use that it might make of those convictions.
>
> (at [12])

7.143 *Jury directions where a defendant of bad character may also lay claim to a good character.* Because the simple absence of criminal convictions may count as evidence of a defendant's good character in English law (see *ante*, paras **6.16** ff), in some cases both a good character and a bad character direction may seem justified on the facts of a case. This phenomenon was explored in *Doncaster* (2008) 172 JP 202. In addition to evidence directly relating to the three counts on the indictment, the Crown had been allowed to adduce evidence of bad character under s 101(1)(d) of the Criminal Justice Act 2003 showing that D, a secondhand car dealer charged with cheating the Revenue and false accounting, had been investigated in 1983, 1990 and 2000 and that these enquiries provided evidence of D's propensity towards persistent and wholesale dishonesty in tax matters. D, however, had only once been convicted of an offence many years earlier and was therefore, to all intents, of good character. The trial judge had directed the jurors that the bad character evidence was relevant to proving D's propensity to commit offences of the type charged and to his propensity for untruthfulness, but had declined to deliver a *Vye* direction inviting them also to take D's good character into consideration in relation to his propensity and his credibility. The Court of Appeal upheld this ruling. In a case such as this, where evidence of D's bad character had been admitted as part of the prosecution's case and the misconduct was similar and relevant to the charges weighing against D, whilst the judge should at least remind the jury that D had no previous convictions, a full good character direction, in the words of Lord Steyn in *Aziz*, would have been a charade or spurious ([1996] 1 AC 41, 53). As Rix LJ explained in *Doncaster*:

> [W]here bad character is admitted under the 2003 Act on the grounds that it is relevant both to propensity and credibility, it would make no sense for the judge to give a standard good character direction, stating its relevance to propensity and credibility in precisely the opposite direction.
>
> (at [42])

The advent of the 2003 Act is likely to have exerted an impact on the rules governing good character evidence. But in any case *Doncaster* is distinguishable from *Aziz* because (i) D's bad character was part of the prosecution case, and (ii) the misconduct was persistent and serious, and not trivial as compared with the offences charged. More generally, Rix LJ suggested how courts might hold the balance, leaving it to the jury to decide between the previous absence of any conviction and the evidence laid before the court of previous misconduct:

> [O]ne way to deal with the difficulties presented in the aftermath of the 2003 Act by a defendant without previous convictions but with evidence of bad character admitted under s 101 is by modifying the bad character direction.... We consider that in the post-2003 Act world, where bad character directions as to propensity have more frequently become necessary, even in the absence of previous convictions, it may be possible similarly to tailor a modified bad character direction, along the following lines. Thus when a judge is directing the jury about the relevance of bad character to propensity or propensities, he could remind them that the defendant had no previous convictions and say that, in the ordinary case, where there was no evidence of bad character, a defendant of no previous convictions would have been entitled to a direction that the jury should consider that that counted in his favour on the questions of both propensity and credibility; as it was, it was for the jury to consider which counted with them more—the absence of previous convictions or the evidence of bad character; and if the former, then they should take that into account in favour of the defendant, and if the latter, then they would be entitled to take that into account against him.
>
> (at [43])

Surviving legislation allowing the Crown to adduce evidence of a defendant's wrongdoing and bad character

7.144 A number of extraneous statutes permit the prosecution to produce in-chief evidence of a defendant's previous offending and/or bad character. In the first instance, it is obvious that a number of offences, of necessity, require that the tribunal of fact learn of the defendant's previous offending. Such offences include driving whilst disqualified contrary to the Road Traffic Act 1988, s 103(1)(b), possession of firearms by those whose previous record debars them from doing so under the Firearms Act 1968, s 21, and prison mutiny contrary to the Prison Security Act 1992, s 1(1). In all such cases proof of a previous offence is either an element of or implicit in the offence concerned. However, two further statutes contain provisions that specifically allow for proof by the prosecution of a defendant's bad character. In logic, the latter statutes ought properly to have been repealed by the Criminal Justice Act 2003, for, to the extent that the 2003 Act founds upon a coherent set of guiding principles, not only are these two survivals exceptions to the general rule but, to a great degree, they also overlap with the provisions of the new Act. It can only be assumed that, because it was realised that they operated in a manner oppressive to accused persons, these statutory provisions were a good thing and deserving of retention.

(i) The Official Secrets Act 1911, s 1(2)

7.145　The Official Secrets Act 1911 states that in proving an offence under the Act, a defendant 'may be convicted if, from the circumstances of the case, or his conduct, or his known character as proved' it appears that he intended to act in a manner prejudicial to the interests and safety of the state. This provision would allow the Crown considerable, if not uncontrolled, latitude in adducing evidence of a defendant's bad character, if he was charged with an offence under this Act. The provision seems not to be used, however; and, significantly, other jurisdictions, like New Zealand, whose legislation used to harbour similar provisions, have repealed them.

(ii) The Theft Act 1968, s 27(3)

7.146　A second statutory provision allows the Crown to adduce evidence of a defendant's other misconduct as part of its case. If the accused is charged with handling stolen goods, but with no other offence, s 27(3) of the Theft Act 1968 allows the prosecution under certain circumstances to prove either:

- that the accused has handled other goods deriving from any theft taking place not more than 12 months before the date of the offence charged. The operative date is that upon which the goods were stolen. Thus, where the accused is charged with handling goods on 1 January 2011, even if on 1 March 2010 he had been found in possession of stolen goods deriving from a theft which occurred on 1 December 2005, this evidence would not be admissible under s 27(3)(a) of the Act. If those other goods had been stolen on 1 February 2010, however, the evidence could be admitted; *or*

- that the accused has been convicted within the previous five years of offences of either theft or handling. If the Crown proposes calling such evidence, it must give the defence seven days' notice of its intention in writing (s 27(3)(b)).

This evidence is only admitted 'for the purpose of proving that [the accused] knew or believed the goods to be stolen goods', and the judge must so direct the jury. If the prosecution does not need to prove guilty knowledge, as for instance in *Duffus* (1993) 158 JP 224, where D admitted that he knew that credit cards in his possession were stolen but, when apprehended, claimed that he was in the process of handing them in to the police, s 27(3) can have no application. D was admitting to guilty knowledge. There was therefore no reason for the Crown to adduce any evidence addressing that issue.

7.147　Although evidence of other handling and/or evidence of previous convictions is admitted for the limited purpose of proving the accused's guilty knowledge, the House of Lords in *Hacker* [1995] 1 All ER 45 determined that s 27(3)(b) should be read in conjunction with s 73(2) of PACE, which provides that where proof of a conviction on indictment is admissible by means of a certificate of conviction, that certificate has to give 'the substance and effect... of the indictment and of the conviction'. Thus, since the nature of the goods may be identified in the certificate of conviction, the judge is not confined to allowing the Crown to prove the fact of the conviction but can also, unless he decides to exercise discretion to exclude it as too prejudicial, permit the Crown to show that the accused's previous conviction related to the same or similar goods to those involved in the offence charged. This, it is argued, may be highly relevant to the question of guilty knowledge. Without question, this is so. However, it is worth bearing in mind that *Hacker* blurred that line between evidence of propensity and evidence which is supposed to be employed for a more restricted purpose. In *Hacker* itself, where H was charged with handling the body-shell of a Ford Escort RS Turbo motor car, the prosecution was allowed to show that H had a previous conviction for handling a Ford RS Turbo motor car. Even allowing for the fact that H ran a garage specialising in these motor cars—a relevant circumstance, it is suggested, but not mentioned in Lord Slynn's speech in *Hacker*—it is obvious that even if a jury is instructed only to use such evidence to assist in deciding whether H knew or believed that the body-shell was stolen, they may be strongly tempted to use such evidence simply as evidence of H's propensity to handle this make of stolen motor car and parts thereof. One cannot help but feel certain misgivings at the efficacy of any direction to a jury (or, indeed, of any direction magistrates are supposed to deliver to themselves and then act upon) which requires them to perform what an American judge first called feats of 'mental gymnastics' (*Nash v US*, 54 F 2d 1006, 1007 (1932) *per* Learned Hand J). After all, to quote another American judge's homespun wisdom, 'A drop of ink cannot be removed from a glass of milk' (*Governor of the Virgin Islands v Toto*, 529 F 2d 178, 183 (1976)). See further Munday (1995) 159 JP Jo 223 and 261.

7.148 It used to be said that s 27(3) was an historical anachronism which, in defiance of the principles governing the admission of all other misconduct evidence in criminal cases, allowed the Crown to adduce proof of an accused's other misdeeds in order to show a general disposition that might or might not cast light on the likelihood of his having possessed guilty knowledge but which might equally arouse prejudice in the tribunal of fact. Indeed, it is revealing that in one case Watkins LJ was so mindful of the dangers that he spoke of the Act conferring on the judge 'a discretion to admit that evidence whenever the demands of justice seem to warrant it' (*Rasini* (1986) Times, 20 March, case no 1136/B/85). However, the Criminal Justice Act 2003 has moved the evidential goalposts. It has both made it easier for the prosecution successfully to apply for leave to adduce much of this bad character evidence under s 101, and also enables the prosecution to use any bad character admitted under s 101 in handling cases for broader purposes than merely proving guilty knowledge, as is permissible under the Theft Act 1968, s 27(3).

7.149 The interrelationship between the Theft Act 1968, s 27(3) and the Criminal Justice Act 2003, s 101 is quite complicated. If one takes evidence of previous handling and theft convictions of a defendant indicted solely for handling, those previous convictions may be admitted for the limited purpose of showing guilty knowledge under s 27(3)(b), provided that seven days' notice in writing has been given to the defence and provided that those convictions occurred during the five years preceding the date of the offence charged. The previous handling convictions may now also be admissible under s 101(1)(d) because they are offences 'of the same description' as the offence charged (ss 103(2)(a) and 103(4)(a)), provided that they relate to any important matter in issue between prosecution and defence and provided that they are not too stale or do not have to be excluded for other reasons (s103(3): this will mean that convictions dating back more than five years may tend to be admitted). Different notice requirements will apply if evidence of previous convictions is tendered, governed by the rules of court applicable to bad character evidence in general (s 111(2)). Apart from being admissible under s 27(3)(b) as evidence of guilty knowledge, the theft convictions may either come to be admitted under those 'categories of offence' prescribed from time to time by the Secretary of State (ss 103(2)(b) and 103(4)(b), and Criminal Justice Act 2003 (Categories of Offences) Order 2004, SI 2004/3346), or may just possibly be admitted as evidence showing 'whether the defendant has a propensity to be truthful' under ss 101(1)(d) and 103(1)(b). It should also be noted that, whereas s 27(3) of the Theft Act 1968 only applies in cases where the defendant is charged with handling, and no other offence, no such restriction applies in cases where the Criminal Justice Act 2003 is invoked. On the contrary, s 112(2) explicitly states that:

> Where a defendant is charged with two or more offences in the same criminal proceedings, this Chapter…has effect as if each offence were charged in separate proceedings; and references to the offence with which the defendant is charged are to be read accordingly.

7.150 From just this brief sketch it will be apparent that, although there may be some situations where it is still appropriate for the Crown to consider employing s 27(3) of the Theft Act, to a great extent the 2003 Act has made the older statute's provisions superfluous. Similarly, if one imagines that there is evidence that a defendant, charged with handling, has handled other stolen goods deriving from thefts taking place not earlier than 12 months before the date of the offence charged, whilst this evidence remains admissible under s 27(3)(a), apart from evidence of a 'propensity to commit offences' it could just conceivably amount to 'other reprehensible behaviour' (s 112) admissible under s 101(1)(d), or even as 'important explanatory evidence' under ss 101(1)(c) and 102. Were it admissible under the 2003 Act, the 12-month restriction on admissibility would not apply. From this brief analysis, it can be seen that in some respects the Theft Act provision is broader in scope than Part 11 of the 2003 Act, in others the Criminal Justice Act renders bad character evidence admissible in circumstances that fall outside the purview of the earlier statute. The Crown, therefore, can now draw on a richer and more varied palette whenever prosecuting handling cases.

Envoi

7.151 On the day that he laid orders before Parliament in conformity with s 103(4)(b) detailing what previous convictions might be treated as 'offences of the same category' under s 103(2) in respect of those charged with theft or with sexual offences involving child victims, the former Home Secretary, Mr Blunkett, was reported to have said:

> Trials should be a search for the truth and juries should be trusted with all the relevant evidence available to help them to reach fair decisions. The current rules are confusing and difficult to apply and can mean evidence of previous misconduct that seems clearly relevant is still excluded from court.
>
> (*Daily Mail*, 26 October 2004)

Making all due allowance for the present writer's literary limitations—and even ignoring the contentious assumptions made in Mr Blunkett's statement—having read this chapter and studied Part 11 of the Criminal Justice Act 2003, perhaps readers might care to ask themselves to what extent, in their opinion, the new rules are straightforward and easy to apply.

II. Similar fact evidence in civil cases

7.152 In criminal cases, prior to the entry into force of the Criminal Justice Act 2003, the purpose of the once highly restrictive similar fact evidence rules was to protect an accused against the risk of wrongful conviction on the basis of inherently prejudicial evidence. These rules could have been said to encapsulate the very essence of fair trial at common law. In civil cases, however, a party frequently is allowed to adduce evidence of his opponent's misconduct on other occasions in order to establish that something was likely to be the case. In *Hales v Kerr* [1908] 2 KB 601, for instance, a client contracted ringworm and brought an action in negligence against a barber, who, having cut him with a razor, had staunched the flow of blood with a towel and a powder puff, any one of which may have been contaminated. The plaintiff was permitted to call two witnesses who had suffered similar experiences at this barber's shop. Such evidence, it was said, gave rise to a 'legitimate inference' that the barber's instruments were not kept clean, which in turn was strongly suggestive of negligence. Again, in *Sattin v National Union Bank Ltd* (1978) 122 Sol Jo 367, where S sought damages following the defendant bank's loss of a diamond he had deposited as security for an overdraft, the Court of Appeal allowed evidence to be admitted of another customer whose jewellery had also been lost when deposited with that bank. As in criminal cases, provided that it is probative of the contested issue in the case, similar fact evidence adduced at a civil trial may relate to incidents either prior to or posterior to the event being litigated; *Desmond v Bower* [2010] EMLR 5.

7.153 In innumerable other situations civil courts admit evidence of misconduct on other occasions as circumstantial evidence logically probative of a fact in issue. As Lord Denning MR explained in *Mood Music Publishing Co Ltd v de Wolfe Publishing Ltd* [1976] Ch 119:

> The criminal courts have been very careful not to admit (similar fact) evidence unless its probative value is so strong that it should be received in the interests of justice; and its admission will not operate unfairly to the accused. In civil cases the courts have followed a similar line but have not been so chary of admitting it. In civil cases the courts will admit evidence of similar facts if it is logically probative, that is, if it is logically relevant in determining the matter which is in issue; provided that it is not oppressive or unfair to the other side; and also that the other side has fair notice of it and is able to deal with it.
>
> (at 127)

Although a court, considering whether to admit such evidence, will follow a broadly similar balancing process to that which used to be employed in criminal courts prior to the 2003 Act when deciding whether to admit 'similar fact evidence', the standard of admissibility is likely to be lower and the court will not think in terms of prejudice to the defendant, but in more general terms of oppression, unfairness and the necessity of furthering the fundamental procedural *desiderata* laid down in the Civil Procedure Rules.

7.154 The civil courts' approach to evidence of similar facts was reviewed by the House of Lords in *O'Brien v Chief Constable of South Wales Police* [2005] 2 AC 534. In *O'Brien*, the House of Lords was concerned to explain how the courts propose integrating into the civil similar fact evidence rules those case management objectives which form the key element of the Civil Procedure Rules. O had brought proceedings against the South Wales Police for misfeasance in public office and malicious prosecution, following the quashing of his 1988 murder conviction. O, who had wrongly spent 11 years behind bars, sought aggravated and exemplary damages in recompense for the despicable treatment meted out to him. In brief, he claimed that he had been framed. A detective inspector, L, was said to have been primarily responsible for fabricating a case against O, whilst a more senior officer, C, had connived with L by giving either express or tacit approval to what was taking place. As part of his case, O wished to introduce evidence of two further trials, which had taken place in 1983 and 1990, that had involved the same investigating officer, and in which similar oppressive misconduct had occurred. L, it was alleged, had engaged in similarly imaginative police work on both occasions, whereas his superior, C, had misconducted himself in like fashion on one of those occasions. The question raised on appeal was, in light of the CPR's overriding objective what is the test of admissibility for similar fact evidence in civil cases today?

7.155 The House of Lords laid down a two-stage test for determining the admissibility of similar fact evidence in civil cases. Initially, in order for it to be considered potentially admissible a party had merely to show that the other misconduct evidence possessed a similar degree of relevance to that demanded of evidence in any other context. In his brief speech, Lord Bingham of Cornhill declared that 'relevance', which simply signifies evidence that is either logically probative or disprobative of a fact which requires proof, ought not to diverge more than is necessary from the logical thought processes of 'rational, objective, fair-minded people called upon to decide questions of fact in other contexts where reaching the right answer matters' (at [4]). Once the similar fact evidence has surmounted this initial hurdle, the case management judge or the trial judge is then left with the sometimes 'finely balanced judgment' to promote the ends of justice, taking a decision that is designed not only to arrive at the correct answer, but also to ensure that it is achieved by a trial process that is fair to all parties. (Although the case management judge may have to anticipate matters, making what Lord Bingham called a 'proleptic ruling in principle on admissibility', the ultimate decision must rest with the trial judge, who bears overall responsibility for the fairness of the trial.) Besides relying upon the intrinsic importance of the evidence itself in the quest for the right answer, the party seeking its admission, as in *O'Brien*, may also urge public interest factors such as the desirability of exposing official misfeasance and protecting the integrity of the criminal trial process, the vindication of an individual's reputation, and the public righting of public wrongs. As against these considerations, the judge will need to weigh such countervailing matters as the problems posed when collateral issues require being determined in a case, the potential for prejudice when other misconduct is introduced, and the burden that similar fact evidence can lay upon a resisting party:

> [T]he burden in time, cost and personnel resources...giving disclosure; the lengthening of the trial, with the increased cost and stress inevitably involved; the potential prejudice to witnesses called upon to recall matters long closed, or thought to be closed; the loss of documentation; the fading of recollections.
>
> (at [6])

The case management dimension of similar fact evidence in civil cases is new, if unremarkable. However, it is meant to contribute to the attainment of the 'over-riding objective' set out in Part 1 of the Civil Procedure Rules: namely, the saving of expense, the treating of cases in accordance with their importance and complexity, their expeditious but fair handling, and the overall consideration of the proper allocation of the court's resources.

FURTHER READING

Criminal bad character evidence

Laudan & Allen, 'The Devastating Effect of Prior Crimes Evidence—and Other Myths of the Criminal Justice Process' (2010) http://ssrn.com/abstract=1670999

Lloyd-Bostock, 'The Effects on Lay Magistrates of Hearing that the Defendant is of "Good Character", Being Left to Speculate, or Hearing that he has a Previous Conviction' [2006] Crim LR 189

Mirfield, 'Character and Credibility' [2009] Crim LR 135

Munday, 'Handling the Evidential Exception' [1987] Crim LR 345

Munday, 'What Constitutes "Other Reprehensible Behaviour" under the Bad Character Provisions of the Criminal Justice Act 2003?' [2005] Crim LR 24

Munday, 'Bad Character Rules and Riddles: "Explanatory Notes" and True Meanings of Section 103(1) of the Criminal Justice Act 2003' [2005] Crim LR 337

Munday, 'Cut-Throat Defences and the "Propensity to be Untruthful" under Section 104 of the Criminal Justice Act 2003' [2005] Crim LR 624

Munday, ' "Round up the Usual Suspects!" or What We have to Fear from Part II of the Criminal Justice Act 2003' (2005) 169 JP Jo 328

Munday, 'The Purposes of Gateway (g): Yet Another Problematic of the Criminal Justice Act 2003' [2006] Crim LR 300

Munday, 'Misconduct that "has to do with the alleged facts of the offence with which the defendant is charged"...More or Less' [2008] J Crim Law 214

Munday, 'Single-Act Propensity' [2010] J Crim Law 128

Perry and Weimann-Saks, 'Stealing Sunshine', 73 Law & Contemporary Problems (2011) forthcoming; also http://papers.ssrn.com/sol3/papers.cfm?abstract_id=1611558

Redmayne, 'Recognising Propensity' [2011] Crim LR 177

Spencer, *Evidence of Bad Character* (2006: Hart Publishing)

Tapper, 'The Criminal Justice Act 2003: Evidence of Bad Character' [2004] Crim LR 533

Civil similar fact evidence

Munday, 'Case Management, Similar Fact Evidence in Civil Cases, and a Divided Law of Evidence [2006] 10 E & P 81

SELF-TEST QUESTIONS

1. Why would a criminal justice system wish generally to exclude evidence of an accused's misconduct on other occasions?

2. What do you understand by:

   (a) 'important explanatory evidence';

   (b) 'reprehensible behaviour';

   (c) 'an important matter in issue between the defendant and the prosecution'; and

   (d) 'evidence to correct a false impression given by the defendant'?

3. Dolly, who is on trial for handling stolen goods, currently works as a masseuse in Soho. She has three convictions for soliciting. Before she begins her testimony, the trial judge notices that Dolly is wearing a lapel badge indicating that she regularly gives blood, and, in the presence of the jury, she is asked to remove it. In her evidence-in-chief Dolly falsely claims that she is employed as a lay sister and also acts as a part-time marriage counsellor. Prosecuting counsel applies to cross-examine Dolly on her criminal record on the ground that she has created 'a false impression' within the meaning of the Criminal Justice Act 2003, s 101(1)(f). Discuss.

4. Herbert, who has a criminal record made up largely of sexual offences, is on trial for armed robbery. In response to the question 'How would you describe Herbert's general reputation in the community?', which is put by Herbert's counsel in cross-examination to Gripe, a prosecution witness, Gripe declares: 'Well, I would emphasise that Herbert has an unblemished reputation. He is kind to old ladies, is a pillar of society, and is committed 110 per cent to good works.' At the close of this cross-examination, Herbert's counsel says to the judge, in open court: 'Obviously, my client wishes unreservedly to disassociate himself from this fulsome and, frankly, embarrassing testimonial from Gripe. Herbert would be the last person to describe himself in these terms.' Discuss.

5. Bob, a builder, is on trial for theft of a bulldozer. Because Ram, the owner of the bulldozer, is now deceased, his evidence is admitted in the form of a written statement

under the Criminal Justice Act 2003, s 116. In his testimony Bob claims that Ram originally stole the vehicle from Bob. The judge not only allows the Crown to cross-examine Bob on his convictions for theft and prison mutiny, but allows the prosecution to bring out the fact that the earlier theft conviction related to other earth-moving equipment. Discuss.

6. Rag, Tag and Bobtail, three animal rights fanatics, are jointly charged with causing criminal damage with intent to endanger life contrary to the Criminal Damage Act 1971, s 1(2). Rag, in evidence, claims that Tag and Bobtail were responsible for the damage. Tag applies to cross-examine Rag on his previous convictions for perjury and perverting the course of justice. Bobtail applies for leave to call a psychologist who has examined all three co-accused and who will be prepared to testify that whereas Bobtail is an easy-going, pacific and tolerant character with excellent impulse control, Rag is an irascible, violent, impulsive and quick-tempered person who employs aggressive language and has an overpowering urge to dominate all those around him. Discuss.

7. When is evidence of an accused's previous acquittals admissible in evidence?

8. Hanzon, a faith healer, is charged in the Crown Court with handling three boxes of surgical stockings on 10 January 2011 knowing or believing them to be stolen contrary to the Theft Act 1968, s 22. The prosecution wish to adduce evidence that:

(i) in 2006 Hanzon was convicted of theft;

(ii) in 2007 Hanzon was convicted of dishonestly diverting electricity contrary to the Theft Act 1968, s 13;

(iii) in 2008 Hanzon was convicted of taking Rita's invalid tricycle without authority contrary to the Theft Act 1968, s 12;

(iv) on 21 January 2011 the police found Hanzon in possession of a fourth box of surgical stockings, stolen the previous day from a local warehouse.

Discuss the following.

(a) How much of this evidence is likely to be admitted?

(b) What direction ought the judge to give to the jury on the purpose for which such evidence is admitted?

(c) Will the prosecution be permitted to introduce in evidence that Hanzon's 2006 conviction relates to the theft of a consignment of surgical trusses?

(d) Would any of your answers be different if Hanzon's defence to the handling charge is that he purchased the surgical stockings knowing that they were stolen but, when arrested, he was on his way to the local hospital to which the stockings belonged hoping to receive a reward for their safe return?

(e) Would your answer be different if the indictment charged Hanzon with one count of handling and another of attempting to pervert the course of justice (following an attempt to bribe the investigating police officer)?

9. In *Michelson v US*, 335 US 469, 486 (1948) Justice Jackson said of American law: 'We concur in the general opinion of courts, text writers, and the profession that much of this law [concerning the exclusion of defendants' bad character] is archaic, paradoxical, and full of compromises and compensations by which an irrational advantage to one side is offset by a poorly reasoned counter-privilege to the other. But somehow it has proved a workable, even if clumsy, system when moderated by discretionary controls in the hands of a wise and strong trial court.'

   To what extent are these remarks applicable today to English law's rules governing the admission of evidence of a defendant's bad character?

8

The opinion rule and the presentation of expert evidence

SUMMARY

The general rule excluding evidence of opinion

Four exceptions to the opinion rule born of necessity

The principal exception to the opinion rule: expert opinion

- Who may qualify as an expert witness?
- Matters on which an expert may deliver opinion evidence
- The expert's field of expertise
- Particular problems posed by opinion evidence proffered by psychiatrists, psychologists, *et simil*
- Cut-throat defences and psychological and psychiatric opinion evidence
- The expert witness and the ultimate issue
- Experts do not testify only to matters of opinion
- Expert evidence and the hearsay rule
- Expert opinion evidence in civil cases
- Expert opinion evidence in criminal cases

Scientific evidence: the presentation of DNA evidence

Scientific evidence: the presentation of Bayes theorem and instructing the jury in mathematical probabilities

We find these pearls of wisdom emanating from the mouth of one whose testimony was being adduced to assist the court and whom we must presume, from the very nature of his profession, has accepted the Hippocratic Oath which, as we all know, is the foundation of medical ethics. In response to the question:

"Is that your conclusion that this man is a malingerer?"

Dr Unsworth responded:

"I wouldn't be testifying if I didn't think so, unless I was on the other side, then it would be post-traumatic condition."

> *Ladner v Higgins*, 71 So 2d 242, 244 (La 1954) *per* Judge Regan

The general rule excluding evidence of opinion

8.1 The so-called 'opinion rule' is one of the major exclusionary rules of the law of evidence. The law draws an important distinction between matters of fact and matters of opinion and, in essence, provides that witnesses may not give evidence of their opinions, but must confine their testimony to matters of fact. To give an example, if W has witnessed a road accident which leads to D being charged with causing death by reckless driving, at D's trial W may describe what she saw. She can relate that she observed a silver Ford RS Turbo, which was being driven at high speed down the middle of the road by a gesticulating man absorbed in conversation on a mobile phone, slam into a child on a pedestrian crossing. She may not, however, tell the court that she thinks that D was driving the car recklessly.

8.2 Why does the law exclude evidence of opinion? Two reasons are commonly put forward.

- It is said that a witness's opinion is simply not relevant. To stay with the example given above, it is not to the point that W may think that D had been driving recklessly. The sole question is whether *the court* forms the opinion that he was.

- A second reason for excluding evidence of opinion is said to be the fear that, unless witnesses are forbidden from stating their opinions, they may unduly influence and even usurp the role of the jury or tribunal of fact. If W were permitted to say in court, 'D was driving his car recklessly', it could appear that W rather than the jury was resolving the ultimate issue in the case.

Neither reason is entirely persuasive, but one can see that a certain crude logic underlies this exclusionary principle.

Four exceptions to the opinion rule born of necessity

8.3 The exclusionary principle proceeds upon two assumptions, neither of which is true in all circumstances. It also assumes that a crisp distinction can be drawn between fact and opinion. Whilst the distinction can often be drawn with confidence, this is not always so. There are situations where, inevitably, a witness's factual evidence will be tainted by an element of opinion. Consequently, the opinion rule is subject to four major exceptions that enable ordinary witnesses, as a matter of necessity, to give evidence which may be coloured with their opinions.

- *Evidence of identity*—Whether identifying persons or things, a witness is likely to be expressing a view that he believes that what he is identifying now is what he saw on some previous occasion. As Parke B remarked in *Fryer v Gathercole* (1849) 13 Jur 542:

  In the identification of a person you compare in your mind the man you have seen with the man you see at the trial. The same rule belongs to every species of identification.

  It is a statement inevitably contaminated with an element of opinion. Since it would otherwise prove impossible to adduce evidence of identification, the law has little option but to allow this important exception to the general exclusionary rule.

- *Evidence of a witness's own feelings, mental or physical condition*—A witness may give evidence on such matters because it is something of which he was conscious and is not based upon inference. But a witness may equally express an opinion as to what particular words a party utters may have meant, if they happen not to bear their ordinary meaning. Thus, in *Hendy* (1850), 4 Cox CC 243, a witness who received a letter from H warning him 'You will suffer as before' was permitted to express his view that this meant that the writer was threatening to burn his house down.

- *Handwriting proved by non-expert*—Where handwriting is disputed in criminal cases, it has been held that parties will be expected to call expert evidence to assist the court (*Tilley* (1961) 45 Cr App R 360). Indeed, if there is a risk that a jury may make comparisons in the absence of expert evidence, it should be warned against so doing (*O'Sullivan* [1969] 2 All ER 237). Section 8 of the Criminal Procedure Act 1865, however, simply states that 'comparison of a disputed writing...shall be permitted to be made by witnesses'. Thus, strictly speaking, even in criminal proceedings, if the evidence is undisputed, handwriting may be proved by witnesses who are not experts.

In civil cases, too, a lay witness familiar with a person's writing may be called to give his opinion on handwriting. Indeed, in one fairly recent civil case, involving an allegedly forged will, unusually the court preferred the opinions of the lay witnesses, who maintained that the will was not a forgery, to that of the professional handwriting expert, who thought the opposite (*Fuller v Strum* [2001] WTLR 677; reversed on other grounds: [2002] 1 WLR 1097). Whilst the Chancery Court felt entitled to take this step in a case involving handwriting, courts are most unlikely to do so in cases involving subjects where the scientific expertise laid before the court is less impressionistic and susceptible to error than handwriting evidence. As Jules Sher QC explained:

> Some expert evidence may amount to no more than the drawing of inferences from facts observable as much by the expert as by a lay witness; and the inferences to be drawn from those facts may be capable of being drawn as much by the expert as by a lay witness. Of course, in such a case, the views of the expert are entitled to be given great weight. After all, the expert's training and experience will have equipped him or her to draw these inferences. But in relation to this type of expert evidence the judge...is entitled to form his own view, having regard to, and balancing, the other evidence available to him in the case.

- *Matters of impression and narrative*—Witnesses may inform the court of the impressions created in their minds by people and events, even though they contain within them elements of opinion. Therefore, a witness can say, 'She was in her mid-twenties', 'He was of athletic build', or even that he felt a person was unfit to drive, provided that the witness also states the facts on which that opinion is based (*Davies* [1962] 1 WLR 1111).

More generally, under s 3(2) of the Civil Evidence Act 1972, a witness in a civil case may state his non-expert opinion on any relevant matter provided that the statement is 'made as a way of conveying relevant facts personally received by him'. Hence, in *Rasool v West Midlands Passenger Transport Executive* [1974] 3 All ER 638, although Finer J had heard no separate argument on this point and made no reference to s 3(2), a witness recounting a traffic accident was rightly permitted to comment that 'the bus driver was in no way to blame' for the accident since the plaintiff had walked straight into the road without looking either way and without using the pedestrian crossing.

The principal exception to the opinion rule: expert opinion

8.4 Although the law notionally proceeds upon the basis that witnesses testify to the facts from which the court then determines what inferences to draw, many questions will fall outside the court's experience and competence. For this reason, the major exception to the opinion rule is that in matters falling outside the ordinary knowledge of the court, opinions may be received from witnesses who are expert in the relevant field. To take an elementary example, if in a murder case witnesses state where the body was found, its temperature, its state of *rigor mortis*, relevant weather conditions and so on, a jury will not be qualified to form an opinion on the possible time of death. Hence, the need to call a pathologist to give an expert opinion on this question, founded on the proven facts. As Lawton LJ commented in *Turner* [1975] QB 834:

> An expert's opinion is admissible to furnish the court with scientific information which is likely to be outside the experience and knowledge of a judge or jury. If on the proven facts a judge or jury can form their own conclusions without help, then the opinion of an expert is unnecessary.
>
> (at 841)

Expert testimony, it needs hardly to be said, is only strictly admissible in relation to matters of fact, not on what are properly questions of law. In *Cockburn* [2008] 2 WLR 1277, for example, where C was charged with setting a mantrap with intent contrary to s 31 of the Offences against the Person Act 1861, Sir Igor Judge P accepted that expert engineering evidence might well have been admissible to show the jury how the contraption worked but expressed reservations as to whether it had been properly admitted to show whether or not that contraption was capable of being an engine 'calculated to destroy human life or inflict grievous bodily harm', as required by the terms of the statute (at [4]).

8.5 Experts are called to testify on any number of matters. In addition to representatives of 'the old-established academically-based sciences such as medicine, geology or metallurgy, and the established professions such as architecture, quantity surveying or engineering', and handwriting and fingerprint experts, amongst the more colourful experts who have appeared in recent times one could mention the following: facial mappers (*Stockwell* (1993) 97 Cr App R 260); an expert in the recognition of Renault 25s (*Browning* (1991) 94 Cr App R 109); a podiatrist expert in gait analysis—in April 2008 John Rigg, who walked bow-legged like John Wayne, was convicted of burglary, partly on the evidence of such a medical expert (*The Times* (2008) 15 April) (see also *Otway* [2011] EWCA Crim 03); experts in the social habits of dolphins, called to testify in a case of outraging public decency through the commission of lewd acts with a bottle-nose dolphin (*Cooper* (1991) Times, 13 December); Pete Townshend, lead guitarist with The Who, who appeared as an expert on the musicianship of a tenor pop saxophonist injured in the 1989 *Marchioness* disaster (*The Guardian*, 19 March 1997); and phoneticians expert in voice identification (*Robb* (1991) 93 Cr App R 161). Nothing, however, is fixed in stone: 'Today's orthodoxy may become tomorrow's outdated learning' (*Holdsworth* (2008) 102 BMLR 112 at [57] *per* Toulson LJ).

8.6 English courts are generally rather receptive to new varieties of expertise. In *Stockwell*, Lord Taylor CJ approved the trial judge's observation that in this field 'one should not set one's face against fresh developments, provided that they have a proper foundation'. However, new areas of 'learning' are sometimes considered too speculative—for instance, in *Stagg* (1994) 14 September, unreported (Central Criminal Court) Ognall J remarked that a prosecutor would face formidable difficulties in showing that psychological profiling evidence ought to be recognised as expert evidence. Again, in *Gilfoyle* [2001] 2 Cr App R 57, a troubling murder case, the Court of Appeal rejected psychological evidence from a prominent expert in criminal psychology which purportedly could have assisted the court in determining whether the victim's alleged suicide note was genuine or questionable. The psychologist had never embarked upon such a task before; there was no substantial body of academic writing approving his methodology—which provoked the Court to remark that unstructured and speculative conclusions were not the stuff of which admissible expert evidence was made; and it was doubtful whether assessing levels of happiness or unhappiness, which lay at the root of his analysis, was a task for an expert rather than for the jurors. In contrast, in *Dallagher* [2003] 1 Cr App R 195, another murder case, the courts were presented with the novelty of two experts in earprints, a Dutch police officer with ten years' experience of earprints and the Glasgow Regius Professor of Forensic Medicine, who each testified that in their opinions left and right earprints left on window glass at the scene of crime were either surely, or highly probably, those of D. Earprint researchers were thin on the ground, the subject being in its infancy. Although fresh expert evidence submitted on appeal cast doubt on the reliability of techniques of identification by earprints, the Court of Appeal once again demonstrated English law's comparatively relaxed attitude to the admission of new, barely tested scientific techniques. D's conviction was quashed and a new trial ordered, owing to the fact that the fresh evidence proffered by defence experts might reasonably have affected the jury's decision. (At the retrial in January 2004 the prosecution offered no evidence, and a formal verdict of not guilty was entered.) However, the notable point remains that for Kennedy LJ the acid test of admissibility of expert opinion evidence was that proposed in *Cross on Evidence* (1999, 9th edn) to the effect that:

> ...so long as the field is sufficiently well-established to pass the ordinary tests of relevance and reliability, then no enhanced test of admissibility should be applied, but the weight of the evidence should be established by the same adversarial forensic techniques applicable elsewhere.
>
> (at 523)

The limitations of new forms of scientific evidence need always to be borne in mind. In *London Borough of Richmond v B* [2010] EWHC 2903 (Fam), for instance, in care proceedings the court considered the admissibility of evidence of hair strand analysis for the purpose of detecting whether a mother was a drinker. Since this science is in its infancy and is known to have serious limitations, the evidence was held only to be admissible as part of the overall evidential picture and could only be used to ascertain whether or not the results were consistent with chronic excessive alcohol consumption. For other purposes—for instance, to determine whether the mother was a moderate drinker or even a teetotaller—detection of the presence of ethyl glucuronide and fatty acid ethyl esters was simply not a sufficiently reliable indicator.

Who may qualify as an expert witness?

8.7 *It is for the judge to determine whether a particular witness can demonstrate sufficient competence within his field to be treated as an expert and to be permitted to give evidence of his opinion.* This will frequently mean that the witness will show the court that he or she possesses relevant professional qualifications. However, the courts are not unduly strict on this point. In *Silverlock* [1894] 2 QB 766 a solicitor who whiled away his leisure hours in the private study of handwriting was allowed to testify as an expert on handwriting. Similarly, in *Oakley* [1979] Crim LR 657 a policeman who had served in the traffic division for 15 years, who had passed a qualifying examination as a traffic investigator and who had attended more than four hundred road accidents was allowed to give an expert opinion on the likely cause of a collision. In *Dallagher*, the earprint case (*ante*, para **8.6**), the Dutch police officer who was allowed to testify as an expert had no formal qualifications but had ten years' experience of earprints, had assembled an archive of six hundred photographs and three hundred earprints, and was conversant with the available literature. The essential question in all these cases is whether study and experience will give a witness's opinion an authority that the opinion of one not so qualified would lack and, if so, whether the witness is skilled and possesses an adequate knowledge.

8.8 More generally, and particularly when a witness's evidence invokes a new or still developing area of scientific endeavour or technical expertise, the court will be required to adjudicate upon whether that particular discipline qualifies as a recognised expertise entitling the witness to testify as an expert. Not so long ago, the Court of Appeal considered the status of evidence given by lip-readers. In *Luttrell* [2004] 2 Cr App R 31, in two conjoined appeals the admissibility of lip-reading evidence of words allegedly spoken by the accused, captured on videotape, was contested. The general principles affecting the admissibility of expert evidence were consequently considered by the court. As Rose LJ explained, two conditions require to be met in order for expert evidence to become admissible:

- *firstly*, it must be demonstrated that study or experience will give a witness's opinion an authority which the opinion of one not so qualified will lack; and

- *secondly*, the witness must be so qualified to express that opinion.

In elucidating the first principle, Rose LJ quoted from King CJ's judgment in the Australian decision of *Bonython* [1984] 38 SASR 45, where it was said:

> [the first condition] may be divided into two parts:
>
> (a) whether the subject matter of the opinion is such that a person without instruction or experience in the area of knowledge or human experience would be able to form a sound judgment on the matter without the assistance of witnesses possessing special knowledge or experience in the area, and
>
> (b) whether the subject matter of the opinion forms part of a body of knowledge or experience which is sufficiently organised or recognised to be accepted as a reliable body of knowledge or experience, a special acquaintance with which by the witness would render his opinion of assistance to the court.
>
> (at 46)

In *Luttrell*, the appellants contended that a further third condition ought to apply: namely, that evidence ought not to be admitted unless it passed a further test, that the evidence can be seen to be reliable because the methods used are sufficiently explained to be tested in cross-examination, and therefore to be verifiable or falsifiable. The problem with lip-reading, it was argued, was its inherent unreliability and the difficulty of judging how accurate or inaccurate it happened to be in any given case. As the court conceded, in the case of lip-reading,

> the information from visible sources is incomplete . . . so speech reading inevitably involves inference from incomplete information. . . . Even the best speech readers achieve only up to 80% correctness when the words are presented in clearly spoken sentences.
>
> (at [30])

Nevertheless, it concluded that whilst such a factor could enter into a judge's calculations when deciding whether to exclude evidence under s 78 of PACE, otherwise it was not a condition of admissibility:

> In established fields of science, the court may take the view that expert evidence would fall beyond the recognised limits of the field or that methods are too unconventional to be regarded as subject to the scientific discipline [see, eg, *Gilfoyle*, *ante*, para **8.6**]. But a skill or expertise can be recognised and respected, and thus satisfy the conditions for admissible expert evidence, although the discipline is not susceptible to this sort of scientific discipline. Thus, in *In re Pinion decd* [1965] Ch 85 the court was willing, indeed felt obliged, to hear expert evidence on the question whether a collection of paintings and other objects had aesthetic worth so that their display would be of educational value and for the public benefit, notwithstanding, as Harman LJ observed, *'de gustibus non est disputandum'*.
>
> (at [34])

Applying the two conventional principles, therefore, Rose LJ upheld both trial judges' decisions to admit the lip-readers' evidence. Although such cases are likely to be fact-sensitive, admissibility being contingent upon such factors as the quality of the video recording and the skill of the lip-reader, and although the number of qualified readers is comparatively small (in this country four *in toto*, it was thought), lip-reading is a sufficiently well-recognised discipline for such evidence to be treated as admissible and for the weight of the evidence then to be assessed by the customary adversarial forensic techniques applicable elsewhere in the law of evidence (see *post*, para **12.22**).

8.9 When deciding whether to allow a particular witness to testify as an expert, the courts will not necessarily refuse to admit an expert whose approach to his subject is contentious in the sense that it does not coincide with the received wisdom in the field. Thus, in *Robb* (1991) 93 Cr App R 161, a kidnapping case, an expert on phonetics was called to lend expert assistance on the issue of voice identification. Contrary to 'the great weight of informed opinion, including the world leaders in the field', this particular phonetician used exclusively auditory techniques unverified by acoustic analysis. Most phoneticians would consider that such a technique affords an unreliable basis upon which to identify a speaker. Although his approach to voice identification may have been unconventional in phonetic circles, the Court of Appeal nevertheless held that since R had had 'ample opportunity to meet and rebut' the expert's evidence, no objection could be taken to the fact that his methods were not those adopted by the majority of phoneticians. (It might be noted that the Northern Irish Court of Appeal subsequently declined to follow this decision in *O'Doherty* [2003] 1 Cr App R 5, taking the view that, save in certain exceptional cases, in the present state of scientific knowledge no prosecution ought to proceed in Northern Ireland in which the Crown relies predominantly on auditory analysis of voice samples. In *Flynn and St John* [2008] 2 Cr App R 20 at [62] the English Court of Appeal confirmed that it was 'neither possible nor desirable' to go as far as its Northern Irish counterpart in excluding expert auditory evidence unless accompanied by expert evidence of acoustic analysis.)

8.10 The comparative ease with which witnesses may be admitted as experts by English courts should not necessarily be thought too alarming. A witness's credentials can be investigated during cross-examination and a paucity of qualifications will result in less weight being given by the court to the witness's opinions. Although the criteria the court applies are relatively relaxed, a witness must still demonstrate a modicum of relevant competence. In *Southwark LBC v Simpson* (1998) 31 HLR 725, Lord Bingham CJ held that although an expert witness did not actually need a medical qualification to testify as to whether a nuisance was prejudicial to health, he did need to have some relevant experience. Therefore, a chartered surveyor who had merely read some articles about damp problems similar to those in the case simply did not make the grade.

8.11 The reliability of some expert evidence laid before criminal courts in recent times has nevertheless aroused concern. Responding to this, in 2009 the Law Commission consulted on *The Admissibility of Expert Evidence in Criminal Proceedings* (CP no 190). In order to combat the lack of peer review in some new scientific disciplines and to allay doubts surrounding the validity of the methodologies employed, it proposed introducing a statutory test for determining the admissibility of expert evidence in criminal proceedings, along with a list of guidelines designed to assist courts in deciding whether particular proffered expert evidence is up to scratch.

Matters on which an expert may deliver opinion evidence

8.12 *An expert may only give an opinion on matters that fall within his particular field of competence.* If a question falls outside the scope of a witness's particular expertise, the opinion ought not to be received. In *Nightingale v Biffen* (1925) 18 BWCC 358, a workmen's compensation case in which the court had to determine a medical question—did the plaintiff contract arsenic poisoning whilst working in his employer's sheep dip?—the court ruled inadmissible the opinion of a research student in toxicology, because he was not medically qualified. In similar vein, in *Cook* [1982] Crim LR 670 C's murder conviction was reduced to one of manslaughter because a doctor expressed what he admitted to be only a *personal* opinion that the blows inflicted upon the victim were not consistent with the assailant having been in a frenzy and hence were inconsistent with C's defence of provocation. Not surprisingly, the cases hold that the expert witness's testimony is to be confined to his professional, *expert* opinion. Personal impressions and opinions are not received under this exception.

The expert's field of expertise

8.13 *The expert's field of expertise must fall outside the ordinary knowledge of the court.* Since the exception which allows experts to give evidence of opinion is justified by the fact that there are matters on which the tribunal of fact is unable to form its own authoritative view, an expert's opinion will not be received on matters where it is felt that the court is perfectly capable of drawing inferences for itself. In matters of ordinary occurrence, therefore, on which ordinary people are qualified to form their own opinions, expert opinion evidence will be excluded. In *Land* [1999] QB 65, L was charged with possessing indecent photographs of an unidentified child. The question was whether the child portrayed in the pictures was under the age of

16. The Court of Appeal held that expert paediatric evidence was unnecessary on this issue because the jury was as well placed as a paediatrician would have been to assess whether someone was under or over the age of 16. For similar reasons, in *esure Ins Ltd v Direct Line Ins plc* [2008] Bus LR 438 it was doubted that a branding consultant possessed the necessary expertise to testify on the likelihood of public confusion in a trade mark registration case. As Butler-Sloss LJ said in *Re M and R (minors)* [1996] 4 All ER 239, in explaining why expert evidence had been excluded in another case involving child abuse:

> The reason for that lay in the fact that the primary evidence did not involve technical matters (such as length of skid marks) that required expert interpretation, but simply the evaluation of eyewitness accounts, on which the so-called expert had nothing to contribute that was outside the competence and expertise of a layman. *His evidence was inadmissible because it was not relevant.*
>
> (at 253: emphasis added)

Finally, in *Ugoh* [2001] EWCA Crim 1381, three defendants were charged with conspiring to rape a female student whom they had encountered in the street in a drunken state. The central issues in the case were whether she had in fact given consent and, assuming that not to be so, whether the defendants knew that she had not consented. Mance LJ held that the trial judge had wrongly allowed a psycho-pharmacologist to give evidence. This expert witness had testified on the effects alcohol produces on the brain and on human behaviour, and had implied in his evidence that he thought that the defendants ought to have known from her behaviour that the victim was not in fact consenting. In the view of the court, which quashed the convictions, this was not a matter on which a jury would have needed to hear an expert opinion:

> The appellants were normal young men, not themselves under the influence of drink or drugs, whose ability or inability to appreciate the complainant's inability to consent was a matter for the jury to assess. Their age, inexperience, tiredness or desires at 3 am on a Saturday night or early Sunday morning were all matters for the jury to assess.
>
> (at [20])

8.14 In addition to falling outside the ken of the average juror or member of the tribunal of fact, the court must also be persuaded that the matter on which the expert is called to testify is within a field in which recognised opinions are validly held. The Civil Evidence Act 1972, s 3 states that expert evidence may be admitted 'on any relevant matter on which [the expert witness] is qualified to give expert evidence', 'relevant' in this context being taken to mean 'helpful' to the court. In the leading case of *Midland Bank Trust Co Ltd v Hett Stubbs & Kemp* [1979] Ch 384, Oliver J rejected expert evidence proffered by legal practitioners on the scope of solicitors' duties when engaged in conveyancing transactions precisely because there was no objective yardstick to which appeal could be made:

> I doubt the value, or even the admissibility, of this sort of evidence...The extent of the legal duty in any given situation must...be a question of law for the Court. Clearly if there is some practice in a particular profession, *some accepted standard of conduct which is* laid down by a professional institute or *sanctioned by common usage*, evidence of that can and ought to be received. But evidence which really amounts to no more than an expression of opinion by a particular practitioner of what he thinks that he would have done had he been placed, hypothetically and without the benefit of hindsight, in the position of the defendants, is of little assistance to the court...
>
> (at 402: emphasis added)

It will sometimes be difficult to distinguish between accepted standards of conduct laid down by an institution or established by common usage and questions that simply turn on the reasonableness of business conduct in specific situations. Oliver J's decision in *Midland Bank Trust Co Ltd* can be contrasted with Evans-Lombe J's judgment in *Barings plc v Coopers & Lybrand* [2001] PNLR 22 at [47], a case arising out of the mind-boggling losses registered by Barings when their employee, L, engaged in increasingly wild derivatives trading, which eventually led to the collapse of that bank. In admitting expert testimony addressing the question, whether a competent derivatives manager, examining the size and profitability of L's reported trading, should have realised that the patterns of risk and reward observed were incredible or, at the very least, so unusual as to merit extensive and detailed examination, Evans-Lombe J found that there did exist a body of expertise with recognised standards in relation to the managers of investment banks conducting or administering the highly technical and specialised business of futures and derivatives trading. His decision was heavily influenced by the fact that traders in futures and derivatives are required to be licensed by a regulator and may be made answerable before a disciplinary tribunal for failure to comply with ordained professional standards of conduct.

Particular problems posed by opinion evidence proffered by psychiatrists, psychologists, *et simil*

8.15 This seemingly inoffensive principle that the expert's opinion must relate to something outside the ordinary ken of the average juror has sometimes posed acute problems when parties have tried to adduce evidence of psychologists and psychiatrists. In one of the best known of the cases illustrating this phenomenon, *Turner* [1975] QB 834, T's defence to a charge of murdering his girlfriend was one of provocation. After she had made certain admissions to him, he claimed to have lost his self-control and beaten her to death in a frenzy with a hammer. The Court of Appeal upheld the trial judge's refusal to allow a psychiatrist to testify to the likelihood of someone reacting as T, who was not mentally disordered or abnormal in any way, had done to the news that his girlfriend had been seeing other men whilst T was in prison, had earned money by this means, and was now pregnant. The court added, for good measure:

> Jurors do not need psychiatrists to tell them how ordinary folk who are not suffering from any mental illness are likely to react to the stresses and strains of life.

Similarly, in *Chard* (1971) 56 Cr App R 268, C, who was charged with murder, wished to call a prison doctor to say that at the time of the offence he considered that C had no intent to kill. Roskill LJ held that it was 'not permissible to call a witness, whatever his personal experience, merely to tell the jury how he thinks an accused man's mind—assumedly a normal mind—operated at the time of the alleged crime with reference to the crucial question of what that man's intention was'.

8.16 In *Turner*, Lawton LJ also rejected the argument that the psychiatrist's evidence should have been admitted simply to assist the jury on the issue of T's credibility, stating:

> [T] had to be judged as someone who was not mentally disordered. That is what juries are empanelled to do. The law assumes they can perform their duties properly. The jury . . . did not need . . . the evidence of a psychiatrist to help them decide whether the defendant's evidence was truthful.
>
> (at p 842)

This theme was taken up by Lord Taylor CJ in *Robinson* (1994) 98 Cr App R 370, when he declared that a party 'cannot call a witness of fact and then, without more, call a psychologist or psychiatrist to give reasons why the jury should regard that witness as reliable.' He added that even if such evidence is admitted to assist in assessing the evidence of someone who is mentally *abnormal*, 'great care would need to be taken . . . not to allow [the expert opinion] to extend to "oath-helping"'. The evident fear is that trial by psychiatrist and psychologist might otherwise come to supplant trial by jury or by magistrates.

8.17 Nevertheless, where a psychiatrist can testify to matters that truly fall outside a juror's normal range of knowledge, the evidence may be admitted. In *C* [2006] EWCA Crim 231, for example, the appellant had been convicted of a number of serious sexual offences against his daughter (V1) and her close school friend (V2) when they were aged between 10 and 15 years. At the time of trial V1 and V2 were 34 and 33 years old respectively. The prosecution revealed to C that V2 had mentioned sexual abuse for first time during a series of recent hypnotherapy sessions. C appealed against the trial judge's refusal to allow him to call an expert witness to testify to the dangers inherent in hypnotically revived memories. To the extent that evidence the expert would have given fell outside the everyday knowledge of jurors, Gage LJ held that C's expert ought to have been admitted. (On some of the problems posed by hypnotically enhanced evidence, see further R Munday (1987) 151 JP Jo 404, 426, and 452.)

8.18   *Turner* is one of a number of cases that betray a certain reserve regarding the evidence of medical witnesses who specialise in the workings of the human mind. Predictably, the relevant professions have felt aggrieved at this treatment. However, decisions like *Turner* do not mean that such witnesses' evidence will always be rejected. If the court is dealing with someone who is not normal, then the testimony of experts will be admitted. The rough-and-ready criterion the courts used to operate in determining whether such expert opinion was admissible was that if the evidence related to someone with an IQ of 69 or below (70, of course, being the lower limit of 'normal'), that person was to be considered abnormal (eg *Masih* [1986] Crim LR 395). But *Raghip* (1991) Times, 9 December and, more especially, *Ward (Judith)* (1992) 96 Cr App R 1, a notorious miscarriage of justice case resulting from a false confession that W had murdered 12 people by placing a bomb on a coach, show that the courts have moderated their position, at least when the genuineness of a confession is in question in the case. Although Glidewell LJ was at pains to stress that the court's decision was not intended as 'an open invitation to every defendant who repents of his confession to seek the aid of a psychiatrist', in *Ward* he did say that expert evidence would be admitted 'if it is to the effect that a defendant is suffering from a condition not properly described as mental illness, but from a personality disorder so severe as properly to be described as mental illness'. The *Masih* test is not dead, however. In *Henry* [2006] 1 Cr App R 6 H, who had an IQ of 71, sought to adduce fresh evidence of mental impairment to shed light on the question of intention. Maurice Kay LJ did acknowledge that, at least in cases concerned with the reliability of confessions, the courts now demonstrated a laxer attitude. However, otherwise the *Masih* test of admissibility applied:

> The cut-off point of 69 has sometimes been criticised as arbitrary but it has psychological significance and . . . it does have the advantage of being "a clean rule", even if "a rather stringent one."
>
> (at [10])

Later his Lordship added:

> Whilst it is true that persons with an IQ as low as that of the appellant form a small part of the population at large, sadly they form a somewhat larger part of those charged with criminal offences. An intention that someone should be killed is a visceral matter of no

great complexity. . . . [I]t is not a matter which, on the authorities, lends itself to expert evidence in relation to a person such as this appellant.

(at [14])

8.19 In *O'Brien, Hall and Sherwood* [2000] Crim LR 676, too, Roch LJ repeated that the abnormality to which an expert may testify need not fall within any recognised category of personality abnormality. Indeed, Roch LJ stated that the limits within which such evidence must fall in order to be admissible are that:

- the abnormality must be both one which might render the defendant's evidence or confession unreliable and which deviates significantly from the norm;
- the defendant's condition must predate his confession or testimony, as the case may be, its history must not be based solely upon the defendant's own account, and it must point to or explain his abnormality.

Additionally, the judge has to tell the jury that they are not obliged to accept the expert's view. Even if Roch LJ's judgment in *O'Brien* does go slightly beyond the earlier decision in *Ward (Judith)*, the intention was not to render such evidence freely admissible: the Court was acutely 'conscious of the need to have defined limits for the case in which expert evidence of the kind we have heard may be used'.

8.20 Whilst the *Turner* principle is now applied a little more flexibly, the admissibility of expert testimony commenting on parties' mental states remains a contentious issue. On 20 December 2000, the Court of Appeal handed down two decisions touching on this theme. In *Gilfoyle* [2001] 2 Cr App R 57, a murder case in which G claimed that his heavily pregnant wife had committed suicide, the court stated, *inter alia*, that a jury did not need a psychologist to inform them how ordinary people were likely to react to the stresses and strains of life. Meanwhile, in *S*, where a 13-year-old boy who had acted as lookout for a robbery pleaded duress, the court again held that the jury did not require a psychiatrist to tell them that S, who suffered from no kind of mental abnormality, was unusually timid or vulnerable. Before admitting such evidence too readily, courts will doubtless bear in mind Lord Hobhouse's firm, cautionary words in *Pendleton* [2002] 1 WLR 272:

[T]he courts should be cautious about admitting evidence from psychologists, however eminent, as to the credibility of witnesses. The assessment of the truth of verbal evidence is save in a very small number of exceptional circumstances a matter for the jury. The suggestibility of some persons is well within the experience of the ordinary members of juries. To admit evidence from psychologists on such questions is not only contrary to the established rules of evidence, but is also contrary to the principle of trial by jury and risks substituting trial by expert.

(at [45])

8.21 Sometimes the nature of the case will involve a highly speculative element. For instance, a series of appeals in high-profile infant death cases, such as those of *Clark (Sally)* [2003] 2 FCR 447 and *Cannings* [2004] 1 WLR 2607, has raised the question: how ought the courts to deal with situations in which experts are deeply divided on something as fundamental as the cause of death? In *Cannings*, at [178] in particular, the Court of Appeal did appear to have stated as a principle that if, in a case involving the killing of children, the trial's outcome hangs exclusively or almost exclusively on a serious disagreement between reputable experts as to cause of death, it will often be unwise or unsafe to proceed in the absence of other cogent evidence tending to support the conclusion that the infant(s) was/were deliberately harmed. As Judge LJ declared:

> [F]or the time being, where a full investigation into two or more sudden unexplained infant deaths in the same family is followed by a serious disagreement between reputable experts about the cause of death, and a body of such expert opinion concludes that natural causes, whether explained or unexplained, cannot be excluded as a reasonable (and not a fanciful) possibility, the prosecution of a parent or parents for murder should not be started or continued, unless there is additional cogent evidence, extraneous to the expert evidence... which tends to support the conclusion that the infant, or where there is more than one death, one of the infants, was deliberately harmed.... [I]f the outcome of the trial depends exclusively or almost exclusively on a serious disagreement between distinguished and reputable experts, it will often be unwise, and therefore unsafe, to proceed.
>
> (at [178])

8.22 Such a proposition would beg all sorts of questions (see excellent commentary by Walker and McCartney in [2005] Crim LR 127–30). However, as Richards LJ later pointed out in the salt-poisoning case, *Gay and Gay* [2006] EWCA Crim 820 at [100], such an interpretation of *Cannings* has been 'knocked firmly on the head by Judge LJ's judgment in *Kai-Whitewind* [2005] 2 Cr App R 31 at [73]–[91],' which stated:

> We understand that *Cannings* is being deployed in many cases by the defence as authority for different arguments running along the lines that whenever there is a genuine conflict of opinion between reputable experts, the prosecution should not proceed, or should be stopped, or that the evidence of the prosecution experts should be disregarded. If so, the single passage found in part of para. 178 in *Cannings*, taken in isolation, is being asked to sustain an unforeseen, and... inappropriate burden...
>
> ... [C]arried to its logical conclusion, the submission would mean that whenever there is a conflict between expert witnesses, the case for the prosecution must fail unless the conviction is justified by evidence independent of the expert witnesses. Put another way,

the logical conclusion of what we shall describe as the overblown *Cannings* argument is that where there is a conflict of opinion between reputable experts, the expert evidence called by the Crown is automatically neutralised. That is a startling proposition, and it is not sustained by *Cannings*.

(at [74] and [84])

As the court proceeded to explain, *Cannings* displayed special features:

In *Cannings* there was essentially no evidence beyond the inferences based on coincidence which the experts for the Crown were prepared to draw. Other reputable experts in the same specialist field took a different view about the inferences, if any, which could or should be drawn. Hence the need for additional cogent evidence.

(at [85])

These features were absent in *Kai-Whitewind*, a case involving only one infant death, where, even if the experts disputed the correct interpretation to be upon the post-mortem findings, their disputes could not diminish the significance of those findings. It was simply for the jury to evaluate the expert evidence and to take into account the findings of the post-mortem in reaching a verdict. (See also *Gian v CPS* [2009] EWCA Crim 2553 at [22] *per* Moses LJ.)

Cut-throat defences and psychological and psychiatric opinion evidence

8.23 Although in *Turner*, and other cases discussed above, the courts rejected the testimony of psychiatrists and psychologists called to explain the behaviour of parties who could be described as 'normal', just occasionally courts have admitted such evidence. This has arisen when, on rare occasions, the courts have allowed psychological or psychiatric evidence of an accused's disposition. As we saw in Chapter 7, in the context of bad character evidence, evidence of a defendant's bad disposition may be admissible if 'it is relevant to an important matter in issue between the defendant and the prosecution' or if 'it has substantial probative value in relation to an important matter in issue between the defendant and a co-defendant' (Criminal Justice Act 2003, s 101(1)(d) and (e)). Take the case of *Lowery and King v R* [1974] AC 85, an Australian appeal to the Privy Council. In *Lowery*, L and K were jointly charged with a particularly sadistic murder. The motive, it was claimed, was that the two men wanted to see what it was like to 'kill a chick'. L and K each blamed the other for the crime. L testified that he was not the sort of person to commit such a brutal offence and, indeed, claimed that he had done what he could to prevent K from doing the deed. K denied the offence and maintained that at the relevant time he was under the influence of drugs and therefore in no position to prevent

L from killing the girl. The Privy Council held that K had been properly allowed to call a psychologist to testify that while K was immature and easily led, L was callous, aggressive and sadistically inclined, thereby opining that by reason of his personality K was the less likely of the two men to have committed a vicious killing. In *Turner*, the Court of Appeal was at pains to stress that *Lowery* was a case that had been decided on its own special facts. The psychologist, who had examined both co-accused, was well placed to offer such evidence to assist the jury and, more importantly, the case involved co-defendants, one of whom, K, was being permitted directly to rebut evidence given by his co-accused, L, that by reason of his personality K was more likely to have killed the girl. At one point in his opinion Lord Morris, however, suggested that this type of evidence would generally be relevant and admissible whenever it tended to show that the version of events put forward by one co-defendant was more likely than that put forward by his co-accused. This broad proposition, although once doubted, now tallies closely with the intentions of s 101(1)(d) and (e) of the 2003 Act.

The expert witness and the ultimate issue

8.24 It used once to be thought that an expert witness could not be invited to give an opinion on 'the ultimate issue' in the case. Otherwise, it was feared, the expert would effectively usurp the role of the fact-finder; in a jury trial, for example, deciding the case for them. If strictly applied, however, an 'ultimate issue rule' could prove highly inconvenient. The law has therefore progressively distanced itself from it.

8.25 In civil cases, s 3 of the Civil Evidence Act 1972 now specifically provides that 'where a person is called as a witness in any civil proceedings, his opinion *on any relevant matter on which he is qualified to give expert evidence* shall be admissible in evidence' (cf *In the Pink Ltd v NE Lincs Council* (2005) 169 JP 385 at [9] *per* Sedley LJ). Although no similar provision governs criminal proceedings, in many criminal cases experts have been permitted to testify to the ultimate issue. As Lord Parker CJ remarked in *DPP v A & BC Chewing Gum Ltd* [1968] 1 QB 159, 164, 'although technically the final question "Do you think he was suffering from diminished responsibility?" is strictly inadmissible, it is allowed time and time again without any objection'. In *A & BC Chewing Gum* a company was prosecuted under the Obscene Publications Act 1959 for publishing cards depicting battle scenes that, it was claimed, would tend to deprave and corrupt the children who bought the gum. Although nominally upholding the ultimate issue rule, Lord Parker CJ was clearly sceptical, particularly as he acknowledged that an impermissible question asking the child psychiatrists whether specific cards would tend to deprave and corrupt children would be allowed, whatever the strict position in law might be.

In *Stockwell* (1993) 97 Cr App R 260, where a facial mapping expert was permitted to say that he thought the photographs strongly supported the view that S was the robber, the Court of Appeal declared that whilst there was a school of thought which considered that an ultimate issue rule existed, 'if there is such a prohibition, it has long been more honoured in the breach than the observance'. The rule today, then, is better regarded as a 'matter of form rather than substance'.

Experts do not testify only to matters of opinion

8.26 Although one tends to asssociate experts with this exception to the opinion rule, it should be noted that experts may also testify to matters of fact. The distinction is important as it affects the terms in which in a criminal trial the judge can direct the jury. Although the instruction does not necessarily have to follow the Judicial Studies Board specimen direction 'slavishly' in every case (*Fitzpatrick* [1999] Crim LR 832), when directing a jury the judge is entitled to tell them that whilst they will no doubt wish to have regard to the opinions expressed by an expert witness, he should also say, something along the lines 'if, having given the matter careful consideration, you do not accept the evidence of the expert, you do not have to act upon it. It is for you to decide whose evidence and whose opinions you accept (if any).' In civil cases, too, there is no rule that a judge ought to prefer the evidence of experts to that of lay witnesses: *Armstrong v First York Ltd* [2005] 1 WLR 2751.

8.27 However, whereas it may be open to the jury to reject an expert's opinions, this judicial direction is not appropriate if the expert has testified to matters of fact. Therefore, in *Anderson v R* [1972] AC 100, a murder case in which a forensic expert basically testified that he had found no human blood on A's boots, the trial judge was wrong to have told the jury that they were entitled to reject that evidence if they wished. The direction in effect invited the jurors to form an opinion in contradiction of the expert and to find a fact proven—that there was blood on the boots—in the absence of any evidence.

8.28 *Experts on foreign law.* Given its distinctly contentious subject matter, it may at first appear surprising that one variety of expert, whose role is strictly confined to testifying to fact, is the expert on foreign law. The role of such an expert before the English court is limited to giving evidence of the content of the rules of the relevant system, not to expressing a view on their application. *Hardy* [2003] EWCA Crim 3092 provides a striking example of this principle at work. The case involved a conspiracy to import large quantities of cocaine. At trial a question arose as to whether the seizure by Dutch police from an Amsterdam hotel room of bags containing cocaine with a street value of over £10m was illegal under the Dutch Criminal Code, thereby amounting to an infringement of H's right to a private life under the ECHR, Article 8. Had the seizure been unlawful, H contended that the English judge ought to have contemplated excluding the evidence under PACE, s 78. A Dutch lawyer had been called to testify before the Crown Court, who had given evidence not only as to what the relevant rules of Dutch law were but had also been allowed to express an opinion on the conclusion that the Dutch examining magistrate had reached in applying those rules to the facts of the case. As Kay LJ pointed out:

> It is clearly right that expert evidence can be given as to the law of a foreign country, as to the procedural requirements involved in that foreign country, but where at the end of the day the foreign law requires the court to make a decision on the facts, we do not see that it is any more appropriate for an expert lawyer to express his view on the facts than it is for any other witness to express a view on the facts; that task is exclusively for the fact-finding body, be it the jury or, as in this instance, the trial judge.
>
> (at [38])

Expert evidence and the hearsay rule

8.29 Much scientific work is collaborative. Scientists tend to work in teams. This can raise evidential problems. It may be, for instance, that in a criminal court an expert witness cannot personally vouch for each item of evidence upon which his opinion rests. Clearly, if the expert relies upon the truth of facts of which he has no personal knowledge, unless witnesses are called who do have such knowledge or unless the evidence falls into an exception to the hearsay rule, the expert's opinion is based upon inadmissible hearsay. From time to time the criminal courts made some effort to reduce the attendant inconveniences. The Court of Appeal drew attention to some of these in *Jackson* [1996] 2 Cr App R 420. J was charged with assault occasioning actual bodily harm. It emerged that the Crown's expert, who gave evidence of blood tests, had relied on work done by others. Strictly speaking, his evidence was therefore tainted by hearsay and those who conducted the experiments had to be called in person to establish the facts upon which the expert's opinion was founded. Because the defence stood upon its rights and refused to admit the relevant facts, the recorder allowed the prosecution to serve notice of further evidence. Two extra days of court time were taken up with hearing these witnesses' testimony. While acknowledging the fundamental premise that primary facts upon which an expert's opinion is based must be proven by admissible evidence, Holland J was not impressed by what had occurred in this case. He drew attention to s 30 of the Criminal Justice Act 1988 which permits experts' reports to be agreed and submitted in written form, admonished counsel (there were in fact three defence counsel in this case) to take points in good time, and finally warned that legal proceedings should not be conducted 'without obvious regard for cost, for time and for the patience of respectively the recorder and, more importantly, the jury'.

8.30 The situation has been eased, however, by the overriding objective (Part 1) and the expert evidence disclosure requirements (Part 33 of the Criminal Procedure Rules 2010 (SI 2010/60)), and by the Criminal Justice Act 2003, s 127, which now provides that where:

(a) a statement has been prepared for the purposes of criminal proceedings,

(b) the person who prepared the statement had or may reasonably be supposed to have had personal knowledge of the matters stated,

(c) notice is given under the appropriate rules [made under PACE, s 81] that another person (the expert) will in evidence given in the proceedings orally or under section 9 of the Criminal Justice Act 1967 base an opinion or inference on the statement, and

(d) the notice gives the name of the person who prepared the statement and the nature of the matters stated...

(s 127(1))

...in evidence given in the proceedings the expert may base an opinion or inference on the statement.

(s 127(2))

When an expert relies upon such a statement, s 127(3) stipulates that 'the statement is to be treated as evidence of what it states'. The opposing party may apply to the court to issue an order that the statement is not to be so used provided that it it considers it in the interests of justice to do so (s 127(4)). Section 127(5) enumerates some of the matters to which the court must have regard in arriving at this decision:

(a) the expense of calling as a witness the person who prepared the statement;

(b) whether relevant evidence could be given by that person which could not be given by the expert;

(c) whether that person can reasonably be expected to remember the matters stated well enough to give oral evidence of them.

8.31 *Abadom* [1983] 1 WLR 126 exemplifies another problem. In order to show that A had committed a robbery, an expert was called to testify that the refractive index of glass fragments embedded in A's shoes matched that of a pane of glass broken at the crime scene and that this refractive index was only found in 4 per cent of glass. He opined that, given the comparative rarity of glass of this refractive index, this was very strong evidence that the fragments in A's shoes came from the crime scene.

The glass fragments had been analysed by another witness, while the 4 per cent figure was based on statistics compiled by the Home Office of which the expert had no personal knowledge but which were generally recognised as an authoritative source of data. Kerr LJ, rejecting the defence's argument that the expert had founded his opinion on analyses of samples of glass of which he had no personal knowledge, held that the expert was not merely entitled to refer to the Home Office statistics but stressed:

> it is part of [his] *duty* to consider any material that may be available in [his] field...The statistical results of the work of others in the same field must inevitably form an important ingredient in the cogency or probative value of his conclusion in the particular case.
> (at 129)

It would distort and diminish the expert's testimony were relevant background information not taken into account, even if it has been assembled and collated by others. Expertise cannot be divorced from the general *corpus* of learning within the expert's relevant field and the expert 'must' therefore take it into account when formulating an opinion. Indeed, as Bingham J held in the civil case of *H v Schering Chemicals* [1983] 1 WLR 143, an expert 'can fortify his opinion by referring to learned articles, publications, and letters as reinforcing the view to which he has come'. He ought also to make reference to sources which support an opinion contrary to his own, in short providing the court with a balanced and reasoned opinion. Additionally, the expert must inform the court of sources upon which he relies, so that the information can be properly tested and evaluated. The admissibility of this sort of evidence in the testimony of experts therefore amounts to an exception to the rule against hearsay. This common law exception has been specifically retained by the hearsay provisions of the Criminal Justice Act 2003, s 118 (1), r 8 of which provides:

> The following rules of law are preserved...Any rule of law under which in criminal proceedings an expert witness may draw on the body of expertise relevant to his field.
> (See further *post*, para **9.67**)

8.32 Subject to the newly expanded exceptions to the hearsay rule (see further, Chapter 9), it remains clear that in some circumstances, where expert evidence is received, the hearsay rule will still hold firm. In *Edwards (Christopher)* [2001] EWCA Crim 2185 E was charged with possession of 28.5 ecstasy tablets with intent to supply. To buttress his defence that they were for his personal use, E claimed that he had already consumed 18 or 20 more ecstasy tablets between lunchtime and his arrest at 1 am the following day. The Court of Appeal held that the trial court had properly rejected the opinion evidence of someone who had been employed in a drug education unit for eight years, who had no formal qualifications and who relied on his personal experience rather than upon any academic materials. In this witness's opinion, it was perfectly possible for a drug user to consume that number of ecstasy tablets within such a short space of time. His opinion was founded upon what unidentified ecstasy users had told him about their consumption. As Henry LJ said, the opinion was based upon 'classic hearsay'; it was 'valueless' and properly rejected (esp at [12] and [14]). Even under the relaxed regime of the Criminal Justice Act 2003, this hearsay evidence would be inadmissible. It would fall outside statements receivable under s 127 (*ante*, para **8.30**) and would not be admissible under s 116 as the informants, although probably unavailable, cannot be 'identified to the court's satisfaction', as required by s 116(1)(b). It would also be most unlikely to be admitted 'in the interests of justice' under s 114(1)(d) of the 2003 Act.

Expert opinion evidence in civil cases

8.33 We have mentioned elsewhere the impact the Civil Procedure Rules (CPR) have had on several areas of the law of evidence (see Introduction). The Rules are important in the context of expert witnesses, too. Although nominally impartial, experts were widely thought of as little better than loyal members of the team calling them—a feeling captured in the quotation from an American federal decision with which this chapter opens. Their testimony all too often reflected the adversarial properties of the civil trial itself. The CPR, and their accompanying Practice Directions, notably now require that the court's leave be sought before expert evidence can be called, encourages the parties to appoint a single joint expert, and compels their experts to exchange information and reports. In short, the CPR are designed to speed matters up, to hone the issues for trial, and to minimise parties' costs. Although the accent is on economy and efficiency, as Brooke LJ pointed out in *ES v Chesterfield and N Derbyshire Royal Hospital NHS Trust* [2004] Lloyd's Rep Med 90:

> [Judges] have a heavy responsibility under the CPR to control the type and number of experts in all cases, and must always be vigilant of their duty under r 35.1 to restrict expert evidence to that which is reasonably required to resolve the proceedings. But the approach cannot be mechanistic and must remain case specific, both by the terms of r 35.1 itself (which refers to 'the proceedings') and by the overriding objective in r 1.
>
> (at [21])

8.34 *Stevens v Gullis* [2000] 1 All ER 527 illustrates the effect of these changes. A defendant, counterclaiming against a builder and suing an architect for negligent work and delay in completion of a contract, employed an expert. Following a meeting of the various expert witnesses involved in the case, the defendant's expert failed to respond adequately to a court order that a memorandum be circulated and agreed by those experts, setting out matters upon which they either agreed or disagreed. The expert then failed to fulfil a further judicial order that he comply with the requirements of the Practice Direction accompanying Part 35 of the CPR, which demands that an expert provide the court with a range of information, including his instructions, and submit a declaration that he understands his duty to the court and that he has acted accordingly. The trial judge, in consequence, ruled that by his conduct the witness had debarred himself from appearing in the case as an expert. On appeal, Lord Woolf MR stressed that, 'in addition to the duty that an expert owes to a party, he is also under a duty to the court'. Notwithstanding that the CPR had only very recently come into force and that the effect of the order would prove 'draconian' for the employer, the expert's refusal to comply with the terms of the Practice Direction showed that he was not an appropriate person to give evidence and he was therefore rightly debarred from doing so. The expert had 'demonstrated by his conduct that he had no conception of the requirements placed upon an expert under the CPR'.

8.35   *Stevens v Gullis* shows that a civil court now has considerable power to control the evidence placed before it and to ensure that expert witnesses apprehend that they owe an overriding duty to the court. As a corollary to this, provided that a party can satisfy the court that its expert witness understands this obligation, the expert may even be one of its own employees. In *Field v Leeds CC* (1999) 32 HLR 618 the Court of Appeal held that it would have been open to the council, defending a claim by one of its tenants that a property was in a state of disrepair, to have called a surveyor employed in its own Housing Claims Investigation Section as an expert witness, provided that he could show that he was fully familiar with the need for objectivity and that he appreciated that his primary duty was to the court.

Expert opinion evidence in criminal cases

8.36   Part 3 of the Criminal Procedure Rules 2010 makes clear that henceforth 'active case management' is an important element in criminal cases, just as it has been for several years in the civil arena (see CPR, r 1.4). Case management will have an impact on many areas of the law of evidence. One of the most obvious perhaps is that of expert evidence, where much unnecessary court time can be taken up with resolving disputes between the parties' expert witnesses. General principles have begun to develop in this context. In *Harris* [2006] 1 Cr App R 5 at [270]–[273] (a shaken baby syndrome case) Gage LJ reminded lawyers of the obligations owed by expert witnesses in both civil and criminal cases, as set out in Cresswell J's judgment in *The Ikarian Reefer* [1993] 2 Lloyd's Rep 68, at 81. Gage LJ summarised the following key points from that judgment:

(1) Expert evidence presented to the court should be and [be] seen to be the independent product of the expert uninfluenced as to form or content by the exigencies of litigation.

(2) An expert witness should provide independent assistance to the court by way of objective unbiased opinion in relation to matters within his expertise. An expert witness...should never assume the role of advocate.

(3) An expert witness should state the facts or assumptions on which his opinion is based. He should not omit to consider material facts which detract from his concluded opinions.

(4) An expert should make it clear when a particular question or issue falls outside his expertise.

(5) If an expert's opinion is not properly researched because he considers that insufficient data is available then this must be stated with an indication that the opinion is no more than a provisional one.

(6) If after exchange of reports, an expert witness changes his view on material matters, such change of view should be communicated to the other side without delay and when appropriate to the court.

To these six points Gage LJ added Wall J's observations in *Re AB (Child Abuse: Expert Witnesses)* [1995] 1 FLR 181, at 192 to the effect that in cases where there is a genuine disagreement on a scientific or medical issue, or where it is necessary for a party to advance a particular hypothesis to explain a given set of facts, that expert 'owes a very heavy duty to explain to the court that what he is advancing is a hypothesis, that it is controversial (if it is), and places before the court all material which contradicts the hypothesis'. Such an expert must also make all his material available to the other experts in the case as that will often serve to reduce the area for forensic disagreement. Gage LJ, in *Harris*, stressed that the new case management powers of criminal judges conferred by the Criminal Procedure Rules now make wide provision for experts to consult together and, if possible, settle points of agreement or disagreement with a summary of reasons. (See also *Holdsworth* (2008) 102 BMLR 112 at [59] *per* Toulson LJ.) Indeed, in *Bowman* [2006] 2 Cr App R 3 at [177] Gage LJ reverted to this theme, decreeing six further 'necessary inclusions' in experts' reports, all of them designed to assist in controlling and managing expert evidence in criminal cases.

Scientific evidence: the presentation of DNA evidence

8.37 Advances in science have led to the introduction of several new types of scientific evidence. Foremost amongst these is DNA profiling evidence, which was described by one New York court as 'the single greatest advance in the "search for the truth"...since the advent of cross-examination' (*People v Wesley* 533 NYS 2d 643, 644 (1988)). The first murder conviction obtained in England thanks to DNA profiling evidence was that of Colin Pitchfork, who was convicted in 1988 for raping and killing two teenage girls in 1983 and 1986. (The DNA evidence completely exonerated the police's prime suspect.) DNA technology now allows the re-opening and solving of cases that have for long lain dormant in police files. In April 2010 DNA evidence led Robert Carpenter to plead guilty to a rape committed in Scunthorpe in March 1979. In 2007, thanks to advances in DNA analysis, John Pope was arrested for murdering a woman in 1996, whom he had trussed up and cast in the River Ely in Cardiff. The woman's former husband had originally stood trial for the offence, but most fortunately had been acquitted. In July 2008 thanks to new DNA technology Derek Mann, a former gardener of the late member of The Beatles, George Harrison, was convicted at Bristol Crown Court for a rape committed in Henley in 1981 as his victim recited the Lord's Prayer (*Henley Standard*, July 22, 2008). It was advances in DNA technology that led to the freeing of Sean Hodgson in March 2009, 27 years after he was jailed for the murder of Teresa de Simone, who was found strangled in her car in Southampton in December 1979.

8.38 The increasing accessibility of DNA evidence explains in part why, under Part 10 of the Criminal Justice Act 2003, subject to the DPP's giving consent, the prosecution may now apply to the Court of Appeal to quash a person's previous acquittal and to order that that person be retried for the relevant offence, provided that 'there is new and compelling evidence' and that the court considers that it is in the interests of justice for a retrial to take place (ss 78 and 79). The new retrial provisions, which were first successfully employed in September 2006 (see *Dunlop* [2007] 1 WLR 1657), apply to a wide range of grave offences that are listed in Schedule 5 of the Act. Quite simply, DNA technology has transformed criminal detection: in January 2006 a Home Office minister reported that in the period 2000–05 the number of crimes detected in England and Wales thanks to DNA evidence had quadrupled, and that as many as three thousand matches were being made each month.

8.39 *What is DNA profiling?* DNA (deoxyribonucleic acid) evidence reposes upon the notion that this chemical, which carries every person's genetic coding, is unique to each individual. The only exception occurs in the case of identical twins. For example, in March 2004, DNA samples, taken following a rape in Michigan, matched two identical twin brothers, each of whom put forward alibis (*USA Today*, 6 March 2004). But even in the case of twins it is not impossible that technology may shortly overcome this identification problem, because tiny mutations are known to occur in DNA as cells divide during every embryo's growth. DNA can be extracted from any cells that contain a nucleus, and most commonly are derived from samples of blood, semen, saliva or hair. But advances continue to be made. Thus, in 2002, John Cook was identified as the murderer of a woman in a nursing home in 1995 thanks to DNA extracted from excrement he had thoughtfully left behind as he descended a fire escape at the scene of crime. And a Tasmanian burglar pled guilty after DNA, extracted from blood taken from a leech found beside a safe at the victim's ransacked home following a break-in in 2001, eight years later matched a sample taken when he was DNA-tested over drug offences in late 2008 (*The Australian* (2009) October 20). DNA evidence requires scientific comparison of samples of DNA, one taken from the crime scene and one taken from the accused. The scientific method is constantly being refined. As Moore-Bick LJ explained in *Bates* [2006] EWCA Crim 1395, esp at [10]–[14], the current process, known as 'SGM Plus', involves the identification of identical repeated blocks of material called 'alleles' at ten different regions, known as 'loci', at which the number of alleles present are known to vary widely from one individual to another, along with a sex indicator. The process involves gel electrophoresis, using an electric current to draw the DNA through the gel separating the alleles. Lasers then detect coloured markers placed in the sample and the data are fed into a computer, which releases its information in the form of a graph. The graph has to be interpreted. (See also *Reed and Reed* [2010] 1 Cr App R 23 [31]-[61] *per* Thomas LJ.)

8.40   When the samples are matched, profiling can indicate the 'match probability'—ie the probability of the accused being the culprit by means of what is known as the random occurrence ratio. (This is a ratio, arrived at by empirical research, showing the statistical likelihood of an individual DNA band being found in the genetic make-up of individuals from particular racial groups.) This type of data, however, has to be carefully explained to juries, who could easily misunderstand it. As was pointed out in *Doheny* [1997] 1 Cr App R 369, when the accused has a profile which matches a crime stain and the random occurrence ratio shows that, say, only one in a million members of the population possesses this DNA profile, that does not mean that there is a million-to-one chance that the accused left the crime stain and is therefore guilty of the offence. If one imagines that this 1:1,000,000 random occurrence ratio means that there are probably 30 males in the country who match the profile in the crime stain, the DNA evidence only signifies that there is a 1 in 30 chance that the accused is the offender. The cogency of the DNA evidence will then depend both on what other evidence in the case links that person to the crime scene and the rigour with which the DNA testing has been conducted. To this end, in *Doheny* the Court of Appeal gave guidance on two matters: (i) the way in which such evidence should be presented; and (ii) the manner in which the jury is to be directed on its use.

- Regarding presentation, Phillips LJ said that when the scientist adduces evidence of the DNA comparisons and his calculations of the random occurrence ratio, the Crown should serve upon the defence sufficient details to allow it to review the basis upon which those calculations were made. Indeed, if so requested, the Forensic Science Service should furnish the defence with the databases upon which the calculations were based. The latter instruction is particularly significant as it is widely accepted that, in regard to access to scientific evidence, the prosecution enjoys a marked advantage over the defence. Phillips LJ also said that:

  ... the scientist should not be asked his opinion on the likelihood that it was the defendant who left the crime stain, nor when giving evidence should he use terminology which may lead the jury to believe that he is expressing such an opinion. (at 374)

  The scientist merely tells the jury about the matching of the samples, the random occurrence ratio and, if he has the data and the relevant statistical expertise, how many people with matching characteristics are likely to be found within a given geographical location.

- Given that few ordinary people are conversant with statistics, the content of the jury direction will be very important when DNA profiling evidence has been adduced. Phillips LJ was at pains to stress that jurors should be directed along the following general lines:

  [I]f you accept the scientific evidence called by the Crown, this indicates that there are probably only four or five white males in the UK from whom that semen stain could have come. The defendant is one of them. If that is the position, the decision you have to reach, on all the evidence, is whether you are sure that it was the defendant who left that stain or whether it is possible that it was one of that other small group of men who share the same DNA characteristics.

8.41 *Partial and mixed samples.* In practice, the process of identification of an offender by means of DNA profiling can be greatly complicated in cases where the DNA sample taken from the scene of crime is only partial or is mixed with other DNA profiles, or in cases even where routinely other fragments of DNA have been generated in the course of preparing a sample for analysis (see *Bates, supra* at [14]–[17]). In *Bates* itself the sample purporting to identify B as the likely murderer, taken from the victim's door handle, was partial in that it showed identical alleles in only two loci. Nonetheless, this was said to show that only 100 members of the male population of the British Isles could have matched this incomplete profile. On appeal it was urged that, since the profile was partial and since it would require only one allele in one of the eight missing loci (or 'voids') to exculpate B, the DNA evidence ought to have been excluded. Moore-Bick LJ rejected this argument, concluding:

> In many cases there is a possibility (at least in theory) that evidence exists which would assist the accused and perhaps even exculpate him altogether, but that does not provide grounds for excluding relevant evidence that is available and otherwise admissible, though it does make it important to ensure that the jury are given sufficient information to enable them to evaluate that evidence properly. Moreover, . . . the significance of DNA evidence depends to a large extent upon the other evidence in the case. By itself such evidence, particularly if based on a partial profile, may not take the matter far, but in conjunction with other evidence it may be of considerable significance.
>
> (at [30])

8.42 In March 2009 the Forensic Science Service announced that, after trials, a new DNA profiling technique DNA Boost, which allows scientists to obtain individual DNA profiles from crime scenes that contain a mix of genetic material from several people, using computer technology to provide identifiable DNA profiles for each suspect, was 'fit for purpose'. The technique could be of use in approximately 1,000 criminal cases each year. Scientists have begun looking through 'cold cases', estimating that DNA Boost could increase the number of provable cases by as much as 30 per cent.

8.43 *'Low Copy Number' profiling.* DNA profiling techniques are persistently being refined and extended. In the Northern Irish case of *Sean Hoey*, who, in December 2007, was cleared of murdering 29 people at Omagh in August, 1998, and of other terrorist charges, one contested issue was the prosecution's use of DNA analysis of a type known as 'Low Copy Number' (LCN). LCN, an extension of SGM Plus, made its first appearance in 1999. It claims to be able to make a match using a simply minuscule trace left behind by a perpetrator. At H's trial the validity of the technique was contested. Weir J pointed out in his ruling, quoting from a report of the House of Commons Science and Technology Committee published in July 2005:

> The absence of an agreed protocol for the validation of scientific techniques prior to their being admitted in court is entirely unsatisfactory. Judges are not well placed to determine scientific validity without input from scientists.
>
> (at [55])

It remains the case in England that there exists 'no single test which can provide a threshold for admissibility' of scientific evidence (*Harris* [2006] 1 Cr App R 5). Following H's acquittal, the CPS in England did briefly suspend the use of LCN, but after review declared in January 2008 that it had unearthed no particular problems and that LCN DNA examination should remain available to the prosecution. More recently, in *Reed and Reed* [2010] 1 Cr App R 23 the Court of Appeal has provided careful guidance on how low template DNA evidence is to be employed, where the quantities fall below the 'stochastic threshold', concluding:

> [W]e consider that the science is sufficiently reliable for it to be within the competence of a forensic science expert to give admissible evidence evaluating the possibilities of transfer in DNA cases where the amount is over 200 picograms and when there is a sufficient evidential basis from the profiles and other material... for it to be done.
>
> (at [122]. See also *Broughton* [2010] EWCA Crim 549.)

8.44 *Eliminating risk of sample contamination.* The *Hoey* case also illustrates the importance of the Crown being able to prove the integrity of the scientific evidence it adduces. In dismissing the 58 charges against H, Weir J held that the prosecution had egregiously failed to establish the integrity and freedom from contamination of each item throughout the entirety of the period between seizure and any examination relied upon:

> It is not my function to criticise the seemingly thoughtless and slapdash approach of police and [scene of crime] officers to the collection, storage and transmission of what must obviously have been potential exhibits in a possible future criminal trial but it is difficult to avoid some expression of surprise that in an era in which the potential for fibre, if not DNA, contamination was well known to the police such items were so widely and routinely handled with cavalier disregard for their integrity. The position so far as [NI Forensic Science] is concerned is even more difficult to comprehend as everyone there must have been very well aware of the risks of improper labelling, storage and examination.
>
> (at [59])

Clearly, if the integrity of the evidence cannot be demonstrated, it risks being declared inadmissible.

8.45 *DNA profiling in conjunction with other evidence in the case.* Phillips LJ's warning in *Doheny* that the strength of DNA profiling evidence has to be gauged in the context of any other evidence in the case implicating the accused was taken to heart in *Lashley* (2000) 8 February 2000, transcript no 99/03890/Y3. The sole evidence linking L with the robbery of a Liverpool post office was DNA evidence from a partly smoked cigarette discarded at the scene of crime. It was estimated that the DNA matched only between seven and ten men in the UK. Nevertheless, in the absence of evidence showing either that L was in the vicinity of Liverpool at the relevant time or that he had participated in or knew of the offence, the Court of Appeal held that the judge ought to have upheld L's submission of no case to answer and withdrawn the case from the jury. *Lashley* may be contrasted with *Smith (Jesse)* (2000) 8 February, transcript no 99/04098/W3, coincidentally another post office robbery, where the court upheld the judge's rejection of S's submission of no case to answer on the basis that, in addition to DNA evidence indicating that only 43 males in the UK matched the profile, the Crown could show that S was in the vicinity of the crime scene, albeit three months after the offence. Lord Hope underscored this point in *Pringle v R* [2003] UKPC 9, stressing that, despite the impressive numbers the prosecution may lay before the tribunal:

> The question whether the statistic points to the defendant as the actual perpetrator will depend on what else is known about him. If it is plain from the other evidence that he could not have committed the crime because he was elsewhere at the time, the fact that the defendant's DNA profile matches that on the sample taken from the crime scene cannot be said to show that he did commit it. That proposition will have been negatived by the other evidence. So the probative effect of the DNA evidence must depend on the question whether there is some other evidence which can demonstrate its significance. And it is for the jury, not the person who gives the DNA evidence, to assess its significance in the light of that other evidence.
>
> (at [19])

Scientific evidence: the presentation of Bayes theorem and instructing the jury in mathematical probabilities

8.46   It is not altogether surprising that the advent of new forms of scientific evidence with a strong statistical content—notably, DNA profiling evidence—should have stimulated wider interest in mathematical theories of proof. On several occasions the Court of Appeal has had to consider the admissibility of the method of evaluating conditional probabilities known as Bayes theorem. The theorem is widely used by statisticians and other professions. Reduced to probably over-simple terms, it predicates that a numerical value can be ascribed to each item of evidence in a case, representing the ratio between the probability of circumstance x in relation to the guilt of the accused. The individual percentages, which are to a great degree themselves going to be matters of personal judgement, are then combined into an overall formula which, exponents of the theorem claim, represents a mathematical representation of the likelihood of the accused's guilt, provided of course those particular items of evidence are accepted by the tribunal of fact. Not surprisingly perhaps, in *Doheny* [1997] 1 Cr App R 369 it was suggested that Bayes theorem could be used to calculate from the DNA profiling evidence and the other items of proof in the case the overall statistical probability that the defendant committed the offence charged.

8.47   In *Adams* [1996] 2 Cr App R 467, a rape case where the Crown relied on DNA evidence which was said to show that the random chance of anyone else's possessing A's genetic profile was 1:200,000,000, the trial judge had allowed the defence to call an expert who explained Bayes theorem to the jury in order to assist them in evaluating the DNA evidence. Rose LJ took the opportunity to state:

> [Bayes theorem] is not appropriate for use in jury trials, or as a means to assist the jury in their task . . . [T]he theorem's methodology requires . . . that items of evidence be assessed separately according to their bearing on the accused's guilt, before being combined in the overall formula. That . . . is far too rigid an approach to evidence of the type that a jury characteristically has to assess . . .

Whilst acknowledging that this was only a 'provisional conclusion', Rose LJ declared that it was wrong for a judge to admit evidence of Bayes theorem without objection, suggesting the following reasons:

- jurors do not evaluate evidence according to mathematical formulae, but by 'joint application of their individual common sense and knowledge of the world to the evidence before them';

- to imagine that juries could evaluate evidence in terms of probability formulae 'would in any event be impossible of sensible achievement';

- there could be disagreements over the cogency of particular pieces of evidence and 'different jurors might well wish to select different numerical figures even when they were broadly agreed on the weight of the evidence in question', presumably having to average out their various figures only in order to arrive at a final figure that would reflect neither party's view;

- finally, the introduction of methods of statistical analysis into the criminal trial 'plunges the jury into inappropriate and unnecessary realms of theory and complexity deflecting them from their proper task'.

Although, technically speaking, it may be that the question has not been finally resolved, it is now most unlikely that the criminal courts will permit juries to be addressed on the subject of Bayes theorem.

8.48   More generally, one senses that the courts are increasingly suspicious of the way in which some statistical evidence is being presented to juries. In the high-profile case of *Clark (Sally)* [2003] 2 FCR 447, where C was wrongly convicted of murdering her two sons, the prosecution case partly rested on a scientist's testimony concerning the contents of a government-funded report on the frequency of multiple cot deaths within the same family. The Crown's expert had suggested, somewhat incautiously, that the probability of double cot deaths occurring in these circumstances was 1:73,000,000—that is, one might anticipate approximately one such occurrence every hundred years. As Kay LJ pointed out:

> Putting the evidence of 1 in 73 million before the jury with its related statistic that it was the equivalent of a single occurrence of two such deaths in the same family once in a century was tantamount to saying that without consideration of the rest of the evidence one could be just about sure that this was a case of murder. If the figure of 1 in 73 million accurately reflected the chance of two cot deaths in the same family, then the whole of the [Care of Next Infant] scheme was effectively wasted effort. Seeking to provide guidance and monitoring against the possibility of a second cot death would be taking precautions against a risk that could effectively be discounted. . . . [T]he evidence should never have been before the jury in the way that it was when they considered their verdicts . . . There is evidence to suggest that it may happen much more frequently than suggested by that figure although happily the risk remains a relatively unlikely one . . . Quite what impact all this evidence will have had on the jury will never be known but we rather suspect that with the graphic reference by Professor Meadow to the chances of backing long odds winners of the Grand National year after year it may have had a major effect on their thinking.
>
> (at [175]–[178])

Although C's appeal succeeded on other grounds, the court noted that the misleading way in which statistics on the occurrence of cot deaths in England and Wales had been presented to the jury would 'in all probability' (at [180]) have also justified the quashing of her conviction.

FURTHER READING

Burns, 'Low Copy Number DNA on Trial' (2008) 158 NLJ 919

Jackson, 'The Ultimate Issue Rule—One Rule Too Many' [1984] Crim LR 75

McKay and Colman, 'Excluding Expert Evidence: A Tale of Ordinary Folk and Ordinary Experience' [1991] Crim LR 800

Munday, 'Excluding the Expert Witness' [1981] Crim LR 688

Roberts, 'Science in the Criminal Process' (1994) 14 OJLS 469

Schauer, 'Can Bad Science be Good Evidence? Lie Detection, Neuroscience and the Mistaken Conflation of Legal and Scientific Norms' 95 Cornell L Rev 1191 (2010)

Spencer, 'Court Experts and Expert Witnesses: Have We a Lesson to Learn from the French?' [1992] CLP 213

Wilson, 'The Law Commission's Proposal on Expert Opinion Evidence: an Onerous Demand on Judges' [2010] 1 Web JCLI

'Isolated in a vast desert', <http://www.nzlawyermagazine.co.nz> (2010) 11 June, issue 138 (illustrating the risks of DNA evidence, like Ozymandias' broken statue in Shelley's eponymous poem)

'The Admissibility of Expert Evidence in Criminal Proceedings in England and Wales' (Law Commission Consultation Paper no 190 (2009)

SELF-TEST QUESTIONS

1. Why does the law normally exclude evidence of a witness's opinion?

2. When will the courts admit non-expert opinion evidence?

3. In *Turner* [1975] QB 834 Lawton LJ said that 'jurors do not need psychiatrists to tell them how ordinary folk who are not suffering from any mental illness are likely to react to the stresses and strains of life'. When will the courts admit evidence of the opinions of psychiatrists and psychologists?

4. How do the rules governing the admissibility of opinion evidence differ according to whether a trial is civil or criminal?

5. In *Adams* [1996] 2 Cr App Rep 467 Rose LJ suggested that '[Bayes theorem] is not appropriate for use in jury trials, or as a means to assist the jury in their task'. Do you agree?

6. Oedipus is on trial, charged with the murder of his father, Rex. The defence wishes to call the following witnesses:

   (i) Dr Rave, who will testify that Oedipus, who is not suffering from any mental illness, like any other rational human being, is likely to have been provoked beyond endurance when his father, a die-hard Everton supporter, let off a canister of pepper spray into the face of his son, a loyal Liverpool fan, when Liverpool scored the winning goal in the annual Merseyside derby in the last minute of injury time; and

   (ii) Dr Morticus, a pathologist, who will testify that although there is external evidence of quite serious injuries on Rex's body, it is his firm personal conviction that Rex actually died of natural causes—namely, shock brought on by the defeat of his beloved football club.

7. What changes has the Criminal Justice Act 2003 made to the rules governing the admissibility of hearsay evidence in cases where a criminal court admits expert evidence?

9

The rule against hearsay

SUMMARY

The rationale underlying a rule against hearsay

I. Hearsay in criminal cases

- Defects in the rule against hearsay prior to the enactment of the Criminal Justice Act 2003
    - Implied assertions
- What constitutes hearsay evidence under the Criminal Justice Act 2003?
- Exceptions to the rule against hearsay (s 114)
    - Unavailable witnesses and business documents
        - (a) Cases where a witness is unavailable (s 116)
        - (b) Statements of witnesses who do not testify through fear (s 116(2)(e))
        - (c) Business and other documents (s 117)
    - Preservation of certain common law categories of admissibility (s 118)
- 'Public information etc' (rule 1)
- 'Reputation as to character' (rule 2)
- 'Reputation or family tradition' (rule 3)
- '*Res gestae*' (rule 4)
- 'Confessions etc' (rule 5)
- 'Admissions by agents, etc' (rule 6)
- 'Common enterprise' (rule 7)
- 'Expert evidence' (rule 8)
    - All parties agree to the statement being admissible (s 114(1)(c))
    - When it is in the interests of justice to admit the statement (s 114(1)(d))

- Admissibility of 'multiple hearsay' (s 121)
- Testing the credibility of makers of statements who do not testify (s 124)
- Stopping the case where hearsay evidence is unconvincing (s 125)
- The court's general discretion to exclude evidence in the interest of case management (s 126)
- Other statutory exceptions to the hearsay rule
  - Proof by written statements admitted under the Criminal Justice Act 1967, s 9
  - Confessions (PACE, ss 76 and 76A)
  - Bankers' books (Bankers' Books Evidence Act 1879)
- Human rights law, the rule against hearsay and its exceptions (ECHR, Article 6(3)(d))
- Anonymous witnesses: the Coroners and Justice Act 2009, ss 86–96

II. Hearsay in civil proceedings

PRENTICE: It's a fascinating theory, sir, and cleverly put together. Does it tie in with known facts?

RANCE: That need not cause us undue anxiety. Civilizations have been founded and maintained on theories which refused to obey facts.

Joe Orton, What the Butler Saw (1969)

The rationale underlying a rule against hearsay

9.1 The rule against hearsay is one of the great exclusionary rules of the law of evidence. The underlying idea seems sound enough. In a system which places a premium on orality, with witnesses delivering their testimony in person, it is an understandable corollary that witness A should be forbidden from giving testimony on behalf of witness B. As Lord Normand explained in *Teper v R* [1952] AC 480:

> The rule against the admission of hearsay evidence is fundamental. It is not the best evidence and it is not delivered on oath. The truthfulness and accuracy of the witness whose words are spoken by another person cannot be tested by cross-examination, and the light which his demeanour would throw upon his testimony is lost.
>
> (at 486)

The rule against hearsay, Lord Bridge was later to claim, is also 'rooted...in the system of trial by jury' and recognises the inability the untrained mind encounters in assessing what weight to attribute to reported evidence:

> The danger against which this fundamental rule provides a safeguard is that untested hearsay evidence will be treated as having a probative force which it does not deserve.
>
> (*Blastland* [1986] AC 41, 54).

Although these justifications carry some weight, writers on evidence (and even the courts) grew increasingly sceptical about the hearsay rule. For example, in *Gilfoyle* [1996] 1 Cr App R 302, Beldam LJ inveighed against a rule that could serve to deprive the tribunal of fact of evidence that is both relevant and probative:

> Those men and women (on the jury) were surely entitled to a rational explanation why, when they were chosen to apply their common sense and experience in the assessment and appraisal of witnesses' evidence, they should be regarded as lacking the ability to discern the difference between speculative rumour and spontaneous truth in statements made out of court.
>
> (at 324)

Not everyone, then, was persuaded by the reasons commonly invoked to justify the continuing existence of the exclusionary rule.

9.2 The hearsay rule, it could be added, has for some time epitomised a considerable rift between the civil and criminal wings of the law of evidence. Whereas, until the entry into force of the Criminal Justice Act 2003, the rule against hearsay retained its vigour, and, in criminal cases, was even capable of extending its empire (eg *Kearley* [1992] 2 AC 228), in the civil arena the hearsay rule has been of little significance since the enactment of the Civil Evidence Acts of 1968 and 1995. As we shall see, the Criminal Justice Act 2003 has considerably expanded the exceptions to the rule against hearsay in criminal cases—or, in the words of Rose LJ in *Joyce and Joyce* [2005] EWCA Crim 1785 at [16], has 'modernised the law'. Nevertheless, it must be noted that the relaxation of the hearsay rule effected by the 2003 legislation does not remotely mean that in criminal cases hearsay issues are now a thing of the past. As Leveson J observed in *Maher v DPP* (2006) 170 JP 441:

> Although the purpose of the hearsay provisions . . . was undeniably to relax the previously strict rules against the admission of hearsay, it is important to underline that care must be taken to analyse the precise provisions of the legislation and ensure that any route of admissibility is correctly identified.
>
> (at [26])

Certainly, the 2003 Act has not brought the criminal and civil branches into exact alignment. It has in fact led to the very term 'hearsay' bearing different meanings according to whether the context is criminal or civil. Hence, in this chapter the rule against hearsay in criminal cases and civil cases will be discussed separately.

9.3 In essence, the principal legislation under discussion in this chapter, which governs the rule against hearsay in criminal cases (Part 11, Chapter 2 of the Criminal Justice Act 2003), grew out of a Law Commission Consultation Paper, *Evidence in Criminal Proceedings: Hearsay and Related Topics*, published in 1995. The policy pursued by the Law Commission was, subject to satisfactory safeguards, to seek to admit relevant evidence whenever this coincided with the interests of justice. By the time that the government began to contemplate which reforms to lay before Parliament in its Criminal Justice Bill, however, there were rival recommendations to consider deriving from Sir Robin Auld's *Review of the Criminal Courts of England and Wales* (2001). Whereas the Law Commission, in its final report (Law Com No 245), broadly recommended the retention of the exclusionary rule along with certain additional exceptions, the far more sparely argued *Auld Review* proposed a radical solution. The object of the law of evidence, Auld argued with beguiling simplicity, should be to 'facilitate rather than obstruct the search for truth and [to] simplify rather than complicate the trial process' (para 11.110). Crudely put, Auld argued that the court should invariably be presented with the best available evidence, even if that evidence happens to be hearsay. (Even more tendentious were Auld's subsidiary arguments concerning the supposed blurring of the distinctions between 'adversarial' and 'inquisitorial' systems so called, and indeed the desirability of such a development.) This more thoroughgoing reform of hearsay, probably by good fortune, did not win approval. Nevertheless, the Criminal Justice Act 2003 does make a couple of changes to the original scheme recommended by the Law Commission. In particular, it has modified the Commission's definition of hearsay, and has given added prominence to the new inclusionary discretion created by s 114(1)(d). Professor Birch pointed out ([2004] Crim LR at 558–9) that, despite the government's sweeping claim to have redesigned the Act after the Auld model, the legislation does nothing of the sort. The 2003 Act continues to require lawyers, as they have had to in the past, to follow a two-stage thought process:

- *first*, they must examine the contested statement to determine whether it is capable of amounting to hearsay, in which case it is *prima facie* inadmissible; then,

- *second*, they have to identify into which exception to the hearsay rule, if any, that statement might fall, in order to justify its admissibility.

Although the amount of evidence that will fall within one or other of the exceptions to the hearsay rule has greatly increased under the new Act, the underlying legal method remains unaltered, and as McCombe J pointed out in *N* [2006] EWCA Crim 3303, at [17], 'the rule remains... an exclusionary one'.

I. Hearsay in criminal cases

Defects in the rule against hearsay prior to the enactment of the Criminal Justice Act 2003

9.4 The old law had many defects. The rule against hearsay was an unusually convoluted, and sometimes outright counter-intuitive, area of the law of evidence. The extent of its failings serves to explain why wholesale reorganisation of the rule was felt appropriate. Those failings are detailed in paras 9.5–9.18 of the fourth edition of this work. Briefly, the main objections were that:

(i) *The rule applied indiscriminately to both prosecution and defence evidence.* The potential relevance of evidence, or the importance of the evidence in the context of the case, offered no guarantee that it would be admitted. Thus, in *Sparks* [1964] AC 964, for instance, a 27-year-old white staff sergeant in the US Air Force was accused of indecently assaulting a three- or four-year-old girl. The child did not appear as a witness at the trial. The defence, however, wished to call the girl's mother to testify that immediately after the offence her daughter had told her that the culprit was a 'coloured' boy. Consoling itself with the sterile thought that 'the cause of justice is... best served by adherence to rules which have been long recognised and settled', the Privy Council ruled this evidence inadmissible. Indeed, Lord Morris of Borth-y-Gest added by way of historical commentary:

> [O]ur law... is firmly based upon the view that it is wiser and better that hearsay should be excluded save in certain well-defined and rather exceptional circumstances.

Similarly, in *Turner* (1975) 61 Cr App R 67, where T wished to adduce in evidence the fact that another party had actually confessed to the offence with which T was charged, Milmo J said that:

> The idea, which may be gaining prevalence in some quarters, that in a criminal trial the defence is entitled to adduce hearsay evidence to establish facts, which if proved would be relevant and would assist the defence, is wholly erroneous.

This view was resoundingly endorsed in the House of Lords case of *Blastland* [1986] AC 41. B, who had been convicted of buggering and murdering a 12-year-old boy, was refused leave to call a witness to testify that, before the boy's body was discovered, a third party had said that the boy had been murdered—suggesting that he knew rather a lot about how the boy met his end. Little wonder, then, that the hearsay rule's indiscriminate application to prosecution and defence evidence alike aroused concern or that courts occasionally admitted that judges sometimes admitted evidence which, technically speaking, was inadmissible hearsay 'as a matter of grace in favour of the [accused]' (*Callan* (1994) 98 Cr App 467, 471).

(ii) *The courts sometimes saw hearsay where none was actually present*—arguably, a kind of paranoia induced by a rule that few found it easy to operate (eg, *The Statue of Liberty* [1968] 2 All ER 195; *Spiby* (1990) 91 Cr App R 186; *R (O'Shea) v Coventry Justices* [2004] EWHC 905 (Admin)).

(iii) *The inherent reliability of a piece of evidence did not justify its admission* if it was technically hearsay evidence. In *Myers v DPP* [1965] AC 1001, a car-ringing case in which the prosecution had to establish that the cars sold on by M were stolen vehicles to which M had given new identities, the prosecution sought to rely upon microfilms of manufacturers' records made up from cards on which unidentified workmen had inscribed engine block numbers. No one doubted their authenticity. However, as Lord Reid, one of the three majority judges in the House of Lords, declared:

> The whole development of the exceptions to the hearsay rule is based on the determination of certain classes of evidence as admissible or inadmissible and not on the apparent credibility of particular evidence tendered. No matter how cogent particular evidence may seem to be, unless it comes within a class which is admissible, it is excluded. Half a dozen witnesses may offer to prove that they heard two men of high character who cannot now be found discuss in detail the fact now in issue and agree on a credible account of it, but that evidence would not be admitted although it might be by far the best evidence available.
>
> (at 1024)

(iv) *The hearsay rule could exert an inhibiting effect* on the evidence parties thought to adduce. Parties might wrongly imagine that evidence was inadmissible hearsay. Lord Hoffmann noted this phenomenon in *Goldson and McGlashan v R* [2000] 4 LRC 460. A woman who had been shot in the jaw at point-blank range while lying in bed alongside her lover, who had been shot dead in the same incident, was interrogated by the police in hospital. Her teeth had had to be wired up and she could not speak. His Lordship said:

> She wrote down some names on a piece of paper. There is no direct evidence of which names she wrote, because *a misguided concern for the hearsay rule* seems to have inhibited the prosecution from leading evidence on the point or producing the paper.

See also *Snowden* [2002] EWCA Crim 923 (4th edn, para 9.8).

(v) *The courts did not always apply the hearsay rule consistently.* Sometimes they displayed generosity in its application, seeking to confine its adverse effects, and sometimes they did not. It then became necessary to construct convoluted arguments to explain away these seeming inconsistencies (eg, *Muir* (1983) 79 Cr App R 153; *Harry* (1987) 86 Cr App R 105. See 4th edn, para 9.9.)

(vi) This process was sometimes taken further when *a court simply appeared not to see a hearsay problem*, particularly in cases where a strict application of the rule would have led to a solution at odds with commonsense (eg, *Rice* [1963] 1 QB 857. See 4th edn, paras 9.10–9.11.) When a court might do this could not be predicted. If the courts applied the rule scrupulously, there might be an outcry. In one notorious decision, *McLean* (1967) 52 Cr App R 80, evidence of a car registration number taken down by witness C at the dictation of witness G soon after a robbery was ruled inadmissible as evidence of the number of the car used by the robbers. The Court of Appeal reluctantly reached this conclusion because G, the victim of the robbery, had not verified what C had written down, and by the time of trial G had no recollection of what he had dictated to C. In these circumstances,

> for C to be allowed to say that what he was told by G was that the car involved was HKB 138D is a contravention of the hearsay rule when that remark is adduced as evidence that the car involved in the robbery was in fact HKB 138D.

Similarly, if the courts bypassed the rule, they left themselves open to criticism. In *Osbourne and Virtue* [1973] QB 678 one witness, Mrs B, had picked O and V out at an identification parade but by the time of trial could not actually recall having picked anyone out. Another witness, Mrs H, somewhat less forgetful, did not believe that the person she had picked out at the parade was present in court. To supplement these deficiencies in the Crown case, the police officer responsible for the parade was permitted to give evidence of the relevant identifications made by the witnesses. The Court of Appeal held that this evidence was properly admitted because 'all the prosecution were seeking to do was to establish the fact of identification'. The truth is that *McLean* and *Osbourne and Virtue* were to all intents indistinguishable. In both cases, a witness sought to prove the truth of another's statement. In both cases, application of the hearsay rule would have proven highly inconvenient. In one case, the court quietly sidestepped the rule.

(vii) Finally, one of the most remarkable features of the old hearsay rule was that it not only outlawed the repetition of express assertions made by parties who were not giving evidence—that is, statements intended by their original makers to be assertive, but additionally the House of Lords, in *Kearley* [1992] 2 AC 228 determined that the hearsay rule rendered inadmissible so-called 'implied assertions'—that is, statements which the maker did *not* intend to be assertive. The House of Lords in *Kearley* [1992] 2 AC 228 held, by a bare majority, that implied assertions fell within the hearsay rule. The majority's ruling was vigorously criticised. The decision has left an indelible mark on the definition of hearsay in the Criminal Justice Act 2003. For this reason, it may be helpful to have an understanding of the problems raised by *Kearley*.

Implied assertions

9.5 What exactly was meant by an 'implied assertion'? At its simplest, one could say that an implied assertion was a piece of circumstantial evidence which the law treated as though it was a direct statement upon whose truth a party intended to rely. Take *Kearley* itself. Police, who had been keeping surveillance on K, a convicted drug trafficker, whom they suspected of renewed drug-dealing, raided K's flat, but found insufficient drugs stashed in a bathroom bin and in the roof of a rabbit hutch to raise the inference that K was a dealer. After taking K into custody, officers remained behind searching K's flat. During the few hours they were there, ten people were reported to have telephoned and a further seven to have called in person at the flat, seven of whom asked specifically for 'Chippie' (K) and offered to buy drugs. For reasons that were not elucidated, the Crown did not call any of these 17 callers as witnesses. Instead, police officers were called to testify to the calls in order to establish K's all-important intent to supply. As Lord Griffiths acknowledged, 'it is difficult to think of much more convincing evidence of [K's] activity as a drug dealer than customers constantly ringing his flat to buy drugs and a stream of customers beating a path to his door for the same purpose'. The defence nevertheless successfully argued before the House of Lords that this evidence was inadmissible both on the ground that it was irrelevant and that it was inadmissible hearsay.

- Regarding relevance, the majority concluded that words spoken when K was not present only provided evidence of the callers' states of mind and thus were irrelevant to the issues in the case. At most, the words established that the callers believed that K was a supplier. Had K been present when the words were spoken and had he accepted their truth, then that would have been another matter (see *Christie* [1914] AC 545).

- As far as hearsay was concerned, the majority held that just as any reported express assertion by a witness who said 'Kearley is a drug dealer' would have been inadmissible under the hearsay rule, so too this evidence which by implication sought to establish that K was a dealer was inadmissible for the same reason: the Crown was relying upon the truth of an assertion *implicit* in the fact that 17 people had called within a short space of time asking for drugs. As Lord Oliver put it:

> I cannot...see any logical difference between evidence of a positive assertion and evidence of an assertion expressed as a question from which the positive assertion is to be inferred. In both cases the opinion or belief of the maker is unsworn and untested by cross-examination and is equally prejudicial. To admit such statements as evidence of the fact would...not only entail a radical departure from the underlying reasoning in *Blastland* and *Myers v DPP* [*ante*, para **9.4(iii)**]...but would involve embarking upon a process of judicial legislation.
>
> (at 277)

9.6 Both rulings were questionable. *Kearley* demonstrated the inconvenience (and some would have said, the plain silliness) of the hearsay rule. Even though implied assertions, as Lord Bridge pointed out, are not motivated by any possible intention to mislead and should therefore be exempt from much of the suspicion which attaches to express assertions, and although they are, in a sense, 'self-authenticating', the majority nevertheless determined that they too were inadmissible hearsay. History, however, is prone to repeat itself. In *O'Connell* [2003] EWCA Crim 502, O had been arrested in the street in possession of drugs. His mobile telephone rang. The call was answered by the police, and a woman asked O to 'sort me out two'—that is, until O, who could not hear the caller but guessed what the call was about, shouted to her that she was talking to police officers. The same thing happened a second time, the caller this time asking 'Can you sort me out one?'; O shouted to him: 'Hang up you stupid wanker, it's the old bill!' Indeed, as Mantell LJ relates—it would be funny, were it not so grave—*en route* to the police station 'the phone hardly stopped ringing'. It was conceded that O's reaction to the calls was admissible as evidence suggestive of his involvement in drug dealing. However, the court followed *Kearley* in ruling that the police witness could not relate the content of the calls because 'what the caller says...is irrelevant unless the person to whom he is addressing his remarks actually hears it' and, of course, is inadmissible hearsay (at [10]).

9.7 From the foregoing, it should be apparent both why the Law Commission was instructed to review the hearsay rule and to make recommendations for its overhaul in criminal cases, and why Part 11 of the Criminal Justice Act 2003 has fundamentally reorganised this area of the law of evidence. This prologue, outlining the faults in the old law, has been necessary because many of the Law Commission proposals that have been integrated into the new statute, more or less unaltered, can be best understood against the background of what went before: the old law, to a degree, has shaped much of the new text.

> 'The hearsay rule with its exceptions resembles an old-fashioned crazy quilt made of patches cut from a group of paintings by cubists, futurists and surrealists.'
>
> Morgan & Maguire, *Looking Backward and Forwards at Evidence*, 50 Harv L Rev 909, 921 (1937)

What constitutes hearsay evidence under the Criminal Justice Act 2003?

9.8 Sections 114 and 115 of the Criminal Justice Act 2003 provide a new definition of hearsay. These provisions lay down which 'statements' are to be treated as inadmissible, as well as how the notions of 'statement' and 'matter stated' are to be construed under the Act. Section 114 sets out the foundational principle that 'statements' which have not been made in oral evidence are inadmissible unless they fall within one of four categories of exception:

> In criminal proceedings a statement not made in oral evidence in the proceedings is admissible as evidence of any matter stated if, but only if...
>
> (s 114(1))

9.9 *Statements.* Section 115(2) proceeds to define what is meant by a 'statement' in the 2003 Act:

> A statement is any representation of fact or opinion made by a person by whatever means; and it includes a representation made in a sketch, photofit or other pictorial form.

It will be noted that the hearsay rule encompasses evidence of a declarant's representation, whether of fact or of opinion, no matter how that may have been expressed. The illustrative examples—sketches, photofits and other pictorial forms—figure amongst the most common instances of representations of fact or opinion made otherwise than in words. To these could be added people communicating by means of signs or gestures. Put at its most elementary, unless the evidence falls within an exception to the hearsay rule, the Act forbids A to repeat in court what B, who is not a witness in the case, has represented as a fact or as his opinion on a matter stated.

9.10 *Matters stated.* Section 115(3) further defines what is meant by the expression 'matter stated', as employed in s 114(1) and throughout Part 11, Chapter 2 of the Act:

> A matter stated is one to which this Chapter applies if (and only if) the purpose, or one of the purposes, of the person making the statement appears to the court to have been—
>
> (a) to cause another person to believe the matter, or

(b) to cause another person to act or a machine to operate on the basis that the matter is as stated.

This provision was inserted with the explicit purpose of reversing the decision of the House of Lords in *Kearley* [1992] 2 AC 228 (*ante*, para **9.5**), which had held that 'implied assertions' fell within the purview of the hearsay rule. The legislature's intention was that only statements that were intended to be assertive by the original maker ought to fall within the hearsay rule. The section is framed in these particular terms (causing another person to believe) owing to concerns that, if otherwise expressed, different solutions might be demanded according to the exact form that the reported speech took. Such an interpretation has been confirmed by the Court of Appeal in *Singh* [2006] 1 WLR 1564, where Rose LJ confessed that, although the interrelationship between ss 114 and 115 is 'deeply obscure', the common law rule against the admissibility of hearsay has been abolished. Read together, ss 114 and 118 abolish the common law hearsay rules (save those expressly preserved by s 118) and create instead a new rule against hearsay which does not extend to implied assertions. What was said by the callers in *Kearley* should now be admissible as direct evidence of the fact that there was a ready market for the supply of drugs from the premises, from which could be inferred an intention by an occupier to supply drugs. The view of the majority of the House of Lords in *Kearley*, in relation to hearsay, has therefore been set aside by the Act. Hence, in *Singh* itself telephone entries, which showed that calls had been made from mobile telephones that were said to have been in S's possession at the time of a kidnap, were not a 'matter stated' within s 115. They were relevant implied assertions, which are now treated as admissible because they are no longer hearsay.

9.11 Section 115(3)(a) provides that a statement is only to be treated as hearsay if:

> one of the purposes, of the person making the statement appears to the court to have been to cause another person to believe the matter.

In each case it will be a matter of determining what the maker of the statement's purposes were when uttering the words. Thus, in *Leonard* (2009) 173 JP 366 the Court of Appeal held that two text messages sent to L, who stood charged with possession of Class A drugs with intent to supply, ought to have been treated as hearsay statements. One correspondent had proclaimed that L's 'gear' was 'well sound' and that he felt 'well wankered today'; the other sender appeared to be moaning about the quantity of drugs with which L had supplied him. The texts, which had not been in oral evidence, contained statements of fact, the purpose in seeking adduce them had been to prove the matters therein stated, and the purpose of whoever had sent the texts had been to cause the recipient to believe the matters stated within them.

9.12 Many illustrations can now be found under the 2003 Act. In *N* (2007) 171 JP 158, for example, the Court of Appeal determined that because a diary kept by the victim of a sexual assault, whose contents might not have been admissible as evidence of the facts under the old law, had been kept for her own purposes and had not been intended to be read by anyone or to cause anyone else to believe anything, it did not constitute hearsay within the meaning of the 2003 Act. This decision has been followed in *Knight* [2007] EWCA Crim 3027, where the aunt of C, a victim of rape and gross indecency committed on a female under 16, was allowed to testify to the contents of C's diary, which C had since destroyed. The aunt's evidence fell outside the hearsay rule as C had never intended that others would read her diary and, the Court declared, was the equivalent of evidence showing the witnessing of a reaction by a particular person to an incident:

> [T]he very point of the decision in *N* and the terms of s 115, namely that the diary entries are not representations but direct evidence, is that [the aunt's] account of that direct evidence is to be thought of as parallel to observing someone fleeing, or lashing out in reaction, or being in an embrace with someone, or blushing at a significant moment: an account of direct evidence by an observer explaining the reactions of the observed person.
>
> (at [19])

In each case, it will be for the party seeking to adduce the evidence to satisfy the tribunal what the purposes of the maker of the statement actually were.

9.13 In a different context, in *MK* (2008) 172 JP 538, a case in which MK was acquitted of being concerned in making an offer to sell amphetamines, the prosecution successfully appealed against a trial judge's terminating ruling on a point of hearsay. The Court of Appeal held that the Crown had been wrongly prevented from adducing a covertly recorded conversation between V (who did not testify at MK's trial) and police officers concerning the price of drugs. MK's name had cropped up in the course of that conversation. The Crown wanted to use the recording to enable the jury to infer that MK must have been the supplier of the drugs. The Court of Appeal held that the trial judge had wrongly ruled that this evidence was hearsay, and hence inadmissible. It was plain that the sole purpose of the police officers' conversation with V was to elucidate the price and availability of amphetamines. Therefore, V's purpose had not been to cause another person to believe that MK was the supplier of the drugs. The Court of Appeal came to a similar conclusion in *Elliott* (2011) 175 JP 39, where evidence of E's membership of the Peckham Young Guns (PYG) gang was partly proved by inferences drawn from letters E had received in prison in which the writers had included references to gangs and drawings of a hand making a 'P' shape (the sign of the

PYG). E argued that the letters were inadmissible hearsay. Holroyde J disagreed: the authors were not making any representation of fact or opinion, nor did they have as a purpose causing E to believe any such representation or to act on the basis that it was correct:

> They were simply expressing the shared support of both writer and reader for the PYG. The contents of the letter could properly be regarded by the jury as being predicated upon a shared involvement in the gang. The jury could infer that the authors did not need to, and did not, represent any fact, or seek to cause the applicant to believe or act upon any such representation, precisely because of that shared involvement.
>
> (at [27])

9.14 The Criminal Justice Act 2003 seems not to have banished all uncertainty when courts try to unravel whether or not particular evidence does potentially constitute inadmissible hearsay. Even the new definition, constructed in terms of causing another person to believe the matter, can present courts with difficulties. In *Olden* [2007] EWCA (Crim) 726 at [35], for example, Dyson LJ, without totally committing himself, expressed serious doubts as to whether the trial judge had been correct to treat certain financial data as hearsay. Auld LJ's judgment in *Isichei* (2006) 170 JP 753, too, exemplifies the problems posed. I had been identified as one of two men who had robbed and assaulted a pair of female students out on the razzle in Manchester. I claimed that it was a case of mistaken identity. The trial judge had allowed the Crown to introduce evidence that, as they were cruising around in the early hours looking for an open nightclub the girls had heard an unidentified companion in their taxi say that he was going to call someone called Marvin. Marvin was I's first name. At the nightclub to which they were eventually admitted, the students for the second time saw the two men, one of whom was later identified as their assailant. On appeal, one question was whether the trial judge had correctly admitted the evidence of the telephone call, which he held did not amount to evidence of a 'matter stated' under s 115(3)(a). The judge held that the word 'Marvin' was not a statement amounting to hearsay because it had not been said for the purpose of making anyone believe anything. On appeal, Auld LJ was somewhat equivocal. Indeed, it is difficult to discern exactly what his Lordship did decide on this point. Section 114(1)(d), however, came to the rescue (see *post*, para **9.76**):

> [T]he judge may have been wrong in concluding that it was not a statement within s 115(3) and so governed by the Act. That would require a semantically correct and somewhat highly artificial application of the provision in this context in an analysis to what was essentially an inconsequential part of the story so far as the speaker on the telephone at the time was concerned. It is common sense that it is a possible inference that he spoke to

Marvin, or someone whom he knew who was at the club, leading, as a result of the conversation, for them all to go there. But even if the man on the telephone had not, in the words of s 115(3)(a), had the purpose of causing the others in the cab to know that he was talking to Marvin, the evidence, if that were the case, would be, if anything, more probative than otherwise. Why should he care, if the story was true, what the others believed as to the truth of the person to whom he was talking or as to what was being said? Their only interest at the time was whether as a result of the telephone call they would be able to find another club to go to which was open. Whatever the position, it seems to us that the evidence about that was clearly admissible in the interests of justice under s 114(1)(d) as part of the story of a common sense series of events, the one leading from the other.

(at [41])

9.15 It should be noted that the hearsay provisions apply only to statements made by persons. They do not therefore apply to statements emanating from machines that are operating automatically. The hearsay rule will only apply where a statement from a machine is based upon information fed into it by a person, one of whose purposes appears to the court to have been

> to cause ... a machine to operate on the basis that the matter is as stated.
> (s 115(3)(b))

In such cases, the matters stated will require to be proved. Broadly speaking, this preserves a distinction that existed under the old law. In *Wood* (1982) 76 Cr App R 23, for example, the Crown needed to prove that metal found in W's possession was similar to the metal which made up a stolen consignment. Chemists had performed analyses, which had then been fed through a computer. Because the chemists had come to court and given oral evidence concerning the work they had done, the figures produced by the computer were held admissible. Had the chemists not given this oral evidence, the computer results would have been inadmissible. Such would still be the case today under s 115(3)(b), because the object of the chemists in making their statements, when feeding data into the computer, was 'to cause ... a machine to operate on the basis that the matter is as stated'. For this same reason, under the 2003 Act, a court would still hold inadmissible evidence rejected by the court in *Coventry Justices, ex p Bullard* (1992) 95 Cr App R 175. The Crown had sought to adduce a computer printout indicating that B was in arrears with his poll tax in order to establish that that was so. The Crown, however, was unable to produce any witness who had actually fed the relevant information into the computer. The court held the printout inadmissible on the ground that it must have been based on data 'implanted' into the computer by human agency, which had not been properly proved. Such evidence would still be hearsay evidence under s 115(3)(b), and inadmissible unless salvaged under s 114(1)(d) (see *post*, para **9.70**).

9.16 *Methodology.* The first critical step, it will have been seen, is to identify potentially inadmissible hearsay evidence. Not all reported speech is automatically treated as hearsay. The law distinguishes between hearsay evidence (as defined in ss 114 and 115), on the one hand, and original evidence, on the other. In essence, the distinction between hearsay and original evidence rests upon the purpose for which the statement was made and, hence, for which evidence is being introduced. If the purpose for which a party leads the evidence is to establish a matter stated by means of a statement which the original maker uttered in order to cause someone else to believe the matter, that *prima facie* will be inadmissible hearsay. Unless it falls within one of the exceptions to the hearsay rule, such evidence ought to be ruled inadmissible. To take a simple case, let us imagine that Vera has been robbed by Dave, an old acquaintance. In the event, the prosecution simply calls PC Walter to report that Vera told him that Dave had robbed her. The prosecution elects not to call Vera as a witness. Since the prosecution's plain objective is to prove the contents of Vera's statement to PC Walter—namely, that Dave robbed her—this would be inadmissible 'hearsay'. Vera's 'statement' will constitute a representation of fact not made in oral evidence in the proceedings whose purpose, when made, was to cause another person (PC Walter) to believe it. 'Original evidence', in contrast, occurs when a party is simply reporting the fact of what someone else has said or written, but is not relying upon the statement as a representation of fact or opinion and the purpose of the original maker of the statement is not to cause another person to believe the matter or to act upon it. Having once established that a particular item does constitute hearsay evidence, the second step is to determine whether that evidence falls within one of the many exceptions to the hearsay rule.

Exceptions to the rule against hearsay (s 114)

9.17 Section 114(1) sets out the four categories of situation in which hearsay evidence becomes admissible under the Act. The provision states:

> In criminal proceedings a statement not made in oral evidence in the proceedings is admissible as evidence of any matter stated if, but only if—
>
> (a) any provision of this Chapter or any other statutory provision makes it admissible,
>
> (b) any rule of law preserved by s 118 makes it admissible,
>
> (c) all parties to the proceedings agree to it being admissible, or
>
> (d) the court is satisfied that it is in the interests of justice for it to be admissible.

We shall consider each of these four exceptions separately, and in the order in which they are set out in the Act.

Unavailable witnesses and business documents

9.18 The Law Commission, in its draft bill, had envisaged that hearsay evidence would be admitted in the following categories of situation:

- it would be automatically admissible in cases where a declarant's oral evidence was, for one of certain specified reasons, unavailable;

- as under the previous law, statements made by witnesses who are in fear could be admitted with the leave of the court;

- as under the old law, there would be an exception allowing for the admissibility of business documents.

These broad categories of admissible hearsay are now reproduced in what May LJ has described as 'the labyrinthine recesses of ss 117 and 116' of the Criminal Justice Act 2003 (*Kordansinki* [2007] 1 Cr App R 17 at [64]). The hearsay exceptions set out in ss 116 and 117 extend to both documentary and oral evidence. We shall consider each category of admissible hearsay in turn.

(a) Cases where a witness is unavailable (s 116)

9.19 *Statements of identified absent witnesses (s 116(1) and s 116(2)(a)–(d))*—The first major exception to the hearsay rule concerns identified witnesses who are unavailable to testify in person. Section 116(1) provides:

> In criminal proceedings a statement not made in oral evidence in the proceedings is admissible as evidence of any matter stated if—
>
> (a) oral evidence given in the proceedings by the person who made the statement would be admissible as evidence of that matter,
>
> (b) the person who made the statement (the relevant person) is identified to the court's satisfaction, and
>
> (c) any of the five conditions mentioned in subsection (2) is satisfied.

Before being admitted, all such statements, whether written or oral, will need to surmount three hurdles.

- *First*, evidence of a statement may only be introduced if the maker could have given admissible oral evidence of the matter in question. This means that two types of statement will be excluded. On the one hand, facts which are simply inadmissible, no matter how they are presented, will remain so. Thus, evidence of bad character that falls outside the provisions of Part 11 of the 2003 Act (see *ante*, Chapter 7) or a confession that has been beaten out of a suspect (see *post*, Chapter 10) cannot of course be adduced under this hearsay exception. On the other hand, admissible facts of which the maker of the statement would not have been permitted to give oral evidence will also fall outside this exception.

Therefore, evidence may not be given of a fact of which the maker of the statement did not have personal knowledge. Equally, a statement will be inadmissible if the maker would not have been competent to testify at the time that he originally made the statement.

- *Secondly*, the statement may only be introduced provided that the maker has been identified to the court's satisfaction. This restriction was included in order to enable an opposing party to challenge the maker's credibility and reliability. The requirement applies equally to prosecution and defence evidence. The notion of admitting the statements of unidentified declarants was thought entirely unsatisfactory. An example of which much was made during the gestation of this section concerned a hypothetical defendant, who called a witness to say that whilst travelling on a train overseas he had overheard a conversation between two strangers. They were discussing how they had carried out the murder for which the defendant currently stood charged, and had further declared that the defendant had not been present at the killing. Even in this situation, it would be necessary under s 116(1)(b) to attribute the statement to a specific individual, together with sufficient detail of that person's identity, in order to satisfy the court that the relevant person actually exists, and to supply the Crown with enough information to enable it to make enquiries about the maker and to test the maker's credibility at trial, if such a course was felt appropriate. (The requirement that the declarant must be identified to the satisfaction of the court also led the Court of Appeal in *Mayers* [2009] 1 WLR 1915 to conclude that the hearsay evidence of anonymous witnesses is completely inadmissible in an English courtroom. Legislation, which has substituted a new regime for the common law rules governing the delivery of evidence by anonymous witnesses, provides only for the identities of individuals who testify at trial to be concealed (see *infra*, paras **9.104–9.114**). As Lord Judge CJ remarked, 'the language of the [2003] Act is quite clear and it requires disclosure of the witness's name, not just confidentially and secretly to the judge, but to the defence' (at [109]). Section 116, therefore, cannot apply to anonymous statements made by parties who do not give evidence at trial.)

- *Thirdly*, s 116(1) requires that the party seeking to adduce evidence of a statement must establish the existence of one of five alternative conditions. In this section, we shall consider the first four, since the fifth (which concerns witnesses who do not testify through fear: s 116(2)(e)) adopts a slightly different *schema* and merits separate treatment.

9.20 Even if evidence has cleared these three hurdles, it may also be desirable for the judge to explain to the jury how to consider such evidence. As Laws LJ noted in

McCoy [1999] All ER (D) 1410, where the victim's written statement was admitted in evidence in lieu of his live evidence,

> If a statement of a critical witness is to be read to a jury, perhaps especially in an alibi case where identification is the true issue, it must be incumbent on the trial judge to ensure that the jury realise the drawbacks which are imposed on the defence if the prosecution statement is read to them. It is not enough simply to say that counsel has not had the opportunity of cross-examining. The lay jury may not appreciate the significance of that fact. The judge must at least explain that it means that they may feel quite unable to attach anything like as much weight to the evidence in the statement, as they might if it were tested in cross-examination; and where appropriate it would be necessary, certainly desirable, for the judge also to indicate to the jury by way of illustration the sort of matters that might well be put in cross-examination in the particular case.
>
> (at [25])

Although *McCoy* was concerned with pre-2003 law, the counsel of prudence enunciated in the judgment is equally applicable to hearsay evidence admitted under the Criminal Justice Act 2003.

9.21 Section 116(2) lays down five facts, which will permit a party to adduce the statements of identified, absent witnesses. The first four alternative conditions laid down by the subsection are:

(a) that the relevant person is dead;

(b) that the relevant person is unfit to be a witness because of his bodily or mental condition;

(c) that the relevant person is outside the United Kingdom and it is not reasonably practicable to secure his attendance; [or]

(d) that the relevant person cannot be found although such steps as it is reasonably practicable to take to find him have been taken...

These conditions are not dissimilar to provisions contained in the earlier Criminal Justice Act 1988, and the courts have sometimes invoked authorities decided under this earlier legislation when interpreting certain of the new provisions.

- *Death*—The first condition, the death of the declarant, is probably self-explanatory.

- *Bodily or mental condition*—The notion of bodily or mental impairments to testifying requires some comment. Paragraph (b) follows quite closely the wording of the 1988 Act. One can therefore assume that the courts are likely to construe the language in the same way as under the previous Act. It is true that the words 'because of his bodily...condition' could have been understood to refer only to the evidence of witnesses who are by reason of their bodily condition completely 'unfit to attend' court—that is to say, this provision might be construed only to allow the reception of the evidence of those who are bed ridden, paralysed, raving and so on. In *Millett* (2000) 21 July, transcript no 99/07705/W2, however, the Court of Appeal ruled that the testimony of a 79-year-old victim of a burglary might be given in documentary form because there was medical evidence indicating a risk that she might suffer transient blindness or even a stroke if she testified in person. The court held that a witness who runs a modest risk of potentially serious, permanent consequences could properly be found unfit to attend by reason of her bodily condition. As regards 'mental condition', this expression too was given a generous reading under the 1988 legislation. In *Setz-Dempsey* (1994) 98 Cr App R 23 it was stated that although, strictly speaking, an amnesiac could in a sense be described as 'fit to attend' court, 'unfitness to attend' referred not to the witness's physical ability to be present in court but to that person's ability to testify capably. An amnesiac's testimony, therefore, might be received in the form of a written statement under this provision. Moreover, the decision whether or not to admit a witness's evidence under this subsection has always been entirely a matter for the judge. Thus, in *Lang* [2004] EWCA Crim 1701, at L's retrial on a burglary charge, owing to a marked deterioration in the principal prosecution witness's mental condition following the first trial, the Crown wished to introduce his evidence under this hearsay exception. Although a doctor's report indicated that, in his opinion, S was technically fit to attend as a witness, the judge conducting the hearing viewed a recent video recording of S being interviewed which left him in no doubt that S was not fit to attend within the meaning of the Act. On appeal, Buxton LJ upheld the decision to admit the transcript of the previous trial:

> [T]he person who makes the decision is the judge. He will be assisted in that by the doctor—but only assisted...It was entirely open to him...to form his own view about S's capacity to give evidence: this is a question not of his abstract mental state, but of whether he can give evidence.
>
> (at [6])

It is important that there is adequate evidence of the person's physical or mental incapacity. In *R (Meredith) v Harwich Justices* (2007) 171 JP 249 Collins J held that a doctor's statement, that it would be in a witness's best interests if she was able to submit written evidence, was neither very positive nor equivalent to proof that she was unfit to attend proceedings owing to her mental condition. Whilst the evidence pointed in that direction, it did not amount to sufficient proof of her unfitness to testify in person.

- *Witness outside the United Kingdom*—This provision, again, resembles an earlier legislative provision. Under the 1988 Act the notion of 'attendance' was given a generous reading. In *Radak* [1999] 1 Cr App R 187 the Court of Appeal held that when the legislation referred to a person outside the UK who had made a statement and 'it is not reasonably practicable to secure his attendance', 'attendance' means not only 'being present in person at the criminal proceedings' but also covers cases where a witness gives evidence by live television link under the Criminal Justice Act 1988, s 32 because, the Court reasoned, such a person:

can be seen and heard live by those involved in the...trial, not least the jury. For all practical present purposes, the witness attends the English criminal trial.

(at 197)

In *C* [2006] EWCA Crim 197, three co-accused were charged with fraud. A key prosecution witness, P, was resident in South Africa. P's name, the Crown contended, had been employed without P's knowledge as a front for the purchase of a property at auction whose value had been artificially depressed thanks to a false lease, which was entirely of the co-defendants' invention. Originally P had agreed to come over to London and testify, but late in the day his solicitor announced that P in fact would give evidence neither in person nor by video link. The Crown applied successfully at a preparatory hearing, held under s 31 of the Criminal Procedure and Investigations Act 1996, to put in evidence under s 116(2)(c) a note of a 30-minute telephone call between P and the building owner's trustee in bankruptcy, together with a transcript of evidence taken at a magistrates' court in South Africa (sworn for purposes of the owner's insolvency proceedings), and a witness statement confirming the answers P had given in that transcript. In reversing the trial judge's ruling, Pill LJ indicated that the expression 'reasonably practicable' was to be given a similar reading as under earlier legislation:

We accept...that the expression 'reasonably practicable' in s 116(2)(c) of the 2003 Act must in this case be judged on the basis of the steps taken, or not taken, by the party seeking to secure the attendance of the witness. That is, however, only the first stage in a ruling upon the admissibility of the statement...The court must also consider whether to exercise its powers under s 126 of the 2003 Act and s 78 of the 1984 Act...

Whether it is fair to admit the statement...depends, in part, on what efforts should reasonably be made to secure the attendance of the witness or, at least, to arrange a procedure whereby the contents of the statements can be clarified and challenged...

(at [23] and [24])

On the facts of the case the Court was not satisfied that the parties had made sufficiently strenuous endeavours to secure P's attendance at court:

> Here, parties had not made great efforts, and each simply hoped that the judge would rule in their favour. Thus, owing to their "lack of flexibility" and the fact that this was a ruling delivered at a preparatory hearing in a fraud case, orders in the prosecution's favour are premature. What further steps should be taken is for the consideration of the parties and then for case management by the trial judge.
>
> (at [26])

- *Witness cannot be found*—The formulation of this exception is slightly different to its predecessor (Criminal Justice Act 1988, s 23(2)(c)). However, even if it does seem to impose slightly less demands on the party seeking to adduce the evidence, it remains the case that it has to be shown that reasonable attempts have been made to secure the attendance of the missing witness. In *Lockley and Corah* [1995] 2 Cr App R 554, under the old law, at the defendants' retrial, a principal prosecution witness was available to testify to a confession that C had allegedly made to her whilst they were sharing a cell. Before L and C's retrial, however, the witness in question had absconded from open prison while on home leave. The Court of Appeal held that the trial judge would have been entitled to admit her evidence under this exception, it having been shown that the police had employed all reasonable endeavours to recapture the witness. In *Adams* (2008) 172 JP 113, a decision handed down under the 2003 Act, the Court of Appeal admonished the prosecution in a case where, apart from one telephonic contact made two months after the date of trial had been set, the sole effort made to ensure an important prosecution witness's attendance at trial was a message left on the voicemail of the latter's mobile 'phone on the final working day before the trial was due to begin. On the day of trial a police officer had also failed to get through to the witness by telephone. Hughes LJ remarked,

> [T]the need to keep in touch, to be alive to the witness's needs and commitments is not less now than it ever was; if anything, it is rather greater now than it used to be. Leaving contact with the witness such as this until the last working day before the trial is not good enough and it certainly is not "such steps as it is reasonably practicable to take to find him."
>
> (at [13])

Noting that it would not have required vast expenditure, the Court suggested that once the message left on the witness's voicemail was not known to have been received, reasonably practicable steps which ought to have been taken could have included a visit to his address and/or to his place of work or agency, or at least contact with those places, perhaps by telephone. Hughes LJ's reference to expenditure echoes concerns expressed under the 1988 Act where courts regularly took a number of factors into account in determining whether or not reasonable steps had been taken to secure a witness's attendance (eg *Medway* [2000] Crim LR 415; *Henry* [2003] EWCA Crim 1296). The types of factor that a court might wish to take into account included expense, the seriousness of the offences being tried, the relative importance of the witness's testimony in the context of the trial, and even the feasibility of securing the witness's attendance at a later date should the parties raise the issue of postponing the trial. *Adams* would indicate that such factors will continue to play a role under the new formulation.

9.22 As was made clear in *DT* (2009) 173 JP 425, whenever a party seeks to introduce a statement under s 116 on the ground that a witness is unavailable or reluctant to testify through fear, the trial court will require either agreed facts or the production of evidence to demonstrate that s 116 is actually engaged on the facts.

9.23 Section 116(5), not surprisingly, provides that s 116(1) and (2) do not apply if a witness's death, bodily or mental state, absence from the United Kingdom or inability to be found is ascribable to the actions of the party seeking to have that person's statement admitted:

> A condition set out in any paragraph of subs (2) which is in fact satisfied is to be treated as not satisfied if it is shown that the circumstances described in that paragraph are caused—
>
> (a) by the person in support of whose case it is sought to give the statement in evidence, or
>
> (b) by a person acting on his behalf,
>
> in order to prevent the relevant person giving oral evidence in the proceedings (whether at all or in connection with the subject matter of the statement).

Whilst s 116(5) clearly applies to defendants who interfere with their own witnesses, the wording, 'person in support of whose case', does not necessarily make clear what the situation is if, having got word that an important prosecution witness has decided to recant on her evidence at trial, a misguidedly zealous police officer knocks her down with his panda car in the hope that her statement will be admitted in evidence under s 116.

(b) Statements of witnesses who do not testify through fear (s 116(2)(e))

9.24 Section 116(2)(e) allows a witness's statement to be given in evidence in place of oral testimony where it can be shown:

> that through fear the relevant person does not give (or does not continue to give) oral evidence in the proceedings, either at all or in connection with the subject matter of the statement, and the court gives leave for the statement to be given in evidence.

This is intended to provide a very broad exception to the rule against hearsay, and is meant to encourage courts to be sympathetic to witnesses who do not testify through fear. The analogous provision under the Criminal Justice Act 1988 was considered of considerable practical importance in alleviating the widespread problem of witness intimidation. Home Office research, derived from the 1998 British Crime Survey, revealed that intimidation of victims and witnesses was likely to have occurred in no less than eight per cent of criminal cases (*Victim and Witness Intimidation: Key Finding from the British Crime Survey*, 2000). The problem of witnesses who are fearful of testifying, it should be said, besets both prosecution and defence. The 1988 Act, too, used to allow the statement of a Crown witness to be read out in court if the party seeking to adduce the documentary evidence could establish beyond reasonable doubt that the witness had failed to give evidence through fear (*Cole* [1990] 2 All ER 108). Whilst the Act made plain that a witness who failed to give any evidence at all through fear fell within this provision, prior to *Ashford Justices, ex p Hilden* [1993] QB 555, in the Divisional Court, and *Waters* (1997) 161 JP 249, in the Court of Appeal, it had been unclear whether the statement of a witness who broke down during the course of testifying but who could still be expected to contribute material evidence was admissible. Endorsing these decisions, the 2003 Act makes clear that the statement of someone who fails to complete giving testimony owing to fear may be admitted under s 116(2)(e) by referring explicitly to a witness who 'does not give (or does not continue to give) oral evidence'. The 2003 provision is broader than its predecessor in another significant respect: in order to become admissible, the witness's statement does not need to have been made to a police officer; it may have been made to anyone.

9.25 A perceived problem under the old law was the difficulty of identifying exactly what would qualify as a motive for 'fear'. Obviously it would cover such a thing as threats of bodily injury, but would it also extend to fear of financial loss, to threats from associates of the defendant rather than necessarily threats made by the defendant himself, or even to the plain notoriety that can attach to a witness who appears in a high-profile criminal case? What would now happen in a situation such as arose in *Parkinson* [2004] EWCA Crim 3195? There, a defence witness was 'apprehensive' of testifying because, when initially interviewed by them, the police had put questions to him on the basis that he might have conspired with P in the handling of stolen goods. He feared what he termed 'police harassment'. As the trial judge said, the witness 'no doubt [anticipated] that giving evidence would not be a very pleasant experience and he [did] not want to be questioned by the police'. Although the concept of 'fear' was undefined in the 1988 Act, the Court of Appeal upheld the judge's ruling that this was not a witness in fear within the meaning of that legislation. Hooper LJ twice referred to the Criminal Justice Act 2003 (which was not in force at the time), but left open how in likelihood this question would be resolved under s 116 of the Act. The intention of the 2003 Act was to lay many such doubts to rest, and to encourage the courts to make wide use of s 116(2)(e), whenever a witness could be shown to have failed to testify owing to fear of almost any sort. To this end, s 116(3) stipulates:

> For the purposes of subsection (2)(e) "fear" is to be widely construed and (for example) includes fear of the death or injury of another person or of financial loss.

This wording wears a slightly casual air, but the general message is clear. Nevertheless, it may well be that a witness, like the hapless fellow in *Parkinson*, remains outside its ambit. (See also Tapper, 'Use of Third Party Confessions: *R v Finch*' (2007) 11 E&P 318, esp at 321.)

9.26 The courts are alive to the risks to which this generous interpretation of 'fear' now lays the law open. In *Davies (Anita)* [2007] 2 All ER 1070, for example, Moses LJ pointed out that under the 2003 Act 'fear' is now to be widely construed and that, in consequence, 'courts are ill-advised to seek to test the basis of fear by calling witnesses before them, since that may undermine the very thing that s 116 was designed to avoid' (at [14]). At the same time, however, Moses LJ was at pains to urge:

> [J]udges must be astute not to skew a fair trial by a too ready acceptance of assertions of fear since it is all too easy for witnesses to avoid the inconvenience and anxiety of a trial by saying they do not want to come.
>
> (at [15]. See also *Nelson* [2009] EWCA Crim 1600)

9.27 One major question, considered by the Law Commission, was whether the statements of witnesses affected by fear should be automatically admissible in the same way as the statements of identified dead persons, those who are unfit to testify, and so on (s 116(2)(a)–(d)). Hesitantly, the Law Commission became persuaded that witnesses in fear had to be treated separately from other types of absent, but identifiable witnesses, if only because:

> There is a very genuine risk that, if the statements of frightened witnesses were automatically admissible, prospective witnesses could give statements to the police in the knowledge that they could at a later stage falsely claim to be frightened, with the result that they could avoid having to go to court and be cross-examined…[I]t would be undesirable to have an automatic exception to the hearsay rule for frightened witnesses.
>
> (para 8.58)

For this mildly implausible reason, the statements of those who do not testify through fear are only admissible with the leave of the court (s 116(2)(e)). Section 116(4) sets out factors to which the court must have regard in determining whether to allow the statement to be admitted:

> Leave may be given under subsection (2)(e) only if the court considers that the statement ought to be admitted in the interests of justice, having regard—

(a) to the statement's contents,

(b) to any risk that its admission or exclusion will result in unfairness to any party to the proceedings (and in particular to how difficult it will be to challenge the statement if the relevant person does not give oral evidence),

(c) in appropriate cases, to the fact that a direction under s 19 of the Youth Justice and Criminal Evidence Act 1999 (special measures for the giving of evidence by fearful witnesses etc) could be made in relation to the relevant person, and

(d) to any other relevant circumstances.

The court is therefore enjoined to have regard to what is contained in the statement, to any risk of unfairness—whether to the defendant, to a co-defendant, or even to the prosecution—taking special account of the difficulty of challenging the statement, and (where appropriate) to the fact that the evidence could be received otherwise than from the witness in person in the courtroom. In determining whether a witness's failure to testify is actuated by fear, it was felt that the court should be encouraged to view matters through the witness's eyes, bearing in mind his or her personal weaknesses, and to assess whether that witness's failure to testify is reasonable in all the circumstances. The phrase 'any other relevant circumstances' in s 116(4)(d), it appears, was intended to encompass the personal traits and circumstances of the individual witness. Obviously, para (d) is not restricted to such matters, but gives the court free rein to take into account any other factor that strikes it as germane to whether it is in the interests of justice to admit the statement. Given that the 2003 Act has extended the range of statements potentially admissible under this provision to both oral statements and to statements made to parties other than police officers, s 116(4) will be important in ensuring compliance with Article 6(3)(d) of the ECHR, which guarantees the defendant the 'right to examine or have examined witnesses on his behalf under the same conditions as witnesses against him'—a point made by Potter LJ in *M (KJ)* [2003] 2 Cr App R 21, by Leveson J in *Arnold* [2004] EWCA Crim 1293, and by Waller LJ in *Sellick* [2005] 2 Cr App R 15 and by Scott Baker LJ in *Al-Khawaja* [2006] 1 WLR 1078 in relation to the 1988 Act (see further, *post* para **9.95** ff).

9.28   In *Doherty* (2007) 171 JP 79, in providing guidance on how to approach s 116(2)(e) and s 116(4), the Court of Appeal took these points to heart. At trial the judge had allowed the evidence of a solicitor, B, who had been returning by train from watching the FA Cup Final when his companion was unlawfully wounded by D, to be read out to the court pursuant to s 116(2)(e). B had been the most important witness to the attack. On appeal, D questioned whether evidence presented to the court to show that B was in fear had been sufficiently cogent to engage s 116(2)(e). There was only evidence of veiled threats, and no clear link could be established between B and D. The Court of Appeal laid down that in deciding whether to allow a witness's statement to be read the trial judge had to balance the subjective element of 'fear' in s 116(2)(e) against the objective element of fairness in s 116(4). Tuckey LJ, however, added that the trial judge would be in the best position to conduct this evaluative, fact-sensitive balancing. Therefore, adopting an approach similar to that employed by the Court of Appeal in relation to the admission of evidence of bad character (see *ante*, para **7.140**), Tuckey LJ made clear that an appellate court would only interfere with a trial court ruling on s 116(2)(e) if it was 'wrong, perverse or unreasonable'.

9.29   Obviously, if a potential witness claims to be in fear of testifying it may be highly relevant to consider who actually did the intimidating. What if it turns out that the party seeking to introduce the statement in evidence was the very party who intimidated the witness? In such cases, no question of discretion will arise. As in the four other situations set forth in s 116(5), where a party has deliberately ensured that a witness is unavailable to testify, such party will not be entitled to rely on that witness's statement (see *ante*, para **9.23**). Section 166(5) is likely to be most often employed in relation to witnesses who do not testify through fear. Thus, a party who can be shown to have been responsible for intimidating a witness with a view to preventing him from testifying will not be allowed to make use of that absent witness's statement.

(c) Business and other documents (s 117)

9.30   Under the previous law, the Criminal Justice Act 1988, s 24 made provision for documents generated in the course of business to be admitted under an exception to the hearsay rule. This general exception has been retained in the Criminal Justice Act 2003, s 117. Section 117(1) lays down that in criminal proceedings a statement contained in a document is admissible as evidence of any matter stated if oral evidence given in the proceedings would have been admissible as evidence of that matter, provided that certain conditions are met.

9.31   The 2003 Act draws a distinction between business documents, properly so called, and documents that qualify as business documents under the terms of s 117 but which have been prepared 'for the purposes of pending or contemplated criminal proceedings, or for a criminal investigation'. Additional conditions must be satisfied before the latter class of documents will become admissible.

9.32   The term 'document' is given a broad definition and, as under the old law, refers to 'anything in which information of any description is recorded' (s 134). Hence, in *Duffy* [1999] 1 Cr App R 307, a video recording of a severely disabled witness giving a statement to the police, which was admitted as a 'document' under the 1988 Act, would similarly be treated as a document under the 2003 Act.

9.33   Section 117(1) renders a statement contained in a document admissible as evidence of any matter stated if oral evidence given in the proceedings would be admissible as evidence of that matter, provided that certain conditions are met. The basic conditions of admissibility, set out in s 117(2), are:

(a) the document or the part containing the statement was created or received by a person in the course of a trade, business, profession or other occupation, or as the holder of a paid or unpaid office,

(b) the person who supplied the information contained in the statement (the relevant person) had or may reasonably be supposed to have had personal knowledge of the matters dealt with, and

(c) each person (if any) through whom the information was supplied from the relevant person to the person mentioned in para (a) received the information in the course of a trade, business, profession or other occupation, or as the holder of a paid or unpaid office.

Section 117, therefore, roughly speaking, covers the archetypal situation where A, who could at least be supposed to have had personal knowledge of the facts, passes that information on to B, who creates a document or receives a document from A as part of his employment or office.

9.34 As we all know, information in modern commercial organisations may pass through a number of hands before a record is created or before it reaches its ultimate recipient or repository. Section 117(2)(c) allows for this eventuality, but provides that if the information was supplied indirectly, it will only be admissible,

if each person…through whom the information was supplied from the relevant person to the person mentioned in para (a) received the information in the course of a trade, business, profession or other occupation, or as the holder of a paid or unpaid office.

The underlying idea is that whilst it must be shown that the facts originated in someone who had or could be taken to have had personal knowledge of them, from thereon it must only be transmitted through a chain of command of parties whose callings require or entitle them to handle such information until the final document is created or filed. Subsection (3) specifies that 'the persons mentioned in paras (a) and (b) of subs (2) may be the same person', meaning that a document created by someone who, in the course of a trade, business etc, records matters of which he might be reasonably supposed to have personal knowledge, also falls within s 117.

9.35 As mentioned above, the Criminal Justice Act 2003 distinguishes between business documents in general and documents generated as part of criminal investigations. Section 117(4) and (5) impose restrictions on the admissibility of 'business documents' if such statements were:

…prepared for the purposes of pending or contemplated criminal proceedings, or for a criminal investigation…

If a statement has been prepared for these purposes—and, most commonly, the provision contemplates statements witnesses have made to the police, it will only be admitted provided that it satisfies the requirements of s 117(5), which provides:

> The requirements of this subsection are satisfied if—
>
> (a) any of the five conditions mentioned in s 116(2) is satisfied (absence of relevant person etc), or
>
> (b) the relevant person cannot reasonably be expected to have any recollection of the matters dealt with in the statement (having regard to the length of time since he supplied the information and all other circumstances).

It was not Parliament's intention that the documentary hearsay provisions would provide a convenient short cut for the prosecution and police, authorising the admission of witness statements taken by the police (or, indeed, other investigating authorities) in circumstances that might prove prejudicial to defendants by dispensing with the need to call the witnesses concerned. The five conditions referred to in s 117(5)(a) have already been considered above (*ante*, paras **9.21–9.29**). Evidently, the object is to have witnesses testify in person, save in cases where this would either prove impossible (eg owing to death, physical or mental incapacity) or impractical (eg where the witness cannot be found, or where a witness does not testify through fear).

9.36 *Statements prepared for pending or contemplated criminal proceedings, or for a criminal investigation, of which the relevant person cannot reasonably be expected to have any recollection.* The requirement in s 117(5)(b) that a person cannot reasonably be expected to retain 'any recollection' of the matters dealt with in the statement predicates that if the supplier of the information harbours any recollection whatsoever of the contents of the statement, s 117 has no application and the statement is not admissible as a business document. As the wording of this provision is identical to that of the previous law, the old case law presumably remains relevant. Collins J's judgment in *Brown v Secretary of State for Social Security* (1994) Times, 7 December, read in conjunction with *Derodra* [2000] 1 Cr App R 41, would indicate that parties seeking the admission of business records under s 117 may be put to searching proof that the 'relevant person' is bereft of any recollection of the matters dealt with in the statement. The provision is certainly not intended to afford an easy way of remedying a witness's minor memory deficiency but is meant to cover cases where a witness could not reasonably be expected to retain any recollection of the matters dealt with in the document. In *Kamuhuza* (2009) 173 JP 55, in order to implicate K in a burglary that had taken place five years earlier the Crown needed to show that K's fingerprints matched those found on the window frame at the scene of the crime. By the time of trial X, who had lifted the fingerprints from the inside of the window-ledge, had left the police service and his whereabouts were allegedly unknown. Whilst Thomas LJ was unconvinced that X 'cannot be found although such steps as it is reasonably practicable to take to find him have been taken', as required by s 116(2)(d)—as he said of the efforts made to trace X, 'It would be kind to describe the actions of the police officer as desultory'—the Court of Appeal was willing to accept under s 117(5)(b) that X could not 'reasonably be expected to have any recollection of the matters dealt with in the statement (having regard to the length of time since he supplied the information and all other circumstances)'. The judge had to consider carefully whether on the materials laid before him, and on his knowledge of the way in which people work—particularly scene-of-crime officers—whether X would not reasonably be expected to have any recollection of the matter. The Court of Appeal upheld the judge's conclusion that in this particular situation s 117(5)(b) was satisfied.

9.37 *Documents of doubtful reliability.* Sometimes the court will have reason to doubt the reliability of the evidence contained in a business document. The 2003 Act provides the court with a general power to exclude such statements, whether or not they have been generated as part of a criminal investigation. However, in place of the complicated discretions that used to operate under the 1988 Act, s 117(6) simply states that a court may issue a direction ordering that a business document, otherwise admissible under s 117, is not to be admitted in evidence. In determining whether or not such a direction is called for, s 117(7) stipulates:

> The court may make a direction under this subsection if satisfied that the statement's reliability as evidence for the purpose for which it is tendered is doubtful in view of—
>
> (a) its contents,
>
> (b) the source of the information contained in it,
>
> (c) the way in which or the circumstances in which the information was supplied or received, or
>
> (d) the way in which or the circumstances in which the document concerned was created or received.

Some of these factors are self-explanatory. Thus, if the contents of the statement are self-contradictory or obviously fragmentary, if the method of transmission looks dubious or the mode of recording is egregiously casual, the court may feel it right to exercise discretion in favour of excluding the documentary evidence. But what of a situation such as arose in *Jisl, Tekin and Konakli* [2004] EWCA Crim 696? Under the previous law, the court was required to have regard 'to any risk, having regard in particular to whether it is likely to be possible to controvert the statement if the person making it does not attend to give oral evidence in the proceedings, that its admission or exclusion will result in unfairness to the accused ...' (Criminal Justice Act 1988, s 26(ii)). Thus, the trial judge in *Jisl* was held to have been within his rights in refusing T leave to adduce the written statement of a party, A, who could reasonably have been assumed to have been a member of the conspiracy to import large quantities of diamorphine into the UK, and whose evidence, because there was no chance that he would ever have come to testify in person, could never have been subjected to cross-examination. Would this now be a case where, under s 117 (7)(b), the court might be persuaded 'that the statement's reliability as evidence for the purpose for which it is tendered is doubtful in view of... the source of the information contained in it'?

9.38 A further provision renders inadmissible business documents created, transmitted or received by persons who do not enjoy full capacity. To this end, s 123(2) lays down:

> (2) Nothing in s 117 makes a statement admissible as evidence if any person who, in order for the requirements of s 117(2) to be satisfied, must at any time have supplied or received the information concerned or created or received the document or part concerned—
>
> (a) did not have the required capability at that time, or
>
> (b) cannot be identified but cannot reasonably be assumed to have had the required capability at that time.

The Act then goes on to specify the requisite level of capability, modelled upon s 53 of the Youth Justice and Criminal Evidence Act (see *ante*, para **3.3** ff):

> (3) For the purposes of this section a person has the required capability if he is capable of—
>
> (a) understanding questions put to him about the matters stated, and
>
> (b) giving answers to such questions which can be understood.

If a question arises in a case as to the capability of a relevant person, the enquiry takes place in the absence of the jury, expert evidence may be heard—as may evidence of the person to whom the statement was made—and the party seeking to adduce the business record must establish capability on a balance of probabilities (s 123(4)).

9.39 The terms of the court's discretion under s 117(7) are deliberately narrower than under the earlier law. Whereas previously the court's task in all cases was to determine whether it was in the interests of justice to admit the documentary evidence, the 2003 Act's exclusionary discretion is concerned solely with the statement's likely reliability. Thus, in determining a document's admissibility a court will no longer be required to investigate the fairness of admitting the evidence. So far as unfairness is concerned, a court may only have recourse to its general discretion to exclude otherwise admissible business or other documents that reflect adversely on the fairness of the proceedings under PACE, s 78.

Preservation of certain common law categories of admissibility (s 118)

9.40 Section 118 of the Criminal Justice Act 2003 retains eight of the old common law exceptions to the rule against hearsay. As s 118(2) then proceeds to state, all other common law exceptions to the hearsay rule (eg dying declarations, declarations by deceased persons against their financial or proprietary interests, and declarations made by deceased persons in the course of duty: see second edition of this work, paras **10.36–10.41**) are henceforth abolished. The following common law exceptions survive.

'Public information etc' (rule 1)

9.41 The first retained rule of common law covers a wide range of documents and sources of public information which the courts have for long admitted without demur. Rule 1 reads:

> Any rule of law under which in criminal proceedings—
>
> (a) published works dealing with matters of a public nature (such as histories, scientific works, dictionaries and maps) are admissible as evidence of facts of a public nature stated in them,
>
> (b) public documents (such as public registers, and returns made under public authority with respect to matters of public interest) are admissible as evidence of facts stated in them,
>
> (c) records (such as the records of certain courts, treaties, Crown grants, pardons and commissions) are admissible as evidence of facts stated in them, or
>
> (d) evidence relating to a person's age or date or place of birth may be given by a person without personal knowledge of the matter.

Technically, the information gleaned from these sources is hearsay in character, in the sense that the individuals who originally recorded the data will not be present in court to testify in person to the matters in question. (Many may have been dead for generations.) Detailed examination of many of these rules is beyond the scope of an introductory text, although some have been mentioned in the context of discussion of judicial notice (eg, see *ante*, para **1.17** ff).

'Reputation as to character' (rule 2)

9.42 Traditionally, at common law evidence of a party's character was only admissible in the form of evidence of reputation. Following *Rowton* (1865) L & Ca 520, a witness speaking to a party's character (good or bad) was not permitted to inform the court of his personal opinion of that person but might only speak to that person's reputation in the community (see *ante*, para **6.18**). Clearly, such an antiquated rule—which is expressly retained, despite s 99 having repealed all other common law rules relating to evidence of bad character—reposes on the most extreme form of hearsay. As an American court wryly observed, 'it is an evidentiary anomaly that—in proving general moral character, the law prefers hearsay, rumour, and gossip, to personal knowledge of the witness' (*Simpkins v State*, 256 SE 2d 65 (Ga Ct App 1979)). To add insult to injury, we know that the rule, restricting character evidence to evidence of reputation, was an error that entered English law, thanks to Lord Ellenborough CJ's irritable intervention at the trial of *Jones* (1809) 31 How St Tr 151, 310 (see Wigmore, *A Treatise on the Anglo-American System of Evidence in Trials at Common Law* (1923, 2nd edn) § 1981). Nevertheless, rule 2 retains:

> Any rule of law under which in criminal proceedings evidence of a person's reputation is admissible for the purpose of proving his good or bad character.

It adds, in a note, that 'the rule is preserved only so far as it allows the court to treat such evidence as proving the matter concerned'.

'Reputation or family tradition' (rule 3)

9.43 The common law has for long accepted the admissibility of a number of forms of declaration by parties who are unavailable to testify at trial. This is a complex and, sometimes, arcane area of evidence. Rule 3 provides for the retention of:

> Any rule of law under which in criminal proceedings evidence of reputation or family tradition is admissible for the purpose of proving or disproving—
>
> (a) pedigree or the existence of a marriage,
>
> (b) the existence of any public or general right, or
>
> (c) the identity of any person or thing.

By way of an example of evidence of reputation at work, take *Phillips* (2010) 174 JP 169. B, a witness to an assault, admitted that until some time after the incident he had not known the surname of the person, P, whom he claimed to be one of two assailants. B had seen P about a couple of times per day, knew that P spoke with a Liverpool accent, belonged to the Support Weapons Flight, and was nicknamed 'Scouse'. Following conviction, P argued that B's evidence, identifying him as one of the assailants, was inadmissible because it was based upon hearsay. The Courts Martial Appeal Court held that whilst the attribution of a surname is invariably based upon what a witness has been told by others, evidence of reputation for the purpose of proving the identity of a person has always been a common law exception to the rule against hearsay, and it has been preserved by s 118(1) r 3(c) of the Criminal Justice Act 2003. Amongst other forms of evidence preserved under s 118, r 3, a declaration made by a deceased relative, whether orally or in writing, has always been admissible to prove matters of family pedigree, provided that that declaration was made before the dispute currently before the court arose. The declaration as to pedigree reposed upon the necessity of admitting evidence which, by its nature, would be known to few people, which would be difficult of direct proof, and which the declarant would have little motive to misrepresent. One rule of law relating to the existence of marriage, which is presumably retained by rule 3, is that evidence of reputation is generally admissible to prove or disprove marriage. However, although evidence of general reputation is considered a sufficient form of proof for many purposes, in some contexts—for example, if a defendant is charged with bigamy—the court will require something more precise than evidence of reputation in order to establish the existence of a marriage.

9.44 Common law rules relating to public and general rights are a notorious legal thicket. Indeed, these rules antedate the hearsay rule itself by several centuries. In essence, the declaration of a deceased person concerning ancient public and general rights, which are incapable of proof by other direct means, are received by the courts on the ground that their truth is guaranteed by the public and general nature of those rights—a circumstance which supposedly tends to reduce the risk of misstatement and bias. As in the case of the declaration as to pedigree, the declaration must have been emitted before the present dispute arose. Rule 3 comes with a note attached, which cautions:

> The rule is preserved only so far as it allows the court to treat such evidence as proving or disproving the matter concerned.

'Res gestae' (rule 4)

9.45 One of the most significant common law exceptions to the hearsay rule—but, which, under the 2003 Act, will be of diminishing importance—was a doctrine known as *res gestae*. The doctrine means literally, 'things done'. Although Lord Wilberforce remarked in *Ratten v R* [1972] AC 378 that 'the expression *"res gestae"*, like many Latin phrases, is often used to cover situations insufficiently analysed in clear English terms', the Latin shorthand ought not to prove too off-putting and deceptive. (There has of late been something of a campaign against legal Latin, but as Lord Rodger of Earlsferry has pointed out, this view, 'which is unfortunately being given effect in the English system today, that the use of legal Latin is simply an objectionable form of elite bilingualism, is not only patronising but simplistic': (2005) 121 LQR 57 at 66n. See further, R Munday, *Does Latin impede Legal Understanding?* (2000) 164 JP Jo 995; *Lawyers and Latin* (2004) 168 JP Jo 775.) Essentially, the *res gestae* exception to the hearsay rule, which divides into several subheads, means that reported words that are so closely connected as to form part of the transaction are treated as admissible.

9.46 Rule 4 now retains:

> Any rule of law under which in criminal proceedings a statement is admissible as evidence of any matter stated if—
>
> (a) the statement was made by a person so emotionally overpowered by an event that the possibility of concoction or distortion can be disregarded,
>
> (b) the statement accompanied an act which can be properly evaluated as evidence only if considered in conjunction with the statement, or
>
> (c) the statement relates to a physical sensation or a mental state (such as intention or emotion).

We shall consider these three varieties of *res gestae* evidence separately.

9.47 *A statement made by a person so emotionally overpowered by an event that the possibility of concoction or distortion can be disregarded (rule 4(a)).* At one time the *res gestae* exception was confined within very narrow bounds. Thus, in *Bedingfield* (1878) 14 Cox CC 341, a notorious case that was only formally overruled in 1987, the Crown sought to adduce the dying words of a laundress (in likelihood, 'See what Harry [Bedingfield] has done'), whose throat had been slit with a razor shortly beforehand. In a decision that was vehemently criticised even in its day (see further Munday [1987] 46 CLJ 303), Sir Alexander Cockburn CJ excluded the laundress's statement on the extraordinary ground that:

> ... it was not part of anything done, or something said while something was being done, but something said after something done. It was not as if, while being in the room, and while the act was being done, she had said something which was heard.

In the latter portion of the twentieth century, the courts began to show greater latitude in interpreting what amounted to the bounds of the transaction. Notably, in *Ratten* [1972] AC 378 Lord Wilberforce, admittedly speaking *obiter*, defined the *res gestae* more generously to include events both preceding and following the central incident, provided that the pressure of events offers some guarantee of the accuracy of the statement. Thus, referring to words spoken before the event, he said:

> If the drama, leading up to the climax, has commenced and assumed such intensity and pressure that the utterance can safely be regarded as a true reflection of what was unrolling or actually happening, it ought to be received.
>
> (at 389–90)

Words uttered after the event might also be admitted provided that the judge could 'satisfy himself that the statement was so clearly made in circumstances of spontaneity and involvement in the event that the possibility of concoction can be disregarded'.

9.48 *Ratten* itself in fact affords an interesting illustration of hearsay. R was charged with having murdered his heavily pregnant wife, whom he had shot at close range. R's defence was that his shotgun went off accidentally while he was cleaning it in the kitchen. The prosecution wished to call a telephonist to testify that shortly before the wife was killed a woman rang the exchange from the house in an hysterical state, sobbing, 'Get me the police, please'. R denied that any such call was made. It was argued that the telephonist's evidence was inadmissible hearsay. The Privy Council determined that this testimony was admissible as original evidence because of its relevance to two purely factual issues. In the first place, it was said that the telephonist's evidence was relevant evidence of fact because it directly contradicted R's claim that no call had been made from the house that afternoon. Secondly, her evidence was relevant in showing the state of mind of a woman who was in fear shortly before the shooting, thereby rebutting R's defence that the gun went off by accident. The deceased's words, therefore, were not being employed testimonially to prove the truth of their contents, as demanded by the common law's former definition of hearsay. Lord Wilberforce, however, went on to add that, even were the woman's words in fact hearsay evidence adduced testimonially as evidence of the facts, they would nevertheless have been admissible as part of the *res gestae*. Were such a case to fall to be decided under the Criminal Justice Act 2003, provided that the wife's words were not considered to be a 'representation of fact or opinion made by a person by whatever means' (s 115(2)), and that the statement was not considered evidence of a matter stated, in the sense that 'the purpose, or one of the purposes, of the person making the statement appears to the court to have been to cause another person to believe the matter, or to cause another person to act on the basis that the matter is as stated' (s 115(3)), the hearsay rule and the *res gestae* exception would similarly not come into play.

9.49 Lord Wilberforce's expanded definition of *res gestae*, which, contrary to the approach adopted by the House of Lords in an earlier case, *Myers v DPP* [1965] AC 1001 (*ante*, para **9.4**), justifies the admissibility of hearsay evidence on the ground that its reliability is largely assured by the conditions of pressure under which the words were spoken, found favour in the House of Lords in *Andrews* [1987] AC 281. In the latter case, before lapsing into unconsciousness, the victim, who was seriously wounded, gave police officers summoned to his flat shortly after he was stabbed A's name as well as the name and address of another man. At A's subsequent trial for murder, the Crown was permitted to adduce evidence of what the deceased had said in order to identify A as one of his attackers. The House upheld this ruling in what is now the leading case on *res gestae*. Lord Ackner, following the lead of the Privy Council in *Ratten*, emphasised that when determining whether to admit hearsay as part of the *res gestae* 'the primary question' for the judge is, 'Can the possibility of concoction or distortion be disregarded?' To satisfy this criterion the event that gave rise to the declarant's utterance must have been:

> so unusual or startling or dramatic as to dominate the thoughts of the victim so that his utterance was an instinctive reaction to that event, thus giving no real opportunity for reasoned reflection.

Provided that the victim's words were (1) approximately contemporaneous with the event and (2) spontaneous, in the sense that they were so closely connected with it that the mind of the declarant could be fairly said still to be dominated by the event when the words were spoken, a court would be entitled to admit the reported words as part of the *res gestae*. In cases where the court cannot be confident that these factors are absent, evidence will be excluded. Thus, in *Harris* [2002] EWCA Crim 1597, the Court of Appeal held that an eight-year-old's telephone conversation with the police was inadmissible as part of the *res gestae* in a threats-to-kill case owing to the fact that, before making the call, the girl had spoken with her mother, and had also spoken to and been urged to make the call by the victim and by a friend. Because there were opportunities for the evidence to become influenced either intentionally or inadvertently when the child spoke to these people, one could not be sure that what she had said had not been concocted or distorted. Under rule 4(a), too, the child's evidence would probably be inadmissible as the possibility of concoction or distortion could not be disregarded.

9.50 Concoction and distortion are not the only factors that may intrude when spontaneous utterances are admitted in evidence. In the heat of the moment, error on the part of the declarant is also possible. Lord Ackner considered this issue, too, in *Andrews*. If the possibility of error simply arises out of what he termed 'the ordinary fallibility of human recollection', this has no bearing on the question of admissibility; it purely affects the weight of the evidence and should be left to the jury. However, Lord Ackner added, some cases present 'special features'. Cases with 'special features' could include those in which the declarant had drunk to excess (as was the case in *Andrews*) or where an identification had been made by a declarant who suffered from defective eyesight. In such circumstances, Lord Ackner said that 'the trial judge must consider whether he can exclude the possibility of error'. If he cannot do so but the court has decided that the evidence is admissible as part of the *res gestae*, the judge must draw the attention of the jury to any risks of concoction, distortion and error, where appropriate, in his summing-up. In the earlier case of *Turnbull* (1984) 80 Cr App R 104 the words of the victim of a stabbing were admitted despite the fact that there was evidence that he had been drinking heavily, and that he mumbled indistinctly in a thick Scots accent. (One witness actually thought that he was speaking Greek; other bystanders could not understand him at all.) Although there was a danger of distortion, this was not the kind of distortion against which Lord Wilberforce had sought to guard in *Ratten* (or to which Lord Ackner was to refer in *Andrews*). The courts' concern is to exclude statements where there is a risk of fabrication or conscious adaptation of the evidence by the speaker. In a case like *Turnbull*, following *Andrews*, the judge may admit the evidence but should warn the jury of the danger of accepting too readily the indistinct words of a haemorrhaging, drunken Scotsman. The wording in rule 4(a), it is suggested, could accommodate this line of cases—and, given that the common law is 'preserved' by s 118, was most probably intended to do so. Nevertheless, the risk of distortion cannot be disregarded.

9.51　*Is res gestae evidence admissible when the maker of the statement is available?* Lord Ackner made the final point in *Andrews* that, technically, *res gestae* evidence is admissible not only when the declarant is dead or unavailable, but also when he is called as a witness. In criminal cases at least, his Lordship made clear that any attempt by the prosecution to use the *res gestae* doctrine to avoid calling a witness who was available would be 'strongly deprecated'. This issue actually came to the fore in *A-G's Reference (No 1 of 2003)* [2003] 2 Cr App R 453. W was charged with committing gbh on his own mother. Although there was considerable *res gestae* evidence in the form of witnesses who had either heard the mother calling out or who had identified W as the person who had thrown her down a staircase and then tried to set her alight, the mother later made a deposition stating that she had fallen accidentally. The Crown had opted not to call the mother but to rely solely upon the *res gestae* evidence. The trial judge refused to admit this evidence, deeming it inadmissible on the ground that the best evidence—that of the mother—was available. On appeal, Longmore, LJ accepted that there was no rule of law disapplying the *res gestae* exception where better evidence was available. However, he upheld the judge's ruling on the different ground that the judge ought to have treated the evidence as technically admissible but then entertained an application by the defence to exclude it under PACE, s 78 on the basis that it might reflect adversely on the fairness of the proceedings because, unless the Crown tendered the mother as a witness for cross-examination, W would have been deprived of the opportunity to challenge the Crown's evidence. Thus, there was a risk that the admission of the *res gestae* evidence, without more ado, might contravene Article 6(3)(d) of the ECHR by denying W his right 'to examine or have examined witnesses against him'—sometimes designated W's 'right of confrontation' (see further *post*, paras **9.95** ff).

9.52 *The duration of the res gestae.* Although *Ratten* and *Andrews* expanded the concept of *res gestae*, it still tends to extend over a relatively short period—for only so long as the speaker's mind is dominated by the event. Thus, in an unreported Court of Appeal decision, referred to in *Andrews*, statements made roughly one hour and one hour and twenty minutes after an old man fell from a window during the course of a burglary were admitted (*O'Shea* (1986) 24 July, unreported). Although the concept is incapable of precise measurement, the period is normally even shorter.

9.53 In addition to situations such as those discussed above, where the impugned statement relates to a relevant event, there are further categories of situation mentioned in rule 4 to which the *res gestae* doctrine applies.

9.54 *A statement accompanying an act which, without it, cannot be properly evaluated (rule 4 (b))*—This exception, which proceeds upon the basis that words cannot always be separated from the deeds they accompany, was probably most clearly stated by Grove J in *Howe v Malkin* (1878) 40 LT 196:

> Though you cannot give in evidence a declaration *per se*, yet when there is an act accompanied by a statement which is so mixed up with it as to become part of the *res gestae*, evidence of such a statement may be given.

Such statements were admitted as an exception to the hearsay rule at common law, *first*, because the statement's contemporaneity with the relevant event was felt to operate in some sort as a guarantee of its reliability and, *secondly*, because the reception of such evidence was a matter of necessity—deriving from the fact that the person best placed to explain an otherwise ambivalent action was the actor himself. Statements accompanying and explaining relevant acts were only admitted for a limited purpose: they only served as evidence of an actor's intention in acting, or supplied his reasons for acting; they were not admissible to prove the existence of any fact mentioned in the statement of those reasons. Thus, at the trial of Dr Palmer, 'the Rugeley Poisoner', in 1856, a witness was allowed to relate that C, who had won a lot of money at Shrewsbury races in company with P, while in bed suffering from symptoms of poisoning, had handed over his money belt to the witness, accompanying the act by words indicating that he believed that P had been dosing him.

9.55 An American judge once cautioned, 'It is not the law that any or all conversation which happens to be going on at the time of an act can be proved if the act can be proved' (*Commonwealth v Chance*, 54 NE 551, 554 (Mass 1899) *per* Holmes CJ) The common law exception governing statements accompanying and explaining relevant acts was acknowledged to have indeterminate contours, which were obviously likely to pose considerable problems when Parliament set about 'preserving' the exception. The old decisions, no matter how questionable, are presumptively retained by a provision that emphatically states in s 118(1): 'The following rules of law are preserved.' (See further R Munday, 'Preservation of the Common Law and the Perpetuation of Error: s 118(1), r 4(b) of the Criminal Justice Act 2003' (2008) 172 JP Jo 348).

9.56 It would seem, nevertheless, that the courts may not be prepared to extend these exceptions beyond their outer bounds at the time of their preservation. In *Lynch* [2008] 1 Cr App R 24 L appealed against his conviction for violent disorder, following an attack launched by a band of feral youths on a father, D. D had tried to talk to L about his bullying of D's son and his son's friend. L did not testify. In a police interview, however, L admitted to talking with D but denied being involved in the attack. The son's friend, A, had taken part in an identification procedure about one year before the trial began. At the procedure four witnesses, including A, had picked out L and each had then been asked the following question on the standard witness form used by the Hampshire Constabulary: 'What exactly did you see this person do?' A's reply was recorded as: 'When another boy knocked [D] to the ground, [L] was swearing at him.' At trial A could not recall who had done what and the trial judge admitted in evidence the statement she had made to the police at the time of the identification procedure. The judge considered that the statement could be admitted under three separate heads, including as a statement accompanying and explaining a relevant act. Prior to the 2003 Act's entry into force, in *McCay* [1990] 1 WLR 645, a police officer who had been present at an identification parade had been permitted to testify that a witness had pointed at the eighth person in the line-up and said 'It is number 8'. The Court of Appeal, perhaps surprisingly, held that this was a statement accompanying and explaining a relevant act, and thus part of the *res gestae*. In *Lynch*, Keene LJ acknowledged that *McCay* remains authority for 'the proposition that some statements made at the time of the identification may be so bound up with the identification as to form part of it.' However, although the Court accepted the authority of *McCay*, it considered that the facts in *Lynch* went 'substantially beyond' the principle expressed in the former case. In *McCay* the witness's statement had clearly been necessary simply to indicate whom it was that the witness was identifying. In *Lynch*, in contrast, the witness's answer to the question posed on the Hampshire Constabulary's form, 'What exactly did you see this person do?' was so remote from being a statement accompanying and explaining a relevant act that Keene LJ considered that 'it is very difficult to see where, if a statement such as this were admissible as part of the *res gestae* of identification, the line could then be drawn.' (at [25])

9.57 *A statement relating to a contemporaneous, relevant physical state (rule 4(c))*. As part of the *res gestae* doctrine the common law admitted evidence of statements made by persons concerning their contemporaneous physical sensation. This was a restricted exception, as demonstrated by Pollock CB's ruling in *Nicholas* (1846) 2 Car & Kir 246, where he declared:

> If a man says to his surgeon "I have a pain in the head", or "in such a part of my body", that is evidence, but if he says to the surgeon "I have a wound", and was to add "I met John Thomas who had a sword and ran me through the body with it", that would be no evidence against John Thomas.
>
> (at 248)

Such evidence, then, is confined to establishing a party's contemporaneous physical sensation and is not to be employed incidentally to prove other matters. Moreover, the contemporaneity requirement is enforced quite strictly.

9.58 *A statement relating to a contemporaneous, relevant mental state (rule 4(d)).* Because there will frequently be no other means of demonstrating someone's state of mind, the common law has for long admitted as an exception to the hearsay rule statements relating to a party's contemporaneous, relevant state of mind. As Lord Bridge stated in *Blastland* [1986] AC 41:

> It is, of course, elementary that statements made to a witness by a third party are not excluded by the hearsay rule when they are put in evidence solely to prove the state of mind either of the maker of the statement or of the person to whom it was made. What a person said or heard may well be the best and most direct evidence of that person's state of mind. This principle can only apply, however, when the state of mind evidenced by the statement is either itself directly in issue at the trial or of direct and immediate relevance to an issue which arises at the trial.
>
> (at 54)

9.59 The two requirements of relevance and contemporaneity have tended to be applied strictly by the courts. Thus, to take the relevance requirement first, in *Blastland*, B, who admitted to having had sexual relations with the victim earlier in the evening, was convicted of buggering and murdering a 12-year-old boy. B described someone resembling another local homosexual (Mark) who, he said, had been lurking in the area. B wished to call witnesses who would testify that in conversations with them Mark had spoken of the murder of a boy before the body had actually been found. Clearly, B wished to suggest that, because Mark had known of the killing before it became public knowledge, Mark was likely to have murdered the boy. The House of Lords took a very restrictive view of 'relevance', holding that evidence from the witnesses that would have shed light on Mark's state of mind at the operative time was insufficiently relevant. There were other perfectly innocent ways in which Mark could have come by his knowledge of the boy's murder. In short, the evidence was deemed too speculative for the jury's consideration. Despite assurances that the police had investigated Mark thoroughly and had seen no reason to suspect his involvement in the murder, this ruling inevitably leaves one feeling uneasy. Rulings of this nature, which disadvantage a defendant, may be vulnerable to challenge under the Human Rights Act. However, as we shall see, such cases can now be catered for by the inclusive discretion created in the Criminal Justice Act 2003, s 114(1)(d), which permits the court to admit evidence otherwise deemed hearsay if 'satisfied that it is in the interests of justice for it to be admissible' (see *post*, paras **9.70–9.80**). It is also worth pointing out that in any case the situation operates less unfairly than might appear from these observations: there has been a long-standing practice amongst prosecutors, wherever it is felt that strict application of the rules of evidence—and, notably, the hearsay rule—might lead to possible injustice:

> to make admissions in relation to facts which "might" point to a third party having committed the crime, which the defendant denies having committed... Of course, the Crown cannot be forced to make admissions if they do not accept that the admission points to the possibility of a third party being the perpetrator.
>
> (*Greenwood* [2005] 1 Cr App R 7 at [40] *per* Waller LJ)

Moreover, as Waller LJ went on to explain in *Greenwood*,

> [I]f [the defendant] has evidence which proves that someone else did the murder, he must be able to adduce it. If he has any evidence that points to another person having a motive to do it, he must be entitled to produce evidence of that motive. If he has any other evidence that would point to the possibility that another person might have done the murder, he should be entitled to produce it.
>
> (at [41(i)])

9.60 Evidence of contemporaneous mental state must be relevant to the issues in the case. In *Gilfoyle* [1996] 1 Cr App R 302, for instance, G, who was accused of murdering his wife, claimed that she had committed suicide. At trial G produced what purported to be a suicide note in his wife's handwriting. Three Crown witnesses could have testified that, shortly before her death, the wife had told them that G, who was an auxiliary nurse, had claimed that he was doing a project on suicide and had asked her to help him in writing examples of suicide notes. The trial judge had excluded this testimony. The Court of Appeal's view, however, was that the wife's statements were admissible on a number of grounds. In addition to one argument that they constituted original evidence and another that they formed part of the *res gestae*, the court noted that 'in any event, hearsay to prove the declarant's "state of mind" is an exception to the (hearsay) rule which has been accepted by the common law for many years'. The witnesses' statements would have shown that the wife was not in a suicidal frame of mind when she wrote the note, but rather had written it in the belief that it would help G in a course at work. This was highly relevant because it directly refuted the defence's contention that the suicide note implied that the wife had taken her own life. (See also *ante*, para **8.6**.)

9.61 Such *res gestae* statements must also refer to contemporaneous states of mind. Generally speaking, this has meant that only statements of present state of mind (eg 'I am afraid') have been admitted. More specifically, declarations of intention have often been excluded from the ambit of this exception. Thus, in *Wainwright* (1875) 13 Cox CC 171 a murder victim's statement that she intended to visit W was rejected on the ground that 'it was only a statement of intention which might or might not have been carried out'. Similarly, in *Thomson* [1912] 3ʾ KB 19 a statement by the victim of an illegal operation that she intended to perform the operation upon herself was ruled inadmissible. In contrast, however, in *Buckley* (1873) 13 Cox CC 293, the court admitted without demur the words of a murdered policeman, who, before going out on patrol, told his superior officer that he had heard that B was up to his old tricks again and that he was going out looking for him. At common law the situation was arguably unclear—although the dominant view seemed to be that such evidence was inadmissible. Nor was England the only jurisdiction to encounter difficulty in determining whether to admit statements of intention. Even Canada, which operates a more flexible approach to the admission of hearsay, has been troubled by this situation. Thus, in *Starr* [2000] 2 SCR 144, while four members of the Canadian Supreme Court would have admitted such evidence, the five judges in the majority held that evidence of present intention had been wrongly admitted by the lower courts. C, the victim of a gangland 'hit', had told a witness, G, that he had to 'go and do an Autopac scam with [S]', the implication being that C could be assumed to have carried out his stated intention and to have met up with S. The majority rejected this evidence on the ground of its inherent unreliability. More specifically, they found that the declaration had been made in 'circumstances of suspicion' when C might have had a motive for lying to G, who happened to be a former girlfriend.

9.62 It will be noted that rule 4(c) of the Criminal Justice Act 2003, s 118 concludes with the words in parentheses, '(such as intention or emotion)'. This phrase might suggest that declarations of intention are now meant to fall within this hearsay exception. However, such a reading seems problematical. Since the section is confined to 'preserving' certain existing exceptions to the hearsay rule, it may prove awkward to construe these words as meaning that the rules governing the admission of declarations of intention are to be expanded. More importantly perhaps, the case of *Buckley* may not be that strong authority for the proposition that declarations of intention may be admitted under this common law exception, given that the police officer's declaration may very well have been admitted under the now abolished hearsay exception relating to statements made by deceased persons in the course of duty. Another decision which might otherwise appear to point in the same direction, *Moghal* (1977) 65 Cr App R 56, is also problematical in that the judgment conveys the very strong impression that Scarman LJ was straining every sinew to avoid the obvious miscarriage of justice were M's murder conviction to stand, given that Crown acknowledged that it was M's domineering mistress, S, who had actually stabbed the victim—and taking into account no less than 12 other helpful concessions the Crown had made in the case. See further R Munday, 'Legislation that would 'Preserve' the Common Law: The Case of the Declaration of Intention' (2008) 124 LQR 46.

'Confessions etc' (rule 5)

9.63 Rule 5 retains:

> Any rule of law relating to the admissibility of confessions or mixed statements in criminal proceedings.

Confessions (see *post*, Chapter 10) and mixed statements (see *post*, paras **10.50–10.53**) are considered elsewhere in this book.

'Admissions by agents, etc' (rule 6)

9.64 The topic of vicarious admissions falls beyond the scope of an introductory work. However, just to satisfy curiosity, rule 6, which retains:

> Any rule of law under which in criminal proceedings—
>
> (a) an admission made by an agent of a defendant is admissible against the defendant as evidence of any matter stated, or
>
> (b) a statement made by a person to whom a defendant refers a person for information is admissible against the defendant as evidence of any matter stated,

broadly refers to situations in which a defendant has been authorised by the defendant, as principal, to make an admission on his behalf. The agent's authority to make the admission must be express. Thus, unlike solicitors involved in civil cases, solicitors representing those accused of crime have no general implied authority to commit their clients, say, by making admissions of fact on their behalf. However, a statement made by his lawyer in the presence of the defendant may be admissible against the latter. In *Turner* (1975) 61 Cr App R 67, in the course of his speech in mitigation on behalf of T, who was about to be sentenced in respect of offence *x*, T's counsel, who was said to be somewhat inexperienced, in T's presence, stated that T had committed offence *y*. This admission was held admissible against T at his subsequent trial for offence *y*. As Lawton LJ explained:

> Whenever a barrister comes into Court in robes and in the presence of his client tells the judge that he appears for that client, the court is entitled to assume, and always does

assume, that he has his client's authority to conduct the case and to say on the client's behalf whatever in his professional discretion he thinks is in his client's interest to say. If the Court could not make this assumption, the administration of justice would become very difficult indeed. The very circumstances provide evidence first, that the barrister has his client's authority to speak for him and secondly, that what the barrister says his client wants him to say.

(at 82)

'Common enterprise' (rule 7)

9.65 It is a well established, if confused, principle of common law that where a number of persons are engaged in a common enterprise, the statements of any one of those persons is admissible against the others if uttered in furtherance of that common enterprise. Three things must be established before such evidence is admitted. The court must be satisfied:

(i) that the utterance or document was made by a conspirator;

(ii) that the statement could be reasonably understood to have been made in furtherance of the conspiracy (although courts nowadays often adopt the less demanding test that the statement was made in the course of the conspiracy: eg *Platten* [2006] EWCA Crim 140, [2006] Crim LR 920); and

(iii) that there exists other evidence beyond the document or utterance itself to prove that the other party was a party to the agreement (*Beard and Smart* [2002] EWCA Crim 772).

9.66 Although conspiracy does not actually have to be the charge, it is essential that the parties should have agreed to commit an offence together. Take the case of *Gray* [1995] 2 Cr App R 100, where a number of accused were charged with offences of insider dealing. Although each of the acts charged related to the accused singly, the Crown's case was that all the offences had been committed in pursuance of a common purpose. For this reason, it put in evidence large numbers of recorded telephone conversations in order to show how the defendants passed information around amongst one another. The Court of Appeal held that, in the absence of evidence that clearly showed the complicity of the other person in a common enterprise and that also clearly delineated the nature of that common enterprise, the jury in *Gray* had been wrongly told that a statement made in the course of a conversation in the absence of another 'conspirator' might be used against the latter. As the Court of Appeal later explained in *Murray* [1997] 2 Cr App R 136, the common enterprise exception cannot apply in situations where defendants are charged with isolated offences, rather than with conspiring to commit a joint offence, nor where the common enterprise is neither clearly defined nor proven. To fall within the common enterprise exception, it should be said, a declaration does not have to have been made by someone who has actually been charged, or even to have been uttered when the defendant against whom it is admissible was either present or aware of its having been made. With a view to preserving what in some ways may appear a less than satisfactory exception to the rule against hearsay, rule 7 retains:

> Any rule of law under which in criminal proceedings a statement made by a party to a common enterprise is admissible against another party to the enterprise as evidence of any matter stated.

'Expert evidence' (rule 8)

9.67   As we saw when we considered opinion evidence (see *ante*, para **8.31**), as part of their evidence, expert witnesses may require to refer to standard works of reference within their field. These works either comprise or are founded on statements of fact, widely accepted as authoritative within an expert's field, but of which the expert has no personal knowledge. The courts have held that it is actually part of the expert's duty to consider any such work which 'must inevitably form an important ingredient in the cogency or probative value of his conclusion in the particular case' (*Abadom* [1983] 1 WLR 126, 129). Although, technically, this vital species of background information may constitute inadmissible hearsay evidence, owing to its obvious utility, it is admitted as an exception. To this end, rule 8 retains:

> Any rule of law under which in criminal proceedings an expert witness may draw on the body of expertise relevant to his field.

One context in which rule 8 can prove important in practice is possession of drugs with intent to supply. Whenever the Crown has to establish that a defendant was in possession of a quantity of drugs greater than would be justified by personal use, it is common to call a police officer experienced in drugs offences. This happened in *Hodges and Walker* [2003] 2 Cr App R 15, where an officer with 16 years' experience in the Drugs Squad in Portsmouth testified to the usual method of supplying heroin (in £20 bags), to the local purchase price in Portsmouth, and to the fact that 14g was more than would have been for personal use alone. Rose LJ held that the officer's evidence had been properly admitted. Once the primary facts had been established—the police observations on the defendants, the finding of the heroin and other drugs paraphernalia—the Drugs Squad officer, testifying as an expert witness, was entitled to draw on the 'work of others as part of the process of arriving at [his] conclusion' (*Abadom* [1983] 1 WLR 126, 131 *per* Kerr LJ). The officer's knowledge—derived from training videos, personal observation, conversations with prisoners and informants, talk with colleagues, attendance at Home Office courses, and records he had kept over the years—qualified him to give expert testimony and to express an opinion based upon his accumulated experience—and 'that [did] not mean...that it [was] necessary to call the various people to whom the witness [had] spoken, before the witness [could] give expert evidence based upon what they [had] said' (at [31]). This reinforces the older *dictum* in *Bryan* (1984) 8 November, unreported, to the effect that:

> Police officers with their experience of dealing with these problems, being on the streets and with their knowledge and meeting with those having a drug problem and those pushing the drugs, have a very wide experience and can give evidence of fact of what takes place on many occasions on the streets.

They may additionally, under *Abadom*, give evidence of opinion, too.

All parties agree to the statement being admissible (s 114(1)(c))

9.68 It is not unusual for uncontested evidence, in the form of written statements or depositions, to be simply read out in court. This device has the merit of avoiding a waste of court's time and the inconvenience of summoning witnesses unnecessarily to testify in person to matters not actually in dispute. It therefore allows the court to focus on the serious points of disagreement in the trial. The Act makes provision for the admission of hearsay statements in cases where all parties agree to admit the statements. As we shall see, this overlaps to a great extent with written statements admitted under the Criminal Justice Act 1967, s 9 (see *post*, para **9.92**).

9.69 Although the expression, 'all parties to the proceedings agree', might suggest that formal or explicit agreement was required, in *Williams v VOSA* (2008) 172 JP 328 it was held that a court may infer agreement from the circumstances of the case. At W's trial for using a vehicle on a road with dangerous parts, the prosecution case relied substantially upon a vehicle examiner's account of what W's driver had told him—namely, that she was employed by W, who was under contract with a local authority to convey schoolchildren in his vehicle. The prosecution had made no application to have this evidence admitted as hearsay. The justices nevertheless relied upon the examiner's account of what the driver had told him. The Divisional Court held that 'agree' was not to be equated with, say, the notion of offer and acceptance in the law of contract; nor did it necessarily mean that there had to be express agreement between the parties. The realities of the criminal trial needed to be taken into account. Since, in practice, one party at trial would often adduce evidence to which the other party lodged no objection, it had to be open to a court to infer that, by failing to raise any objection, a party might be 'agreeing' to the admission of the hearsay evidence. Such inferences, of course, were not to be lightly drawn. The drawing of such an inference would be most improbable if a party was not legally represented. In the *Williams* case, the Divisional Court held both that the justices had been entitled to draw the inference that the parties were agreed on the admission of the hearsay and that there was no injustice to W since the prosecution had made advance disclosure before trial that it intended calling this evidence, and at no time had W signified that he objected (cp *ante*, para **7.39**).

When it is in the interests of justice to admit the statement (s 114(1)(d))

9.70 Section 114(1)(d) enacted a 'limited inclusionary discretion', recommended by the Law Commission in order to prevent potential injustice which might be provoked by the exclusion of hearsay evidence:

> [O]ur purpose is to allow for the admission of reliable hearsay which could not otherwise be admitted, particularly to prevent a conviction which that evidence would render unsafe.
>
> (Report, para 8.133)

As the Law Commission later explained, 'Our view is that all courts would regard the safety-valve as an exception to be used in very limited circumstances' (para 8.143). The inclusionary discretion, however, is not by any means confined to defence evidence, but may be exercised by the judge whenever 'the court is satisfied that it is in the interests of justice for [a hearsay statement] to be admissible'.

9.71 It has been suggested by some commentators that the inclusionary discretion is so all-encompassing that, despite its having been proposed by the Law Commission as a safety-valve, it could actually be converted into the prime moving force governing the admission of hearsay statements. In view of its genesis and its positioning in s 114(1), this seems an ambitious, not to say unwarranted, interpretation of parliamentary intention. Nor is it clear that the courts view s 114 in this manner. In *ED* (2010) 174 JP 289 at [17], for example, a case in which it was held that the statement of an available witness was wrongly admitted under s 114(1)(d) in place of her live testimony, Pitchford LJ indicated that courts would not countenance the use of s 114(1)(d) 'to circumvent the requirements of other gateways to admissibility higher up the s.114(1) hierarchy'.

9.72 *Factors the court must weigh.* As has become fashionable in modern legislation, the statute tells judges what factors they *must* take into account in determining to admit any given statement under s 114(1)(d). The statutory list is not exclusive, however. The court may also have regard to 'any others it considers relevant'. Section 114(2) provides:

> In deciding whether a statement not made in oral evidence should be admitted under subs (1)(d), the court must have regard to the following factors (and to any others it considers relevant)—
>
> (a) how much probative value the statement has (assuming it to be true) in relation to a matter in issue in the proceedings, or how valuable it is for the understanding of other evidence in the case;
>
> (b) what other evidence has been, or can be, given on the matter or evidence mentioned in para (a);

(c) how important the matter or evidence mentioned in para (a) is in the context of the case as a whole;

(d) the circumstances in which the statement was made;

(e) how reliable the maker of the statement appears to be;

(f) how reliable the evidence of the making of the statement appears to be;

(g) whether oral evidence of the matter stated can be given and, if not, why it cannot;

(h) the amount of difficulty involved in challenging the statement;

(i) the extent to which that difficulty would be likely to prejudice the party facing it.

9.73 How is the judge meant to approach the nine factors to which he 'must have regard'? In *Taylor* [2006] 2 Cr App R 14, two prosecution witnesses, who had seen the attack that led to a charge of causing gbh with intent, each named T as a participant in the attack after having been told his name by someone else. The trial judge admitted this hearsay evidence via s 114(1)(d) but was unable to reach a concluded view on some of the factors listed in s 114(2). On appeal, the Court of Appeal was required to decide whether a judge had to arrive at a clear view on each of the various factors. Concerned at the protracted enquiries that might need to be undertaken were this necessary, Rose LJ held that s 114(2) does not impose an obligation on the judge to reach a conclusion on each listed factor. What is required of the judge is:

> the exercise of judgment, in the light of the factors identified in the subsection. What is required of him is to give consideration to those factors. There is nothing in the wording of the statute to require him to reach a specific conclusion in relation to each or any of them. He must give consideration to those identified factors and any others which he considers relevant . . . It is then his task to assess the significance of those factors, both in relation to each other and having regard to such weight as . . . they bear individually and in relation to each other. Having approached the matter in that way, he will be able . . . in accordance with the words of the statute, to reach a proper conclusion as to whether or not the . . . evidence should be admitted.
>
> (at [39])

Although s 114(1)(d) states that the court '*must* have regard' to these factors, the Court of Appeal has sometimes been prepared to overlook a trial judge's failure to comply with this requirement where the need to admit hearsay evidence in the interests of justice is sufficiently self-evident—and especially where the defence has been unnecessarily obstructive (eg, *R v S* [2008] 2 Cr App R 26).

9.74 *The nature of s 114(1)(d).* The Law Commission suggested three examples of cases where it could envisage the inclusionary discretion being needed. It suggested, firstly, the sort of problem that arose in *Sparks* [1964] AC 964, where an adult male

Caucasian defendant, facing an indecent assault charge on a child too young to test-ify, wished to introduce a statement that the child had originally claimed that 'a little coloured boy' committed the offence. Secondly, it proposed the situation that arose in *Thomas* [1994] Crim LR 745, where the Crown needed to fix the time of death in a case in which T denied having killed his girlfriend. A child of eight had told the police that she had seen the victim leaving her house after the time when it is alleged she was already dead. By the time of trial, the child could recall nothing of the inci-dent. Finally, it suggested a case like *Cooper* [1969] 1 QB 267, where a third party, T, admitted to a friend that he in fact had committed the assault with which C was charged. C and T happened to look very similar to one another. T's confession to a friend might have been admitted under the inclusionary discretion.

9.75 Although all three examples concern evidence proffered by the defence, it bears repeating that the Crown is equally entitled to take advantage of this provision. Some writers (eg Ormerod in [2006] Crim LR at 640–1) argue that there is no reason to treat s 114(1)(d) simply as a 'safety valve', and that 'the fact that it appears last in the list of exceptions in s 114(1)...does not substantiate such a narrow interpretation'. This argument is coupled with the practical point that, in view of the long list of factors that must be weighed in accordance with s 114(2), it will often be easier for a judge to resort to the other exceptions which have the virtue of leading to virtually automatic admis-sion of hearsay evidence or which are tried and trusted friends. Sometimes, of course, it will not, in which case the judge is afforded another easier route: namely, s 114(1)(d). Whilst it is perfectly correct that 'no...limitation is imposed by the statutory wording' expressly indicating that s 114(1)(d) was meant to operate only as a last-ditch safety valve, this writer agrees with Birch that the natural reading of s 114—together with the history of the provision—indicate that the intention was that this provision would apply only in cases where the hearsay evidence fell into no other recognised hear-say exception and it was in the interests of justice to admit it (see [2004] Crim LR 5556, 559–60). The courts' attitude also seems divided. Sometimes they will refer to s 114(1)(d) as a species of safety valve: eg, *J(S)* [2009] EWCA Crim 1869 at [24] *per* Hooper LJ; *Freeman* [2010] EWCA Crim 1997 at [26] *per* Moses LJ. On other occa-sions, as, in *Sak v CPS* (2008) 172 JP 89, they give the provision a wider construction.

9.76 Interestingly, what is emerging in the reported case law is that s 114(1)(d) appears to afford assistance to the prosecution more frequently than it does to the defence, and that the Court of Appeal shows itself ready to employ this provision as a second line of argument, buttressing rulings of which it is not otherwise entirely confident (eg *Isichei* (2006) 170 JP 753 and *Singh* [2006] 1 WLR 1564 at [15] *per* Rose LJ).

9.77 Potentially, s 114(1)(d) has some radical properties. In *M* [2007] EWCA Crim 219, for instance, it was held that under s 114(1)(d) a court could even hold that one co-defendant's out-of-court statement might be admitted in support of another co-accused's case. On the other hand, in *Smith* [2007] EWCA Crim 2105 at [24], whilst acknowledging that co-defendants' guilty pleas admitted under PACE, s 74 might also 'in strict legal terms' be admissible under s 114(1)(d), the Court of Appeal insisted that such evidence would still have to meet 'the interests of justice' standard set out in s 114(2), which presumably means that evidence that would not satisfy the criteria for admissibility under s 74 would also fail to meet the requisite standard under s 114(2). (On PACE s 74, see *ante*, paras **1.40** ff; on the prosecution's right to use s 114(1)(d) to adduce evidence of a third party's statement as part of its case, see *post*, paras **10.54–10.59**.) The key in every case, then, is that it must be demonstrated to be 'in the interests of justice' to admit the statement. Moreover, as Hughes LJ explained in *Marsh* [2008] EWCA Crim 1816, even when a defendant invokes s 114(1)(d),

> the interests of justice . . . are not wholly synonymous with the interests of the defendant. They mean the public interest in arriving at the right conclusion in the case, including of course the acquittal of anyone about whose guilt there is proper doubt.
>
> (at [24])

9.78 *Reluctant witnesses and the relationship between s 114(1)(d) and the other hearsay exceptions.* The Court of Appeal has made clear that s 114(1)(d) is not to be employed simply as a means of circumventing s 116 and of routinely making available evidence that otherwise fails tests of admissibility set out elsewhere in the hearsay provisions (see *Freeman* [2010] EWCA Crim 1997 at [26] *per* Moses LJ.) Indeed, s 114(1)(d) must not be used to allow evidence to be adduced in place of witnesses who are simply reluctant to testify (*ibid* at [29] and [31]). That said, once in a blue moon a reluctant witness's testimony may be admitted under s 114(1)(d). In *Sadiq and Hussain* (2009) 173 JP 471, most unusually, testimony given by the paralysed victim of an attempted murder at a first trial was read out under s 114(1)(d) at the retrial when the victim indicated a reluctance to testify afresh. With difficulty, the victim could have done so but he indicated that he had found the first experience too demanding and that he did not wish to submit to it again. The appellants argued that s 114(1)(d) ought not to apply without good reason, that the witness was available, that he would provide vital identification evidence, and that he was a hardened criminal whose testimony needed to be properly tested in cross-examination. Keene LJ acknowledged that it is not normally in the interests of justice that an important witness's evidence should be given under the hearsay provisions of the 2003 Act when he simply refuses to testify and will not provide a good reason for his refusal. However, there were countervailing circumstances in this particular case: the victim's demeanour would be of little help as he was paralysed; and he had already been cross-examined at the first trial at which the same judge had presided.

> [T]he interests of justice under section 114(1)(d)…bring in the public interest in crimes being tried as well as the interests of the accused.… In the present case…the prejudice to [S and H] from the admission of this evidence in this particular form was very slight indeed, and was outweighed by the public interest in it forming part of the total evidence put before the jury.
>
> (at [29] and [30])

9.79 In each individual case the court will have to weigh all the relevant factors in order to determine overall what is in the interests of justice. By way of illustration, in *Seton* (2010) 174 JP 241 S, who was charged with murder, accused P of having been the true culprit. P, at the time of S's trial, was already in prison for another murder. P declined to cooperate with the police. The trial judge concluded that it would have been a fruitless exercise for S to call P, who would have had to be warned of his right to exercise the privilege against self-incrimination; all that the defence could have obtained was the advantage of having him brought up before the jury, who would presumably have seen his obduracy. The Court of Appeal held that the judge had been entitled to allow the Crown to adduce evidence of recordings of telephone calls P had made to his son and his wife denying all knowledge of the murder under s 114(1)(d). Before admitting the recordings, the judge had addressed the factors listed in s 114(2). Under s 114(2)(a) he had found that the evidence possessed extremely strong probative value as P appeared to be expressing genuine outrage at being implicated in a murder in which he denied involvement; under para (b) P could not be called because he refused to testify, although police enquiries had confirmed his lack of involvement in the killing; under para (c) the evidence was extremely important; under paras (d) and (e), whilst the judge took into account that P's statements were likely to be self-serving (P would have known that his calls were being recorded), overall the jury could consider these points in assessing the weight to be attached to P's denials—they did not furnish grounds for excluding the evidence; under para (f) the statements were reliable as they had been recorded; under para (h) the defence had already cross-examined a police witness as to P's criminal record and the details of the murder for which he was serving a sentence of life imprisonment; in relation to para (i) the judge did not consider that the appellant suffered any real prejudice from the tapes being played. Additionally, the defence had had, and had employed, an opportunity to tell the jury that P's statements were self-serving, having been made by a serious criminal who knew that his calls were being recorded. In conclusion, Stanley Burnton LJ considered that the decision to admit the recordings was not marred by legal error;

all relevant matters had been taken into account, and the decision to admit the recordings was not one that no judge could sensibly have made.

9.80 *Appealing against s 114(1)(d) rulings.* Once a court has decided to admit evidence under s 114(1)(d), the Court of Appeal has stated that it 'will not readily interfere with a trial judge's decision to admit evidence under s.114(1)(d). It will do so, in general, only if his decision is marred by legal error, or by a failure to take relevant matters into account or it is such that the judge could not sensibly have made': *Z* (2009) 173 JP 145 at [25].

Admissibility of 'multiple hearsay' (s 121)

9.81 The Law Commission was of the firm view that a distinction needed to be drawn between first-hand and multiple hearsay. The term 'first-hand hearsay' essentially refers to situations where B recounts what A has said, when A has personal knowledge of those reported facts. In the case of 'multiple hearsay' (or second-hand hearsay), in contrast, B is reporting what A has said when A has no personal knowledge of the facts but has been informed about them by C, who did have personal knowledge. There are several reasons for drawing such a distinction between these two categories of situation. *First*, whereas in the case of first-hand hearsay it is said to be possible to cross-examine B in order to test the accuracy of A's statement, such a course is not open in the case of multiple hearsay. *Second*, there may be reason to fear that if evidence more remote than first-hand hearsay were to become generally admissible, it would become too easy to manufacture evidence. *Finally*, if admitted, multiple hearsay would require complicated jury directions, a disproportionate amount of time would be spent discussing the admissibility of such evidence, and the jury might be even be 'misled or distracted'. Whereas the unavailability of the declarant might militate in favour of admitting multiple hearsay, the Law Commission considered that the risk of admitting unreliable evidence was too great to justify extending the hearsay exceptions to multiple hearsay.

9.82 Whilst 'multiple hearsay' would exclude evidence where A has no personal knowledge of the facts C had recounted to him, the question arises as to whether the same rule ought to apply in cases where A, had he been available to testify, would have been permitted to do so because his testimony in turn would have fallen within an exception to the hearsay rule. To give a concrete example, let us imagine that C has witnessed a stabbing. C tells A about the stabbing immediately after the event in circumstances that fall within the *res gestae* exception to the hearsay rule (see *ante*, paras **9.45–9.53**). Had A been an available witness, A could have repeated what C had told him and it would have been treated as evidence of the facts stated. A, however, who has subsequently told B what C told him, is now raving mad and therefore unfit to appear as a witness within the terms of s 116(2)(b).

Can one make cumulative use of the two hearsay exceptions in order to allow B to report what A stated that C had told him about the stabbing? The question, in this context, is whether it is enough to justify the admission of the evidence that A could have given oral evidence of the fact stated, even if that evidence would itself have been—albeit admissible—hearsay? Alternatively, ought it to be necessary that the declarant could have given oral evidence without resort to a hearsay exception? The Law Commission gave a qualified answer to this question, suggesting that it should depend upon the hearsay exception upon which A would have relied.

9.83 Adopting this broad analysis, s 121 now provides:

(1) A hearsay statement is not admissible to prove the fact that an earlier hearsay statement was made unless—

(a) either of the statements is admissible under s 117, 119 or 120,

(b) all parties to the proceedings so agree, or

(c) the court is satisfied that the value of the evidence in question, taking into account how reliable the statements appear to be, is so high that the interests of justice require the later statement to be admissible for that purpose.

Obviously, if all sides are agreeable, there can be no reason to object to the admission of multiple hearsay (s 121(1)(b). On 'agreeing', see *ante*, paras **9.68–9.69**). The thinking behind s 121(1)(a) is rather more complex. This paragraph is the product of compromise. It was felt, for example, that in the case of statements admissible under s 117 (business documents), the presumption that business documents are reliable is so powerful that it outweighs by far the risks which otherwise are attendant upon the admission of multiple hearsay. Similarly, in the case of a witness's previous inconsistent statements (s 119) or in the case of previous statements admitted to rebut a charge of fabrication, to refresh memory, or to prove a victim's complaint (s 120), the fact that B is available for cross-examination adequately compensates for the fact that A's statement is in the form of multiple hearsay. In contrast, if the reason for A's not testifying is simply his non-availability (s 116) or if A's evidence falls within one of the preserved common law exceptions, such as *res gestae* (s 118, r 4), it was felt that the dangers attendant upon multiple hearsay exceeded the comparable benefits to be gleaned from admitting the evidence for, in the words of the Law Commission,

with each additional step in the chain, the risk of error or fabrication increases...[T]here comes a point where the need to exclude potentially unreliable evidence must come before the desirability of allowing the court to hear the best evidence available.

(para 8.22)

9.84 Section 121(1)(c) provides the court with an additional means of admitting multiple hearsay in situations where, because all the parties are unwilling to agree to its admission, taking into account its apparent reliability, the court feels that it would nevertheless be in the interests of justice to admit the multiple hearsay. Section 121(1)(c), however, does not provide a particularly easy route to admissibility. As Richards LJ underlined in *Scorah* [2008] EWCA Crim 1786 at [32], 'The test for admissibility under [s 121] is more onerous than the general test in s 114.' Although one might once have anticipated that this inclusive discretion was most likely to be exercised at the defence's behest, as in the case of s 114(1)(d) (see *ante*, para **9.76**), this has not proven to be the case. In *Maher v DPP* (2006) 170 JP 441, for example, Mrs D witnessed M's car collide with a stationary vehicle in a supermarket car park. M stopped to inspect the damage, then drove off. Public-spiritedly, Mrs D left a note of the appellant's registration number on the windscreen of the damaged car. The girlfriend of the driver of the damaged vehicle gave the police the appellant's registration number over the telephone, and police recorded the number in the police incident log. In consequence, M was traced but denied having been involved in any collision. By the time of her trial for careless driving and for failing to stop and report the accident the original note had been lost. The justices had admitted the log in evidence as a 'business or other' document under s 117 of the Criminal Justice Act 2003 in order to establish the identity of the offending car. On appeal, Scott Baker LJ concluded that the evidence of the log had not been properly admitted under s 117 since the requirement in s 117(2)(c), that each individual through whom information is transmitted must have received it in the course of a trade, business, etc, was not satisfied in the case of the driver's girlfriend. However, it was held that the log's evidence could have been rightly admitted as multiple hearsay under s 121(1)(c). Given that it would have been extraordinary had there been an error in transmission, and yet the number of the vehicle recorded on the police log just happened to coincide exactly with the number and description of a vehicle that was in the car park at the time and seen by the witness, the reliability of the evidence was so high as to require its admission in the interests of justice. Interestingly, noting the use of similar phraseology ('the interests of justice') in both ss 114(1)(d) and 121(1)(c), the court also observed that, at least in the circumstances of this case, the provisions about the interests of justice in s 121 ought to have been considered cumulatively with the interests of justice criteria enumerated in s 114(2) (*ante*, para **9.72**).

9.85 Multiple hearsay may give rise to complex evidential issues. With respect, Rose LJ was right to emphasise in *Joyce and Joyce* [2005] EWCA Crim 1785 that:

> it will...be essential, when the hearsay relied on is the product of multiple hearsay, to give a most careful direction that that is so in order that juries may be in a position properly to evaluate the weight which they ought to give to such hearsay evidence.
>
> (at [30])

Testing the credibility of makers of statements who do not testify (s 124)

9.86 Given that the Criminal Justice Act 2003 has considerably enlarged the classes of absent witnesses whose evidence will be received under exceptions to the hearsay rule, it is important that their evidence can be effectively tested even if the witnesses themselves will not be subject to cross-examination. Section 124 of the Act makes provision for various types of evidence to be adduced whenever a statement not made in oral evidence in the proceedings is admitted as evidence of a matter stated and the maker of that statement does not give oral evidence in connection with the subject matter of the statement. The intention is to permit the credibility of makers of statements admitted under Part 11 of the Act to be tested as effectively as can be managed. To this end, s 124(2)(a) allows for the testing of such persons' capability and credibility by providing that:

(a) any evidence which (if he had given such evidence) would have been admissible as relevant to his credibility as a witness is so admissible in the proceedings;

(b) evidence may with the court's leave be given of any matter which (if he had given such evidence) could have been put to him in cross-examination as relevant to his credibility as a witness but of which evidence could not have been adduced by the cross-examining party;

(c) evidence tending to prove that he made (at whatever time) any other statement inconsistent with the statement admitted as evidence is admissible for the purpose of showing that he contradicted himself.

9.87 A number of points might be noted. The distinction between paras (a) and (b) reflects the fact that in respect of some matters it is possible to rebut a witness's denial (eg bias), whereas in others a witness's replies must be taken as final (eg collateral matters). In the case of the former, para (a) allows the evidence to be adduced to demonstrate the witness's lack of credibility. In the case of the latter, the court has discretion whether or not to allow evidence to be called on a matter which, had the witness testified in person, would have been considered collateral. Leave is required in such cases in order to exclude evidence either which might be unfair to the maker of the statement (who would not be present to repulse attacks on his credibility) or which might make the trial unduly protracted. Paragraph (c) allows an opposing party to adduce evidence of any inconsistent statement, whether made before or after the time when the statement produced in court was uttered, but only in order to show that that person has contradicted himself. At first, this appears to contrast with the wording of s 119(1), which states that where a witness gives oral evidence, previous inconsistent statements are admitted 'as evidence of any matter stated of which oral evidence by him would be admissible'. However, s 119 (2) provides that:

> If in criminal proceedings evidence of an inconsistent statement by any person is given under s 124(2)(c), the statement is admissible as evidence of any matter stated in it of which oral evidence by that person would be admissible.

9.88 In the case of business documents admitted under s 117, where information may have passed through the hands of a chain of persons acting in the course of a trade, profession, etc (s 117(2)(c)) before a statement is actually created or received, s 124(4) makes provision for the testing of the credibility of each party in the chain, enacting as follows:

> In the case of a statement in a document which is admitted as evidence under s 117 each person who, in order for the statement to be admissible, must have supplied or received the information concerned or created or received the document or part concerned is to be treated as the maker of the statement for the purposes of subss (1) to (3) above.

9.89 In all cases in which the credibility of the maker of a hearsay statement has been attacked, the party adducing the statement may wish to rehabilitate the maker's credibility. Alternatively, the party may desire to adduce additional evidence to counteract the effect of that evidence or to reinforce his case. Section 124(3) provides:

> If as a result of evidence admitted under this section an allegation is made against the maker of a statement, the court may permit a party to lead additional evidence of such description as the court may specify for the purposes of denying or answering the allegation.

In order to ensure that the pursuit of collateral issues does not unnecessarily protract trials, the court has been left with discretion whether or not to permit such evidence to be led.

Stopping the case where hearsay evidence is unconvincing (s 125)

9.90 English law normally demarcates sharply the respective roles of the judge and the trier of fact in the criminal trial. Matters of law are for the former, matters of fact for the latter. This strict division of functions is embodied in *Galbraith* [1981] 1 WLR 1039, the leading case that lays down when it is permissible for a judge to uphold a defence submission of no case to answer. In essence, *Galbraith* holds that the judge may only stay a case if (a) there is no evidence that the defendant committed the offence or (b) the judge feels that, taking the prosecution evidence at its highest, a jury, properly directed, could not reasonably convict on it. There are exceptions to this principle. The risks posed by identification evidence are recognised to be so great that a judge is entitled to stop the case if he believes that the quality of the identification evidence is poor (*Daley v R* [1994] 1 AC 117: see *post*, para **12.8**). So, too, a judge, after a *voire dire*, is entitled to reject a defendant's confession if he has not been persuaded by the party seeking to adduce the confession that it was obtained in the absence of oppression or things said and done that might render a confession unreliable (see *post*, Chapter 10). Hearsay evidence, it was concluded, could pose similar risks. Therefore, another exception to the *Galbraith* principle was created and, without prejudice to any other existing powers courts have to direct an acquittal or to discharge a jury (s 125(4)), s 125(1) provides:

> If on a defendant's trial before a judge and jury for an offence the court is satisfied at any time after the close of the case for the prosecution that—
>
> (a) the case against the defendant is based wholly or partly on a statement not made in oral evidence in the proceedings, and
>
> (b) the evidence provided by the statement is so unconvincing that, considering its importance to the case against the defendant, his conviction of the offence would be unsafe,
>
> the court must either direct the jury to acquit the defendant of the offence or, if it considers that there ought to be a retrial, discharge the jury.

In *Joyce and Joyce* [2005] EWCA Crim 1785 at [19], Rose LJ recognised that this provision acts as 'an additional safety valve obliging a judge to direct an acquittal where the . . . statements are particularly unpersuasive'. However, as the court's ruling shows, this power is only to be exercised in extreme circumstances. In *Joyce*, the court was confronted with the statements of three witnesses, who knew the defendants (who stood accused of homicide) and who had viewed the shootings in full daylight in summer. As Rose LJ said, rejecting Js' invitation to apply s 125:

> It would have been an affront to the administration of justice, on a trial of offences based on this terrifying conduct, if the jury had not been permitted by the judge to evaluate, separately and together, the quality of the three witnesses' oral evidence and to be able to rely, if they thought fit, on the terms of their original statements.
>
> (at [27])

The court's general discretion to exclude evidence in the interest of case management (s 126)

9.91 Section 126 introduces a new judicial discretionary power to exclude hearsay evidence admitted under the Act. The discretion operates in addition to the court's customary power to exclude evidence under PACE, s 78 and its other powers to exclude evidence, at its discretion, whether by preventing questions from being put or otherwise. Unlike conventional discretions in criminal cases, the discretion created by s 126 is not a response to the weakness of proposed evidence but is exercised for motives of case management. (On case management in criminal cases, see *ante*, Introduction, pp 14–16.) It is meant to protect the court from wasting its time over pieces of superfluous hearsay, whose value as evidence does not justify their admission. Thus, it is provided:

> (1) In criminal proceedings the court may refuse to admit a statement as evidence of a matter stated if—
>
> (a) the statement was made otherwise than in oral evidence in the proceedings, and
>
> (b) the court is satisfied that the case for excluding the statement, taking account of the danger that to admit it would result in undue waste of time, substantially outweighs the case for admitting it, taking account of the value of the evidence.

Clearly, s 126 was prompted by the fear that increases in the amount of hearsay evidence that may be presented to the court could make trials unduly inefficient and unwieldy. For obvious reasons, it is a discretion to which courts are likely to have cautious recourse.

Other statutory exceptions to the hearsay rule

Proof by written statements admitted under the Criminal Justice Act 1967, s 9

9.92 Although in English criminal procedure the accent is still just about on orality, with witnesses giving their testimony in person, the Criminal Justice Act 1967, s 9 provides a procedure whereby evidence may be laid before the court in written form. If the parties so agree, evidence may be presented at trial in documentary form under the Act. Such written statements are 'admissible as evidence to the like extent as oral evidence to the like effect by that person' (s 9(1)). Witnesses' services, therefore, in practice can be conveniently dispensed with if their evidence is non-contentious. The section simply requires that in order to be admissible the statement:

- must have been signed by the maker;
- must contain a declaration by the maker that it is true to the best of his knowledge and belief, and must acknowledge that the maker knows that he is liable to penalties if he has wilfully told falsehoods;

- must have been tendered to all other parties in advance of the hearing; and

- no party on whom the statement was served must within seven days of service have given notice of an intention to object to the statement.

A party seeking to adduce such a statement must comply strictly with the requirements of s 9; otherwise, the statement will be inadmissible: eg, *Guttentag v DPP* [2009] EWHC 1849 (Admin) at [14] *per* Cranston, J. As noted above, there is now an overlap between this provision and s 114(1)(c) of the 2003 Act, which allows hearsay statements to be admitted where all parties consent thereto (*ante*, para **9.68**).

Confessions (PACE, ss 76 and 76A)

9.93 Confessional evidence, which will be considered in the next chapter, constitutes another statutory exception to the hearsay rule. The rules regulating this species of evidence were expressly retained by s 118, r 5 (*ante*, para **9.63**).

Bankers' books (Bankers' Books Evidence Act 1879)

9.94 Special rules have applied to the admission of evidence of the contents of bankers' books since Victorian times. The provisions of the Bankers' Books Evidence Act 1879, which remains undisturbed by the Criminal Justice Act 2003, are considered in a later chapter (see paras **13.10–13.13**).

Human rights law, the rule against hearsay and its exceptions (ECHR, Article 6(3)(d))

9.95 The principles of the European Convention on Human Rights can have an important bearing on the question whether or not to admit hearsay statements in place of live witness evidence. Article 6(3)(d) of the Convention guarantees to a defendant the minimum right 'to examine or have examined witnesses against him.'

This does not signify that the prosecution may never rely on hearsay evidence. However, it does mean that the prosecution must take appropriate steps to palliate the effects of introducing the evidence of parties who will not appear in person at trial. As the Commission has noted:

> Art 6(3)(d)...does not grant the accused an unlimited right to secure the appearance of witnesses in court. Its purpose is rather to secure equality between the defence and the prosecution as regards the summoning and examining of witnesses...It does not exclude the possibility that witnesses residing abroad whose presence at the trial cannot be enforced by the trial court are examined on commission by a court at their place of

residence. This...well-established practice...is to assure to the greatest possible extent the availability of evidence which cannot be collected otherwise.

(*X v Germany* (1988) 10 EHRR 521, 523)

Lord Bingham of Cornhill, in *Grant v The Queen* [2007] 1 AC 1, characterised this minimum right as:

the need for a fair balance between the general interest of the community and the personal rights of the individual...the rights of the individual must be safeguarded, but the interests of the community must also be respected.

(at [17])

9.96 To the extent that European human rights organs have considered the question, the English hearsay rule, in principle, ought not normally to risk violating Article 6(3)(d) of the Convention. Thus, in *Blastland v UK* (1987) 10 EHRR 528 (see *ante*, para **9.4(i)**) the Commission declared that it was legitimate for English law to exclude hearsay evidence with a view both to ensuring that the best evidence was placed before the jury and to avoiding undue weight being attributed to evidence which had not been tested in cross-examination. Indeed, one might once have said that English law's reluctance to admit hearsay evidence, an attribute that it did not share with the majority of European criminal jurisdictions, meant that it broadly complied with Article 6(3)(d)'s requirement that the accused enjoy the right 'to examine or have examined the witnesses against him'. It is, however, important to be aware that Article 6(3)(d) raises some vexed questions. More particularly, in view of the increasing number of cases in which English law will now allow hearsay evidence to be given, alleged infringements of Article 6 are becoming more frequent in English criminal cases. It is true, on the one hand, that in *Saidi v France* (1993) 17 EHRR 251 the European Court of Human Rights held that:

the taking of evidence is governed primarily by the rules of domestic law and...it is in principle for the national courts to assess the evidence before them. The Court's task...is to ascertain whether the proceedings in their entirety, including the way in which evidence was taken, were fair.

(at [43])

However, as the Law Commission concluded after a thorough examination of that court's decisions on the matter (see *Evidence in Criminal Proceedings: Hearsay and Related Topics*, Consultation Paper No 138), English law in this context could yet find itself in violation of Article 6.

9.97 When the prosecution, at trial, relies upon a statement made by a witness whom the defence has had an opportunity to question during the pre-trial phase, the

European Court holds that such evidence complies with the Convention. Thus, in *Kostovski v Netherlands* (1989) 12 EHRR 434, the ECtHR declared:

> In principle, all the evidence must be produced in the presence of the accused at a public hearing with a view to adversarial argument...To use as evidence...statements obtained at a pre-trial stage is not in itself inconsistent with [Article 6(3)(d), art. 6(1)], provided that the rights of the defence have been respected. As a rule, those rights require that an accused should be given an adequate and proper opportunity to challenge and question a witness against him, either at the time the witness was making his statement or at some later stage of the proceedings.
>
> (at [41])

It will be readily seen that not all statements admitted under ss 116 and 117 of the Criminal Justice Act 2003 will necessarily comply with this basic human rights requirement as the Act does not demand, as a condition of admissibility, that the defence should have been afforded an opportunity to challenge the witness. The effective demise of committal proceedings, where D had an opportunity (rarely seized) to question and challenge Crown witnesses, and their replacement under the Criminal Procedure and Investigations Act 1996 by a paper committal which has 'drastically reduced' the scope for defence intervention at the pre-trial phase of indictable offences (*R v DPP, ex p Lee* (1999) 163 JP 569, 579 *per* Kennedy LJ) mean that English criminal courts on occasion could be skating on thin ice in this context.

9.98 Although it is permissible to use witness statements which the defence has not had an opportunity to challenge if, for instance, this would have been impossible, the ECtHR has regularly taken the view that a conviction will not be fair if founded 'mainly' on such evidence (eg *Unterpertinger v Austria* (1986) 13 EHRR 175 at [33]). In *PS v Germany* [2002] Crim LR 312, application no 33900/96, for example, PS, a private music teacher, had been convicted of a sexual assault on his pupil, S. The court had convicted PS on the following evidence: (i) S's mother's testimony (who related S's complaint); (ii) evidence of S's behaviour after the music lesson; (iii) evidence of S's general character; and (iv) the evidence of a police officer who had questioned S shortly after the incident. The ECtHR found that there had been a violation of Article 6(3)(d). Whilst there are exceptions to the general principle that all evidence must be produced at a public hearing, in the presence of the accused, with a view to adversarial argument—for instance, as here, to protect juvenile witnesses—the accused must be granted an adequate opportunity to challenge and question a witness against him. If it is strictly necessary to restrict the defence's rights, any restrictions must be sufficiently counterbalanced by the procedures followed by the judicial authorities. In this case, S had never been questioned by a judge; PS and the court had had no opportunity to observe S's demeanour; the trial court had even refused to receive psychological evidence regarding S's credibility. In these circumstances, PS had been deprived of his right to a fair trial, for, as the ECtHR explained:

> Where a conviction is based solely or to a decisive degree on depositions that have been made by a person whom the accused has had no opportunity to examine or have examined, whether during the investigation or at the trial, the rights of the defence are restricted to an extent that is incompatible with the guarantees provided by Article 6...
>
> (at [24])

(See also *Lucà v Italy* [2001] Crim LR 747, application no 33354/96; Potter LJ's judgment in *M (KJ)* [2003] 2 Cr App R 21 at [56] ff, and Waller LJ's judgment in *Sellick* [2005] 2 Cr App R 15 at [34] ff.) The use of witness statements may however be condoned if supplemented by other legitimate forms of evidence.

9.99 In theory at least, nothing prevents an English court from convicting solely on a witness statement which the accused has not had an opportunity to contest. In *D* [2003] QB 90, a challenge was mounted against the admission of a witness statement partly on the ground that it would offend against Article 6(3)(d). At the preparatory hearing the trial judge had ruled admissible a video recording of an interview conducted with an 81-year-old woman who suffered from delusions and the onset of Alzheimer's disease. D, who denied indecent assault and rape, unsuccessfully argued before the Court of Appeal that since he had never been afforded an opportunity to challenge the woman's statement before the trial and since the trial would not cure that deficiency as she was unfit to testify within the meaning of s 23(2)(a) of the Criminal Justice Act 1988 (see now Criminal Justice Act 2003, s 116(2)), he had been deprived of his right 'to examine...witnesses against him'. In the words of the court, in dismissing D's argument:

> ...if the court has concluded that it is in the interests of justice that a statement should be admitted, and if the court carries out its duty to consider the risk so far as the appellant is concerned, it is most unlikely that there will be a breach of art 6(3)(d). There is no absolute right that witnesses should be available for cross-examination and the essential question is whether the trial process is fair. The important point that has to be remembered...is that a victim, or possible victim, has rights which have to be balanced against those of a defendant.
>
> (at [41])

9.100 Witnesses, however, may not testify in person for a wide variety of reasons, and in those cases where the defendant himself is responsible for this situation 'he is in no position to complain that he has been denied a fair trial if a statement from that witness is admitted'. In determining whether it is consistent with a fair trial to admit such evidence, it has been suggested that '[f]actors that will be likely to be of concern to the court are identified in s 114(2) of the [Criminal Justice] Act' (*Cole and Keet* [2007] 1 WLR 2716 at [21] *per* Lord Phillips of Worth Matravers. See *ante*, para **9.72**).

9.101   Sometimes, however, a court will exclude hearsay precisely because it is effectively the only evidence against an accused. In *CPS (Durham) v CE* [2006] EWCA Crim 1410, esp at [14], the Court of Appeal upheld a trial judge's refusal to admit the videotaped statement of a rape complainant, who did not testify in person. The judge's ruling had not been unreasonable given that the complainant's statement constituted 'the sole or decisive evidence' against CE, was an 'uncross-examined and untested video statement' and, had CE been convicted, admission of the statement would have been 'likely to result to result in a successful appeal against conviction'.

9.102   *Where hearsay constitutes 'the sole or decisive prosecution evidence'*. Quite recently, in *Al-Khawaja and Tahery v UK* (2009) ECHR 26766/05 the ECtHR held that there had been breaches of Article 6 of the ECHR in both appealed cases as each conviction had been based to a sole or decisive degree on the statements which A-K and T had had no opportunity of challenging (in one case, a deceased witness, in the other, a fearful witness). Adopting an earlier statement in *Lucà v Italy* (2001) 36 EHRR 807 at [40] to the effect that 'where a conviction is based solely or to a decisive degree on depositions that have been made by a person whom the accused has had no opportunity to examine or to have examined, whether during the investigation or at the trial, the rights of the defence are restricted to an extent that is incompatible with the guarantees provided by Art. 6', in *Al-Khawaja* the ECtHR advanced the proposition that if hearsay is the sole or decisive evidence in the case, there will necessarily be a breach of Article 6(3)(d) if the defendant is denied the right to confront the witness, at least unless the case is one of fear.

In *Horncastle* [2009] 2 Cr App R 15, a five-man Court of Appeal considered this ruling and declined to apply it on the grounds that the ECtHR had not been true to its own case law and that the Criminal Justice Act 2003 offers 'a crafted code intended to ensure that evidence is admitted only when it is fair that it should be' (at [16]). To the extent that English law is not bound by ECtHR decisions but only 'obliged to take account of them so far as they are relevant' *(R (Alconbury) v Secretary of State for the Environment* [2003] 2 AC 295 *per* Lord Slynn), Thomas LJ, speaking for the court, concluded that in *Al-Khawaja* the ECtHR had misinterpreted its own case law. The court questioned whether any of the decisions prior to *Al-Khawaja* had gone so far as to examine evidence from an identified witness who was absent for good reason, but where such evidence can be assessed as reliable or tested in a manner that respects the rights of the defence (at [47]). The ECtHR in *Al-Khawaja* was said to have proceeded under two misapprehensions: it had assumed, first, that all hearsay evidence which is critical to a case will be potentially unreliable in the absence of testing in open court and, second, that fact-finders cannot be trusted to assess the weight of such evidence. Thomas LJ went on to explain why the Court of Appeal had arrived at the conclusion that there ought to be no rule that counterbalancing measures can never suffice where hearsay is the sole or decisive evidence in the case:

> *First*, such a requirement was rejected by the Law Commission...and...by Parliament.... *Second*, the code set out in the Criminal Justice Act 2003 provides...rigorous conditions for admissibility.... *Third*, explicit provisions are made which enable the defence to test the credibility and reliability of the evidence by s 124 of the Criminal Justice Act 2003.... *Fourth*, such a rule...has principled and practical objections. The essential considerations are whether there is a justifiable reason for absence...and whether the evidence can be assessed and tested so that it is safe to rely upon it—a consideration which the ECtHR has not, it appears, fully considered. *Fifth*, s 125 of the Criminal Justice Act 2003 provides an overriding safeguard which goes to the essence of the evidence so admitted – its reliability. *Sixth*, the difficulties facing a defendant when an application is made to admit hearsay evidence are well understood by the courts...; the statutory conditions in the Criminal Justice Act 2003 are rigorously applied. *Seventh*, we consider that the decision of the ECtHR in *Al-Khawaja* does not, on the analysis which we endeavour to set out in the light of a fuller consideration of the Criminal Justice Act 2003, justify us in departing from the decisions of this court prior to that decision.
>
> (at [58]

9.103 In *Horncastle* [2010] 2 WLR 47 appeal was taken to the Supreme Court. Having passed in review the law of other Commonwealth jurisdictions where, in line with English law, the 'sole or decisive test' has no place, in a judgment plainly composed in order to initiate what he termed 'valuable dialogue between this court and the Strasbourg Court' (at [11]), Lord Phillips described the ECtHR's declaration in *Lucà v Italy* as 'a startling proposition' (at [46]). Indeed, the 'sole or decisive' test was said to present a kind of paradox:

> It permits the court to have regard to evidence if the support that it gives to the prosecution case is peripheral, but not where it is decisive. The more cogent the evidence the less it can be relied upon.
>
> (at [91])

As Lord Phillips noted, 'if applied rigorously [the sole or decisive test] will in some cases result in acquittal, or failure to prosecute, defendants where there is cogent evidence of their guilt' (at [105]). In an appendix to the judgments, in order to demonstrate the fairness of English law's stance, Lord Judge analysed a catalogue of

Strasbourg cases, endeavouring to show that if one applied the various safeguards presently available under English law to Strasbourg cases where Article 6 has been held to have been violated, in almost all such cases English law, too, would have excluded the evidence of the absent or anonymous witnesses concerned. This permitted the conclusion:

> The cases suggest that in general [English] rules of admissibility provide the defendant with at least equal protection to that provided under the continental system.
>
> (at [93])

The Supreme Court's pugnacious conclusion was:

> The jurisprudence of the Strasbourg Court in relation to Article 6(3)(d) has developed largely in cases relating to civil-law rather than common-law jurisdictions and this is particularly true of the sole or decisive rule.... [T]that case law appears to have developed without full consideration of the safeguards against an unfair trial that exist under the common-law procedure. Nor, I suspect, can the Strasbourg Court have given detailed consideration to the English law of admissibility of evidence, and the changes made to that law, after consideration by the Law Commission, intended to ensure that English law complies with the requirements of Article 6(1) and (3)(d).
>
> (at [107])

Thus, the Supreme Court, agreeing with the Court of Appeal, declined to follow *Lucà v Italy*, concluding instead that the 2003 Act:

> strike[s] the right balance between the imperative that a trial must be fair and the interests of victims in particular and society in general that a criminal should not be immune from conviction where a witness, who has given critical evidence in a statement that can be shown to be reliable, dies or cannot be called to give evidence for some other reason.

Lord Hope, too, emitted 'the hope that the Grand Chamber will clarify the law upon hearsay evidence and recognise that [English] domestic law is compatible with Art. 6' (at [121]). At the time of writing the decision of the Grand Chamber is still awaited.

Anonymous witnesses: The Coroners and Justice Act 2009, ss 86–96

9.104 Just as human rights law can play an important role where evidence is supplied by absent witnesses, broadly similar considerations apply when witnesses testify 'anonymously'. The issue was carefully considered by the House of Lords in *Davis*

[2008] 3 WLR 125, a murder case in which the prosecution case had been heavily reliant on evidence given by anonymous witnesses. Given the level of intimidation present in certain communities nowadays, in order for some trials to proceed at all, two alternative sets of devices have been employed: either resort has been had to witness protection programmes—which will often be impractical—or various devices have been adopted in court so as to reassure witnesses—these include voice modulation machines, screening, false names, and outright concealment of identity. In *Davis* seven witnesses had claimed to be in fear for their lives if it became known that they had given evidence against the appellant. Three of them were the only witnesses in the case to identify D as the gunman. To ensure the safety of those three witnesses, the trial judge had ordered (i) that they might give their evidence under a pseudonym, (ii) that their addresses and any personal details or particulars that might identify them were to be withheld from D and his legal advisers, (iii) that D's counsel was forbidden to ask these witnesses any question that might enable any of them to be identified, (iv) that these witnesses were to testify behind screens so that they could be seen by the judge and the jury but not by D, and (v) that the witnesses' natural voices were to be heard by the judge and the jury but were to be heard by the appellant and his counsel subject to mechanical distortion so as to prevent recognition by D. On appeal, it was argued that these restrictions were contrary to the common law of England, and inconsistent with Article 6(3)(d) of the European Convention on Human Rights. In the Court of Appeal these arguments failed. However, in five interlocking judgments, which elicited an immediate government response in the form of a Criminal Evidence (Witness Anonymity) Act 2008, the House of Lords reversed this decision, quashed D's conviction and remitted the case to the Court of Appeal. The 2008 Act was subject to a 'sunset clause'. Its provisions were renewed in the Coroners and Justice Act 2009, and further protections were created in the form of 'investigation anonymity orders' that may be made by magistrates to protect individuals' identities during the course of police investigations in homicide cases where a firearm or knife has been employed (s 76).

9.105 The obvious disadvantages for a defendant who is unaware of who is testifying against him were set out by the ECtHR in *Kostovski v Netherlands* (1989) 12 EHRR 434:

> If the defence is unaware of the identity of the person it seeks to question, it may be deprived of the very particulars enabling it to demonstrate that he or she is prejudiced, hostile or unreliable. A testimony or other declaration inculpating an accused may well be designedly untruthful or simply erroneous and the defence will scarcely be able to bring this to light if it lacks the information permitting it to test the author's reliability or cast doubt on his credibility.
>
> (at [42])

As Lord Bingham put it, the practice of allowing witnesses to testify anonymously compels the defence 'to take blind shots at a hidden target' (*Davis*, at [32]).

9.106 Lord Mance analysed the ECtHR's position on evidence given by anonymous witnesses, noting that that Court had repeatedly stated that the use of anonymous evidence was 'not under all circumstances incompatible with the Convention'. Thus, in *Doorson v Netherlands* (1996) 22 EHRR 330 a drug smuggler's conviction had been secured in significant part upon the statements of two anonymous witnesses, who had been questioned by the investigating judge. The applicant's advocate had been absent, but did personally question the two witnesses at the appeal hearing. The ECtHR observed, since witnesses' interests coming within Articles 2 (the right to life) and 8 (respect for family and private life) are protected along with the defendant's Article 6 right to a fair trial, contracting States must organise their criminal proceedings in such a way that those interests are not unjustifiably imperilled. Against this backdrop, principles of fair trial additionally require that in appropriate cases the court must balance the interests of the defence against those of witnesses or victims called upon to testify. Although there are indications that there could be circumstances in which even decisive testimony may be given anonymously (eg, *Krasniki v Czech Republic* (Application no 51277/99) February 28, 2006, unreported), the current understanding seemed to be that whenever witness anonymity has been granted, a conviction must not be based solely or to a decisive extent on the evidence of such persons, 'even when "counterbalancing" procedures are found to compensate sufficiently the handicaps under which the defence labours' (*Doorson* at [76]). (The relevant ECtHR 'jurisprudence', it should be said, is confused because the cases tend to be concerned primarily with pre-trial statements made by (identified) witnesses who are not subsequently called for cross-examination at trial rather than with the testimony of anonymous witnesses *stricto sensu*: see Lord Mance at [89].) According to Lord Bingham in *Davis*, 'this is the view traditionally taken by the common law of England' (at [25]).

9.107 The House of Lords' decision in *Davis* sparked instant controversy. There was consternation that up to forty prisoners currently languishing in gaol would become entitled to appeal their convictions for serious offences. Lord Mance, however, concluded in *Davis* that there was scope within the ECHR for 'a careful statutory modification of basic common law principles' (at [98]). At electrifying speed the government introduced legislation enabling evidence to be given in criminal trials, under controlled conditions, by witnesses whose identities were concealed to varying degrees.

9.108 The Criminal Evidence (Witness Anonymity) Act 2008, and its successor the Coroners and Justice Act 2009, abolished the common law rules and instituted a new regime governing the testimony of anonymous witnesses in criminal trials. Under the Act application may now be made to the court by either prosecution or defence for a 'witness anonymity order' (s 87(1)). The order will specify what measures may be taken to ensure that a particular witness's identity remains undisclosed. Section 86(2) lists the sort of measures that may be required, but does not exclude the possibility of other measures being employed (s 86(3)). These are:

(a) that the witness's name and other identifying details may be—

  (i) withheld;

  (ii) removed from materials disclosed to any party to the proceedings;

(b) that the witness may use a pseudonym;

(c) that the witness is not asked questions of any specified description that might lead to the identification of the witness;

(d) that the witness is screened to any specified extent;

(e) that the witness's voice is subjected to modulation to any specified extent.

In the case of screening and voice modulation, the witness must remain visible and his or her natural voice be audible to the judge, the jury, interpreters, and to other persons appointed by the court to assist the witness (s 86(4)).

9.109 The Act places prosecution and defence applications on separate footings. The prosecution need only inform the court of the identity of any witness whose identity it wishes to protect; it is not required to reveal the identity or any information that might serve to identify the witness to any other party to the proceedings or to any other party's legal representatives. The court may even direct that the prosecution can withhold a Crown witness's identity from it—one presumes, typically in cases where national security is a factor (s 87(2)). Because it is likely that such defence applications will only be made in cases where there are multiple defendants, the defence, in contrast, must inform both the court and the prosecution of the identity of its witness, but may withhold the information from any co-accused and the latter's legal representatives (s 87(3)). In all cases, whenever an application is made, all parties have the right to be heard—although the court may hear parties in the absence of the defendant and his or her legal representatives 'if it appears to the court to be appropriate to do so in the circumstances' (s 87(7)).

9.110 Section 88 stipulates that a court may only grant a witness anonymity order if three conditions (A–C) have been met:

Condition A requires that the measures specified by the court must be either:

'necessary...to protect the safety of the witness or another person or to prevent any serious damage to property' (s 88(3)(a))

or

'necessary . . . to prevent real harm to the public interest (whether affecting the carrying on of any activities in the public interest or the safety of a person involved in carrying on such activities, or otherwise)' (s 88(3)(b)).

In the case of s 88(3)(a) it should be noted that there is no need to show that the witness or any other party has actually been threatened. Nevertheless, s 88(6) does stress that in determining whether the measures are necessary:

the court must have regard (in particular) to any reasonable fear on the part of the witness—

(a) that the witness or another person would suffer death or injury, or

(b) that there would be serious damage to property,

if the witness were to be identified.

Section 88(3)(b) is primarily concerned to protect the identities of police officers and security personnel who may be unable to take part in future undercover operations if their identities become known.

Condition B, mindful of Article 6 of the ECHR, requires that the court must be satisfied that, 'having regard to all the circumstances, the taking of those measures would be consistent with the defendant receiving a fair trial' (s 88(4). Eg, *Khan* [2010] EWCA Crim 1692).

Finally, *Condition C* requires that 'the importance of the witness's testimony is such that in the interests of justice the witness ought to testify' and either the witness would not otherwise testify or there would be 'real harm to the public interest' if the witness were to testify in the absence of such an order (s 88(5)). In *Mayers* [2008] EWCA Crim 2989 at [26] and again in *Powar* [2009] EWCA Crim 594 at [56], it was said to be more logical in most cases for a court to begin by considering Condition C.

9.111 In determining whether Conditions A–C have been met—and all three must be satisfied before an order can issue—in addition to 'such other matters as the court considers relevant' (s 89(1)(b)), the court must have specific regard to the following considerations:

(a) the general right of a defendant in criminal proceedings to know the identity of a witness in the proceedings;

(b) the extent to which the credibility of the witness concerned would be a relevant factor when the weight of his or her evidence comes to be assessed;

(c) whether evidence given by the witness might be the sole or decisive evidence implicating the defendant;

(d) whether the witness's evidence could be properly tested (whether on grounds of credibility or otherwise) without his or her identity being disclosed;

(e) whether there is any reason to believe that the witness—

(i) has a tendency to be dishonest, or

(ii) has any motive to be dishonest in the circumstances of the case,

having regard (in particular) to any previous convictions of the witness and to any relationship between the witness and the defendant or any associates of the defendant;

(f) whether it would be reasonably practicable to protect the witness's identity by any means other than by making a witness anonymity order specifying the measures that are under consideration by the court.

(s 89(2))

9.112   If there has been a material change of circumstances—eg, if a witness has a change of heart, deciding that he does not object to his identity being revealed—parties to the proceedings may apply to the court to have a witness anonymity order discharged. The court may discharge an order 'if it appears . . . appropriate to do so in view of the provisions of ss 88 and 89 that applied to the making of the order.' Alternatively, the court may discharge an order on its own initiative (s 91(2)(b)).

9.113   If the trial takes place before a jury, the judge 'must give the jury such warning as [he] considers appropriate to ensure that the fact that the order was made in relation to the witness does not prejudice the defendant' (s 90(2)).

9.114   In conclusion, as the Court of Appeal declared in *Powar*:

> [T]he calling of anonymous witnesses must not become a routine event in the prosecution of serious crime but we reject the submission that witness anonymity orders should be confined to cases of terrorism or gangland killings. The intimidation of witnesses has become an ugly feature of contemporary life; as has been said (by Royce J in *Mayers* at [101]), "the climate of fear in these cases is like a cancer"; this fear serves "to silence, blind and deafen witnesses; without witnesses justice cannot be done' (*per* Judge LJ in Davis . . .).
>
> (at [63])

II. Hearsay in civil proceedings

9.115   *The rule against hearsay has been abrogated to all intents in civil proceedings*—In contrast to its criminal counterpart, the hearsay rule has little or no application in civil proceedings. The opening words of the Civil Evidence Act 1995, s 1(1) set the tone:

> In civil proceedings evidence shall not be excluded on the ground that it is hearsay.

'Hearsay', in this context, still means hearsay in the traditional, common law sense of the term. Whereas the Criminal Justice Act 2003, ss 114–115 have introduced a new statutory definition of 'hearsay', in civil proceedings 'hearsay' still largely retains its old meaning. The formula proposed in *Cross & Tapper on Evidence* is most often accepted as an authoritative statement of the rule at common law:

> An assertion other than one made by a person while giving oral evidence in the proceedings is inadmissible as evidence of any fact or opinion asserted.

9.116 Although the intention of the Civil Evidence Act, in implementing recommendations of the Law Commission, presumably was 'to abrogate the rule of evidence whereby evidence of a hearsay nature may not be adduced in civil proceedings as evidence of the facts asserted' (Law Com no 216, Cm 2321 (1993) para 4:1), there was an argument that it had not done so. The Act defines 'hearsay' in s 1(2)(a) as:

> ... a *statement* made otherwise than by a person while giving oral evidence in the proceedings which is tendered as evidence of the matters stated; and
>
> (b) references to hearsay include hearsay of whatever degree.

It was suggested that use of the word 'statement' could actually exclude from the operation of the Act implied assertions of the type found in *Kearley* [1992] 2 AC 228, in as much as implied assertions cannot properly be described as 'statements'. This view, which is still of relevance given that in civil proceedings the old common law definition of hearsay will continue to apply, flies full in the face of the indisputable purpose of the statute. It also assumes that a civil court would adopt the kind of literal reading of s 1(2)(a) and the obsessive logic-chopping that has typified much discussion of the hearsay rule, especially in criminal cases. It would be most strange were the Civil Evidence Act held to cover clear cases of hearsay involving express assertions whilst the strongly disputed category of implied assertions remained subject to the hearsay rule. In view of the fact that, as we have seen, implied assertions of the sort that the House of Lords decreed in *Kearley* were to be treated as hearsay no longer fall within the hearsay rule in criminal cases following enactment of the Criminal Justice Act 2003, s 115(3) (see *ante*, para **9.10**), it is most unlikely that the civil courts would choose to adopt this literal construction. (Moreover, if the courts did so, the Civil Procedure Rules Committee might be expected to exercise their extensive powers under the Civil Procedure Act 1997, Sch 1, para 4 to 'modify the rules of evidence as they apply to proceedings in any court' to restore a degree of sanity to the law.)

9.117 Hearsay evidence is now generally admissible in civil cases, but its admission is hedged about with conditions. Although s 1(4) provides that:

> ... the provisions of ss 2 to 6 (safeguards and supplementary provisions relating to hearsay evidence) do not apply in relation to hearsay evidence admissible apart from this section, notwithstanding that it may also be admissible by virtue of this section ...

the majority of hearsay evidence will be subject to safeguards set out in the Act. Thus, to avoid unfairness—and, in particular, to enable an opposing party, with the leave of the court, to call and cross-examine the relevant witness just as if he had been called in the first place by the party adducing his hearsay evidence—advance notice must be given by a party intending to adduce hearsay evidence (s 3 and Civil Procedure Rules, r 33.2)—not that a failure to comply with this requirement will always be treated as a fatal flaw: eg *Polanski v Condé Nast Publications Ltd* [2004] 1 All ER 1220 at [19] *per* Simon Brown LJ. Part 33 of the Civil Procedure Rules 1998 sets out the form such notice must take, and indeed provides detailed procedures for the admission of hearsay evidence generally (SI 1998/3132, as amended). Under s 2 of the Act, unless the parties have agreed to dispense with the requirement or it has been waived, a party proposing to adduce hearsay evidence must give:

(a) such notice... of that fact, and

(b) on request..., such particulars of or relating to the evidence,

as is reasonable and practicable in the circumstances for the purpose of enabling him... to deal with any matters arising from its being hearsay.

Failure to comply with this requirement will not lead to exclusion of the hearsay evidence, but notably can affect the weight it is accorded.

9.118　The 1995 Act enumerates factors to which the court is to have regard in evaluating the weight of evidence presented in the form of hearsay. Thus, s 4 states:

(1) In estimating the weight (if any) to be given to hearsay evidence in civil proceedings the court shall have regard to any circumstances from which any inference can reasonably be drawn as to the reliability or otherwise of the evidence.

The provision then suggests that:

(2) Regard may be had in particular to the following—

(a) whether it would have been reasonable and practicable for the party by whom the evidence was adduced to have produced the maker of the original statement as a witness;

(b) whether the original statement was made contemporaneously with the occurrence or the existence of the matters stated;

(c) whether the evidence involves multiple hearsay;

(d) whether any person involved had any motive to conceal or misrepresent matters;

(e) whether the original statement was an edited account, or was made in collaboration with another or for a particular purpose;

(f) whether the circumstances in which the evidence is adduced as hearsay are such as to suggest an attempt to prevent proper evaluation of its weight.

This list is neither exhaustive nor mandatory, and the court is at liberty to take other factors into account as well. It is to be noted that s 4(1), '(if any)', allows a judge to discount hearsay evidence entirely, if sufficiently dubious of its reliability. As Mance LJ pointed out in *Solon South West Housing Association Ltd v James* [2005] HLR 24 at [19], practically speaking, this may be little different from a power to exclude evidence:

[T]here is very little, if any, relevant difference between asking a judge to exclude evidence...and asking him not to rely upon it, since under s 4 a judge could determine evidence was not worthy of particular weight even after it had been admitted.

(see also para 1.58, *ante*)

9.119 Just as criminal courts have had to consider whether there are circumstances in which a conviction can be secured solely on the strength of hearsay evidence, in civil cases too this question has arisen. In *Welsh v Stokes* [2008] 1 WLR 1224 W's action for negligence following a horse-riding accident succeeded against the owners of the yard where she had been employed as a trainee. Apart from the testimony of an expert who said that the account was 'credible', the sole evidence in the case was that of Mr Welsh who reported what Mr Wragge had reported to him that an unidentified witness to the accident, X, had told him that he had seen. On appeal, it was argued that this uncorroborated and untested double hearsay evidence of an unidentified motorist carried insufficient weight to allow the court to make specific findings of fact based upon it. Dyson LJ upheld the judge's decision to rely upon this hearsay evidence in delivering judgment in favour of the claimant because the judge had had proper regard to all the factors listed in s 4(2) of the 1995 Act, had been entitled to give weight to the expert's view of the plausibility of the account of the incident given by the motorist, and had plainly been alive to the difficulty of assessing the reliability of the account given by the unidentified eyewitness. Dyson LJ then went further, adding:

Even if the hearsay evidence were the only evidence on which the claim was based, I would not accept that this was necessarily a reason for giving into weight. It would depend on all the circumstances. I accept that there will be cases where it is so unfair to hold a defendant liable solely on the basis of hearsay evidence that a court should place little or no weight on the evidence. Consideration of the factors stated in s 4(2) will point the way, but will not necessarily be determinative....Where a case depends entirely on hearsay evidence, the court will be particularly careful before concluding that it can be given any weight. But there is no rule of law which prohibits a court from giving weight to hearsay evidence merely because it is uncorroborated and cannot be tested or contradicted by the other party.

(at [22] and [23])

9.120 After the general manner of s 124 of the Criminal Justice Act 2003 (*ante*, paras **9.86–9.89**), evidence may be adduced attacking or supporting the credibility of persons whose hearsay evidence has been received as if they had given evidence in person. Similarly, any inconsistent statements they may have made can be introduced (s 5(1)). However, the principle of collateral-finality (see *ante*, paras **4.42–4.49**) is preserved by s 5(2), which provides that 'evidence may not be given of any matter of which, if he had been called as a witness and had denied that matter in cross-examination, evidence could not have been adduced by the cross-examining party'.

9.121 Like the Criminal Justice Act 2003, s 118, the Civil Evidence Act 1995 also retains a number of existing common law rules, which permit the admission of hearsay evidence. Thus, s 7(2) preserves the following rules.

- *Firstly*, it provides that 'published works dealing with matters of a public nature (for example, histories, scientific works, dictionaries and maps) are admissible as evidence of facts of a public nature stated in them' (s 7(2)(a)).

- *Secondly*, it provides that statements contained in public documents are admissible as evidence of the truth of their contents (s 7(2)(b): see *post*, para **13.3**). This well-established exception to the hearsay rule was explained by Lord Blackburn in *Sturla v Freccia* (1880) 5 App Cas 623:

  In many cases, entries in the parish register of births, marriages and deaths, and other entries of that kind, before there were any statutes relating to them, were admissible, for they were "public" then, because the common law of England making it an express duty to keep the register, made it a public document in that sense kept by a public officer for the purpose of a register, and that made it admissible.

- *Thirdly*, 'records (for example, the records of certain courts, treaties, Crown grants, pardons and commissions) are admissible as evidence of facts stated in them' (s 7(2)(c)).

- *Fourthly*, 'evidence of a person's reputation is admissible for the purpose of establishing his good or bad character' (s 7(3)(a)).

- *Fifthly*, the common law rule is preserved that 'evidence of reputation or family tradition is admissible for the purpose of proving or disproving pedigree or the existence of marriage' (s 7(3)(b)(i)). Whilst statements of fact concerning pedigree and the fact of marriage are now admissible under s 1 of the 1995 Act in the normal way, s 7 is needed to admit evidence of reputation concerning such matters, which is still subject to the common law conditions of admissibility set out in *The Berkeley Peerage Case* (1811) 4 Camp 401.

- *Sixthly*, 'evidence of reputation or family tradition is admissible for the purpose of proving or disproving the existence of any public right or general right or of identifying any person or thing' (s 7(3)(b)(ii)). For the purposes of the Act, such evidence 'shall be treated…as a fact and not as a statement or multiplicity of statements about the matter in question' (s 7(3)(a)). This provision allows the evidence of reputation to be used as evidence of the fact reputed. Thus, if evidence is given that by local tradition a particular public right exists, although proof of the fact that this is the general reputation is unproblematic, s 7(3)(a) allows it to be used to prove the underlying fact, the existence of the public right itself.

9.122 The legitimacy of admitting hearsay material in civil proceedings has been tested in the lower courts in light of the Human Rights Act 1998. In *Clingham v Kensington and Chelsea London Borough Council* (2001) 165 JP 322 a local authority sought an ASBO against C under the Crime and Disorder Act 1998. The local authority was unable or unwilling to disclose the identities of its informants. It therefore relied upon complaints made by unidentified individuals concerning C's anti-social behaviour. On appeal, it was argued that the admission of this hearsay evidence, with C unable to cross-examine his accusers, meant that C had been denied a fair trial under Article 6(1) of ECHR. Schiemann LJ held, not altogether surprisingly, that 'the fact that some of the evidence [was] hearsay does not have the automatic result that the trial is not a fair trial.…Even in the context of a criminal case there is no such automatic exclusion' (at [11]). It was, however, essential to evaluate the weight to be accorded to this evidence in light of the considerations set out in s 4 of the Civil Evidence Act 1995 (see *ante*, para **9.118**). The House of Lords subsequently affirmed the Divisional Court's ruling (see [2003] 1 AC 787 especially at [36] *per* Lord Steyn).

FURTHER READING

Birch, 'Hearsay: Same Old Story, Same Old Song?' [2004] Crim LR 556

Evidence in Criminal Proceedings: Hearsay and Related Topics (Law Commission Report 245)

Munday, 'The Judicial Discretion to Admit Hearsay Evidence' (2007) 171 JP Jo 276

Munday, 'Legislation that would 'Preserve' the Common Law: The Case of the Declaration of Intention' (2008) 124 LQR 46

Munday, 'Preservation of the Common Law and the Perpetuation of Error: Section 118(1), r. 4(b) of the Criminal Justice Act 2003' (2008) 172 JP Jo 348

Smith, 'Proving Conspiracy' [1996] Crim LR 386

Smith, 'More on Proving Conspiracy' [1997] Crim LR 333

Spencer, 'The Common Enterprise Exception to the Hearsay Rule' (2007) 11 E&P 106

SELF-TEST QUESTIONS

1. What do you understand by the terms 'hearsay,' 'original evidence' and *res gestae*'?

2. What are the principal exceptions to the hearsay rule in criminal cases, following the entry into force of the Criminal Justice Act 2003?

3. What were considered to be the principal defects of the hearsay rule prior to the enactment of the Criminal Justice Act 2003? Do you believe that this legislation has cured them?

4. In *Kearley* [1992] 2 AC 228 a majority of the judges in the House of Lords held police evidence inadmissible on the grounds both of irrelevance and of infringement of the hearsay rule. How would an identical case be decided today, following the entry into force of the Criminal Justice Act 2003?

5. 'No matter how cogent particular evidence may seem to be, unless it comes within a class which is admissible, it is excluded': *Myers v DPP* [1965] AC 1001, 1024 *per* Lord Reid. Discuss this statement in light of the Criminal Justice Act 2003.

6. Bishop discovers his friend, Haze, suffering from acute poisoning in the car park of a public house. Bishop had gone looking for Haze when he failed to return from the toilets. Haze, who was pretty inebriated before setting off for the toilets, tells Bishop in a slurred voice: 'It was Tarwater what done it. I thought that I saw him slip something into my ale. But don't worry about me. There is nothing much you can do. Just get the police and the emergency services as quick as you can.' Dr Quack, a local GP who has been drinking heavily in the public house that evening, arrives on the scene shortly afterwards. When he asks Haze what appears to be the trouble, Haze replies: 'I've got a hell of a pain in my guts. Tarwater poisoned me. I'm 110 per cent positive.' Finally, an ambulance and a police car arrive in the car park. PC Panda gets out of his police car and asks Haze: 'Good evening, sir. What seems to be the problem?' Haze answers: 'Just as I told Bishop and the doctor, Tarwater has done me in.' Haze lapses into unconsciousness and dies shortly afterwards in the ambulance. Tarwater is charged with Haze's murder. At his trial Tarwater wishes to call his sister, Gabrielle, to give evidence that she later heard someone, whom she does not now recollect, in the same public house mention that Polonius had subsequently confessed to having spiked Haze's beer with arsenic. Discuss.

7. 'You know damned well that you won't be allowed to testify to it in court. What someone who is now dead may have told you—unless the person it affects was present—isn't evidence, and you know it.' (Dashiell Hammett, *The Golden Horseshoe*, Black Mask (November 1924)) Discuss.

8. Following an accident at his watersports centre in which a jet-ski, driven by a novice, left the portion of a lake dedicated to jet-skiing and collided with a power-boat killing a water skier whom it was towing, Drip was convicted on various charges brought under the Health and Safety at Work Act 1974, and notably for failing to make a suitable and sufficient risk assessment contrary to s 33. Since the prosecution had to prove that the separate parts of the lake used for waterskiing and jet-skiing respectively were not sufficiently clearly demarcated, the principal contested issue at trial was what

amounted to good practice at other similar water sport facilities. In order to establish what amounted to generally recognised levels of good practice, an expert hired by the local authority had sent a questionnaire to other local authorities enquiring how they managed similar facilities. It was not certain who had supplied the information contained in the 18 or so questionnaires—either council officers or other unidentified parties answering from their personal knowledge or someone simply responding on the basis of information derived from telephone conversations with the relevant facilities. The trial judge admitted this evidence under the Criminal Justice Act 2003, s 117. Advise Drip, who is considering an appeal.

9. In what ways, if any, may the hearsay rule come into conflict with the principles of human rights law?

10. In what circumstances will the concealment of the identity of witnesses in likelihood be held to be compatible with an accused's right to a fair trial?

11. What are the principal rules governing the admissibility of hearsay evidence in civil proceedings?

10

Confessions

SUMMARY

What constitutes a 'confession' under PACE, s 82(1)?

At common law an accused's silence may amount to an admission

Can a denial ever amount to a 'confession' under PACE, s 82(1)?

The conditions of admissibility of confessions under PACE

- A confession must be excluded if it has been obtained by oppression

- A confession must be excluded if it has been made in consequence of things said or done which might render it unreliable

- A confession may be excluded if its admission might reflect adversely on the fairness of the proceedings (PACE, s 78)

- A confession may be excluded under common law discretion retained in PACE, s 82(3) if the prejudicial effect of admitting it is likely to exceed its probative value

What if the accused, having first made an inadmissible confession, later makes a further confession which is obtained by proper methods?

Confessions made by mentally handicapped persons (PACE, s 77)

The admissibility of evidence discovered in consequence of an inadmissible confession

Using an inadmissible confession to show that the accused speaks, writes or expresses himself in a particular way

The status of 'mixed statements'

An accused's statement to the police is not normally evidence against other co-accused

An accused's right to use his co-accused's confession (PACE s 76A)

Confessions by third parties, the prosecution and the hearsay rule

"You do not have the slightest proof."

"That does not worry me," Aubry replied. "I shall have as much as I want once we have got her to speak at the police station."

I stared in perplexity at this man whose reasoning was vulgar, but effective.

Silvina Ocampo and Adolfo Bioy Casares, *Los que aman, odian* (1946)

10.1 Confessions constitute an important exception to the hearsay rule. They are attractive to police officers, for obvious reasons, and can impress juries. However, experience also teaches that confessions can prove unreliable and, regrettably, even lead to miscarriages of justice. The source of a confession's unreliability may lie in the methods used to extract it: if obtained by coercion, which can cover forms of pressure as varied as torture at one extreme to far more subtle means of inducement presented to the suspect at the other, there is a plain risk that the confession may prove untrue; and this is quite apart from any further consideration that, as a matter of policy, the law cannot simply be seen to have any truck with confessions obtained by especially devious or overreaching methods. Alternatively, a confession's unreliability may stem from the constitution of the suspect: that person may be unusually suggestible, or may happen to be interviewed while in a vulnerable frame of mind or an impaired state, or may actually be suffering from a mental illness or identifiable personality disorder. In all these cases it has been found advisable to be circumspect about admitting confessional evidence. Unreliability, then, is far from being the only reason for which improperly obtained confessional evidence is excluded in English law. As Lord Griffiths observed in *Lam Chi-Ming v R* [1991] 2 AC 212, 220:

> ...[T]he more recent English cases established that the rejection of an improperly obtained confession is not dependent only upon possible unreliability but also upon the principle that a man cannot be compelled to incriminate himself and upon the importance that attaches in a civilized society to proper behaviour by the police towards those in their custody.

10.2 Whilst it is true that confessional evidence may prove highly convincing, at the same time it is unusual for prosecutions to be brought if the Crown has to rely solely upon the evidence of a confession. *Greenwood* [2005] 1 Cr App R 7, a murder case, is an unusual instance of a successful prosecution for murder in such circumstances—although G's conviction was subsequently quashed on the ground that the trial judge had wrongly prevented G from adducing evidence suggesting that a former boyfriend with a motive could equally have committed the murder. More recently, in *K (Julie)* [2010] EWCA Crim 914 a murder conviction was upheld by the Court of Appeal, unusually, where the only Crown evidence consisted of confessions which K later either denied making or denied were true. (The New Zealand case of *Pauga* affords an even more alarming example of a conviction obtained solely on the strength of confessional evidence. P's videotaped confession, later disavowed, led to his conviction for rape in the total absence of any other evidence that a crime had even been committed: see Munday, 'Convicting on Confessional Evidence in the Complete Absence of a Corpus Delicti' (1993) 157 JP Jo 275.) Lest anyone doubts the potential perils of admitting in evidence a confession extracted from a suspect by improper means, they need only contemplate the case of Trevor Campbell, who was convicted of the murder of an elderly woman in March 1985, for which he served 14 years in prison. His conviction was quashed by the Court of Appeal in October 1999 because what Lord Bingham CJ described as 'the bedrock of the case against him' was a confession made by Mr Campbell only after he had been threatened by members of the now infamous West Midlands Serious Crimes Squad (see further, *Murray* [2003] EWCA Crim 27 at [17]–[29] *per* Kennedy LJ). This sorry episode affords a salutary cautionary tale. Again, there is the case of Stephen Downing, who, having spent 27 years in prison protesting a wrongful conviction, which rested predominantly on confessional evidence, was finally freed by the Court of Appeal in February 2000 and saw his conviction quashed in January 2002 ([2002] EWCA Crim 263)—although the police have since made known, pointedly, that there is no other suspect in the case. Additionally, one could mention the palpably unsafe double murder conviction of Peter Fell, a suggestible 'serial confessor' who was pressured and denied legal advice while in police custody, and whose case was referred to the Court of Appeal by the Criminal Cases Review Commission 16 years later (see [2001] EWCA Crim 696); the case of Ian Lawless, later described as having a 'pathological need for attention', whose conviction for fire-bombing the house of a suspected paedophile was set aside in June 2009; the case of Andrew Evans, convicted of murder in 1973 but only freed in December 1997; the case of Ashley King, tried for murder in 1986 and set free in December 1999; and, in Northern Ireland, the conviction of Iain Gordon, for the murder of the daughter of a High Court judge a full 47 years ago on the basis of confessional evidence bullied out of him, was finally set aside (*The Guardian* (2000) 20 December). It is a wretched chronicle.

10.3 In view of such considerations, a number of legal requirements, both procedural and evidential, have been introduced to reduce the risks of miscarriages of justice provoked by unreliable confessional evidence. Notably, PACE Code of Practice C lays down detailed procedures that the police and various other investigating organs must observe when interrogating suspects. Section 58 of PACE, buttressed by para 6 of Code C, further confers on defendants extensive rights to legal advice when they are held in custody 'in a police station or other premises'; and as Guidance Note 6D makes explicit, on such occasions 'the solicitor's only role in the police station is to protect and advance the legal rights of his client'. The likely authenticity and accuracy of defendants' statements when adduced in evidence in court is increased by s 60 of PACE, which provides for the tape recording of interviews, a practice which is regulated in PACE Code E. Indeed, video recording of interviews is now sometimes required (see further, para **10.39**).

10.4 In addition to provisions such as these, however, the conditions under which evidence of a confession may be admitted in a criminal trial are tightly restricted. In particular, the prosecution may be required to prove beyond reasonable doubt that a confession it seeks to adduce was not obtained in a manner that might cast doubt on its reliability. This chapter will examine these latter rules, which are designed to prevent against the admission of unreliable confessions.

What constitutes a 'confession' under PACE, s 82(1)?

10.5 Section 82(1) of PACE states that the term 'confession':

> ... includes any statement wholly or partly adverse to the person who made it, whether made to a person in authority or not and whether made in words or otherwise.

The definition is very broad. Notably, it encompasses statements which would not necessarily be referred to as confessions in ordinary parlance. By expressly including statements which are 'partly adverse', the statutory definition includes under the umbrella of confession 'mixed statements' which include only portions which implicate D in the commission of an offence. Thus, the accused's statement may be a 'confession' under s 82(1) even if it consists in the main of denials. Similarly, whilst containing admissions, a statement may still constitute a 'confession' within the meaning of s 82(1) even if it is designed primarily to diminish the involvement or criminality of parties other than the defendant (eg, *Hudson* [2007] EWCA Crim 2083 at [23] *per* Sir Igor Judge P, where 'the context [served] to show that the confession could properly be treated as an admissible confession by someone who was guilty himself, but who was seeking to exculpate other members of his family').

10.6 Thus, if any statement made by the defendant contains a concession that could be considered 'adverse', it will qualify as a 'confession' and will be subjected to the rules of admissibility set out in s 76 of the Act. All manner of statements may therefore qualify as 'confessions'. Retracted admissions or vacated guilty pleas, for example. In *Johnson* (2007) 171 JP 574, J, who had been charged with two counts of illegally importing drugs, had initially pleaded guilty to one of those counts on a written basis of plea. Later, however, J successfully applied to have his guilty plea vacated. At trial, J's co-accused, C, as part of her case was allowed to introduce J's vacated guilty plea as a 'confession' under s 76A of PACE (see *post*, paras **10.60** ff). Although it did seem for a while that the courts might adopt an even more expansive construction of this provision (see *post*, paras **10.15–10.16**), the House of Lords has made clear that only statements that are *ex facie* inculpatory wholly or in part will qualify as 'confessions' under s 82(1).

10.7 Prior to PACE, confessions were restricted to admissions that had been made to 'persons in authority' (by which was meant someone who was in a position to affect the course of a prosecution). It now makes no difference to whom a confession has been made. The same rules of admissibility apply. Indeed, it would seem that a confession does not need to have been made to another human being: in January 2008 at David Henton's trial for murdering his partner, the prosecution was permitted to adduce secretly taped recordings of the accused allegedly confessing the crime to his cats (*The Sun*, 17 January 2008). Nor will the law concern itself with the defendant's motive for confessing. In March 2009 James Brewer, who believed that he was dying, confessed in Oklahoma to the murder of Jimmy Carroll 32 years earlier in Tennessee. Brewer subsequently recovered his health and has since been charged. There is no ground for thinking that English law would not follow suit.

10.8 Although a confession will normally be spoken or written, it need not be; a confession may for instance result from conduct. Thus, if the suspect nods in answer to questioning, thereby indicating acceptance of an accusation, or if he participates in a police re-enactment of a crime acting out his role therein, such actions will constitute confessions under s 82(1) to the extent that they are statements adverse to the accused made otherwise than by words. Merely looking shifty and guilty, on the other hand, will not suffice as demeanour could hardly be described as a 'statement'. Similarly, running away and hiding from the police will not qualify as a confession, no matter how suspicious the behaviour may appear. Yet, just how far removed the legal notion of 'confession' can sometimes be from ordinary parlance is illustrated by *Ward, Andrews and Broadley* [2001] Crim LR 316 where, bizarrely, a motorist's replies to a police officer that he was in fact W were treated as confessions and therefore admissible as evidence identifying W as one of those involved in a conspiracy to steal under this exception to the hearsay rule. This case, it should be noted, antedates the hearsay provisions of the Criminal Justice Act 2003 (see *ante*, Chapter 9).

At common law an accused's silence may amount to an admission

'If I ask my son whether he saw a movie that I had forbidden him to watch, and he remains silent, the import of his silence is clear.'

Mitchell v US, 526 US 314, 333 (1999) *per* Justice Scalia

10.9 A more complex situation arises where an accused maintains silence when accused of an offence. Self-evidently, silence falls outside the ambit of s 82(1) as it cannot plausibly be described as a 'statement'. Nevertheless, a defendant's silence can appear suspicious, even strongly suggestive of guilt. The Criminal Justice and Public Order Act 1994 (see further *post*, Chapter 11) made provision for adverse inferences to be drawn in certain circumstances from the accused's silence—or rather, the accused's failure to mention facts or to give certain explanations—during police interrogation. However, at common law, too, it has been held that a defendant's silence is capable of grounding an adverse inference in certain circumstances. Indeed, ss 34(5), 36(6) and 37(5) of the 1994 Act expressly preserve the common law rules alongside the statutory regime.

10.10 At common law, provided that the accused and his accuser were 'on even terms' at the time and, more importantly, provided that in the circumstances an accusation might reasonably have been expected to have elicited a response from the defendant, the fact that he remained silent in the face of that accusation may be left to the tribunal of fact which can then decide whether or not to draw an adverse inference from it. The 'even terms' criterion was one of two formulations of the test devised by Cave J in an *extempore* ruling on assize in *Mitchell* (1892) 17 Cox CC 503. It produced some fairly strange reasoning in *Chandler* (1976) 63 Cr App R 1, where Lawton LJ held that a suspect who was accompanied by his solicitor was 'on even terms' with the police sergeant questioning him. Lawton LJ even suggested that the same might be true in the case of a civic dignitary being questioned by a junior police officer. The calculus of 'even terms' looks to be flawed. It is preferable to consider that, as a matter of principle, contrary to the ruling in *Chandler*, a policeman is not on even terms with a suspect he is interrogating. The better course, it is suggested, is to ignore 'even terms' and to apply only the second limb of Cave J's test in *Mitchell*: namely, to ask simply whether in the circumstances an accusation might reasonably have been expected to elicit a response from the suspect. *Parkes* (1977) 64 Cr App R 25 exemplifies the point. The mother of a girl, who had been stabbed, confronted P and twice asked him why he had done it. P made no reply. The Privy Council held that the jury was entitled, if it so wished, to draw an adverse inference from P's failure to respond to this face-to-face confrontation. In the circumstances, the jury could legitimately conclude that a normal person would have said something, and that P's failure to deny anything signified acceptance of the mother's accusation. (It might be noted that in this case the 'even terms' test would hardly have contributed much to the analysis.)

10.11 The factual context is important. Whereas one might be expected to repel accusations made face-to-face, charges made by correspondence are likely to prove another matter. As Lord Esher MR remarked in a civil case, 'It is the ordinary and wise practice of mankind not to answer such a letter …' (*Wiedemann v Walpole* [1891] 2 QB 534). The Court of Appeal acknowledged in *Edwards* [1983] Crim LR 539 that, while a court might on rare occasions admit as evidence of admissions letters to which a defendant had not replied, a court will need to be very careful in admitting such evidence. Reverting to what it was suggested was the more serviceable prong of the test in *Mitchell*, the critical thing is to ask whether in the circumstances one would have reasonably anticipated a response from the accused.

10.12 More problematical is the type of situation that arose in *Collins and Keep* [2004] 1 WLR 1705, where the Crown sought to argue that C's failure to contradict a lie told by B, another of his confederates, amounted to adoption of that lie (from which an adverse inference might be drawn: on permissible inferences drawn from lies told by defendants: see *post*, paras **11.75–11.80**). C and K stood trial on charges of kidnapping and possession of a firearm with intent. Having ruled that it would be wrong to convict them solely on the evidence of the victim in the absence of supporting evidence, the trial judge suggested that a lie told by B in the hearing of C, and not contradicted by the latter when he was afforded an opportunity to do so in interrogation, might be used as supporting evidence by the jury. The Court of Appeal considered *Mitchell*, *Christie* [1914] AC 545 and *Parkes*, and ruled that 'similar principles are applicable where circumstances arise where an important question is asked in the presence of the accused and answer given and the issue arises as to whether he has joined in the answer'. The appropriate course in such cases, it was said, is for the trial judge to invite the jury to consider whether in all the circumstances B's proven lies called for some response from C, and then to ask itself whether C's reaction amounted to an adoption of B's false statement. In *Collins and Keep* the court decided that C's silence when asked about B's false story that at the relevant time they had both been in a pub chasing girls could not have provided sufficient evidential basis for leaving to the jury the question of whether C's reaction amounted to an adoption of B's answer:

> Mere silence could have been the exercise of his right to silence in the response to the question asked, particularly when the question was asked by a police officer and the parties were not on equal terms.
>
> (at [36])

Nevertheless, *Collins and Keep* left open the possibility that, if the court adjudges the parties 'on even terms', an 'important lie' or a false alibi given by a third party in the presence of the defendant, which is thought to have required a response, may be treated as having been adopted by the latter and may ground an adverse inference. Subsequently, in *O (Stevie)* [2005] EWCA Crim 3082, Lord Phillips of Worth Matravers CJ held, in a murder case, that a trial judge had been entitled to leave to the jury the fact that O had smirked and walked away with his two companions, after they had been challenged by an acquaintance two days after the incident. Whilst it was one of O's companions who had actually replied that the victim had been struck over the back of the head with a wooden stake 'cos we don't like Asian people', on the facts O could have been said to have acquiesced in what his companion had said. Although it was eventually doubted whether evidence of racial motivation was sufficiently relevant, seemingly this was a situation where it would otherwise have been open to the jury to infer that O had adopted his companion's statement.

Can a denial ever amount to a 'confession' under PACE, s 82(1)?

10.13 A question arises: what exactly is meant by 'adverse' in s 82(1)? If a suspect makes a statement to the police denying everything and giving an alibi for his whereabouts at the time of the offence being investigated, if the alibi is subsequently shown to be false, is the defendant's statement 'adverse' within the meaning of s 82 (1)? In the context of the trial it will undoubtedly be 'adverse' to the accused's interests to be shown to have been lying (see *post*, paras **11.75-11.80** and the direction jurors receive on lies told by an accused: JSB specimen direction no 23). Although it declined to rule formally on the question, the Court of Appeal in *Sat-Bhambra* (1988) 88 Cr App R 55 inclined to the view that purely exculpatory statements fall outside the ambit of s 82(1), Lord Lane CJ remarking:

> The section is aimed at excluding confessions obtained by word or deeds likely to render them unreliable, ie admissions or partial admissions contrary to the interests of the

defendant and welcome to the interrogator. They can hardly have been aimed at statements containing nothing which the interrogator wished the defendant to say and nothing apparently adverse to the defendant's interests. If the contentions of the appellant in the present case are correct, it would mean the statement: "I had nothing to do with it" might in due course become a "confession", which would be surprising with or without s 82(1).

(at 61)

Subsequently, *Park* (1993) 99 Cr App R 270 endorsed this interpretation. P, who was charged with burglary, when stopped and questioned about the contents of his car, told the police a pack of lies which, on their face, appeared exculpatory. When these were shown to be untrue, although at trial the impact of P's lies was unquestionably adverse, Kennedy LJ declined to treat P's lies as confessions within the meaning of the Act.

10.14 While *Sat-Bhambra* and *Park* conclude correctly that it would be a strange use of language to treat an accused's false denials and lies as 'confessions', from a policy standpoint the opposing view is not devoid of merit. The object of s 76 is to exclude adverse statements made by the accused, which, it is feared, could be unreliable owing to the manner in which they have been elicited. Just as illegitimate pressure may cause the accused to make untrue admissions, so too it may induce him to lie—through panic, fear or confusion. Since the prosecution is entitled to rely upon adverse inferences drawn from the accused's proven lies, there is something to be said for giving PACE a generous reading and for excluding false denials when they result from improper pressure which jeopardises their reliability. After all, no conviction ought to rest on evidence of acknowledged unreliability. Some recent research warns that 'average citizens may not understand the potential link between psychologically coercive interrogation and false confessions'. (Leo and Liu, *What Do Potential Jurors Know about Police Interrogation Techniques and False Confessions?* (University of San Francisco School of Law Research Paper No. 2009–17: <http://ssrn.com/abstract=1404078>.))

10.15 In Z [2003] 1 WLR 1489 the meaning of 'confession' in PACE, s 82(1) fell to be considered again. Z had set up a defence of duress to a charge of burglary. Crown counsel desired to cross-examine Z about the contents of an off-the-record statement Z had later made to the police in which he appeared to suggest that the relevant threats had not been made until after the burglary had taken place. Because the off-the-record interview did not concern Z's own case, none of the conventional safeguards that accompany interrogation—a caution, a contemporaneous record of anything said, and so on—had been observed by the police when this conversation took place. Z argued, *inter alia*, that the cross-examination on his interview ought to be excluded on the ground that it would not be admissible as a 'confession' under PACE, s 76. This introduced the question as to whether or not Z's statement, which was on its face exculpatory, ought nevertheless to be considered 'adverse' within the meaning of s 82(1). On appeal, it was argued that, following the ECtHR's decision in *Saunders v UK* (1997) 23 EHRR 313, *Sat-Bhambra* can no longer be regarded as good law. Notably, it was urged, in *Saunders* the European Court had stated:

> ...bearing in mind the concept of fairness in Article 6, the right not to incriminate oneself cannot reasonably be confined to statements of admission of wrongdoing or to remarks which are directly incriminating. Testimony obtained under compulsion which appears on its face to be of a non-incriminating nature—such as exculpatory remarks or mere information on questions of fact—may later be deployed in criminal proceedings in support of the prosecution case, for example to contradict or cast doubt upon other statements of the accused or evidence given by him during the trial or to otherwise undermine his credibility.
>
> (at [71])

In light of this, it was said that a confession should now be regarded as any statement which turns out to be self-incriminating, even if the accused's remarks were intended to be exculpatory at the time that they were made. Reminiscent of the song first popularised by Jimmy Lunceford and his Orchestra, 'Taint what you do (It's the way that cha do it)', what counts according to this analysis is the manner in which the statement is sought to be employed, not its formal content. In *Z* the Court of Appeal accepted this argument. Preferring an approach to this issue previously taken by Canada's Supreme Court (*Piche* (1970) 11 DLR 700) and by Warren CJ in *Miranda v Arizona*, 384 US 436, 477 (1975), Rix LJ rejected the literal interpretation of s 82(1) hitherto adopted by the Court of Appeal in *Sat-Bhambra* and *Park*, as well as by most of the legal pundits, concluding:

> *Prima facie* one would have thought that the test [whether a statement is "adverse"] is to be made at the time when it is sought to give the statement in evidence...[T]he prosecution bear the criminal burden of proving that the confession was *not* obtained in...circumstances [contrary to s 76(2)]. If therefore an accused is driven to make adverse statements by reason of oppression, why should he lose the protection of s 76(2) just because, although he may have sought to exculpate himself, in fact he damned himself?
>
> (at [37])

The overall tone of Rix LJ's judgment in *Z*, nevertheless, appeared tentative, and his Lordship was at pains to restrict interpretation of the term 'adverse' to the narrow category of case before the court, making explicit that:

> We can...leave open to another day whether "I did not do it" is a confession. This case is of an accused who says "I did do it, but under duress"; and the duress which he claims,

so the prosecution seek to prove, is an incoherent one because it only operates from a time after the burglary.

(at [38])

10.16   On appeal, *sub nom Hasan* [2005] 2 WLR 709, the House of Lords reversed Rix LJ's ruling. Only Lord Steyn spoke to the question of neutral or wholly exculpatory statements extracted from a defendant; the other four members of the Appellate Committee concurred. Not surprisingly, Lord Steyn rejected the Court of Appeal's argument that *Saunders v UK* (1997) 23 EHRR 313 was relevant to the question; after all, that decision was concerned exclusively with evidence obtained under coercion, and in *Hasan* the issues were inadvertent deception by the police and the absence of almost all the customary safeguards that accompany the interrogation of suspects, not outright compulsion (at [61]–[62]). In *Hasan* Lord Steyn boldly asserted that, when the relevant provisions of PACE are read together:

> It is…clear that section 76, as read with section 82(1), and section 78, are designed to provide in a coherent and comprehensive way for the just disposal of all decisions about statements made by accused persons to the police. There is no gap in the procedural safeguards of the relevant provisions of PACE.
>
> (at [53])

His Lordship laid particular emphasis on the fact that:

> …any evidence obtained by the police by oppression is liable to be excluded under s 78. It would cover the case where the police by oppression obtained a wholly exculpatory but plainly false statement from an accused such as to damage his credibility at trial.
>
> (at [53])

For the same reason—namely, 'the unrestricted capability of section 78 to avoid injustice by excluding any evidence obtained by unfairness (including wholly exculpatory or neutral statements obtained by oppression)'—Lord Steyn rejected the suggestion in Rix LJ's judgment that ss 76(1) and 82(1) were incompatible with the ECHR, Article 6 (see esp [2005] UKHL at [62]). The decision in *Hasan* doubtless settles the question whether or not s 82(1) extends to non-inculpatory statements made by a suspect. One can perhaps regret the fact that Lord Steyn viewed the question uniquely from the viewpoint of s 76(2)(a) (oppression: see *post*, paras **10.23–10.25**), seemingly ignoring the more difficult issue of cases—like *Hasan* itself—where things have been said or done that might render a 'confession' unreliable and where one cannot be so confident that s 78 will operate to prevent the admission of adverse evidence (see *post*, paras **10.26–10.31**). It would also have been reassuring had the speech remained less aloof from the practical policy issues and been less concerned to affirm what Lord Steyn termed Lord Widgery's 'characteristically analytical' judgment in *Sat-Bhambra* (at [54]), whose discussion, it might be noted, actually ends with the uncharacteristically analytical words, 'we do not need to come to any firm conclusion on this aspect of the case' ((1989) 88 Cr App R 55, at 62).

The conditions of admissibility of confessions under PACE

> The coercion inherent in custodial interrogation blurs the line
> between voluntary and involuntary statements …
> *Dickerson v US*, 530 US 428, 435 (2000)

10.17 A number of rules, statutory and common law, regulate the admissibility of confessions. In essence, before it may be admitted in evidence a confession has to clear four legal hurdles, which we shall now consider in turn. The most important rules governing confessions are to be found in PACE. Under s 76(1) of PACE a confession may be given in evidence against an accused only 'in so far as it is relevant to any matter in issue in the proceedings and is not excluded by the court in pursuance of this section'. The prosecution therefore cannot introduce the accused's confessions to offences unrelated to those charged in the proceedings in hand since they will not be 'relevant to any matter in issue'. The subsection also draws attention to the fact that the court may exclude confessions in certain circumstances.

10.18 It should perhaps be stressed that the rules under discussion in this chapter relate to the circumstances in which a confession has been obtained—in essence, its voluntariness and the fairness of admitting it. The rules do not concern questions of fact—whether a confession was actually made and the authorship of that confession. These are matters for the tribunal of fact. By way of example, in *Bailey* [2008] EWCA Crim 817 esp at [46]-[48] B was one of six co-accused originally charged with murder. One of B's grounds of appeal was that his co-accused had alleged that he had sent an email message, signed 'Mifer', to a condolence chat-room website that read 'Yeah me and Ma Bredrins bunned him up but I didn't kill him and whoeva try say Im a shockhed is gonna get murdered. So watch ureself n ewayz Poets was a dickhed.' B denied having ever written this message. Gage LJ held that, even though the message could have been composed and submitted to the website by virtually anyone, the trial judge had properly allowed the co-accused to question B about it, and had left it to the jury then to decide whether they believed that this amounted in fact to a confession authored by B.

10.19 *Raising the issue of admissibility.* It will normally be for the defence to contest the admissibility of a confession. PACE s 76(2) requires that a party must 'represent to the court' that the confession may have been extracted in breach of s. 76. Although not further defined in PACE, it has been held that 'a statement by responsible counsel, upon the basis of documents or a proof of evidence in his possession at the time of speaking' to this effect qualifies as a representation for these purposes (*Dhorajiwala* (2010) 174 JP 401 at [23] *per* Aikens LJ). Whilst responsibility will normally rest with the defence to set matters in motion, the court also may raise the issue of its own motion (s 76(3)).

10.20 Once the issue has been raised, s 76(2) then lays down that a court must exclude a confession if the prosecution fails to prove beyond reasonable doubt that it has not been obtained either (i) by oppression of the defendant or (ii) as a consequence of things said or done which might render a confession unreliable. Section 76(2) reads:

> If, in any proceedings where the prosecution proposes to give in evidence a confession made by an accused person, it is represented to the court that the confession was or may have been obtained
>
> (a) by oppression of the person who made it; or
>
> (b) in consequence of anything said or done which was likely, in the circumstances existing at the time, to render unreliable any confession which might be made by him in consequence thereof,
>
> the court shall not allow the confession to be given in evidence against him except in so far as the prosecution proves to the court beyond reasonable doubt that the confession (notwithstanding that it may be true) was not obtained as aforesaid.

The enquiry into whether the Crown can show that the confession it proposes introducing in evidence was not obtained by forbidden means is conducted in the form of a *voire dire*, sometimes referred to as a trial within a trial (*ante*, para **1.3**). And that is exactly what it is: a mini-trial that takes place before the judge, in the absence of the jury, with evidence being called by prosecution and defence in turn. When the evidence has been called and the legal submissions made, the judge delivers his ruling on the admissibility of the confession. The jury then returns into court, and the trial proper resumes. A *voire dire* must be held whenever there are allegations such as reasonably require investigation and testing by consideration of the evidence. In *Dhorajiwala* (2010) 174 JP 401, where an employee was prosecuted for theft from her employer, it was held that even though counsel had made no request, the trial judge had been wrong to dismiss allegations that private investigators had interrogated her in a questionable manner without conducting a *voire dire*.

10.21 If, following a *voire dire*, the judge rules that a defendant's confession is admissible because he considers that the Crown has established beyond reasonable doubt that the confession was obtained in compliance with PACE s 76, that is not necessarily the end of the matter. The circumstances in which the confession was extracted may be ventilated afresh before the jury when the trial resumes. Because it would be wrong to allow the jury to make use of any confession which *they* believed had been obtained improperly, in *Mushtaq* [2005] 1 WLR 1513 the House of Lords laid down that the judge is required to direct the jury that if, contrary to the judge's findings, they conclude that the defendant's confession was in fact obtained by oppression or other improper means, then they must disregard it. Such a direction will be required only in cases where 'there is a possibility that the jury may conclude (i) that a statement was made by the defendant, (ii) the statement was true but (iii) the statement was, or may have been, induced by oppression' (*Wizzard* [2007] UKPC 21 at [35] *per* Lord Phillips of Worth Matravers).

10.22 The jury ought not to be made aware that a *voire dire* has taken place at which the admissibility of a confession has been considered. As Lord Steyn, pointed out in *Mitchell* [1998] AC 695,

> The decision on the admissibility of a confession after a *voire dire* is the sole responsibility of the judge. There is no logical reason why the jury should know about the decision of the judge. It is irrelevant to the consideration by the jury of the issues whether the confession was made and, if so, whether it is true. [I]n modern English practice the judge's decision after a *voire dire* is never revealed to the jury.
>
> (703)

Were this information made available to them, there would be a risk that, if jurors once knew that the judge had admitted a confession, they might take the view that because the judge believed the prosecution witnesses, disbelieving the defendant's account of impropriety, so should they:

> [T]he jury, or some of them, may be diverted from grappling properly and independently with a defendant's allegations of oppression so far as it is relevant to their decision. And such an avoidable risk of prejudice cannot be tolerated in regard to a procedure designed to protect a defendant.
>
> (703–4)

A confession must be excluded if it has been obtained by oppression

10.23 Under s 76(2)(a), if the prosecution is unable to establish beyond reasonable doubt that the confession was not made as a result of oppression, the accused's confession will be held inadmissible even if there is ample additional evidence in the case confirming its reliability. The purpose of the paragraph is automatically to exclude confessions obtained by the more extreme means. This is borne out by the definition of 'oppression' provided in s 76(8), which states that oppression 'includes torture, inhuman or degrading treatment, and the use or threat of violence (whether or not amounting to torture)'. Curiously, however, when the Court of Appeal had to determine what 'oppression' meant in *Fulling* [1987] QB 426, no reference was made to s 76(8). Instead, the court referred to one of the meanings given to the word in the *Oxford English Dictionary*, and claimed to derive assistance from half a sentence lifted from a sermon on self-deceit delivered by an eighteenth-century prelate, Bishop Butler. More recently, Stanley Burnton LJ has claimed, oddly perhaps, 'while subs (8) is not a definition of that term, it indicates what kind of conduct may amount to oppression' (*JA* [2010] EWCA Crim 1506 at [25]). It is hard to think of any like provision that the courts decline to treat as a statutory 'definition'.

10.24 *Fulling* concerned a woman charged with making a false insurance claim who, at her third interview over a period of two days, made a confession. F claimed that she had only confessed in order to get out of the police station after the police had told her that her lover had been having an affair with the woman in the next-door cell. Somewhat improbably, the court had to decide if this conduct on the part of the police amounted to oppression. The dictionary defined oppression as 'exercise of authority or power in a burdensome, harsh or wrongful manner; unjust or cruel treatments of subjects, inferiors, etc; the imposition of unreasonable or unjust burdens', while the bishop intoned: 'There is not a word in our language which expresses more detestable wickedness than oppression.' (Evidently, the Court of Appeal was unaware that Bishop Butler's sentence continues, 'yet the nature of this vice cannot be so exactly stated, nor the bounds of it so determinately marked, as that we shall be able to say in all instances, where rigid right and justice ends, and oppression begins'!) Concluding that the police conduct had not amounted to oppression in this case, Lord Lane CJ said that he found it 'hard to envisage any circumstances in which such oppression would not entail some impropriety on the part of the interrogator'.

10.25 *Fulling* makes clear that 'oppression' requires very wrongful treatment on the part of the interrogator. As was held in *Emmerson* (1990) 92 Cr App R 284, a policeman who, three-quarters of the way through an interview, raises his voice and uses bad language may be 'rude and discourteous' but will not have acted oppressively. Rougher treatment is demanded. For instance, in *Paris, Abdullahi and Miller* (1992) 97 Cr App R 99, a miscarriage of justice case involving 'The Cardiff Three', M, who was almost mentally handicapped, was interviewed in a bullying and hectoring manner, only confessing to having murdered a prostitute after denying the offence 300 times: 'the officers...were not questioning him so much as shouting at him.'

Lord Taylor CJ was 'horrified' by the police tactics, remarking that 'short of physical violence, it is hard to conceive of a more hostile and intimidating approach by officers to a suspect'. It was held that, on grounds of oppression, M's confession had been wrongly admitted. Again, in *Ridley* (1999) 17 December, transcript no 9806973/W4, a church welfare worker, who had originally gone to the police to complain that he was being blackmailed by two members of the youth club, was eventually charged with indecently assaulting the youths. The Court of Appeal, which declared itself 'dismayed' at the manner in which R's interview had been conducted, held that R's confession ought not to have been admitted: the confession was the product of a three-hour police interrogation, which had exploited R's naiveté with questioning which was 'tendentious, persistent, aggressive and prurient'.

A confession must be excluded if it has been made in consequence of things said or done which might render it unreliable

10.26 Although in practice a great majority of cases under either limb of s 76(2) will involve alleged police misconduct of some sort, as the Court of Appeal has pointed out, subs (2)(b) does not actually require any impropriety to be shown on the part of the questioner. As Potter LJ observed in *Walker* [1998] Crim LR 211, a case where, unknown to the police, W was suffering from a personality disorder:

> Whereas the questions asked by the police at interview were not in any sense improper and would not, on the face of them, have constituted undue pressure by the police on an ordinary person in full possession of their faculties, they were, nonetheless, questions which could lead a suggestible or fantasising personality into admissions which . . . could not be taken at face value.

Subsection (2)(b) does however lay down that, once its admissibility is questioned either by the defence or the court, a confession must be excluded from evidence if the Crown is unable to establish beyond reasonable doubt that, 'notwithstanding that it may be true', it was not obtained 'in consequence of anything said or done which was likely, in the circumstances existing at the time, to render unreliable any confession which might be made by [the defendant] in consequence thereof'.

10.27 Section 76(2) requires the court, in reaching this determination, to disregard the fact that it may be known that the confession was actually true. The test it must apply is therefore hypothetical. In *McGovern* (1990) 92 Cr App R 228, for example, M made a confession admitting to complicity in a homicide under the following conditions. When first questioned, she had been denied access to a solicitor, contrary to PACE, s 58; the police had made no contemporary notes at her interview, in breach of PACE Code C; M was peculiarly vulnerable, later being rated practically subnormal by a psychologist; and finally, M, who was six months pregnant, was in a highly emotional state when interrogated. M's low IQ was treated as part of the background which the court has to take into account as a 'circumstance existing at the time'. Denying M access to a solicitor, however, was held to be something said or done which tended to render M's resulting confession unreliable, despite the fact that the court knew, thanks to a later confession M had made in the company of her solicitor, that M's first confession was in fact true. As Farquharson LJ noted: 'The fact that the confession was in substance true is expressly excluded by the Act as being a relevant factor.'

10.28 *McGovern*, of course, also illustrates a further proposition: namely, that where a first tainted interview has taken place, any subsequent interview, even if it has been conducted in full conformity with PACE, may also have to be treated as contaminated and therefore be excluded from evidence. This is not to say that where a series of interviews, some lawful and others unlawful, has taken place, the courts will consider that in all such cases there exists what might be termed a compulsive sequence. As Laws LJ showed in *Ahmed* [2003] EWCA Crim 3627 at [14], in each case it will be a question of determining whether the subsequent interview was in fact freely made. In *McGovern*, it was significant that M was someone of limited intelligence. In *Ahmed*, on the other hand, A was not abnormal and his admissions at the later interview were freely made. The irregularities that may have compromised his first interview did not therefore affect the integrity of the second, properly conducted interview.

10.29 Subsection (2)(b) refers to 'anything said or done'. This poses the question, by whom must these things have been said and done? In *Goldenberg* (1988) 88 Cr App R 285, five days after his arrest on a drugs charge, a heroin addict requested an interview with police officers and confessed. On his behalf it was later claimed that G only confessed because he was desperate to get bail and anxious to gain credit for helping the police. The court held that G's confession was rightly admitted because 'anything said or done' in para (b) did not include things said or done by the maker of the confession. The section's use of the expression 'in consequence of' showed that a causal link had to be established between what was said or done and the subsequent confession. What was therefore needed was 'something external, something likely to have an influence on [G]'. The decision in *Goldenberg* has prompted courts sometimes to go further. For instance, in *Crampton* (1990) 92 Cr App R 369 it was doubted whether the police's merely interviewing a drug addict who was undergoing symptoms of heroin withdrawal amounted to 'something done' within the meaning of the Act which:

> ... seem[s] to postulate some word spoken by the police or acts done by them which were likely to induce unreliable confessions ... What ... subs 2(b) is concerned with is the nature and quality of the words spoken or the things done by the police which are likely

to, in the circumstances existing at the time, render the confession unreliable in the sense that it is not true.

(at p 372)

The court, then, will be primarily concerned to assess the actions and words of the interrogators (and sometimes, it should be added, even what may have been said or done by third parties like solicitors and family who may also induce the suspect to make a confession that could be unreliable).

10.30 Section 76(2)(b) requires the court to take into account 'the circumstances existing at the time'. Thus, in *Everett* [1988] Crim LR 826 it was held that the judge should have taken into account the circumstance of E's mental condition: although 42 years old, he had a mental age of eight. Similarly, in *Walker* [1998] Crim LR 211, in determining whether a prostitute's confession to robbery ought to have been admitted in evidence, it was a relevant circumstance that W suffered from a severe personality disorder that meant that she might make unreliable statements and embellish events without appreciating the implications. It did not matter in these cases whether the interrogating officers had actually spotted E's mental age or W's personality disorder. The Act sets an objective test: did E have a mental impairment; did W have a personality disorder? Section 76(2)(b), it should also perhaps be emphasised, disregards the concerns or motives of the person making the confession—unless, of course, these affect its reliability. Although the decision antedates PACE, a passage from Lord Lane CJ's judgment in *Rennie* (1982) 74 Cr App R 207 is regularly cited, in which he said:

> Very few confessions are inspired solely by remorse. Often the motives of an accused person are mixed and include a hope that an early admission may lead to an earlier release or a lighter sentence. If it were the law that the mere presence of such a motive...led inexorably to the exclusion of a confession, nearly every confession would be rendered inadmissible. That is not the law...commonly the presence of such a hope will, in part at least, owe its origin to something said or done...There can be few prisoners who are being firmly but fairly questioned in a police station to whom it does not occur that they might be able to bring both their interrogation and their detention to an earlier end by confession.
>
> (at p 212)

For this reason, in *Wahab* [2003] 1 Cr App R 232, Judge LJ held that even had W's mind been influenced by the possibility that if he confessed to conspiring to supply Class A drugs, members of his family might be released from police custody, the trial judge had been correct to discount W's motives for confessing. W had instructed his solicitor to make the initial approach, the police had acted properly, and W knew precisely what he was doing when he confessed at the fourth interview. His desire to help his family was just 'one factor among several which served to explain his decision to confess' and, palpably, did not affect the reliability of the confession (at [45]).

10.31 As can be seen, s 76(2)(b) requires the court to take into account a number of factors, and the question it must address is quite complex. *Barry* (1991) 95 Cr App R 384 therefore provides useful guidance on the method to be followed when a court assesses the admissibility of a confession under s 76(2)(b). B, who was arrested in connection with an international fraud, on the day of his arrest was concerned to get bail as he feared his wife might otherwise gain custody of their child. B was charged and appeared before the magistrates the next day, where his counsel advised him to exercise his right of silence. Later, however, in the absence of his solicitor, and in return for a chance of bail, B began to give the police assistance and eventually made a full confession. The Court of Appeal, which determined that B's confession had been wrongly admitted at trial, explained that s 76(2)(b) demanded that the court do the following:

- the court must identify everything said and done extending back to the date of B's arrest and to the interview at which B had been told that it might be of some good to him if he helped the police;

- the court should then look at what had been said or done, against the background circumstances, and ask whether that was likely to render any confession made by B unreliable—bearing in mind that this test was hypothetical and that it related to *any* confession that might be made, not the particular confession in the case;

- the court should decide whether the Crown had proven beyond reasonable doubt that the confession had not been made as a result of things said or done; and finally

- while, as we shall see in the next section, breaches of the PACE Codes may lead to exclusion of a confession under s 78 of that Act, they may also have some bearing on the question, was the confession likely to be reliable? Thus, in *Barry*, in breach of PACE Code C:11.5 police interviews had taken place of which no record had been made. This led to disagreement as to what had occurred on these occasions, and in turn had an indirect bearing on the likely reliability of B's confession.

A confession may be excluded if its admission might reflect adversely on the fairness of the proceedings (PACE, s 78)

10.32 Even if a confession does not infringe s 76 of PACE, the court additionally possesses discretion to exclude it under PACE, s 78 'if it appears to the court that, *having regard to all the circumstances in which the evidence was obtained*, the admission of the evidence would have such an adverse effect on the fairness of the proceedings that the court ought not to admit it'. In most instances 'the circumstances in which the evidence was obtained' will involve breaches by the police of the PACE Codes of Practice.

10.33 Section 67(11) of PACE provides that if any provision of one of the Codes of Practice promulgated under PACE 'appears to the court...to be relevant to any question arising in the proceedings it *shall* be taken into account in determining that question'. Therefore, in exercising this discretion the court will take into account any breaches of PACE Code C, which lays down detailed procedures that must be followed when a suspect is in custody or being questioned by police officers.

10.34 *Who is bound to comply with the PACE Codes of Practice?* The police, it should be said, are not alone in being under a duty to comply with the PACE Codes. Section 67(9) ordains that:

> Persons other than police officers who are charged with the duty of investigating offences or charging offenders shall in the discharge of that duty have regard to any relevant provision of such a code.

Hence, Customs officers have been held bound to observe the Codes when questioning suspects. In *Sanusi* [1992] Crim LR 43, Customs officers failed to inform S, a foreigner with no previous convictions who was assumed not already to be familiar with the rights enjoyed by suspects in police interviews, of his rights. The Court of Appeal held that the Customs officers were bound to comply with Code C and that, in view of the substantial nature of their breaches of the Code, S's replies to questions ought to have been excluded from evidence under s 78. Similarly, an investigator employed specifically to look into copyright breaches on behalf of the Federation Against Copyright Theft was under an obligation to comply with PACE Code C (*Joy v FACT* [1993] Crim LR 588).

10.35 Cases involving tax offences illustrate how important it is to identify the exact role that the relevant official filled. In *Doncaster* (2008) 172 JP 202, for instance, a case involving cheating the Revenue and false accounting, it was held that tax inspectors whose task was merely to investigate taxpayers' liabilities and who, the moment they detected serious fraud, handed matters over to the Revenue's separate Special Compliance Office, did not fall within PACE, s 67(9). In contrast, in *Gill* [2004] 1 WLR 469 Code C had been held to apply to Inland Revenue 'special compliance officers'. Although at the time of the interview the latter had not initiated criminal proceedings against him, they had told G that they reserved the right to do so. The officers had conducted a so-called 'Hansard interview'. This type of interview, which forms part of a civil proceeding to recover unpaid tax, follows the procedure recommended by the Chancellor of the Exchequer in a parliamentary reply, published in 1990. A Hansard interview, however, does not meet the exacting standards of Code C. G was later charged with cheating the Revenue. The Court of Appeal determined that the Revenue's special compliance officers had in fact been bound to observe Code C. Even if the Revenue remains free to agree a financial settlement, compounding its differences with the taxpayer, tax fraud still involves the commission of criminal offences. Therefore, unless they give the taxpayer an unequivocal undertaking that criminal proceedings will not subsequently be instituted, special compliance officers can be said to be conducting a criminal investigation and are bound to comply with PACE Code C.

10. 36   In contrast to cases like *Sanusi, Joy* and *Gill*, the Divisional Court has decided that, although the investigation of offences may form a part of such a person's job, a head teacher investigating an assault complaint made by a parent against a supply teacher at his school was not a person 'charged with the duty of investigating offences' (*DPP v G* (1997) Times, 24 November). Similarly, in *Welcher* [2007] 2 Cr App R (S) 83 it was held that a disciplinary interview conducted by a chief engineer investigating corrupt practices within his company fell outside s 67(9) because he was not under a duty to investigate offences. By the same light, the Court of Appeal more than once has held that prison officers enquiring into offences committed by prison inmates do not fall directly within s 67(9) (eg *Taylor* (2000) 16 March, case no 99/1413/Y4; *Ristic* [2004] EWCA Crim 2107. In the latter case, however, Hallett J emphasised that 'the question of whether or not someone is a person or body charged with a duty of investigating offences, or charging offenders, very much turns on the particular facts of the case' (at [12]). This sentiment echoed *Bayliss* (1994) 98 Cr App R 235, where Neill LJ held that a store detective might be a person 'charged with the duty of investigating offences', depending on the terms of his employment and the circumstances of the case.

10.37   Nevertheless, even though particular parties may not be bound in strict law to comply with the Codes of Practice, the principles embodied in the Codes may still be relevant in determining whether confessions they have received should be excluded under s 78. Thus, in *Smith* (1994) 99 Cr App R 233, R, who was responsible for supervising S's bank on behalf of the Bank of England, interviewed S, the bank's chairman. In the course of this interview S acknowledged financial misconduct, and R made a note of this. The note was not shown to S. Although R was not bound by s 67(9) to adhere to Code C, the Court of Appeal did observe that the principles underlying Code C have a wider application and may be of assistance when considering whether to exclude confessional evidence under s 78. The Court of Appeal adopted a similar approach in *Elleray* [2003] 2 Cr App R 11. E had just been convicted of indecent assault. He admitted to probation officers, who were questioning him preparatory to submitting a pre-sentence report, that on several occasions he had actually raped the victim while she was incapacitated through drink. Whilst acknowledging the admissibility of the officers' evidence, the Court of Appeal stressed that:

> In deciding whether to exclude the evidence it is perfectly appropriate for the court to have in mind the contrast between the position that exists where an offender is interviewed by the police and that which exists when the offender is interviewed by a probation officer. The court should bear in mind the need for frankness between the offender and the probation officer; the fact that there may not be a reliable record of what was said; that the offender has not been cautioned; and that the offender has not had the benefit of legal representation. The protection which the court can provide under s 78 in the majority of cases should be sufficient to ensure that no unfairness occurs to an offender.
>
> (at [11])

10.38 Reverting to cases where the investigator is bound to comply with the Codes, *not every breach of a provision of a Code will justify the exclusion of an accused's confession under s 78*. The court must assess its gravity in the context of the individual circumstances of the case. As was held in *Absolam* (1988) 88 Cr App R 332, only if the breaches are 'significant and substantial' ought the court to conclude that admission of the confession may reflect adversely on the fairness of the proceedings. The court will not only consider how flagrant was the police misconduct or how fundamental the right infringed, but may also take on board the strength of the case against the suspect. Thus, in *Keenan* [1990] 2 QB 54 the court offered the view that 'in cases when the rest of the evidence is weak or non-existent, that is just the situation where the temptation to do just what the provisions are aimed to prevent is greatest, and the protection of the rules most needed'.

10.39 Code C is intended to safeguard a number of rights, which the courts consider important and whose breach may lead to the exclusion of a confession under s 78. Although breaches of these rights will not inevitably lead to the rejection of confessional evidence, it may be instructive to examine those situations where the admissibility of confessions is typically contested following breach of Code C.

  • *Being informed of one's rights*—Suspects should be informed of their rights prior to an interview taking place. In *Beycan* [1990] Crim LR 185 an unsophisticated interviewee, who was being investigated in connection with a conspiracy to supply heroin and whose native tongue was not English, was asked by a police officer if he was 'happy to be interviewed in the normal way we conduct these interviews without a solicitor, friend or representative'. H agreed to this. Not surprisingly, the Court of Appeal decided that the confession H subsequently made ought to have been excluded from evidence, observing:

> It would seem to us that a complete failure to inform a defendant of what his rights are is no less serious than a denial to accord those rights having informed him what they are ... [W]e

understand it to have been the intention of Parliament that these Codes of Practice should have teeth and should not merely be of an exhortatory nature with all but the most flagrant breaches being overlooked.

- *The right to legal advice*—PACE provides suspects with a right to legal advice. Section 58, subject to certain narrow exceptions, accords a person arrested and held in custody the right 'to consult a solicitor privately at any time'. Section 58, which was variously described in *Samuel* (1987) 87 Cr App R 232 as 'precise and unambiguous', as 'perhaps the most important right given... to a person detained by the police' and as 'one of the most important and fundamental rights of a citizen', is reinforced by the detailed provisions of Code C, para 6. In *Samuel*, a confession obtained from S, after his request to consult a solicitor had been improperly turned down by police investigating an armed robbery, was ruled inadmissible. However, not all confessions made by suspects deprived of legal advice will be excluded. In each case the court must judge what effect the with-holding of legal advice had on that particular defendant and then determine if the breach is sufficiently 'significant and substantial' to reflect adversely on the fairness of the proceedings. Thus, in *Alladice* (1988) 87 Cr App R 380, a case that followed hard upon the heels of *Samuel*, Lord Lane CJ seemed to distin-guish *Samuel* on the ground that there was evidence suggesting that the solici-tor, had he been present, would have advised S not to answer further questions (ie, the presence of the solicitor could very well have prevented S from making the confession that he did), whereas in *Alladice*, A, who displayed unusual 'cand-our' in the witness box by admitting that he was well able to cope with police interviews and knew and understood his rights, claimed that he had actually said nothing after answering the first few police questions and acknowledged that he only really wanted the lawyer present as some sort of check on the police during interview. In these circumstances, the court held that although there had undoubtedly been a breach of s 58, it had not had such an impact as to reflect adversely on the fairness of the proceedings. In a bid to reconcile the authorities, in *Walsh* (1989) 91 Cr App R 161 Saville J, having pointed out that the purpose of s 58 and related provisions of Code C is to achieve fairness *both* for D *and* for the police—against whom there will be less unfounded allegations of malprac-tice, stated:

[I]f there are significant and substantial breaches of s 58 or the provisions of the Code, then *prima facie* at least the standards of fairness set by Parliament have not been met. So far as a defendant is concerned, ... to admit evidence against him which has been obtained in circumstances when these standards have not been met, cannot but have an adverse effect on the fairness of the proceedings. This does not mean, of course, that in every case of a significant or substantial breach of s 58 or the Code of Practice the evidence concerned will automatically be excluded. Section 78 does not so provide. *The task of the court is not*

merely to consider whether there would be an adverse effect on the fairness of the proceed-
ings, but such an adverse effect that justice requires the evidence to be excluded.

(at 163: emphasis added)

The final statement in the passage quoted is, of course, of general application to all cases where appeal is made to exclude evidence under s 78.

In *Wahab* [2003] 1 Cr App R 232, the Court of Appeal indicated its view of the purpose of legal advice given to suspects undergoing interrogation. W had argued that advice given by his solicitor had contributed to inducing him to confess and that therefore his confession ought not to have been admitted. Judge LJ explained:

Advice properly given to the defendant by his solicitor does not normally provide a basis for excluding a subsequent confession under s 76(2). One of the duties of a legal advisor, whether at a police station, or indeed at a pre-trial conference, or during the trial itself, is to give the client realistic advice. That emphatically does not mean that the advice must be directed to "getting the client off", or simply making life difficult for the prosecution. The advice may, and sometimes ought to, be robust, sensibly considering the advantages which the client may derive from evidence of remorse and a realistic acceptance of guilt, or the corresponding advantages of participating in a "no comment" interview. The exercise of professional judgment in circumstances like these is often very difficult, often dependent on less than precise instructions from the defendant.

(at [42])

The judge acknowledged that if a solicitor, who was acting for two clients, per-suaded one to confess in order to obtain an advantage for the other, or if a solici-tor were found to have been in cahoots with the police, those circumstances would necessitate that a judge considered whether or not to exclude the confes-sion under s 78 of PACE, notwithstanding that the reliability of the confession might not be in doubt. Otherwise, however, it is highly unlikely that the reason for excluding a confession will derive from the nature of the legal advice given by the solicitor.

One further point perhaps deserves to be made. A number of cases have suggested that withholding legal advice from a suspect will be considered less serious if that suspect is an experienced villain, who can be taken to know the ropes. In *Dunford* (1990) 91 Cr App R 150 D, who on this occasion was convicted of conspiracy to rob and attempted robbery of a supermarket during which three policemen had been shot, had previous convictions and, by initially refusing to answer questions, appeared clearly to understand that he had a right to remain silent. Taking what he termed 'an overall and practical view', Macpherson J concluded that in this case 'the solicitor's advice would not have added anything to this particular appellant's knowledge of his rights':

> If a man shows...that he knew that he could answer "no comment" and could refuse to sign an interview, and if a man has experience of arrest, we do not believe that a judge...can simply pay no attention to these facts.... [I]t must be open to the court, even where breach of s 58 is established, to balance all the circumstances and to decide whether or not there exists *such* an adverse effect upon the fairness of the proceedings that justice requires the evidence to be excluded.
>
> (at 154)

While such an analysis was plausible in the days when an accused both still enjoyed an unqualified right to silence and jurors would not be directed that they could draw an adverse inference from his refusal to answer police questions—and more specifically from his failure to mention facts, it is doubtful whether such an approach would be appropriate today following the introduction of the silence provisions in the Criminal Justice and Public Order Act 1994 (see *post*, Chapter 11). The new caution (Code C:10.4) is not readily intelligible (see Fenner, Gudjonsson and Clare, 'Understanding of the Current Police Caution (England and Wales) among Suspects in Police Detention' (2002) *Journal of Community and Applied Social Psychology*, 83–93, which, alarmingly, discovered that although more than 96 per cent of the police detainees and jobcentre attendees who participated in their experiment claimed to have understood the caution fully after it had been presented to them as it would be by the police, on further investigation it emerged that none of them actually did). The risk that inferences may be drawn under s 34 of the 1994 Act if, in interrogation, the accused fails 'to mention any fact relied on in his defence...which in the circumstances existing at the time the accused could reasonably be expected to mention when so questioned', has in fact radically altered matters. It is no longer simply a question for a suspect either to speak or to remain silent. Section 34, along with the other silence provisions in that Act, has made the presence of a legal adviser during questioning all the more important as a suspect's every decision not to answer a question is likely to involve a delicate legal calculation.

Finally, it might be mentioned that a different regime applies in the case of interviews conducted under the Terrorism Act 2000. Under para 8 of Sch 8 of that Act a police officer of at least the rank of superintendent may authorise a delay in permitting a detained person to consult a solicitor provided that he has reasonable grounds for believing, for instance, that others who have not been arrested at that juncture may be alerted, that legal advice will make it more difficult to prevent an act of terrorism or that it may make more difficult the apprehension, prosecution or conviction of persons connected with terrorism. Interviews conducted under these conditions are known as 'safety interviews'. Safety interviews are intended to help the police to protect life and to prevent serious damage. In *Ibrahim et al* [2008] 2 Cr App R 23 the question arose as to whether the Crown had properly been allowed to make use of statements the appellants had made at their safety interviews—in this case, false statements that contradicted the defence they had advanced at trial to the effect that their bombs were simply hoaxes. The Court of Appeal upheld Fulford J's decision to admit the evidence. The relevant legislation did not preclude the admission of evidence that emerged at safety interviews; in this case, the appellants were under no illusions as to the purpose of their safety interviews or as to the potential risks of not revealing elements of their defence at that stage; access to a lawyer was only denied for a relatively short period (8 hours, at the outside), and in no case was the defence so complicated as particularly to demand the services of a lawyer. In principle, then, the fruits of safety interviews were admissible at the appellants' subsequent trials subject to the ordinary principles governing a fair trial, and to the overarching control of PACE, s 78.

- *Cautioning*—Code C requires the police to caution a suspect at various points, informing him:

  > You do not have to say anything. But it may harm your defence if you do not mention when questioned something which you later rely on in court. Anything you do say may be given in evidence.

Notably, a caution must be delivered before the suspect is interviewed regarding his involvement or suspected involvement in any offence. (He must also normally be cautioned upon arrest and upon being charged or informed that he may be prosecuted for an offence.) The failure to caution, again, may lead to the exclusion of any confession the suspect subsequently makes. However, as was pointed out in *Pall* [1992] Crim LR 126, although the police's failure to caution is in most cases bound to be 'significant', this may be counteracted by the individual circumstances. Thus, in *Pall*, because P had already been cautioned in connection with another matter, the failure to caution him in regard to the conspiracy to defraud enquiry was said not to have misled or lulled P into a sense of false security.

Rather more serious is the sort of situation which arose in *Kirk* [2000] 1 WLR 567, where the police arrested K and questioned him about the snatching of a shopping bag from an elderly woman in the street who fell and sustained injuries from which she died in hospital. The police omitted to tell K of the lady's death or of the risk that he might be charged with robbery or manslaughter. K, who had declined legal advice, was only told of the lady's death after having confessed to theft of the shopping bag, at which point he sought to retract his confession. The court noted that Code C:10.1 envisages that a suspect in custody should at least be made aware of the true nature of the police investigation. Notably, in order that he may properly weigh whether or not to seek legal advice, the suspect should know both why he is in custody and, when interviewed, in general terms at least the level of offence of which he is suspected. The police's failure to observe these basic principles, which led K not to seek legal advice and to give critical answers which he might not otherwise have given, meant that the confession ought to have been excluded under s 78 of PACE as its admission would have 'a serious adverse effect' on the fairness of the proceedings. K's convictions for robbery and manslaughter were therefore quashed. The position in *Kirk* is in fact reinforced by Article 5(2) of the European Convention on Human Rights, which provides:

> Everyone who is arrested shall be informed promptly, in a language that he understands, of the reasons for his arrest and of any charge against him.

That 'elementary safeguard that any person arrested should know why he is being deprived of his liberty' by prompt disclosure under Article 5(2) (*Fox, Campbell and Hartley v United Kingdom* (1990) 13 EHRR 157, 170, at [40]) therefore leads to an identical conclusion.

In assessing the gravity of the breach, the court may also have regard to the purpose of PACE Code C. In *Gill* [2004] 1 WLR 469, because he took the principal purpose of Code C:10.1 to be to ensure so far as possible that interviewees do not make admissions unless they wish to do so, and that they are aware of the consequences of their so doing, Clarke LJ chose to differentiate interviews where uncautioned suspects can be shown to have told lies and those where they have made admissions, concluding that:

> We do not think that the principal purpose of the Code is to prevent interviewees from telling lies.
>
> (at [46])

Lies, of course, will not automatically be admissible whenever a breach of Code C occurs. Each case will depend upon its own facts. Nevertheless, whereas a court is unlikely to allow the prosecution to rely upon admissions made by an accused in the course of an interview conducted in breach of Code C:10.1 (cf *Allen* [2002] 1 AC 509), a suspect's lies during questioning are said by Clarke LJ to present less of a dilemma.

- *Keeping contemporaneous records*—Code C:11.7 lays down that 'an accurate record must be made of each interview with a person suspected of an offence'. As the Court of Appeal stressed in *Canale* (1989) 91 Cr App Rep 1, a case where police officers were found to have flagrantly and cynically breached this rule:

> ...the importance of the rules relating to the contemporaneous noting of interviews could scarcely be over-emphasized. The object is twofold: not merely to ensure, so far as possible that [D's] remarks are accurately recorded and that he has an opportunity when he goes through the contemporaneous record afterwards of checking each answer and initialling each answer, but likewise it is protection for the police, to ensure, so far as

is possible, that it cannot be suggested that they induced the suspect to confess by improper approaches or improper promises.

Moreover, the court added, if no contemporaneous record is made, that deprives the judge of the very evidence which normally enables him to determine the admissibility of the confessional evidence. In *Bryce* (1992) 95 Cr App R 320, a case in which B alleged entrapment, a police officer's account of conversations he had had with B regarding a stolen Saab was excluded because of the absence of a neutral, reliable record of the officer's call to B's mobile (on entrapment, see *ante* paras **1.55–1.61**).

The importance of obtaining reliable records is endorsed by Code of Practice E on Audio Recording of Interviews with Suspects. This Code, last amended in May 2010, notably requires that 'audio recording shall be used at police stations for any interview with a person cautioned under Code C, in respect of an indictable offence, including an offence triable either way...which takes place as a result of an interviewer exceptionally putting further questions...when an interviewer wants to tell a person [after charge etc]...about any written statement or interview with another person.' Note 3A adds that Code E does not preclude audio recording at police discretion of interviews at police stations in other classes of situation. Although audio recording will not always be practicable for interviews conducted elsewhere than in the police station, Code E underlines the importance of accurate, contemporaneous records of interviews.

The recording of police interviews has since been taken a stage further. In August 2004 Code F came into effect for the Visual Recording with Sound of Interviews with Suspects (last revised in May 2010), should interviewing officers decide that they wish to video record an interview. As Code F makes clear: 'There is no statutory requirement under PACE to visually record interviews.' Nevertheless, Code F:3.1 does suggest six specific situations in which a visual recording of an interview may be deemed desirable. Thus:

[I]f an interviewing officer decides to make a visual recording these are the areas where it might be appropriate:

(a) with a suspect in respect of an indictable offence...

(b) which takes place as a result of an interviewer exceptionally putting further questions to a suspect about an offence described in sub-para (a) above after they have been charged with, or informed they may be prosecuted for, that offence...;

(c) in which an interviewer wishes to bring to the notice of a person, after that person has been charged with, or informed they may be prosecuted for an offence described in sub-para (a) above, any written statement made by another person, or the content of an interview with another person...;

(d) with, or in the presence of, a deaf or deaf/blind or speech impaired person who uses sign language to communicate;

(e) with, or in the presence of anyone who requires an "appropriate adult"; or

(f) in any case where the suspect or their representative requests that the interview be recorded visually.

This list is not exhaustive, however (Note 3A).

- *The mentally disordered and mentally vulnerable*—Certain classes of suspect are considered to be particularly at risk during interview. For this reason, Code C:11.15 provides that normally 'a juvenile or a person who is mentally disordered or otherwise mentally vulnerable must not be interviewed regarding their involvement…in a criminal offence…, or asked to provide or sign a written statement under caution or record interview, in the absence of the appropriate adult' as defined in Code C:1.7. In *Aspinall* (1999) 49 BMLR 82, upon being arrested for conspiracy to supply heroin, A told the police that he was a schizophrenic. Despite his medical condition having been confirmed by two doctors, A was interviewed, in the absence of a solicitor and with no appropriate adult present and after a delay of 13 hours, whereupon he made important admissions as well as telling some lies. The Court of Appeal held that A's confession had been wrongly admitted in evidence, notably because the trial judge had failed to give adequate weight to the police's omission to provide either an appropriate adult or a legal representative to assist and advise him.

A confession may be excluded under the common law discretion retained in PACE, s 82(3) if the prejudicial effect of admitting it is likely to exceed its probative value

10.40 Although the two varieties of discretion overlap to such an extent that it is difficult to see much of a role for the old common law discretion, which pre-PACE enabled a judge to exclude evidence whose prejudicial effect was considered to exceed its probative value, courts do from time to time refer to the common law discretion, which was expressly preserved by s 82(3) of PACE, as though the two species of discretion are to be exercised separately (eg *Park* (1993) 99 Cr App R 270; *H* [1995] 2 AC 596). Indeed, in one case, the common law discretion was described by the Court of Appeal as the judge's power 'to take such decision as he thinks fit to ensure fairness both to the prosecution…and to the defendant' (*Sayer* (1988) 22 March, unreported)).

10.41 There is, indeed, one situation in which arguably the common law discretion preserved in s 82(3) may prove useful. As the Court pointed out in *Sat-Bhambra* (1988)

88 Cr App R 55, s 78 of PACE refers only to situations in which the Crown 'proposes to give in evidence' an accused's confession. Section 78 does not apply to cases where the court at first admits a confession but then changes its mind and decides that it ought to be excluded, since at this juncture one cannot say that the confession is any longer evidence which the Crown 'proposes to give'. Given the problematical direction which a judge would require to deliver to the jury in any case where it was determined to exclude from their consideration a confession of which they had been made aware—instructing them to disregard the fact that they know that the defendant has acknowledged his guilt—the most likely outcome in such situations will always be for the judge to stop the case and to declare a mistrial. However, on the rare occasions upon which the judge feels that such a course is practicable, provided that the prejudicial effect of the confession exceeds its probative value, the surviving common law discretion permits the exclusion of a confession previously admitted in evidence.

What if the accused, having first made an inadmissible confession, later makes a further confession which is obtained by proper methods?

10.42   This is what occurred in *McGovern* (*ante*, para **10.27**). Having first confessed in circumstances which offended against s 76(2)(b), M, the next day, made a confession in compliance with the provisions of PACE. Did the presence of a solicitor and the absence of emotional stress at the second interview counteract the shortcomings of the first interview? Or was the second confession to be viewed as a direct consequence of the first, and thus tainted by what had occurred at the first interrogation session? The Court of Appeal held:

> ...when an accused person has made a series of admissions as to...her complicity in a crime at first interview, the very fact that those admissions have been made are likely to have an effect upon her during the course of the second interview. If...the first interview was in breach of s 58,...the second interview must be similarly tainted.
>
> (at 234)

10.43   It is sometimes argued that where interviews have initially taken place under conditions that breach Code C and which therefore merit the exclusion of confessional evidence, police compliance with the Code in subsequent interviews can cure this defect. It is however for the court to consider the individual circumstances. Hence, in *Ismail* [1990] Crim LR 109 I, who was not a strong personality and who, besides, understood little English, had six police interviews concerning a series of indecent assaults. The police breached all manner of Code provisions in the third, fourth and fifth interviews—notably denying I legal advice, failing to keep a record of his interviews and at the third interview, where the interviewing officer actually deceived the custody officer as to his intentions, being adjudged by the trial judge to have employed oppression. The sixth and final interview, however, was impeccably conducted. In the final analysis, the Court of Appeal decided that the earlier breaches were such that they could not be cured by a properly conducted interview because by then I's will had been affected.

Confessions made by mentally handicapped persons (PACE, s 77)

10.44 Mentally handicapped persons who make confessions during interrogation enjoy additional protection under the Act. Section 77 of PACE provides that where the prosecution case against a mentally handicapped person relies wholly or substantially on a confession that was not made in the presence of an independent person, the court shall warn the jury of the special need for caution before convicting the accused in reliance on the confession. The sort of independent person envisaged by this section includes solicitors instructed by the suspect, but expressly excludes police officers and those employed for or engaged on 'police purposes' within the meaning of the Police Act 1996 (s 77(3)).

10.45 Any failure to comply with s 77 is a serious matter. On the one hand, the police may fail to ensure that an independent person is present during interrogation. Thus, in *J* [2003] EWCA Crim 3309 a manslaughter conviction was set aside principally because the Court of Appeal concluded that, in addition to J's interviews having been conducted in the absence of a solicitor, had the trial judge known that it was likely that the police were actually aware of J's mental subnormality and very high suggestibility, the judge would 'undoubtedly' (at [45]) have excluded J's confessions under PACE, s 76(2)(b), owing to this significant failure to comply with s 77.

10.46 The Court of Appeal is also inclined to take a dim view of a trial judge's failure to deliver the requisite warning under PACE, s 77. In *Lamont* [1989] Crim LR 813, L had the reading age of a child of eight and an IQ of 73. His conviction for attempted murder was set aside because no warning had been delivered, the court remarking that this direction was 'an essential part of a fair summing-up'. More generally, as was held in *Bailey* [1995] 2 Cr App R 262, 'what is required of a judge in summing up in such cases . . . is a full and proper statement of the mentally handicapped defendant's case against the confession's being accepted by the jury as true and accurate.'

The admissibility of evidence discovered in consequence of an inadmissible confession

10.47 Even if a court rules a confession inadmissible, evidence uncovered in consequence of an inadmissible confession, if relevant, may still be admissible. Let us imagine that, following a beating from a police officer, Dahlia confesses that, having slit her husband's throat, she proceeded to bury his corpse under the buddleia in the back garden. As we have seen, the confession will be inadmissible under s 76(2)(a) of PACE, having been extorted by oppression. However, if the police dig up the garden and find the corpse under the buddleia, precisely where Dahlia said it would be, the finding of the corpse is admissible evidence because PACE, s 76(4)(a) provides:

> ...the fact that a confession is wholly or partly excluded in pursuance of this section shall not affect the admissibility in evidence of any facts discovered as a result of the confession.

The prosecution may not reveal that the corpse was found in consequence of a statement made by Dahlia; it may only prove the facts unearthed in consequence of Dahlia's confession. This may deprive the subsequently discovered facts of much of their probative force as other means will have to be found of linking Dahlia to the offence.

10.48 Since situations may conceivably arise in which it could be in Dahlia's interests to make known that facts were discovered in consequence of a statement she has made, s 76(5) confers on Dahlia the option of revealing that she was the source of the police's information:

> Evidence that a fact...was discovered as a result of a statement made by an accused person shall not be admissible unless evidence of how it was discovered is given by him or on his behalf.

Using an inadmissible confession to show that the accused speaks, writes or expresses himself in a particular way

10.49 An inadmissible confession may be admissible for other limited purposes. Thus, if the Crown wishes to adduce a confession, not as evidence of D's admissions, but 'where the confession is relevant as showing that the accused speaks, writes or expresses himself in a particular way', it may introduce 'so much of the confession as is necessary to show that he does so' (s 76(4)(b)). In *Voisin* [1918] 1 KB 531 a paper on which V had written, at the police's request, the words 'Bladie Belgiam' was admitted in evidence despite the fact that this had not been done under caution.

This writing showed that V misspelled the words 'bloody Belgian' in this singular fashion. (In his memoirs, it is concerning that the investigating officer proudly recounts that Voisin had to be induced to make several attempts before producing a satisfactory writing!) The selfsame reasoning was employed in *Nottle* [2004] EWCA Crim 599. N was charged with having committed criminal damage to 83 cars in a compound. N had a grievance against the owner's son, Justin. On some of the cars the offender, clearly neither a master criminal nor a scholar, had petulantly scratched the words, 'F*** you Jutin'. In interview, a police officer had asked N to write out these words 12 times, saying: 'It does not matter how you spell it.' On each occasion N wrote 'Jutin' for 'Justin'. Simon J held that the evidence of how N spelt 'Justin' had been properly admitted under s 76(4)(b).

The status of 'mixed statements'

10.50   A statement a suspect makes to the police, which may be a confession within the meaning of PACE, s 82(1), along with inculpatory admissions, may also contain self-serving elements favourable to his case. In these circumstances, one is in the presence of what is known as a 'mixed statement'. Whilst no one ever doubted that those parts of the statement in which an accused made admissions could be treated as evidence against him, the question remained: what is the evidential status of those portions of the statement in which he sought to exculpate himself? As we have seen, purely self-serving statements are not generally admissible as evidence of the facts (see *ante*, para **5.1**).

10.51   In *Sharp* [1988] 1 All ER 65, the House of Lords resolved that the jury was to be told that it could consider the whole mixed statement in deciding where the truth lies. Where appropriate, however, the judge may add that 'the incriminating parts are likely to be true (otherwise why say them?), whereas the excuses do not have the same weight'. Additionally, if the accused elects not to testify, the House in *Aziz* [1996] AC 41 has held that a judge may also make more obvious adverse comment on the self-serving parts of the statements, pointing out that the accused has not been cross-examined on them.

10. 52   *What constitutes a 'mixed statement'?* In *Papworth and Doyle* [2008] 1 Cr App R 36 Hooper LJ observed that although the principle can be clearly stated, there is little reported authority on the issue of what actually amounts to a mixed statement. The problem, which was first identified by Evans LJ in *Garrod* [1997] Crim LR 445, is that:

> it is almost impossible to conceive of any series of answers—i.e. something more than a bare denial—which cannot be regarded as containing some admissions of relevant fact as well as a statement of innocence and denial of guilt (the so-called 'exculpatory' part of

a mixed statement). The question is how to identify the kind of interview which contains enough in the nature of admissions to justify calling it a 'mixed' rather than an 'exculpatory' statement.

The House of Lords cannot have intended to permit virtually any exculpatory statement made by the accused to be admitted as evidence of the facts on the ground that it also contained some utterly trivial concession. The test formulated by Evans LJ in *Garrod*, and since endorsed in *Papworth and Doyle*, is that:

> where the statement contains an admission of fact which [is] significant to any issue in the case, meaning those which are capable of adding some degree of weight to the prosecution case on an issue which is relevant to guilt, then the statement must be regarded as "mixed" for the purposes of this rule.

Hooper LJ sought to put this principle in more concrete form in *Papworth and Doyle*:

> The admission in interview of an ingredient of the offence will often constitute a significant admission for the purposes of the *Garrod* test, but not necessarily. The fact that a defendant on trial for murder accepted in interview that the victim was dead is not likely to be a significant admission. Likewise, in the absence of an admission of an ingredient of the offence, it will be more difficult to conclude that the admissions which were made convert the statement into a mixed statement.
>
> (at ([15])

10.53 Hitherto, the courts have been concerned with the prosecution's entitlement to have a mixed statement admitted in evidence. Lord Steyn, however, did remark *en passant* in *Aziz* [1996] AC 41, 50: '*Sharp* does not warrant the introduction by a defendant of a mixed statement as part of his case.' The Court of Appeal adopted this proposition in *Tine* [2006] EWCA Crim 1788 at [26], where T had unsuccessfully argued that one of his police statements, which the prosecution did not put in evidence, ought to have been admitted for the defence because it contained both admissions and a statement exculpating T. Crane J held that only the Crown might tender in evidence a mixed statement.

An accused's statement to the police is not normally evidence against other co-accused

10.54 Although, arguably, the proper place for this point is the chapter on hearsay, it does not hurt to repeat that if in the course of D1's statement to the police, D1 makes allegations implicating a co-accused, D2, in the commission of the offence, the conventional view is that this statement cannot be adduced by the Crown as evidence against D2. D1's statement, made in D2's absence implicating D2 cannot be evidence against D2, and if it becomes revealed to them the jurors must be instructed to disregard it as evidence against D2. Although such an outcome will only rarely arise, D1's statement might be admissible by virtue of s 114(1)(d) of the Act if 'the court is satisfied that it is in the interests of justice for it to be admissible'. Section 114(1)(d) is regularly invoked to justify the admission of Crown evidence (*ante*, para **9.77**), and has actually led to one co-accused's out-of-court statement being adduced in support of another co-accused's case: *M* [2007] EWCA Crim 219. As Hughes LJ remarked in that case:

> If hearsay evidence is admitted in the interests of justice the jury is by law entitled to consider it, to determine its weight and to make up its mind whether it can or cannot rely upon it . . . There is no doubt that if and when hearsay evidence of this kind is ruled admissible it becomes evidence in the case generally.
>
> (at [20])

10.55 It may be virtually axiomatic that co-accused D1's out-of-court statements are inadmissible against co-accused D2—for instance, if D1 has told X, in D2's absence, 'D2 and I did the job'. But this does not mean that in other circumstances D1's statements can never be of any effect against D2. In *Hayter* [2005] 1 WLR 605 H appealed his conviction for murder. The Crown alleged that H had acted as a middleman between his two co-accused, R and B, in setting up the contract killing of B's husband. R had admitted to V that he had committed the murder; B was reported to have said that she intended to get someone to kill the victim. There was evidence that H had passed money from B to R. The trial judge told the jury that if they were sure that R was the killer, they could employ that 'fact' as part of the case against H. On appeal, it was objected that since the jury could only convict R on the basis of his out-of-court statements to V, there was no evidence admissible against H that R was the killer, and the jury had in effect been invited to convict H on the strength of R's admissions. The Court of Appeal having rejected this argument ([2003] 1 WLR 1910), on further appeal the following question was certified for consideration by the House of Lords:

> In a joint trial of two or more defendants for a joint offence is a jury entitled to consider first the case in respect of defendant R which is solely based on his own out-of-court admissions and then to use their findings of R's guilt and the role R played as a fact to be used evidentially in respect of co-defendant H?

The House of Lords, too, dismissed H's appeal, by a majority of 3–2. Lord Brown of Eaton-under-Heywood, with whom Lord Bingham allied himself, admitted that an affirmative answer to this question would inevitably involve 'some modification' (at [80]) to 'the universal rule which excludes out-of-court admissions being used to provide evidence against a co-accused, whether indicted jointly or separately' (*Spinks* (1981) 74 Cr App R 263, 266). This is because, even when the trial judge tells the jury that V's evidence is only evidence against R, and is no evidence against H, it is still an ineluctable fact that the task of establishing R's guilt (using V's evidence) is a key staging post along the road to establishing H's guilt.

10.56   The critical question was 'whether this modest "erosion" of the basic principle ought properly to be countenanced' (at [81]). Adopting the view that confessions are admitted as an exception to the hearsay rule owing to their inherent reliability (subject, of course, to the safeguards of PACE, s 76), Lord Brown confessed to being unable to see the logic of insisting that a confession could never be admitted as evidence against another party merely because the statement was not made in the presence of that party. Indeed, were this to prove such a problem:

> Why should not the jury be directed instead to assume in H's favour that, had he been present when R made his confession, he would have resolutely denied it if and insofar as it might otherwise have been thought to constitute evidence against him?
>
> (at [83])

Lord Brown was careful to stress that his intention was not to abrogate the general rule, as stated in *Spinks*, so as to render one co-accused's confession admissible against other co-accused for all purposes (at [86]). The exception was to be strictly confined to the type of factual situation that had arisen in *Hayter*. In such cases the jury would need to be told that before convicting H:

(i)   they must be sufficiently sure of the truthfulness of R's confession to convict R solely on the strength of it; and

(ii) when determining the case against H, they must entirely disregard everything said out of court by R which might otherwise be thought to incriminate H.

This is a pretty tall order, and it is not altogether surprising that one dissenting judge remarked that under such a regime 'the jury's supposed powers are incoherently selective' (Lord Rodger of Earlsferry at [48]). In response to the argument that there is no relevant difference between portions of R's confession that implicate R and any parts that implicate H, Lord Brown argued that it is wrong to equate the two elements in such a confession. Those portions of R's 'confession' implicating H ought to be excluded when the jury comes to consider the case against H for the reason that they are not declarations against R's interests and are thus less likely to be true: R, after all, may well have an interest in seeking to implicate H.

10.57 Like Lord Steyn (at [21]–[23]), and indeed like Mantell LJ in the Court of Appeal ([2003] 1 WLR 1910 at [18]), Lord Brown was seduced by the notion that this 'modest erosion' of legal principle was broadly consistent with the expressed will of Parliament, as evidenced in the reversal by PACE, s 74 of the rule in *Hollington v Hawthorn* (see *ante*, paras **1.40–1.46**):

> It is now twenty years since PACE s 74 was enacted and with it the prosecution's right to adduce in evidence against an accused another person's prior conviction. True it is that s 74 has no direct application to a case like the present where both accused stand trial together. But it is hardly to be thought that Parliament, had it turned its mind to the comparatively rare case like the present where the question arises of using evidentially against [H] the jury's already formed conclusions that [R] is guilty, would have proposed a different approach.
>
> (at [90])

With respect, this train of thought is largely wishful thinking. We *know* from the debates and from the statements of the minister responsible for the legislation that Parliament had no particular understanding of what it was doing when it enacted PACE, s 74—nor, in likelihood, did the CLRC from whose 11th Report the section stems (see Munday, 'Proof of Guilt by Association under s 74 of PACE' [1990] Crim LR 236). Provided always that one is confident that juries can cope with this suggested form of direction (eg Lord Steyn at [19]), the majority's conclusion may well accord with certain dictates of common sense. But to portray the decision as slipping easily into a consciously willed parliamentary development of the English rules of criminal evidence is to practise virtual history.

10.58 More convincing perhaps, if one wishes to adopt a more philosophic stance—or simply to state the majority's position at its simplest—is the point made in Lord Rodger's dissenting speech:

> [T]he Crown are in substance asserting that the jury have a power to turn inadmissible evidence into admissible evidence, and to convict a defendant by using evidence that is inadmissible against him.
>
> (at [47])

To this, the other dissentient, Lord Carswell, added:

> Such alchemy should not form part of the criminal law. Nor is it desirable that juries should be given directions which require them to draw such difficult distinctions and which are bound to cause confusion in their minds and understanding. Those concerned with reform of the law of evidence regularly state that the requirements for a rational law are simplicity, certainty and fairness. The approach adopted by the courts below would certainly fail to meet either of the first two criteria.
>
> (at [73])

Lord Rodger of Earlsferry also delivered another thoughtful observation. He pointed out that, when reporting on the hearsay rule (which, of course, lies at the root of the problem in *Hayter*), the Law Commission had specifically recommended that, in view of the gravity of the consequences in criminal cases, no change be made to the principle that a hearsay admission is only evidence against the person who made it. More significantly, s 118(1) of the Criminal Justice Act 2003 has just specifically preserved any common law 'rule relating to the admissibility of confessions or mixed statements in criminal proceedings'. Before the relevant portion of the 2003 Act had even been brought into force, the majority's ruling in *Hayter* appears to have punctured a principle that Parliament, a matter of months earlier, had *explicitly* determined to leave unchanged. One might just wonder how this can be reconciled with the majority's argument that their decision dovetails elegantly into the presumed will of the legislature.

10.59 Finally, in contrast to Lord Steyn's lofty reading of the majority's decision in *Hayter* as 'a principled evolution in keeping with modern developments, statutory and judge-made, which [have] corrected some of the worst absurdities of the law of evidence of a bygone era' (at [25]), there is an alternative interpretation of this case. It seems obvious that the real difficulty lay in the tactics selected by the Crown, which decided to proceed against all three defendants simultaneously. Had it first jointly prosecuted B and R for the husband's murder, once R was convicted it is highly likely that the Crown could then have legitimately employed PACE, s 74 in order to prove R's conviction at H's subsequent trial for murder. Lord Brown's approach was to assert that, given that a conviction admitted under PACE, s 74 might be founded on identification evidence, out-of-court statements or even a guilty plea, 'the particular evidential basis on which the jury finds [R] guilty should equally make no difference merely because, for obvious good reason, [R and H] are tried jointly' (at [90]). As Lord Carswell commented, however, in these circumstances, where the prosecution has deliberately chosen to adopt a particular course, 'to modify the common law rule to fill the gap left in the evidence against [H] would be an undesirable erosion of accepted principles' (at [77]). It is interesting to note that in *Persad v Trinidad and Tobago* [2007] UKPC 51 the Privy Council declined to apply *Hayter*: see esp at [85] *per* Lord Brown of Eaton-under-Heywood.

An accused's right to use his co-accused's confession (PACE s 76A)

10.60 We have seen that the prosecution will not be allowed to make use of the contents of D1's confession either if it has been obtained in breach of s 76 of PACE or if the judge exercises discretion and excludes it. However, even if the prosecution cannot take advantage of an inadmissible confession, the co-accused, D2, may still have reason to wish to make use of D1's confession. It can obviously be to D2's advantage to be able to show that on another occasion D1 has admitted his guilt. D1's confession may undermine D1's denials in court or may provide evidence tending to exculpate D2. At common law, D1's confession was of dubious admissibility until the House of Lords, in *Myers* [1998] AC 124, decided that D2 might put a statement made voluntarily by D1, if relevant to D2's defence, to a witness to whom it was made, even if it did incriminate D1 as its maker and even though it had not been used by the Crown. *Myers* itself, it could be added, left several important questions unanswered (see second edition of this work, paras **11.34–11.36**). Following up on a recommendation made by the Law Commission in its report *Evidence in Criminal Proceedings: Hearsay and Related Topics* (1997, Cm 3670), however, the Criminal Justice Act 2003, s 128 has now amended PACE, s 76 in order to regulate the admissibility of confessions made by a co-accused. The new provision (s 76A) confers upon a defendant an entitlement to proffer evidence that a co-accused has made a confession when this is relevant to his defence. Such entitlement, however, is subject to conditions of admissibility that closely resemble those facing the Crown when it seeks to adduce confessional evidence.

10.61 It might be noticed that in other contexts, whenever co-accused are jointly tried, a trial dynamic comes into play, different from that which operates when a defendant is tried alone. Whereas the Crown is bound by many evidential rules which, broadly speaking, are intended to ensure that the prosecution does not take unfair advantage of defendants, in joint trials the law is driven by other concerns. In the case of PACE s 76A, it is possible to see potentially contradictory forces at work. On the one hand, there is the principle, embodied in s 76A, that any defendant has the right to defend himself and that, in so doing he ought not to be hamstrung by the same procedural niceties that bind the Crown. But on the other, there is a seemingly conflicting principle that every defendant is entitled to receive a fair trial, which really means that no defendant ought to be deprived of procedural safeguards designed to prevent either his being convicted on the basis of unreliable evidence or even his co-accused's being acquitted on the basis of shaky evidence. The new statutory provision seeks to reconcile these competing *desiderata* by insisting that D2 shows that the confession was not obtained in an inappropriate manner, either as a result of oppression or of anything said or done that might render the confession unreliable.

10.62 Section 76A(1) of PACE now provides:

> In any proceedings a confession made by an accused person may be given in evidence for another person charged in the same proceedings (a co-accused) in so far as it is relevant to any matter in issue in the proceedings and is not excluded by the court in pursuance of this section.

The situations in which a court must exclude such confessions are enumerated in s 76A(2). These are identical, in all respects bar one, to the conditions which its sister provision, s 76, imposes whenever a defendant contests (s 76(2)) or the court of its own motion questions (s 76(3)) the admissibility of a confession that the Crown wishes to lead in evidence. Section 76A(2) now provides:

> If, in any proceedings where a co-accused proposes to give in evidence a confession made by an accused person, it is represented to the court that the confession was or may have been obtained—
>
> (a) by oppression of the person who made it; or
>
> (b) in consequence of anything said or done which was likely, in the circumstances existing at the time, to render unreliable any confession which might be made by him in consequence thereof,
>
> the court shall not allow the confession to be given in evidence for the co-accused except in so far as it is proved to the court on the balance of probabilities that the confession (notwithstanding that it may be true) was not so obtained.

As in the case of s 76, under s 76A(2) it must be shown that there was no 'oppression' and nothing was said or done that might render a confession unreliable, notwithstanding that it may be true. Equally, if for some reason D1 does not question the admissibility of his confession, the court may of its own motion require D2 to show that D1's confession was not obtained in these ways (s 76A(3)). The significant difference between s 76A(2) and its counterpart, s 76(2), is that whereas under s 76(2) the prosecution is required to establish the absence of 'oppression' or 'anything said or done' beyond reasonable doubt, a defendant who wishes to adduce evidence of a co-accused's confession has only to satisfy the court of the absence of these factors on a balance of probabilities. As we saw when we considered the burden of proof, the convention is that whenever the defence is required to prove something, it is set a less demanding standard of proof than the prosecution (*ante*, paras **2.23** ff). Otherwise, it is stated that the purpose of s 76A was 'to ensure that the defendant whose confession was being put before the [court] should be provided with similar protection against unfairness, whether that confession was introduced by the prosecution or by one of his co-defendants' (*Ibrahim et al* [2008] 2 Cr App R 23 at [142]).

10.63 One comment might be hazarded concerning the way in which courts could apply the test concerning 'anything said or done' under s 76A(2)(b). It does seem to some commentators that when the Crown seeks to have confessions admitted in evidence, there has often been a blurring between cases where confessional evidence is excluded under s 76(2)(b) on grounds of unreliability and cases where such evidence is excluded under the broad discretion conferred on judges by PACE, s 78 (*ante*, paras **10.32** ff). Notably, where the defendant's principal procedural protections under PACE have been violated by the police (the right to legal advice, the contemporaneous recording of statements, etc), the courts' tendency has been to proceed under s 78 rather than to consider the reliability test of s 76(2)(b). Given that s 78 only applies to evidence that the prosecution proposes adducing, courts might be expected to focus more determinedly upon s 76A(2)(b) when D2 applies to have D1's confession admitted in evidence and D1 invokes the likely unreliability of a confession obtained under conditions such as he endured. If only for the sake of consistency, in turn this might even induce them to have more frequent recourse to s 76(2)(b) in similar cases when the prosecution seeks to adduce such evidence.

10.64 More generally, PACE, s 78 can only lead to the exclusion of a confession which the prosecution proposes introducing if the court considers that its admission would reflect adversely on the fairness of the proceedings. In *Johnson* (2007) 171 JP 574 (*ante*, para **10.06**), where the co-accused was permitted to employ J's vacated guilty plea in support of her defence, it is striking that whereas the prosecution would almost inevitably have been refused leave to adduce this type of evidence on grounds of unfairness under PACE, s 78, a court has no power to intervene and prevent a co-accused from so introducing such a confession in so far as the confession is relevant to any matter in issue in the proceedings. As Pill LJ observed,

> We understand the frustration of a defendant who is permitted to vacate a guilty plea but not then permitted to enjoy the fruits of vacation by way of a trial unencumbered by the earlier plea. On the evidence, however, the issue at this trial was essentially between the two defendants and the decision in *Myers* [1998] AC 124, and s. 76A of the 1984 Act, are designed to ensure a fair trial in that situation.
>
> (at [22])

10.65 A further feature of s 76A(2) potentially raises serious problems, owing to the similarity of wording in the new provision and in s 76(2). Section 76A(2) requires a court to exclude D1's confession 'notwithstanding that it may be true'. Whilst such a requirement may make sense when the Crown is seeking to have a confession admitted that has been extracted by things said or done, it does seem hard to reconcile with any notion of fair trial that D2 must be refused leave to introduce D1's putatively reliable confession in evidence, even if it is relevant to D2's defence, if it has been obtained by illicit means. A provision that prevents a defendant point blank from adducing reliable evidence that could exonerate him can hardly be treated as compatible with the right of fair trial guaranteed by Article 6 of the ECHR. It is far from obvious that reading it down can save this provision under the Human Rights Act 1998, s 3. Although the courts treat declarations of incompatibility as the nuclear option—'a measure of last resort... [to] be avoided unless it is plainly impossible to do so' (*R v A (No 2)* [2002] 1 AC 45 at [44] *per* Lord Steyn; see also appendix to Lord Steyn's judgment in *Ghaidan v Godin-Mendoza* [2004] 2 AC

557)—in this respect the new s 76A may simply have to be declared incompatible with human rights law under s 4 of the 1998 Act.

10.66 Section 128(3) of the Criminal Justice Act 2003 spells out that, when the term 'confession' is used in s 76A, it bears exactly the same meaning as it does in PACE, s 76. Indeed, as s 128(2) makes clear, no statement of D1 may be treated as amounting to a confession under s 76A unless it would also so qualify under s 76. Therefore, the House of Lords' decision in *Hasan* [2005] 2 WLR 709 will apply, and the term 'confession' will not extend to statements made by D1 that are either neutral or wholly exculpatory (see *ante*, para **10.16**). The scope of the term 'confession' is not wholly settled, however. In *Finch* [2007] 1 Cr App R 33 at [12], Hughes LJ left open for another day the question of whether, when the contents of a co-accused's police interviews, which 'go beyond admission of the offence but in some way serve the interests of someone else, remain within the meaning of the word "confession"'. F and R had originally been jointly charged with possession of a prohibited firearm and possession of ammunition without a firearms certificate. The items were found by police under the front passenger seat of a car driven by R. F had been in the passenger seat. At his police interview, R admitted that the gun and the ammunition items were his but said that F knew nothing about them. R pleaded guilty to the two offences; F was therefore tried alone. R was available to be called as a witness, but was reluctant to testify for F. Instead of calling R, F applied to introduce R's 'confession' into evidence on the grounds that it exculpated him. The court ruled that R's confession was not admissible under the new s 76A of PACE 1984 because R, once convicted, was neither 'an accused person' nor 'another person charged in the same proceedings', as required by that provision. (F's application to have R's statement admitted under s 114(1)(d) of the Criminal Justice Act 2003 was also unsuccessful.) In *Nazir* [2009] EWCA Crim 213, however, in a case where M had made a confession admitting full responsibility for the murder of N's sister and exculpating N, Stanley Burnton LJ held:

> [S]tatements made in an interview that are partly inculpatory of the interviewee and also in part exculpatory of another person are nonetheless a confession within the statutory definition.
>
> (at [23])

10.67 In similar manner, s 76A(7) defines 'oppression', as used in s 76A, in terms identical to those found in PACE, s 76(8). 'Oppression' under the two provisions is therefore said to include:

> torture, inhuman or degrading treatment, and the use or threat of violence (whether or not amounting to torture).

Given that the courts, in applying s 76, have persistently ignored the statutory definition of 'oppression', supplied in s 76(8), (see *Fulling* [1987] QB 426, *ante*, paras **10.23–10.25**), what does reiteration of the statutory definition in s 76(7) signify? On the one hand, it might indicate a parliamentary resolve that the statutory definition ought at last to be respected and applied by the courts. Yet, on the other, given that s 76A, as a whole, is just a very lightly amended restatement of s 76, one could as easily conclude that repetition of the definition conveys no particular message and, if anything, might be portrayed as a signal that the current state of affairs to be tolerated.

10.68 As is the case under s 76 when the prosecution seeks to rely upon confessional evidence, if D2's application to have D1's confession declared admissible fails, the confession may still be admissible for other purposes. Thus, employing identical phraseology to s 76(4), s 76A(4) allows subsequently discovered facts to be admitted although the means by which they came to light may not be revealed; similarly, it allows a confession to be used by D2 to the extent necessary to show that D1 expresses himself in a particular manner (cp *ante*, para **10.49**). Again, as in s 76(5) and (6), s 76A(5) and (6) prevent D2 from introducing the fact that any subsequently discovered facts which may be admitted came to light as a consequence of D1's having made a confession, which the court has ruled wholly or partly inadmissible (*ante*, paras **10.47–10.48**). Only the maker of the statement, D1, is entitled to make this known to the tribunal, should he so choose (s 76A(5)).

10.69 The new s 76A poses several problems. As we have already seen, in so far as it constrains the court to exclude confessions that could be considered reliable, it may well infringe ECHR, Article 6. Additionally, s 76A may turn out to possess another defect. It was noted above that the common law discretion to exclude evidence that the court deems more prejudicial than probative was expressly retained by PACE s 82(3), and that this discretion may still come into its own when a court, having once ruled admissible a confession tendered by the Crown, changes its mind and resolves to declare the confession inadmissible instead (*ante*, para **10.41**). It is not clear that a court could take similar action in the case of the confession of a co-accused, which at first the court was minded to admit but which later it determined did not satisfy the conditions of admissibility laid down in s 76A(2). Admittedly, such cases will be far from common. However, let us imagine that at a *voire dire*, D2 has initially satisfied the court on a balance of probabilities that D1's confession, which is relevant to 'a matter in issue in the proceedings', has not been obtained by illicit means, and that the confession has been ruled admissible and given in evidence. Evidence subsequently emerges suggesting that, contrary to what had previously been assumed, D1's confession was in fact obtained in violation of PACE, s 76A(2). The judge cannot rely upon PACE, s 78 since this discretion only applies to 'evidence upon which the prosecution proposes to rely'. The judge almost certainly cannot have recourse to the old common law discretion, retained by PACE, s 82(3), as it too only ever covered evidence the prosecution sought to have admitted. Although it is true that s 82(3) does declare in general terms that 'nothing in this Part of the Act shall prejudice any power of a court to exclude evidence... at its discretion', the strong implication is that this refers to existing powers to exclude evidence rather than to any more extensive power the court might subsequently arrogate to itself to exclude otherwise admissible evidence. Joint trials, of course, tend to be controlled by other means. Thus, judges may sever indictments under the Indictments Act 1915, s 5(3) if they are of the view that D1 and/or D2 would be 'prejudiced or embarrassed in [his/their] defence' if tried jointly. The judge also possesses a far-reaching power to stay proceedings and to order a retrial if the fairness of the proceedings has been compromised—probably the most satisfactory solution in this eventuality. It is also open to judges who have changed their minds simply to deliver a warning to the jury to disregard the confession.

Confessions by third parties, the prosecution and the hearsay rule

10.70 Traditionally, in English law a confession has largely been treated as evidence only against the party who made it. Statements in X's confession implicating another person, Y, have not been generally admissible as evidence against Y. As we have seen, in the case of co-accused PACE, s 76A now permits one co-accused, D1, to pray in aid the confession of another co-accused, D2, provided that it is relevant to D1's defence and the conditions of admissibility laid down in s 76A are satisfied (see *ante*, paras **10.60–10.69**). However, the hearsay provisions of Part 11 of the Criminal Justice Act 2003 (see *ante*, Chapter 9) have additionally allowed the *prosecution* in certain limited circumstances to put in evidence X's confession at the trial of Y if X's confession happens to implicate Y.

10.71 In *R v Y* [2008] 1 WLR 1683 Y stood trial, alone, for murder. Another man, X, who had subsequently pleaded guilty to the offence, had made a confession implicating Y in that murder. The Crown applied unsuccessfully to have X's statement admitted at Y's trial in the interests of justice under s 114(1)(d) of the Criminal Justice Act 2003. (On s 114(1)(d), see *ante*, paras **9.70–9.80**.) The trial judge was of the view that s 114(1)(d) had no application to a hearsay statement contained in the confession of someone other than the accused, and any such statement was therefore inadmissible. It was argued on behalf of Y that because s 118, r 5 had preserved the common law rules governing the admissibility of confessions, s 118 had also preserved the common law principle that a confession was only evidence against its maker, not against third parties. The Court of Appeal held that this reasoning betrayed a misunderstanding of the scope of s 114(1)(d). As Hughes LJ explained, the Law Commission's report, upon which the hearsay provisions of the Criminal Justice Act 2003 were closely modelled, demonstrates conclusively that, in proposing what became s 114(1)(d), the Commission meant to grant the court a residual judicial power to admit hearsay evidence which would not otherwise be admissible. Indeed, one example furnished in the Commission's report (Law Com no 245, 1997, para 8.147) shows that one of the situations in which it was contemplated that that residual power might be exercised occurred where the hearsay was contained in a non-defendant's confession, which would neither be admissible at common law, nor under any other provision of the 2003 Act, nor under PACE, s 76A. Viewing the four categories of exception to the hearsay rule set out in s 114(1) of the 2003 Act, the Court concluded that hearsay contained in another party's confession, in law, is as open to admission under s 114(1)(d) as any other item of hearsay.

10.72 Although the decision in *R v Y* recognises in principle that the prosecution may be entitled to adduce evidence of X's confession at Y's trial in order to implicate Y, Hughes LJ stressed that this does not signify that hearsay contained in, or associated with, third party confessions will be routinely admitted under s 114(1)(d). Admission of such evidence will be conditional upon the perceived interests of justice, as defined in the nine factors listed in s 114(2) of the 2003 Act (see *ante*, para **9.72**). The nature of the vehicle which carries that statement (and whether it is associated with a confession or otherwise) is going to be most pertinent to the question whether it is in the interests of justice to admit it. A bare accusation against someone, whether associated with a confession by the maker or not, is perfectly capable of falling within s 114(1)(d). Moreover, the rules of admissibility are identical whether the prosecution or the defence is seeking admission of the evidence. Neither the fact that the hearsay is an accusation against the defendant rather than an admission against interest by the maker, nor the fact that it is the Crown rather than the defence which seeks to adduce the evidence, can rule out the application of s 114(1)(d) as a matter of law. However, those two factors, together with any other material considerations, will be highly relevant to the exercise of judicial judgment under s 114(2). As Hughes LJ pointed out,

> [The judge] will of course remember that the statute does not render hearsay automatically admissible, and the reasons why it is not. Put broadly, they are that hearsay is

necessarily second best evidence, and that it is for that reason much more difficult to test and to assess. The jury never sees the person whose word is being relied upon. That person cannot be asked a single exploratory or challenging question about what he said. Those very real disadvantages of hearsay evidence, which underlay the common law rule generally excluding it, remain critical to the assessment of whether the interests of justice call for its admission.

(at [56])

In a case such as *R v Y*, the interests-of-justice test requires that heed be paid to the difference between a declarant's admission against interest and an accusation made against someone else. It does not necessarily follow that the interests of justice will point in the same direction upon an application by the Crown as they might upon an application made by a defendant:

[T]he greatest care must be taken, before admitting an out-of-court statement under s 114(1)(d), to ensure that the s 114(2) factors are fully considered and that overall it is genuinely in the interests of justice that the jury should be asked to rely on the statement without seeing its maker and without any question being addressed to him about it. It is not the effect of s 114(1)(d) that out-of-court statements, whether by co-accused or any-one else, are routinely to be admitted.

(at [62])

Just to underline the point, Hughes LJ stressed that the decision in *R v Y* was not intended to provide the Crown with a ready means of putting in evidence all manner of allegations third parties might make against eventual defendants in the course of police enquiries:

The existence of s 114(1)(d) does not make police interviews routinely admissible in the case of persons other than the interviewee, and . . . the reasons why they are ordinarily not admissible except in the case of the interviewee are likely to continue to mean that in the great majority of cases it will not be in the interests of justice to admit them in the case of any other person

(at [57]. See also *Ibrahim et al* [2008] 2 Cr App R 23 at [144]–[152])

FURTHER READING

Choo, 'Corroboration of Disputed Confessions' (1991) 107 LQR 544

Gudjonsson, *The Psychology of Interrogations, Confessions and Testimony* (1992, Chichester) chs 4–7 and 10–12

Hartshorne, 'Defensive Use of a Co-accused's Confession and the Criminal Justice Act 2003' (2004) 8 E & P 165

Hirst, 'Confessions as Proof of Innocence' [1998] CLJ 146

Kassim and Kiechel, 'The Social Psychology of False Confessions: Compliance, Internalization, and Confabulation' (1996) 7 Psych Sci 125

Mirfield, 'Successive Confessions and the Poisonous Tree' [1996] Crim LR 554

Mirfield, *Silence, Confessions and Improperly Obtained Evidence* (1998, Oxford) chs 2–8 and 10

Munday, 'Adverse Denial and Purposive Confession' [2003] Crim LR 850

Munday, 'The Court, the Dictionary, and the True Meaning of "Oppression": A Neo-Socratic Dialogue on English Legal Method' [2005] 26 Statute Law Review 103

Pattenden, 'Should Confessions be Corroborated?' (1991) 107 LQR 317

SELF-TEST QUESTIONS

1. Ought false denials to be treated as confessions within the meaning of PACE, s 82 (1)?

2. ' "I am trying," Rowe said with a flash of anger, "to tell you all I know. . . . In English law isn't a man supposed to be innocent until you prove him guilty? I'm ready to tell you everything I can remember about the murder, but I'm not a murderer." The plump man began to smile. He drew out his hands and looked at his nails and tucked them back again. "That's interesting, Mr Rowe," he said. "You mentioned murder, but I have said nothing about murder to you, and no paper has mentioned murder. . . yet." ' (Graham Greene, *The Ministry of Fear* (1943))

   Assume that, following his interrogation by the plump detective, Rowe has been charged with murder and that, as part of its case, the Crown wishes to adduce in evidence what Rowe said to him on this occasion. Could Rowe contest the admissibility of this exchange under s 76 of PACE on the ground that his words constituted a 'confession' within the meaning of s 82(1)?

3. Whilst at work, Helot's gold Rolex watch disappears from a drawer of his desk during the lunch hour. Helot works in a secure area of the company, entry to which is by swipe card only. Immediately upon learning of the possible theft of the watch, Helot's employer, Draco, posts notices and sends an internal email to all employees in which he says that there is great concern at the loss and that the police will be informed at close of business if the missing watch is not retrieved. The notice and the email also remind staff that the swipe card system in force in this area enables one to know exactly who was in that particular area at the relevant time, adding that theft is an automatic sacking offence under the terms of their contracts of employment. Within ten minutes of circulation of the email, a fellow employee, Ooze, calls upon Draco

and says: 'Look, I was in the area at the time. But so were a lot of other people. I want you to know the disappearance of that watch had nothing to do with me.' The watch is never found, but eventually various items of circumstantial evidence point to Ooze as the culprit and he is charged with theft. Advise the prosecution which, at the trial, wishes to include in its case evidence of Ooze's reaction to Draco's messages. Discuss.

4. What constitutes 'oppression' under s 76(2)(a) of PACE?

5. Chump, who has had no previous dealings with the police, is being questioned at the police station by PC Brisket, who suspects him of shoplifting. PC Brisket has cautioned Chump twice as Chump said that he did not understand the caution the first time the policeman parroted it. Chump is very agitated and asks to see a lawyer. PC Brisket explains that while that can be arranged, it does unfortunately tend to delay matters. 'Most suspects,' PC Brisket adds, 'do not understand what their lawyer is telling them anyway. Frankly, nor does the lawyer!' Chump says: ' Look, my mum is really ill in hospital. I've got to see her. The doctor's put me on pills. Let's just get this over with. I'll say whatever you like.' PC Brisket switches on the tape recorder, the interview commences and Chump confesses to shoplifting. PC Brisket goes round to Chump's flat and, just as Chump claimed, finds stolen goods concealed behind a partition in the bathroom. Discuss.

6. When do breaches of the PACE Codes of Practice typically lead to confessions being ruled inadmissible by the trial judge?

7. ' "Did he, Sherry?" I barked into the still face. The dead or dying man didn't move. I cautiously moved my fingers again so that his dead or dying head nodded, twice. Then I made his head jerk back, and let it gently down on the floor again. "Well," I said, standing up and facing Ringgo, "I've got you at last." '

   In this story by Dashiell Hammett ('The Farewell Murder', first published in *Black Mask* in February 1930), a private detective seeks to extract a confession to murder by manipulating a dying or, more likely, dead witness's head so as make it appear that the latter is nodding in assent. At the time the killer, Ringgo, says nothing; but later, under police interrogation, Ringgo confesses to the slaying. How would an English court approach the admissibility of this evidence? (Consider, *inter alia, Christie* [1914] AC 545 and evidence deriving from statements made in the presence of a party.)

8. In *Dunford* (1990) 91 Cr App R 150 McPherson, J took what he termed 'an overall and practical view' and ruled a confession admissible in a case where a suspect with form had been wrongfully deprived of legal advice during interrogation. Is there any reason to think that a court today might treat a similar case differently?

9. What classes of person are bound under s 67(9) of PACE to comply with the PACE Codes of Practice?

10. What role does the old common law discretion, expressly retained by s 82(3) of PACE, arguably play today in the law relating to confessions?

11. Where co-accused are jointly tried, if D1's confession is ruled inadmissible under s 76 of PACE, what use, if any, may D2 make of D1's confession?

12. 'A killer dubbed the Fat Ripper owned up to murdering three women after he was given cash to buy Mars Bars. Police say 20st Philip Smith, 36, moaned about £400 seized from his flat. He was given it back to buy hundreds of bars while in jail. At trial he finally admitted his Midlands killing spree. Police have just revealed the rant. They hope Brummie Smith will now admit to more murders.' (*The Sun*, 4 January 2005, 28).

   Discuss the admissibility of this confession to three murders, imagining that Smith had recanted before trial.

11

Drawing adverse inferences from a defendant's omissions, lies or false alibis

SUMMARY

I. Inferences drawn from the defendant's silence

- Erosion of English law's traditional right of silence

- The right of silence and European human rights law

II. The silence provisions of the Criminal Justice and Public Order Act 1994

- Section 34: the effect of the defendant's failure to mention facts when questioned or charged

  - The underlying purposes of s 34

  - Legal advice

- Failure to mention facts following legal advice

  - Failure to mention facts and legal professional privilege

  - Rebutting charges of recent fabrication

  - When will waiver be held to have taken place?

  - 'Circumventing' s 34: the pre-prepared statement

  - 'Circumventing' s 34: declining to be questioned

- Section 34 only applies to facts upon which the defendant subsequently relies at trial

  - What constitutes a 'fact'?

  - Uncontested facts

  - Must the defendant's failure be independent of the issue of guilt?

- Directing the jury on s 34
  - Failures to mention facts following legal advice
  - Instructing a jury not to draw an inference
- The relationship between s 34 of the 1994 Act and s 78 of PACE
- Section 36: the effect of a defendant's failure or refusal to account for objects, substances or marks
- Section 37: the effect of a defendant's failure or refusal to account for his presence in a particular place
- Section 35: drawing an adverse inference when the defendant elects not to give evidence at trial
  - Section 34 and s 35 directions distinguished
- The silence provisions: an envoi
- The effect of a defendant's silence at common law
- The right of silence and evidence obtained under compulsion

III. Inferences drawn from lies told by the defendant: *Lucas* directions

IV. Inferences drawn from false alibis put forward by the defendant

---

On what grounds? Lucas was caught within two minutes after the shot, standing over the body with a recently-fired pistol in his pocket. He never denied having fired it; in fact he refused to make any statement at all, even to me, his lawyer—the lawyer he himself sent for.

William Faulkner, *Intruder in the Dust* (1949)

I. Inferences drawn from the defendant's silence

Erosion of English law's traditional right of silence

11.1 Those familiar with William Faulkner's powerful novel, *Intruder in the Dust*, will be aware that Lucas was innocent and, despite being discovered in what appeared to be the most incriminating situation, had the strongest motives for saying nothing. A suspect's silence in response to questioning may be suspicious: the normal reaction to an accusation, it is commonly thought, is to volunteer a response. Only the guilty have anything to hide. Alternatively, silence may be ambiguous—even deceptive. There are often good, and sometimes noble reasons to explain why a particular defendant may have kept silent. Nevertheless, rather after the manner of confessions, in given circumstances a defendant's silence, either during the investigative phase of criminal proceedings or at his trial, may ground an adverse inference.

When the decision was taken in 1994 to introduce legislation formally enabling the tribunal of fact, if it thought fit, to draw an adverse inference from the defendant's failure to respond to questioning, the Act had to thread its way through a veritable minefield of motivational and procedural considerations. The relevant provisions are predictably complex.

11.2 Prior to the enactment of the Criminal Justice and Public Order Act 1994, English law recognised that an accused had a right of silence in the sense of a privilege against self-incrimination. As Lord Mustill has pointed out, the expressions 'privilege against self-incrimination' and 'right of silence' actually refer to several loosely linked rules or principles of immunity (*R v Director of Serious Fraud Office, ex p Smith* [1993] AC 1, 30–1). They may refer to the fact that the defendant ought not to be compelled to undergo inquisition by the prosecution or the court at his trial, a procedure which would be inconsistent with English law's notions of fairness. Alternatively, these terms can refer to pre-trial investigations and to prohibitions imposed on the questioning of suspects who have not been cautioned or who have already been charged. This second category of prohibitions is made up of what Lord Hoffmann has termed 'prophylactic rules designed to inhibit abuse of power by investigatory authorities and to preserve the fairness of the trial by preventing the eliciting of confessions which may have doubtful probative value' (*R v Hertfordshire County Council, ex p Green Environmental Industries Ltd* [2000] 2 AC 412, 419). Finally, there is a general privilege not to be compelled to answer questions put by persons in authority, a principle founded upon what Lord Mustill in *ex p Smith* called 'the common view that one person should so far as possible be entitled to tell another person to mind his own business'.

11.3 Although these various privileges are subject to a variety of exceptions, they used to mean that a suspect could exercise a so-called 'right of silence' during police interrogation. While it was not uncommon for a jury to learn that he had made no comment during interview, the jury would not be directed by the judge to consider drawing an inference adverse to the defendant by reason of his having taken this course. Similarly, the defendant was entitled not to give evidence at his trial and, again, the jury would not be instructed that they could assume the worst from his omission to testify. Indeed, judges sometimes took the opposite tack, emphasising that the onus of proof in a criminal case lies squarely on the Crown and informing the jury that the defendant may simply sit back and say, 'Prove your case'. Thus, at the trial of Dr Bodkin Adams, Devlin J directed the jury in the following terms:

> The law on this matter reflects the natural thought of England. So great is, and always has been our horror at the idea that a man might be questioned, forced to speak and perhaps to condemn himself out of his own mouth that we grant to everyone suspected or

accused of crime at the beginning, at every stage and until the very end the right to say: "Ask me no questions. I shall answer none. Prove your case".

Patrick Devlin, *Easing the Passing* (1985, Oxford) p 176

11.4 The Royal Commission on Criminal Justice, chaired by Lord Runciman, which reported in 1993, examined the use made of the right of silence and concluded that, contrary to suggestions from some quarters, the right was not being widely abused by professional criminals and that, if it were removed, there would actually be a risk of increasing the number of miscarriages of justice. Responding to the blandishments of persistent lobbyists like the Association of Chief Police Officers and anxious to appear tough on law and order, the government however ignored the Royal Commission's opinion and proceeded to enact ss 34–38 of the Criminal Justice and Public Order Act 1994. Whether portrayed as an act of political courage or of ill-judged pig-headedness, the product is an unusually intricate piece of legislation. The Act soon yielded a dense crop of appellate case law and has encountered predictable difficulty in satisfying the overriding requirement of 'fair trial' imposed by Article 6 of the European Convention on Human Rights.

11.5 Sections 34, 36 and 37 of the 1994 Act, which overlap with one another to a degree, set out to transform English evidentiary culture in relation to the investigation of crime. Whereas before the 1994 Act a suspect was under no more than a civic obligation to assist the police with their enquiries and could freely decline to answer questions without fear of legal reprisal, the new provisions proceed upon the assumption that a suspect as a rule ought to cooperate with the investigating authorities. It is intrinsically suspicious if he does not do so. Unless he has good reason for withholding cooperation, a defendant's refusal to respond to certain requests for information is capable of grounding an adverse inference if the tribunal of fact feels it appropriate to draw one. Buttressing these provisions, s 35 additionally permits the tribunal of fact to draw an adverse inference from the defendant's failure to give evidence at trial in most circumstances.

11.6 Sections 34, 36 and 37, it should be said, provide for the drawing of inferences in four distinct situations:

- when a court is hearing an application for dismissal of a serious fraud charge under the Criminal Justice Act 1967, s 6;

- when applying for dismissal of a charge falling under the notice of transfer provisions of the Criminal Justice Act 1991;

- when a court determines whether there is a case to answer; and finally

- when the court or jury is determining whether the accused is guilty of the offence charged.

For the sake of simplicity, discussion of these provisions will be confined to the fourth class of situation, where the court is concerned to determine the accused's guilt. Also, although the 1994 Act applies with equal force to both Crown Court and magistrates' courts, this chapter will concentrate almost exclusively on jury trials.

The right of silence and European human rights law

11.7 Recognising that the silence provisions of the 1994 Act have undermined an established common law right—a right which had almost acquired constitutional sanctity—the Court of Appeal has signalled the spirit in which this legislation ought to be interpreted. In *Bowden* [1999] 1 WLR 823 Lord Bingham CJ warned that since ss 34–38 'restrict rights recognized at common law as appropriate to protect defendants against the risk of injustice they should not be construed more widely than the statutory language requires'. In *Birchall* [1999] Crim LR 311 his Lordship further cautioned:

> The drawing of inferences from silence is a particularly sensitive area. Many respected authorities have voiced the fear that s 35 and its sister sections may lead to wrongful convictions. It seems very possible that the application of these provisions could lead to decisions adverse to the United Kingdom at Strasbourg under article 6(1) and 6(2) of the European Convention on Human Rights unless the provisions are the subject of very carefully framed directions to juries.

Lord Bingham CJ's remarks in *Bowden* have since been strongly endorsed by the House of Lords in *Webber* [2004] 1 Cr App R 40, where it was said that, bearing in mind that in the former case the remarks were made with particular reference to legal professional privilege,

> It is indeed important, if the statutory provisions are not to be an instrument of unfairness and abuse, that the statutory safeguards are strictly observed, the jury directions are carefully framed and, in cases under s 34, that care is taken to identify the specific facts relied on at trial which were not mentioned during questioning.
>
> (at [27])

11.8 These latter remarks allude in part to the European Court of Human Rights' decision in *Murray v UK* (1996) 22 EHRR 29, a terrorist case from Northern Ireland, a jurisdiction whose silence provisions quite closely resembled those of the 1994 Act. *Murray v UK* was concerned with whether M had received a 'fair trial' under Article 6 of the European Convention on Human Rights, given that the trial court had drawn an adverse inference from the fact that M had declined to answer police questions. It may be premonitory that, in rejecting the claim that Article 6 had been breached, a majority of the judges of the European Court of Human Rights appeared to derive comfort, on the one hand, from the strength of the evidence the prosecution had assembled against M even discounting any inferences that might be drawn from his silence during police questioning and, on the other, from the additional consideration that the trial was presided over by an experienced judge (sitting without a jury) who gave a reasoned judgment explaining the role the inferences had played in his ultimate decision. One might infer from this that had inferences from silence played a bigger part in the prosecution case and/or had the tribunal of fact been a jury of laypersons handing down an inscrutable verdict, the Court might well have felt justified in coming to a different conclusion on whether Article 6's requirement of fair trial had been met in the case. As the ECtHR indicated in the subsequent case of *Condron and Condron v UK* (2000) 8 BHRC 290, these are indeed factors to be taken into account in determining whether a particular defendant has received a fair trial. In *Condron v UK*, the Court stated:

> [T]he fact that the issue of the applicants' silence was left to a jury cannot of itself be considered incompatible with the requirements of a fair trial. It is, rather, another relevant consideration to be weighed in the balance when assessing whether or not it is fair to do so in the circumstances.
>
> (at [57])

11.9 Significantly, in *Murray v UK*, the European Court explicitly declared:

> [T]he right to remain silent under police questioning and the privilege against self-incrimination are generally recognized international standards which lie at the heart of the notion of a fair procedure under Article 6.

As both *Murray v UK* and *Condron v UK* make clear, the right of silence is not absolute. Indeed:

> Whether the drawing of inferences from an accused's silence infringes Article 6 is a matter to be determined in the light of all the circumstances of the case, having regard to the situations where inferences may be drawn, the weight attached to them by the national courts in their assessment of the evidence and the degree of compulsion inherent in the situation.
>
> (at [47])

Yet, the right of silence is so central to the concept of fair trial that 'particular caution was required before a domestic court could invoke an accused's silence against him'. Moreover, in the context of jury trial, the safeguards provided for in the 1994 legislation and in the directions which judges are bound to give to juries in their summings-up are all the more important. As the court stressed in *Condron*, because it is impossible to gauge how important is the role played by inferences derived from silence in an inscrutable jury verdict and since additionally their decision is not subject to review on the facts, 'it [is] thus even more compelling to ensure that the jury [is] properly advised on how to address the issue of [the accused's] silence' (at [62]). Significant judicial failures to deliver the prescribed directions, therefore, 'must be seen as incompatible with the exercise by [the defendant] of [his] right to silence at the police station'. The ECtHR has followed this approach in other cases, such as *Beckles v UK* (2002) 13 BHRC 522, where the trial judge's failure to direct the jury fully in a case in which B had declined to answer police questions on the explicit advice of his solicitor was adjudged to have infringed B's right to a fair trial:

> Having regard to the fact that it is impossible to ascertain the weight, if any, given by the jury to [B's] silence, it was crucial that the jury was correctly directed on this matter.
>
> (at [65])

The full import of the ECtHR's stance becomes apparent if one considers a domestic case like *Bristow and Jones* [2002] EWCA Crim 1571. J, who had been hired to commit a contract killing, had made no comment when interviewed by the police. The trial judge delivered a defective direction to the jury on how to approach the drawing of inferences under s 34, notably omitting to tell them that silence alone could not prove guilt or to deliver a direction on reasonable expectations (*post*, paras **11.34–11.36**). Even though the Court of Appeal admitted that it was 'unlikely' that J's silence played a significant role in the jury's decision to convict, nevertheless the ECtHR's decision in *Condron and Condron* compelled it to hold that these defects in 'what was otherwise an admirable summing-up' amounted to a material irregularity and to quash J's conviction, on the ground that 'the jury may have convicted on a basis which did not give effect to the qualified protection to the right of silence provided by the law'.

11.10 Following adverse rulings and minatory rumblings in the ECtHR, the Youth Justice and Criminal Evidence Act 1999, s 58 sought to make the silence provisions more human rights-compatible. It amended the 1994 legislation, decreeing that no adverse inference might be drawn under ss 34, 36 and 37 unless the accused first has had an opportunity to consult a solicitor. Section 59 of the 1999 Act, it might be added, also restricted the use to which answers and statements made by the defendant under compulsion may be put, following the ECtHR's decision in *Saunders v UK* (1996) 23 EHRR 313 (*post*, para **11.65**).

II. The silence provisions of the Criminal Justice and Public Order Act 1994

'What the jury may infer, given no help from the court, is one thing. What it may infer when the court solemnizes the silence of the accused into evidence against him is quite another.'
Griffin v California, 380 US 609, 614 *per* Justice Douglas

Section 34: the effect of the defendant's failure to mention facts when questioned or charged

11.11 As Waller LJ remarked in *Bresa* [2005] EWCA Crim 1414 at [51]; [2006] Crim LR 179: 'Section 34 is a very difficult area.' Section 34 of the Criminal Justice and Public Order Act 1994 provides:

(1) Where . . . evidence is given that an accused—

(a) at any time before he was charged with the offence, on being questioned under caution by a constable trying to discover whether or by whom the offence had been committed, failed to mention any fact relied on in his defence in those proceedings; or

(b) on being charged with the offence or officially informed that he might be prosecuted for it, failed to mention any such fact,

being a fact which in the circumstances existing at the time the accused could reasonably have been expected to mention when so questioned, charged or informed, as the case may be, subs (2) below applies.

(2) Where this subs applies—

. . .

(d) the court or jury, in determining whether the accused is guilty of the offence charged,

may draw such inferences from the failure as appear proper.

As Rose LJ pointed out in *Roble* [1997] EWCA Crim 118, s 34 is intended to achieve two purposes:

• it is meant to discourage an accused from fabricating a defence late in the day; and

• it is also designed to encourage the accused to make speedy disclosure of any genuine defence or any fact which may go towards establishing a genuine defence.

It is crucial to have these purposes in mind when interpreting this convoluted provision.

The underlying purposes of s 34

11.12 Section 34 sets out to achieve the two objectives set down in *Roble*, by allowing the tribunal of fact to 'draw such inferences...as appear proper' from the defendant's unreasonably failing to mention facts upon which he subsequently relies in his defence. The propriety of drawing these inferences is dependent upon whether, in the circumstances existing at the time, the defendant could reasonably have been expected to mention particular facts when questioned, charged or informed that he might be prosecuted. The issue of what the defendant might reasonably have been expected to mention may arise in two ways under the provision.

- The defendant may seek to argue that it would have been completely unreasonable to have expected him to mention something at the relevant time. The fact in question, for instance, may have been unknown to him at the relevant time or, even if known, its significance would not have been properly appreciated. Evidently, if the Crown has no proof that at the relevant time the defendant was aware of a fact upon which he subsequently relies at trial, it will be inappropriate to direct a jury to consider drawing an adverse inference from his failure to have mentioned it. In *B (MT)* [2000] Crim LR 181, B, who was indicted for sexual offences with two girls, at interview had claimed that he knew of no motive for their making false allegations against him, but at trial testified that one of the girls hated him because he had come between her and her mother. Since the Crown had not explored at trial whether B actually knew of the girl's hatred at the time of his interview, it could not show that B's testimony was anything more than speculation, and certainly the Crown could not demonstrate that this was a fact which B ought reasonably to have mentioned at interview.

  Equally, owing to circumstances such as extreme mental impairment, the defendant's condition at the relevant time may make it impossible to draw any conclusion as to what it would have been reasonable for him to have mentioned at interview, when charged, etc. In such cases, the question for the judge is whether it is even appropriate to instruct the jurors that they are entitled to draw an inference from the accused's failure to mention facts, should they deem it 'proper' under s 34(2). Thus, in *R v Central Criminal Court, ex p S and P* (1998) 163 JP 776, 786–9 we learn incidentally that, after a *voire dire*, a youth court refused to apply s 34 in the case of one co-accused who had an IQ of only 51.

- Alternatively, the judge may determine that it is open to the jury to draw an inference, in which case the jury must be carefully instructed on how to approach the question, to infer or not to infer. The judge will need to give the jury guidance on what 'circumstances existing at the time' must be taken into account. This may include a very wide range of factors. For instance, the extent to which the police have disclosed information to the suspect or his legal adviser prior to interview may affect what it would have been reasonable for the suspect to mention at interview. Rose LJ specifically adverted to this possibility in *Roble*, when he said:

Good reason may well arise if…, the interviewing officer has disclosed to a solicitor little or nothing of the nature of the case against the defendant, so that the solicitor cannot usefully advise his client.

In similar manner, the personal health and state of mind of the defendant may have a bearing on what he might reasonably have disclosed. (JSB specimen direction no 40 suggested a model that judges should adopt in their summings-up.) In *Argent* [1997] 2 Cr App R 27, Lord Bingham CJ enumerated the sort of circumstances that might be relevant in this context:

Like so many other questions in criminal trials this is a question to be resolved by the jury in the exercise of their collective common sense, experience and understanding of human nature. Sometimes they may conclude that it was reasonable for the defendant to have held his peace for a host of reasons, such as that he was tired, ill, frightened, drunk, drugged, unable to understand what was going on, suspicious of the police, afraid that his answer would not be fairly recorded, worried at committing himself without legal advice, or some other reason accepted by the jury.

(at 33)

Legal advice

11.13 The drawing of an inference under s 34 is conditional upon the defendant having previously been afforded an opportunity to take legal advice. The Youth Justice and Criminal Evidence Act 1999 added a new s 34(2A), which states:

Where the accused was at an authorised place of detention at the time of the failure, subss (1) and (2) above do not apply if he had not been allowed an opportunity to consult a solicitor prior to being questioned, charged or informed as mentioned in subs (1) above.

'Authorised place of detention' essentially refers to police stations (s 38(2A)).

Failure to mention facts following legal advice

11.14 An accused will not infrequently have failed to mention facts following legal advice. This will not necessarily avail him. An argument commonly put forward in a bid to prevent or counter the drawing of adverse inferences is that, when he refused to answer police questions, the defendant was simply acting on legal advice. The argument has some force. PACE clearly stipulates—notably, in s 56 and Code C:6—that a suspect is generally entitled to legal advice before and during police interrogation. Given the difficulty of deciding when it is still tactically open to a suspect to decline to answer particular questions under the complex silence provisions of the 1994 Act, it is unquestionably more important than ever that a suspect should possess and, indeed, exercise this right to legal advice. To confuse matters, when the 1994 Act was first introduced the Law Society informed its members that they could still advise clients not to answer questions in police interrogation. Clearly, in view of these circumstances, if his solicitor tells the suspect 'You do not need to respond to the police officer's question', it might be difficult to portray the latter's consequent failure to mention facts as unreasonable. Indeed, in the context of police interrogation, it might appear distinctly unreasonable for a suspect to ignore the advice of the solicitor sitting at his elbow. If the suspect does act upon his lawyer's advice and omits to mention facts upon which he subsequently relies at trial, one could argue that it is wholly unfair to visit upon the suspect the omissions of the lawyer. It is true that the lawyer is acting for him. But even if the lawyer's advice to keep silent is completely dotty, the reasonable course for a suspect, assuming that he is unskilled in the perplexities of criminal evidence, is still to comply with the instructions of the solicitor.

11.15 The Court of Appeal has grappled with these difficulties more than once. Notably, in *Argent* [1997] 2 Cr App R 27 Lord Bingham CJ declared:

> Under s 34, the jury is not concerned with the correctness of the solicitor's advice, nor with whether it complies with the Law Society's guidelines, but with the reasonableness of the [defendant's] conduct in all the circumstances which the jury have found to exist. One of those circumstances, and a very relevant one, is the advice given to a defendant. There is no reason to doubt that the advice given to the [defendant] is a matter for the jury to consider. But, neither the Law Society by its guidance, nor the solicitor by his advice can preclude consideration by the jury of the issue which Parliament has left to the jury to determine.
>
> (at 35–36)

Thus, while legal advice is a relevant factor for the jury to take into account in deciding whether actually to draw an inference from the accused's omission to mention a fact, it will not render him immune from a judicial direction inviting the jury to consider the question. The paradoxical implication of *Argent* is that the courts consider that, despite the pains Parliament took when enacting PACE to guarantee a suspect a right to legal advice before and during interrogation, it can still be inherently unreasonable for the suspect to take that advice! It is difficult to suppress a wry smile. (See further, *Hoare and Pierce, post*, para **11.40**.) In Hughes LJ's words in *Daha Essa* [2009] EWCA Crim 43:

> [T]he significance of s 34 does not lie in silence in interview, it lies in reliance at trial on something that should have been said in interview. … [I]t is important to remember that the acid question in any s 34 case is not: was it reasonable to rely on the solicitor's advice?

Rather it is: could the appellant reasonably have been expected to say what he now relies upon at trial? The first question must be answered *en route* to the second, but the second is the one that matters.

(at [15])

Failure to mention facts and legal professional privilege

11.16 Suspects not infrequently exercise their right to have access to a lawyer prior to or during interrogation. If the lawyer advised the suspect not to answer particular questions, at trial the defendant may try to inhibit the jury from drawing an adverse inference from his failure to put his cards on the table at interview by revealing that his silence was dictated by legal advice. However, if the defendant does give this as his reason for failing to answer questions, the gambit is liable to lead to waiver of his legal professional privilege. The courts adopt the line that it would be all too easy for a defendant simply to claim that he was acting under legal instructions not to answer questions. If the court required no more of him than the statement that the solicitor advised him to maintain silence, the effect would be to drive a coach-and-four through s 34. Solicitors could routinely advise their clients to stay silent and the latter would incur no risk of adverse inferences being drawn. Such cannot have been the intention of the 1994 Act. Not surprisingly, therefore, the courts have repeatedly held that a defendant will invariably need to do more than merely assert that he was acting on legal advice in order to avoid the jury's being invited to consider drawing an adverse inference.

11.17 This raises delicate issues. As we have seen, communications between lawyer and client are privileged. A court cannot compel their disclosure unless the client waives that privilege (see *ante*, para **3.47**). But if the defendant is to convince the court not to draw an adverse inference from his failure to mention facts falling within s 34, he may have no option but to waive privilege. The Court of Appeal first discussed this issue in *Condron* [1997] 1 WLR 827. The court began with the proposition that an accused's bare assertion that he acted on legal advice 'is unlikely by itself to be regarded as a sufficient reason for not mentioning matters relevant to the defence'. Therefore, to prevent the court from drawing the inference he will need to 'state the basis or the reason for the advice'. Indeed, it is not unlikely that the defendant will actually wish to call his solicitor to testify as to why the latter gave this advice, allowing the prosecution then to explore in cross-examination the reasons for the advice. More particularly, the prosecution will wish to investigate whether the advice was prompted simply by tactical considerations—in which case, of course, the drawing of an inference may still be justified. Does this procedure amount to a waiver by the defendant of legal professional privilege?

11.18 Legal professional privilege, defined in PACE s 10, has been termed 'a fundamental condition on which the administration of justice as a whole rests' and, incongruously, was even recognised in one case as a right protected under the ECHR (*R v Derby Magistrates' Court, ex p B* [1996] AC 487, 507 *per* Lord Taylor CJ; see generally *ante*, paras **3.33–3.50**). The principle is so fundamental that a rule under the Civil Procedure Rules purporting to restrict its ambit was declared *ultra vires* and unenforceable (*General Mediterranean Holdings SA v Patel* [2000] 1 WLR 272). It is thought vital that an accused should be able to consult freely with his lawyer. Legal professional privilege, however, attaches to the client. As Lord Bingham CJ explained in *Bowden* [1999] 1 WLR 823:

> A waiver ordinarily occurs when a client chooses to...reveal the effect of a communication protected by the privilege: he cannot claim privilege for that which he has voluntarily revealed. It makes no difference whether the revelation is made by the client or by the legal adviser acting within the scope of his authority as agent on behalf of the client. Nor does it matter when the disclosure is made.
>
> (at 828)

Rebutting charges of recent fabrication

11.19 Not every revelation will amount to a waiver. If a defendant merely seeks to rebut Crown suggestions that his story is a recent fabrication by calling his lawyer to say that the client did indeed communicate the relevant facts to him at an earlier stage, there is authority that holds that the defendant will not necessarily be treated as having waived legal professional privilege. In this situation, the lawyer is said to be 'in the same position as anyone else' called to rebut an allegation of recent concoction (*Condron*; cf *Benjamin* (1913) 8 Cr App R 146, *ante*, paras **5.22–5.25**). More therefore is required. As Lord Bingham CJ explained in *Bowden*:

> If, at trial, the defendant or his solicitor gives evidence not merely of the defendant's refusal to answer pre-trial questions on legal advice but also of the grounds on which such advice was given, or if (as here) the defence elicit evidence at trial of a statement made by the defendant or his solicitor pre-trial of the grounds on which legal advice had been given to answer no questions, the defendant voluntarily withdraws the veil of privilege which would otherwise protect confidential communications between his legal adviser and himself, and having done so he cannot resist questioning directed to the nature of that advice and the factual premises on which it had been based.
>
> (at 829–30)

In *Bowden*, B, who was convicted of robbery, had declined to answer questions at three police interviews and, more particularly, had omitted to reveal until the trial that his mother had paid for a holiday he took in the Canary Islands only four days after the robbery. At the third interview, B's solicitor informed the police that he had instructed his client to say nothing. At trial B did not lead evidence of the solicitor's statement, but elicited this information during cross-examination of a police officer. It was held that the trial judge had rightly allowed the Crown to cross-examine B about what he had told his solicitor about the holiday; privilege had been waived.

When will waiver be held to have taken place?

11.20 Until recently, the case law on waiver of legal professional privilege engendered considerable confusion. In *Seaton* [2011] 1 Cr App R 2 at [43], however, Hughes LJ reviewed the authorities and instilled order by reinterpreting one leading case, *Wilmot* (1989) 89 Cr App R 341, and by reducing the subject to eight broad propositions. These are (a)–(h):

> (a) *Legal professional privilege is of paramount importance.* There is no question of balancing privilege against other considerations of public interest.

This proposition, of course, is enshrined in *Derby Magistrates' Court, ex p B* [1996] AC 487, *ante* para **3.33**.

> (b) [I]*n the absence of waiver, no question can be asked which intrudes upon privilege....* [I]f a suggestion of recent fabrication is being pursued at trial, a witness, including the defendant, cannot, unless he has waived privilege, be asked whether he told his counsel or solicitor what he now says is the truth. Such a question would require him either to waive his privilege or suffer criticism for not doing so. If any such question is asked by an opposing party (whether the Crown or a co-accused) the judge must stop it, tell the witness directly that he does not need to answer it... For the same reasons, in the absence of waiver, the witness cannot be asked whether he is willing to waive.

> (c) *[T]he defendant is perfectly entitled to open up his communication with his lawyer,* and it may sometimes be in his interest to do so. One example of when he may wish to do so is to rebut a suggestion of recent fabrication. Another may be to adduce in evidence the reasons he was advised not to answer questions. If he does so, there is no question of breach of privilege, because he cannot be in breach of his own privilege. What is happening is that he is waiving privilege.

> (d) *If the defendant does give evidence of what passed between him and his solicitor he is not thereby waiving privilege entirely and generally,* that is to say he does not automatically make available to all other parties everything that he said to his solicitor, or his solicitor to him, on every occasion. He may well not even be opening up everything said on the occasion of which he gives evidence, and not on topics unrelated to that of which he gives evidence. *The test is fairness and/or the avoidance of a misleading impression.* It is that the defendant should not... be able both to "have his cake and eat it."

As Lord Millett explained in *B v Auckland District Law Society* [2003] 2 AC 736 in relation to disclosure of documents:

> It does not follow that privilege is waived generally because a privileged document has been disclosed for a limited purpose only.... It must often be in the interests of the administration of justice that a partial or limited waiver of privilege should be made by a party who would not contemplate anything which might cause privilege to be lost and it would be most undesirable if the law could not accommodate it.
>
> (at [68])

> (e) *If a defendant says that he gave his solicitor the account now offered at trial, that will ordinarily mean that he can be cross-examined about exactly what he told the solicitor on that topic,* and if the comment is fair another party can comment upon the fact that the solicitor has not been called to confirm something which, if it is true, he easily could confirm.

> (f) *A defendant who adduces evidence that he was advised by his lawyer not to answer questions but goes no further than that does not thereby waive privilege.* This is the ratio of *Bowden* and is well established. After all, the mere fact of the advice can equally well be made evident by the solicitor announcing at the interview that he gives it then and there, and there is then no revelation whatever of any private conversation between him and the defendant.

As Maurice Kay LJ had explained in *White, Thomas and Graves* [2004] EWCA Crim 1988, a conspiracy-to-rob case in which the trial judge had invited the jury to speculate on the fact that the solicitor had not been called to testify:

> It is a matter for a defendant whether or not he answers questions, whether or not he accepts legal advice, whether or not he waives his privilege and gives evidence about the reasons for that legal advice, and whether or not he calls his solicitor to give evidence. In the present case the appellants gave evidence that they were advised to remain silent but not... as to the reasons proffered for that advice, nor as to what information or instructions they had imparted to their solicitors. In other words, they drew the line at the point of legal professional privilege in accordance with the authority of *Bowden*.
>
> (at [19])

> (g) *[A] defendant who adduces evidence of the content of, or reasons for, such advice, beyond the mere fact of it, does waive privilege* at least to the extent of opening up questions which properly go to whether such reason can be the true explanation for his silence: *Bowden*. That will ordinarily include questions relating to recent fabrication, and thus to what he told his solicitor of the facts now relied upon at trial: *Bowden* and *Loizou* [2006] EWCA Crim 1719.

(h) The rules as to privilege and waiver…are the same whether it is the Crown or a
co-accused who challenges the defendant.

11.21 Exercise of legal professional privilege by defendants can undoubtedly frustrate
a tribunal of fact, which may well feel that it needs more information. In *Loizou*
[2006] EWCA Crim 1719 at [25], Hooper LJ noted: 'a claim for privilege will
often deny a court the best evidence available to determine a particular issue, but,'
his Lordship was careful to add, 'that has never been a reason for saying that privilege has impliedly been waived.' All the same, it will be seen from the foregoing
that if a defendant chooses to use the gambit that his failure to mention facts
under the 1994 Act was dictated by legal advice, in all likelihood this will mean
that he has to sacrifice legal professional privilege and allow the prosecution to
explore the reasons for the advice, including the instructions upon which it was
based.

'Circumventing' s 34: the pre-prepared statement

11.22 Not surprisingly, given the complexity of the provision, the ingenuity of lawyers
has discovered at least one way in which to neutralise s 34, permitting the suspect to refuse to answer questions without fear that the jury may be invited
to draw an adverse inference—the 'pre-prepared statement'. The legitimacy of
this device was first upheld by the Court of Appeal in *Ali (Sarfraz)* [2001]
EWCA Crim 863. A and five other family members were jointly charged with
offences arising out of a brutal assault committed against K. A's defence was
alibi. Although A declined to answer any questions put to him by the police at
interview, he did hand in a prepared statement in which he claimed that he had
not been present when the attack on K took place; he had been at home asleep.
Disregarding the contents of the prepared statement, the trial judge had invited
the jury to draw an adverse inference from A's failure to mention his alibi to
the police at interview. As Mantell LJ put it, allowing A's appeal, A's prepared
statement had 'flagged up the defence of alibi' (at [33]). Indeed, in the court's
view:

> The wording of s 34…makes it clear that any available adverse interest depends upon
> any failure to mention any fact relied upon by the defendant in his defence. Here,…the
> essential facts had been disclosed in the prepared statement. Accordingly,…there
> was no such failure and…it was not appropriate for the jury to be permitted to draw an
> adverse inference on the basis of any such failure.
> (at [34])

The decision in *Ali (Sarfraz)*, in one sense, is true to the purposes which were
declared by the Court of Appeal in *Roble* to underlie s 34 (see *ante*, para **11.11**). A

prepared statement guards against the late concoction of defences by an accused and operates as an early disclosure of his defence as effectively as answers given to the police in interrogation.

11.23 *Ali (Sarfraz)*, however, also sidestepped an important debate as to whether or not s 34 does not additionally serve a further purpose: namely, that of enabling the court also to draw an adverse inference from the fact that the accused had been reluctant to expose himself to questioning on a particular topic. This possibility was suggested by Otton LJ in *Daniel* [1998] 2 Cr App R 373, who said of a trial judge's summing-up that 'It would, however, have been "desirable" to include a passage to the effect that despite the evidence relied on to explain his reticence, if the jury concluded that his reticence could only sensibly be attributed to the appellant's unwillingness to be subjected to further questioning', they might draw an adverse inference. Similarly, in *Beckles and Montague* [1999] Crim LR 148 Henry LJ held that s 34 was 'also apt to cover a reluctance to be subject to questioning and further enquiry by Customs when in a compromising position'. The language of s 34(1)(a), too, conceivably implies that the facts a defendant is expected to mention ought to be mentioned in the course of interrogation, not *via* a pre-prepared statement: 'Where...evidence is given that the accused at any time before he was charged with an offence, on being questioned under caution by a constable...failed to mention any fact relied on in his defence ...' Because it had not addressed the argument specifically on this possible clash of approaches to s 34, the Court of Appeal in *Ali (Sarfraz)* declined to attempt to resolve this conflict. Subsequently, in *Knight* [2004] 1 Cr App R 9, the Court of Appeal affirmed Mantell LJ's interpretation of s 34 in *Ali (Sarfraz)*, Laws LJ coming to 'the clear conclusion that the aim of s 34(1)(a) does not distinctly include police cross-examination of a suspect upon his account over and above the disclosure of that account'. Indeed, if such had been the legislature's intention, the statute would doubtless have expressed this objective more clearly—leaving to one side the fact that this 'significantly greater intrusion into a suspect's right of silence' would simultaneously have run the risk of infringing the suspect's right of fair trial under ECHR, Article 6. (See also *T v DPP* (2007) 171 JP 605.)

11.24 Additionally, in *Knight*, Laws LJ reflected on the purpose persistent police cross-examination of a suspect might serve in the context of the trial. Its sole purpose would be to suggest that a suspect's account of events, as related to the police, was unworthy of belief. But if the defendant testified at trial, the veracity of his account would be tested in cross-examination anyway, and he would therefore be assessed on his performance in court. Even if the defendant declined to testify, irrespective of what may have happened at police interview, the jury might in any case be invited to draw adverse inferences against him under s 35 of the 1994 Act. In neither circumstance, therefore, would police cross-examination have any obvious role to play:

> If (having given in full his account at the earliest stage by way of a pre-prepared statement) he acquits himself well in the witness box in the eyes of the jury, it would surely be neither realistic nor fair for them then to draw back from that conclusion in light of the fact that he did not subject himself to police cross-examination in interview. If, on the other hand, the defendant declines to give evidence at his trial, then adverse inferences may be drawn against him where appropriate under s 35. In that situation there can surely be no sensible room for further inferences under s 34.
>
> (at [17])

One could even add that the legislature's use of the rather casual term 'mention' in s 34(1)(a) hardly suggests that the most detailed account of events is demanded of suspects.

11.25 Whilst there may be no place for an adverse inference where an accused has given a full account of his defence to the police in a pre-prepared statement from which he does not depart in evidence, the protection afforded by the pre-prepared statement is not necessarily 100 per cent teflon-coated. As Scott Baker LJ remarked in *Turner (Dwaine)* [2004] 1 Cr App R 24,

> Of itself the making of a preprepared statement gives no automatic immunity against adverse inferences under s.34 ... It may be incomplete in comparison with the defendant's later account at trial or it may be inconsistent with that account. This court notes a growing practice, no doubt on advice, to submit a preprepared statement and decline to answer any questions. This...may prove to be a dangerous course for an innocent person who subsequently discovers at the trial that something significant has been omitted. No such problems would arise following an interview where the suspect gives appropriate answers to the questions.
>
> (at [25])

For this reason, in *Mohammad* [2009] EWCA Crim 1871 esp at [25], a case of wounding with intent to cause gbh, the Court held that the trial judge had probably not been wrong to deliver a s 34 direction in a case where, in the course of M's cross-examination, additional details of the incident emerged which were broadly relevant to self-defence.

11.26 This cluster of cases provides an important reminder of the relative fragility of s 34: taken to its logical conclusion, these decisions undermine one commonly understood purpose of the section, which is to encourage suspects actively to participate in interrogation. In as much as the cases permit a 'pre-prepared' statement to substitute for interrogation, the authorities provide suspects with a device with which to avoid answering police questions altogether without running the accompanying risks.

'Circumventing' s 34: declining to be questioned

11.27 At first blush, it might appear that there exists a further way in which suspects may successfully circumvent s 34. Because s 34(1)(a) refers specifically to a suspect who is 'being questioned under caution by a constable trying to discover whether or by whom the offence had been committed', in *Johnson and Hind* [2005] EWCA Crim 971, [2006] Crim LR 253, the Court of Appeal was required to consider whether the provision has any application to the situation where a suspect in custody flatly refuses to come out of his cell to be interrogated. The Crown argued that because the House of Lords in *Webber* [2004] 1 Cr App R 40 at [33] had asserted that the object of s 34 was 'to bring the law back into line with common sense', s 34(1)(a) ought to be given a broad reading in order to prevent suspects from so easily circumventing the requirement to provide early disclosure of their account of events. Treacy J, however, pointed out that, even if this legislation ought not to be read too pedantically, 'the language of the statute cannot be ignored' (at [27]). Therefore, the trial judge had correctly ruled that H's refusal to emerge from his cell to be questioned meant that his omission to mention facts upon which he subsequently relied could not be made the subject of adverse comment under the Act. Moreover, in Treacy J's view, the Crown's gloomy prognostications that such a decision would drive a coach-and-four through s 34 were not justified. In the first place, s 34(1)(b), which allows inferences to be drawn when a suspect is 'officially informed that he may be prosecuted for [an offence]' might afford an alternative avenue in such cases. Secondly, Code C:12.5 and Code E:3.4 of PACE specifically provide for interviews to take place in police cells, if necessary. Therefore, in cases like *Johnson and Hind* the police can easily take effective countermeasures in respect of a suspect who declines to leave his cell, and the prosecution may subsequently rely upon failures to mention facts under s 34 of the 1994 Act.

Section 34 only applies to facts upon which the defendant subsequently relies at trial

11.28 It is significant that s 34 refers to a defendant's failure to mention 'any fact relied on in his defence'. His failure to mention anything other than facts at interview will therefore fall outside the ambit of the section. In *Nickolson* [1999] Crim LR 61, N, who was charged with indecently assaulting a nine-year-old child, was asked at trial if he could think how semen had found its way onto the girl's nightdress. N suggested one possible explanation, which he had not mentioned during his police interview. The trial judge wrongly decided that this omission fell within s 34, and gave the jury a direction entitling them to draw an inference from N's failure to advance the explanation at interview. The Court of Appeal pointed out that N was simply being invited by counsel to propose 'a theory, a possibility, or a speculation only'. Section 34 is not concerned with theories, only with facts that the defendant unreasonably fails to mention (see also *B (MT)* [2000] Crim LR 181; *ante*, para **11.12**).

What constitutes a 'fact'?

11.29   The Court of Appeal has considered what exactly is meant by the expression 'any fact relied on in his defence' in s 34(1)(a) in a number of cases. The prevailing view is that this expression is not to be given a narrow construction. In *Milford* [2001] Crim LR 330, for example, in a passage which has found favour in subsequent cases, Potter LJ suggested:

> . . . the words "any fact" do not fall to be read only in the narrow sense of an actual deed or thing done but in the fuller sense contemplated by the *Oxford English Dictionary* of "something that . . . is actually the case . . . hence, a particular truth known by actual observation or authentic testimony, as opposed to what is merely inferred, or to a conjecture or to fiction".

Moreover, if one looks to the purpose of the provision and to the context and stage of proceedings with which s 34 is concerned, Potter LJ reasoned:

> [T]he questioning of a suspect [occurs] at a stage when the facts available to the prosecution without the benefit of any explanation of the defendant, give rise to a suspicion or inference of his involvement in the crime under investigation, and the questioning is being directed to establishing whether such suspicion or inference is well founded in fact. The facts relevant to establishing whether or not the defendant is guilty of the crime in respect of which he is being interrogated go far wider than the simple matter of what might have been observed to happen on a particular occasion and frequently involve what reasons or explanations the defendant gives for his involvement in the particular event observed which, if true, would absolve him from the suspicion of criminal intent or involvement which might otherwise arise.
>
> (Transcript no 00/04778/Y4 at [32])

11.30   In *Bowers, Taylor and Millen* (1998) 163 JP 33 at [43]–[44] Rose LJ stated that a 'fact' may be raised within the terms of s 34(1)(a) either by the defendant himself in evidence, by a witness called the defendant, or by a prosecution witness in evidence-in-chief or in cross-examination. Again, in *Chenia* [2003] 2 Cr App R 83 Clarke LJ accepted that s 34(1)(a) 'expressly contemplates that a fact may be relied upon by the defendant which is not put in evidence on his behalf' (at [25]). Yet, even this list may not be exhaustive. In *Ashton, Lyons and Webber* [2002] EWCA Crim 2782 at [47], Mantell LJ was called upon to consider whether two specific situations fell within this provision—namely, one situation where a co-accused gave evidence that was subsequently adopted in the other defendant's closing speech, and another where suggestions were made to a witness in cross-examination that were not accepted by the witness. Mantell LJ's rulings, that these did fall within the terms of s 34, were subsequently affirmed by the House of Lords (see *Webber* [2004] 1 Cr App R 40). Notably, the House affirmed that a 'fact' under s 34 could include a positive suggestion put to a witness by a defendant, even if that suggestion was not accepted by the witness. As it duly noted, s 34 'does not...refer to establishing a fact, but simply to relying upon it' (at [23]). The word was therefore wide enough to cover any alleged fact that was in issue having been put forward by counsel, on instructions, as part of the defence case. The court distinguished this sort of questioning from situations in which counsel was merely 'asking questions intended to probe or test the prosecution case'; the latter variety of questioning would not fall within s 34 (at [34]). Since positive suggestions will plant the defendant's version of events in jurors' minds, the House reasoned, common sense would tell us that jurors ought to be free to ask themselves whether, if that version of events were true, the defendant would not have mentioned it earlier when he was being questioned by the police. Furthermore, since s 34(2)(c) allows proper inferences to be drawn by the court when determining whether there is a case to answer—ie, before the defendant will have had an opportunity to give positive evidence in his own behalf—this provision would imply that the court is entitled to determine what inferences to derive from a defendant's failures by having regard to the nature of the questions put to prosecution witnesses during cross-examination. It would certainly be a little odd if s 34(2)(c) only applied in cases where the witness accepted the defendant's suggestions. The House of Lords' decision looks correct in principle, as it serves to fulfil the purposes of s 34, as identified by the Court of Appeal in *Roble* [1997] Crim LR 449 (*ante*, para **11.11**).

Uncontested facts

11.31 A direction on s 34 is only appropriate if the accused has failed to mention at interview a fact which the prosecution wishes to challenge. If the object of s 34 is to allow the jury to draw an adverse conclusion from a defendant's introducing late in the day a fact which he omitted to mention at interview and which he could reasonably have been expected to have mentioned, s 34 must be primarily concerned with discouraging the concoction of evidence and encouraging speedy disclosure. In *Wisdom and Sinclair* (1999) 10 December, case no 98/04544/Y2, a case involving possession of heroin, although this was her story at the trial S had not mentioned in interview that she had made the fateful trip from Sheffield to Liverpool on the spur of the moment. Her family, however, corroborated this version of events, and the prosecution made no attempt to contest the claim. In the circumstances, the trial judge was held wrongly to have given a s 34 direction, the Court of Appeal stating that S's failure to mention a 'true fact' should not lead to a s 34 direction. Similarly, if the accused admits at trial a fact asserted by the Crown, even if he failed to mention it during interview, this admission ought not to form the basis for a s 34 direction. In *Betts and Hall* [2001] 2 Cr App R 16, H was jointly charged with inflicting grievous bodily harm upon C, presumptively as punishment for having had a fling with the wife of someone called Jason. In his evidence H agreed with the Crown's contention that he knew C to be Jason's best friend, and that he knew of the affair. H had not mentioned this during his two police interviews. As Kay LJ pointed out:

> ...to hold against a defendant that an inference could be drawn against a person who did not make an admission in interview but made it at trial would effectively be to remove his right to silence.
>
> (at [34])

To give effect to the decisions of the European Court of Human Rights, which on more than one occasion have recognised that the right of silence 'lies at the heart of the notion of a fair procedure guaranteed by Article 6' (at [49]), a court therefore had to guard against drawing inferences where the Crown relied upon no more than an admission made by H of a fact asserted by the prosecution.

Must the defendant's failure be independent of the issue of guilt?

11.32 It was once believed to be impermissible to invite the jury to draw an inference if they could not reject the reason for which a defendant had not mentioned a fact without also rejecting the truth of the fact itself. The Court of Appeal had held on more than one occasion that the question whether an adverse inference could be drawn from the defendant's failure to mention facts had to be capable of being resolved as an issue independent of his guilt. Thus, in *Gill* [2001] 1 Cr App R 160, a drugs supply case, G had failed to mention at police interview that he was only a customer for drugs and that his co-accused was in fact the supplier. At trial he explained that he had not mentioned this before because he did not then wish to implicate anyone else. Whether or not the co-accused was the supplier was the key question in the case. There was therefore no independent basis upon which the jury could determine whether G's omission to mention that fact meant that this fact was untrue without actually determining the case itself. The truth of each issue depended on the truth of the other. The Court, therefore, relying upon the authority of an earlier ruling in *Mountford* [1999] Crim LR 575, resolved that the trial judge had been wrong to invite the jury to draw inferences under s 34 from G's omission to mention this fact.

11.33 In *Hearne and Coleman* (2000) 4 May, case no 99/04240/Z4, however, Mantell LJ pointed out that such an interpretation of s 34 could have the effect of 'emasculating the section and to defeat the very purpose for its enactment'. Lord Woolf CJ subsequently took up the cudgels in *Gowland-Wynn* [2002] 1 Cr App R 569 declaring that:

> Particularly where a defendant does not comment, when he could be expected to comment about something which goes right to the heart of his defence, it seems to us that s 34 has the largest and most significant part to play.
>
> (at [9])

G-W had been convicted of complicity in the smuggling of cigarettes in consignments of timber. He made no comment whatsoever at his first two police interviews. At his third interview, in a pre-prepared statement, he disclaimed the cigarettes altogether. At trial, his testimony also cast the blame upon H, a colleague who had earlier been discharged. Although the Lord Chief Justice's judgment is not especially clear on the principle's application to the facts, and mysteriously fails to refer to Potter LJ's decision to similar effect in the earlier case of *Milford* [2001] 2 All ER 609 esp at [34]–[35], Lord Woolf does make clear that cases like *Gill* and *Mountford* are now 'consigned to oblivion' (at [9]). As Potter LJ expressed matters in *Milford*:

> [T]he clear statutory intention of s 34, manifest from its wording, that the jury should, in respect of any fact relied on by the defendant in his defence, but not mentioned at interview, first resolve the issue whether he could in the circumstances existing at the time have been expected to mention it and, second, if the jury so concludes, it should draw such inference or inferences from that failure as seem proper, subject to [the] limitation imposed by s 38(3) that such inferences are alone insufficient for a finding of guilt. Whilst this requirement raises difficulties as to the directions to be given to the jury in order to define and emphasise the need for evidence from elsewhere, . . . the basic general approach should be one which does not defeat the general width of the statutory intention.
>
> (at [35])

Directing the jury on s 34

11.34 The direction, which a judge is expected to deliver to jurors explaining how they should approach their task under s 34, is complex and troublesome. In *Bresa* [2005] EWCA Crim 1414 Waller LJ confessed:

> It is a matter of some anxiety that, even in the simplest and most straightforward of cases, where a direction is to be given under s 34, it seems to require a direction of such length and detail that it seems to promote the adverse inference question to a height it does not merit.
>
> (at [4])

So troublesome is the direction that the Judicial Studies Board's *Crown Court Bench Book* explicitly stated that it was 'desirable' that judges discuss with counsel beforehand the exact form their direction ought to take. The commentary on specimen direction no 40 actually enumerated no less than five matters on which judge and counsel ought to confer. The Court of Appeal 'has repeatedly emphasised the importance of accurate directions in the face of a defendant's silence', thereby underlining the desirability for the judge to confer with counsel before summing up (eg *Gowland-Wynn* [2002] 1 Cr App R 569 at [5] *per* Lord Woolf CJ). In *Compton* [2002] EWCA Crim 2835 Buxton LJ explained why this should be:

> We would wish strongly to reinforce the importance of correct directions being given in respect of failures under both s 34 and s 36, not least because this is an area that has attracted the concern of the ECtHR. It is perhaps more important here than in respect of some other issues in a summing-up that the guidance given both by this court and by the JSB is closely mirrored in what the judge says.
>
> (at [37])

11.35 This has sometimes been assumed to mean that if a judge fails to deliver a correct direction on s 34, any ensuing conviction will inevitably be quashed on appeal. Whilst it is true that this has been the pattern in many cases, appeals in such circumstances will not always succeed. Even though the ECtHR and English courts acknowledge that it is most important that judges adhere closely to the prescribed form of s 34 direction, Waller LJ pointed out in *Boyle and Ford* [2006] EWCA Crim 2101 at [14] that 'an absolutist approach' is not called for and convictions will not automatically be quashed simply because a defective direction was delivered. In *Adetoro* [2006] EWCA Crim 1716, for example, Tuckey LJ explained that each appeal would turn on its own facts. In *Adetoro* itself, although the misdirection had been serious, the appeal was dismissed: the Crown's case against A was very strong; A had no reason for refusing to reply to the police questions concerning his alleged involvement in a string of armed robberies other than the reason that made up his general defence, that he was involved only in car theft—an explanation which the jury had clearly rejected; and, quite fortuitously, the judge had given a *Lucas* direction (see *post*, paras **11.75–11.80**), quite unnecessarily, which meant that jurors would have reached their verdict by following the same thought processes as they would have had to pursue if the proper s 34 direction had been given.

11.36 The direction ought to begin with the point that the caution the police administered to the suspect will have warned him of the consequences of failure to mention facts. As is now well known, the caution runs:

> You do not have to say anything. But it may harm your defence if you do not mention when questioned something which you later rely on in court. Anything you do say may be given in evidence.

(PACE Code C:10.4—This caution is anything but straightforward. One therefore discovers with interest that Note for Guidance 10C adds: 'If it appears that a person does not understand what the caution means, the officer who has given it should go on to explain it in his own words.')

Next, the judge will specify any fact, relied upon by the accused at trial, which, it is alleged, he failed to mention earlier. The judge will state that the prosecution's contention is that this omission variously shows that the fact was invented subsequently by the defendant, that it was tailored to fit the prosecution's case, or that the defendant realised that it would not stand up to scrutiny. If the jury, whose attention must be drawn to any reason the defendant may have given for not having mentioned a particular fact, is sure that the accused ought reasonably to have mentioned this fact, then they may draw such inference from this as appears proper. Whilst a failure to mention a fact on its own cannot prove guilt, and the jury must not convict wholly or mainly on the strength of any adverse inference they may choose to draw, they may take the inference into account in supplementing the prosecution case 'as some additional support for the prosecution's case and when deciding whether his [evidence/case] about these facts is true'. The jury may only draw an adverse inference if they think that it is a fair and proper conclusion, and are satisfied of three things:

- *first*, they must be satisfied that, when interviewed, the defendant could reasonably have been expected to mention the facts on which he presently relies;
- *second*, they must be satisfied that the only sensible explanation for the defendant's failure to mention the facts in question was that he had no answer at the time or none that would stand up to scrutiny; and
- *third*, they must be satisfied that, apart from his failure to mention those facts, the prosecution's case against the defendant is so powerful that it clearly calls for an answer from him.

The judge has to remind the jury of any reason the defendant has put forward to explain his failure to mention the relevant fact. If that reason does not offer an adequate explanation and the jury is sure that the real reason for the failure was that the accused had no innocent explanation to offer or none that he believed would stand up to questioning or investigation, then the jury may hold that failure against the defendant.

Failures to mention facts following legal advice

11.37 Regarding the defendant's reasons for not mentioning facts, in *Betts and Hall* [2001] 2 Cr App R 16, Kay LJ specifically acknowledged that 'directions pursuant to s 34 of the Act are never easy for a trial judge, particularly where reliance is placed on legal advice' (at [57]). In this case, the court even went so far as to draft the sort of direction that might be appropriate in such cases. The direction, subsequently incorporated into the JSB's specimen direction no 40, § 5, stresses that the jury may only draw an adverse inference if they conclude that the defendant was simply hiding behind the legal advice:

> The defendant has given evidence that he did not answer questions on the advice of his solicitor/legal representative. If you accept the evidence that he was so advised, this is obviously an important consideration: but it does not automatically prevent you from drawing any conclusion from his silence. Bear in mind that a person given legal advice has the choice whether to accept or reject it; and that the defendant was warned that any failure to mention facts which he relied on at his trial might harm his defence. Take into account also [here set out the circumstances relevant to the particular case, which may include the age of the defendant, the nature of and/or reasons for the advice given, and the complexity or otherwise of the facts in which he relied at the trial]. Having done so, decide whether the defendant could reasonably have been expected to mention the facts on which he now relies. If, for example, you considered that he had or may have had an answer to give, but genuinely relied on the legal advice to remain silent, you should not draw any conclusion against him. But if, for example, you were sure that the defendant had no answer, and merely latched onto the legal advice as a convenient shield behind which to hide, you would be entitled to draw a conclusion against him, subject to the direction I have given you.

11.38 Genuine reliance on legal advice, then, is not meant to lay a defendant open to the risk of an adverse inference being drawn. The strength of this proposition, however, may be open to question. In *Betts and Hall* Laws LJ went out of his way to stress, that 'does not give a licence to a guilty person [*sic*] to shield behind the advice of his solicitor'. In *Howell* [2005] 1 Cr App R 1, Laws LJ further explained:

> [Section 34] is one of several enacted in recent years which has served to counteract a culture, or belief, which has been long established in the practice of criminal cases, namely that in principle a defendant may without criticism withhold any disclosure of his defence until the trial. Now, the police interview and the trial are to be seen as part of a continuous process in which the suspect is engaged from the beginning... This benign [*sic*] *continuum* from interview to trial, the public interest that inheres in reasonable disclosure by a suspected person of what he has to say when faced with a set of facts which accuse him, is thwarted if currency is given to the belief that if a suspect remains silent

on legal advice he may systematically avoid adverse comment at his trial. And it may encourage solicitors to advise silence for other than good objective reasons. We do not consider, *pace* the reasoning in *Betts and Hall*, that once it is shown that the advice (of whatever quality) has genuinely been relied on as the reason for the suspect's remaining silent, adverse comment is thereby disallowed.

(at [23]–[24])

Indeed, Laws LJ felt that it should not be treated as reasonable *per se* for a suspect to follow his solicitor's advice to remain silent. He proceeded to suggest that, on the contrary:

... the kind of circumstance which may most likely justify silence will be such matters as the suspect's condition..., or his inability genuinely to recollect events without reference to documents which are not to hand, or communication with other persons who may be able to assist his recollection. There must always be soundly based objective reasons for silence, sufficiently cogent and telling to weigh in the balance against the clear public interest in an account being given by the suspect to the police. Solicitors bearing the important responsibility of giving advice to suspects at police stations must always have that in mind.

(at [24])

11.39 It will be seen that Laws LJ's judgment makes some odd assumptions. Section 34 makes no reference to any notion of a 'clear public interest', just as the reasonableness of a suspect's silence has nothing much to do with whether his solicitor's advice took this 'clear public interest' into proper account. Indeed, the most telling moment in Laws LJ's judgment, it is suggested, is an excerpt taken from H's cross-examination at trial: when asked by the Crown whether he knew that, despite his solicitor's advice to remain silent, he was at liberty to answer the police's questions if he so wished, H replied: 'Well, what was the point of me having a solicitor there, if I wasn't going to actually take his advice?' (Crown counsel's ill-judged reply, that if H had been innocent he would not have wanted a solicitor to advise him at all, almost beggars belief.) Does Laws LJ realistically believe that it will only rarely be reasonable for a suspect to take the advice of the legal adviser who is sitting at his elbow throughout the interview? What of course is pointed up by *Howell* is the confused philosophy underlying s 34: Laws LJ wishes to give full effect to the policy behind the statute, but as is increasingly well understood fulfilment of this policy is to a high degree frustrated by the suspect's undoubted, but inconvenient, right to legal representation.

11.40 The debate concerning what might be meant by genuine reliance in this context rumbles on. Everyone agrees that it is ultimately a matter for the jury to decide what was reasonable in the circumstances. However, one might take the simple route and say that this just entails deciding whether the suspect genuinely relied upon his lawyer's advice in not answering questions. In *Hoare and Pierce* [2005] 1 WLR 1804 Auld LJ clearly could not stomach the idea that any but an innocent defendant or a defendant who falls within one of the categories of situation enumerated by Lord Bingham CJ in *Argent* (*ante*, para **11.12**) could reasonably (and genuinely) heed his solicitor's advice to remain silent. Thus, in what Lord Woolf CJ later described as a 'helpful judgment' (*Beckles* [2005] 1 WLR 2829 at [44]), Auld LJ declared:

> The whole basis of s 34, in its qualification of the otherwise general right of an accused to remain silent and to require the prosecution to prove its case, is an assumption that an innocent defendant—as distinct from one who is entitled to require the prosecution to prove its case—would give an early explanation to demonstrate his innocence. If such a defendant is advised by a solicitor to remain silent, why on earth should he do so, unless because of circumstances of the sort aired by the court in *Roble, Argent* and *Howell*, he might wrongly inculpate himself?
>
> (at [53])

In consequence, although conceding that an accused cannot reasonably be expected to assess the reasonableness or quality of legal advice he receives ('to second-guess it' (at [58])) and that legal advice is 'a very relevant circumstance' (at [59]), Auld LJ concluded both that legal advice cannot preclude the drawing of an adverse inference and that there is in fact no inconsistency between the approach of Kay LJ in *Betts and Hall* and that of Laws LJ in *Howell*.

> Even where a solicitor has in good faith advised silence and a defendant has genuinely relied on it in the sense that he accepted it and believed that he was entitled to follow it, a jury may still draw an adverse inference if it is sure that the true reason for his silence is that he had no or no satisfactory explanation consistent with innocence to give. That is of a piece with Laws LJ's reasoning in *Howell* ... that genuine reliance by a defendant on a solicitor's advice to remain silent is not in itself enough to preclude adverse comment ... Legal entitlement is one thing. An accused's reason for exercising it is another. His belief in his entitlement may be genuine, but it does not follow that his reason for exercising it is ... The question in the end ... is whether regardless of advice, genuinely given and genuinely accepted, an accused has remained silent not because of that advice but because [he] had no or no satisfactory explanation to give.
>
> (at [51], [54] and [55])

The Lord Chief Justice later endorsed this line of reasoning in *Beckles* [2005] 1 WLR 2829, where he concluded:

> [I]n a case where a solicitor's advice is relied upon by the defendant, the ultimate question for the jury remains under s 34 whether the facts relied on at the trial were facts which the defendant could reasonably have been expected to mention at interview. If they were

not, that is the end of the matter. If the jury consider that the defendant genuinely relied on the advice, that is not necessarily the end of the matter. It may still not have been reasonable for him to rely on the advice, or the advice may not have been the true explanation for his silence...[T]he fact that [the defendant followed his lawyer's advice] because it suited his purpose may mean he was not acting reasonably in not mentioning the facts. His reasonableness in not mentioning the facts remains to be determined by the jury. If they conclude he was acting unreasonably they can draw an adverse inference from the failure to mention the facts.

(at [46])

Instructing a jury not to draw an inference

11.41 As has already been noted, not every failure by a defendant to mention a fact during interrogation allows the jury to draw an adverse inference under s 34. In such cases the jury ought now to be told in the summing-up that they are not entitled to draw an inference. This was laid down in *McGarry* [1999] 1 Cr App R 377. The Court of Appeal argued that s 34 has altered the established rules of the common law and there is a consequent risk that, unless they are told not to do so, the jury will in fact draw unwarranted inferences adverse to the defendant simply because the latter has failed to mention something at police interview. If the judge concludes that the defendant has not failed to mention facts subsequently relied upon by him at trial within the terms of s 34, the jury must be positively told that they must not in any way hold the defendant's silence against him. As Hutchison LJ put it:

> The common law rule requiring that juries should receive a direction against holding an accused's silence after caution against him plainly recognises that a jury, without such guidance, may treat silence as probative of guilt. The jury should not, therefore, ... be left in some no-man's-land between the common law principle and the statutory exception, without any guide to tell them how to regard the defendant's silence.
>
> (at 383–4)

Such a direction may assume great importance because, in all but exceptional cases, any request made to the judge by defence counsel that the jury be not invited to draw an adverse interest from the accused's silence is made in the absence of the jury at the conclusion of evidence (see, eg, *Condron and Condron* [1997] 1 WLR 827). In short, the jury will already have heard, possibly during pointed cross-examination, that the defendant has failed to answer questions. Unless warned against it, they may therefore be tempted to draw an inference, even in cases where such a course is not justified. Whether a trial judge's failure to deliver such a direction justifies the quashing of a conviction, however, will depend very much on the circumstances of the individual case (*Smith (Brian)* [2004] EWCA Crim 2414 at [34] *per* Scott Baker LJ).

The relationship between s 34 of the 1994 Act and s 78 of PACE

11.42 Since failures under s 34 constitute 'evidence on which the prosecution proposes to rely', PACE, s 78 applies to render inadmissible failures consequent upon breaches of PACE and its Codes of Practice if their admission would reflect adversely on the fairness of the proceedings. But, more boldly, it has been claimed that inferences may no longer be drawn under s 34 if questioning is no longer permitted under PACE Code C, and more specifically from the moment when the police have sufficient evidence to charge the suspect. A complex case law has grown up involving defendants who have failed to mention facts in interviews conducted after the investigating authorities have sufficient evidence to justify charging them. One line of authority suggested that failures occurring in such circumstances could not ground an adverse inference under s 34. Thus, in *Pointer* [1997] Crim LR 676, a police officer admitted that before interviewing P he already had 'sufficient evidence to charge the person' in accordance with PACE, s 37(7). Had the police complied with PACE and charged P when they had sufficient evidence to do so, the 1994 Act would no longer have applied, as s 34(1) only permits inferences from failures which occur 'at any time before [the accused] was charged with any offence'. For this reason, it was held that the jury had been wrongly invited to draw an adverse inference from P's omission to mention a fact upon which he later relied at trial. The position is not, however, so clear-cut. *Odeyemi* [1999] Crim LR 828, for example, distinguished *Pointer* on its facts, and the Court of Appeal noted:

> [It is] desirable that officers should have the chance to question suspects in order that explanations could be put forward which showed that either no offence had been committed or that the offence had been committed by someone else.

11.43 It is of course true that Code C:11.4 used to say that questioning had to cease if the officer in charge believed that a prosecution ought to be brought; that when the suspect has said all he wishes to say, the police officer must without delay bring him before the custody officer, who then decides whether he should in fact be charged (Code C:16.1); and that further questions may only be put to the suspect in certain clearly defined circumstances (Code C:16.5). However, as was pointed out in *Ioannou* [1999] Crim LR 586, it would be 'nonsense' to interpret these provisions so that a prospective defendant would not be afforded an opportunity to give any explanation in cases where the evidence against him appeared overwhelming. In *Elliott* [2002] EWCA Crim 931 a soldier convicted of assault occasioning actual bodily harm had omitted to refer to self-defence in an interview that had been conducted after the interviewing officer admitted that he thought that he had sufficient evidence to charge E. Nelson J carefully reviewed the authorities and concluded:

Notwithstanding the interviewing officer's belief that there was sufficient evidence at the time when he sought to question to justify charging him, he was not prohibited from offering [the defendant] the opportunity to put forward his own account of the incident…Section 34 applies where an officer is 'trying to discover whether or by whom the offence has been committed.' Whether an offence has been committed depends…as much on the availability of defences as it does on the proof of *actus reus* and *mens rea*.

(at [31] and [32])

Therefore, it may be that only in cases where, to adopt Nelson J's language, 'a fixed decision to charge the [defendant], irrespective of anything he may have said, has been reached' (at [31]) that failures to mention facts will fall outside the ambit of s 34.

11.44 A further problem may arise in cases where the trial judge has determined that evidence of a defendant's interview is inadmissible. Section 34(1) permits inferences to be drawn from the defendant's failure to mention a fact in two alternative situations:

(a) at any time before he was charged with the offence, on being questioned under caution by a constable trying to discover whether or by whom the offence had been committed…; or

(b) on being charged with the offence or officially informed that he might be prosecuted for it…

In *Dervish* [2002] 2 Cr App R 105, on account of serious breaches by the police of PACE Code C, D's 'no comment' interviews had been excluded from evidence by the trial judge under PACE, s 78. Section 34(1)(a) therefore had no application. However, the judge did direct the jury that they might draw an adverse inference from D's failure to mention facts shortly after interview, when charged, under s 34(1)(b). Kay LJ rejected counsel's arguments that para (b) was only intended to cover cases where no interview had taken place (say, owing to the trivial nature of the charges or to the fact that the police had a settled intention to charge) and that Parliament cannot have intended that the police should have a back-up inference in the event that evidence of the interview was excluded. The Court of Appeal held that, 'subject only to any issue of unfairness' (at [49]), in cases where a judge was unable to leave an inference to the jury under s 34(1)(a), it was still open to him to do so under s 34(1)(b). 'Unfairness' meant either that the drawing of a s 34(1)(b) inference would 'nullify the safeguards contained in the 1984 Act' or that the police had cynically taken advantage of the fact that they could safely breach PACE Code C in interrogation and still fall back upon s 34(1) (b). A similar strategy was adopted in *Goodsir* [2006] EWCA Crim 852. Because no questions had been asked, as required by the provision, inferences could not be left to the jury under s 34(1)(a): see at [13]. However, inferences were left to the jury under s 34(1)(b) because para (b) did not require the police to put questions to G.

Section 36: the effect of a defendant's failure or refusal to account for objects, substances or marks

11.45 Adopting a similar pattern to s 34, s 36 provides that the court or jury may be directed to 'draw such inferences...as appear proper' (s 36(2)) from the defendant's failure to account for objects, substances or marks when requested to do so by a constable investigating an offence. The provision sets out a number of conditions that must be met before this inference becomes permissible. These are that:

(a) a person is arrested by a constable, and there is—

(i) on his person; or

(ii) in or on his footwear or clothing; or

(iii) otherwise in his possession; or

(iv) in any place in which he is at the time of his arrest,

any object, substance or mark, or there is any mark on any such object; and

(b) that or another constable investigating the case reasonably believes that the presence of the object, substance or mark may be attributable to the participation of the person arrested in the commission of an offence specified by the constable; and

(c) the constable informs the person arrested that he so believes, and requests him to account for the presence of the object, substance or mark; and

(d) the person fails or refuses to do so...

11.46 The defendant's failure to account for substances etc must relate to one of the matters set out in s 36. In *Abbas* [2010] All ER (D) 79 (Jan) A was charged with engaging in sexual activity with a child under 16, a promiscuous 15 year old who had absconded from a care home. A's DNA was found in the crotch of the girl's underwear. The victim could not recall a sexual encounter with A. The police had purported to ask A under s 36 to account for the presence of his DNA on the girl's underwear, and his failure to do so was wrongly left to the jury at his trial. The semen staining did not fall within any of the circumstances enumerated in s 36(1)(a)(i)-(iv).

11.47 As in the case of s 34, the Youth Justice and Criminal Evidence Act 1999 has added s 36(4A), which imposes an additional condition that if the defendant was at an authorised place of detention (essentially, a police station) at the time of his failure or refusal, no inference may be drawn unless he was afforded an opportunity to consult a solicitor before the request was made that he account for the object, substance or mark.

11.48 Because s 36 requires the suspect 'to account for the presence of the object', the judge determines whether a suspect's explanation is capable of being interpreted as a statement that fails to account for the presence of an object. In *Compton* [2002] EWCA Crim 2835 at [32], Buxton LJ held that the 'bare statement' of one defendant, who was being questioned about various drugs offences, to the effect that large sums of cash that had been found in his safe were the product of a legitimate antiques business and that much of this cash was contaminated with heroin simply because he was a heroin user 'in the circumstances...far from accounted for' the object. The trial judge had therefore been entitled to hold that it could be left to the jury to determine whether C had in fact failed to account for the money within the terms of s 36(1)(c) and (d). If the judge finds that the requirements of s 36 have been satisfied, the judge must then deliver a direction along the general lines of JSB specimen direction no 41. Let us take the example of a suspect asked to explain his possession of a particular object. The jurors must first decide whether the prosecution has proved so that they are sure that on arrest the defendant had something in his possession, that the policeman reasonably believed that it was attributable to his participation in a specified offence, that the police told the defendant this and asked him to explain the presence of the object (at the same time, cautioning him), and that the defendant declined to account for its presence. The court must then explain to the jury that the prosecution contends that, in view of the warning the police officer gave to the defendant, the latter could reasonably have been expected to have provided an innocent explanation for the incriminating article, if he had had one, and that his silence may signify that he had no explanation for it. If the jurors are sure of this, they may draw such inferences as appear proper. Failure to explain the presence of objects cannot on its own prove guilt (s 38(3)). However, if, without taking the defendant's failure into account, the jury is sure that there is a case to meet, any inference they then choose to draw may be taken into account as additional support for the Crown case. The judge must remind the jury of any reasons the defendant may have given to explain why he failed to respond to the policeman's enquiry. Only if they are sure that his failure can be ascribed to the fact that he had no adequate explanation to offer may the jury go on and draw an inference adverse to the defendant. It would be idle to pretend that this direction is straightforward, let alone readily intelligible.

Section 37: the effect of the defendant's failure or refusal to account for his presence in a particular place

11.49   Section 37 is another provision that allows for inferences to be drawn from a defendant's failure or refusal, when so requested, to account for his presence in a particular place. It stipulates that such inferences as appear proper may be drawn:

> ...where—
>
> (a) a person arrested by a constable was found by him at a place at or about the time the offence for which he was arrested is alleged to have been committed; and

(b) that or another constable investigating the offence reasonably believes that the presence of the person at that place and at that time may be attributable to his participation in the commission of the offence; and

(c) the constable informs the person that he so believes, and requests him to account for his presence; and

(d) the person fails or refuses to do so...

As in the case of s 36, an inference may only be drawn once all of these conditions have been met. The Youth Justice and Criminal Evidence Act 1999 added that if the defendant is held at 'an authorised place of detention' at the time of his failure or refusal, no adverse inference may be drawn unless he had previously been given an opportunity to consult a solicitor. The defendant cannot be convicted solely on the evidence of a failure or refusal (s 38(3)), and the judicial direction no 42 follows the general pattern of the direction judges ought to deliver in respect of s 36 (see *ante*, para **11.48**).

Section 35: drawing an adverse inference when the defendant elects not to give evidence at trial

11.50 Although it retains the traditional common law principle that the accused is not compellable to give evidence on his own behalf (s 35(4)), s 35 of the Criminal Justice and Public Order Act 1994 does permit an adverse inference to be drawn by the tribunal of fact under certain circumstances if he elects not to go into the witness box to give evidence. Section 35 sets out a procedure which must be followed by the court—a procedure which is detailed in *The Consolidated Criminal Practice Direction*, IV.44. In a nutshell, at the close of the Crown case the court will ascertain either from the defendant's counsel or, if he is unrepresented, from the defendant himself whether he proposes to give testimony. A defendant's decision not to testify can prove portentous. For this reason, in *Ebanks v R* [2006] 1 WLR 1827 Lord Rodger of Earlsferry issued the following powerful reminder:

> Since it appears that even experienced counsel are still failing to follow the practice, their Lordships wish to emphasize yet again that, where it is decided that the defendant will not give evidence, this should be recorded in writing, along with a brief summary of the reasons for that decision. Wherever possible, the record should be endorsed by the defendant.
>
> (at [17])

The Consolidated Criminal Practice Direction provides appropriate forms of words a judge 'should' use in a trial on indictment, in the presence of the jury, enquiring of the accused's legal representative (or of the accused himself, if unrepresented) in clear—not to say peremptory—terms, whether he is aware that the time has come when he may give evidence and asking both whether he intends doing so and whether he realises that 'the jury may draw such inferences as appear proper from his failure to do so' (IV.44.3). This direction puts flesh on the bones of s 35(2), which requires that the court satisfy itself that the defendant is aware:

(i) that the time has come when he may give evidence;

(ii) that he has the option whether or not to testify; and

(iii) that his failure to give evidence at all or his failure to answer specific questions if he does elect to testify will entitle the court 'to draw such inferences as appear proper.

This procedure is important. Indeed, since s 35(2) expressly requires the court 'at the conclusion of the evidence for the prosecution, to satisfy itself... that the accused is aware' that the time has come when he may give evidence, it has been held in *Gough* [2002] 2 Cr App R 121, that if a defendant absconds during the course of his trial before a judge can so satisfy himself either by asking the defendant or his counsel (assuming that the latter was in a position to take instructions from the defendant), the judge ought not to direct the jury that they are entitled to draw adverse inferences from the accused's failure to testify.

11.51 In cases to which s 35 applies—ie all criminal cases save those where the defendant's guilt is not in issue or where his physical or mental condition is such as to persuade the court that it would be undesirable for him to give evidence (s 35(1)(a) and (b))—s 35(3) lays down:

> Where this subsection applies, the court or jury, in determining whether the accused is guilty of the offence charged, may draw such inferences as appear proper from the failure of the accused to give evidence or his refusal, without good cause, to answer any question.

Section 35 puts pressure on an accused to testify and, should he elect to do so, to induce the accused to answer all questions put to him. Only if an accused has good cause not to answer a particular question will the court not inform the jury that it may draw an adverse inference from the defendant's reticence. For good measure s 35(5) provides that a defendant's failure to answer questions is presumed to be 'without good cause' unless the accused either is entitled under statute not to answer particular questions or enjoys a legal privilege not to answer them or, alternatively, 'unless... the court in the exercise of its general discretion excuses him from answering it'.

11.52 Section 35(1)(b) provides that no adverse inference may be drawn if:

> it appears to the court that the physical or mental condition of the accused makes it
> undesirable for him to give evidence.

This involves 'a wide question for the judgement of the judge.' The mere fact that a defendant may have 'extreme difficulty in giving evidence' will not make it 'undesirable for him to give evidence'. As Aikens J explained in *Ensor* [2010] 1 Cr App R 18:

> That is quite common among defendants and other witnesses who give evidence in
> criminal trials. That does not in itself make it "undesirable" that that person should give
> evidence. . . . There is no degree of certainty that the experience of giving evidence will
> adversely affect the mental health of [E] so that it is therefore "undesirable" that [E] should
> have given evidence.
>
> (at [35]. See also *Tabbakh* (2009) 173 JP 201 at [11] *per* Hughes VP)

Evidence must be adduced and considered on a *voir dire*. In *Charisma* (2009) 173 JP 633 C, who claimed to be suffering from amnesia, declined to testify at his trial for serious sexual assaults. There was no consistent medical view that C genuinely suffered from memory loss and, even if he did, Lord Judge CJ pointed out that C could have said so in testimony, been cross-examined on his claim, and if they believed it the jurors could have taken his amnesia into account. No one suggested that giving evidence would have had lasting consequences to C's health, and C had not lost his memory through trauma following interview. In the circumstances, the trial judge had been entitled to deliver a s 35 direction.

11.53 Sometimes a s 35 direction will not be called for. Thus, Maurice Kay LJ, in *Barry* [2010] 1 Cr App R 32 at [20], proposed the case of a defendant, pleading diminished responsibility, who suffered from delusions or was 'on the border of insanity.' Equally, if the defence advanced did not relate to the defendant's conduct or state of mind but concerned, say, causation or whether a particular exhibit was or was not a firearm or a controlled drug, s 35 would not be engaged (at [24]).

11.54 In *Cowan* [1996] QB 373, Lord Taylor CJ devised a direction to enable judges to explain this complex provision to juries. The general form of direction proposed by Lord Taylor CJ received the approval of the House of Lords in *Becouarn* [2005] 1 WLR 2589. *Cowan* requires that jurors be told the following things:

- the burden of proof remains on the prosecution, and the jurors must be told what the required standard is;
- the defendant has the right to remain silent and is entitled to sit back and let the prosecution prove its case;

- the jury must not assume guilt just because the defendant omits to testify: any inference drawn from the defendant's silence cannot on its own prove guilt (this is specifically spelt out in s 38(3));

- the jury, therefore, must first have decided that the defendant has a case to meet before turning to consider whether any inference should be drawn from the defendant's failure to testify. At that point, they must effectively ask themselves, if the defendant had had any answer to the Crown's evidence, would he not have gone into the witness box to make it known to the jury? Lord Bingham CJ in *Birchall* [1999] Crim LR 311 stressed that:

> Inescapable logic demands that a jury should not start to consider whether they should draw inferences from a defendant's failure to give oral evidence at his trial until they have concluded that the Crown's case against him is sufficiently compelling to call for an answer by him... There is a clear risk of injustice if the requirements of logic and fairness in this respect are not observed.

As Pill LJ pointed out in *Milford* [2002] EWCA Crim 1528 at [38], the words 'sufficiently compelling', employed by Lord Bingham CJ in *Birchall*, have to be read in the context of the phrase that follows them, 'to call for an answer', which simply means that 'there must be a case which is fit to go to the jury and on the basis of which they would be entitled to convict'. The evidence 'must be of a strength sufficient to call for an answer by the [defendant]'. It will be observed that this fourth restriction is 'a necessary and logical consequence' of the earlier requirement that the jury must not simply assume guilt from the defendant's failure to testify (*Whitehead* [2006] EWCA Crim 1486 at [30] *per* Pill LJ).

- Taking into account any evidence which might explain why the defendant chose not to give evidence, if the jurors are satisfied that the only sensible reason for his not having testified is that he had no answer to the charge, or at least none that would bear examination, they may draw an inference against the defendant in additional support of the prosecution case. The notion of having no answer to the charge can also include a defendant's concern that he may give himself away if he does take the stand. Thus, in *Dalligan* [2001] EWCA Crim 1051, a drug-smuggling case, the prosecution was held properly to have suggested to the jury that D had not testified because he feared that they might thereby identify him as one of the speakers on a covert tape recording of a conversation between the smugglers which had been put in evidence in the case.

11.55 Lord Taylor CJ, in *Cowan*, described an accused's failure to testify as 'a further evidential factor in support of the prosecution case'. The logical corollary of this is that if the jury is already persuaded by the evidence of a defendant's guilt, strictly speaking there is no need for them then to have regard to the defendant's omission to testify or to answer particular questions put to him in court. This has been described as 'a real [problem] and one to which there is no simple answer':

> If the jury are sure of the reliability of [the prosecution evidence], reference to the defendant's silence is unnecessary. Parliament has intended that a jury should be entitled to bear silence in mind in cases in which they have not already decided upon guilt. Clearly, the jury should start with a consideration of the evidence and not with the defendant's silence. They must conclude that it is sufficiently cogent to call for an explanation before considering the implications of the defendant's silence. Having crossed that threshold, the jury are entitled to consider the defendant's silence, as a further evidential factor, in the words of Lord Taylor, and in the context of the evidence as a whole. The fourth essential is not really a separate point but is the necessary and logical consequence of the third. It amplifies and spells out what is in any event inherent in the third, . . . that failure to give evidence cannot on its own prove guilt.
>
> (*Whitehead* [2006] EWCA Crim 1486 at [48] *per* Pill LJ)

11.56 On occasion a defendant may claim that tactical considerations have led him to refrain from testifying at trial, and that for this reason the trial judge ought not to deliver a *Cowan* direction. In *Becouarn* [2005] 1 WLR 2589 B argued that the trial judge was wrong to have delivered a *Cowan* direction in view of the fact that B had not entered the witness box in order to avoid being cross-examined concerning his previous convictions under the (now repealed) Criminal Evidence Act 1898. Such situations are less likely to arise under the Criminal Justice Act 2003. Nevertheless, the House of Lords' response to B's argument is instructive. Lord Carswell stated, to exempt B from the operation of s 35 would be effectively to privilege him because he had a criminal record, thereby creating an 'unjustifiable distinction between defendants with previous convictions and those with none' (at [23]). Furthermore, in such cases it would also be inappropriate to require a judge to direct the jury that the defendant might have had some compelling reason for not testifying: not only would such a direction invite the jury to indulge in 'unfounded speculation' (at [24]), but in any given case a defendant might well have other distinct motives for not testifying.

11.57 Naturally, if no inference is warranted under s 35—for instance, because the accused has a mental handicap or, as occurred in *Brown (Leroy)* [2002] EWCA Crim 2708, an accused suffers from epilepsy and the judge accepts that the condition of the accused makes it 'undesirable for him to give evidence' (s 35(1)(b))— the judge must direct the jury not to hold his failure to testify against him. As we have seen, such a direction will only be called for if there exists evidence that it is undesirable for the accused to give evidence.

Section 34 and s 35 directions distinguished

11.58 The reader will have noticed that the structure of the judicial directions respecting ss 34 and 35 are not identical. The Court of Appeal explained the differences between the two directions in *Doldur* [2000] Crim LR 178, case no 98/08076/W2. D appealed against his conviction for grievous bodily harm with intent. Although he had not mentioned this during police interview, at trial D claimed that it was his associate, A, who had actually kicked the victim and who had been wearing the red shirt witnesses said was worn by the assailant. D complained that the trial judge had failed to direct the jury that before it could draw an adverse inference from D's failure to mention a fact relied on later at trial, it had to be satisfied that there was, on the Crown's evidence, a case to answer. Such a direction, it was urged, is required by *Cowan* when a jury is being instructed how to apply s 35, and also conforms to s 38(3), which states that a person may not be convicted solely on an inference drawn under either s 34 or s 35. Auld LJ pointed out that in the case of s 35 a jury is restricted to consideration of the prosecution case in deciding whether it should draw an adverse inference from an accused's failure to testify. Under s 34, on the other hand, a jury would almost always have to consider both prosecution and defence evidence as it was the contrast between the accused's earlier silence and his subsequent reliance on a fact which may justify the drawing of an adverse inference. Therefore, there is no reason to limit the jury to consideration of the prosecution evidence when directing them on s 34. Further, there is no need to tell them to consider whether the prosecution has established a case to answer before turning to the question of whether it is appropriate to draw an inference from the accused's omission to mention facts at interview upon which he subsequently relies at trial.

11.59 Only an accused's failure to testify falls within s 35. Thus, even though she may be compellable for the defence, an accused's spouse may still not be called to testify for the defendant. PACE, s 80A expressly provides that this 'shall not be made the subject of any comment by the prosecution' (*ante*, para **3.22**). Nor would a judge normally invite a jury to draw any inference from this. On the contrary, as the case of *C (T)* (2000) 14 January, case no 98/01431/Y3 shows, the judge may be obliged to do precisely the opposite. C was charged with the rape of his daughter. It was obvious to everyone that the girl's mother was present in the public gallery. The mother could easily have commented on C's relationship with his daughter, but she was not called. This was because the defence knew that the mother had forbidden C to bathe the girl, owing to concerns she had about C. The Court of Appeal held that the trial judge ought to have directed the jury both that C was under no obligation to call any particular witness and that it must not speculate on the reasons why the mother had not been called.

The silence provisions: an envoi

11.60 It will be apparent from the foregoing that the failures provisions contained within the 1994 Act are complex in the extreme. They demand a meticulously crafted jury direction and, not altogether surprisingly, have given rise to large numbers of appeals. As May LJ remarked in *Adinga* [2003] EWCA Crim 3201, a case in which it was noted that a judge's 'complicated and extensive' s 34 direction took up between five and six pages of the transcript:

> This series of statutory provisions has caused a considerable amount of thought and some trouble. In the result, the Judicial Studies Board have produced a quite extensive model form of directions which in appropriate circumstances judges are encouraged to give when this question arises in cases before juries. The model form of direction covers more than a page of closely-typed material and extends to five numbered paragraphs.
>
> (at [27])

The direction has not been without its critics, and judges have occasionally sought to simplify it. In *Bashier and Razak* [2009] EWCA Crim 2003 Scott Baker LJ said:

> As the judge pointed out, the...direction is long and complex and he had seen jurors' eyes glaze over in other cases when it was referred to in detail. He had to try and tailor it to the circumstances of each defendant in the present case in order to do justice to them all in respect of their failures to mention something that arose in each instance in a different context....[H]e should not be criticised for trying to simplify the direction and tailor it to the particular circumstances of the case.
>
> (at [19])

11.61 In view of the problems these provisions occasion, Professor Birch felt impelled to write,

> one might sometimes be forgiven for wondering whether the game of drawing inferences from silence is worth the candle...these statutory provisions continue to provide an extraordinarily rich source of problems, out of all proportion to the value of the evidence generated for the prosecution.
>
> ([1999] Crim LR 78)

Such a view would seem to have been reinforced by the findings of a Home Office Research Study, published in April 2000. This extensive research found that there had been no discernible rise in either charging or conviction rates since the coming into force of the 1994 Act. Defendants, it would appear, continued to decline to answer police questions, although the percentage who did so had declined somewhat, presumably in the hope that the Crown would fail to gather sufficient other evidence. The proportion of suspects providing admissions at police interview remained unchanged at 55 per cent, and, as before the Act, only about one in three suspects availed him- or herself of legal advice at the police station (Zander suggests that this may have risen to approximately one in two suspects: see (2010) 174 CL&J 629). There were some suggestions from the Crown Prosecution Service that barristers are reluctant to draw attention to a defendant's omission to answer questions in case the jury infers from this that the prosecution case is weak. Perhaps the most puzzling Home Office finding was that the proportion of silent suspects who were actually charged had fallen. The study brought little comfort to those who adhere implacably to that obsessive dreamer, Jeremy Bentham's simple creed that 'innocence claims the right of speaking, guilt invokes the privilege of silence' (see *The Right of Silence: The Impact of the Criminal Justice and Public Order Act 1994*, Home Office Research Study no 199).

11.62 The courts, too, have added their voice to this reaction against s 34. Hedley J appended an observation to his judgment in *B (Michael)* [2004] EWCA Crim 310,

> discouraging prosecutors from too readily seeking to activate the provisions of section 34 . . . [W]e would counsel against the further complicating of trials and summings-up by invoking this statute unless the merits of the individual case require that that should be done.
>
> (at [57])

Hughes LJ endorsed this advice more recently in *Maguire* (2008) 172 JP 417, a case in which M's account of events in interview and at trial were at variance with one another. Having noted that the prosecution had always been able to rely upon an accused's deliberate lies as part of its case (see *post*, paras **11.75–11.80**), Hughes LJ suggested that 'the s 34 direction is simply a rather formalised way of saying precisely the same' (at [9]) in situations where the defendant omits to mention a fact at interview upon which he later relies in his defence, for example. Although an altered story may technically qualify as an omission to mention such a fact,

> [P]rosecutors should be cautious about too readily seeking to invite formalised directions under s 34. We respectfully add our discouragement to anything which over-formalises commonsense. We would caution advocates against making submissions which seek such unnecessary formalism from judges in their directions, and equally judges against employing it, unless it becomes essential.
>
> (at [11])

The effect of a defendant's silence at common law

11.63 Section 34(5) provides:

> This section does not—
>
> (a) prejudice the admissibility of the silence or other reaction of the accused in the face of anything said in his presence relating to the conduct in respect of which

he is charged, in so far as evidence thereof would be admissible apart from this section; or

(b) preclude the drawing of any inference from any such silence or other reaction of the accused which could properly be drawn apart from this section.

In the previous chapter, we referred to the circumstances in which under common law an accused's silence in the face of an accusation may be treated as evidence of an admission (*ante*, paras **10.9–10.12**). These rules are unaffected by the 1994 Act. Thus, in *Johnson and Hind* [2005] EWCA Crim 971, the Court of Appeal ruled that a trial judge had been in error to allow a jury to draw an adverse inference at common law from the fact that H had flatly refused to leave his cell to be questioned by the police. Treacy J observed that, prior to the 1994 Act, at common law a judge had not been entitled to comment adversely on an accused's failure to respond to police questioning or to volunteer his account of events prior to trial (see *Gilbert* (1966) 50 Cr App R 166, 169 *per* Viscount Dilhorne). In terms of common law, therefore, Treacy J concluded that in this case 'in reality [H] was in an emphatic way exercising his right to silence'.

The right of silence and evidence obtained under compulsion

'One looked like a politician, bit tubby, with a baby face. He just spoke real quiet, like. He says, "You have no right to silence under the ASIO Act."
"What do you mean?" I say.
"You can go to jail for up to five years for not answering our questions." '

Richard Flanagan, *The Unknown Terrorist* (2006)

11.64 Reverting to Lord Mustill's observation in *R v Director of Serious Fraud Office, ex p Smith* concerning the different meanings attributable to the expression 'right of silence' (*ante*, para **11.2**), although suspects are not in general compelled to answer questions put to them by investigating authorities, a number of statutes do exceptionally require parties to reply to questions and even inflict penalties if they fail to comply. In such cases Parliament will be held, expressly or impliedly, to have overridden the privilege against self-incrimination. As Dillon LJ noted in *Bishopsgate Investment Management Ltd v Maxwell* [1993] Ch 1, 20:

[I]f Parliament, in the public interest, sets up by statute investigatory procedures...to find out if there have been infringements of certain sections of the Banking Act 1987 which have been enacted for the protection of members of the public who make deposits, Parliament cannot have intended that anyone questioned under those procedures should be entitled to rely upon the privilege against self-incrimination, since that would stultify the procedures and prevent them achieving their obvious purpose.

In *R v Hertfordshire County Council, ex p Green Environmental Industries* [2000] 2 AC 412, a case before the House of Lords, the applicants had been served with notice by a local authority under s 71(2) of the Environmental Protection Act 1990 requiring them to provide information concerning the provenance, transporting, handling and disposal of over 100 tonnes of surgical waste which had been discovered by inspectors discarded on two unlicensed sites. Under s 71(3) of the 1990 Act, a party who fails without reasonable excuse to provide answers demanded under s 71(2) may be prosecuted. Not altogether surprisingly, the House determined that, in the interests of protecting public health and the environment, the policy of the Act was to deprive parties of their right to refuse to answer questions on the ground that any answers they gave might otherwise tend to incriminate them. The question that this sort of enactment then poses is, may the prosecution adduce as evidence in subsequent criminal proceedings answers obtained from defendants under statutory coercion during the course of such extrajudicial enquiries?

11.65 *Evidence obtained by coercion.* The European Court of Human Rights first considered this question in *Saunders v UK* (1996) 23 EHRR 313. S's convictions on counts of dishonesty had been secured in part by the Crown's use of transcripts of answers S had provided to questions put by inspectors appointed to investigate the affairs of the bidding company during Guinness's contested takeover bid for the Distillers Company. Under s 434 of the Companies Act 1985, S had been compelled to answer the inspectors' questions. Additionally, the Act provided that such answers could be used in any subsequent criminal proceedings. Whilst the ECtHR saw no inherent objection to legislation which compels parties to answer questions in the course of non-judicial enquiries, it did however hold that:

> . . . the public interest cannot be invoked to justify the use of answers compulsorily obtained in a non-judicial investigation to incriminate the accused during the trial proceedings.
> (at [74])

The court therefore adjudged that S's right against self-incrimination had been infringed and that S had thereby been deprived of his right of fair trial under Article 6 of the Convention. (Subsequently, the appeals of three of S's co-defendants in the Guinness trial succeeded on identical grounds before the Strasbourg Court: see *IJL, GMR and AKP v UK* (2000) 33 EHRR 225.) In the wake of *Saunders v UK*, the Attorney-General issued guidelines intended to prevent the Crown from using so-called 'derivative evidence' obtained in extrajudicial investigations (see (1998) 148 NLJ 208). Subsequently, the Youth Justice and Criminal Evidence Act 1999, Schedule 3 amended those provisions, like s 434 of the Companies Act 1985, which formerly purported to render admissible in subsequent criminal proceedings evidence procured by compulsion during such investigations.

11.66 *When the prosecution may legitimately use evidence obtained by coercion.* The ECtHR has had to reconsider the issue of defendants who have been coerced into furnishing evidence against themselves. In *O'Halloran and Francis v UK* (2008) 26 EHRR 21 two motorists invoked the privilege against self-incrimination in contesting convictions arising out of driving their motorcars in excess of the speed limit. Section 172 of the Road Traffic Act 1988 entitles the police to require the registered keeper of a vehicle to furnish the name and address of the person driving at the relevant time. Failure to comply is a criminal offence. O, who had admitted that he had driven at 69mph in a 40mph zone, argued that this admission had been wrongly admitted by the justices as it breached his privilege against self-incrimination. F, in contrast, had declined to supply the information requested, had been convicted of breaching s 172 and contested the conviction before the ECtHR. A majority of the ECtHR held that although s 172 directly compelled suspects to provide information which might incriminate them, it was 'unable to accept' that the right to remain silent and the right not to incriminate oneself are absolute rights (at [53]).

11.67 The majority developed arguments formulated in the earlier decision of *Jalloh v Germany* (2006) 44 EHRR 667, where the ECtHR had stated that 'in examining whether a procedure has extinguished the very essence of the privilege against self-incrimination, the Court will have regard, in particular, to the following elements: the nature and degree of the compulsion, the existence of any relevant safeguards in the procedures and the use to which any material so obtained is put' (at [101]). The Court in *Jalloh* added that it had:

> consistently held...that the right not to incriminate oneself is primarily concerned with respecting the will of an accused person to remain silent. As commonly understood in the legal systems of the Contracting Parties to the Convention and elsewhere, it does not extend to the use in criminal proceedings of material which may be obtained from the accused through the use of compulsory powers but which has an existence independent of the will of the suspect...
>
> (at [102])

The Court concluded in *Jalloh* that the evidence at issue in the case—drugs swallowed by J which were retrieved by the forcible administration of emetics—could be considered to fall into the category of material having 'an existence independent of the will of the suspect', the use of which is generally not prohibited in criminal proceedings (esp at [113]). Applying similar logic to the case of *O'Halloran and Francis*, the ECtHR indicated that when gauging whether Article 6 had been violated a court had to weigh various factors in the balance. Thus, in determining whether the extent to which a rule infringed the privilege against self-incrimination was proportionate, account had to be taken of:

- the degree and directness of the compulsion—although the compulsion was direct in the case of s 172 of the Road Traffic Act 1988, the relevant penalties were relatively mild involving either a maximum fine of £1000, a period of disqualification or three penalty points on the license;

- the fact that the requirement forms part of a general regulatory scheme to which all motorists voluntarily submit whenever they take the wheel (see also *Brown v Stott* [2001] 2 WLR 817, where Lord Bingham pointed out, 'All who own or drive motor cars know that by doing so they subject themselves to a regulatory regime. This regime is imposed not because owning or driving cars is a privilege or indulgence granted by the State but because the possession and use of cars (like, eg, shotguns …) are recognised to have the potential to cause grave injury');

- the fact that the law imposes a simple, specific and limited requirement; that the offence of failing to furnish information incorporates a defence—in the case of s 172, a motorist who fails to supply the information requested may plead a defence of due diligence—conviction is not simply a self-fulfilling prophecy;

- that the information demanded might not be the only evidence the prosecution needed to adduce—in O's case, in addition to evidence of who was driving the car the Crown also needed to prove that O was speeding.

In these circumstances the majority of the ECtHR concluded that 'the essence of the applicants' right to remain silent and their privilege against self-incrimination has not been destroyed' (at [62]).

11.68 In contrast to *O'Halloran and Francis*, in *K(A)* [2010] 2 WLR 905 a statute placing parties to a divorce under a duty to disclose their finances was held to breach the right to a fair trial. In the course of disclosure, data emerged suggesting that K had committed tax evasion. K was prosecuted for cheating the public revenue and this evidence was used against him. The Court of Appeal declared:

> A restriction of an accused person's right not to incriminate himself will not infringe his right to a fair trial provided that the compulsion under which the information is obtained is of a moderate nature and the use of the evidence obtained by it represents a proportionate response to a pressing social need.
>
> (at [41])

Here, the compulsion had been strong: failure to disclose the information could have led to prosecution for contempt of court. The protection of the public revenue is an important social objective, but the admission of evidence obtained from K under threat of imprisonment is not a reasonable and proportionate response to that social need.

11.69 It is clear from *O'Halloran and Francis v UK* that the ECtHR no longer considers that rules allowing the Crown to use evidence coerced from suspects by the state inevitably violate the privilege against self-incrimination guaranteed under Article 6. In *O'Halloran* the ECtHR did not engage fully with its earlier decisions. For example, in *Saunders* the Court had declared that the public interest could not be invoked to justify the use of answers compulsorily obtained. In *O'Halloran*, it is obvious that the Court has resiled somewhat from this position. In *Saunders* the Court also made clear that the protection of the privilege against self-incrimination applied across the board to all criminal proceedings, no matter how trivial or grave they might be (at [74]). The factors enumerated in *O'Halloran* indicate that courts may now take violations of the privilege against self-incrimination less seriously where less is at stake.

11.70 *When an accused's right to silence is undermined by someone acting as an agent of the State: Allan v UK.* The ECtHR has had an opportunity to consider the extent of a defendant's right not to be coerced or oppressed into incriminating himself in a different context in *Allan v UK* (2003) 36 EHRR 12. *Allan* concerned the admissibility of statements allegedly made by A to an informer, H. The police infiltrated the informer, whom they had previously schooled, into a police cell along with A, who was under intensive interrogation concerning an armed robbery. The informer had instructions to 'push for what you can'. Although in interrogation A had maintained silence, he made a number of incriminating remarks to his cellmate, H, which were tape recorded. The recordings were admitted in evidence at A's trial. As the court explained, the privilege against self-incrimination extends beyond blatant coercion and compulsion to a wider range of cases where the freedom of the suspect to speak or not to speak to the authorities is undermined:

> While the right to silence and the privilege against self-incrimination are primarily designed to protect against improper compulsion by the authorities and the obtaining of evidence through methods of coercion or oppression in defiance of the will of the accused, the scope of the right is not confined to cases where duress has been brought to bear on the accused or where the will of the accused has been directly overborne in some way. The right, which the Court has previously observed is at the heart of the notion of a fair procedure, serves in principle to protect the freedom of a suspected person to choose whether to speak or to remain silent when questioned by the police. Such freedom of choice is effectively undermined in a case in which, the suspect having elected to remain

silent during questioning, the authorities use subterfuge to elicit, from the suspect, confessions or other statements of an incriminatory nature, which they were unable to obtain during such questioning and where the confessions or statements thereby obtained are adduced in evidence at trial.

(at [50])

The ECtHR laid down that whenever the subterfuge to which the authorities resort in order to cause a suspect who has elected to remain silent to speak is 'the functional equivalent of interrogation', the privilege against self-incrimination will have been infringed:

[T]he right to silence would only be infringed where the informer was acting as an agent of the State at the time the accused made the statement and where it was the informer who caused the accused to make the statement. Whether an informer was to be regarded as a State agent depended on whether the exchange between the accused and the informer would have taken place, and in the form and manner in which it did, but for the intervention of the authorities...whether the conversation...was the functional equivalent of an interrogation, as well as on the nature of the relationship between the informer and the accused.

(at [51])

11.71 In *Allan* itself, the ECtHR considered that although 'no factors of direct coercion' could be identified, A would have been subjected to psychological pressures which impinged on the 'voluntariness' of the disclosures purportedly made by A to H. The conversations H alleged that he had had with A were therefore 'the functional equivalent of interrogation, without any of the safeguards which would attach to a formal police interview, including the attendance of a solicitor and the issuing of the usual caution' (at [52]). The Court of Appeal later accepted that the ECtHR had 'correctly analysed the case', and determined that H's evidence was in consequence largely inadmissible ([2004] EWCA Crim 2236 at [117]). Indeed, Hooper LJ proceeded to explain why this conclusion was logically inescapable:

It would be strange if the law were otherwise than as decided by the ECtHR. One of the functions of the caution is to make it clear that what a suspect says may be used in evidence. The presence of a solicitor or friend should additionally ensure that the suspect understands the questions, knows the importance of his answers and the seriousness of the occasion. The requirements of audio recordings introduced to overcome problems associated with actual (or unfounded allegations of) 'verballing' by police officers now ensure an accurate record of questions and answers...Allowing an agent of the state to interrogate a suspect in the circumstances of this case bypasses the many necessary protections developed over the last twenty years.

(at [122])

11.72 It should be noted that cases like *Saunders v UK* and *Allan v UK* are concerned solely with a defendant's responses to questioning. Thus, *Saunders* did not outlaw:

> ...the use in criminal proceedings of material which may be obtained from the accused through the use of compulsory powers but which has an existence independent of the will of the suspect such as, *inter alia*, documents acquired pursuant to a warrant, breath, blood and urine samples and bodily tissue for the purpose of DNA testing.
>
> (at [69])

This distinction was later endorsed by the Court of Appeal in *A-G's Reference (No 7 of 2000)* [2001] 1 WLR 1879, where a bankrupt had been ordered, under the threat of a penalty, to deliver up all books and papers relating to his estate and his affairs under the Insolvency Act 1986, s 291. Criminal charges followed. Rose LJ ruled that while European human rights jurisprudence protected an individual's right to remain silent in order not to incriminate himself, the use of compulsory powers to locate and take possession of pre-existing documents did not infringe Article 6. Such articles are therefore admissible, subject only to the judicial discretion to exclude them under PACE, s 78. Aikens J expanded on this point in *Kearns* [2002] 1 WLR 2815:

> [I]f the evidence was already in existence and the only effect of the use of the compulsory powers was to bring such evidence to the attention of the court, then its production could not be...objectionable [under human rights law.] That is because the existence and quality of such evidence are independent of any order to produce it that is made against the will of the accused person. Therefore the production of such pre-existing and "independent" evidence could not render a trial unfair and so breach Article 6...There is a distinction between the compulsory production of documents or other material which had an existence independent of the will of the suspect or accused person and statements that he has had to make under compulsion. In the former case there was no infringement of the right to silence and the right not to incriminate oneself. In the latter case there could be, depending on the circumstances.
>
> (at [52]–[53])

This distinction, however, will not always be of easy application. Thus, in *S and A* [2009] 1 Cr App R 18 the Court of Appeal made somewhat heavy weather of deciding whether, in a terrorism case, encryption codes giving access to the defendants' computers would always exist separate from their wills.

11.73 Reverting to *ex p Green Environmental Industries Ltd* (*ante*, para **11.64**), although the statute did not expressly provide that answers, respecting the provenance, transporting, handling and disposal of surgical waste which had been dumped on unlicensed sites, which had been exacted under threat of prosecution under the

Environmental Protection Act 1990, would be admissible in later proceedings, as Lord Hoffmann acknowledged, the judge at any subsequent criminal trial at which the prosecution might seek to adduce such evidence will now be required under the Human Rights Act 1998 to consider whether such derivative evidence conforms to the fair trial requirements of Article 6(1), as interpreted in cases llike *Saunders v UK* (and now *O'Halloran and Francis v UK*).

11.74 It is evident that caution needs to be exercised. The privilege against self-incrimination is readily invoked. The privilege does not, however, serve wholly to exclude the use of coercion by the state to compel the production of potential evidence. In *R (Bright) v Central Criminal Court* [2001] 1 WLR 662, for example, two newspapers were requested to surrender materials relevant to police enquiries into whether David Shayler, by revealing purported details of a failed attempt by the British security services to assassinate the Libyan head of state, had contravened the Official Secrets Act 1989. The newspapers' editors contended that judicial production orders made under PACE, instructing them to hand over materials, infringed their privilege against self-incrimination. Although Judge LJ accepted this argument, the other two members of the Court of Appeal adopted a more nuanced approach. Maurice Kay J, for instance, emphasised that 'the privilege or right (against self-incrimination) is not an absolute one', adding 'there are numerous examples of legislation interfering with it' (at 693). This echoes Lord Mustill's observation in *R v Director of Serious Fraud Office, ex p Smith* [1993] 1 AC 1, at 40, that 'statutory interference with the right is almost as old as the right itself'. A court certainly ought not to conclude too readily that Parliament intended to override the privilege. However, it is equally plain that where suitable procedural safeguards have been put in place (as in the case of production orders under PACE, ss 8 and 9), the courts will not assume that such orders 'fly in the face of the privilege against self-incrimination'.

III. Inferences drawn from lies told by the defendant: *Lucas* directions

> . . . and when she pleaded grace for the mighty lie which Tom had told in order to shift that whipping from her shoulders to his own, the judge said with a fine outburst that it was a noble, a generous, a magnanimous lie—a lie that was worthy to hold up its head and march down through history breast to breast with George Washington's lauded Truth about the hatchet!
>
> Mark Twain, *The Adventures of Tom Sawyer* (1876) chap xxxv

11.75 Thus far we have considered cases where, because the uncommunicative conduct of the defendant at various stages in the criminal process arouses suspicion, the law allows the tribunal of fact, if it so wishes, to draw an adverse inference. Other conduct of the defendant may also arouse suspicion. Notably, if the defendant is shown to have told lies, the jury may be prepared all too readily to infer guilt merely from this circumstance. A defendant of course may tell lies for a variety of reasons, not all of which signify guilt. In order to guide juries in their approach to the matter of lies told by the accused, the judge in many cases is obliged to deliver a special direction, known as a *Lucas* direction (see *Lucas* [1981] QB 720).

11.76 The *Lucas* direction is intended to warn juries against jumping too readily to the conclusion that any lies told by a defendant can be equated with guilt. However, as Beldam LJ pointed out in *Harron* [1996] 2 Cr App R 457, 462, the rules now governing inferences derived for the defendant's lies are complex. The case law is so profuse that it induced Judge LJ, in *Middleton* [2001] Crim LR 251, to say that rather than trawling through 'the steady and almost unstoppable stream of reported decisions' and learned commentaries which have 'tended to obscure the essential simplicity of the principle', it is best for the court to analyse whether a warning needs to be given in the context of each individual case. In a sense, this echoes Kennedy LJ's remarks in *Burge and Pegg* [1996] 1 Cr App R 163, when he cautioned against unnecessary recourse by judges to *Lucas* directions:

> If a *Lucas* direction is given where there is no need for such a direction (as in a normal case where there is a straightforward conflict of evidence) it will add complexity and do more harm than good. Therefore...a judge would be wise always, before speeches and summing-up...to consider with counsel whether, in the instant case, such a direction is required, and if so, how it should be formulated.
>
> (at 173. See also *Codsi* [2009] EWCA Crim 1618 esp at [27] *per* Rix LJ)

11.77 The first question to arise is: when is it actually necessary for a judge to deliver a *Lucas* direction? The Court of Appeal in *Burge and Pegg* provided guidance, suggesting four categories of case where a *Lucas* direction is most commonly called for:

- where the defence relies upon an alibi which is shown to be false (see *post*, para **11.80**);

- where, having determined in his discretion, under *Makanjuola* [1995] 3 All ER 730, that a full corroboration warning is called for in respect of a particular suspect witness's testimony, the judge suggests to the jury that lies told by the defendant may serve to confirm the evidence of the suspect witness (on *Makanjuola* and judicial warnings, see *ante*, paras **1.64–1.68**);

- where the prosecution seeks to show that something the defendant said, either in or out of court, in relation to a separate and distinct issue was a lie, and the prosecution relies on that lie as evidence of guilt in relation to the charge(s) laid against the defendant. This would apply, for example, in a case with facts similar to *Blick* (1966) 50 Cr App R 280. In *Blick*, in a bid to explain why he had been apprehended as a suspected robber after a Keystone Kops chase in a certain locality, B claimed that, as he emerged from a local public lavatory, he had been mistaken for the robber, chased and arrested. It emerged at trial that that particular public lavatory had been closed on the relevant day. If the prosecution sought to rely upon this lie as indicative of B's guilt, it would now be mandatory for the judge to deliver a *Lucas* direction;

- where, although the prosecution's strategy is not actually to rely on the defendant's having told a lie as part of its case, the judge reasonably envisages that there is a real danger that the jury will be tempted to draw an inference unless warned not to do so.

In all these cases the jury will need to be given guidance on how to approach the lies told by the accused.

11.78 From the above it will be seen that a *Lucas* direction does not have to be given in every case, merely because there is a clash between the prosecution and defence versions of events. As Glidewell LJ said in *Liacopoulos* (1994) 31 August, unreported:

> ...where a jury, as is so frequently the case, is asked to decide whether they are sure that an innocent explanation given by a defendant is not true, where they are dealing with the essentials in the case and being asked to say that as a generality what the defendant has said in interview about a central issue, or agreed in evidence about a central issue is untrue, then that is a situation that is covered by the general direction about burden and standard of proof. It does not require a special *Lucas* direction.

Not all inconsistencies and lies, then, attract a *Lucas* direction. Take the case of *Barnett* (2002) 166 JP 407. B, an electrical dealer, was charged with handling a stolen painting. At various times, B gave three different (and bizarre) innocent explanations as to why the police should have found a £40,000 stolen painting under his bed. The trial judge told the jury that the Crown had invited them to infer from this that B was not telling the truth and that it was blindingly obvious that B knew the picture was stolen given that he had told three different and wholly inconsistent stories. The judge omitted to deliver a *Lucas* direction. Jackson J endorsed the view that the mere fact that a defendant has made inconsistent statements does not automatically trigger the need for such a direction. More specifically, the Court of Appeal reasoned, in this case the Crown was not relying upon the details of particular lies told by B to establish an inference of guilt, but was arguing more generally that B's inconsistencies could establish the central plank of the prosecution case, namely that B was lying when he claimed that he did not know that the painting was stolen property. The case did not fall within any of the four categories set out in *Burge and Pegg* (*ante*, para **11.77**) and there was therefore no danger that the jury would follow the forbidden line of reasoning. Moreover, it could be said that:

> In almost every contested handling case, the defendant denies knowing or believing that the relevant goods were stolen, and the prosecution assert that that evidence is a lie. It would be absurd to suggest that every handling case requires a *Lucas* direction.
>
> (at [30])

Unless there is a real perceived risk that the jury may treat a lie, without more ado, as evidence of guilt, a full *Lucas* direction is not called for. This is notably the case where there are merely minor inconsistencies in the accused's account of events (*Hill* [1996] Crim LR 419) or if his lies only affect the defendant's credibility. Thus, in *Smith* [1995] Crim LR 305 S, who was charged with having murdered her husband, had pleaded diminished responsibility. The prosecution were using S's various lies and dishonesty in her fiscal affairs in order to undermine this defence. The lies related uniquely to S's credibility, and there was no real risk that a jury would infer that she had murdered her husband because she had set out to deceive the revenue services. Therefore, the Court of Appeal concluded that there had been no need for the trial judge to deliver a *Lucas* direction.

11.79 In cases where a *Lucas* direction is required, the judge must first tell the jury that before they proceed further they must decide whether they are sure that the defendant actually told the relevant lie. If they are sure that he did deliberately lie, they must next ask themselves why the defendant lied. People lie for all kinds of reasons, some perfectly innocent—for instance, to bolster a true defence, to protect someone, out of panic or confusion, or to conceal some disgraceful conduct other than commission of the offence charged. The judge will refer to whatever explanation the accused has advanced to explain why he lied. Particularly in cases where the accused claims to have lied in order to avoid responsibility for an offence, the courts emphasise the importance of the judge telling the jury only to draw an adverse inference from the lies if they are sure that these were not told for some purpose other than guilt. In *Richens* (1994) 98 Cr App R 43, for example, where the question was whether R had committed a murder under provocation, Lord Taylor CJ held that the trial judge had been wrong to invite the jury to reject R's account of provocation on the basis that he had told lies. The judge ought to have drawn to the jury's attention that someone facing the most serious of charges may have strong motives for lying. Only if they could be sure that that was not R's motive for lying might they draw an adverse inference. Indeed, in *Woodward* [2001] EWCA Crim 2051, Kennedy LJ had to admit that, since in most instances it will be impossible to say what the defendant's motive in lying may have been, in the majority of cases the defendant's lies will lack potential probative force. Finally, the judge will tell the jury that only if they are sure that the defendant did not lie for an innocent reason may they treat the lie as evidence supporting the prosecution case.

IV. Inferences drawn from false alibis put forward by the defendant

11.80 One particular form of untruth put forward by accused persons is the false alibi. In cases where the accused has advanced a false alibi, the judge must direct the jury that even if they find an alibi to be false, that does not entitle them without more ado to convict the defendant. It is something that the jury may take into account, but they should bear in mind that false alibis are sometimes put forward to bolster genuine defences. Lord Widgery CJ discussed this issue in the context of 'supporting evidence' in cases of contested identifications in *Turnbull* [1977] QB 224. He declared:

> Care should be taken by the judge when directing the jury about the support for an identification which may be derived from the fact that they have rejected an alibi. False alibis may be put forward for many reasons: an accused, for example, who has only his own truthful evidence to rely on may stupidly fabricate an alibi and get lying witnesses to support it out of fear that his own evidence will not be enough. Further, alibi witnesses can make genuine mistakes about dates and occasions like any other witnesses can. It is only when the jury are satisfied that the sole reason for the fabrication was to deceive them and there is no other explanation for its being put forward can fabrication provide any support for identification evidence.
>
> (at 230)

It is suggested that these words, which were cited with approval in *Pemberton* (1993) 99 Cr App R 228, apply with equal force to any case where the prosecution invites the jury to draw an adverse inference from the false alibi or where there is a real risk that the jury may assume guilt because the accused concocted a false alibi. Failure to deliver a direction along these general lines may lead to a conviction being quashed as unsafe. In *Pemberton*, as a defence to a charge of mugging a taxi driver, P called his grandmother as an alibi witness. In cross-examination, the grandmother admitted that she was unsure about her dates. Because the crumbling alibi, which may have been a product either of deliberate lies or of an elderly lady's understandable uncertainty about dates, may have exerted 'a significant impact' upon the jury's deliberations, the judge's failure to instruct them on how to approach such evidence was held to have rendered the verdict unsafe.

FURTHER READING

Ashworth and Emmerson, 'Silence and Safety: The Impact of Human Rights Law' [2000] Crim LR 879

Azzopardi, 'Disclosure at the Police Station, the Right of Silence and *DPP v Ara*' [2002] Crim LR 295

Birch, 'Suffering in Silence: A Cost–Benefit Analysis of s 34 of the Criminal Justice and Public Order Act 1994' [1999] Crim LR 769

Cape, 'Incompetent Police Station Advice and the Exclusion of Evidence' [2002] Crim LR 471

Choo, 'Prepared Statements, Legal Advice and the Right to Silence: *R v Knight*' [2004] E & P 62

Dennis, 'Silence in the Police Station: The Marginalisation of Section 34' [2002] Crim LR 25

Jackson, 'Silence and Proof: Extending the Boundaries of Criminal Proceedings in the UK' (2001) 5 E & P 145

Kemp & Balmer, 'The Justice Lottery? Police Station Advice 25 Years on from PACE' [2011] Crim LR 3

Mirfield, *Silence, Confessions and Improperly Obtained Evidence* (1997, Oxford) ch 9

Munday, '*Cum Tacent Clamant*: Drawing Proper Inferences from a Defendant's Failure to Testify' [1996] CLJ 32

Munday, 'Inferences and Explanations' (2002) Archbold News No 2, 6–9

Munday, 'Failures to Mention Facts, the "Pre-prepared Statement", and the Reality of Legal Representation', The Criminal Lawyer, January 2004, 3

Redmayne, 'Rethinking the Privilege against Self-incrimination' (2007) 27 OJLS 209

Redmayne, 'English Warnings' (2008) 30 Cardozo L Rev 1047

Sedley, 'Wringing out the Fault: Self-incrimination in the 21st Century' [2001] 52 NILQ 107

Skennis, 'The Right to Legal Advice in the Police Station: Past, Present and Future' [2011] Crim LR 19

Wolchover, 'Serving Silent Suspects' 2011 (175 Ch & J 71 and 86

Zander, 'What's the Matter in Police Stations?' (2010) 174 CL&J 629

SELF-TEST QUESTIONS

1. Professor Birch has said of the silence provisions in the Criminal Justice and Public Order Act 1994 that 'one might sometimes be forgiven for wondering whether the game of drawing inferences from silence is worth the candle' ([1999] Crim LR at 78). Do you agree?

2. What impact has the European Convention on Human Rights exerted on the English law governing the drawing of adverse inferences *both* from the silence of a person accused of crime *and* from answers given to questions under compulsion?

3. PC Scuffer is questioning Slimeball at the police station concerning the rape of his neighbour's 20-year-old daughter, Lolita. Lolita claims that Slimeball attacked her when she came to his house to deliver a birthday card. Slimeball's solicitor, Bent, is present during the interrogation. At the beginning of the interview, and after caution, Slimeball declares: 'On the categorical advice of Mr Bent, I refuse to answer any of your questions. I merely wish to say that Lolita has made all this up. She is a highly imaginative young lady.' At his trial, Slimeball's defence is that Lolita consented to intercourse with him. Discuss.

   Would your answer be any different if at interview Slimeball had handed in a statement, drafted by his solicitor, Bent, in which it was stated that Lolita had agreed to have sex with Slimeball?

4. If an accused claims that he remained silent on legal advice, in what ways can that affect legal professional privilege?

5. What must the trial judge tell the jury when directing them on the proper inferences they may draw from an accused's silence under s 34 of the Criminal Justice and Public Order Act 1994?

6. What is a *Cowan* direction? What form does it take?

7. Research would suggest that, despite the entry into force of the 1994 Act, no more than half of suspects take advantage of their right to legal advice when interrogated by the police. To what extent, if any, might this statistic be considered disturbing?

8. 'Innocence claims the right of speaking, guilt invokes the privilege of silence' (Jeremy Bentham). Discuss.

9. What is a *Lucas* direction? When is a trial judge obliged to give such a direction?

12

Identification evidence

He talked of going to Streatham that night. Taylor: "You'll be robbed, if you do: or you must shoot a highwayman. Now I would rather be robbed than do that; I would not shoot a highwayman." Johnson: "But I would rather shoot him in the instant when he is attempting to rob me, than afterwards swear against him at the Old Bailey, to take away his life, after he has robbed me. I am surer I am right in the one case, than in the other. I may be mistaken as to the man when I swear. I cannot be mistaken if I shoot him in the act."

James Boswell, *The Life of Samuel Johnson* (1791)

The inherent unreliability of evidence of identification

12.1 Following two grave miscarriages of justice arising out of mistaken identifications, a Departmental Committee was set up in the mid-1970s under the chairmanship of Lord Devlin to report on identification evidence and identification procedures. The Committee concluded:

> We are satisfied that in cases which depend wholly or mainly on eye-witness evidence of identification there is a special risk of wrong conviction. It arises because the value of such evidence is exceptionally difficult to assess; the witness who has sincerely convinced himself and whose sincerity carries conviction is not infrequently mistaken. We have found no forensically practical way of detecting this sort of mistake...

Ever since Lord Devlin reported in 1976, it has been received wisdom that identification evidence—that is, evidence of witnesses, who may have only caught a fleeting glance of an offender, purporting to identify the defendant as the culprit—can prove extremely unreliable. Indeed, mistaken identifications have undoubtedly accounted for a significant number of miscarriages of justice. The trial of Adolf Beck in 1896 affords a notorious example (see 'The Trial of Adolf Beck', Watson (ed), *Notable British Trials* (1924)). But even in comparatively recent times, in *Mattan* (1998) Times, 5 March, the Court of Appeal was compelled posthumously to quash the murder conviction of an appellant who was hanged 42 years earlier on the strength of flawed identification evidence.

12.2 Since 1976 both the courts and the legislature have embarked upon a number of initiatives designed to reduce the risk of wrongful convictions following mistaken identifications. The rules outlined in this chapter—particularly those regulating the identification procedures in PACE, Code D—might seem to carry detail almost to the point of obsession. However, readers who doubt the utility of 'concrete, enforceable rules' should ponder the ordeal three Duke University student lacrosse players underwent between March 2006 and April 2007, following an exotic dancer's false accusations of rape. True, some of these events might not have occurred within our own jurisdiction. Nevertheless, the flawed identification procedures and weak evidentiary protection afforded to those accused of serious crime make for uncomfortable reading. See Robert B. Mosteller, 'The Duke Lacrosse Case, Innocence, and False-Identifications: A Fundamental Failure to "Do Justice"', 76 Fordham L Rev 1337 (2007).

Check out

The Court of Appeal's decision in *Turnbull*

12.3 Although the Devlin Report made a number of recommendations, before Parliament had an opportunity to consider them, 'a specially constituted Court of Appeal of exceptional strength' (*pace Forbes* [2001] 2 WLR 1 at [5] *per* Lord Bingham), summoned in *Turnbull* [1977] QB 224, jumped the gun and issued a set of guidelines. These were designed to reduce the risk of miscarriages of justice resulting from the admission of unreliable identification evidence. In essence, *Turnbull* obliges the court *either* to halt cases where the Crown case relies pretty much exclusively on weak identification evidence *or* in a wide range of circumstances to deliver a warning to the jury, now known as a '*Turnbull* direction', underlining the dangers inherent in identification evidence.

12.4 *Turnbull directions: identification and recognition.* The utility of a *Turnbull* direction is perhaps self-evident in cases where a witness claims to identify a stranger whom he has never seen before the incident. However, as the court noted in *Turnbull*, 'even when the witness is purporting to recognise someone whom he knows, the jury should be reminded that mistakes in recognition of close relatives and friends are sometimes made' (at 228). The fact that the witness has some prior acquaintance with the suspect does not therefore automatically dispense with the need to deliver a *Turnbull* direction (*Fergus* [1992] Crim LR 363). Indeed, as Lord Taylor CJ stressed in *Bentley* (1991) 99 Cr App R 342:

> The recognition type of identification...[is not] straightforward and trouble-free...Each of us...has had the experience of seeing someone in the street whom we know, only to discover later that it was not that person at all. The expression "I could have sworn it was you" indicates the sort of warning which the judge should give, because that is exactly what the witness does...He may nevertheless have been mistaken even where it is a case of recognition rather than one of identification.
>
> (at 344)

In *Capron v R* [2006] UKPC 34, Lord Rodger of Earlsferry reviewed the practice of the Privy Council in such situations, concluding:

> [E]ven in a recognition case, the trial judge should always give an appropriate *Turnbull* direction unless, despite any defence challenges, the nature of the eyewitness evidence is such that the direction would add nothing of substance to the judge's other directions to the jury on how they should approach that evidence.
>
> (at [16])

In *Capron* itself the jury had heard from two eyewitnesses who had known C for many years before the murder. The incident had occurred in the morning, in full daylight. One witness was standing about 40 feet from where the gun was fired; the other said that he was very close indeed when C fired at the deceased and that he was facing C when the latter proceeded to point the gun at him. In these circumstances Lord Rodger was satisfied that the nature of the eyewitnesses' evidence was such that giving a full *Turnbull* direction would have added nothing of substance to the general directions which the judge actually gave the jury. As Scott Baker LJ sagely remarked in *Ley* [2007] 1 Cr App R 25:

> There are...recognition cases and recognition cases. The degree of familiarity of the witness with the person he...is identifying is very relevant just as are the circumstances of the identification itself.
>
> (at [19])

Cases that must be withdrawn from the tribunal of fact

12.5   In some circumstances, it is considered simply too dangerous for the court to admit visual identification evidence at all. If the prosecution case relies upon identification evidence of poor quality—for example, a fleeting glimpse made in difficult conditions—and there is no other evidence in the case to support the correctness of the identification or identifications, it is the judge's duty to withdraw the case from the jury and to direct an acquittal (*Turnbull* [1977] QB 224, 230). This places a heavy onus on the judge, who must decide objectively whether, in the absence of other supporting evidence, the quality of the identification evidence alone justifies leaving the case to the jury (eg, *Shervington* [2008] EWCA Crim 658 esp at [20]; [2008] Crim LR 581). The need to withdraw the case from the jury will sometimes be obvious. In *Daley v R* [1994] AC 117, it could not be established that a shopkeeper, who had identified D as the murderer of his wife, had had adequate opportunity of viewing the killer from his hiding place. There was essentially no other evidence implicating D in the crime. The Privy Council held that in these circumstances the judge ought to have withdrawn the case from the jury.

12.6 The identifying evidence of more than one witness may turn out to be 'poor'. As a full Court of Appeal remarked in *Weeder* (1980) 71 Cr App R 228:

> The identification evidence can be poor, even though it is given by a number of witnesses. They may all have had only the opportunity of a fleeting glance or a longer observation made in difficult conditions, eg the occupants of a bus who observed the incident at night as they drove past.
>
> (at 231)

12.7 It was perhaps predictable that once it was settled law that a court had to withdraw a case from the jury if there was only weak identification evidence identifying the defendant as the culprit, it would be argued that if a judge decided that the identification was of such poor quality that he would not have left the case to the jury in the absence of supporting evidence, did that place the judge under an obligation then to direct the jury that they should not convict on the evidence of identification alone, in the absence of supporting evidence? In *Ley* [2007] 1 Cr App R 25, Scott Baker LJ rejected this argument, stating:

> [T]he jury has to consider its verdict in the light of the whole of the evidence, it being a matter for them what evidence they accept and what evidence they reject.
>
> (at [31])

12.8 *Withdrawing weak identification cases and submissions of no case to answer.* In *Daley*, Lord Mustill reflected upon the unusual power granted to a court to stay a proceeding where the quality of the identification evidence gives serious grounds for concern. More particularly, he sought to explain its relationship to a court's general power to uphold a submission of no case to answer under the principles laid down by the Court of Appeal, a few years after *Turnbull*, in *Galbraith* [1981] 1 WLR 1039 (*ante*, para **2.27**). In essence, when a defendant submits at the close of the Crown case that there is no case to answer, the court must uphold this submission and stay the case only if, taking the prosecution evidence at its highest, it feels that a properly directed jury could not reasonably convict. This is not exactly the principle applied by a court when it determines to withdraw a case from a jury on the ground that the prosecution is placing unduly heavy reliance upon weak identification evidence. If a submission of no case is made, the court has no real regard for the quality of the evidence adduced by the Crown. Under *Turnbull*, however, the court stays the proceedings precisely because the quality of the evidence gives grounds for serious concern. Lord Mustill argued that it was inconceivable that in *Galbraith* the Court of Appeal cannot have had in mind recent decisions of the Court of Appeal in identification evidence cases. The two lines of authority could be reconciled in one of two alternative ways.

The first might be simply to concede that *Turnbull* is an exception to the general principle laid down in *Galbraith*, created:

> to eliminate the "ghastly risk"...run in certain types of identification case. The risk may well be seen as serious enough to outweigh the general principle that the functions of the judge and jury must be kept apart.

However, the Board concluded that the two principles did not conflict on another ground. Whereas *Galbraith*'s purpose is to prevent the judge from substituting his opinion on the credibility of the Crown's evidence for that of the jury—something that Lord Widgery CJ had said was just not the judge's job—*Turnbull* pursues a rather different goal:

> [I]n the kind of identification case dealt with by *Turnbull* the case is withdrawn from the jury not because the judge considers that the witness is lying, but because the evidence, even if taken to be honest, has a base which is so slender that it is unreliable and therefore not sufficient to found a conviction: and indeed, as *Turnbull* itself emphasised, the fact that an honest witness may be mistaken on identification is a particular source of risk. When assessing the "quality" of the evidence, under the *Turnbull* doctrine, the jury is protected from acting upon the type of evidence which, even if believed, experience has shown to be a possible source of injustice.

The need to deliver a warning in the summing-up: the *Turnbull* direction

12.9 Otherwise, in cases where the judge does not stay the prosecution on account of the Crown's heavy reliance upon inherently weak identification evidence, a *Turnbull* direction must be delivered whenever the prosecution case:

> depends wholly or substantially on the correctness of one or more identifications of the accused which the defence alleges to be mistaken.
>
> (at 228)

Moreover, the identification need not always be an identification of the accused himself. In *Bath* [1990] Crim LR 716, for instance, a shopkeeper, from whom B had obtained money by deception in respect of stolen goods, had identified one of the two children who had accompanied B on his visit to the shop. Since, as Lord Taylor CJ noted, 'to identify the accused's companion as being present at the scene alongside the offender is, practically speaking, to identify the latter as the accused', in this category of situation, too, a *Turnbull* direction is required.

12.10 The appellate courts do not require of trial judges the 'incantation of a formula' (*Mills v R* [1995] 3 All ER 865, 872, *per* Lord Steyn). As Scarman LJ indicated in *Keane* (1977) 65 Cr App R 247:

It would be wrong to interpret or apply *Turnbull*...inflexibly. It imposes no rigid pattern, establishes no catechism, which a judge in his summing-up must answer if a verdict of guilty is to stand. But it does formulate a basic principle and sound practice. The principle is the special need for caution when the issue turns on evidence of visual identification: the practice has to be a careful summing-up, which not only contains a warning but also exposes to the jury the weaknesses and dangers of identification evidence both in general and in the circumstances of the particular case.

(at 248)

In all cases in which a *Turnbull* direction is called for, however, the judicial warning must convey the following points:

- the judge must warn of the special need for caution before convicting an accused on the strength of evidence of identification(s);

- the judge must explain why special caution is required when considering identification evidence, and more particularly tell the jury that a convincing identifying witness can still be a mistaken one. There is no necessary correlation between confidence and accuracy;

- the judge must remind the jury of the circumstances in which the identification was made, in short commenting on the quality of the evidence: How long did the witness have the suspect in view? At what distance? In what light? How often did the witness see the suspect? Did the witness have any special reason to remember the accused? Were there discrepancies between the witness' original description of the suspect and the latter's actual appearance? The judge should also remind the jury of any specific weaknesses affecting the identification evidence in the case.

12.11 If the judge considers that the quality of the identification evidence is good, as for example when the identification has been made after a long period of observation or where the identification has been made by a close friend, a neighbour or a workmate, then he may allow the case to proceed even in the absence of any other evidence tending to support the correctness of the identification, provided that the above warning is delivered in the summing-up. However, if the judge feels that the quality of the identification evidence is poor but sees that there is other evidence which could support the correctness of the identification, the judge must additionally point out to the jury any items of evidence capable of supporting the identification—leaving it to the jury, of course, to determine whether those items of evidence do in fact support it. Just as importantly, the judge should also warn the jury about any pieces of evidence which, he feels, they might mistakenly be tempted to treat as supportive (*Forbes* [1992] Crim LR 593).

12.12 *Supporting evidence.* What sort of things amount to 'supporting evidence' for this purpose? Essentially, supporting evidence signifies items of evidence which independently confirm that the witness' identification is unlikely to be mistaken. The evidence must derive from a source independent of the identifying witness, which of course may include the accused. Pieces of evidence that can potentially support the correctness of an identification include items of circumstantial evidence materially linking the accused to the offence, and lies told or false alibis furnished by the accused. A burglar who, having been identified by the householder who caught a glimpse of him, is also found in possession of articles taken from the house, is clearly more likely to have been correctly identified. Similarly, the suspicious behaviour of an accused who concocts a false alibi to put himself elsewhere at the time of the crime will tend to confirm the correctness of a witness's identification. It may be presumed that inferences the tribunal of fact may draw from the defendant's silence during interrogation or from his failure to testify at trial under the Criminal Justice and Public Order Act 1994 can also offer support for an identifying witness's evidence. It might once have been a moot point whether propensity evidence admitted under s 101 of the Criminal Justice Act 2003 ought to qualify as potential 'supporting evidence'. However, since the courts have now admitted such evidence to identify an accused as a perpetrator of an offence, it seems obvious that other misconduct evidence can qualify under this head (see *Eastlake and Eastlake* [2007] EWCA Crim 603 and *ante*, paras **7.52–7.53**). It is to be noted that several of these common types of supporting evidence (notably, lies, false alibis and the defendant's silences) will also require the judge to deliver additional warnings within the summing–up (see *ante*, eg paras **11.34–11.36** and **11.75–11.80**). Curious coincidences, too, may serve to support an identification—as, for example, in *Penny* [1992] Crim LR 184, where a witness to a robbery just happened to have picked out at an identification parade someone who owned one of four cars in the relevant area which was of the right model and colour, and which bore the correct two digits from a partly obscured number plate of which the witness had made a contemporaneous note.

12.13 More controversially perhaps, given that the Devlin Report argued that, owing to its inherent unreliability, convictions ought not to be based exclusively upon visual identification evidence, a full Court of Appeal in *Weeder* (1980) 71 Cr App R 228 held that where the judge considers the quality of the identification evidence good, even if there is no other evidence to support it, a trial judge may 'if so minded' direct the jury that the identification of one witness can support that of another provided that the jury are told that even a number of honest witnesses can be mistaken. The court's principal reason for adopting this line appears to have been that to demand that trial judges instruct juries to treat identifying witnesses' testimony separately would be to impose upon them:

> an obligation to pronounce a wholly useless incantation in the course of their summing-up. No jury, urged to use their common sense, could realistically be expected to follow,

let alone understand, the reasoning of such direction. Take the simple case of violence at a football match. If a dozen witnesses, all of whom had in satisfactory conditions a good opportunity of observing who was committing the particular act of violence complained of, all identified the accused, is their evidence not to be viewed as capable of supporting each other?

(at 231)

It is worth recalling that one of the most notorious miscarriages of justice in our legal history, that of Adolf Beck in 1896, was a result of multiple mistaken identifications (see *ante*, para **12.1**).

12.14 From the foregoing, it will be readily appreciated that *Turnbull* directions can be lengthy and complicated. Nevertheless, in *Nash* [2004] EWCA Crim 2696 at [8]; [2005] Crim LR 232, Hedley J emphasised that in disputed identification cases JSB specimen direction no 30 was 'the briefest permissible summary of the dangers inherent in identification evidence'. This raises a question that frequently troubles those who reflect on the law of evidence: do these directions actually achieve their purpose? How much can jurors realistically be expected to take in? And does the generally positive tone of the warning not reinforce the identification evidence rather than alerting jurors to 'the ghastly risk run in cases of fleeting encounters' (*Oakwell* [1978] 1 All ER 1223, 1227 *per* Lord Widgery CJ)? In an experiment conducted in the 1970s conviction rates were measured amongst groups of jurors who heard a rape case. At that time, the complainant's evidence required a corroboration warning, which was not dissimilar in structure to a *Turnbull* direction. Contrary to the researchers' expectations, conviction rates amongst juries who sat in the cases where a warning was given were higher than amongst those where no warning was given concerning the danger of acting on the uncorroborated evidence of a sexual complainant. Were these experimental findings—which, admittedly, involved only small numbers of surrogate 'jurors'—to be replicated in the real world, and if we could assume that the *Turnbull* direction would produce broadly similar results, such findings still make some sense. Although one might at first assume that a warning is likely to make a jury more cautious and thus less likely to convict, the directions in question are perfectly capable of introducing a very different dynamic into the decision-making process. First, by their very length such directions may serve to focus attention on the suspect piece of evidence, thereby increasing its significance in the jury's eyes. Second, if one examines the structure of that common form of *Turnbull* direction where the judge refers the jury to items of potential supporting evidence in the case, it can be seen that whilst the direction opens with words cautioning the jury against trusting identification evidence too readily, the latter portion of the direction is more upbeat and emphasises all the other items of evidence in the case that might serve to confirm the correctness of the identification. Whatever the truth, one needs to appreciate that the elaborate precautions sometimes taken to control the way in which the tribunal of fact employs suspect evidence may not always achieve the exact purpose we imagine (see Cornish and Sealy, 'Juries and the Rules of Evidence' [1973] Crim LR 208).

12.15 The Court of Appeal normally views failures to deliver *Turnbull* directions seriously. The Court is not unlikely to consider unsafe and to quash convictions returned in such circumstances. Indeed, in *Turnbull* itself Lord Widgery CJ had made explicit:

> A failure to follow these guidelines is likely to result in a conviction being quashed and will do so if in the judgment of this court on all the evidence the verdict is...unsafe.
>
> ([1977] QB 224 at 231)

It has been acknowledged that in certain circumstances a court may dispense with the *Turnbull* warning. In *Freemantle v R* [1994] 1 WLR 1437, the Privy Council indicated that with this statement 'the door was deliberately left ajar for cases encompassed by special circumstances', which will include cases where the visual identification evidence is exceptionally good. In *Shand v R* [1996] 1 All ER 511, for instance, the Privy Council stated that a warning would not be needed if the sole issue in a case was the credibility of the identifying witness. However, since this is the sort of situation where, say, a sane and sober witness purports to identify someone whom he has known for many years and had good opportunity to study at close quarters during the relevant incident but is claimed by the defence to be lying, such cases 'will constitute a very rare exception to a strong general rule' (*Beckford* (1993) 97 Cr App R 409, 415 *per* Lord Lowry).

12.16 The *Turnbull* guidelines were only intended to apply to visual identification of people. Therefore, the judge need not deliver this warning, for example, when a witness purports to identify a motor car implicated in an offence (*Browning* (1991) 94 Cr App R 109), when forensic evidence, like a palm print which could be used to identify the offender, is contested (*Atkinson* (1987) 86 Cr App R 359) or when—as in *Abbott* [2006] EWCA Crim 151, where two witnesses said that intruders, who had entered a restaurant wearing full balaclavas that made it impossible to identify any of their features apart from their eyes, and that they had light-coloured or blue eyes—the case is simply not one in which eyewitness identification plays any part. In *Abbott*, references in the evidence to the description of the men who carried out the robbery, and whom the police later saw running away from a car, were no more than part of the general description of the events. They were not put before the jury as evidence identifying any particular appellant. Similarly, the *Turnbull* warning need not be delivered where the defendant's presence at or near the scene of crime is not in issue, but where the only question is what exactly he was doing there. As

Rose LJ pointed out in *Slater* [1995] 1 Cr App R 584, 589, whether a direction is required in such cases will depend upon the individual circumstances: thus, if the possibility exists that a witness may have mistaken one person for another, a direction will of course be called for. In another case, *Conibeer* [2002] EWCA Crim 2059, C admitted that he had been at the scene of a burglary in the company of his brother, who subsequently pleaded guilty to the offence. C's defence to the burglary charge was that he had been imbibing liberally on the day in question, had had no idea what his brother had been up to, but that when he saw his brother running away he guessed that his brother had got himself into mischief and thought that it would be wiser for him to run away too. In one sense, the witnesses who testified to having apprehended C, after a Keystone Kops chase, were identifying him as the culprit. However, since C admitted that he had been at or near the scene of crime at the relevant time, the real issue was not whether he had been correctly identified, but whether he had been there committing a burglary along with his brother. The Court of Appeal upheld the trial judge's decision not to deliver a full *Turnbull* direction.

Voice identification evidence and adapted *Turnbull* directions

12.17 The visual identification guidelines have found fresh applications in other contexts. First, courts now require trial judges to deliver a special warning to the jury in cases where the Crown relies upon voice identification evidence. In *Hersey* [1998] Crim LR 281, where a robber's identity was established by a witness who had recognised his voice, the Court of Appeal held that when directing juries in such cases trial judges should deliver a 'suitably adapted' *Turnbull* direction. The direction, Swinton Thomas LJ said, should be 'tailored for the purposes of voice identification or recognition':

> Above all, it is vital that the judge should spell out to the jury the risk of a mistaken identification, the reason why a witness may be mistaken, pointing out that a truthful witness may yet be a mistaken witness, and dealing with the particular strengths and weaknesses of the identification in the instant case.

12.18 Voice identification evidence comes in two principal forms: expert evidence, given by forensic specialists with particular scientific competence in the field (*ante*, para **8.9**), and non-expert evidence, delivered by people who have simply acquired familiarity with the target's voice. The reliability of the latter form of voice identification evidence came under intense scrutiny in *Flynn and St John* [2008] 2 Cr App R 20, where the Court of Appeal quashed two convictions that rested heavily on the voice identification evidence of two police officers who claimed to recognise the appellants' voices on poor-quality covert recordings. Whilst the Court had no wish to cast doubt on the admission of evidence of properly qualified voice experts, it was anxious about the practice of police officers, who had had contact with suspects during the course of an investigation, subsequently being called at trial to testify that they recognised the defendants' voices on covert recordings made during the enquiry.

12.19 The Crown regularly resorts to what is termed 'lay listener evidence' from police officers. In *Robb* (1991) 93 Cr App R 161, for example, in addition to practically orthodox expert voice identification evidence (*ante*, para **8.9**), Bingham LJ held that two police officers, who had travelled in the same car as R from Keighley to London, had properly been allowed to testify that R's voice was identical to the one on a tape recording made of the voice of the kidnapper. The policemen, who had listened to R talking incessantly throughout the journey, were not, according to Bingham LJ, expert witnesses giving opinion evidence but merely witnesses of fact giving evidence of what was termed 'recognition based on familiarity'. Such evidence, Gage LJ stressed in *Flynn and St John*, should be employed 'with great caution and great care' (at [63]). Gage LJ made some important general observations on the subject of voice identification evidence, noting that—

- Identification of a suspect by voice recognition is more difficult than visual identification;

- Identification by voice recognition is likely to be more reliable when carried out by experts using acoustic and spectrographic techniques as well as sophisticated auditory techniques, than lay listener identification;

- The ability of a lay listener correctly to identify voices is subject to a number of variables. There is at present little research about the effect of variability but the following factors are relevant:

    (i) the quality of the recording of the disputed voice or voices;

    (ii) the gap in time between the listener hearing the known voice and his attempt to recognise the disputed voice;

    (iii) the ability of the individual lay listener to identify voices in general. Research shows that this ability varies from person to person;

    (iv) The nature and duration of the speech sought to be identified is important. Some voices are more distinctive than others, and the longer the sample of speech the better the prospect of identification;

    (v) The greater the familiarity of the listener with the known voice the better his chance of accurately identifying a disputed voice.

- Whereas an expert in speech analysis is able to draw up an overall profile of an individual's speech patterns, in which the significance of each parameter is assessed separately, backed up with instrumental analysis and reference research, the lay listener's response is 'opaque' in the sense that he cannot know and has no way of explaining to which aspects of a speaker's speech patterns he is responding.

([2008] 2 Cr App R 20 at [16])

2.20 In *Flynn and St John* the Court considered that the voice identification evidence of two police officers, who had spoken with the appellants after their arrest and who had later listened to a covert recording made in a van prior to an aborted robbery, ought to have been excluded by the judge under PACE, s. 78. The quality of the covert recording was poor; the police officers had had little opportunity to acquire familiarity with the defendants' voices; unlike the police officers, other experts were unable to make identifications; the police officers had used quite basic equipment to listen to the covertly taped voices; one police officer's transcript of the taped conversation contained words which an independent forensic consultant could not distinguish as words at all; there was no proper record showing how much contact each officer had had with the appellants; before listening to the tape, one police officer was allowed to see a transcript of the conversation made earlier by the other officer; and the Court took into consideration that even those with considerable familiarity with the parties can still make mistakes. The evidence was 'self-evidently very prejudicial' (at [52]). Gage LJ also made the following telling point:

> [F]or obvious reasons, it is highly desirable that such a voice recognition exercise should be carried out by someone other than an officer investigating the offence. It is all too easy for an investigating officer wittingly or unwittingly to be affected by knowledge already obtained in the course of the investigation.
>
> (at [54])

Where the prosecution seeks to rely upon such evidence in future, it is desirable that the expert is instructed to give an independent opinion on the validity of the voice identification evidence and that 'great care' is taken by police officers to record the procedures which form the basis for their evidence. 'Whether the evidence is sufficiently probative to be admitted will depend very much on the facts of each case'. In every case the judge must deliver a careful direction to the jury warning it of the danger of mistakes in such cases (at [63]) (Cp *Hussain* [2010] EWCA Crim 1327, esp at [46]–[47] *per* Pitchford LJ and *Tamiz et al* [2010] EWCA Crim 2638).

2.21 The Court of Appeal considered one further matter in *Flynn and St John*. Earlier cases had been divided over whether, once voice identification evidence had been admitted, the jury should be invited to compare the voices on the covert recording and the voices of the co-accused when they gave evidence. The Court took the view that such an instruction was permissible provided that the judge also told the jurors that that they should listen to the tapes guided by the evidence of the voice recognition experts, whether expert or lay listeners (at [56]).

Lip-reading and adapted *Turnbull* directions

12.22 It has been held in *Luttrell* [2004] 2 Cr App R 31, that a special warning, not alto-gether dissimilar from a *Turnbull* warning, also needs to be given whenever the Crown relies upon lip-reading evidence (see *ante*, para **8.8**). Proceeding from the general tenet that a special warning is necessary if experience, research or common sense indicates that a certain type of evidence requires the delivery to the jury of a warning of its attendant dangers and the need for caution, tailored of course to meet the needs of the particular case, Rose LJ laid down:

> [I]ts precise terms will be fact-dependent, but in most, if not all cases, the judge should spell out to the jury the risk of mistakes as to the words that the lip-reader believes were spoken; the reasons why the witness may be mistaken; and the way in which a convinc-ing, authoritative and truthful witness may yet be a mistaken witness. Furthermore, the judge should deal with the particular strengths and weaknesses of the material in the instant case, carefully setting out the evidence, together with the criticisms that can prop-erly be made of it because of other evidence. The jury should be reminded that the quality of the evidence will be affected by such matters as the lighting at the scene, the angle of the view in relation to those speaking, the distances involved, whether anything interfered with the observation, familiarity on the part of the lip-reader with the language spoken, the extent of the use of single syllable words, any awareness on the part of the expert witness of the context of the speech and whether the probative value of the evidence depends on isolated words or phrases or the general impact of long passages of conversation.
>
> (at [44])

Clearly, this is yet a further example of what looks very much like a modified *Turnbull* direction.

Identifying animals, identifying from photographs, etc

12.23 The courts do not inflexibly insist upon the delivery of a *Turnbull* direction in every case in which a witness claims to identify something. In *Huddart* [1999] Crim LR 568, for example, a prosecution under the Dangerous Dogs Act 1991, where H claimed that the dog which had bitten the victim was not his docile, affectionate rottweiler 'Winston', who 'was blind in one eye, had eczema and bad back legs and hips', but someone else's vicious cur, it might be noted that Pill LJ left open the question whether a *Turnbull* direction was required when a witness purported to identify the offending dog.

12.24 Nowadays, it is becoming increasingly common for photographs, videotapes and even photofits to assist in identifying offenders. In such cases it is the court itself which is called upon to make the identification. Here, too, since the jurors are not at the mercy of fallible eyewitnesses, no *Turnbull* direction is required. The judge needs merely to warn the jurors of the risk of mistaken identification, and of the need to exercise particular care in any identifications which they make for themselves. However, if deemed appropriate, the judge may additionally warn the jurors about the quality of the photographic evidence, although such matters should be obvious to them anyway (*Blenkinsop* [1995] 1 Cr App R 7).

2.25 More generally, it might just be noted that in a growing range of situations judges are now required to deliver cautionary directions to juries. Recently created categories include not only voice identification and lip-reading testimony, but also cases involving 'cell confessions' (see *Pringle v R* [2003] UKPC 9, *ante*, para **1.69**), lifestyle evidence (JSB specimen direction no 36), identification by DNA evidence (JSB specimen direction no 30a), special measures directions (JSB specimen direction no 22a), and so on.

Identification procedures and PACE, Code D

2.26 PACE, Code D provides a second means of reducing the risk of miscarriages of justice deriving from mistaken identifications. This Code, of which the latest version came into force on 31 January 2008, sets out detailed procedures with which the police must comply for identification of suspects by witnesses during the investigation of crime. Notably, whereas under the earlier versions the identification parade was unquestionably the preferred method, under later revisions of Code D the preferred form of identification procedure in most circumstances is the video identification.

2.27 The decision to override the old principle that an identification parade was the most reliable method of identifying suspects was largely a response to the high proportion of costly identification parades which had to be cancelled. Whereas police records revealed that roughly half of the identification parades they organised were being called off, only about five per cent of video parades used to suffer a similar fate. Video identifications, of course, can also be organised very speedily. The VIPER (Video Identification Parade Electronic Recording) system was first introduced as part of a drive against street crime. Under this procedure, police forces make a video of their suspect at one of the many studios around the country, and then send the images to West Yorkshire, where a central body compiles a video portfolio with footage of eight similar-looking foils. The video compilation is then sent back to the original force. Witnesses, under this system, can take part in a video identification within a matter of hours of the crime. From the outset, police forces that availed themselves of this service reported an increase in both the number of procedures organised and in the percentage of positive identifications. Now, all police forces make use of the VIPER system, which, it is claimed, 'can turn around urgent parades in one hour'. In December 2004 the Home Office reported:

> By 2004/2005, 98 per cent of ID parades were conducted using video technology, resulting in a 65 per cent saving on time spent on ID parades for uniformed staff time and a 71 per cent reduction for administrative staff. On current trends and projected usage, this will represent a saving of £143 million over five years from April 2002.

12.28 Some research has actually suggested, improbably perhaps, that video identifications can prove more reliable than identification parades—although counsel did venture a contrary opinion in *George (Barry)* [2002] EWCA Crim 1923 ('A video parade provides an inferior opportunity to examine and assess a suspect': at [33]). Code D meticulously regulates the procedures that must be followed when the police conduct an identification procedure—notably in Annexes A, B and C. The Annexes set out how video identifications, identification parades and group identifications must be conducted, specify how identifications are to be made, and also require *inter alia* that a video recording or, if that is impracticable, a colour photograph be taken of the parade to show that the line-up was indeed conducted fairly (avoiding the sort of problem that came to light in *Kamara* (2000) 9 May, case no 99/2799/X4, where, unlike the foils, K, whose conviction dated from 1981, had appeared on an identification parade in ill-fitting prison clothing—something now expressly contrary to para 6 of Annex A).

When must an identification procedure be held?

12.29 The Code requires that an identification procedure must be held in the following circumstances:

> Whenever
>
> (i) a witness has identified a suspect or purported to have identified them prior to any identification procedure set out in paras 3.5 to 3.10 having been held; or
>
> (ii) there is a witness available, who expresses an ability to identify the suspect, or where there is a reasonable chance of the witness being able to do so, and they have not been given an opportunity to identify the suspect in any of the procedures set out in paras 3.5 to 3.10,
>
> and the suspect disputes being the person the witness claims to have seen, an identification procedure shall be held . . .
>
> (para 3.12)

Additionally, an identification procedure may be held 'if the officer in charge of the investigation considers that it would be useful' (para 3.13). It is notable that video identifications are now listed (paras 3.5–3.6) ahead of identification parades (paras 3.7–3.8) in Code D, thereby underlining the altered hierarchy of methods of identification. Whilst the officer in charge of an investigation can resort to other procedures in specified circumstances under the Code, para 3.14 states:

> If, because of para 3.12, an identification procedure is to be held, the suspect shall initially be offered a video identification … unless:
>
> (i) a video identification is not practicable; or
>
> (ii) an identification parade is both practicable and more suitable than a video identification; or
>
> (iii) para 3.16 (group identifications) applies.

2.30 A video identification is defined as 'when the witness is shown moving pictures of a known suspect, together with similar images of others who resemble the suspect' (para 3.5), whereas an identification parade occurs 'when the witness sees the suspect in a line of [at least, eight] others who resemble the suspect' (para 3.7). The hierarchy set out in para 3.14 is plain. In future, resort will be had to identification parades only if a video identification is considered unsuitable or if, for some reason, a parade is to be preferred. The third option, the group identification, which is 'when the witness sees the suspect in an informal group of people' (para 3.9; examples given in Annex C, §§ 4 and 5), may be offered initially by the officer in charge if he considers that it would be 'more suitable than a video identification or an identification parade and the identification officer considers it practicable to arrange' (para 3.16). The suspect may refuse the method of identification offered by the police and may make representations that another method be adopted. However, it is up to the officer in charge whether or not to offer the suspect another form of identification procedure 'which [he] considers suitable and practicable' (para 3.15). A suspect is warned that if he does not cooperate in a video identification, an identification parade or a group identification, his 'refusal may be given in evidence in any subsequent trial and police may proceed covertly without their consent or make other arrangements to test whether the witness can identify them' (para 3.17(v)). If none of the three above-mentioned options is 'practicable', the officer in charge may resort to a confrontation, 'when the suspect is directly confronted by the witness' (para 3.23).

2.31 An identification procedure must be held:

> unless it is not practicable or it would serve no useful purpose in proving or disproving whether the suspect was involved in committing the offence. For example, when it is not disputed that the suspect is already well known to the witness who claims to have seen them commit the crime.
>
> (para 3.12)

One question posed by para 3.12 is what qualifies as 'serving no useful purpose'. By way of example of how this exception might be interpreted, in *Harris* [2003] EWCA Crim 174 victims of a robbery claimed to know one of their aggressors, having attended the same school until two years previously: although they had not been in the same class and only knew H, who would have been 14 years old at the time, by his distinctive forename (Tristan), the trial judge had held that this case fell within the terms of Code D, where the police were not obliged to hold an identification procedure. Potter LJ, however, noted that the example furnished in the version of Code D then in force (para 2.15) insisted that '*it is not in dispute* that the suspect is already well-known to the witness'. (As the House of Lords had earlier indicated in *Forbes*, these italicised words were important, given that the purpose of the parade was not merely to afford an opportunity to the eyewitness to identify the suspect but also to allow the suspect an opportunity, if he so desired, to test the reliability of the eyewitness identification: [2001] 2 WLR 1 at [19] and [26(4)]].) In *Harris*, the suspect had contested that he was well known to the victims. Therefore, the case fell outside the express terms of the example given in para 2.15 (now para 3.12), and an identification procedure therefore ought to have been arranged. In contrast, the court in *H v DPP* [2003] EWHC 133 (Admin) held, not unexpectedly, that it would have served no useful purpose for the police to have organised an identification parade in H's case given that it was undisputed that the victim, prior to an assault which had lasted a full seven minutes, had known her aggressor well for a period of 18 months.

12.32   Whilst Code D imposes a duty to hold an identification procedure in a wide range of circumstances—and failure to do so and to warn the jury of the gravity of that failure may lead to the quashing of convictions (eg, *Gojra* [2010] EWCA Crim 1939)—it should be noted that the Code does not give a suspect a general right to call for a parade to be held whenever he contests his guilt. *Nicholson* (1999) 164 JP 29, for example, illustrates a situation where, in the words of the former Code D:2.15, '*there is no reasonable possibility that a witness would be able to make an identification*'. N pleaded an alibi to charges of wounding, indecent assault and robbery. Because the victim, who had been attacked from behind, had said that she would be unable to identify her assailant, the police decided not to hold an identification parade. The Court of Appeal rejected N's contention that in these circumstances it was mandatory to hold a parade under Code D if N requested one. It is the case that a defendant is entitled to rely at trial upon the fact that a witness has failed to pick him out at an identification procedure. As Lord Bingham subsequently pointed out in *Forbes* [2001] 1 AC 473, 482, 'If the eyewitness fails to identify the suspect, that will ordinarily strengthen his position during the investigation and at trial.' However, a mere assertion by N that he required a parade, simply so that at trial he could rely upon the witness's failure to recognise him, did not trigger an obligation on the police to indulge in the trouble and expense of organising a parade. More specifically, Potter LJ declared that 'there must have been what amounts to a purported visual identification by a witness before the terms of [Code D] come into operation'. This situation it is suggested, will continue to be one where, in the words of para 3.12, an identification procedure 'would serve no useful purpose in proving or disproving whether the suspect was involved in committing the offence'.

How Code D is generally to be interpreted

12.33 At one time the courts did allow for one exceptional category of case that was said to fall outside the literal wording of Code D. Problems had arisen in the situation where a suspect had already been identified by a witness under another permissible method of identification. In *Popat* [1998] 2 Cr App R 208, P, who was charged with serious sexual offences, had been identified by a witness from her front window while looking out for the suspect in the company of a police officer. Such a procedure was provided for in Code D, allowing a police officer to take the witness to a particular neighbourhood to see whether she can identify the suspect there. This procedure continues to figure in Code D, which provides:

> In cases where the suspect's identity is not known, a witness may be taken to a particular neighbourhood or place to see whether they can identify the person they saw. Although the number, sex, age, race, general description and style of clothing of other people present at the location and the way in which any identification is made cannot be controlled, the principles applicable to the formal procedures under paras 3.5 to 3.12 shall be followed so far as practicable.
>
> (para 3.2)

In *Popat* no further identification procedure took place and, in essence, the question for the Court of Appeal was whether a suspect who had already been identified but continued to contest the correctness of the identification was entitled to an identification parade. Hobhouse LJ held that if there has been an 'actual and complete' identification, there is no need to hold a further identification procedure. What precisely 'actual and complete' meant in this context was unclear, but it was plainly intended to include a one-to-one identification under good conditions and to exclude identifications which there may be reason to suspect are unreliable. As the court put it, 'The mandatory obligation in the first sentence of para D:2.3 [now para 3.12] relates to a situation where a suspect is being produced by the police to a witness not by a witness to the police'. Whether in cases where the police feel that there has been an 'actual and complete' identification it is necessary in addition to hold a parade for other witnesses was therefore said to be 'a matter of discretionary judgement exercised in the light of the purpose of the Code and the interests of justice' (*El-Hannachi* [1998] 2 Cr App R 226 at 238).

12.34 The House of Lords considered whether the 'actual and complete' exception created by Hobhouse LJ in *Popat* was good law in *Forbes* [2001] 1 AC 473. More importantly, however, the House of Lords settled the way in which the provisions of Code D are to be interpreted. The House reasoned that Code D is 'an intensely practical document', designed to give police officers clear instructions on when to hold identification procedures. Therefore, it only makes sense 'to read the Code as meaning what it says'. Transposing the House's argument into the terms of the current version of Code D, para 3.12 states clearly that a parade is to be held whenever 'the suspect disputes being the person the witness claims to have seen': this is a mandatory requirement and there is no warrant for reading additional exceptions into it. In *Forbes*, the Law Lords could see no justification either in the Code or in the earlier case law for drawing the distinction, suggested by Hobhouse LJ, between cases where the suspect is produced by the police for the witness and those where the suspect is produced by the witness. The very notion of a 'fully satisfactory', or of an 'actual and complete', or of an 'unequivocal' identification is problematical for a number of reasons. First, in the words of the court, 'it replaces an apparently hard-edged mandatory obligation with an obviously difficult judgmental decision'. In this context, a clear rule is preferable to a vague discretion. Second, under *Popat* the decision as to whether a 'fully satisfactory' procedure has already taken place is entrusted to a police officer, whose view on this question may not be entirely neutral. Finally, the House reminded itself of the policy underlying Code D: namely, the need to prevent against wrongful conviction following mistaken identification of a suspect. The House of Lords felt that *Popat* overlooked the fact that grave miscarriages of justice have in the past resulted from identifications which were thought to be 'fully satisfactory'. Thus, *Forbes* reaffirmed the literal reading of Code D, which requires that a parade be held 'whenever a suspect disputes an identification'.

12.35 Although the wording and content of the Code may have been modified—notably, in 2003—the interpretative approach the House of Lords advocated in *Forbes* must remain good law. One sees this perhaps in *Marcus* [2004] EWCA Crim 3387; [2005] Crim LR 384. In this case, it emerged that, owing to a suspect's unusual features and to a lack of similar images in the VIPER picture library, the police, following the advice of the CPS, had organised two separate video parades for witnesses. In one, the witnesses had viewed the videotape of nine individuals who, by a 'somewhat crude procedure', had certain key facial features masked; in the other, the masking was removed, thereby facilitating identifications of M. Even the officer in charge of the parade admitted that this procedure was 'blatantly unfair'. The Court of Appeal, not surprisingly, disapproved the police's inventiveness, and quashed those of M's convictions that arguably had been contaminated by this very clear violation of Code D.

12.36 Of course, the question remains: what exactly qualifies as an 'identification'? In *Akinyemi* [2001] EWCA Crim 1948, [2001] All ER (D) 47 (Aug), for instance, where the victim of an attempted robbery kept A in view continuously while the police chased and eventually apprehended him, the Court of Appeal held that the police had been under no obligation to hold an identification parade: A had been in view at all times, and therefore this was not a case of identification within the terms of Code D. As Latham LJ put it, the situation:

> ...was no different from [the victim's] having been able to overcome A himself and then been joined by the police. The only distinction is in point of time and the extent to which the jury could be satisfied that [the victim] and the police were correct in their evidence as to what was described by the judge as continuity. This was the true issue for the jury, not identification.
>
> (at [14])

It is perfectly possible that this would still be a situation where, in the words of revised Code D:3.12, to hold an identification procedure 'would serve no useful purpose in proving or disproving whether the suspect was involved in committing the offence'.

Identification evidence and evidence of description

12.37 The question whether or not to qualify something as an identification can arise in another way. Witnesses not infrequently describe suspects' clothing, appearance and so on, rather than claiming to recognise their visual features. Such evidence, in a sense, 'identifies' the suspect; but is it an identification such as to require the witness to take part in an identification procedure? As the Court of Appeal suggested in *Gayle* [1999] 2 Cr App R 130, there is a:

> qualitative difference between identification evidence and... "evidence of description". The special need for caution before conviction on identification evidence is because, as experience has so often shown, it is possible for an honest witness to make a mistaken identification. But the dangers of an honest witness being mistaken as to distinctive clothing or the general description of the person he saw (short or tall, black or white, etc, or the direction in which he was going) are minimal. So the jury can concentrate on the honesty of the witness in the ordinary way.
>
> (at 135)

The House of Lords, too, in *Forbes* conceded that Code D need not be construed to cover all situations where a suspect might be described as having been 'identified' by a witness. Thus, if a witness says that he cannot identify the suspect, the House accepted that there is 'very probably' no necessity to hold a parade.

12.38 Finally, it might be mentioned that in *Gummerson and Steadman* [1999] Crim LR 680 the Court of Appeal ruled that Code D does not actually require in express terms that a 'voice identification parade' be held in cases where voice identification arises. It is suggested, however, that it will normally be desirable for the police to arrange such a test of the witness's ability to pick out the suspect's voice from a number of foils if the witness claims to be able to recognise the culprit's voice. This, it should be stressed, is an issue distinct from a witness attending an identification parade who requests that a member or members of the parade be invited to speak. In the latter event, Code D, Annex B, § 18 lays down:

> When the request is to hear members of the parade speak, the witness shall be reminded that the participants in the identification parade have been chosen on the basis of physical appearance only. Members of the identification parade may then be asked to comply with the witness's request to hear them speak...

See 'Voice identification Parades', discussed *post*, para **12.42**.

Code D and the various methods of identification

12.39 Code D regulates the various methods of identification: video identification (where the witness picks the suspect out by viewing nine persons, including the suspect, on videotape), identification parades, group identifications (where the witness picks the suspect out from an informal group, either with or without the suspect's consent—for example, from amongst pedestrians passing through a shopping centre, passengers at a railway or bus station, people waiting in queues or groups in public places, people leaving an escalator, and so on—see Annex C, § 4), and confrontations (confronting the witness with the suspect, in the presence of the latter's solicitor, interpreter or friend, normally at a police station). Code D additionally regulates the showing of photographs to witnesses (see Annex E) and the taking of fingerprints—and their destruction if those individuals from whom they have been taken are no longer suspected of having committed an offence (Code D:4 and Annex F).

12.40 The police are under a strict duty to comply with the procedures laid down in Code D (*Quinn* [1995] 1 Cr App R 480), and any serious breaches of these rules, if they result in potentially significant prejudice to the accused, will lead judges to exclude the identification evidence under s 78 of PACE. Nevertheless, in each individual case the question will be to determine whether the breach of the Code D procedures is 'significant and substantial' in the context of the trial. For this reason, in

Nelson [2004] EWCA Crim 447, for example, the Court of Appeal upheld a trial judge's decision to admit evidence of identification despite the police's failure to note down N's objections to six of the nine videotaped foils shown to witnesses at the video parade. Inadvertent omissions by the police will tend to be disregarded if they could not have affected the outcome (*Middleton* [2005] EWCA Crim 692). In *Kingdom* [2009] EWCA Crim 2935, where a witness in hospital accidentally saw a photograph of K and spontaneously exclaimed 'That's him!' before taking part in a video parade at which he eventually picked K out, the judge was held rightly to have admitted evidence of the successful identification accompanied by a warning that the later identification was tainted and that the hospital incident was not to be treated as evidence of an identification.

12.41   The fact that Code D may not technically apply to a particular method of identi-fication does not necessarily mean that the Code will not exert influence on the procedures that, the courts will insist, must be observed when such forms of identi-fication are employed. In *Smith (Dean Martin)* [2009] 1 Cr App R 36, for instance, as now happens very frequently, police officers viewed a CCTV recording to try to make identifications of people involved in a shooting outside a nightclub. Whilst recognising that police officers in this situation do not stand in the same shoes as witnesses asked to identify someone they have seen committing a crime, it was accepted that 'safeguards which [Code D] is designed to put in place are equally important in cases where a police officer is asked to see whether he can recog-nise anyone in a CCTV recording.' As in the case of other forms of identification, record-keeping is important. As Moses LJ explained:

> The mischief is that a police officer may merely assert that he recognised someone with-out any objective means of testing the accuracy of such an assertion. Whether or not Code D applies, there must be in place some record which assists in gauging the reliabil-ity of the assertion... [I]f the police officer fails to recognise anyone on first viewing but does so subsequently those circumstances should be noted. The words that officer uses by way of recognition may also be of importance. If an officer fails to pick anybody else out that also should be recorded, as should any words of doubt. Furthermore, it is necessary that if recognition takes place a record is made of what it is about the image that is said to have triggered the recognition.
>
> (at [67]–[68])

'Voice identification parades'

12.42   Although Code D does not regulate this form of identification procedure, the Home Office has issued a non-mandatory circular, as an example of good practice, prescribing the way in which voice identifications parades ought to be conducted ('Advice On The Use Of Voice Identification Parades', no 057/2003). The circular 'may ultimately go forward for inclusion in Code D' (para 2). For the time being, however, Code D simply says that the police are not precluded from employing them 'where they judge that appropriate' (para 1.2). Sensibly, the circular declares that 'under no circumstances should an attempt be made to conduct a live voice identification procedure, using live suspect and foils' (para 7). Instead, along with 'a representative sample' of the suspect's recorded speech, no less than 20 other persons' samples should be sent to a police-approved expert in phonetics or linguistics, and the latter should select eight of these to accompany that of the suspect. The nine samples are copied onto three videotapes, each displaying the sample numbers. The suspect's solicitor must be given an opportunity to be present at the voice procedure (para 22), which is itself videotaped (para 23). Owing to its inherent unreliability, Ormerod argues that 'trial judges ought to adopt an ultra-cautious approach to such evidence' (note to *Robinson* [2006] Crim LR 427, 428). This is not necessarily the courts' perspective. In *Robinson* [2006] 1 Cr App R 13, Smith LJ remarked: 'it seems to us that these problems are no different in their general nature from the problems frequently encountered with visual identification...in fleeting glimpse cases' (at [21]).

Dock identifications

12.43 Dock identifications, something of a charade where witnesses formally identify suspects for the first time in the courtroom, used to be common practice. They are still technically admissible in the discretion of the judge. It is sometimes said that this form of identification is more readily permitted in the magistrates' courts (*Barnes v Chief Constable of Durham* [1997] 2 Cr App R 505), in the sense that in certain situations dock identifications are unavoidable. For example, if a police officer stops the driver of a car, who then fails to produce documents evidencing his identity as required and who at trial subsequently claims that he was not in fact the driver, the justices may feel that they have little option but to allow the prosecution to call the police officer to identify the defendant in the dock as the driver. In the words of Popplewell J:

> If in every case where the defendant does not distinctly admit driving there has to be an identification [procedure], the whole process of justice in a magistrates' court would be severely impaired.
>
> (at 512)

12.44 Although in *North Yorkshire Trading Standards Department v Williams* (1995) 159 JP 383 it was said that the same principles must apply in the case of non-arrestable offences as in the most serious cases—and, indeed, this message is implicit in *Forbes* [2001] 2 WLR 1, where Lord Bingham clearly indicated that the strict requirement to hold identification parades in all save exceptional circumstances (under the old version of Code D) applied to courts across the board—it is acknowledged that magistrates' courts present particular problems (see, eg, Conner (2001) 165 JPJo at 842). The following principles, it is suggested, apply in the magistrates' courts:

- dock identifications are not *ipso facto* inadmissible (*R v Horsham Justices, ex p Bukhari* (1982) 74 Cr App R 291);
- justices have a discretion whether or not to admit such evidence, weighing the prejudicial effect of admitting it against its probative value;
- unless a defendant gives notice to the prosecution of his intention to raise the issue of identity, a dock identification may be permitted in order to counter an ambush defence (*Barnes v Chief Constable of Durham, supra*). Moreover, there are clear indications that such a notice requirement is unlikely to be held to infringe a defendant's right of fair trial under ECHR, Article 6 (*Karia v DPP* (2002) 166 JP 753 esp at [26]–[27] and [40] *per* Stanley Burnton J);
- if they do allow a dock identification, the justices—just like jurors—will have to be reminded of the dangers inherent in identification evidence.

12.45 Otherwise, speaking of criminal courts more generally, a dock identification is normally only allowed if a witness has already identified the accused at a prior identification procedure conducted in accordance with Code D. In other circumstances, save where justified by unusual circumstances (eg *Reid* [1994] Crim LR 442, a recognition case, where the witness had had a chance to view the suspect for a total period of about three hours; and *Gardner* [2004] EWCA Crim 1639, another recognition case where it was not initially obvious that identification would be an issue in the case and where there was ample supporting evidence), dock identifications are considered a most unsatisfactory method of identifying a suspect. As Lord Carswell remarked in *Edwards v R* [2006] UKPC 23 at [22], unless he has already been identified by the witness by other means, the dock identification is 'an undesirable practice in general and other means should be adopted of establishing that the defendant in the dock is the man who was arrested for the offence charged'.

Police photographs

12.46 When the police are still looking for a suspect, it may be necessary to show a witness albums of mugshots. Since the presence of a suspect's photograph in such a collection indicates that person has a criminal record, the courts will normally hold that the prosecution may not lead in-chief that the witness identified the accused after having been shown photographs (*Lamb* (1980) 71 Cr App R 198).

Such evidence is considered simply too prejudicial to the defendant. However, it may be admitted if the disclosure will not occasion prejudice—for example, if the jury already know that the accused has a criminal record (*Allen* [1996] Crim LR 426), or if the defendant has refused to participate in any identification procedure and there is no other means of establishing that he was actually identified (*Lamb*). Alternatively, such evidence may be led to refute a defence suggestion, say, that the witness' identification is a recent error—as in *Bleakley* [1993] Crim LR 203, where B had claimed that the robbery victim had only identified him because B had visited the victim's newsagents the evening before the robbery. This position has not altered since the entry into force of Part 11 of the Criminal Justice Act 2003, which renders a defendant's bad character admissible in a wider range of situations than before: *Green* [2006] EWCA Crim 776 (see further Chapter 7, *ante*). Indeed, *Green* makes clear that such prejudice cannot realistically be averted even by adopting the subterfuge of saying that the witness identified the defendant from what are called pictures of 'local males'.

Identifications made from photographs and videotape

12.47 It is now commonplace for the Crown to adduce as part of its case photographs and films taken by surveillance or security cameras. When the Crown introduces photographic evidence, in addition to allowing the tribunal of fact to examine the photograph or film to decide for itself whom it depicts (*Dodson and Williams* (1984) 79 Cr App R 220), the proper procedure is to call a witness familiar with the defendant to identify him as the person portrayed in the photograph or film. Although close acquaintance is obviously desirable, the witness need not have known the defendant especially well. The extent of the witness's acquaintance with the defendant will simply affect the weight of his evidence. In *Blenkinsop* [1995] 1 Cr App R 7, a violent disorder case arising out of an incident in which a hunt saboteur had died, the Crown produced police video and photographs taken at the scene which showed someone resembling B. At trial, a policeman, who had interviewed B for approximately three minutes, was allowed to relate that he had viewed the photographs two months after the interview and that he recognised B on the basis of this short acquaintance. As Simon Brown LJ pointed out in *Caldwell and Dixon* (1993) 99 Cr App R 73, 76:

> The plain fact is that recognition evidence of this kind is, subject always to the discretion of the trial judge to exclude it, *prima facie* admissible...Recognition, all would surely agree, is generally more reliable than identification of a stranger and accordingly it ordinarily deserves greater evidential weight.

12.48 Particular problems may arise when an identification purports to be made, say, by police officers who 'recognise' the accused. There is an obvious risk that the use of policemen to make such identifications may prejudice the accused. Although the point appears not to have been taken in this case, in *Taylor v Chief Constable of Cheshire* [1986] 1 WLR 1479 no less than three police officers were allowed to testify that they had viewed a video taken by a security camera, showing someone they recognised as the defendant shoplifting. This was the sole identification evidence in the case as the staff at the store, to which the police had returned the videotape, had thoughtfully erased the film. The fact that T was well known to a number of policemen could easily have implied that T had had other brushes with the law. In other words, evidence given in this form can carry the implication that a defendant has a criminal record, a course which is normally to be avoided unless such evidence is admissible as other misconduct evidence (see generally Chapter 7, *ante*). The courts' treatment of such evidence has not always been too sure-footed. Whilst in *Fowden and White* [1982] Crim LR 588, the Court of Appeal held that a police officer's evidence that he recognised a pair of shoplifters ought to have been excluded because it was based upon his having seen them commit similar offences a week earlier, in *Caldwell and Dixon* (1993) 99 Cr App R 73 another Court of Appeal more realistically observed that such an attitude unduly favours those with criminal records or with other offences to their credit. It might be noted that the view in *Caldwell and Dixon* that there is no reason to advantage those with criminal records has since found favour in *Hardy* [2002] EWCA Crim 296, where a trial judge's decision to admit the evidence of four policemen who had recognised H from an indistinct still photograph of a robbery was upheld. Of course, the defendant's acquaintance with the forces of law and order may be perfectly innocent. If an officer's ability to identify D is explicable on other grounds—in *Grimer* [1982] Crim LR 674, for instance, a security officer could identify G because they knew one another socially, having played football together for a number of years—it ought to be sufficient for the judge specifically to direct the jury's attention to the nature of their acquaintance.

Photographic identification and the expert *ad hoc*

12.49 Identification by means of photographs and videotape has even given rise to a novel form of quasi-expert witness. In *Clare and Peach* [1995] 2 Cr App R 333, the Court of Appeal formulated a new role for police officers in identifying offenders from photographs, creating a category of witnesses designated 'experts *ad hoc*'. C and P, who had denied guilt by claiming mistaken identity, were convicted of violent disorder following a fracas between rival football supporters. CCTV cameras had filmed the incident in monochrome. Because the incident was brief and the scene confused, with large numbers of young men milling around, a police witness was called who had carefully viewed the film forty or so times and who had also studied good-quality colour photographs taken of supporters at and before the match. The officer was allowed to talk the jurors through the video as it was being shown, explaining what he *thought* was happening and who he *thought* was involved. He identified C and P amongst those committing acts of violence. On appeal, Lord Taylor CJ held that 'whether or not the tag (expert *ad hoc*) is appropriate' and regardless that it might constitute 'an extension of established evidential practice', because the police officer had, by lengthy and studious application, acquired special knowledge that the court did not possess, this entitled him to give the evidence he did in the character of an 'expert *ad hoc*'. Such a course, it was claimed, coincides with interests of economy, convenience and dispatch, for 'to afford the jury the time and facilities to conduct the same research would be utterly impracticable'. This decision does seem to raise some difficulties. It might be questioned whether, solely to save time and money, it is really desirable to convert evidence, which a court is perfectly capable of viewing for itself, into identification evidence presented by an interested third party dressed up as an expert for the day. Similarly, one cannot help wondering why, if police officers can by repeated study of a piece of film footage turn themselves into experts *ad hoc*, the defendant too, in deference to equality of arms, ought not to be allowed to produce a similar 'expert' witness who is prepared to claim the contrary. Equally, if one recalls what Bingham LJ, in *Robb* (1991) 93 Cr App R 161, described as witnesses of fact giving evidence of what was termed 'recognition based on familiarity', it is not necessarily easy to see the distinction between the policeman in *Clare and Peach*, who pored over the video and photographs and thereby turned himself into an expert *ad hoc*, and the two officers in *Robb* who endured R's relentless chatter on a long journey and who thereby acquired familiarity with R's voice but no *ad hoc* expertise.

Facial mapping

12.50   With the spread of CCTV cameras in our urban areas and a proliferation of private security cameras, photographic evidence figures ever more prominently in criminal prosecutions. In its wake, a further form of identification evidence, facial mapping, has been growing more common in recent years. This device allows a suitably qualified expert witness to give opinion evidence of identification based on a comparison between images taken, say, at a scene of a crime by a video or stills camera and a reasonably contemporary photograph of the accused, provided that both are available to the jury so as to enable them to form their own judgement on the basis of the photographs and the expert testimony (eg, *Stockwell* (1993) 97 Cr App R 260). A conviction has even been upheld where the prosecution case in one robbery trial rested solely on the testimony of a facial mapping expert (*Mitchell* [2005] EWCA Crim 731).

12.51   In *Gray* [2003] EWCA Crim 1001, it might be noted, the Court of Appeal did sound a word of caution regarding the way in which facial mapping evidence is laid before the courts. Concerned at the fact that no database or agreed formula exists from which the probabilities deriving from perceived similarities in facial characteristics can be objectively calculated, Mitting J warned:

> In their absence any estimate of probabilities and any expression of the degree of support provided by particular facial characteristics or combinations of facial characteristics must be only the subjective opinion of the facial imaging or mapping witness. There is no means of determining objectively whether or not such an opinion is justified. Consequently, unless and until a national database or agreed formula or some other such objective measure is established, this court doubts whether such opinions should ever be expressed by facial imaging or mapping witnesses. The evidence of such witnesses, including opinion evidence, is of course both admissible and frequently of value to demonstrate to a jury with, if necessary, enhancement techniques afforded by specialist equipment, particular facial characteristics or combinations of such characteristics so as to permit the jury to reach its own conclusion—see *A-G's Reference (No 2 of 2002)* [2003] 1 Cr App R 21; but…such evidence should stop there.
>
> (at [16])

However, as Waller LJ noted in *Gardner* [2004] EWCA Crim 1639 at [10], this does not mean that the expert is debarred from referring to studies he has done himself when indicating the likelihood that the two images are of the same person.

12.52 In *Clarke* [1995] 2 Cr App R 425 the Court of Appeal made clear that the courts will not be at all averse to receiving evidence of other more developed identification methods where photographic material is available, for:

> It is essential that our criminal justice system should take into account modern methods of crime detection…It would be entirely wrong to deny to the law of evidence the advantages to be gained from new techniques and new advances in science.
>
> (at 429–30)

The Court ruled admissible video superimposition evidence, a slightly more sophisticated form of facial mapping. Although such evidence is real evidence to which no general rules were said to apply, it was additionally held that, as in the case of fingerprints (*ante*, para **1.14**), expert evidence was needed to make video superimposition evidence intelligible to the jury. Such an approach to scientific advances coincides with a more general attitude visible in Lord Taylor CJ's remarks in *Clare and Peach* [1995] 2 Cr App R 333, where he said of the admission of evidence given by identification expert witnesses *ad hoc*:

> If admitting evidence of this kind seems unfamiliar and an extension of established evidential practice, the answer must be that as technology develops, evidential practice will need to be evolved to accommodate it. Whilst the Courts must be vigilant to ensure that

no unfairness results, they should not block steps which enable the jury to gain full assistance from the technology.

(at 339)

12.53 *Presentation of facial mapping evidence.* In *Atkins and Atkins* (2009) 173 JP 529 the
Court of Appeal returned to the method of presenting facial mapping evidence,
holding that it must be made crystal clear to the jury that a facial mapper's conclusion on identity is not based upon a statistical database recording the incidence
of the features compared as they appear in the population at large. Nevertheless,
where a qualified photographic comparison expert testifies to similarities and/or
dissimilarities between a photograph and a known person, he may express his conclusion as to the significance of his findings, and may do so by use of conventional
verbal formulae, not a numerical scale that might mislead the jury into believing
that it represents an established, measurable scale. It must be made clear to the
jury that it is an expression of subjective opinion. In *T* [2010] EWCA Crim 2439
at [95] the Court of Appeal recently held that, in the absence of a sufficiently reliable statistical database, expert evidence of footwear marks was not to be expressed
in statistical likelihood ratios but as an evaluative opinion, such as the footmark
'could have been made' by the footwear. Similar methods of expressing conclusions on a scale, running from 'highly likely' to 'highly unlikely' are employed by
voice identification experts (*Yam* [2010] EWCA Crim 2072 at [37]).

12.54 The photographs upon which facial mapping evidence relies, often taken by CCTV
cameras, can be of poor quality. It is for the judge to determine in each case whether
the images are of good enough quality to be left to the jury. The fact that prosecution and defence expert witnesses disagree as to the quality of the photographic
evidence, however, does not of itself mean that the judge is bound to exclude the
evidence. As Moses LJ observed in *Ciantar* [2005] EWCA Crim 3559, a case in
which only one of six witnesses successfully identified C as the murderer and where
facial mapping supplied the only other evidence in the case:

> The experts are permitted to give their evidence because they have experience, sophis-
> ticated equipment, time and skill in such identification techniques. The judge is not con-
> cerned with the task of favouring one, or more than one, expert witness over another in a
> way which a jury may do. There may, of course, be cases where the expert's views are so
> outlandish, or the way in which he gives his evidence so over-confident or tentative that
> the judge rejects the evidence, but the judge's essential task is logically prior to that. He
> must determine whether the evidence is such as to entitle the jury to consider it. Thus if
> there is expert evidence capable of acceptance it is not for the judge to withdraw it from
> the jury merely because there is other evidence which contradicts it. He is not deciding
> which witness to accept or reject.
>
> (at [28])

Photographic evidence

12.55 The general position regarding photographic identification evidence is quite complex. In a bid to clarify the circumstances in which a tribunal of fact may be invited to conclude from photographic evidence that the defendant was indeed the culprit, in *A-G's Reference (No 2 of 2002)* [2003] 1 Cr App R 21, Rose LJ proposed the following summary:

> In our judgment, on the authorities, there are...at least four circumstances in which, subject to the judicial discretion to exclude, evidence is admissible to show and, subject to appropriate directions in the summing-up...a jury can be invited to conclude, that the defendant committed the offence on the basis of a photographic image from the scene of the crime:
>
> (i) where the photographic image is sufficiently clear, the jury can compare it with the defendant sitting in the dock (*Dodson and Williams* (1984) 79 Cr App R 220);
>
> (ii) where a witness knows the defendant sufficiently well to recognise him as the offender depicted in the photographic image, he can give evidence of this (...*Blenkinsop* [1995] 1 Cr App R 7); and this may be so even if the photographic image is no longer available for the jury (*Taylor v Chief Constable of Cheshire* [1986] 1 WLR 1479);
>
> (iii) where a witness who does not know the defendant spends substantial time viewing and analysing photographic images from the scene, thereby acquiring special knowledge which the jury does not have, he can give evidence of identification based on a comparison between those images and a reasonably contemporary photograph of the defendant, provided that the images and the photograph are available to the jury (*Clare and Peach* [1995] 2 Cr App R 333);
>
> (iv) a suitably qualified expert with facial mapping skills can give opinion evidence of identification based on a comparison between images from the scene, whether expertly enhanced or not, and a reasonably contemporary photograph of the defendant, provided the images and the photograph are available for the jury (*Stockwell* (1993) 97 Cr App R 260).
>
> (at [19])

Other assorted means of identification, including tracker dogs

12.56 Other than visual identification, which has been the primary focus of this chapter, the prosecution may have resort to a range of other means of identifying the accused as the perpetrator of the offence(s) charged. Some are discussed elsewhere in this book. Thus, we have considered the admissibility of fingerprint evidence (*ante*, para **1.14**) and the admissibility of proof deriving from DNA profiling (*ante*, paras **8.37–8.45**). Voice recognition, which, Laws LJ has warned, 'can be at least as problematical as visual identification, if not more so' (*Erskine and Dale* [2001] EWCA Crim 2513 at [17]), figures earlier in this chapter (*ante*, para **12.17**). One further type of identification evidence merits a passing mention: identification by tracker dog.

12.57 A number of potential evidential problems arise whenever it is claimed that a suspect has been traced by a trained dog which has followed his scent. First, there is a hearsay argument (on the hearsay rule, see Chapter 9): reliance, it is said, is being placed upon a dog handler's evidence of the actions and reactions of his dog, which of course cannot be cross-examined. Secondly, a question mark hangs over the general reliability of such evidence. On September 30, 2009 *The Houston Chronicle* carried an editorial drawing attention to errors made following 'scent line-ups' at which dogs had purportedly sniffed out culprits at canine identification parades:

> Earlier this year, based on scent matches from [dog handler PK's] dogs, a man was charged with rape and robbery... —but DNA evidence later cleared him. After a 2006 PK scent line-up, a man was named the prime suspect in a Victoria murder—but then someone else confessed to it. Yet another PK scent line-up, following a 2007 string of Houston burglaries, led to an incorrect arrest ...

12.58 The Court of Appeal addressed these concerns in *Pieterson and Holloway* [1995] 2 Cr App Rep 11 in the context of dogs tracking by scent. Largely ignoring the hearsay issue, Lord Taylor CJ held that tracker dog evidence may be admitted:

> if a dog handler can establish that a dog has been properly trained and that over a period of time the dog's reactions indicate that it is a reliable pointer to the existence of a scent of a particular individual.

Admissibility, however, is subject to two important safeguards. First, detailed evidence will be required demonstrating the reliability of the dog. In *Pieterson and Holloway*, evidence of the police dog's abilities was somewhat perfunctory, giving no account either of the sort of training the German shepherd had received or of the results of any tests conducted under controlled conditions to test the dog's reliability. Lord Taylor therefore rejected the tracker dog evidence because the Crown had not displayed 'scrupulous care' in laying a proper foundation for its admission. (In the context of US drugs enforcement, the saga of Officer Lujan and his trusty hound, Bobo, offers a further cautionary tale of a handler who failed to keep proper records evidencing the reliability of the dog: *United States v Florez*, 871 F Supp 1411 (N Mex, 1994); *United States v Kennedy*, 131 F 3d 1371 (10th cir, 1997).) Secondly, according to *Pieterson and Holloway*, if tracker dog evidence is admitted, the trial judge must warn the jury to treat such evidence with care and to look with circumspection at the evidence of tracker dogs, having regard to the fact that a dog may not invariably be reliable and cannot be cross-examined.

FURTHER READING

Bull, 'Earwitness Testimony' (1999) NLJR 216

Costigan, 'Identification from CCTV: The Risk of Injustice' [2007] Crim LR 591

Cutler and Penrod (eds), *Mistaken Identification—The Eyewitness, Psychology and the Law* (1995, Cambridge)

Heaton-Armstrong and Wolchover, *A New Look at Eye-Witness Testimony* (1994, British Academy of Forensic Sciences)

Molloy, 'Facial mapping expert evidence' [2010] 74 J Crim Law 20)

Munday, 'The Admissibility of Hypnotically Refreshed Testimony' (1987) 151 JP 404 and 426

Munday, 'Hypnosis and the Enhancement of Witness Recall' (1987) 151 JP 452

Munday, 'Videotape Evidence and the Advent of the Expert *ad hoc*' (1995) 159 JP 412

Ormerod, 'Sounds Familiar?—Voice Identification Evidence' [2001] Crim LR 595

Ormerod, 'Sounding out Expert Voice Identification' [2002] Crim LR 771

Shaw, 'The Quasi-Expert Witness: Fish or Fowl?' [2009] 73 J Crim Law 146

Report to the Secretary of State for the Home Department on Evidence of Identification in Criminal Cases (Devlin Report), 1976, HMSO

SELF-TEST QUESTIONS

1. Why ought we often to be suspicious of identification evidence?

2. What were the principal modifications made to PACE, Code D in March 2003?

3. Do you agree with Latham LJ's approach to the meaning of 'identification' for the purpose of Code D in *Akinyemi* [2001] EWCA Crim 1948?

4. What is a *Turnbull* direction? When must it be delivered? What form does it take?

5. What do you understand by (a) 'supporting evidence' and (b) 'experts *ad hoc*' in the context of contested identification evidence?

6. What principles govern the admission of contested voice identification evidence?

7. What rules, if any, govern the conduct of voice identification parades?

8. In what ways was the House of Lords' decision in *Forbes* [2001] 2 WLR 1 important?

9. What evidential problems may arise when evidence of tracker dogs is adduced?

10. When are dock identifications permissible?

11. How do the courts approach the evidence of (i) lip-readers and (ii) facial mappers?

Documents

SUMMARY

What is a 'document'?

Proof of 'public documents' and 'judicial documents'

Proof of 'private documents' by primary evidence

Proof of 'private documents' by means of copies

Proof of 'private documents' by means of other forms of secondary evidence

Bankers' books

Mr Oliver QC (counsel for Victor Chandler International Ltd) properly disavowed that he was a document: the repository of information must be inanimate: neither a person nor A P Herbert's 'Negotiable Cow' (referred to in *Uncommon Law,* p 201) can constitute a document. It matters not whether the information is in writing or some other form capable of being assimilated by the eye or by the ear or (as in the case of braille) by the touch; nor whether apparatus (such as a tape recorder or microdot reader) is required for this purpose. Information of itself cannot constitute a document, and the transmission of information of itself cannot constitute the transmission of a document.

Victor Chandler International Ltd v Customs and Excise Commissioners
[1999] 1 WLR 2160 at [11] *per* Lightman J

13.1 English law could once boast rules that were both complex and restrictive respecting the admissibility of documentary evidence. Such restrictions, however, have progressively been whittled away. It is impossible in a brief chapter in an introductory work to detail all the relevant rules. This account will therefore simply provide an outline of the subject, focusing on just one or two features of the law relating to the admissibility of documentary evidence.

What is a 'document'?

13.2 Although the term 'document' conjures up the idea of a writing on paper, as Darling J made clear in *Daye* [1908] 2 KB 333, 340, it actually covers 'any written thing capable of being evidence' and which furnishes information, no matter what it may happen to be written upon. In *Daye* itself, for example, the term 'document' was held to cover a sealed packet. In other cases, documents have included such disparate things as microfilm records, photographs and information stored on computer hard disk. A number of statutes actually supply definitions of what is meant by 'document' in particular contexts. For instance, PACE, s 118(1), as amended by the Civil Evidence Act 1995, now defines a 'document' as 'anything in which information of any description is recorded' (see also *ante*, para **9.32**). The Civil Evidence Act 1995, s 13 meanwhile adds for good measure that, so far as copies are concerned:

> "Copy", in relation to a document, means anything onto which information recorded in the document has been copied, by whatever means and whether directly or indirectly.

The topic of documentary evidence, then, has a wide ambit.

Proof of 'public documents' and 'judicial documents'

13.3 Broadly speaking, when it comes to proving documents a distinction must be drawn between 'public documents' and 'judicial documents' on the one hand, and 'private documents' on the other. 'Public documents' refer to documents made by a public officer for purposes of public record, enabling the public to make use of them or to refer to them (*Sturla v Freccia* (1880) 5 App Cas 623, 643 *per* Lord Blackburn). This class of documents includes such things as Acts of Parliament, government orders, statutory instruments, and registers of births and deaths. On the whole, the law does not require that public documents have to be proved by production of the originals. Thus, the Civil Evidence Act 1995, s 9(1) lays down that any document that can be shown to form part of the records of a public authority is admissible in civil proceedings 'without further proof'. In criminal cases, too, broadly similar rules, either at common law or under statute, apply to various classes of public document.

13.4 Rather after the manner of 'public documents', the law also makes special provision for proving 'judicial documents', which include such things as evidence of criminal convictions or acquittals and court judgments. Thus, to take an important example, proof of convictions and acquittals in all proceedings, whether civil or criminal, is governed by PACE, s 73. This provision lays down that such matters are proved simply:

(i) by production of the party's certificate of conviction or certificate of acquittal, and

(ii) by proof that the person named is the person whose conviction or acquittal is to be proved.

It should also be noted, however, that s 73(4) additionally retains other pre-existing methods of proving convictions. For instance, a conviction can still be proved by admissions made by the relevant party (*R v Derwentside Justices, ex p Heaviside* [1996] RTR 384; *Moran v CPS* (2000) 164 JP 562). Similarly, the Criminal Justice Act 1948, s 39 provides:

> A previous conviction may be proved against any person in criminal proceedings by the production of [a certificate purportedly signed on behalf of the Commissioner of Metropolitan Police, or on behalf of the governor of the prison or remand centre where any person is being detained, etc.] and by showing that his fingerprints and those of the person convicted are the fingerprints of the same person.

Section 39(5) further provides, for good measure, that this method of proving a previous conviction 'shall be in addition to any other method of proving the conviction'. Indeed, as Newman J stressed in *Pattison v DPP* (2006) 169 JP 51 at [16], laying to rest growing misconceptions concerning the permissible methods of establishing the identities of those with previous convictions, 'the identity of a person on a memorandum of conviction is capable of being proved by the same multiplicity of ways in which any other essential fact can be proved in a criminal case.' (See also *Burns* [2006] 1 WLR 1273.)

Proof of 'private documents' by primary evidence

13.5 In the case of all other 'private documents', however, the law of evidence develops from the general proposition that a private document must be proved by primary evidence. To all intents, this means that the original ought to be produced before the court. This principle, it should nevertheless be noted, is applicable only to written documents; it does not apply to such things as tapes and films. This distinction was drawn in *Kajala v Noble* (1982) 75 Cr App R 149. In that case the admissibility of a videotape, showing an incident which had given rise to a charge under the Public Order Act 1936, was contested on the ground that it was only a copy of an original film shot by the BBC. As a matter of policy, the BBC informed the court that it did not allow originals of its films to leave its premises. The Divisional Court held that, although only a copy, the videotape was admissible in evidence. Notably, it was pointed out that the rule decreeing that documents must be proved by primary evidence applies exclusively to written documents in the strict sense of the term. Parties, of course, do not always have literally to produce original 'documents' in court. For example, if it is physically impossible or extremely inconvenient to produce a 'document'—take, for example, an inscription on a wall—it is highly likely that a party will be absolved from the need to produce the document itself.

Proof of 'private documents' by means of copies

13.6 If the original of a document cannot be produced, often it will be permissible to prove the document by means of a copy. Although it is a common saying that there are no degrees of secondary evidence and that a party is free to produce any form of admissible, trustworthy evidence to prove a document, secondary evidence does tend to take a number of distinct forms. Thus, copies are a very common form of secondary evidence. In civil proceedings, in particular, the situation is relatively relaxed, as documents may be proved either by production of the original or by production of an authenticated copy. The Civil Evidence Act 1995, s 8 lays down that, no matter how many removes there may be between the original and the copy:

> Where a statement contained in a document is admissible as evidence in civil proceedings, it may be proved—
>
> (a) by the production of that document, or
>
> (b) whether or not that document is still in existence, by the production of a copy of that document . . . ,
>
> authenticated in such manner as the court may approve.

Many documents may become admissible under the hearsay provisions of the Criminal Justice Act 2003. That legislation makes provision for their production either in the form of originals or of copies. Thus, after the manner of its civil counterpart, s 133 provides:

> Where a statement in a document is admissible as evidence in criminal proceedings, the statement may be proved by producing either—
>
> (a) the document, or
>
> (b) (whether or not the document exists) a copy of the document or of the material part of it, authenticated in whatever way the court may approve.

"Copy", in relation to a document, means anything on to which information recorded in the document has been copied, by whatever means and whether directly or indirectly.
(s 134(1))

13.7   Distinguishing between what is counted an original and what should be considered a copy is not always entirely straightforward. In *DPP v Hutchings* [1991] RTR 380, for instance, a drink-driving case, because a first printout from a Lion Intoxemeter inexplicably disappeared from the charge room where it had been left lying on a table, the police officer who had breath-tested H simply ran off another printout from the machine. Rejecting H's argument that this print-out was not an original document, the court determined that since it was produced by a second operation of the device in relation to the same material, it was as much an original document as the first printout. More generally, it can be said that where there are duplicate originals of a document, all are treated as originals, and therefore as primary evidence (*Forbes v Samuel* [1913] 3 KB 706).

Proof of 'private documents' by means of other forms of secondary evidence

13.8   A party will not always be able to produce the original copy of a document or indeed an authentic copy. Thus, the questions will often arise: when is it permissible to prove a document by means of secondary evidence? And what forms of secondary evidence are permissible? The relevant rules used once to be quite strict. Not surprisingly, perhaps, they also were treated as though they were closely connected with the so-called 'best evidence rule' (see *ante*, para **1.15**). In recent years, however, the courts have considerably relaxed the legal requirements. In what ought now to be counted the leading case, *Springsteen v Masquerade Music Ltd* [2001] EMLR 654, the musician, Bruce Springsteen, claimed relief against MM and others for infringements of his copyright in nineteen recordings made in the 1970s. The performer was unable to produce the original written assignments relating to the copyrights to establish his rights in these recordings. He therefore sought to adduce secondary evidence in the form of the oral testimony of a New York lawyer who had been involved in the relevant transactions. MM contended that because S could not show that he had conducted an exhaustive search for the documents, he was not entitled to rely upon secondary evidence. Having carefully reviewed the authorities, Jonathan Parker LJ, for his part, suggested that the best evidence rule has now ceased to have any influence, even in cases involving the production of documents (cf *Garton v Hunter* [1969] 2 QB 37, 44 *per* Lord Denning MR, *ante*, para **1.15**). Moreover, the judge went on to endorse the 'without any difficulty' test, first propounded by Lloyd LJ in the Divisional Court in *R v Governor of Pentonville Prison, ex p Osman* [1990] 1 WLR 277. In that case Lloyd LJ had said:

> What is meant by a party having a document available in his hands? We would say that it means that a party who has the original of the document with him in court, or could have it in court without any difficulty. In such a case, if he refuses to produce the original and can give no reasonable explanation, the court would infer the worst. The copy should be excluded.
>
> (at 308)

Bruce Springsteen's efforts to locate the original company minute books recording the assignments may not have been exhaustive, but 'the only requirement was for him to provide a reasonable explanation for his non-production of the minutes'. There had been no allegations of impropriety or bad faith on his part and genuine attempts had been made to find the items. The trial judge, therefore, had been within his rights to find that the 'without any difficulty' test had been satisfied and to allow the singer to prove the assignments by means of secondary oral evidence.

13.9   As the *Springsteen* case shows, secondary evidence may take the form of oral testimony. However, a party may equally make an admission acknowledging the existence of a document. Alternatively, a document may be proved by circumstantial evidence—for example, where a document has been lost but the parties have always conducted themselves as though the document existed. Hence, in *R v Inhabitants of Fordingbridge* (1858) 27 LJMC 290, the court was prepared to infer from the testimony of witnesses concerning the conduct of the parties the existence of an apprenticeship, even though the original indenture was lost. Also, when we considered the hearsay rule, we saw that certain classes of statement made by deceased persons are admissible (see *Pritt v Fairclough* (1812) 3 Camp 305, and *ante*, esp para **9.21**).

Bankers' books

13.10   One significant statutory exception to the general principles governing the admission of documentary evidence stated above deserves to be mentioned: namely, the Bankers' Books Evidence Act 1879. This statute was introduced in order to reduce inconvenience and disruption for banks, which otherwise would all too frequently be requested by courts to produce their original records or to make their staff available as witnesses. As Lord Bingham of Cornhill said of the broadly similar legislation in force in the British Virgin Islands, in *Wheatley and Penn v Commissioner of Police of the British Virgin Islands* [2006] 1 WLR 1683:

> The purposes of the Act were threefold: to enable a banker's books to be inspected and copied despite the duty of confidentiality owed by banker to customer; to relieve the

banker of the need to produce his books in court; and to provide that duly authenticated entries in such books should be received as *prima facie* evidence not only of the entries but of the transactions recorded.

(at [14])

The Act achieves this objective by means of two devices: on the one hand, it allows the production of copies of relevant entries from bankers' books; on the other, it regulates parties' rights to inspect bankers' books and restricts the situations in which bankers can be compelled to appear and testify in court.

13.11 'Bankers' books', as defined in the statute, refer to a wide category of documents, and include 'ledgers, day books, cash books and other records used in the ordinary business of the bank'. Although this terminology now has an antiquated air, the definition covers such records, whether they are retained in the form of writings, microfilms, magnetic tapes or 'any other form of mechanical or electronic data retrieval mechanism' (s 9(2); see further *Williams v Williams* [1988] QB 161, 167 ff *per* Lord Donaldson MR). Section 3 of the 1879 Act provides:

Subject to the provisions of this Act, a copy of any entry in a banker's book shall in all legal proceedings be received as *prima facie* evidence of such entry, and of the matters, transactions, and accounts therein.

Section 4, however, qualifies this rule by stipulating that a copy of any such entry may only be admitted in evidence provided that four conditions have been met:

- it has to be proved that the book was at the time when the entry was made 'one of the ordinary books of the bank';
- the entry must have been made 'in the usual and ordinary course of business'; and
- the book is in the custody or control of the bank.

An officer of the bank may prove these matters, and his or her evidence may be given either orally or by affidavit. Additionally, a copy of an entry may only be received:

- if it has also been proved that the copy has been compared with the original entry and found to be correct.

Plainly, these provisions make an important inroad into the general principle that originals of documents ought normally to be produced in court. But they also afford a vital timesaving device. As Caulfield J noted in *Barker v Wilson* [1980] 1 WLR 884:

[S]ection 4 enables evidence to be admissible in a court by the production of copies of entries, as distinct from the original books which would be maintained by the bank. That section is obviously necessary, otherwise—certainly in 1879—the business of the bank would probably be held up for days while the books were at court, which would be an absurd situation. One can see the reason for s 4. Section 4 operates today, as it always has done, enabling banks to produce copies of their entries, as long as those copies are certified by an officer of the bank, within the meaning of that term as used in the Bankers' Books Evidence Act 1879.

(at 886–7)

13.12 Often, a party to a legal proceeding will wish to gain access to information that is held by a bank. Section 7 provides that such a party has to apply to the court for leave to inspect and to take copies of entries in bankers' books. Although the section provides no guidance on how a court is to exercise this discretion, in the oft-cited case of *Williams v Summerfield* [1972] 2 QB 512, Lord Widgery CJ cautioned:

One must . . . recognise that an order under s 7 can be a very serious interference with the liberty of the subject. It can be a gross invasion of privacy. It is an order which clearly must only be made after the most careful thought and on the clearest grounds.

(at 518)

Thus, unless the party has waived its rights—in which case an order would be unnecessary (*Wheatley and Penn v Commissioner of Police of the British Virgin Islands* [2006] 1 WLR 1683 at [14])—the court must reflect long and hard before granting leave. 'Fishing expeditions' by parties are strongly discouraged. Lord Denning MR explained in *Grossman* (1981) 73 Cr App R 302 that a court must normally respect the confidence of a bank account, only issuing an order if the public interest in helping the prosecution outweighs the private interest in maintaining confidentiality. For the same reasons, Lord Widgery CJ, in *R v Marlborough Street Magistrates' Court Metropolitan Stipendiary Magistrate, ex p Simpson* (1980) 70 Cr App R 291, added that any order made under s 7 must both be framed in clear words so that the bank knows exactly what is to be done and also should specify the period of time covered by the disclosure. Such considerations will not have lost any of their impact following the entry into force of the Human Rights Act 1998.

13.13 For the sake of completeness, it may be noted that s 6 declares that bankers and officers of the bank are exempt from the normal rules regarding compellability of witnesses. They can only be compelled to produce any banker's book, the contents of which may be proved under the Act, or to appear as a witness if the judge so orders 'for special cause'.

SELF-TEST QUESTIONS

1. How may a party's previous convictions be proved?

2. In relation to documentary evidence what is meant by the saying, 'there are no degrees of secondary evidence'?

3. What is the test for the admissibility of secondary evidence of a document? Is this principle in any sense related to the best evidence rule?

4. What are the principal dispensations granted to banks and their staff by the Bankers' Books Evidence Act 1879? Why were they granted?

Index